CISTERCIAN FATHERS SERIES: NUMBER SEVENTY-TWO

# The Great Beginning of Cîteaux
A Narrative of the Beginning of the Cistercian Order

CISTERCIAN FATHERS SERIES: NUMBER SEVENTY-TWO

# The Great Beginning of Cîteaux
## A Narrative of the Beginning of the Cistercian Order

### The *Exordium Magnum*
### of
### Conrad of Eberbach

Translated by
Benedicta Ward, SLG, and Paul Savage

Edited by
E. Rozanne Elder

Foreword by
Brian Patrick McGuire

Cistercian Publications
www.cistercianpublications.org

LITURGICAL PRESS
Collegeville, Minnesota
www.litpress.org

A Cistercian Publications title published by Liturgical Press

Cistercian Publications
Editorial Offices
Abbey of Gethsemani
3642 Monks Road
Trappist, Kentucky 40051
www.cistercianpublications.org

A translation of the critical edition of Bruno Grießer,
*Exordium magnum cisterciense sive Narratio de initio cisterciensis ordinis*,
Series Scriptorum Sacri Ordinis Cisterciensis, volume 2
Rome: Editiones Cistercienses, 1961

Translation © 2012 Benedicta Ward and Paul Savage

Introduction © 2012 Paul Savage

| 1 | 2 | 3 | 4 | 5 | 6 | 7 | 8 | 9 |
|---|---|---|---|---|---|---|---|---|

**Library of Congress Cataloging-in-Publication Data**

Konrad, Abbot of Eberbach, d. 1221.
    [Exordium magnum Cisterciense. English]
    The great beginning of Cîteaux : a narrative of the beginning of the
Cistercian order : the Exordium magnum of Conrad of Eberbach /
translated by Benedicta Ward and Paul Savage ; edited by E. Rozanne Elder.
        p. cm. — (Cistercian fathers series ; no. 72)
    Includes index.
    ISBN 978-0-87907-172-1 (hardcover) — ISBN 978-0-87907-782-2
(e-book)
    1. Cistercians—History—Sources.  I. Ward, Benedicta, 1933-  II. Savage,
Paul.  III. Elder, E. Rozanne (Ellen Rozanne), 1940-  IV. Title.

BX3406.3.K6613  2012
271'.12—dc23                                          2011052980

To the memory of

M. Basil Pennington, OCSO

A. M. (Donald) Allchin

*Et quod miratur in patribus, ipse sequatur*

# Contents

# Abbreviations

Bibliographic details are cited in the bibliography.

| | |
|---|---|
| Acta SS | *Acta Sanctorum.* |
| BHL | *Bibliotheca Hagiographica Latina antiquae et mediae aetatis.* |
| Canivez | Canivez, Josephus-Maria, ed. *Statuta Capitulorum Generalium Ordinis Cistercienses, 1116–1786.* 8 vols. |
| Cap | *Capitula.* Included in the *Exordium Cistercii* and the *Summa Cartae Caritatis*, in Waddell, *Narrative and Legislative Texts from Early Cîteaux*, 398–413. |
| CC | *Carta caritatis.* In Waddell, *Narrative and Legislative Texts from Early Cîteaux*, 442–52. |
| CCCM | *Corpus Christianorum, Continuatio Mediaevalis.* Turnhout: Brepols, 1966–. |
| CCP | *Carta caritatis posterior.* In Waddell, *Narrative and Legislative Texts from Early Cîteaux*, 498–505. Citations are made according to traditional chapters, with Waddell's line numbers in parentheses. |
| CCSL | *Corpus Christianorum, Series Latina.* |
| CF | Cistercian Fathers Series. Cistercian Publications. |
| Cottineau | Cottineau, Laurent H. *Répertoire topo-bibliographique des abbayes et prieurés.* |
| CS | Cistercian Studies Series. Cistercian Publications. |
| CSEL | *Corpus scriptorum ecclesiasticorum latinorum.* |
| DHGE | *Dictionnaire d'histoire et de géographie ecclésiastiques.* Paris: Letouzey et Ané, 1912–. |
| EC | *Exordium cistercii.* In Waddell, *Narrative and Legislative Texts from Early Cîteaux*, 298–404. |
| EM | Conrad of Eberbach. *Exordium magnum cisterciense sive Narratio de initio cisterciensis ordinis.* |

| | |
|---|---|
| EO | *Ecclesiastica Officia.* |
| EP | *Exordium parvum.* In Waddell, *Narrative and Legislative Texts from Early Cîteaux*, 416–40. |
| *Gallia Christiana* | *Gallia Christiana in provincias ecclesiasticas distributa.* 16 volumes. Paris: Regia, 1725–1899. |
| Grießer | *Exordium magnum cisterciense sive Narratio de initio cisterciensis ordinis.* Edited by Bruno Grießer. Rome: Editiones Cistercienses, 1961. |
| *Le Grand Exorde* | *Conrad d'Eberbach, Le Grand Exorde de Cîteaux ou Récit des débuts de l'Ordre Cistercien.* Studia et documenta 7. |
| Inst | *Instituta Generalis Capituli* / Institutes of the General Chapter. In Waddell, *Narrative and Legislative Texts from Early Cîteaux*, 453–97. |
| Janauschek | Janauschek, Leopold. *Originum Cisterciensium Tomus I.* |
| LM | Herbert of Clairvaux. *Liber miraculorum.* |
| PL | Migne, J.-P., ed. *Patrologia cursus completus, Series Latina.* |
| RB | *Regula Benedicti.* The Rule of Saint Benedict. |
| RM | *Regula magistri.* The Rule of the Master. |
| S-Bland | Caesarius of Heisterbach. *The Dialogue on Miracles.* Translated by H. von E. Scott and C. C. Swinton Bland. |
| SBOp | *Sancti Bernardi Opera.* 8 vols. |
| SBS | *St. Bernard's Sermons for the Seasons and Principal Festivals of the Year.* |
| SCh | Sources Chrétiennes. |
| SCC | *Summa Cartae Caritatis.* In Waddell, *Narrative and Legislative Texts from Early Cîteaux*, 398–413. |
| Strange | Caesarius of Heisterbach. *Dialogus miraculorum textum.* Edited by Joseph Strange. |
| *Textes de Cîteaux* | Van Damme, Jean Baptiste, and Jean de la Croix Bouton. *Les plus anciens textes de Cîteaux.* Achel, 1974. |
| Tubach | Tubach, Frederic C. *Index exemplorum: A Handbook of Medieval Religious Tales.* |
| Vita Bern | *Vita prima sancti Bernardi.* The First Life of Saint Bernard. |
| Williams | Williams, Watkin. *Saint Bernard of Clairvaux.* |

The Works of Bernard of Clairvaux
English translations are noted in the bibliography.

| | |
|---|---|
| Abb | *Sermo ad Abbates.* SBOp 5:288–93. |
| Adv | *Sermo in adventu domini.* SBOp 4:160–96. |
| Apo | *Apologia ad Guillelmum abbatem.* SBOp 3:63–108. |
| Asc | *Sermo in ascensione domini.* SBOp 5:123–60. |
| Asspt | *Sermo in assumptione BVM.* SBOp 5:228–61. |
| Circ | *Sermo in circumcisione domini. Sermones per annum.* SBOp 4:273–91. |
| Conv | *Sermo de conversione ad clericos.* SBOp 4:69–116. |
| Csi | *De consideratione libri v.* SBOp 3:393–493. |
| Ded | *Sermo in dedicatione ecclesiae.* SBOp 5:370–98. |
| Dil | *Liber de diligendo Deo.* SBOp 3:119–54. |
| Div | *Sermones de diversis.* SBOp 6/1:59–406. |
| Ep | *Epistles.* SBOp 7 and 8. |
| Epi | *Sermo in epiphania domini.* SBOp 4:291–309. |
| 5 HM | *Sermo in cena domini.* SBOp 5:67–72. |
| Hum | *Liber de gradibus humilitatis et superbiae.* SBOp 3:13–59. |
| Humb | *Sermo in obitu domni Humberti.* SBOp 5:440–47. |
| James | James, Bruno Scott, trans. *The Letters of St. Bernard of Clairvaux.* |
| Mich | *Sermo in festo sancti Michaelis.* SBOp 5:294–303. |
| Miss | *Homelium super* Missus *est in laudibus virginis matris.* SBOp 4:13–58. |
| Mor | *Epistola de moribus et officii episcoporum.* SBOp 7:100–131. |
| OS | *Sermo in festivitate Omnium Sanctorum.* SBOp 5:327–70. |
| Par | *Parabolae.* SBOp 6/2:259–303. |
| Pasc | *Sermo in die paschae.* SBOp 5:73–111. |
| P Epi | *Sermo in dominica I post octavam epiphaniae.* SBOp 4:314–26. |
| Pre | *Liber de praecepto et dispensatione.* SBOp 3:243–94. |
| QH | *Sermo super psalmum* Qui habitat. SBOp 4:382–492. |
| Quad | *Sermo in Quadragesima.* SBOp 4:353–80. |

| | |
|---|---|
| SC | *Sermo super Cantica canticorum*. SBOp 1 and 2. |
| Sent | *Sententiae*. SBOp 6/2:3–255. |
| Sept | *Sermo in Septuagesima*. SBOp 4:344–52. |
| T pl | *Liber ad milites templi (De laude novae militae)*. SBOp 3:207–39. |
| V Mal | *Vita sancti Malachiae*. SBOp 3:297–378. |
| V Nat | *Sermo in vigilia nativitatis domini*. SBOp 4:197–244. |

### Works by Other Medieval Authors

| | |
|---|---|
| Ælred, Orat past | Ælred of Rievaulx. *Oratio pastoralis* [The Pastoral Prayer]. CCCM 1. |
| Ælred, Serm | Ælred of Rievaulx. *Sermones I–XLVI. Collectio Claravallensis prima et secunda*. CCCM 2A. |
| Ælred, Spec car | Ælred of Rievaulx. *Speculum caritatis* [The Mirror of Charity]. CCCM 1. |
| Cassian, Inst | John Cassian. *De institutiones* [The Institutes]. SCh 19. |
| Gregory, Dial | Gregory the Great. *Dialogorum libri iv* [The Dialogues]. SCh 251, 260, 265. |
| Gregory, Mor | Gregory the Great. *Moralia in Job*. CCSL 143–43B. |
| Guerric, Nat | Guerric of Igny. *Sermo in nativitate domini* [Christmas Sermon]. SCh 166. |
| Guerric, Pent | Guerric of Igny. *Sermo in die sancto pentecostes* [Pentecost Sermon]. SCh 202. |
| Guerric, Pur | Guerric of Igny. *Sermo in purificatione BVM* [Sermon for the Feast of the Purification of Mary]. SCh 166. |
| Guerric, Rog | Guerric of Igny. *Sermo in rogationibus* [Rogationtide Sermon]. SCh 202:260–71. |

# Foreword

## The Cistercian Love of Story

The *Exordium magnum* is a notoriously difficult Latin text but rewards close reading. Conrad of Eberbach may have been too ambitious in terms of trying to impress his readers with his embellished language, but he does manage to convey a passion he shared with many other Cistercians: a love of story. The Cistercians had begun a century earlier with a narrative about the foundation of one monastery, Cîteaux, and its founding, in turn, of daughter houses. By the end of the twelfth century there were hundreds of houses that called themselves Cistercian, either begun from scratch or moved from other monastic orientations into the Cistercian Order.

This development, known to anyone interested in European medieval history, has been traced in terms of institutional, political, social, and legal developments. But behind all the official sources, there is the informal story repeated time and again of brothers banding together to live a more perfect and complete monastic life and associating themselves with like-minded houses. For Conrad, as with his near-contemporary Caesarius of Heisterbach, the story needed to be told again and again. They considered themselves to be building on the narrative already enshrined by about 1150 in the *Exordium parvum*, which by 1200 had become an official record of the beginnings of the Cistercian Order.

It is ironic that monks who spent so much of their lives in being silent were at the same time such great lovers of story. Conrad shows this attachment by beginning not with Cîteaux in 1098 but by going back to the story of Jesus and his apostles, whom he saw as the first to live the "form of perfect penance" that is the basis of monastic life. He does not call the apostles "monks," but he sees them as the inspiration behind what became monasticism. We thus find the Cistercian story as continuing the gospel narrative, the Good News concerned with finding a way of life that provides a preparation for heaven. From the New Testament, Conrad moved easily to Antony in the desert and Benedict and his Rule (EM 1.3-4).

If Conrad had concentrated on his stories and had devoted less attention to Latin style, his work might have become better known than it is today. For the contemporary reader, it is necessary to get behind the rhetoric and listen to the stories themselves, many of which, but not all, were taken from Herbert, monk of Clairvaux, whose *Liber miraculorum* dates from the late 1170s and early 1180s. Conrad wanted to show that it was not only well-known abbots such as Bernard who had distinguished themselves in Cistercian life but also humble choir monks and lay brothers. The Cistercian Order, as R. W. Southern once pointed out, was the first movement within the Christian Church that offered the possibility of salvation to peasants, who in the Early Middle Ages were more or less forgotten. Peasants could join the monastery as lay brothers and through prayer and hard work find their way to God. For Conrad, as for his brethren, the humble lay brother had just as good a chance of reaching salvation as his abbot did—if not a better one! The Cistercians transformed a hierarchical social world into one in which salvation was available to everyone.

As an illustration of this new attention to men of modest social origins we can look at the fourth *distinctio* in the *Exordium magnum*, where there are many stories about lay brothers. Chapter 34 concerns a lay brother of Clairvaux, Lawrence, at a time soon after Bernard's death. He was sent by his prior to the king of Sicily, Roger, but when he got to Rome, Lawrence discovered that Roger had recently died. He was taken aback and did not know what he should do. He turned in prayer to Saint Bernard and asked him for guidance. That same night Bernard appeared to him and told him to continue on his journey and all would be well: "And in this you should know that I am sending you."

The next morning Brother Lawrence resumed his trip and quickly found a companion to accompany him. He gained an audience with the new king of Sicily and not only accomplished his mission but received from the regent funds for building a new church at Clairvaux. Once back in Rome he was given ten bison to take back to his monastery. He apparently amazed onlookers who saw an old man with two small boys accompanying him managing to cross the Alps and avoiding robbers and brigands and able to drive the big animals ahead of them. There is no doubt for Conrad that it was the protection of Saint Bernard that made this journey possible.

This story combines an assertion of Bernard's spiritual power with recognition of the courage of a lay brother. This was once noticed back in the 1940s by a novice at the Trappist-Cistercian monastery of Gethsemani, Frater Chrysogonus Waddell. He was thumbing through the Latin version of the *Exordium* and came upon the story. It changed his understanding of the Cistercians, away from the Trappist emphasis on austerity and toward an appreciation of the monastic love of story. Waddell went on to become one of the leading Cistercian scholars of the second half of the twentieth century and at the same time an unforgettable storyteller himself.

The Cistercian devotion to edifying narratives can be seen as a continuation of gospel stories, positing the presence of God transforming human life. Conrad insisted on a narrative wholeness, beginning with Christ and the apostles and continuing through his own time. In the first Cistercian century he discovered a layer of stories that emphasized the power of God and the efforts of the first generations of monks and lay brothers. Behind the ambitious rhetoric with which Conrad clothed his narrative, we find men who found meaning and joy in reciting stories that encouraged them to live their lives.

The Cistercian foundation narratives and their continuation in the *Exordium magnum* are remarkable, not only because they bear witness to medieval culture, but also because they are still important in our time for new generations of monks and nuns. These look back to the first Cistercians for inspiration. In the story of Lawrence the lay brother and his arduous journey with bison over the Alps, I find a pioneering spirit and the beginnings of a monastic experiment that continues in our time.

Brian Patrick McGuire

# Preface

THE *EXORDIUM MAGNUM CISTERCIENSE* is a massive and complex Latin work by Conrad, abbot of Eberbach, who wrote near the end of the twelfth century. It reflects his admiration for a glorious Cistercian past but also shows that the glory he saw in those early days had been gained at a price. Both madness and apostasy were not unknown among the early Cistercians, and even in the records of miracles that Conrad presented in praising the Cistercian Order there were instances of negative reactions to unendurable stress. Ministering to those suffering psychological stress seems to have included the use of miracle stories to show the rewards in heaven, the help of God on earth, and the terrors in store for those who failed. This kind of shock treatment was apparently applied in the early days of the Order by Bernard himself and by Achard, the first novice master at Clairvaux.

For his part, Conrad was first of all concerned with the increase of what he called *negligentia*, a vice that he believed had by his own day crept into his Order. This concern with slackness was familiar to other reformers, notably in the treatises of Peter Damian and the rhetoric of the Gregorian Reform. Conrad saw a similar negligence among the Cistercians, whom he urged to imitate their predecessors by providing examples of the miracles granted to them in response to their fervor and discipline. Conrad's book can be seen, therefore, as a kind of internal propaganda aimed at the brothers themselves.

Cistercian miracles served also as external propaganda. The writer of the *Exordium* was concerned with more than encouraging Cistercians. He was thinking of another audience: the black monks (the Benedictines), mostly those living in the provinces of Germany, who "will not stop criticizing our sacred Order wherever and to whomever they can" (EM 1.10). His book, when seen partly as a reply to the black monks' polemic, included both the early documents of the Order and its miracles to show that the Cistercians had from the first been "approved equally by divine and human judgment" (EM 1.10). The *Exordium* is thus, Conrad says, "a two-branched candlestick" meant to shed light upon the darkness of those who were opposing the Order from outside and those who were failing it from within.

A distinctive mark of the twelfth-century Cistercian miracle collections is that they are miracles not of a holy individual but of the holy Order. They were seen as rewarding not some great feat of individual asceticism but the keeping of the rules and customs that regulated the Order's daily life. The Cistercians had their holy men, particularly holy abbots, but even such men as Stephen Harding and Alberic were seen by Conrad primarily within the context of the Order as a whole.

The miracles of the Order were seen too within an even more specialized context. The author of the *Exordium magnum* recounted the emergence of the Cistercians as the fitting culmination of the monastic tradition, which, he says, began with Christ and was followed by Saint John the Baptist, the apostles, and the early monks Antony, Pachomius, and Basil, about whom he may have known through Cassian's *Conferences*, recommended by Benedict in the closing chapters of his Rule. Conrad then selected incidents from the lives of Western monks, including Benedict and early abbots of Cluny, to show that they had been true monks and that they had observed the very customs for which the Cistercians were now being criticized by their successors. Following this, there are books of miracles taken from the life and writings of Bernard and the records of the early monks at Cîteaux and Clairvaux, including the lives of the lay brothers.

The intention, therefore, is to present the Cistercians as those monks who follow the most ancient customs of the Church; they are not innovators but preservers of what had been later obscured, secure in the authority of history. With this perspective, the Cistercians could see themselves as approved by God; they saw such approval expressed by miracles and visions. And so, presented as an extensive *apologia* for the Cistercian way of life, with the whole fabric of its observance set forth in terms of the power and protection of God, Conrad's book became the first history of the Order.

The *Exordium magnum* shows Conrad's concept of history as a demonstration of the work of God in events, rather than as simply a chronology of established facts and deeds, and when it is read with this in mind it can shed light on Cistercian history and ideology. It is not an easy text to appreciate. Conrad's Latin is not easy to understand, and his mixture of pompous affirmation and vehement condemnation is even more difficult to translate into a form that is acceptable today. In this translation we have attempted to preserve the polemic tone of the work but also to make it comprehensible to modern readers. As Conrad says, perhaps echoing Origen's precept that translation should be by the sense and the word, "we have been careful to restate summaries in suitable language" (EM 6.10).

Regarding particular Latin words, first, we have consistently translated *conversus* as "lay brother." Sometimes Conrad also refers to a *monachus laicus*, which we have rendered as "lay monk." Lay monks were not ordained priests but were nevertheless part of the monastic, not the lay brother, community. They sang in choir and were members of the chapter. Lay brothers, on the other hand, performed manual labor at the monastery or worked on the granges. Second, the Latin *religio*/religion often refers to the quality of one's religious life or observance. Thus, in our translation, a phrase that would literally be "advanced in religion" becomes "advanced in religious life," or "advanced in monastic observance." Third, with few exceptions we have translated the word *conversio*/conversion as "conversion of life," that is, a conversion to monastic life. Finally, in keeping with Conrad's ideas, we have chosen to render *clericus* as "clerk" rather than "cleric."

In Psalm citations, we have used the Vulgate/Douay-Rheims numbering. Thus, our references to the Psalms are those according to the Septuagint and Vulgate versions and the number will generally (i.e., Psalm 10 to 147) be one lower than those found in contemporary translations. We have not, however, used four books of Kings (as does Douay-Rheims). Instead Kings I and II are here cited as Samuel I and II, followed by Kings I and II. In the footnotes, we sought to merge useful references found in previous editions—Latin, French, and German—citing the various editors. To these we have added many notes of our own, with special attention to sources and translations in English.

Paul Savage and I would like to thank Brian Patrick McGuire for putting us in contact with one another and for conversations with various colleagues at Kalamazoo; Rozanne Elder, for her remarkable patience, wit, and wisdom; and librarians at the Bodleian and at the University of Utah and Brigham Young University Libraries. For its hospitality, we thank Saint Stephen's House, Oxford, and the fellows and librarians of Harris Manchester College, Oxford. We are especially thankful for those living in community with us: the Sisters of the Love of God and Maureen Wilson.

Benedicta Ward, SLG
Oxford
2011

# Introduction

IN THE CLOSING DECADES of the twelfth century the Cistercian Order found itself in a world rather different from the one commonly associated with Cistercian life of the period. The Order was justifiably proud of its achievements and unparalleled diffusion across Europe, and in 1215 the papacy would impose the Cistercian system of General Chapters on all religious Orders, another sign of the Order's success. By the early thirteenth century the Cistercian Order had expanded greatly, become an important ecclesiastical and economic power in Europe, and developed an institutional structure meant to sustain a large, widespread organization.[1] Yet, in 1153 it had lost its influential spokesman, Bernard of Clairvaux, and as the century drew to a close religious sensibilities were changing. These would become obvious in the first decades of the thirteenth century when the same papacy that enthusiastically ratified Cistercian organization authorized the new mendicant Orders. The Franciscans and Dominicans, and the impulses they embodied, were to shift the center of gravity in Christian religious life for centuries to come.

It was in this transitional period that Conrad of Eberbach gradually—between the 1180s and 1215—compiled the *Exordium magnum cisterciense: The Great Beginning of Cîteaux*.[2] It is a book of history and lore, often with miraculous stories, meant to continue a great spiritual tradition, and it is also a book meant to justify and repair the Order. As Conrad continued to work, the book took a

---

[1] Cistercian Statutes, the decisions of the annual General Chapter of abbots, were codified in 1202. Begun as early as 1116, they grew in size and scope quickly after the 1150s. See Constable, *Reformation of the Twelfth Century*, 39n172. See the bibliography for bibliographical details for this and other works cited in the text and footnotes.

[2] On the identification of Conrad as the author, see below, "The Question of Authorship."

unique form which reflects the needs of the time, a time in which the ostensibly successful Cistercian Order was reexamining its past with some anxiety. The *Exordium magnum* was in part an effort to provide a historical and formative context for those who were to be Cistercians in the thirteenth century.[3]

The author's conscious decision to provide this historical and formative context gives the book its unique character. It is the largest Cistercian text of its day and the first to weave together varied strands of Cistercian history and lore: narrative historical accounts, documentary sources, and, above all, stories that were circulating in Cistercian houses. These *exempla*, edifying stories told orally and later written down, were meant primarily to instruct and were central in the monastic formation of the time—and the telling of them no doubt did much to form a sense of community within the cloister.[4] They reflect concerns inside the monastery, and because of their wide-ranging subject matter and attention to everyday life, they lend themselves to many kinds of inquiry. The uniqueness of the *Exordium magnum* lies in how it combines the most thorough history of the Order until that time with one of the most extensive *exempla* collections to date.

The *Exordium* shows a remarkably strong historical sensibility. It begins with a narrative that brings a thousand years of monastic life together with gospel accounts of Jesus and John the Baptist. As the work continues, however, the historical orientation gives way to overt edification and instruction. Books 5 and 6 show little historical sensibility at all. Between these two groupings, books 3 and 4 contain *exempla* loosely organized around time and place. They constitute an informal group biography of laudable Cistercians from the abbey of Clairvaux. While this large collection of *exempla* does not form a well-ordered, chronological narrative, it

[3] On this anxiety, see Freeman, *Narratives of a New Order*, 127–31.

[4] The *exempla* genre of literature can be traced back to hagiographical texts like Gregory the Great's *Dialogues* and became immensely popular in twelfth-century monastic circles. Many of these stories eventually found their way into the sermon collections and pastoralia of subsequent centuries. See Bremond and LeGoff, *L' "exemplum"*; and McGuire, "Cistercian Storytelling." McGuire writes (287) that "the *exemplum* is at the very heart of the monastic experience."

clearly begins with a deliberate historical orientation that should be considered when interpreting the book as a whole. Among Cistercian *exempla* collections, the *Exordium magnum* falls within the period between the earlier *Liber miraculorum* (LM) of Herbert of Clairvaux[5] and the later *Dialogus miraculorum* of Caesarius of Heisterbach, both of which are wholly edifying works and lack the *Exordium magnum*'s chronological structure and its sense of alarm over monastic formation.

Because of the book's singular structure, the *Exordium magnum* has often been approached with some ambivalence. There are no monographic studies of it. It has often been considered a work of pious hagiography, and certainly its stories may be read at this level. Yet selected parts of the text have been treated as historical sources,[6] and at least one writer has noted Conrad's historical awareness.[7] The challenge in approaching the *Exordium magnum* as more than a near-random collection of stories is the book's combination of genres. Conrad, in crafting a presentation of the Cistercian past designed both as a defense of the early Cistercian Order and as a means of reforming what he considered the Cistercians' increasingly lax observance, attempted to reconcile documentary history, miraculous *exempla*, and instructive exhortation. Hortatory passages often occur as he introduces or concludes his stories and, on a few occasions, as commentary within his narrative. His purposes—defense, formation, and reform—therefore overlap.

In the *Exordium* Conrad's monastic history defends Cistercian legitimacy but also provides a basic pattern of how a monk should live. The *exempla* illustrate how monks should conduct themselves, but they also assert the legitimacy of Cistercian life and give readers a strong sense of a glorious past. All of it is meant to inspire

---

[5] Herbert is also known as Herbert of Mores. The *Liber miraculorum* text, now being critically edited, is available in PL 185:1273–1384.

[6] In *The White Monks* (1953), Louis Lekai included EM in a section on hagiography (154); in *The Cistercians* (1977), he used the EM as a source in his treatment of the lay brotherhood.

[7] The best study of the EM is McGuire, "Structure and Consciousness in the *Exordium Magnum Cisterciense*." See also his "An Introduction to the *Exordium Magnum Cisterciense*."

readers with the greatness of God's work. To grasp Conrad's overall purpose and achievement, readers need to embrace the book's unique character and remember the singular period that prompted its creation. The history it contains provides a deliberate framework for the stories and this both sets the book apart from other *exempla* collections and provides the key to understanding it. As a result, the *Exordium magnum* becomes a door through which we may enter the Cistercian past and better understand it.

## READING THE *EXORDIUM MAGNUM*

The basic structure of the *Exordium magnum* mirrors Conrad's concerns as well as the sense of accomplishment and anxiety within the Cistercian Order. Books 1 through 4, begun while Conrad was a monk at Clairvaux,[8] are centered on the communities of Cîteaux and Clairvaux. Books 5 and 6, written later, almost certainly at the German abbey of Eberbach, from which Conrad receives his cognomen, reflect a greater concern with the individual monk's way of life and his subsequent salvation. Books 1 through 4 are roughly chronological in nature, beginning with a brief, though well-elaborated, monastic history. Quite unlike these, book 5 contains a wide-ranging series of stories that function as warnings about unmonastic behaviors, betraying an increased concern with personal formation at all phases of monastic life that continues in the sixth, and final, book, which focuses on sacramental aspects of monastic life and emphasizes the "last things": the Eucharist, confession, and the communion of saints. This understanding of the book's form came about only in the twentieth century through the

---

[8] While it is clear that Conrad began the EM at Clairvaux, one should keep open the possibility that these books did not take their final form there. Herbert of Clairvaux had finished the LM by 1181, and after that Conrad could well have referred to it while at Eberbach and revised his earlier text. With the reappearance of the *Codex Eberbachensis* (see below, "Textual Tradition"), such a possibility deserves further research.

manuscript studies of Bruno Grießer. The following chart shows each book's relative size[9] and subject matter:

SCHEMA OF THE *EXORDIUM MAGNUM*

| BOOK 1 | BOOK 2 | BOOK 3 | BOOK 4 |
|---|---|---|---|
| 35 chapters<br>53 pages | 34 chapters<br>50 pages | 34 chapters<br>76 pages | 35 chapters<br>49 pages |
| Monastic History from Christ to Cîteaux: Apostles, Desert Fathers, Benedict, Cluny, and the first five abbots of Cîteaux | History of Clairvaux and stories of its first eight abbots. Concentration on Bernard and his circle | Stories about senior monks of Clairvaux, includes some who became abbots of daughter houses | Stories about common monks, illiterate lay monks, and lay brothers, mostly at Clairvaux |

| BOOK 5 | BOOK 6 |
|---|---|
| 21 chapters<br>66 pages | 10 chapters<br>32 pages |
| Stories about the dangers of disobedience, conspiracy, discord, voluptuousness, negligence | Stories about Eucharist, Confession, and an extensive final summation |

In addition to this structure, there are three elements that are helpful for understanding the *Exordium magnum* as a whole: Conrad's sense of purpose in writing; his intended audience; and his understanding

---

[9] Unless otherwise noted, all references to Grießer in the notes refer to page numbers in Grießer's original 1961 edition. See bibliography for details on the publishing history.

of the uses of—and connections between—narrative, history, and *exempla*. Conrad refers specifically to his purpose in four places: the introductory prologue, brief summaries at the ends of books 2 and 4, and the final summation (EM 6.10). These passages also confirm that he wrote the work in two distinct phases.

The prologue introduces the text, signals how the author intended to structure the historical background of monasticism, and focuses the reader's attention on what Conrad intended readers to learn from his text. It is analogous to the *exordia*, which prefaced many twelfth-century histories,[10] and a close reading reveals that it was written to introduce a work of only four books or, in Conrad's terminology, *Distinctiones*. Having addressed his intended audience—those seeking salvation, i.e., monks—Conrad describes what readers should expect in the coming pages:

> Here you are duly taught how the desert of Cîteaux,
> Till then long sterile, produced sublime flowers.
>
> > [i.e., *Distinctio* I]
>
> These pages will teach you that the perfect mother has produced
> A perfect offspring who has fulfilled her hopes,
> For the renowned house of Cîteaux brought forth a noble scion,
> And produced from the womb of its dutiful love the Clear
>    Valley [Clairvaux],
> Twice, yea thrice, blessed, a true sun for the world.
>
> > [i.e., *Distinctio* I / II]
>
> Here are described the venerable deeds of the fathers
> Who, as we shall show, governed each of these houses.
>
> > [i.e., *Distinctio* III]
>
> Reading this then gives witness
> To the exertions of the senior monks of Clairvaux;
> When read and reread it is profitable to those

---

[10] John Ward, "Some Principles of Rhetorical Historiography in the Twelfth Century," in *Classical Rhetoric and Medieval Historiography*, ed. Ernst Breisach, illustrates how *exordia* can be used to show the variety of twelfth-century approaches to writing history (160ff.).

Against whom the temptations of the flesh have not prevailed.

[i.e., *Distinctio* IV][11]

As the bracketed notations indicate, books 1 through 4 of the *Exordium magnum* correspond neatly with what Conrad describes in his prologue. That there will be "readings that witness to the vigor of the senior monks of Clairvaux" can only refer to book 4, which is a general selection of edifying stories (*lectiones testes*) about monastic life at Clairvaux.

As we observed earlier, the subject matter of books 5 and 6 is utterly different from that of book 4. Here the stories focus not on the "vigor of the senior monks of Clairvaux" but on the consequences suffered by sinful monks, generally not from Clairvaux (book 5), and on the sacraments, the communion of saints, and discord within the Order (book 6). Nothing in the prologue describes the material in books 5 and 6. If manuscripts of the *Exordium magnum* contained only the first four books, no one reading the prologue would suspect anything was missing. Clearly, at some point Conrad decided to expand the scope of his book.

Near the end of book 4 Conrad signals his intention to add *exempla* more focused on personal monastic formation by writing:

> Just as we learned [in EM 3–4] from the aforementioned fathers how generous God's mercy is toward his saints . . . in the same way we will show in the following examples [EM 5–6] with what goodness he pardons sinners and yet with what severity he punishes transgressors.[12]

As Conrad shifts his emphasis in book 5 from the "fathers" and "saints" of the Order to the "sinners," he makes an insightful distinction between "sinners" (*peccatores*) and "transgressors" (*delinquores*). Saints are those monks who keep the mandates by living according to the established observances of monastic life; God has mercy on them and they will be saved. For those who do not live

---

[11] EM Prol. (lines 65-66; 70-74; 77-78; 81-83 in Grießer's critical edition). The bracketed references above have been added.
[12] EM 4.35.

according to these observances, God's mercy is uncertain. "Sinners" who recognize and repent of their sin and do penance (especially within sacramental confession, a major theme in book 6) will be forgiven; "transgressors," those who are delinquent either because they are not truly contrite or do not seek penance—those people who appear in most of book 5—will be punished.

In his final summation (EM 6.10), Conrad most clearly states his twofold purpose. First, he wanted to "hand down a certain knowledge of our Order from its inception to our brothers . . . in the more remote parts of the world" so they would appreciate the holiness of the early Cistercian fathers and be moved to imitate their way of life. There is a growing sense of urgency that Cistercians, especially those far from the Order's Burgundian home, needed to have "certain knowledge" of their history and way of life so they could live it properly and defend it. Second, he wanted to put an end to the statements of Benedictine monks, especially those "living in the provinces of Germany," "who openly slander our Order to seculars and to those ignorant of the facts."[13] This makes it seem that the Cistercians' knowledge of their shared history and common way of life had diminished with the Order's growth and that Conrad sought to put this right.[14] His concern is similar to that of mid-twelfth-century Cistercians who had felt a need to educate communities closer to home as they experienced rapid expansion, sometimes by affiliating entire non-Cistercian communities with the Order.[15]

The author's comments in the prologue and the final summation also reveal something about how he conceived his audience. The opening lines of the prologue—"Whoever . . . hastens in the fruitful contest of the monk to strive"—suggest that Conrad was addressing those new to monastic life. Yet, while the book's utility for

[13] EM 6.10 and 1.10 .

[14] See Brian Patrick McGuire, "An Introduction to the *Exordium Magnum Cisterciense*."

[15] Chrysogonus Waddell, "The *Exordium Cistercii* and the *Summa Cartae Caritatis*," notes evidence in liturgical texts of an increased need for documentation and history about the Order after 1147, when Obazine and Savigny were incorporated into the Cistercian Order (45). See also Chrysogonus Waddell, *Narrative and Legislative Texts*, 227–31.

novices is almost self-evident in its historical and didactic passages, at various points he addresses monks at all levels—not only novices, but also priests, senior monks, cellarers, the occasional abbot, and even illiterate lay brothers who had occasion to hear it read aloud.[16] Book 5, for example, contains a remarkable story about a particularly egregious sinner who murders his confessor and thus needs to find a more discerning one. The unfortunate victim is held accountable because his harshness in hearing confession drove the penitent to greater sin. Conrad exhorts priests to realize that their attitude in confession may literally save or damn a penitent.[17] Such a story was not intended for the edification or socialization of novices; it served as an *exemplum* to ordained monks to give serious attention to their priestly office. Many, but by no means all, such stories occur late in the *Exordium magnum*, when Conrad's focus had shifted more toward issues of formation and the maintenance of discipline.

## *NARRATIO* AND *EXEMPLA*

Inherent in Conrad's sense of purpose and audience is his perception of history and *exempla*. This is an elusive distinction in the *Exordium magnum*, and indeed in many medieval texts, because historiographic assumptions generally went unspoken and must be inferred contextually.[18] The *Exordium magnum* is largely a miracle collection, but the book's initial conception is so historically informed that the author and his audience probably saw these miraculous stories as a meaningful way in which to order and remember their past. The distinction between such exemplary stories and documentary evidence is more rigid in our time than it was in Conrad's.[19] A medieval audience accepted miracles as valid evidence in a narrative construction of the past. The *Exordium*

---

[16] See EM 5.5, in which he hopes anyone who "reads or hears" (*legerit vel audierit*) an *exemplum* will go to confession.

[17] See EM 5.12. See also 5.14.

[18] See McGuire, "Introduction," 284–92.

[19] Freeman (*Narratives of a New Order*, 3–7) surveys various positions about what constitutes "history" in a medieval Cistercian sense. In the process she makes clear that while we today limit history to "non-saintly narratives," we do

*magnum* presents, in effect, a temporal and spiritual history of the Cistercians by combining narrative and didactic elements. Conrad did not consider the *Exordium magnum* solely an edifying work; in the prologue he wrote that he would use "sound reasoning" throughout the text, and in the final summation he claimed the book provided "certain knowledge."[20]

The title Conrad chose for his work emphasizes the historical-narrative element and its importance in reading and interpreting his book. In fact, the book was originally known as *Narratio de initio cisterciensis ordinis* (*A Narration of the Beginning of the Cistercian Order*), and the generation immediately after him read it as such.[21] Perceptions change, however, and by the last third of the thirteenth century Cistercians themselves seem to have considered it less a narrative about their past and more a miracle collection. Another title, *Book about the Illustrious Men of the Cistercian Order*, appears in the manuscripts of the late thirteenth century.[22] Scholars who followed this later way of classifying the text have all too often ignored the EM's uniquely historical dimension.[23]

---

so in part as a matter of convenience. See Felice Lifshitz, "Beyond Positivism and Genre: 'Hagiographical' Texts as Historical Narrative," *Viator* 25 (1994): 95–113.

[20] EM Prol.: "And now [reader], pay heed and carefully examine / The text of this volume, / By which I shall plainly and with compelling reasoning [*valida ratione*] disclose / The origin of this celebrated way of life, / Which to the joys of heaven gives birth / and on earth prepares the seeds of salvation."

[21] Immediately after the prologue, in EM 1.1, Conrad writes, "In the name of our Lord Jesus Christ—here begins the narrative of the origins of the Cistercian Order." The title in the Oxford manuscript (Bodleiana Cod. Laud. Misc. n. 238, fol. 1r.) is "Book about the beginning of the holy Cistercian Order" (*Liber de s. ord. cisterc. initio*). For more on the title, see Grießer, EM, 26. The smaller *Exordium parvum* has been known by this name only since 1666, when Bertrand Tissier labeled it in his edition of Cistercian texts; in Conrad's day it was known as *Exordium cisterciensis coeniobii*. See Waddell, *Narrative and Legislative Texts*, 416.

[22] *Liber de viris illustribus Cisterciensis ordinis*; see Grießer, EM, 26 and 12; *idem*. "Probleme der Textüberlieferung des Exordium Magnum," *Cistercienser-Chronik* 52 (1940): 162. During the same period the story of Robert disappears from the manuscript tradition of the Cistercian foundation, significantly diminishing its narrative quality; see Grießer, 10–11.

[23] See McGuire, "Structure and Consciousness," 37, 89. See also Freeman, *Narratives of a New Order*, 128–30, on the connection between *exempla*, history, and identity.

The Latin *narratio* came out of the rhetorical tradition of the ancient world and carried shades of argumentative meaning not found in our word "narration." Cicero considered the *narratio* especially important in cases where facts were in dispute,[24] and Quintilian regarded it as perhaps the orator's most important tool in making his case.[25] As Isidore of Seville summarized the matter, *narratio* was the second of rhetoric's four components. It came immediately after the introduction of the subject of debate and "unfolded the sequence of events"[26] before the argument was made and the conclusion drawn. Yet Isidore also used the word in his definition of history: "a narration of events through which what happened in the past" becomes known.[27] Narration was so closely associated with history that in medieval Latin usage a *narrator* could be either a teller of tales or an advocate. In the *Exordium magnum* Conrad was both.

His vocabulary (*narratio* and *res gestae*, deeds) implies a historical continuity between Christ, his apostles, the desert tradition, Benedict, the Cluniacs, and the first Cistercians. To counter the accusation that the founders had left the monastery of Molesme against their abbot's will he intersperses chronologically ordered documents within historical events and commentary to "bring the events into focus"[28] and enable him to label the black monks' charges "a shameless lie." The many *exempla* serve the author's historical-narrative purposes by showing that Cistercian life remains true to its historic monastic roots. Conrad no doubt also considered *exempla* an engaging tool for teaching proper conduct, but in a

---

[24] Cicero, *De oratore* 2.80–81; May and Wisse, *On the Ideal Orator*, 212–14.

[25] Quintilian, *Institutiones oratoriae* 4.2.116–19; Russell, *The Orator's Education*, 2:276–79. See also *Institutiones oratoriae* 2.18.5.

[26] Isidore of Seville, *Etymologiarum* 2.7: "secunda [i.e., *narratio*] res gestas explicat."

[27] Isidore of Seville, *Etymologiarum* 1.41: *Historia est narratio rei gestae, per quam ea, quae in praeterito facta sunt, dinoscuntur. Narratio* was used within the Cistercian world to denote works of history; see Freeman's discussion of the *Narratio de fundatione Fontanis monasterii* (*Narration about the Foundation of Fountains Monastery*) in *Narratives of a New Order*, 151–68. Also in Conrad's time schoolmen like Thierry of Chartres and Peter Helias lectured on *narratio* and assumed that the historian's narrative method was essentially the same as the orator's; see Roger Ray, "Rhetorical Skepticism," 68–69 96–97n56.

[28] EM 1.10.

twelfth- and thirteenth-century context *exempla* were an established means of persuasion and served much the same purpose as
rhetorical narration.[29] Stories are powerful: they can prove a claim
and provide a mirror. Taken as a whole, they form a remembered
past and an important part of the shared culture of the monks who
read or heard them.

Like any historical source, *exempla* and miracle stories were
subject to a certain degree of scrutiny. Conrad often mentions
the origin of his stories in order to establish their authority, as
did Herbert of Clairvaux. If a story's content agreed with general
expectations and its authority was sound, there was no reason to
doubt the events it described.[30] Conrad's book can therefore be
read as a history of the Cistercians. The events he narrated include
what we would identify as institutional, social, or economic realities, but for Conrad these reflect persistent spiritual realities and
had spiritual import. At one point, he even warns his audience
against reading his stories "like a chronicle of events or the annals
of a king, solely out of curiosity for information."[31] These spiritual
realities show themselves in the four periods of the monastic past
he delineates in book 1: (1) the biblical, which begins with John the
Baptist and continues through the apostolic communities described
in Acts and the letters of Paul and Peter; (2) the age of the fathers
(Antony, Pachomius, Benedict); (3) the Cluniac period, especially
Odo's abbacy; and (4) the Cistercian period. Presented in discreet
sections virtually unconnected by a causal narrative, these periods
are tied together by Conrad's sense of the waxing and waning of
the monastic ideal.[32] Each successive era comes to have a specific
typological importance central to Conrad's vision of the monastic

---

[29] Bremond, et al., *L' "exemplum,"* 83.

[30] Partner, *Serious Entertainments*, 191, remarks that there was rarely a rigorous
distinction between "trustworthiness" and "accuracy," or between "possibility"
and "probability."

[31] EM 6.10.

[32] Conrad's notion of an ideal waxing and waning over time is a common
historical sensibility; see de Lubac, *Medieval Exegesis*, 2:69–82, 143–53, 207–16.

ideal and its culmination at Clairvaux, and the *exempla* then reinforce and further delineate these themes.[33]

For Conrad, the common life, and therefore monasticism, began not with the Desert Fathers or Saint Antony but in the events of the New Testament. Each time a new stage of monastic history begins, the Spirit is active. Conrad says little about the Spirit during the gospel period; whenever Christ is mentioned, the Spirit, by implication, is also active. After Christ's ascension, the Spirit's presence defined the first apostolic communities, which Conrad viewed as essentially monastic in nature: then, "as the crowd of believers was multiplying, the splendor of the same life in the Spirit which we have called perfect penance began to shine ever more brightly."[34]

The same Spirit that moved the apostles to a life of perfect penance guided the early monks, to whom Conrad refers as "instruments of the Holy Spirit," to establish an institutional form of a common life guided by rule. Antony of Egypt had the law of charity written in his heart, "not with ink and letters, but by the Spirit of the living God."[35] The same Spirit guided Pachomius to write the first rule in ink, which, according to a long-standing tradition, "an angel had dictated" to him.[36]

Conrad makes no clear distinction between the age of the Desert Fathers and the time of Benedict.[37] Both desert hermits and European cenobites are included within a single phase of history, and

---

[33] See Morrison, *History as a Visual Art*, 69: "Events . . . have typological rather than historical value. History thus becomes a structure of doctrinal precepts illustrated by examples, whose real, typological coherence is disclosed, not to the eye that sees only the outward distinctions of phenomena, but rather to the vision enlightened by inward contemplation of spiritual unities."

[34] EM 1.2, in Grießer, 49.

[35] EM 1.20. This reference comes from EP 15; on Antony, see EM 1.3. See also Jer 36:18 and 2 Cor 3:3.

[36] EM 1.3, in Grießer, 51: *Pachomius vero, cum factus esset apostolica gratia insignis, scripsit monachorum regulas, quas angelo dictante didicerat.* See Armand Veilleux, trans., *Pachomian Chronicles and Rules*, 125. EM 1.3 appears to be original to Conrad.

[37] Conrad credits Western monasticism entirely to Benedict and says nothing about Jerome, Athanasius, Cassiodorus, Martin of Tours, or the many other monastic legislators whose rules were abandoned at imperial behest in the early ninth century.

because monastic expansion into the West is of central importance to his narrative, Conrad extends the early tradition by identifying the Spirit as the real author of Benedict's Rule:

> He, our most reverend father, wrote a Rule for monks, which by the daily exercise of virtue he had learned not through men but by the anointing of him who teaches men knowledge. In it that marvelous craftsman [*artifex*], the Holy Spirit, joined the greatest perfection with the most measured discernment in a connection so subtle that any close observer of the Rule discovers in it the means of making progress, and equally any fainthearted person finds there a remedy for his weakness.[38]

The presence and activity of the Spirit, for Conrad, linked early monastic communities with apostolic communities and linked both directly with Christ.

Cluny's second abbot, Odo (926–44), Conrad writes, reformed monastic discipline "according to the grace of the Lord which was given him"—which implies the Spirit's activity in this third monastic age—and Odo acted "by the grace of God and the aid of holy Father Benedict."[39] Several stories about Cluniac miracles reinforce the monastery's connection with the primitive monastic ideal, especially a story about an apparition of Benedict sending Odo to reform a monastery in Francia.[40] Just as miracles will affirm the legitimacy of the Cistercian observance, they did the same at Cluny. Conrad, however, believed that Cluny's observance eventually became lax and this had brought about the need for a fourth phase of reform.

In this culminating fourth phase, the Holy Spirit is especially prominent. Several brothers at the Benedictine monastery of Molesme, convinced that the community had deviated from a proper observance of the Rule, were called by God, who "sent his Holy Spirit from the depths of heaven . . . into [their] hearts."[41]

---

[38] EM 1.4.
[39] EM 1.6.
[40] EM 1.6.
[41] EM 1.10.

Obedient to the Spirit's guidance, they left Molesme and founded Cîteaux. Conrad then draws a parallel between the establishment of Cîteaux and Christ's incarnation:

> Just as at the beginning of grace, when Christ our Lord and Savior was born, the world, while it knew him not, received a pledge of new redemption, of ancient reconciliation, of eternal happiness, so too in these last days, when charity is cold and iniquity everywhere abounds, the almighty and merciful Lord planted the seed of that same grace in the wilderness of Cîteaux. Watered by the rain of the Holy Spirit, it gathered an incredibly plentiful harvest of spiritual riches, growing and developing into a great tree, so surpassingly beautiful and fruitful.[42]

This revealing passage, by bringing together Christ, the Holy Spirit, and Cîteaux, links the Cistercians to the very foundations of Christian life. The Spirit is directly responsible for the establishment of both monastic life and the Cistercian Order; thus, the Spirit validates, justifies, and vivifies the Cistercians. Once this powerful image of the Spirit's role in the Order's foundation has been drawn, any mention of the Spirit—or God's grace—is informed by it.

Not only is the *Exordium magnum* unique in Cistercian writing, there is little precedent for it in the whole of monastic historiography.[43] Monastic chronicles usually begin with the foundation of the house in which they were produced, and while a few begin with Christ's birth, they do not integrate earlier events into the larger text.[44] Conrad did not merely allude to the past; he used it actively and consciously to define and defend his view of Cistercian life and to place the Cistercians center stage in this history of monasticism.

The *Exordium magnum* provides evidence of how Cistercian culture developed in the late twelfth and early thirteenth centuries. It

---

[42] EM 1.13.

[43] For an excellent overview of Cistercian historical writing with useful bibliography, see Freeman, *Narratives of a New Order*.

[44] Leclercq, "Monastic Historiography," discusses the various forms of monastic history in the period preceding the EM. See also van Houts, *Local and Regional Chronicles*, 29. Cf. Taylor, *English Historical Literature*, 40: "the vast majority of fourteenth-century chronicles were accounts of contemporary history."

reveals, for example, the long-lived tension between the black and white monks over Robert of Molesme's place in monastic history.[45] It makes clear that Cîteaux's foundation was viewed retrospectively by some Cistercians with a degree of anxiety. Because Conrad lived and wrote at what was then the Order's geographic periphery, one suspects that Cistercian anxiety became all the more pronounced as one traveled farther away from the Order's original Burgundian homeland.[46] It also suggests a lack of consistent formation within, and historical knowledge about, the Order at a time of growth and new challenges. The remedies Conrad offered amount to a conservative call for fidelity to an ancient spiritual ideal, a rigorously penitential life lived according to the customs of the Order.

Conrad's book also betrays an expanded sense of charity (a deeply resonant word for monks who called their monasteries "schools of charity"), which is increasingly social and communal in nature.[47] Strong images of monastic friendship are found throughout the EM, but especially in books 5 and 6.[48] This very tangible and inclusive sense of spiritual kinship includes everyone from lay monks and lay brothers to monastic superiors, not only the brothers with whom one lives, but also those saints and brothers who have died and for whom the Cistercian now prays and who he trusts pray for him.

Finally, the *Exordium magnum* laid out its model for the narrow path of monastic reform at the very time when the thrust of religious culture was toward increased activity in the world. Yet the Cistercians did not escape the temper of the times; a broadening into society occurred within the Cistercian Order only twenty-four

---

[45] See Brian Patrick McGuire, "Who Founded the Order of Cîteaux?"

[46] One should be careful not to identify Eberbach itself as a "peripheral" monastery; it was likely the most important and wealthiest Cistercian abbey in the Germanic territories. Still, there are overt concerns about outlying monasteries, and further study is needed on the relationship between core and peripheral abbeys.

[47] See Newman, *Boundaries of Charity*; and Savage, "History, *Exempla*, and *Caritas* in the *Exordium Magnum*."

[48] See "friendship" in the index; and McGuire, *Friendship and Community*.

years after Conrad died with the establishment of the Cistercian College of Saint Bernard in Paris.[49]

## CONRAD'S SOURCES

To accomplish his purpose, Conrad drew on sources ranging from the Bible, early Christian texts, and Cistercian foundation documents to *exempla* collections circulating during his lifetime. He also drew on an oral tradition that existed within the monasteries of Clairvaux and Eberbach and came from daughter houses as far north as Sweden. The *Exordium magnum* shows that a lively network of monastic storytelling existed and that *exempla* were becoming part of the Order's sense of its past.

Like any twelfth-century monastic author, Conrad of Eberbach quoted liberally from the Bible. While nearly every book is represented, he was notably fond of the Psalms, Sirach, Isaiah, the gospels, and several of Paul's letters. The passages were often quoted from memory, and numerous biblical allusions come directly from liturgical texts. Conrad also made use of texts of the Church Fathers, notably Augustine, Jerome, and Gregory the Great, the most quoted of the Fathers.[50] There are a few references to the *Lives of the Fathers* and the Rule of the Master and—not surprisingly— dozens to the Rule of Saint Benedict. Among later Benedictine authors, Conrad made use of works by Odo of Glanfeuil and Peter the Venerable, the *Life of Hugh of Cluny* by Raynald of Vézelay, and the *Life of Odo of Cluny*. He includes references to works by the canons regular Hugh and Richard of Saint Victor and a remarkably early reference to Anselm of Havelberg's *Dialogues*.[51] While direct citations of classical texts are few and far between, there are eleven quotations from Horace, five from Virgil, four from Ovid, and one from Persius. As it is unlikely that Conrad would have had at hand

---

[49] Lekai, *The Cistercians*, 236–37. Graduates of the college routinely returned to the cloister, often to administrative positions.

[50] Smalley, *The Study of the Bible*, 79–80, notes an interesting Cistercian augmentation of the biblical text. Some biblical and patristic passages may have been heard at the Night Office.

[51] EM 1.3.

a copy of the entire *Aeneid* (to say nothing of Ovid's works); these quotations were almost certainly taken from collections known as *florilegia*, which were common in monastic libraries.[52]

Cistercian texts comprise the bulk of Conrad's written sources. These include the Cistercian founding documents—primarily the *Exordium parvum* (EP), with occasional allusion to the *Exordium cistercii* (EC) and the *Cartae caritatis*[53]—as well as the narrative *Vita prima sancti Bernardi* and Herbert of Clairvaux's *Liber miraculorum* (LM).[54] Additionally, Conrad made use of many works by Bernard of Clairvaux and other Cistercian fathers, such as Aelred of Rievaulx, Guerric of Igny, and Nicholas of Clairvaux.

The *Exordium parvum* forms the basis of Conrad's documentary history, and almost all of it is incorporated into book 1. Although portions of the *Vita prima* are scattered throughout the EM, it is most frequently cited in the chapters about Bernard in book 2. Herbert's *Liber miraculorum* supplied many, but by no means all, the miracles in books 1 to 4, centered on Clairvaux. Relatively little of book 5 and none of book 6 can be traced to the LM, which further suggests that those books were written at a later time and with a different emphasis.

Conrad's use of early Cistercian sources must today be interpreted carefully because these sources have become among the most contentiously debated documents of twelfth-century monastic history. At issue is when the documents were written and therefore what historical circumstances, concerns, and aspirations they reflect. Until the mid-twentieth century Cistercians and scholars considered the *Exordium parvum* to be the work of Stephen Harding, one of the three founders of Cîteaux, while the *Exordium cistercii* was considered a later abridgment of it. This interpretation has been challenged, and the *Exordium parvum*, the *Exordium cistercii*,

---

[52] See Leclercq, *The Love of Learning*, 228–32.

[53] For critical editions of these texts, see Waddell, *Narrative and Legislative Texts.*

[54] *Vita prima Bernardi*; PL 185:225–416; Herbert of Clairvaux, LM, PL 185:1273–1384. For more on Conrad's Cistercian sources, see Grießer, 35–41; McGuire, "Structure and Consciousness," 33–90; and *Le Grand Exorde*, 405–9: "Les sources de Conrad d'Eberbach."

and the various versions of the *Cartae caritatis* have become the focus of academic debate.[55] In the mid-twentieth century, a young scholar, J.-A. Lefèvre, first raised questions about the chronology of early Cistercian documents and claimed that the *Exordium parvum* had been prepared in 1152/53, nearly twenty years after Stephen's death, for the Cistercian pope Eugene III and had its roots in an earlier document that dated possibly from 1119.[56] While no one any longer defends the whole of Lefèvre's thesis, a consensus has been building that a later date for the *Exordium parvum* is correct, and most scholars now place the received text between 1134 and 1150.[57] The background of the *Exordium cistercii* remains unclear: some date it as early as *c.* 1123/24; others maintain that it could not have been begun before Stephen Harding's death in 1134.[58]

The received version of the *Exordium parvum*, therefore, seems clearly to be the later document. This interpretation is bolstered by Chrysogonus Waddell's argument that the *Exordium cistercii* and the *Exordium parvum* should be understood as introductory material in Cistercian customaries sent to far-flung new abbeys.[59] If we

[55] For bibliography of the earliest phase of the debate, see Lekai, *The Cistercians*, 21–32, 477–80; and Waddell, "The *Exordium Cistercii* and the *Summa Cartae caritatis*," 30–61.

[56] J.-A. Lefèvre, "Que savons-nous du Cîteaux primitif?" *Revue d'Histoire Ecclésiastique* 51 (1956): 5–41. On the history of the various editions of these documents, see Knowles, *Great Historical Enterprises,* 198–222.

[57] For a comprehensive overview, along with a new working hypothesis that the EP is "a hybrid work" that evolved between 1112 and 1148, see Waddell, *Narrative and Legislative Texts*, 197–231. Constable (informed by Waddell), *Reformation of the Twelfth Century*, 38n171, provides a concise explication of the various positions. Dating the EP remains contentious; Berman (*The Cistercian Evolution,* 12–15, 62–68) has dated the EP to the 1170s, which would make it virtually contemporaneous with the EM. For responses to Berman, see Waddell, "The Myth of Cistercian Origins"; Freeman, "What Makes a Monastic Order?"; and Casey, "Bernard and the Crisis at Morimond."

[58] Waddell (*Narrative and Legislative Texts*, 147–61) provides a convincing case and excellent bibliography for the later date. Compare Newman, *The Boundaries of Charity*, 257n1.

[59] Waddell first proposed this in "*Exordium Cistercii* and the *Summa Cartae Caritatis*," 30–35, and uses it effectively throughout the introductory material in *Narrative and Legislative Texts*.

compare the relatively defensive tone of the later *Exordium parvum*, the "small beginning," with the *Exordium magnum*, the "great beginning," we discern a growing Cistercian anxiety about their origins. The EC hints at strife between Molesme and the New Monastery[60] but speaks well of Molesme, a monastery "of great renown and outstanding in religious fervor." It makes the move to Cîteaux seem more evolutionary than revolutionary: the monks who left to found Cîteaux "realized that, although life in that place was a godly and upright one, they observed that the Rule they had vowed to keep in a way fell short of their desire and intention."[61] The *Exordium parvum*, by contrast, comments that at Molesme the Rule of Saint Benedict was observed "poorly and neglectfully"; that Alberic, Cîteaux's second abbot, as prior at Molesme had "had to suffer many insults, prison, and beatings";[62] and that proper observance could not be reinstated without overcoming "many obstacles."[63] It also spends a great deal of energy showing that Cîteaux had been founded canonically.

The author of the *Exordium magnum* used the EP text most widely circulated in the latter half of the twelfth century, the one that displayed an increased level of hostility toward Molesme,[64] and created another in a series of determined defenses of the Cistercian's early history. The greatest impetus for this defense was likely a desire to reassure novices entering the Order and, since parts of Conrad's work are directed toward the entire community, monks at various levels of seniority.

The increasing emphasis on monastic formation in books 5 and 6 signals another perceived need: to reinforce the ever-expanding

---

[60] "New Monastery," *Novum monasterium*, is the name first used by the founders for what became known as Cîteaux. Only around 1119 does the name *Cistercium* take its place in the documentation. See Marilier, "Le vocable *Novum Monasterium*"; Marilier, *Chartes et documents*, 24–26; and Elder, ed., *The New Monastery*.

[61] EC 1; Waddell, *Narrative and Legislative Texts*, 179; translation by Bede K. Lackner, Lekai, *The Cistercians*, 443.

[62] EP 9.

[63] EP 2.

[64] Waddell, *Narrative and Legislative Texts*, 141–43, questions how much to make of the "polemical" EP versus the more objective EC.

Statutes of the General Chapter with practical examples of proper monastic behavior.[65] To provide these *exempla*, Conrad turned to Herbert of Clairvaux's *Liber miraculorum*, the first draft of which was completed in 1181.[66] Unlike the *Exordium magnum*, the *Liber* is a haphazard collection of miracle stories, with little, if any, sense of structure. Herbert was still living at Clairvaux when Conrad arrived, but it is impossible to know what effect his presence or activity had on the younger monk. Nonetheless, Conrad was clearly sympathetic to Herbert's outlook and almost certainly had the *Liber miraculorum* with him at Eberbach.[67] He mined it for stories and expanded Herbert's sense of purpose in three important ways: Conrad consciously gave the *Exordium magnum* a historical structure; he selected and arranged his stories in what he considered to be a sound pedagogical order; he editorialized extensively on the text. Because of this, the *Exordium magnum* has a scope and sense of purpose not present in the *Liber miraculorum* or in any Cistercian work before it.

Conrad also used other collections of miracle stories, one of which he refers to in book 5.[68] Two of these previously unidentified collections have come to light since Bruno Grießer's critical edition of the *Exordium magnum cisterciense* was published in 1961.[69] Brian Patrick McGuire's work with the *Liber visionum et miraculorum* suggests that more will come to be known and that the *Exordium*

[65] See above, n. 1. See Canivez, *Statuta Capitulorum Generalium*; and, for this period, Waddell, ed., *Twelfth-Century Statutes*. On Conrad's place among Cistercian *exemplum* writers, see McGuire, "Structure and Consciousness."

[66] Grießer, "Herbert von Clairvaux und sein *Liber miraculorum*," 29. Relatively little critical work had been done on Herbert's *Liber* until the publication of Kompatscher-Gufler's *Herbert von Clairvaux und sein Liber miraculorum*, which includes a critical edition based on two manuscripts and a commentary. See also Casey, "Herbert of Clairvaux's *Book of Wonderful Happenings*."

[67] Later passages (EM 5.1–6; EM 5.14; EM 6.3; and EM 6.5) include stories that can be referenced to the LM.

[68] EM 5.19.

[69] The *Liber visionum et miraculorum*, now available in a critical edition with a corrected title, *Collectaneum exemplorum et visionum Clarevallense e codice Trecensi 946*, ed. Olivier Legendre, Exempla medii aevi, 2, CCCM 208; and the *Liber miraculorum* written by Goswin. See below, "Structure and Consciousness."

*magnum* will figure prominently in studies of the broader *exemplum* tradition.[70] Finally, it is clear that Conrad used various oral sources.[71] One must be careful here, however, because Conrad sometimes quotes verbatim Herbert of Clairvaux's description of his source along with Herbert's version of the story. Thus readers can get the mistaken impression that Conrad is relating a story he heard when, in fact, he is quoting Herbert. Yet some of Conrad's stories clearly come from conversations with people whom he knew and who had witnessed the events he described. He heard the account of the lay brothers' revolt at Schönau, for example, directly from Theobald, his abbot at Eberbach, who had been sub-cellarer at Schönau when the revolt took place.[72]

The variety of Conrad's sources make his text as much a compilation as an original composition. He worked on it for nearly thirty years and did not conceive of its present form, conceptually or in writing, until at least the late 1190s or early 1200s, when he began the two final books. The earliest manuscript of Conrad's work, the *Codex Eberbachensis*,[73] makes clear that he reworked the text, and this could well have happened more than once. Much of the Clairvaux material is taken from written sources that the author could have consulted at any time. Conrad refers to his selection process toward the beginning of his chapter on Abbot Fastrad of Cîteaux: "I have inserted into my narrative . . . stories about other seniors of Clairvaux . . . so that what was scattered here and there, and mixed up with other stories, could better enlighten and better profit

[70] McGuire, "A Lost Clairvaux Exemplum" and "The Cistercians and the Rise of the 'Exemplum.'" See also Mula, "Twelfth- and Thirteenth-Century Cistercian Exempla Collections"; and Mula, "A New Twelfth-Century Cistercian Exempla Collection? Paris BNF lat. 14657," a paper delivered at the Thirty-Fifth International Congress at Kalamazoo (May 4–7, 2000).

[71] Conrad mentions knowing contemporaries of Bernard, among them Dom Gerard, prior of Clairvaux and abbot of Eberbach; Bernard's secretary, Geoffrey of Auxerre; Dom Hugh of Mont-Félix; Dom Peter of Châlons; see EM 2.29; 5.3; and 6.10. See also McGuire, *The Difficult Saint*, 166. In "A Lost Clairvaux Exemplum Found," 38–51, McGuire studies how multiple authors may have shared oral sources.

[72] EM 5.10.

[73] On the *Codex Eberbachensis*, see below, "Textual Tradition."

anyone reading it."[74] While Conrad made clear that he ordered the stories he chose to a purpose, we have already seen that Conrad altered his initial schema for the work during the years he spent compiling it. As his concern with Cistercian laxness increased, he added more and more *exempla*, and as he did so the EM's original and most unique aspect, its historical orientation, became increasingly less pronounced.[75]

The anxiety of Conrad, and the Cistercians, at century's end may seem surprising because the Order's expansion established it as a powerful voice within the Church.[76] Yet the Cistercians were by no means alone in being criticized. Monastic Orders were all being criticized on one count or another: the Cluniacs for "hypocrisy and dissimulation," the Cistercians for "cupidity and robbery," the Carthusians for "litigiousness."[77] Broader tensions over the growth of all monastic institutions and debates over what constituted the

---

[74] EM 1.32.

[75] McGuire ("A Lost Clairvaux Exemplum Found," 42) suggests that Conrad may have found inspiration for widening the scope of the EM from reading the *Liber visionum et miraculorum*. Many of Conrad's stories about lay piety, he notes, are found in this earlier collection, and he thinks that some of the EM's stories "on dangers" may have originated here as well.

[76] Cistercian success was remarkable. By 1180 they could count from their ranks one saint (Bernard, canonized in 1174), one pope (Eugene III, 1145–53), ten cardinals, and over sixty bishops. See Newman, *Boundaries of Charity*, 3 and appendix, 247–51. Joel Lipkin, "The Entrance of the Cistercians into the Church Hierarchy, 1098–1227," *The Chimera of His Age: Studies on Bernard of Clairvaux*, ed. E. Rozanne Elder and John R. Sommerfeldt, CS 63 (Kalamazoo, MI: Cistercian Publications, 1980), 62–64, notes (without giving dates) that six of these bishops were eventually canonized and another five beatified. Lipkin counts nineteen Cistercian cardinals and 151 bishops and archbishops before 1227. The Cistercian system of regular General Chapters became the model for other Orders, mandated in canon 12 of the Fourth Lateran Council; see *Decrees of the Ecumenical Councils*, ed. Norman Tanner, vol. 1 (Washington, DC: Georgetown University Press, 1990), 240–41.

[77] The quotations are taken from a sermon by Stephen of Tournai found in Constable, *The Reformation of the Twelfth Century*, 32. Compare EM 5.20 in which a woman criticizes the Cistercians for "too much land [and] luxurious buildings." See, too, Gerald the Welshman, *The Journey through Wales* 1.3; *The Journey through Wales and the Description of Wales*, trans. Lewis Thorpe (New York: Penguin, 1978), 103–7.

"apostolic life"—prayer and the worship of God or preaching to and succouring the world—presaged the rise of mendicant Orders of the thirteenth century.[78]

## THE QUESTION OF AUTHORSHIP

Throughout this introduction we have attributed the authorship of the *Exordium magnum* to Conrad of Eberbach, and while the evidence for his authorship is not conclusive, it is compelling enough that virtually all scholars now accept it.[79] His name appears in scribal additions to two early manuscripts of the *Exordium magnum*. The first, in an early fourteenth-century hand, occurs in a codex from the Abbey of Foigny: "A certain abbot, Conrad of Eberbach, who was a monk in Clairvaux, composed this book."[80] In the second, now at Paris, a late fourteenth-century addendum to the title reads, "The book of illustrious holy men of the Cistercian Order by the monk, Dom Conrad." On the verso, immediately before the prologue, the same scribe wrote that the book "is said to have been produced by brother Conrad, a monk and senior member of Clairvaux."[81]

When or where Conrad was born we do not know; nor do we know when or under what circumstances he entered monastic life. From the text of the EM we can be certain that he was at Clairvaux by the late 1170s, perhaps as early as 1168. There is no evidence to place him in that monastery after 1195. In his Final Summation (EM 6.10), he reminisces about life at Clairvaux and

---

[78] McGuire (*Difficult Saint*, 154) notes that the twelfth century was largely suspicious of growth and that monastic expansion specifically often brought criticism.

[79] Among modern scholars, Hermann Bär and Karl Rossel both accepted Conrad's authorship; see Bär-Rossel, 532n14. So too G. Hüffer, *Der heiligen Bernard von Clairvaux*, 535n17; and Grießer, 5–6.

[80] Grießer, 20. The manuscript, Laon, Bibl. Mun. 331, has been partially mutilated, and the clause placing Conrad at Clairvaux is no longer visible. Grießer, working in 1939, was unable to consult the Laon manuscript and recorded the passage from Bertrand Tissier's seventeenth-century edition in *Bibliotheca Patrum Cisterciensium*, 1:13–246 (Grießer, 19).

[81] MS Paris, Bibl. Nat. Nouv. acq. 364, folio 2r, 2v. This manuscript, *Codex Parisinus*, is of Germanic provenance, probably from the north; see Grießer, 17–18, 33.

says specifically that he had experienced it under the abbots Peter Monoculus (1179–86) and Garnier of Rochefort (1186–93) and had seen there disciples of Saint Bernard, including the prior, Dom Gerard, and Bernard's one-time secretary, Geoffrey of Auxerre.[82] While the abbatial dates place him at Clairvaux during the 1180s, his claim to have heard a particular story from Dom Gerard somewhat complicates the dating,[83] both because Gerard was associated with the same two monasteries as Conrad and because the dates of his tenure at Clairvaux are problematic. He was certainly prior until 1171, when he became third abbot of Eberbach, where he remained until 1177. Some have assumed that Gerard died that year because his name is not found in any official records after that. There is, however, a manuscript that states he later returned to Eberbach to be abbot a second time.[84] If this was the case, he probably spent the interim at Clairvaux, and it is entirely possible (some say likely) that Conrad met him then.[85] If he knew Gerard as prior, Conrad must have entered the abbey under either Abbot Pons (1165–70) or Abbot Gerard (1170–75)—not to be confused with Gerard the prior but another Gerard who had previously been abbot of Fossanova. There are numerous stories in the *Exordium magnum* about abbots Pons and Gerard, whom the author appears to have respected. Grießer was convinced that Conrad entered Clairvaux in 1169/70.[86] By the time of Bernard's canonization in 1174, Clairvaux had a well-developed tradition of preserving stories about its great abbot and about many of its other spiritually

---

[82] Geoffrey retired to Clairvaux around 1188 after an eventful career; see Joseph Gibbons, "Introduction," *Geoffrey of Auxerre: On the Apocalypse*, CF 42 (Kalamazoo, MI: Cistercian Publications, 2000), 7–13. Precisely when Conrad met him is not clear.

[83] See EM 2.29: "We heard about this revelation from Dom Gerard of pious memory, formerly prior of Clairvaux, afterward abbot of Eberbach, who, as those acquainted with him knew, was a man of great truth, purity, and innocence."

[84] Troyes MS 1402 (late thirteenth or early fourteenth century); Grießer, EM, 39–40n5.

[85] Bär-Rossel, 312, gave 1177 as Gerard's date of death. McGuire ("Structure and Consciousness," 37–40) thinks it probable that Gerard returned to Clairvaux as prior in 1177, and that it was then that Conrad heard the story.

[86] Grießer, EM, 33.

noteworthy monks. As a monk of Clairvaux at this time, Conrad would have been steeped in this oral and written tradition.[87]

The only reference to Conrad independent of the *Exordium magnum* identifies him as abbot of Eberbach, a daughter house of Clairvaux near Mainz. It is contained in a letter confirming a transfer of property between Eberbach and the abbey of Val-Dieu.[88] Issued under the authority of Abbot William of Clairvaux, it was signed by Conrad, abbot of Eberbach, as well as by James, abbot of Fontenay; Henry, abbot of Himmerod; Christian, abbot of Schönau; and Philip, abbot of Otterburg. The dating clause provides specific information on Conrad's tenure as abbot: "Enacted in the year of grace 1221, in the month of May, at the time in which the lord Abbot Conrad of Eberbach began to function as abbot."[89]

Eberbach had become Clairvaux's first Germanic daughter house between 1131 and 1135 and by Conrad's day was an extremely important monastery.[90] The combination of his having received monastic formation at the Order's epicenter and later serving as abbot in a prominent Germanic house would help explain the wide-ranging concerns of the *Exordium magnum*'s author. During the last half of the twelfth century Kloster Eberbach's development in many ways mirrored that of the Cistercian Order. Between 1145

---

[87] In addition to Herbert's *Liber miraculorum*, there is the *Liber visionum et miraculorum*, and another *Liber miraculorum* written by Goswin; see McGuire, "Structure and Consciousness," 41.

[88] See Grießer, EM, 34.

[89] See Bär-Rossel, 523–27. Bär constructs his narrative of Conrad's election, which contains many unique details but cites no additional sources. Bär-Rossel (225–26) make the point that such a group of abbots would have assembled at Eberbach only for the installation of a new leader for that community. This letter contradicts the assertion in *Gallia christiana* 5:656 that Conrad was abbot from 1213–26, the dates found in some secondary works, e.g., Williams, *Monastic Studies*, 58.

[90] Eberbach, only six miles northwest of the cathedral city of Mainz, was originally founded in 1116 for Augustinian canons; monks from Clairvaux arrived in 1131 at the request of the archbishop (Janauschek, 21). For more information, see A. Schneider, "Eberbach," in *Dizionario degli Istituti di perfezione*, vol. 3, ed. G. Pelliccia and G. Rocca (Rome: Edizioni Paoline, 1974–), 1006–7; and Lekai, *The Cistercians*, 37.

and 1180, it established four daughter houses of its own,[91] and in 1186 its large Romanesque church was consecrated. Less than three kilometers from the Rhine, it is to this day in the center of the Rheingau's finest vineyards, many of which were donated to the monastery in the 1100s and early 1200s.[92] By 1162 the monastery had acquired a house and a cellar in Cologne; by 1232 its holdings formed the hub of a wine trade of some sixty thousand gallons annually.[93] By the 1190s, with its four foundations and a community of sixty monks and two hundred lay brothers, Eberbach was clearly the preeminent Cistercian abbey in the Rheinland.[94] This is probably when Conrad arrived from Clairvaux, and it was here that he altered the focus of his work to match his new circumstances.

The evidence all points to Conrad, monk of Clairvaux and abbot of Eberbach, as the likely author of the *Exordium magnum*. As we have shown, EM falls into two parts: the first four books, centered on the traditions of Cîteaux and Clairvaux,[95] and the last two, concerned with the monks' formation, way of life, and

---

[91] Eberbach's daughter houses were Schönau (1145), Otterberg (1145), Arnsburg (1174), and Val-Dieu (1180); Janauschek, 81, 82–83, 169–70, 179–80.

[92] The monastery overlooks Steinberger, one of Germany's most renowned vineyards, which was acquired by the monastery between 1135 and 1232. Its wine is still occasionally referred to as *Kloster Eberbach*; see Alexis Lichine, "Steinberger," *Alexis Lichine's New Encyclopedia of Wines and Spirits*, 4th rev. ed. (New York: Alfred A. Knopf, 1985), 455. For a study of Eberbach's place in the wine trade, see J. Söhn, *Geschichte des wirtschaftlichen Lebens der Abtei Eberbach in Rheingau,* Veröffentlichungen der historische Kommission für Nassau VII (Wiesbaden: Bergmann, 1914). The abbey is now owned by a not-for-profit foundation, the Stiftung Kloster Eberbach. A virtual tour of the monastery is available on the Kloster Eberbach website: http://www.kloster-eberbach.de/content/stiftung_bereich/index_ger.html.

[93] Lekai, *The Cistercians*, 316–17. By this time, Eberbach's wine was transported on duty-free barges and traded in Cologne, Mainz, and Frankfurt.

[94] Lekai (*The Cistercians*, 343) gives this figure as the monastery's population "in the twelfth century."

[95] The words "begun at Clairvaux" are carefully chosen. While it is clear that Conrad began the EM 1–4 at Clairvaux, one should keep open the possibility that these books did not take their final form there. Herbert of Clairvaux finished the LM by 1181, and from that point on, Conrad could well have referred to it at Eberbach and revised an earlier text. With the reappearance of the *Codex Eberbachensis* (see below, "Textual Tradition"), such a possibility deserves further research.

salvation.[96] The best evidence for the completion date of the *Exordium magnum*, between 1206 and 1221, comes from Conrad's references to the lay brothers' revolts at Schönau and Eberbach. His source for the Schönau revolt was Abbot Theobald, and Theobald was not at Eberbach until 1206.[97] The revolt at Eberbach itself took place during Theobald's abbacy, sometime between 1208 and 1210.[98]

Having become Eberbach's fifth abbot sometime around May 1221, Conrad died on 18 September the same year.[99] That he was the fourth abbot to come from Clairvaux testifies to the close association between the two houses and to their shared Cistercian tradition. Although Conrad did not see himself as an innovator, preferring to look back into history for his models, his combination of a historical sensibility and the edifying *exempla* makes the *Exordium magnum* a remarkably innovative book. Its unique combination of genres—*narratio* and *exempla*—is conceivable only within the intellectual world of the twelfth or early thirteenth centuries, before *exempla* collections came to be complied solely for edifica-

---

[96] Williams (*Monastic Studies*, 58–59) was one of the first to suggest this, basing his hypothesis solely on the different tone of the two sections. See Grießer, EM, 33–34; and McGuire, "Structure and Consciousness," 39–40, who argues that distinctions 1 through 4 were written at Clairvaux between 1181–96.

[97] The date of the Schönau revolt is difficult to determine. Grießer, EM, 292n1, thought *c.* 1179 most likely. Donnelly, *The Decline of the Medieval Cistercian Laybrotherhood*, 34n74, placed it *c.* 1168; as does Newman, *Boundaries*, 105; cf. Bär-Rossel, 409n14. Maximilian Huffschmid ("Beiträge zur Geschichte der Cisterzienserabtei Schönau bei Heidelberg," *Zeitschrift für die Geschichte des Oberrheins* 45 [1892]: 97) noted, however, that it is said to have occurred at the beginning of the abbacy of Geoffrey, who took office only in 1182. We are grateful to James France for this reference and for pointing out in support of the later date that the first reference in the Cistercian Statutes to such a disturbance occurs in 1190. For a recent study of the lay brothers' discontent, see Brian Noelle, "Expectation and Unrest among Cistercian Lay Brothers in the Twelfth and Thirteenth Centuries," *Journal of Medieval History* 32 (2006): 253–74.

[98] On Theobald and the revolt at Eberbach, see McGuire, "Structure and Consciousness," 38–40. Compare Grießer, 292n1 and 297n1.

[99] F. J. Worstbrock, "Konrad von Eberbach," *Die deutsche Literatur des Mittelalters Verfasserlexikon*, vol. 5 (Berlin: Walter de Gruyter, 1985), 156–57. Worstbrock's source for the date is a necrology (see Bär-Rossel, 554n42). This date is also accepted by Kolumban Spahr, "Konrad," in *Neue Deutsche Biographie*, vol. 12 (Berlin: Duncker & Humblot, 1980), 536.

tion or use in sermons.[100] *The Great Beginning of Cîteaux* is therefore
a revealing book and an excellent place to begin more detailed
study of the Cistercian Order between 1174 and the middle of
the thirteenth century.

## THE TEXTUAL TRADITION

This translation has been made from the critical edition of Bruno
Grießer, *Exordium magnum cisterciense sive Narratio de initio cisterciensis ordinis*, published in Rome in 1961 and reprinted, with some
emendations, in the series *Corpus Christianorum* in 1994 and again
in 1997. This critical edition came at the end of a long and che-
quered textual history.

The first printed edition of the *Exordium magnum*, collated and
edited under the direction of Ignatius de Ybero, Cistercian abbot
of Fitero, was published at Pamplona in 1621 and attributed to an
anonymous monk of Clairvaux.[101] Into a large lacuna in book 1,
between chapters 14 and 20, de Ybero placed passages from the
*Exordium parvum*.[102] The Pamplona edition came to be used as the
model for subsequent editions and for information on Saint Bernard.

In 1641 Jacob Merlo-Horstius, a priest and scholar from Cologne, published what the great Maurist Jean Mabillon called "the
best and most accurate" edition of Bernard's *Opera* in six volumes,[103]
the fifth of which contained several books about, but not by, Bernard. This section, known as *Vita et Res Gestae libris septem comprehensae*, contained a selection *ex Exordio magno* taken from the
Pamplona edition, specifically EM 2.1-19; 1.25; 4.12, 13, 16, 19,

---

[100] See Chris Given-Wilson, *Chronicles: The Writing of History in Medieval England*
(New York: Hambledon and London, 2004), xix–xxiii, 12–20, on the nature of
historical writing in the period.

[101] Grießer, 8: "by a thus far anonymous monk of Clairvaux."

[102] The lacuna between EM 1.14–20 is in many manuscripts and is discussed
below, pp. 32–33.

[103] Jacob Merlo-Horstius, also referred to as Jacob Merler (1597–1644), was a
prominent doctor of theology known as an effective preacher. Among his scholarly
activities, he edited the works of Salvian, Gregory the Great, and Peter Damian.
Mabillon's comments on his work can be found in the preface to his edition of
Bernard's *Opera*, PL 182:17–20.

28; 2.20; 3.17; and 6.10. Mabillon included the *Vita et Res Gestae* in his edition of Bernard's works, which was reprinted in the PL and is easily accessible today.[104]

The Pamplona edition was also used the following year by Ángel Manrique as a source for his scholarly treatment of Cistercian history, the *Annales Cistercienses*.[105] Manrique included material from Herbert of Clairvaux's *Liber miraculorum*, which he thought had been written by the same author as the *Exordium magnum*.[106]

In 1871 the Pamplona edition was reprinted at Rixheim under the auspices of Ephrem van der Meulen, abbot of Ölenberg. The accuracy of the reprint is uneven, but despite its several deviations from de Yerbo's original work, Grießer considered it basically a faithful reprint.[107] Having examined the Rixheim edition at Ölenberg, and the annotations made by its editors on occasional differences between manuscripts, Grießer commented that it was regretful these had not been included in the final printing.[108]

Both Grießer and Migne considered superior to both the Pamplona and Rixheim editions a second, independently compiled edition of the *Exordium magnum* produced in 1660 under the direction of Bertrand Tissier, prior of Bonnefontaine. As the basis for his text, Tissier used another incomplete manuscript, a manuscript from the Abbey of Foigny which at one point[109] refers to the author as Conrad and abbot of Eberbach.[110] The Foigny manuscript contained material missing in the Pamplona edition but lacked a folio that had been cut out of book 6. Consequently, Tissier's edition breaks off near the end of EM 6.10 at the line "Let us be afraid that from such negligence and careless sloth deadly wicked-

---

[104] PL 185:415–54.

[105] Manrique (1577–1649) studied at Salamanca and was provost of the Cistercian College of Loreto; see Lekai, *The Cistercians*, 243.

[106] Grießer, 8.

[107] Grießer included the Pamplona and Rixheim editions as a single unit in his *apparatus criticus*.

[108] Grießer, 9.

[109] EM 6.10.

[110] The manuscript, Laon. Bibl. Mun. 331, may date from as early as 1225; Grießer, EM, 19–20. Foigny was the third daughter house of Clairvaux, founded in 1121.

ness and iniquity will enter."[111] In 1854, J.-P. Migne published the Tissier edition in the *Patrologia Latina*.[112] There are serious textual discrepancies between the PL printing and the original Tissier; most notably, for several chapters in the second book Migne substituted sections taken from the Mabillon edition of the *Vita et Res Gestae libris septem comprehensae*.[113] For these chapters the *Patrologia* reader is simply referred by note to the earlier work, published elsewhere in the PL. As a result, neither the complete *Exordium magnum* nor even Tissier's text is available in Migne.

Scholarly work done in the late nineteenth and early twentieth century on Eberbach in general and the *Exordium magnum* in particular led to a three-volume *Diplomatische Geschichte der Abtei Eberbach* which put a wealth of material in the hands of researchers and renewed interest in one of Germany's most prestigious abbeys.[114] The first volume was a chronological narrative of the abbey's history written by Hermann Bär (1742–1814), a priest and bursar of Kloster Eberbach. In the course of his work Bär reviewed Conrad's tenure as abbot and cited him as the author of the *Exordium magnum* without giving any indication that there was reason to doubt the attribution, which may reveal that the tradition of Conrad's authorship was still alive at Eberbach. Bär's work was prepared for publication by Karl Rossel, along with Rossel's own edition of the abbey's collected charters and documents.

During the early twentieth century, notable work on the *Exordium magnum* was done by Tiburtius Hümpfner, a Cistercian of the Hungarian Abbey of Zirc. Scholars since Merlo-Horstius had realized that material was missing from book 1, and Hümpfner was able to bring attention to a manuscript that contained it.[115] Bruno Grießer brought

---

[111] See below, EM 6.10. See Williams, *Monastic Studies*, 59, about this folio.

[112] PL 185:995–1198.

[113] Grießer, EM, 9.

[114] See, for example, F. Otto, "Das Exordium Magnum Ord. Cist. des Klosters Eberbach im Rheingau," *Neues Archiv* 6 (1881): 603–5; and G. Hüffer, *Vorstudien zu einer Darstellung des Lebens und Wirkens des heiligen Bernard von Clairvaux* (Münster, 1886)—direct precedents to Grießer's work; see Grießer, 12–13.

[115] MS Innsbruck, Universitätsbibliothek 25. See Hümpfner, "Der bisher in den gedruckten Ausgaben vermisste Teil des Exordium Magnum"; the manuscript was used by Grießer in his critical edition; see Grießer, 13–14, for his comments.

Hümpfner's work to completion. After thirty years of archival work and manuscript studies, Grießer published what is now the standard critical edition of the *Exordium magnum*.[116] He not only produced the first complete printed text but also, because he had collated ten manuscripts and consulted over two dozen others, enabled scholars for the first time to consider the transmission of the text.[117] Grießer divided the manuscripts into four families that he separated into two groups: complete manuscripts (those that contained all of book 1) and shortened manuscripts (which have a lacuna between EM 1.14 and 1.20). He also determined that still other sections of Conrad's original had fallen out of the tradition altogether. The prologue, rendered in 106 lines of verse, which appears in only two complete manuscripts, had never been included in printed editions and seems to have been unknown before the twentieth century.

The more widespread tradition of shortened manuscripts suggests that many, indeed most, copies of the *Exordium magnum* failed to contain Conrad's disparaging comments about the Order's founder abbot, Robert of Molesme (EM 1.15-16). Grießer doubted that this was intentional and attributed it to the loss of one or more folios. Whatever the cause, the effect of the shortened manuscripts was to reinforce the centrality of Bernard and Clairvaux in early Cistercian history. The reader of a shortened manuscript learned virtually nothing about the original founders of Cîteaux, and Bernard appeared by implication the sole reason for the Order's success.[118]

Of Grießer's complete manuscripts, the most enticing is the *Codex Eberbachensis.* The codex's story is remarkable, and, although it was unavailable to him, Grießer considered it the exemplar for all four manuscript families. It has disappeared twice, only to resurface rather uneventfully both times. Its provenance is Conrad's last abbey, Eberbach: it was marked *liber sancte Marie in Eberbach* and was still in

---

[116] Grießer's earlier manuscript studies contain some material not incorporated into his edition and are therefore useful in their own right: "Probleme der Textüberlieferung des Exordium Magnum," *Cistercienser-Chronik* 52 (1940): 161–68, 177–87; and 53 (1941): 1–10; 84–85.

[117] The transmission and use of the *Exordium magnum* in the thirteenth through seventeenth centuries has yet to be studied.

[118] McGuire, "Structure and Consciousness," 43–44. Compare Grießer, 10–11.

the monastery's library when Hermann Bär prepared his history in the mid-eighteenth century. For reasons unknown, the manuscript was not identified when the monastery was dissolved in 1803, but it surfaced in the hands of a bookseller in Mainz. Fortunately for Grießer, a few eighteenth- and nineteenth-century scholars had left reasonably good descriptions of the manuscript, which had last been consulted around 1880 by G. Hüffer in the Verein für Altertumskunde und Geschichtsforschung in Wiesbaden.[119] Hüffer considered the *Codex Eberbachensis* the autograph copy and described large strike-overs in the manuscript that he thought were the author's direct emendation of the text.[120] Grießer considered this doubtful but suspected that the *Codex* was not far removed from the original. The Eberbach manuscript was again lost sometime between 1905 and 1911, when the contents of the Verein's library were turned over to the Landesbibliothek and Staatsarchiv in Wiesbaden.

In 2001, Ferruccio Gastaldelli located the *Codex Eberbachensis* at the Hessische Landesbibliothek,[121] which had purchased it in 1965 from an antiquarian book dealer. Gastaldelli, working from microfilm of the manuscript, describes some of the larger emendations, calls for further manuscript studies, and provisionally considers it "probable" that the manuscript is indeed in Conrad's hand.[122] While Gastaldelli's work is something of an indictment of the *Corpus Christianorum* reprint of Grießer, it shows how solid was Grießer's research.[123] Additional study of the manuscripts may yet reveal more about how the EM was compiled.

Paul Savage

---

[119] Grießer, 11, lists the accounts left by Bär-Rossel, Otto, Hüffer, et al.

[120] G. Hüffer, "Vorstudien zu einer Darstellung des Lebens," cited in Grießer, 12.

[121] Wiesbaden, Hessische Landesbibliothek, MS 381.

[122] Ferruccio Gastaldelli, "A Critical Note on the Edition of the *Exordium Magnum Cisterciense*," 318.

[123] Among the complete manuscripts, Grießer considered two to be the most authoritative: Bodleian Library, Oxford, Cod. Laud. Misc. 238; and the Staatsbibliothek, Munich, Lat. 7992. Gastaldelli's article bears this out, especially in regard to the Bodley codex.

# The Great Beginning of Cîteaux

*Exordium magnum cisterciense*

## Prologue in Verse to the Following Work

W hoever longs to reach eternal life
And hastens in the fruitful contest of the monk to
strive,[1]
Avoiding byways and holding to the true path [RB 73.4]
Should follow in the footprints of the ancient fathers.[2]
This narrow way, trodden with a careful moderation,
Shall yield the joys of the kingdom promised by the grace of Christ.

Yet if you begin rashly to go down a dubious path,
You supply arms to the robbers who steal souls,
And you seem to hold a murderous dagger to your own throat.

Thus the holy Father Benedict rightly exhorts
That a monk do nothing save what the fathers held [RB 7.55].[3]
For what is more apt to destroy the pattern of justice
Than monks who spurn the sacred undertakings of their
predecessors
Only to perish by abandoning themselves unbridled to a wanton
life?

Those who hold these mandates inviolate, therefore,
And worthily exert themselves in the triumphal contests,[4]

---

[1] The spiritual "contest" is an image Conrad uses often; it has some basis in 1
Cor 9:24. Compare EM Prol.; 1.10, 16; 3.4, 19; 4.21, 23, 27; and 5.2.

[2] Bernard of Clairvaux, Sent 3.116 (SBOp 6/2:210; CF 55:389) uses the
phrase "footprints of their predecessors" (*vestigia praecedentium*). In recalling his
first meeting with Bernard, William of Saint Thierry (Vita Bern 7.34) describes
him as walking along *antiquorum Ægytiorum monachorum patrum nostrorum antiquas
semitas, et in eis nostri temporis hominum recentia vestigia.*

[3] Benedict of Nursia, author of the Rule followed by Western monks, lived in
sixth-century Italy and is primarily associated with the monasteries of Subiaco
and Monte Cassino. For a complete discussion of his life and Rule, see RB *1980*,
65–112.

[4] Here "contests" takes on a military tone, common in monastic texts. Such
militaristic imagery has roots in Job 7:1; 2 Cor 10:4; 2 Tim 2:3; RB Prol.; RB
2.20; and other texts. It is also present in Bernard of Clairvaux, Apo 22 (SBOp
3:99; CF 1:58), Ep 113 (SBOp 7:10–11; James, Ep 1, pp. 8–10), Ep 254.1 (SBOp

Shine before God, wreathed with a bright garland,
Doubly pleasing because they lay claim to heaven for themselves,
And give to succeeding generations a model for living well
    [RB 73.5-6].
Conversely, those who foolishly burn with love for the world,
Susceptible to faults, rejecting noble acts of virtue,
Dull in pious work, and shrewd only for their own advantage—
Them the fearsome ruthlessness of death snatches away.

And so a well-deserved confusion ravages their seared souls.
For by striving after the fleeting pleasures of the body,
They forthwith descend to the wretched depths of the inferno.
While they were living ill, they left behind foul footprints,
And obstruct for those who follow them the pathway of austerity.

Indeed though a murky plague of wickedness oft obscures
The lofty paths of justice, yet Christ again
To those he deems his friends [John 15:14-15] points out the
    direct path.
This the reasoning of the present time proves to you.
Therefore, attend with acute perception, why we set forth this
    discourse.

While—as you will read—a wantonness has so corrupted them,
Confusing what was law, what custom, what uprightness,
That their splendor had scarce survived;
And try though you may, you scarce find among the many
One who once having become a monk perseveres in being one.

E'en so, the fostering goodness of God,
Having taken pity on the ruination of mankind,
Aims to level for his own the way of dutiful love.

---

8:156–57; James, Ep 329.1, p. 408–9), and Miss 4.10 (SBOp 4:55–56; CF 18:56).
In Conrad, see especially EM 4.30; but also EM 3.11; 4.4; and index entries for
"arms," "contest," "battle," "soldier." Martha Newman (*Boundaries of Charity*, 19–41)
argues that the early Cistercians added "aggressive and militaristic connotations
to the idea of caritas" (19).

Hence, the Cistercian Order shines brightly for you, fulfilling your
   desires;
You see it gleam by spreading its light in the darkness,
That through it Christ, the most high, may gain many thousands
   of souls,
And the devil's cunning be annihilated.

For while he torments and inordinately taunts
All worshipers of Christ
He assaults most of all those professed in the Cistercian Order.
He yearns to entrap those whom the grace of Christ defends,[5]
For he sees them bewailing his own tyrannical law.
He gnashes his teeth,
And racked with impatience, he weaves a furtive net;
But he will gain nothing,
Nor will he defeat the fear-inspiring host.

While Mother Church will always be splendid beyond measure
With various states of life, you should not refuse to be in the first
   rank.
These the safeguards of their way of life commend;
Those who are defended by a large company are more fruitful.

Within this order the Cistercian brothers stand out,
Abased by holy labor and crowned by dutiful penance.
Here, here—if you are wise—you will seek the holy footprints
Of monastic life, for here is the surest hope of salvation
And here the undefiled way [Ps 17:31] which leads on high.

And now, pay heed and carefully examine
The text of this volume,
By which I shall plainly and with compelling reasoning disclose
The origin of this celebrated way of life,
Which to the joys of heaven gives birth
And on earth prepares the seeds of salvation.

---

[5] The "grace of Christ" is a Pauline phrase: see Rom 1:7; 16:20, 24; 1 Cor
16:23; 2 Cor 8:9; 2 Cor 13:13; Gal 1:6; 6:18.

Here you are duly taught how the desert of Cîteaux,
Till then long sterile, produced sublime flowers.[6]
Its honey-laden fruit, sent out into the regions of the world,
Fed the people and revived the dying,
That they might grasp the heavenly life they well deserved.

These pages will teach you that the perfect mother has produced
A perfect offspring who has fulfilled her hopes,
For the renowned house of Cîteaux brought forth a noble scion,
And produced from the womb of its dutiful love the Clear Valley,
Twice, yea thrice, blessed, a true sun for the world.[7]
The most illustrious of abbots by his merits made this valley clear,
A succor for the wretched, salvation for sinners.

Here are described the venerable deeds of the fathers
Who, as we shall show, governed each of these houses,
Both of whom by their actions showing that they bore the marks
    of Christ [Gal 6:17],
And that their works were in harmony with their words.

Reading this then gives witness
To the exertions of the senior monks of Clairvaux;
When read and reread it is profitable to those
Against whom the temptations of the flesh have not prevailed.

Here is the mystic garden where the Bridegroom summons the
    bride [Song 5:1].
Here one breathes in the perfume of sundry virtues.

---

[6] The "desert" of Cîteaux is a common Cistercian image, well-known from EP 3.2 and 6.5-6. The image of a place once barren also has many precedents; see Isa 54:1; 1 Sam 2:5; Gal 4:27; EC 2.10; and William of Saint Thierry, VP 1.3.18 (PL 185:237).

[7] "Clear valley" (*clara vallis*) is a wordplay on the Latin for Clairvaux (*Claraevallis*), which Conrad continues for eighteen lines. He concludes with a final reference to the valley made fertile (*vallis optima*) by Clairvaux, which is itself a reference to Wis 5:1. See also William of Saint Thierry, Vita Bern 1.7.35 (PL 185:247–48), trans. Pauline Matarasso, *The Cistercian World* (London, New York: Penguin Books, 1993), 31, who uses the same wordplay: "Entering the clear valley from over the ridge." Additional instances occur in EM 4.6; 4.28; 4.35; 6.2; and 6.4.

Here new fruits give off the aroma of holy zeal.
Thence gleam the roses of patience, the lilies of chastity shine,[8]
The purple of the violets give off a sweet gentleness,[9]
And the whole nursery bed of the heavenly Father flourishes,
Infused from above, sprouted by this fertile Valley
Which makes men blessed by the merits of their virtues.

May their lifestyle be to you, I pray, a living lesson;
May you amend your wicked habits according to this standard,
That, having redirected your attachments, you may deserve
To be joined among the empurpled throngs beyond the stars.[10]

In that place is true salvation, youth without death,
Unquenchable light [Sir 24:6], the soothing song of the heart,
The sweet love of Christ, giving joy with everlasting peace.
There true life will destroy all that is sad.
Whoever now wishes to direct his attention to these writings
Must therefore prove by his life and conduct that they will be
    grace-giving to him,
And that what he admires in the fathers he is himself following.

If, on the other hand, you are lazy and lethargic, sluggishly snoring,
Aspiring with a withered heart only to idleness;
If sacred and fervent studies are a burden to you—
May this little book fly far from your hands.

---

[8] Bernard of Clairvaux, SC 71.14 (SBOp 2:223–24; CF 40:61–62).

[9] Bernard of Clairvaux, Sent 2.147 and 3.122 (SBOp 6/2:52, 230; CF 55:171, 421–22).

[10] Literally, "purple throngs," alluding to those with robes washed in the blood of the lamb; see Rev 7:14; 18:12-16.

## In the name of our Lord Jesus Christ[1]

Here begins the narrative of the origins of the Cistercian Order. It tells how our fathers left the monastery of Molesme in order to restore the purity of the Order according to the meaning of the Rule of Saint Benedict, and how they founded the fruitful church at Cîteaux, which is the mother of us all [EP 3.1; 15.3]. From this, as from a most pure fountain, flow the streams of our Order's many churches. This also describes some of the venerable persons, outstanding in their religious observance, who have given luster to Cîteaux and Clairvaux.

---

[1] Col 3:17.

# Book One

## The Rise
## of the Monastic Order
## and the First Cistercians

## CHAPTER ONE

*How the Lord Jesus Gave the Pattern*
*of Perfect Penance in His Teaching*

The Eternal God, Son of the Eternal God, our Lord Jesus Christ, Creator of all things,[1] Redeemer of all the faithful, while in the days of his humiliation he wrought his salvation in the midst of the earth, preached to the world the saving way of perfect penance, saying, "Do penance, for the kingdom of heaven is at hand" [Matt 3:2; 4:17; Mark 1:15]. Give thanks to the inestimable mercy of God, who with a lenient gaze looked upon the children of Adam, made wretched by the strictness of the law—which mercilessly demanded an eye for an eye and a tooth for a tooth [Matt 5:38]—and all sorts of punishments for each shortcoming. By the incarnation of his Word, he tempered this law, saying, "Do penance." And lest frail human beings should take fright at this word "penance," which seems to mean punishment, he took care to temper the severity of its meaning by a word of consolation, a word worthy of full acceptance, adding, "for the kingdom of heaven is at hand." For who, knowing health, be he sickly or delicate, will not patiently, indeed joyfully, bear the weight of momentary punishment in the present, not only to avoid an eternity of punishment in the future, but to be made a partaker of the kingdom of heaven without end? Surely John, the blessed baptizer and precursor of the Lord, preached this repentance when in his office as precursor he urged people to bring forth fruit worthy of repentance [Luke 3:8]; so how much more ought we to seek the model of perfect penance that will help us bring forth this worthy fruit.

Where may we more properly seek this model than in the words and actions of the Teacher of all teachers, our Lord Jesus Christ

---

[1] This line occurs in the Ambrosian hymn *Deus, creator omnium*, sung at Vespers. See *Le Grande Exorde*, 5n2.

himself?[2] For when a certain man who had many possessions asked the Lord what he should do to obtain eternal life, the Lord replied that he should obey the commandments. And once he said that he had observed all of them from his youth, the Lord then added, "One thing you still lack: if you would be perfect, go sell all that you have, distribute it to the poor, come and follow me; you will have treasure in heaven" [Matt 19:21; Luke 18:22]. Clearly, this man was used to offering, not himself, but his goods—and then not all of those but a part, and a middling part: tithes, firstfruits, and other offerings of the law. And he had thought that this was a great thing. Hearing the word of thoroughgoing righteousness, he drew back and, turning his heart back to earth, he went away sorrowful. No doubt, as Truth testifies, those who dearly love the riches they have can be saved only with difficulty. How differently blessed Peter was affected; how drenched with the abundant dew of heavenly grace was he. Peter was cool to the heat of worldly desire, when—with as much humility as faith—he spoke to the Lord about himself and his fellow disciples, saying, "Look, we have left everything and followed you" [Matt 19:27]. Here, plainly, we have found the model of perfect penance that the Savior commended to those seeking advice about salvation, and that also drew disciples to follow him, although we shall read that some lived a chaste and humble life among all the riches and glory of the world.[3] But the privileges of the few do not constitute the norm, and of those who attempted to pursue heavenly perfection in a surer way, many obeyed the call of the Lord in the gospel: "If any of you does not renounce all that he possesses, he cannot be my disciple" [Luke 14:33].

---

[2] On the twelfth-century background of the word *magister*, see M. T. Clanchy, *Abelard: A Medieval Life* (Oxford / Cambridge, MA: Blackwell, 1997), 65–67. See RB Prol. 46.

[3] See, for example, EM 2.31, on Henry, abbot of Clairvaux, who became cardinal-bishop of Alba.

CHAPTER TWO

## How the Tradition of Common Life Began in the Primitive Church and How the First Institutions of Monastic Observance Continued It [4]

Surely it was fitting that the Wisdom of the most high Father, who had come to establish the pattern of perfect righteousness, should at once impress this strongly on the tiny flock [Luke 12:32] of the newborn Church. All those who were stirred by this example decided to follow the hard and narrow path [5] formed by the teaching of such great majesty. Strengthened by the example of such fathers, they ran the way of the Lord with hearts expanded [RB Prol. 49]; as the psalmist says, "According to the words of your lips, O Lord, I have kept to the hard paths" [Ps 16:4], knowing that you will repay them a hundredfold as you have promised and, moreover, add eternal life [Matt 19:29]. After the Lord had suffered in the flesh, after he had risen from the dead and ascended into heaven, he sent the Holy Spirit to his disciples as he had promised. As the crowd of believers was multiplying, the splendor of the same life in the Spirit which we have called perfect penance began to shine ever more brightly, as Luke bears witness: "the multitude of believers were of one heart and mind, nor did any of them say anything was his own, but they had all things in common" [Acts 4:32-35]. Those who had lands and houses sold what they possessed and laid the price at the

---

[4] The phrase "primitive Church," *ecclesia primitiva*, has roots in Heb 12:23 and the counsels of perfection; see Matt 19:12, 21; 1 Cor 7:38-40; Acts 21:23. On its medieval context, see Glenn W. Olsen, "John of Salisbury's Humanism," *Gli Umanesimi Medievali*, ed. Claudio Leonardi (Florence: SISMEL Edizioni del Galluzzo, 1998), 447–68; and Glenn W. Olsen, "The *Ecclesia Primitiua* in John Cassian, the Ps. Jerome Commentary on Mark, and Bede," in *Biblical Studies in the Early Middle Ages*, ed. Claudio Leonardi and Giovanni Orlandi, Millennio medievale, 52 (Florence: SISMEL Edizioni del Galluzzo, 2005), 5–27.

[5] That the monk remain on the "straight and narrow way" is often mentioned in the EM: see Prol., 1.12, 22; 2.1, 23; 4.20, 23, 31; 6.10. Precedents for the phrase include Matt 7:13-14; RB Prol. 48; RB 5.11; and EP 6.

apostles' feet. Luke bears witness to the respect that their way of life generated in the hearts of unbelievers when he says, "Of the rest no one dared join himself to them, though the people highly esteemed them" [Acts 5:13]. Not only in Jerusalem was this school of the primitive Church instituted in this heavenly discipline, but also in Antioch under the teachers Paul and Barnabas it flourished most gloriously, and there the disciples were first called Christians [Acts 11:26]. That most eloquent Jew, Philo, in his book that he titled *On the Contemplative Life*, had many things to say about their great zeal for the Lord.[6]

That the name, the way of life, and the customs of monks and cenobites took their beginning from these things is evident. Moreover, with the sowing of the word of God through every region [Matt 13:23; Acts 13:49], the sound of the apostles' preaching went out into all lands [Ps 18:5]. It was inevitable that the ark of holy Church, having by the strict observance of its stronger members achieved to within one cubit [Gen 6:15][7] the reputation of being the most perfect religion, now needed to expand its heart in charity to the weaker and more fainthearted and carry the less fit to the heights of perfection. For the mercy of Almighty God most graciously willed to save from the defilement of their infirmities not only human beings but also the very beasts of burden, that is, those who by their weakness are polluted by the dust of their earthly goods. Now this was a noble republic[8] that the Lord Jesus Christ instituted and the Holy Spirit strengthened; in it no one possessed anything, yet no one among them had need [Acts 4:34].

---

[6] Philo of Alexandria was a philosopher and theologian associated with the Jewish contemplative movement of the first century after Christ; see Jerome's *Liber de viris illustribus* 11 (PL 23:625–30); and *Philo of Alexandria: The Contemplative Life, The Giants, and Selections*, trans. David Winston, Classics of Western Spirituality (New York: Paulist Press, 1987).

[7] For Origen's comments on the single cubit, see *In Genesim homilia* 2 (PG 12:162–63), trans. Ronald E. Heine, *Homilies on Genesis and Exodus*, Fathers of the Church 71 (Washington, DC: Catholic University America Press, 1982), 72–74.

[8] Conrad's use of "republic," *res publica*, mirrors Cluniac language. In his letters, Peter the Venerable referred to Cluny and its dependencies as an *ordo*, *congregatio*, and *res publica*. See Giles Constable, *The Reformation of the Twelfth Century* (Cambridge: Cambridge University Press, 1996), 175n30.

Private goods started to be given away, and Christians began to use their property freely, not so that they might be given preference in the heavenly country, but that by distributing their temporal goods appropriately, they might more easily get to heaven.

## CHAPTER THREE

*How the Monastic Order Was Established by Blessed Antony and Other Holy Fathers and How It Shone in Its Excellence*

Although Mother Church, coming down to the level of the many who were imperfect, slackened the reins to allow a more lenient way of life, nevertheless, from the very birth of the Church to our own times there has been no lack of those with inner strength who are fervently ablaze with divine love. Rejecting the enticements of a more remiss life, they held with devout and unflagging purpose to the integrity of the common life, which alone is the stable foundation of the perfect penance preached by the Lord Jesus, and they passed it on to their successors through many rules and examples of holy living. Among these the first and foremost were Antony, Pachomius, and Basil.[9] Of these the first was Antony who showed

---

[9] Antony the Great (251–356), hermit and early Egyptian monk. See *Athanasius of Alexandria: The Life of Antony; The Coptic Life and the Greek Life*, trans. Tim Vivian and Apostolos N. Athanassakis, CS 202 (Kalamazoo, MI: Cistercian Publications, 2003). Pachomius (*c.* 292–346) is often considered the founder of cenobitic monasticism in Egypt; see Armand Veilleux, trans., *Pachomian Koinonia*, 3 vols., CS 45, 46, 47 (Kalamazoo, MI: Cistercian Publications, 1980, 1981). Volume 1 contains the lives of Pachomius. For the general context of Pachomius, see Philip Rousseau, *Pachomius: The Making of a Community in Fourth-Century Egypt* (Los Angeles: University of California Press, 1985). Basil (*c.* 329–79) was bishop of Caesarea and composed ascetic writings which form the basis of Eastern monastic discipline; see PG 29–32; and translation by Monica Wagner, *The Ascetical Works of Saint Basil*, Fathers of the Church (Washington, DC: CUAP, 1950), 223–337. Basil's Rule is also mentioned by Benedict, RB 73.5-7. For background on Basil, see Augustine Holmes, *A Life Pleasing to God: The Spirituality of the Rules of St. Basil*, CS 189 (Kalamazoo, MI: Cistercian Publications, 2000).

by his utterly perfect way of life that the law of charity had been written in his heart, not with ink and letters, but by the Spirit of the living God [2 Cor 3:3]. He left behind perfect disciples—Macarius, Paphnutius, Pambo, Isidore, and many more.[10] These fathers formed monasteries throughout Egypt and the Thebaid; they led innumerable crowds of monks away from the world and into the ways of perfect penance and triumphed most gloriously over the prince of hell and all his train. Pachomius, made eminent by apostolic grace, wrote down a rule for monks that an angel had dictated,[11] and in his communities he brought together an infinite multitude of living stones [1 Pet 2:25] to be polished for rebuilding the walls of the heavenly Jerusalem. Blessed Basil, the bishop of Caesarea and an outstanding teacher of the holy Church, also wrote a rule for monks, which, as our blessed Father Benedict testifies [RB 73.5], is the most direct guide for human life and by which we may come without stumbling to the heavenly homeland. As a result of the

---

[10] Macarius the Egyptian (*c.* 300–390) was a camel driver trading in Nitria. Ordained priest, he lived as an anchorite in a village before going to Scetis and settling there. He is considered as one of the greatest of the hermits; see *The Sayings of the Desert Fathers*, trans. Benedicta Ward, CS 59 (Kalamazoo, MI / Oxford: Cistercian Publications, 1975), 124–38. Paphnutius, a well-known hermit in Egypt and a disciple of Macarius, became the second spiritual leader of the monks of Scetis. He was specially known for his love of solitude; see Ward, *Sayings*, 202–4. Pambo (*c.* 303–74) was an illiterate Egyptian peasant. He joined Amoun (considered, with Antony and Pachomius, the third founder of Egyptian monasticism) in Nitria, was taught the Scriptures, and became both a priest and a monk. Jerome considered him one of the masters of the desert. See Ward, *Sayings*, 195–98. Regarding Isidore, there were at least three hermits of this name in Egypt, but this is probably Isidore the Priest, another companion of Macarius in Scetis; see Ward, *Sayings*, 96–98. For more details on the desert monks, see Metropolitan Anthony and Benedicta Ward, Ward, *Sayings*, xiii–xxxi. See also *The Lives of the Desert Fathers, The* Historia monachorum in Ægypto, trans. Norman Russell, CS 34 (Kalamazoo, MI: Cistercian Publications, 1981). It seems probable that Conrad knew the Desert Fathers through a Latin translation of the Greek apophthegmata, the *Vitae Patrum*, translated into English by Benedicta Ward, *The Desert Fathers: Sayings of the Early Christian Monks* (London: Penguin Books, 2003).

[11] See the account in Veilleux, *Pachomian Koinonia*, vol. 2: *Pachomian Chronicles and Rules*, 125. Also, Bede, *De temporum ratione* 43.416; trans. Faith Wallis, *Bede: The Reckoning of Time* (Liverpool: Liverpool University Press, 1999), 118, which includes the story of angelic dictation to Pachomius.

teachings of the venerable fathers and their examples of virtue, then, the entire Eastern Church flourished at that time. This was proven again recently by Anselm of blessed memory, first bishop of Havelberg, then archbishop of Ravenna, in the dispute he had with the Greeks about the evils of their schism and that he wrote up in an elegant style.[12] He tells how Lothar, the most Christian emperor of the Romans, sent him as an ambassador to Calojohn, emperor of the city of Constantinople.[13] He examined discreetly the statutes of various religious houses. In the monastery of Pantocraton—that is, "the Almighty"—he said he saw nearly seven hundred monks doing battle for the Lord under the rule of the blessed Antony. In another monastery, which is called Philoanthropon—that is, "Lover of Man"—he said he saw about five hundred monks serving the Lord under the rule of holy Pachomius. He also saw many monasteries that bore the sweet yoke of the Lord [Matt 11:30] under the rule of blessed Basil.[14]

[12] Anselm of Havelberg, a Premonstratensian, was bishop of Havelberg from 1129 to 1155 and of Ravenna from 1155 until his death in 1158. In 1135–36 he was legate to Constantinople on Lothar III's behalf. It is not known whether Conrad used Anselm's *Dialogues* 1.10 (PL 188:1156C-D; trans. Ambrose Criste and Carol Neel, *Anselm of Havelberg, Anticimenon: On the Unity of the Faith and the Controversies with the Greeks*, CS 232, Praemonstratensian Texts and Studies 1 [Collegeville, MN: Cistercian Publications, 2010]) or had heard an oral report of them.

[13] Calojohn (sometimes Caloyan) is a name given to the Byzantine emperor John II Comnenus (r. 1118–43). Conrad uses the word *apocrisarius* (ambassador), a Byzantine diplomatic title which by the fifth century referred specifically to representatives of the papacy to the imperial court at Constantinople. Anselm used the term in his account of the mission; see Jay T. Lees, *Anselm of Havelberg* (New York: Brill, 1998), 43; see F. X. Murphy, "Apocrisarius," *New Catholic Encyclopedia*, 2nd ed., 15 vols. (Washington, DC: Catholic University of America Press, 2003), 1:548.

[14] These large numbers of monks are clearly not accurate; Lees, *Anselm of Havelberg* (n. 12), 213n156, places the figures at no more than eighty monks in Pantocraton and forty in Philanthropon. Pantocraton was established by John II Comnenus, while Philanthropon was founded at the beginning of the twelfth century by Irene Ducas, wife of Alexis I Comnenus (r. 1081–1118).

CHAPTER FOUR

*Of the Institution and Importance of the Rule of Our Holy*
*Father Benedict;*
*How It Flourished by the Grace of God*
*and Still Flourishes Today*

Our Lord Jesus Christ, who enlightened the East by the presence of his most sacred humanity, sent into the West in his stead those in his Church whom he held more worthy and sublime, to wit, the most blessed princes of the apostles, Peter and Paul. Thereby the people of the West learned the precious mystery of faith—the faith that Peter received not from flesh and blood but by the inspiration of the most high Father, and also the very gospel that Paul learned not from men or through men but by the revelation of Jesus Christ [Gal 1:12]. Instructed by the authoritative teaching of the Holy Spirit, the people of the West came together with the peoples of the East in the fullness of the same faith, and so from all of them was created the one bride of the Lord Christ, having no spot or wrinkle [Eph 5:27]. That same grace which in the East brought together the aforementioned holy fathers to establish and maintain the discipline of the monastic way of life, by his merciful condescension singled out in the West a man of no less merit, that is, our most holy Father Benedict. Filled not only with the spirit of Antony, Pachomius, and Basil but also—as the blessed Pope Gregory bears witness[15]—with the spirit of all the just [Heb 12:23], and like the purest and brightest star, by the privilege of his outstanding holiness, by the extraordinary purity of his way of life, and by the inestimable glory of his signs and miracles, he so shone from East to West that whatever diverse spiritual gifts the East rejoiced in having divided among different fathers, the West could glory, not without cause, in having brought together by the Spirit of all the just in its one very holy Father Benedict. He, our most reverend father, wrote a rule

---

[15] Dial 2.8; SCh 260:161; PL 66:150B; BHL 1102

for monks, which by the daily exercise of virtue he had learned not through men but by the anointing of him who teaches men knowledge. In it that marvelous craftsman, the Holy Spirit, joined the greatest perfection with the most measured discernment in a connection so subtle that any close observer of the Rule discovers in it the means of making progress, and equally any fainthearted person finds there a remedy for his weakness.[16] If someone is tenacious, as it were, in righteousness, if someone is ablaze for holy religion, he may, if he is led by grace, ascend the twelve degrees of humility that are set out in the Rule [RB 7]. And if by increasing merit he progresses as far as the sixth and seventh degrees, that is, to the last of the first six, and the first of the second six—for six is a number signifying perfection, and it is doubled in these degrees of humility—he shows he has learned the love of God and of neighbor, which is the sum of perfection through the Rule.[17] If he then thinks about it without pretense, if he diligently clips all the corners of known weakness, if—I say—he then measures his strength and acknowledges his defects with unremitting mourning, will he not exclaim with the Apostle, when a man thinks himself "to be something whereas he is nothing, he then deceives himself" [Gal 6:3]? On the other hand, if someone is delicate and weak, let him observe the Rule—that is the fasts, vigils, manual labor, and the other obligations with well-moderated discernment—will he not find in it a remedy suited to the weakness of his condition? Now this same legislator says in the last chapter of the Rule that it does not contain the whole observance of righteousness, and he calls it "a little rule for beginners" and directs those who want to attain the height of perfection to the teachings and rules of the ancient fathers. He did this, as blessed Bernard testifies,[18] out of humility, lest

---

[16] Discernment—*discretio*—is often mentioned by Conrad (EM 1.9, 29, 32; 2.24, 28, 30, 32; 5.3, 5, 12, 13; 6.2, 9); see RB 64.17-19. *Discretio* emerged from the tradition of Cassian and Egypt. Bernard called discernment "the mother of virtues" in Div 91.4 (SBOp 6/1:343); SC 49.5 (SBOp 2:75–76; CF 31:25–26); and Csi 4.IV.12 (SBOp 3:457; CF 37:123–24). See also Sent 3.29 (SBOp 6/2:84; CF 55:216).

[17] Bernard of Clairvaux, Hum 2.3 (SBOp 3:18; CF 13:31–32).

[18] See Bernard of Clairvaux, Mor 33–34 (SBOp 7:127–29; CF 67:77–79).

in outlining his Rule he seem arrogantly to equate his Rule with those of the ancient fathers, and in this way he took care to guard the humility of his own conscience. Blessed Gregory, moreover, a man apostolic in his life no less than office, commended the Rule in his *Dialogues* as being especially outstanding for its discretion.[19] And by his authority Gregory implicitly urged monks to leave the customs of other, perhaps less discerning, institutions so that with their whole hearts they might accept the preeminently discerning Rule of our Father Benedict, beloved of God, and completely conform the ordering of their life to his pattern. At a council that was later convened in Gaul, a decree was sanctioned by all, by which the monks in the provinces of Gaul and Germany should cease following other rules and receive the Rule of the aforesaid Father in all their monasteries and observe the pattern he prescribed in their entire way of living.[20] The pattern of the holy Rule corrected many monasteries throughout Italy as well, and many new ones were built by the venerable father, and in them all a multitude of monks served the Lord in the spirit of humility [Dan 3:39] as they, like true Israelites [John 1:47], produced fruits worthy of repentance.

CHAPTER FIVE

*How Blessed Benedict Received a Request from the Bishop of Le Mans and So Sent His Holy Disciple Maur to Found Monasteries in the Regions of Gaul*

Not only Italy but also the three parts of Gaul, having caught scent of the good odor of this holy religious life, yearned with

---

[19] Dial 2:36; SCh 260:242; PL 66:200.

[20] This refers to the so-called Monastic Capitulary of the Synod of Aachen, 817, ed. J. Semmler, *Corpus Consuetudinum Monasticarum*, vol. 1: *Initia Consuetudinis Benedictinae* (Siegburg: Francis Schmitt, 1963), 423–582. For context, see Mayke de Jong, "Carolingian Monasticism" *New Cambridge Medieval History*, vol. 2: c. 700–c. 900 (Cambridge: Cambridge University Press, 1995), 629–34.

praiseworthy desire to accept the light and gentle yoke of the Lord [Matt 11:3], that is, the statutes of the holy Rule. So it came about that an eminent man, the bishop of the city of Le Mans, sent his legates to the venerable Father Benedict; they were Flodegard, the archdeacon, and Harderad, his vicar.[21] They asked, with very deferential insistence, whether he would be willing to send some brothers from his monastery to establish communities in the regions of Gaul according to the statutes of the Rule of the holy Father. Then blessed Benedict, summoning his disciple Maur, whom he had brought up from infancy in the fear of the Lord, sent him with some other observant brothers to the region of Gaul.[22] There he soon built a monastery that was equally famous for its religious observance and its wealth. Accomplished in signs and adorned with virtues, this father of a great multitude of monks rested in peace. It is said that in this monastery there is reserved even to this day the portion of bread and the measure of wine[23] that holy Benedict had sent with them, kept in memory of earlier days and out of reverence for so great a father. From there, through all the regions of Gaul the monastic observance according to the Rule of Saint Benedict increased and multiplied into an army of Christ the true king [RB Prol. 3]. Many flocked to the life, inspired by divine grace, and by undertaking the exertions of this holy discipline they brought forth from the ground of the heart the fruit of good works with patience [Luke 8:15]. When in later times the barbarians overran

---

[21] Odo of Glanfeuil, *Life of Saint Maurus*, 3.16; *Acta SS* Jan. 2.334–35; trans. John B. Wickstrom, *The Life and Miracles of Saint Maurus: Disciple of Benedict; Apostle to France*, CS 223 (Collegeville, MN: Cistercian Publications, 2008), 59–99, here 72. For background on Odo and the Abbey of Glanfeuil, see Herbert Bloch, *Monte Cassino in the Middle Ages*, 3 vols. (Cambridge, MA: Harvard University Press, 1986), 2:969–77; and Wickstrom, *The Life and Miracles*, 11–55.

[22] The tradition that Maur brought Benedictine life to France and founded Glanfeuil (Saint-Maur-sur-Loire) was based on the *Vita sancti Mauri*; purportedly written by Faustus of Monte Cassino, but more generally attributed to Abbot Odo of Glanfeuil (ninth century); see Herbert Bloch, "The Schism of Anacletus II and the Glanfeuil Forgeries of Peter the Deacon of Monte Cassino," *Traditio* 8 (1952): 182–90; John B. Wickstrom, "Cluny, Cîteaux, and Blessed Maurus of Glanfeuil," *Revue Bénédictine* 113 (2003): 124–34; and Wickstrom, *The Life and Miracles*, 11–55.

[23] RB 39.4 and 40.3: Benedict's allotment of bread and wine.

Gaul—after the Lord resolved to chastise his people for their sins by pagan invasions—many communities of saints were consumed by fire or razed to the ground in some other way.[24] Those that remained were reduced to such negligence and desolation that scarcely a trace of the ancient religious observance could be found in any monastery.[25] Yet, thanks be to our Lord Jesus Christ, although he may allow his Church to be chastised by various tribulations when she grows cold in charity and rich in iniquity [Matt 24:12], he does not shut up his bowels of mercy forever [Luke 1:78; Col 3:12; 1 John 3:17]. And he does not abandon the monastic life when human weakness corrupts it but continually hastens at opportune times to restore it through men of virtue.

CHAPTER SIX

*How Blessed Odo, Abbot of Cluny,*
*When the Monastic Order Had Collapsed,*
*by the Grace of God Repaired It Energetically*

Hence, blessed Odo, the outstanding leader of that most noble monastery of Cluny, advanced to such a pinnacle of sanctity that, according to the grace of the Lord which was given him, he restored the completely ruined monastic way of life of his times to the ancient vigor of holy observance.[26] Let us mention briefly a few things about the ruined monasteries of those times. When the venerable father

[24] Grießer (EM, 54n1) believed that the text actually refers to the invasions of the Normans in the ninth century.

[25] For negligence as a theme in the EM, see entries in the index. See also Brian Patrick McGuire, "Structure and Consciousness in the *Exordium Magnum Cisterciense*: The Clairvaux Cistercians after Bernard," *Cahiers de l'Institut du Moyen-âge Grec et Latin* 30 (1979): 33–90. Bernard writes on negligence in Sent 3.98 (SBOp 6/2:160–61; CF 55:319–20); and Div 10.1 (SBOp 6/1:121–24).

[26] Odo of Cluny (d. 942); see *Vita s. Odonis* 1.32 (PL 133:57) and 2.23 (PL 133:73), trans. Gerard Sitwell, *St. Odo of Cluny: Being the Life of St. Odo of Cluny*

Odo had begun in his monasteries to keep firmly to the strictness of regular discipline, as is appropriate, certain other monks were moved to inordinate anger at noticing how some of the brothers were cleaning their sandals and oiling them themselves, performing other servile offices, carefully keeping silence, and, when it was necessary, using signs for words. "You despicable fellows," they said. "What are you doing?[27] What law or what way of life insists on such vile and servile work? Where does Scripture command that hands be used instead of tongues? Surely you convict the Creator of wrongdoing when you refuse the natural use of the tongue and the organ of the voice, and irrationally create an uproar with your hands!" But the blessed man made light of the silly chattering of these disparaging pseudo-monks and warned his brothers by word and by example to learn a profitable lesson from this. If he was called to go anywhere by men in vows he quickly proceeded either to recall the dissolute monastery to stricter order or to make a new foundation.[28]

To show how firmly his disciples held to monastic discipline, we would like to describe one example of their virtue that shows the steadfastness of soul to which we have referred.[29] While some of them were on a journey, in the middle of a dark night at some place or other they were surrounded by robbers and captured with all their goods, dragged away, stripped, treated with scorn, and finally chained together. The robbers were both amazed and indignant because after so much ill treatment they had not been able to extract from them a single solitary word. The monks endured it all in silence, unprovoked by either contempt or scorn, as if they were dumb and speechless, until

---

by John of Salerno and the Life of St. Gerald of Aurillac by St. Odo (New York: Sheed and Ward, 1959), 33 and 66–70.

[27] Regarding Cluniac customs of washing sandals and hands after manual labor, see Peter the Venerable, Statute 28 (PL 189:1034). Regarding the use of sign language, see Robert A. Barakat, *The Cistercian Sign Language: A Study in Non-verbal Communication*, CS 11 (Kalamazoo, MI: Cistercian Publications, 1975); and Scott E. Bruce, "The Origins of the Cistercian Sign Language," *Cîteaux: commentarii cistercienses* 52 (2001): 193–208.

[28] See Bernard of Clairvaux, Ep 254 (SBOp 8:156–60; James, Ep 329, pp. 408–11).

[29] *Vita s. Odonis*, 2.12 (PL 133:67–68; Sitwell, *St. Odo of Cluny*, 54–56).

dawn spread with its rays and it was time for the solemnity of Vigils and Lauds. Then with a praiseworthy discernment they loosed their tongues, which earlier they had restrained with a still more praiseworthy severity out of fear of God and the discipline of their way of life.

Not only in Gaul did Odo repair the state of the holy life but also in Italy. Especially Saint Benedict's community in Francia, where they say his most sacred body rests,[30] Odo ruled at the invitation of the most blessed Father Benedict himself, as is found in the account of his life.[31] One day, as the monks of that place were sitting in the cloister, shamelessly busying themselves with quarrels and gossip, the holy Father Benedict appeared visibly to a certain monk at the door of the monastery and said to him, "Go and tell these brothers how very much they grieve me by their wayward habits, for I have already hastened to bring a man after my own heart [1 Sam 13:14] from Aquitaine to correct those sinners and restore the discipline of the Order in this, my monastery." Astounded, the monk ran swiftly to the brothers, and when they heard what the father had specifically commanded, everyone reacted with consternation and astonishment. They asked themselves with great amazement who the holy father had spoken of, and they speculated, with some trepidation, that it be blessed Odo, which turned out to be the case. When Father Benedict's devoted disciple Odo came to the aforesaid place, he had to suffer great tribulation and scorn from those who liked their pernicious liberty more than the strictness of regular life. But at length, by the grace of God and the aid of holy Father Benedict, he laudably reformed the discipline of life in that monastery.

---

[30] This refers to the monastery of Fleury (Saint-Benoît-sur-Loire). There is continued debate about whether Benedict's relics were at Fleury or Monte Cassino, with one legend maintaining that they were removed to Fleury after the Lombard invasion. See Benedicta Ward, "The Miracles of St. Benedict," in *Benedictus: Studies in Honor of Saint Benedict of Nursia*, ed. E. Rozanne Elder, Studies in Medieval Cistercian History 8 (Kalamazoo, MI: Cistercian Publications, 1981), 1–14; H. E. J. Cowdrey, *The Age of Abbot Desiderius* (Oxford: Clarendon Press, 1983), 14–16n.95; and Kassius Hallinger, "Development of the Cult of Devotion to St. Benedict," *American Benedictine Review* 36 (1985): 193–215.

[31] *Vita S. Odonis*, 3.8 (PL 133:80–81; Sitwell, *St. Odo of Cluny*, 79–80).

Especially beloved of God is Odo's monastery that is called Cluny and that shines even to this day with the greatest nobility, the greatest number of brothers, and the noblest lands, wealth, and glory. But so too was the monastery that Father Odo, with some of his brothers, left for Cluny, and we know from the written tradition how these men, mature and worthy in God, shone in full religious observance from the very beginning. So I am pleased to insert into this little work two joyful and miraculous excerpts, that from these two the judicious reader may be able to add the rest.

## CHAPTER SEVEN

*About the Brother in Whose Hand Crumbs of Bread Were Changed into Precious Pearls*[32]

There was a rule in the monastery that when the meal was finished the brothers sitting at table should carefully collect and eat the crumbs that had fallen from the broken bread [RM 25.1-12], lest anyone be found negligent before God in this matter. As it happened one day, one of the brothers, who was not careless in matters of conscience, was seated with the rest at the table after the meal. He held the crumbs he had collected in the palm of his hand, according to the custom, and enclosed by his fingers while he listened wholeheartedly to the sweetness of the reading. But before he could eat them, all at once, at a sign from the prior, the reader stopped reading [EO 76.42]. Coming to himself, the brother was bewildered and with some apprehension realized the culpability of his negligence. But what could he do? He was allowed neither to throw the crumbs away nor to eat them now, and either way he would run the peril of deceit. So he held them in his clenched hand, thinking that it was not possible to cancel this fault except by the remedy of confession and penance. After grace had been

---

[32] *Vita S. Odonis,* 1.35 (PL 133:58; Sitwell, *St. Odo of Cluny,* 36).

said, he drew the prior aside by making the sign for confession, and falling on his face and acknowledging his negligence, he asked pardon with great simplicity of heart. The prior inquired about his fault, to see if he deserved reproof, and asked him what he had done with the crumbs. He said, "Here they are, my lord, in my hand." The prior ordered that he show them to him. The monk stretched out his arm and opened his hand, and lo, the crumbs in the palm of his hand had become precious pearls. If only the praiseworthy fervor of that brother would come to the attention of those negligent brothers who, if, when the reading is finished, they happen to have in their hand a bit they want to eat or if anything remains in the cup that they want to drink, are not afraid to do so, with no regard for the fear of God, even though the customary of the holy way of life requires that, once the reader begins to say, "But thou, O Lord," no one ought to take any food or drink whatever.[33] But what are we to make of Almighty God willing to do such a glorious miracle when it was least needed and with the least of things? Surely on this account: that he might make known in front of everyone how pleasing to him it is that a community of brothers be so fervent in spirit that out of fear of him they carefully keep what is commanded and take care not only in great things but in those that are least.

## CHAPTER EIGHT

### *About a Brother Who Was Dying and Saw a Multitude in White Robes Coming for Him*[34]

There was a certain brother at Cluny who had reached the end of his life in fervor and devotion to monastic observances. Stricken by

---

[33] At both the Divine Office and at meals, readings customarily ended with the phrase *Tu autem, Domine, miserere nobis* ("But thou, O Lord, have mercy upon us").

[34] The story also appears in Peter the Venerable, *De miraculis* 1.20 (PL 189:887; CCCM 83:58–63).

a sudden infirmity, he was nearing his end. As he was in his death throes he opened his eyes and saw a great multitude of monks coming toward him, all of them clad in white garments, the same sort as those robes that in ecclesiastical usage are called albs, which it is the custom of the professed community of that Order to wear on very solemn occasions. When he saw them he thought they were brothers from chapter, and he could not understand why they were coming to see him dressed like that. He said with a certain indignation to the infirmarian who was looking after him, "Dearest brother, what is this I see? Since when has it been a custom in our community to come to a dying brother in vestments?" The infirmarian replied, saying that the brothers of the community had not come yet, and the monk said, "What are you talking about? Surely you can see the great crowd of brothers all around me, all vested in pure white albs, coming together ahead of time to celebrate my funeral." When the infirmarian heard this but saw nothing of the sort, he understood that his brother in religion was seeing a vision of the spirits of the blessed. A little while after this, that holy soul was set free from the bonds of the flesh and, as we believe, passed happily out of the vale of weeping, from the tents of Kedar,[35] that is, from the blackness of sin to the whiteness of the heavenly city of Jerusalem, which he had deserved to see while living in the flesh.

Indeed, after the most reverend father Odo, the aforesaid monastery of Cluny was governed by abbots outstanding in monastic observance, of whom Majolus and Odilo were preeminent in holiness and dignity before God, and in recent times there was also blessed Hugh.[36] All of them, propagating the Order of Cluny far and wide through all the lands and islands of Europe, handed down to those under them the uncontaminated pathway of the monastic way of life. In that great and observant house, among other very

[35] Kedar, or Cedar, was the second son of Ishmael, whose name was given to a tribe and to the place where they lived. In a figurative sense, Cedar signifies especially nasty enemies; see Gen 25:13; Ps 119:5; and especially Song 1:4.

[36] Majolus (abbot 965–94), Odilo (994–1048), Hugh (1049–1109). See Joan Evans, *Monastic Life at Cluny, 910–1157* (Oxford: Clarendon Press, 1931; reprint, New York: Archon Books, 1968).

salutary exercises of the spiritual life, there prevailed custom replete with devotion: that is, that entire holy brotherhood conscientiously kept vigil for the deliverance of the souls of the faithful departed, offering devout prayers and celebrations of Masses that they might either mitigate the punishment that they deserved or obtain for them entry into rest. Over and above the daily prayers and psalms in that same house, the pious inventiveness of the fathers decreed that in that house at certain times during the year there should be solemn Offices for the faithful departed. The custom of the universal Church in celebrating the feast of All Souls after the feast of All Saints is said to have had its origins at the church of Cluny.[37]

CHAPTER NINE

*How Blessed Hugh, Abbot of Cluny, Cured a Paralytic*

Blessed Hugh, who ruled the monastery of Cluny so well in modern times, we have already mentioned, and we are going to record for its usefulness to readers one of his miracles.[38] Let them rejoice the more because it happened in recent times, and I know it to be true from the testimony of the venerable man William, who was formerly subprior of Saint Geneviève in Paris, and later abbot of the Paraclete, a house in the Order of Saint Victor.[39] There was in the city of Paris a community of canons regular, and in it one of the brothers

[37] The feast of All Souls was instituted during Odilo's abbacy on 2 November 998. See Evans, *Monastic Life at Cluny*, 23; and Jotsaldus, *Vita Odilonis* 2.13 (PL 142:927A–C).

[38] *Vita Hugonis*, by Raynald, 2.10; *Acta SS* Apr 3:660; and PL 159:897.

[39] See Grießer, EM, 58n1. William of Æbelholt was one of the first canons regular at Saint Geneviève in 1148. He became subprior (*De sancto Wilhelmo*, *Acta SS* Apr 1:620F) before being called in 1165 to Denmark, where he was elected founding abbot of Saint Thomas of the Paraclete (Æbelholt) in 1175. From 1193 to1196 he was back in France, in part for the marriage of King Philip to Ingeborg, daughter of the king of Denmark. In 1196 he was held captive in Dijon and Châtillon, but the abbots of Cîteaux and Clairvaux obtained his release and

of the congregation was so crippled by paralysis that he could not get out of bed without someone's help. By chance, the venerable Hugh, abbot of Cluny, went there. At his arrival the brothers got very excited, conceiving no small hope of the sick brother's recovery. They approached the man of God and pleadingly entreated him to be good enough to obtain by his prayers before Almighty God the recovery of the brother daily laboring under this sickness. Now there was in the same monastery half of the cloak of Saint Peter the apostle, which, as is appropriate, was held in great veneration by the brothers. The saint of the Lord could not refuse what the brothers asked out of charity, but with a deeply felt sense of loving-kindness besought the mercy of God to heal the sick brother. Then, as he was celebrating the most holy mysteries, he went up to the altar and reverently picked up the aforementioned piece of Saint Peter's cloak, and coming to the sick man and covering him with the holy garment, he took his hand and began in a moderated voice to chant the antiphon, "The apostle Peter said to the paralytic,"[40] but changing two words in it; that is, he put "he says" for "he said," and for "Aeneas" [Acts 9:34], he said "Robert," because the sick man was named Robert. While holding his hand he sang to him, "Peter the apostle [says] to the paralytic, '[Robert], arise and make your bed.'" At once the brother got up, all weakness fled from his limbs, and all who were there glorified God, who had deigned to make clear the power of his blessed apostle Peter through the merits of the venerable Hugh. The holy abbot was able to obtain so glorious a miracle from the bounty of God because he attributed it not to his own merits but to the special virtue of his patron, blessed Peter the apostle. It was by that revered name that the noble church of Cluny was glorified, and he took care that all the brothers should with utter devotion venerate the saint.

Under such holy fathers, all conspicuous for their religious observance, the Order of Cluny gleamed brilliantly and spread to many the fragrance of life-giving life [2 Cor 2:16]. So it was that

---

he went back to Paris. On his career and personality, see Brian Patrick McGuire, *The Cistercians in Denmark*, especially 92–98.

[40] Antiphon for Nineteenth Sunday after the Octave of Pentecost; PL 78:844.

blessed Henry, the emperor of the Romans, the second of that name,[41] whose memory is held in benediction before God and men [Sir 45:1], hearing the fame of their religious observance, went to Cluny and offered gifts and revenues—as became his imperial magnificence—and commended himself most earnestly to the prayers of the brothers.[42] Now if one could choose, one would be free to exclaim and say to the Lord with the blessed Saint Peter, "Lord, it is good for us to be here" [Matt 17:4]. It was indeed good that all should come to that apex of monastic observance, so that the discipline of the life should be renewed and brought back into line by the holy fathers and should endure, renewed and un-trammeled, that deadly negligence should be cast out and that the fervor of holy religion flourish in every place and every way. But what are we to do when, as the wise man laments, nothing under the sun continues in the same state [Job 14:2; Eccl 2:11]? What are we to do when negligence, so prone to vice, can, alas, be detected even in the conduct of those under a rule? Woe once, twice, and thrice woe to you, negligence, mother of all dissipation, rust of the mind,[43] moth of the heart, corruption of conduct, which puts discipline to flight, subverts religious observance, and weakens virtue. You are an evil beast, a very cunning little fox [Song 2:15]; so perfidiously do you hide your traces that no one feels it when you bite, no one sees your destructiveness, no one becomes aware of you until you have inflicted the gravest damage. How much evil you have done; how much evil you are doing! How much more evil—God forbid—will you not shrink from doing? O detestable negligence: in the eyes of men you seem so slight, so meager, and of so little account that you are not considered worthy of reproof! But someone who underestimates you even a little, little by little will

---

[41] Henry II, Holy Roman Emperor, 973–1024.

[42] See *Vita Henrici* 4.33 (*Acta SS* July 3:730E); and *Vita Meinwerci* (bishop of Paderborn) 4.26 (*Acta SS* Jun 1:512F).

[43] Bernard uses the "rust of the mind" metaphor in Ep 338.1 (SBOp 8:277; James, Ep 249, p. 328); Sent 3.121 (SBOp 6/2:229; CF 55:420); and 5 HM 2 (SBOp 5:69). Similar usages include "moth of holiness, blinker of hearts" (Isa 6:10) in QH 6.4 (SBOp 4:407; CF 25:146), and "gnaw at the heart" in Guerric of Igny, Pent 1.4 (SCh 202:291; CF 32:113).

fall [Sir 19:1]. Who would believe, if experience did not vouch for it, that a droplet, when it first begins falling gently on a stone, will penetrate its hardness? Or who, seeing a new, solid ring on a finger would think it could be worn away by use? But it is true, as they say, that "a drop wears away a stone, and use consumes the ring."[44]

We cannot say this without great sorrow of heart, but little by little the inroads of negligence wear away monastic observance. The wise man says, "The horseleech has two daughters who cry, 'Give me, give me'" [Prov 30:15].[45] O, how many there are who are seen to take to the broad way of the world which leads to death and disregard the straight and narrow way that leads to life![46] And because they refrain so little from embracing this worst of the horseleeches, this detestable prostitute, that is, negligence, from the poisoned seed of the serpent they beget two daughters worse than their mother, voluptuousness and vanity, who without ceasing and without changing their tune cry out to their unhappy mother, "Give me, give me." These are animal men who hold themselves aloof, "having not the spirit" [Jude 19]; they wear the habit of religion, but they are known by their tonsure to be lying to God. They are enclosed in a sheepfold not of the Lord but of themselves [John 10:16], having as their law the indulgence of their desires [RB 1.7-8]; they who should be brought up on delicacies embrace dunghills [Lam 4:5]. Put out in a good pasture, they change from pasture to pasture until they die of hunger. Their food is the root of junipers [Job 30:4] and the husks of swine [Luke 15:16]; their wine is the gall of dragons [Deut 32:33] pressed from the bitter grapes of deceit. They have professed purity of body and sanctity of the spirit yet are not ashamed to be like the wicked and shameless woman who ate in secret and wiped her mouth, saying, "I have done nothing wrong" [Prov 30:20]. They rejoice in these things and tally up pleasures under the briars of dissoluteness [Job 30:7]. And what will these unhappy men do when

---

[44] Ovid, *Ex Ponto* 4.10.5.

[45] See Bernard of Clairvaux, Div 21.2 (SBOp 6/1:169).

[46] Matt 7:13-14; see also EM Prol. (where Conrad simply uses "narrow"), 1.12, 22; 4.20, 23, 30; 6.10. See also Bernard of Clairvaux, Ep 385.1 (SBOp 8:351; James, Ep 423, p. 491).

God begins his scrutiny? Indeed experience shows us these things: that not for no reason did the prophet lament that the gold had become dim, its incomparable color changed, and the stones of the sanctuary been cast down at every street corner [Lam 4:1]. But it is not for us to carp viciously at the faults of others, lest it perhaps be said of us that with our dim eyes we are blind to our own shortcomings and discern too sharply the faults of our friends.[47] Let anyone who will read the blessed Abbot Bernard's *Apologia*, which he wrote to the venerable William, abbot of Saint Thierry.[48] There, one will discover how tarnished the gold had become, how the incomparable color changed [Lam 4:1]. There, I say, one will find how that noble observance of the Order of Cluny—concerning which we have already said a great deal—had degenerated because of foreign and adulterating customs, indeed had been darkened and veiled by desolation from the pristine integrity of its purity and sanctity. Why do we pay attention to the religious observance of the other Order, formerly the most perfect and afterward the worst, which we with our own eyes see today repeating and teaching its dissolute ways? No doubt it commands our attention so that we, who by the grace of God are fighting for the Lord in the monastic Order [RB Prol. 3] reformed and directed to the pathway of truth by the Cistercian fathers, having been made somewhat cautious by their ruination, may wash our hands in the blood of sinners [Ps 57:11] and always remember that our blessed Father Benedict taught in his Rule that we should flee utterly all negligence and forgetfulness [RB 7.10]. Let us continually reflect on that apostolic word: "Let the one who stands take heed lest he fall" [1 Cor 10:12], knowing most certainly that "it is our concern when our neighbor's house is on fire."[49]

[47] Horace, *Satires* 1.3.25-26.

[48] Bernard of Clairvaux, Apo 1.3–2.4 (SBOp 3:82–84; CF 1:36–38); 5.10–6.12 (SBOp 3:90–93; CF 1:45–49); and 10.26–12.30 (SBOp 3:102–7; CF 1:61–68). The theme of monastic decline is also seen in Ep 1 (SBOp 7:1–11; James, Ep 1, pp. 1–10).

[49] Horace, *Epistles* 1.18.84; also used by Bernard of Clairvaux, Ep 342.2 (SBOp 8:285; James, Ep 387.2, p. 457).

CHAPTER TEN

*How the Brothers Who Founded the Cistercian Order*
*Were Enlightened by Divine Grace While They Were Living*
*at Molesme*[50]

I judge it worthwhile now to describe carefully for future generations how the Cistercian Order made its beginning and how it was
showered by the abundant blessings of God's grace from the outset.
This we have learned in part from the written accounts handed
down to us from the holy men who were the first founders of our
sacred religious observance and in part from the accounts of our
predecessors. We do this so that those who have, by the grace of
God, been found worthy to be called to our Order in these latter
days may—if they read the paltry pages that we have worked out
for their consolation—consider how they have been suckled at the
noble breasts of kings [Isa 60:16] and blush to be found to be degenerate sons. But not devotion alone or the usefulness of the task
lead us in this undertaking; indeed, no small necessity compels us,
for monks of the black order, mostly those living in the provinces
of Germany, will not stop criticizing our sacred Order wherever
and to whomever they can, asserting that our holy fathers left the
monastery of Molesme scandalously and disobediently, against the
will of their abbot.[51] That this is a shameless lie will be clearly shown
in the following narrative, which brings the events into focus. Our
proposal, then, is, with the help of divine grace, to stop the mouths
of those speaking wicked things [Ps 62:12], not only by the clearest reason, but also by the weightiest authority, and to provide my
own brothers, who may until now perhaps have had no reliable

---

[50] EM 6.10.

[51] "Black monks" refers to the Benedictines, whose habits were dyed, as distinct
from the undyed garments of the Cistercians (hence "white monks" and sometimes "grey monks," depending on the natural color of the wool). See Constable,
*The Reformation of the Twelfth Century*, 188–93, on the significance of color and
the type of cloth used by monks of the eleventh and twelfth centuries.

means of refuting the false stories of this malicious criticism with arguments based on true and sincere evidence.

O ever-blind wickedness of stupid jealousy, which sees with its own eyes that the Cistercian Order is approved equally by divine and human judgment and set high on the candlesticks of virtue and honor to give light to all [Matt 5:15] who are in the house of the Lord, yet tries by clandestine whisperings to turn love and respect away from the Order whenever possible, as if it could accrue honor to itself in proportion to its censure of the good reputation of its neighbors. Truly, as the wisdom of the Apostle puts it, "he who commends himself is not approved, but he whom the Lord commends" [2 Cor 10:18]. We will show by letters from the pope, the cardinals, and the bishops who handled the negotiations how reasonably and how authoritatively the beginnings of the Cistercian Order were tested and approved by human judgment and afterward take pains to show how it was approved by divine judgment. For it is obvious to all wise persons that Almighty God approves a religious observance when he pours forth on its beginnings so many blessings of grace and in which he deigns to raise up so many Nazarites[52] of such perfection and sanctity. But who can accurately appraise, I do not say describe, how the vigor of sacred observance radiates in various parts of the world, where the Cistercian Order has houses, not only in large, but also in small houses; how outstanding they were in virtues; how serious and humble the leaders were in their habits; and equally how very patiently the subordinates bore voluntary poverty for Christ and carried out every good work [2 Tim 3:17] prepared for them; how the observant members of the Order were glorified by numerous revelations and heavenly visitations; and how many died happily, having been tried in the narrow path of voluntary tribulation, and—a thing very rare in the race of humankind—passed without purgatorial fire into the land of the living [Ps 26:13], to see the God of gods in Sion [Ps 83:8]. Lest it seem that we speak lightly of the abundance of such

---

[52] In the Old Testament, Nazarites were those who had taken a special vow and consecrated themselves to God; see Num 6:1-21; Judg 13:5; and Amos 2:11.

famous men[53] after we have carefully described the foundation of
our holy Order to cheer the devout and curb the carpers and false
speakers, we will briefly relate something of the strivings toward
virtue of some very revered fathers, that is, the abbots of Cîteaux
and Clairvaux and of those seniors who left behind at Clairvaux
the memory of their lives as followers of the very purest monastic
observance as a blessing to those who came after them. May this be
a strength to the faithful and devout, and may it purge envy from
the invidious eye of the heart of the faithless detractor, that he may
never speak ill of this religious Order but strive harder to imitate
the devotion of its monastic observance, or he will certainly groan,
wasting away as the rays of truth openly shine forth, taking from
him any pretext on which to base malicious detraction. If anyone
is upset because we have mentioned the seniors at Clairvaux more
than those at Cîteaux, let him understand that we were formed in
the community at Clairvaux and so could investigate with more
familiarity and thoroughness the sacred endeavors of our seniors.
What we have described in fulfilling our promise about the heartfelt way of life and joyful consummation of the few is not to slight
the holiness of the innumerable servants of God who at Cîteaux
and in the whole Order strove mightily in the contests of the Spirit.

When, then, as we said above, the monastic life had fallen into
such a torpor of negligence that it seemed in many places as if those
seeking conversion of life [RB 58.1] were coming closer to peril
than to progress and that there was no hope of restoration anywhere, Almighty God—who foreknows his servants from eternity,
in time calls and justifies them [Rom 8:30] that in eternity he may
glorify them—in the midst of silence sent his Holy Spirit from the
depths of heaven, out from his royal throne [Wis 18:15][54] into the
hearts of certain brothers who were living in a monastery called
Molesme in the territory of Burgundy.[55] These servants of God,
though few in number, burned intensely with that fire which the
Lord Jesus sent onto the earth and willed should be vehemently

---

[53] Ovid, *Met.* 3.466.

[54] Introit for Mass and *Magnificat* antiphon on the Sunday after Christmas.

[55] See *Le Grande Exorde*, 22n13, for the use of this passage in the Divine Office.

stoked [Luke 12:49].When they listened to the daily readings from the Rule in chapter and carefully pondered how they were obeying another rule and following customs other than those of their way of life, they were very seriously dismayed, for they saw that they and the other monks who had solemnly promised at profession to keep the Rule of the blessed Father Benedict were not living according to its instructions.[56] At first they deplored this privately, discussing their transgressions rather often among themselves, and they sought carefully for a way to remedy so great an evil. Later they spoke about it publicly. And then the others—who were carnal and could not say with the prophet, "From on high he has sent fire into my bones and taught me" [Lam 1:13]—made fun of the servants of God and began to harass them in any way they could to make them abandon so holy a purpose. But they were led by the Spirit of God [Rom 8:14] and were therefore free and paid no attention to their malicious insults.Turned back heart and soul to God, they prayed with unremitting persistence that the Lord's loving-kindness would deign to lead them to some place where they might fulfill the vows of their lips[57] that they had made according to the Rule but did not keep.Then pondering what the Apostle warns of, that not all spirits are to be believed [1 John 4:1] and that the Rule they wanted to keep perfectly in every way teaches that no one should presume to do anything without the permission of the abbot [RB 67.7], they went humbly to their abbot.They explained their concern about not keeping the Rule and told him of their fervent desire to keep their vows and entreated him to let them carry out, with his counsel and help, what the Holy Spirit had put into their minds. By God's will, the abbot, at that moment pierced to the heart, praised the proposal of the servants of God. He not only offered his advice and help but also promised very firmly to be their future companion in carrying out so holy a proposal. At hearing this these brothers, humble in spirit, were marvelously strengthened and understood for the first time that this desire truly came from

---

[56] EO n.130–32; EO annex 15.2; EP 3.6.
[57] Bernard of Clairvaux, Ep 7.18 (SBOp 7:44; James, Ep 8, p. 37), see Ps 49:14-23.

God and that they were not following a dream of their own hearts but that it was the right hand of the living God working in them.

CHAPTER ELEVEN

*How the Abbot, Dom Robert,*
*and the Brothers Who with Him Wanted*
*to Renew Monastic Observance,*
*Went to the Legate of the Apostolic See*[58]

These great-hearted men, who were to be leaders and standard-bearers of innumerable soldiers of Christ [2 Tim 2:3; RB Prol. 3; EM 5.7], desiring to offer the whole world not so much novel as great things, assiduously consulted among themselves how they could in some suitable way bring into effect what they so devoutly desired; deliberatively and prudently by the judgment of reason they realized that they ought not to presume to change either place or way of life without the consent of the Apostolic See. There was at the time in the territory of the Gauls a legate of the Apostolic See, the venerable Hugh,[59] archbishop of Lyon, a man revered for his piety, prudence, and authority. To him went the aforesaid abbot and the brothers who were burning with the desire for a renewed kind of monastic observance. They laid humbly before him the passion and promise in their hearts, complained of the discrepancy between the customs of their life and the Rule they had professed, and sorrowfully acknowledged that they had committed the crime of perjury. Then they added that they wanted to order their whole life from beginning

---

[58] Parts of this chapter are taken from EP 1 and 3. The title "Dom," *Dominus*, for monks and regular canons began in the twelfth century; see Constable, *The Reformation of the Twelfth Century*, 28–29. On its use for Cistercian abbots, see the detailed note by André Duchesne in *Bibliotheca Cluniacensis, notae*, ed. Martin Marrier and André Duchesne (Paris, 1614; reissued Mâcon, 1915), 148–49.

[59] Hugh of Lyon (Hugh of Die, *c.* 1040–1106) was an archbishop, papal legate to France (1075–87), and an important figure in the Gregorian Reform.

to end according to the prescriptions of the Rule of their holy Father Benedict, and they persistently entreated the legate to set them free to pursue their intention with the support of his apostolic authority. The lord legate, who was both prudent and discerning, considered their claims carefully and pronounced their motives praiseworthy. He approved their auspicious promises and exhorted them by letter to put into effect what they had conceived in their minds.

CHAPTER TWELVE

*The Letter of the Archbishop, Dom Hugh,*
*Legate of the Apostolic See,*
*by which the Beginning of the Cistercian Order Was Founded*
*by His Authority*[60]

Hugh, archbishop of Lyon and legate of the Apostolic See, to Robert, abbot of Molesme, and to those brothers who desire with him to serve God according to the Rule of Saint Benedict.[61] Be it known to all who rejoice in the advance of holy Mother Church that you and some of your sons, brothers of the monastery of Molesme, who stood in our presence at Lyon, want to observe more strictly and perfectly the Rule of Saint Benedict, which you have professed and which is kept somewhat tepidly and negligently in that monastery. Because many obstacles prevent you from doing this at the aforesaid place, we give you leave to go to another location which the bounty of God will show you, there to serve the Lord more wholesomely and in greater quiet. We do this for the salvation of both parties, both those who go and those who remain. At that time then we advised you who were present—abbot Robert, with the brothers Alberic, Odo, Stephen, John, Letald, and Peter—and any others

---

[60] EP 2–3.

[61] For excerpts from Robert's *Vita* as well as other accounts of his life, see *The New Monastery*, CF 60:15–30.

whom you decide to ally to yourselves in accordance with the Rule and by your common consent to carry out those holy proposals. And we have commanded that you persevere in this, and by apostolic authority we confirm this in perpetuity by the impression of our seal.

Relying on such great authorization, Abbot Robert and his brothers returned to Molesme and chose as their associates from that congregation of brothers those who rejected the enticements of a lax life, those who burned with eager minds to keep the holy Rule purely and simply. Of those who had attended the legate at Lyon and those who were called out of the community, there were twenty-one monks who set out in the desire of keeping to the straight and narrow way [Matt 7:13-14] of the more perfect life and Rule of the holy Father Benedict.[62]

CHAPTER THIRTEEN

*How and in What Year of the Incarnation of the Lord*
*the Holy Fathers of the Cistercian Order Left Molesme*
*and Came to the Wilderness of Cîteaux*

In the year of the Incarnation of the Lord 1098, Dom Robert, the abbot of the Abbey of Molesme founded in the diocese of Langres [EP 1.2], and with him went those brothers whose hearts God had touched [1 Sam 10:26], set out from Molesme, making the same choice as their father Saint Benedict, to tire themselves out in working for God rather than settling down in a comfortable way of life.[63] They hurried eagerly to that place which by the grace of God had been offered them beforehand as suitable to their endeavor, that is, to the wilderness called Cîteaux [EP 3.2].

---

[62] See Chrysogonus Waddell, *Narrative and Legislative Texts* 400n7, for comments on the number of monks, which varies between sources.

[63] Gregory, Dial 2.1.

Situated in the diocese of Chalon,[64] it was at that time a place but seldom approached by human beings because of the woods and dense briars and inhabited only by wild beasts [EP 3.3]. The men of God arrived at this place of horror and vast solitude [Deut 32:10; EC 1.8] and thought it quite suitable for the sort of religious observance which they had long had in mind and for which they had come, all the more so when they realized that the density of woods and briars would make the monastery remote and cut off, quite forgotten by and inaccessible to the world. So by the will of the bishop of Chalon and the consent of the person to whom the place belonged, they began to build there in the year we have mentioned, on 21 March,[65] that is, on the solemnity of the birth [to eternal life] of Saint Benedict, which was also Palm Sunday and therefore celebrated with double joy, to the rejoicing of angels [Luke 15:10] and the casting down of demons [Matt 21:12]. So the house at Cîteaux, and through it the observance of the whole Cistercian Order, took its beginning by means of men deeply versed in Christian philosophy. By a happy omen, those who had decided to arrange the ordering of their life and the guidelines for divine services according to the form prescribed in the Rule began this undertaking on the birthday of the very person who had, through the life-giving Spirit, given the saving law to many.

Take note: the supreme and eternal shepherd, who by the condescension of his grace deigned to leave the flock of the blessed on the mountains, in the green pastures [Ps 22], and came down to seek the one straying [Matt 18:11-14] in this vale of tears, has, by a new ordering of his mercy, built sheepfolds of loving devotion and raised over them the sign of salvation, so that any of the little flock who are diseased or sick, caught by the thorns of greed and fleshly desires or wandering through the woods of sin,[66] may hear the voice of the turtledove [Song 2:12-14] inviting them into the sheepfolds of loving devotion and may enter into the inn of the

---

[64] Chalon-sur-Saône.

[65] Literally, "the twelfth of the Kalends of April": the Feast of Saint Benedict on the medieval calendar.

[66] Bernard of Clairvaux, Sent 3.53 (SBOp 6/2:95; CF 55:230).

good Samaritan [Luke 10:29-37], so that their wounds may be healed by the wine of penitence and the oil of forgiveness, and that they may at last truly take up the sign of salvation.[67] Just as at the beginning of grace, when Christ our Lord and Savior was born, the world, while it knew him not, received a pledge of new redemption, of ancient reconciliation, of eternal happiness,[68] so too in these last days, when charity is cold and iniquity everywhere abounds [Matt 24:12], the almighty and merciful Lord planted the seed of that same grace in the wilderness of Cîteaux [EP 3.2]. Watered by the rain of the Holy Spirit, it gathered an incredibly plentiful harvest of spiritual riches, growing and developing into a great tree [Luke 13:19] so surpassingly beautiful and fruitful that people of various nations, tribes, and tongues [Rev 5:9] delighted to rest in its shade and satisfy themselves with its fruits. Yet although this fruit makes bitter the stomach of carnal desire by the work of repentance, it is as sweet as honey in the mouth of the developing conscience. Moreover, the lord archbishop, legate of the apostolic see, acknowledged this solid foundation by his blessing, advice, and authority. Taking note of the poverty of the servants of God, moreover, and the fact that in the barren place they were living in they were able neither to subsist nor to construct a building unless they had the support of some powerful person, he wrote to the illustrious prince Odo, then Duke of Burgundy, asking and urging him to support the poor men of Christ who were so zealous for the Rule and monastic way of life, and to grant them his protection and come to their help with what they needed, as becomes the generosity of a prince.[69] To this request and advice Lord Odo, Duke of Burgundy, agreed, and he was delighted by the fervor and devotion of the brothers; at his

---

[67] *Le Grande Exorde*, 26n6, notes a relationship between this "taking the cross" imagery and that of "taking the cross" by going on Crusade.

[68] Second responsory of the Office of Vigils for Christmas.

[69] Odo of Burgundy (1078–1122) was the principle benefactor of early Cîteaux and was called the "founder of the place" (*fundator loci*) in the first land grant made to the monastery. He died in the Holy Land but had directed that his heart be returned and buried at the monastery (Waddell, *Narrative and Legislative Texts*, 401n2 and 421n7). The "poor in Christ" is a long-standing image based in part on Matt 5:3 and 1 Cor 8:9; see EP 12.8; 15.9; 17.5; EC 1.4-6.

own cost he completely finished the wooden monastery they had begun in their poverty, procured for them everything they needed, and supported them abundantly with lands and livestock [EP 3.7].

Chapter Fourteen

*How by the Consent of the Bishop of Chalon,*
*to Whose Diocese They Belonged,*
*the Place Was Canonically Raised to an Abbey,*
*and about the Departure of the Abbot Who Had Gone There*

At that time the abbot who had settled there received from the bishop of Chalon,[70] to whose diocese they belonged, the pastoral staff and the cure of souls by order of the aforementioned legate,[71] and he caused the monks who had come with him to swear stability according to the Rule in that same place [EP 4.2; RB 61.5]. And so that church, strengthened equally by divine and human favor and fortified as well by apostolic authority, was raised to an abbey according to the Rule of Saint Benedict. But not very long afterward, the monks of Molesme, with the approval of Dom Geoffrey their abbot—who had succeeded Robert—sent messengers to the Roman court to ask for the return of the aforesaid Robert to his place of origin, that is, to the church at Molesme [EP 5.2]. The Lord Pope,[72] moved by their importunity, ordered his legate, that is, the venerable Hugh, that the abbot be sent back, if it could be arranged, and that the monks who loved the wilderness be left in peace [EP 5.3].[73] This is the gist of the letter which the Apostolic See sent about this matter:

---

[70] Walter of Chalon (bishop 1080–1120).

[71] Hugh of Die.

[72] Urban II (1088–99).

[73] There is a lacuna in most manuscripts of the EM from this point to the beginning of EM 1.21, the election of Stephen Harding. See the introduction for the manuscript tradition.

### The Letter of Pope Urban[74]

Bishop Urban, servant of the servants of God, to our venerable brother and fellow bishop, Hugh, vicar of the Apostolic See, health and apostolic blessings.[75] We have heard in council a great outcry from the brothers at Molesme, vehemently petitioning for the return of their abbot. They say that religious observance in their house has been overturned and that because of the absence of their abbot they are being held in contempt by the nobles and other neighbors. Compelled at length by our brothers, we command Your Grace by this present document that we should be pleased to have that abbot returned from the wilderness to the monastery, if it is possible. But if you are unable to bring this about, it should be your responsibility to see that those who love the wilderness live there quietly, and those in the community follow the discipline of the Rule.

Having read this apostolic letter, the legate called together authoritative and religious men, and in their presence having consulted them about this business, he issued the decree which follows.

## CHAPTER FIFTEEN

### The Decree of Dom Hugh, Archbishop and Legate of the Apostolic See, about the Whole Affair of the Brothers of Molesme and Cîteaux[76]

Hugh, servant of the Church at Lyon, to our well-beloved brother Robert, bishop of Langres, greetings.[77] We find it necessary to notify Your Fraternity what we have recently decided

---

[74] EP 6.

[75] Urban II, formerly a monk and prior at Cluny, was an important reforming pope, perhaps best known for his role in preaching the first crusade. See Robert Somerville, "Pope Bl. Urban II," *The New Catholic Encyclopedia*, 14:335–36.

[76] EP 7.

[77] Robert of Langres (*c.* 1085–19 Oct 1110), also known as Robert of Burgundy, bishop of the diocese in which Molesme was located.

in council at Port d'Anselle[78] in the business of the church at Molesme. The monks of Molesme came before us there with your letter, showing how their house had gone to rack and ruin since the departure of Abbot Robert, petitioning urgently that he be returned to them as their father. Otherwise they see no hope whatever of peace and quiet being restored to the church at Molesme, or of the vigor of monastic order being restored there to its original state. Brother Geoffrey, whom you installed as abbot of that community, came into our presence and said he would willingly surrender his place as father to Robert if it should please us to return him to the church at Molesme. Having heard your petition and that of the Molesme community; and having read again the letter from the Lord Pope directing that this whole affair be subject to our arbitration; and having sought the advice of many religious men, bishops, and others, who have been with us; and heeding their advice and the entreaties of the church at Molesme: we decree that he should return to them. But before he does so, he shall go to Chalon, and return the crozier and abbatial charge into the hand of our brother, the bishop of Chalon; and he shall freely and entirely release from their oath of profession and obedience those who made profession and promised obedience to him as abbot; and he shall receive from him release from his profession as abbot which he made at the church at Chalon.

And we have given leave to all the brothers of the New Monastery[79] who followed him there to return with him on condition that neither side dare to entice or to receive any of the rest, except as blessed Benedict prescribes for the receiving of monks from a known monastery [RB 61]. After he has done all these things, we release him to your charge, so that you may reinstate him as abbot at the community of Molesme; in such a way however, that if, with his usual fickleness, he should leave that same community again, no one should be put in his place during the lifetime of Abbot Geoffrey without the consent of

---

[78] The exact location of Port d'Anselle is not known.

[79] Until *c.* 1119, the monastery was referred to as "The New Monastery"; *Cistercium* referred to the freehold on which it was built. See Waddell, *Narrative and Legislative Texts*, 400n8.

you and me and Geoffrey.[80] We order all this as having been ratified by apostolic authority.

Regarding the chapel furnishings and the other things which Robert brought with him when he left the church at Molesme and handed over to the bishop of Chalon and the New Monastery: we decree that they shall all belong to the brothers of the New Monastery.

This is witnessed by the bishops Norgaud of Autun; Walter of Chalon; Gerard of Mâcon; Pons of Belley, and by the abbots Peter of Tournus; Lawrence of Dijon;[81] Jocaran of Ainay; Peter the secretary of the Lord Pope, and many other men of honest and good repute.

And so the abbot, weary of the horror and desolation of the wilderness and discontentedly mindful of his earlier honor and ease, although he could have excused himself in accordance with the gist of the letter sent by the apostolic legate if he had loved the poverty of the wilderness, praised everything set out above and carried it out, releasing the Cistercians from the obedience they had promised to him either there or at Molesme. And Walter, bishop of Chalon, released the abbot from responsibility for the church at Cîteaux. So he returned to Molesme, along with certain monks who did not love the wilderness. So for this reason and by apostolic dispensation the two churches, Molesme and Cîteaux, lived in fraternal peace and complete independence. It was not those who came to Cîteaux from Molesme who disgraced the beginnings of the Cistercian observance with the stain of contempt and disobedience—as monks of the other way of life now falsely slander them—but those who went back to Molesme from Cîteaux, for by choosing a greater good

---

[80] Robert of Molesme's reputation in the twelfth century is the subject of debate, as the term "usual fickleness" (*solita levitate*) implies. Brian Patrick McGuire ("Was Alberic the Real Founder of Cîteaux?") suggests "flakey" as a translation (148). William of Malmesbury characterized Robert as "delicately reared" (see *The New Monastery*, CF 60:54). The *Vita Sancti Roberti* 1.1-13 (PL 157:1271–79), written to help secure his canonization, describes a man who had gone to, and left, several monasteries.

[81] Laurence was abbot of Saint-Bénigne, Dijon.

they made the lesser good unlawful for themselves[82] and did not escape the stigma of apostasy, however much they tried to excuse the vice of lukewarmness to which they had weakly succumbed, by reference to the authority of an apostolic letter, [83] by which they were not ordered to go back but permitted to go back. As Holy Scripture teaches and daily experience proves—and even more the things I have been speaking of—we are shown men, who, sadly for them, lost stamina [Sir 2:16]. How greatly did that abbot lose stamina when he was lured away to a life of temporal convenience, even of pleasure, refusing the squalid conditions of the wilderness, and how wretchedly did he curry fleeting honor by alluring those carnal brothers away from the wilderness? Is there any doubt that because of all this he had lost the great privilege of God's grace which he had had earlier? By that grace, if only he had maintained his stamina and not fallen into lukewarm ways, would he not have deserved to be called the first father, the first abbot, the devoted founder and respected author of the holy Order of Cîteaux? But if, nay rather because, it is true that "events are judged by their results,"[84] one must acknowledge that that abbot and those brothers, who with him abandoned the strictness of the regular life so quickly and ill-advisedly, had never sought the wilderness with their whole hearts, though at the time they believed [they did] and though claiming to share in the sufferings of Christ by patient endurance [RB Prol. 50], in a time of temptation they fell away [Luke 8:13]. So according to the teaching of the gospel truth, the fresh wine of a renewed religious observance should never have been committed to the old

---

[82] On the theme of the greater and lesser goods, see Gregory the Great, *Regula pastoralis* 3.27 (SCh 382:456–570; *The Pastoral Care*, trans. Henry Davis, Ancient Christian Writers 11 [Westminster, MD: Newman Press, 1950], 192). This is also implied in Gregory's *Dial*, 2.Prol. and 2.1. For twelfth-century references, see Bernard of Clairvaux, Ep 1 (SBOp 7:1–11; James, Ep 1, pp. 1–10); Ep 94.1 (SBOp 7:243; James, Ep 168, p. 237); Ep 313 (SBOp 8:243–46; James, Ep 169, pp. 237–40). See also Hélinand of Froidmont, Sermon 8 (PL 212:548B); and below EM 1.35.

[83] On apostasy, see Bernard of Clairvaux, Ep 313.3 (SBOp 8:244–45; James, Ep 169.3, pp. 238–39). For references to tepidity, see RB 5.14; RB 18.25; Bernard of Clairvaux, Asc 3.7 (SBOp 5:135; SBS 2:247–48); and the index.

[84] Ovid, *Heroides* 2.85.

containers [Matt 9:17] of lukewarm men who very lovingly clung to their former customs. It should not have been necessary to take the new wine from them with such difficulty; but rather the new wine ought to have been put into the new containers of brothers fervent with sublime devotion, who were so tightly joined together by the grace of the Holy Spirit that not the slightest crazing of luke-warmness would have cracked them, and so both would have been preserved. The reason why that same abbot, stung momentarily by the holy intention, was seen to acquiesce was so that the Cistercian life, which was to have such authority in the Church of God, and through which the goodness of God was to produce such fruit of godly piety, should have in its beginning no blemish which could be reproved—as they would have had if the brothers had presumed to leave without the consent and permission of their abbot.

## CHAPTER SIXTEEN

*About the Election of Dom Alberic of Blessed Memory,*
*the First Abbot of Cîteaux,*
*How He Obtained Confirmation of the Privileges*
*of the Order from the Apostolic See,*
*and about the Statutes of the Order Which He Introduced*

Widowed of their shepherd, the tiny flock of the Lord [EP 9.2; Luke 12:32] that was at Cîteaux mourned sorrowfully, because although they had quite tenaciously fixed the anchor of their hope to the firmest rock, that is, to Christ, nevertheless the ill-considered departure of the abbot and the instability of the monks who went back with him made them more worried about their own perse-verance. What is more, the monks of Molesme and other monks in their province mocked and scoffed at the servants of God, who longed to be gathered and polished by discipline as living and ra-tional stones [1 Pet 2:5] to be the means of building up the ruins of the heavenly Jerusalem; just as once upon a time godless men who were far from the truth scoffed at the people of God who were hurrying to repair the ruins of the earthly Jerusalem, saying, "Let them build! If a wolf comes he will leap over the stones of their walls" [Neh 4:3]. Surely in this way the scorn of such lukewarm men, who were monks only in name and not in works of virtue, acted for these servants of God as a fire to purge them [Ps 65:10], cooking them in the oven of the Holy Spirit like the barley cake brought out of the ashes that rolled forcefully into the camp of Midian [Judg 7:13] so that the wicked power of the tyrant of the air [Eph 2:2; 6:12] was overthrown by the grace of God, and many thousands of Israelites were delivered from his cruelty.[85] Thanks be to the incomprehensible mercy of God which, over and above anything that the human mind dares to ask or is able to guess, bestows the largess of his grace on unhappy mortals! For who would have believed in those days—when first the servants of God began to cultivate the wilderness and were held in contempt and execration by other monks, as even the aforementioned legate wrote to the Lord Pope out of pity for their tribulations—who would then have believed, I ask, that in so short a space of time their observance would spread so widely that not only bishops, archbishops, and cardinals, but even the supreme universal pontiff of the Apostolic See would be chosen from their Order?

Deprived of its spiritual father, then, as we said, the newly founded church of a new monastic way of life[86] came together in the name of the Lord to discuss the substitution of a pastor better and more experienced in spiritual exercises. These holy men had no difficulty at all in this business, suffering neither from greed nor invidious honor, but by proper election procedure they quickly put forward as abbot a much respected man named Alberic. He was clearly a learned man, assiduous in divine and human affairs, a lover of the Rule and of the brothers. He had previously held the

---

[85] Bernard of Clairvaux, Sent 3.92 (SBOp 6/2:147; CF 55:299) also mentions the powers of the air.

[86] This is similar to the phrase used by William of Saint Thierry in Vita Bern 1.3.8 (PL 185:231): "In the course of his inquiry, he [Bernard] ran to Cîteaux, a new planting of renewed monastic observance."

office of prior in the church at Molesme for a long time and had later been very active and worked long and hard as a true athlete of God in transferring the brothers from Molesme to that place. For his share in that affair he had endured much blame from false brothers, as well as blows and imprisonment for the name of Christ [RB 64.1; EP 9.2-3]. How truly beautiful and how just are the judgments of God, that someone who had been laboring harder than all of them in this conscientious work of bringing the most precious pearl of pure monasticism out of the dunghill of vice should deserve to receive glory in place of shame, the thanks of God and man in place of humiliating and undeserved blows and in place of having been confined in prison, the fullest freedom.[87] So now, accepted by God and much needed to give light to souls, he was freely elected to the highest power in that holy matter— the one whom tepid men, ignorant of the fervor of holiness, had tried to cut off at the very root. After considerable resistance, he agreed to receive the pastoral charge, and, being a man of marvelous foresight, he began to consider what storms of tribulation he believed could trouble his household and when they would break. Taking thought for the future, with the council of his brothers and other creditable persons, he sent two monks to the Roman Curia [EP 10.2]. Through their agency he humbly entreated Lord Pope Pascal[88] to deign to receive the new church into his protection and by apostolic authority to guarantee in perpetuity their peace and liberty from the pressure of all persons, ecclesiastical and secular.

At that time there were living in Gaul two cardinals of the Roman Curia, the venerable men John and Benedict, who had been sent to those parts by the supreme pontiff. Hearing with pleasure the reputation of the new monastic way of life, they visited the place,[89] eager to examine the affair with the weight of the authority and wisdom of Rome [EP 10.3]. They realized that the

[87] See Bernard of Clairvaux, Sent 3.92 (SBOp 6/2:144–49; CF 55:295–304).
[88] Paschal II (1099–1118).
[89] According to Louis Lekai (*The Cistercians: Ideals and Reality* [Kent, OH: Kent State University Press, 1977], 16), the papal legates John of Gubbio and Benedict were "passing through Burgundy and happened to visit Cîteaux."

brothers were truly seeking God and keeping the ways of the holy Rule with faithful and sincere devotion, and they rejoiced at it. And they encouraged them in a kindly way to seek the confirmation, protection, and liberty of the Apostolic See for the place and the way of life. So the brothers who were to set out for Rome departed, armed with letters of intercession from the two cardinals, from Dom Hugh, archbishop of Lyon (whom we mentioned earlier), and from Dom Walter, bishop of Chalon, to the end that they might obtain from the Lord Pope what they devoutly sought more easily for seeming to be strengthened by the support of the authority of such venerable fathers interceding for them. How touched by charity these great persons were is quite obviously shown by the letters they wrote and sent. We have thought it necessary to insert them into this little book [EP 10.4] to remember with great admiration and spiritual joy how the holy Church received the Cistercian Order from the holy womb of grace, our mother, and received it with congratulatory hands, rejoicing and praising.[90] It was as if the Church had foreknown by the spirit of prophecy how greatly it would be strengthened and confirmed by the same Order, and so it strove to promote their affairs and protect their beginning through the highest and most distinguished persons that it had.

CHAPTER SEVENTEEN

*The Letter the Two Cardinals Sent the Lord Pope about the Cistercians*[91]

To our lord and father, Pope Paschal, worthy of the greatest praise everywhere, greetings from John and Benedict who are entirely his:[92]

---

[90] See note below on "grace, our mother" at EM 3.13.

[91] EP 11.

[92] John was Cardinal Priest of Saint Anastasia; Benedict was Cardinal Deacon of Saint Peter in Chains. Waddell (*Narrative and Legislative Texts*, 430) notes that the two were not well received in their new posts.

Whereas it is your province to provide for the care of all the churches, to extend your hand to those making requests by righteous prayers, and because the Christian religion, supported by the help of your justice, should increase: we therefore earnestly entreat Your Holiness to deign to turn the ears of Your Lovingkindness to the bearers of these letters, which on our advice have been sent to Your Paternity by certain religious brothers. They are asking that, by the privilege of your authority, the decree regarding the quiet and stability of their religious observances which they received from your predecessor, the Lord Pope Urban of blessed memory, and which was also defined in the injunctions of the Archbishop of Lyon, then legate, and other fellow bishops and abbots, between them and the abbey of Molesme concerning the religious observance which caused them to leave, should remain unchanged in perpetuity. We have seen them and give good report of their monastic observance.

## CHAPTER EIGHTEEN

### *The Letter of Hugh, Archbishop of Lyon*[93]

To the most reverend lord and father Pope Pascal, Hugh, servant of the church at Lyon and in every way yours, greetings:

The brothers who bring these letters to your exalted Paternity passed by here on the way, and because they have their residence within our province, that is, in the diocese of Chalon, they requested a letter of our lowliness to commend them to Your Exaltedness. You should know then that they are from that place which is called the New Monastery; they went there to live when they left the community of Molesme with their abbot in order to follow a stricter and holier way of life in accordance with the Rule of Saint Benedict, which they proposed to keep, leaving behind the customs of certain monasteries which had judged that in their weakness they were incapable of sustaining

[93] EP 12.

so great a burden. The brothers of the church at Molesme and certain other neighboring monks would not stop troubling and disturbing them, for they thought they themselves would be held in disrespect and despised by the world if these new and singular monks were seen living among them. In this matter, we humbly and confidently beseech Your very ardently desired Paternity that, as is your custom, you will look kindly on these brothers who place their whole hope in you, after God, and who therefore flee to your apostolic authority; and that you will defend their privileges by your authority, so that their place may be free from trouble and disquiet. For these poor ones of Christ have prepared no defense of riches or power against their enemies but place their only hope in God and in your clemency.[94]

## Chapter Nineteen

### *The Letter of Walter, Bishop of Chalon*[95]

To his venerable father, Pope Paschal, Walter, bishop of Chalon, offers salutations and homage.

Whereas Your Holiness ardently desires that the faithful progress in true religion, it is not opportune that they should lack the shadow of your protection, the balm of your consolation. Therefore, we suppliantly beseech you to approve what was done about those brothers who left the church at Molesme on the advice of holy men to seek a stricter life and whom God's loving-kindness gathered together in our diocese; the bearers of these letters come to you from them. We ask that you deign, by the privilege of your authority, to confirm the decree of your predecessor and what has been defined and written down by the archbishop of Lyon, the legate of the Apostolic See, and

---

[94] On the importance of "the poor of Christ" as a theme in a medieval context, see Michel Mollat, *The Poor in the Middle Ages*, trans. Arthur Goldhammer (New Haven: Yale University Press, 1986), 74–81, 102–23.

[95] EP 13.

his fellow bishops and abbots, which we and others witnessed and confirmed; and that you approve of the abbey remaining independent in that place in perpetuity, saving the canonical reverence for our rights and those of our successors. Both the abbot whom we ordained in that same place and the rest of the brothers with all their strength entreat that you, of your loving-kindness, confirm the protection of their peace.

Fortified by the support of these letters, the brothers who had been sent came to the Roman pontiff, found grace in his eyes, and quickly had their pious petition put into effect. On their return they brought back his apostolic privilege, written in line with the wishes of the abbot and their brothers [EP 10.3]. The gist of the privileges of these letters we have thought it worthwhile to include, so that those who come after us may know how, right from the beginning of its foundation, by what grace of the apostolic see the privileges and liberties of the church at Cîteaux were guaranteed and by what weight of mature counsel and grave authority the observance of the Cistercian Order was founded and propagated [EP 10.4]. Nor would it have been fitting that this very appropriate and very holy way of life, by which so many thousands of men have been snatched from the peril of sin and death and called back to life, should not be approved by the judgment of the universal Church. For if the craft of the devil, the hammer of the whole earth [Jer 50:23], had discovered that the Cistercian Order had not begun on the firm foundation of reason and authority but instead—God forbid!—had been built (as it was not) on the shifting ground of presumption, he could easily have contrived the ruination of the building with the hammer of malice. And so he would have cut off the salvation of many souls who have evaded the snares of the cruel hunter.

Let it be noted, moreover, that this period when by the grace of God the Cistercian Order made its beginning was indeed a time of grace, a time when the Lord deigned to console his Church—which had long been mourning because the wicked Saracens had trampled the holy city of Jerusalem underfoot—and to heap up an increase of graces for many afflictions. With the Christians contending manfully for the law of their God [Neh 10:29], and by the might of Christ powerfully overcoming the devil's might in the

Saracens and casting out the tyrannous enemy, the holy city was restored to those to whom it legally belonged, that is, to the true worshipers of the Lord Christ, in the second year of the foundation of the monastery at Cîteaux. And the Lord, from the depths of his grace, gave rise to the three holier ways of life in the Church—that is, the eremitical, the monastic, and the canonical—renewed and restored to the model of their ancient ways of life: the eremitical by the Carthusians, the monastic by the Cistercians, and the canonical by the Premonstratensians.[96] These three Orders, though their beginnings were separated from one another by a few years, arose at this time and by their holy and unsullied way by which to go to God [RB 58.8] very brightly illumined the world, and even today the fragrance of their life leads many men to life, for they are the good fragrance of Christ in each place [2 Cor 2:14-16].

Now we want the reader to be apprised of that privilege which removed from the Cistercian church all unjust power that weighed down rather than fostered the life and gave it complete liberty. It had been granted and confirmed before Pope Paschal, who gave it, was placed in captivity by the emperor and sinned by granting the emperor the right of investing bishops with staff and ring, which was contrary to justice and decreased the dignity of the supreme priesthood.[97] Thus no one, being moved by a dark suspicion, should

---

[96] The semi-eremetical Carthusian Order was founded by Saint Bruno in 1084 near the present site of the Grande Chartreuse. The Order's observances combine their interpretation of Benedictine monasticism with an ascetic solitary life. The Premonstratensians, also known as the "white canons" or "Norbertines," were founded by Saint Norbert of Xanten at Premontré, near Laon, in 1120. They followed the Rule of Saint Augustine, and they became arguably the most cloistered of the canons regular; see François Petit, *Spirituality of the Premonstratensians*, trans. Victor Szczurek, Premonstratensian Texts and Studies 2, CS 243 (Collegeville, MN: Cistercian Publications, 2011). See C. H. Lawrence, *Medieval Monasticism*, 3rd ed. (New York: Longman, 2001), 146–71. For Bernard's opinion on clerics with a monastic rule and communal life, see Sent 3.116 (SBOp 6/2:210–12; CF 55:389–92). See also *Libellus de diversis ordinibus et professionibus qui sunt in aecclesia*, ed. and trans. with an introduction by Giles Constable and Bernard Smith (Oxford: Clarendon Press, 1972).

[97] The Roman Privilege was dated at Troia on 19 October 1100 (Grießer, EM, 74n1). On 12 February 1111, the pope was captured by King Henry of Germany

think that he gave it at that time when it seemed that the intrusion of deceit had lessened the authority and ability of the Holy See.

## CHAPTER TWENTY

### *The Privilege of the Lord Pope Paschal, by Which He Gave Liberty to the Cistercians in Perpetuity*[98]

Bishop Paschal, servant of the servants of God, to the venerable Alberic, abbot of the New Monastery which is situated in the diocese of Chalon, and to his rightfully appointed successors in perpetuity.

A desire shown for a religious undertaking and the salvation of souls, and with God as its author, should be fulfilled without delay. Therefore, without any hindrance, we grant all that you ask in your petition, my sons, most beloved in the Lord, for we rejoice with fatherly affection in your religious observance. We decree that the place in which you have chosen to dwell for the sake of the peace of monastic order shall be safe and free from the intrusion of all human interference and that the abbey there shall always be held under the special protection of the Holy See, saving only canonical reverence to the church of Chalon. By the writ of these present decrees we forbid any person whomsoever to make any change in your way of life, either by receiving monks of your community, which is called the New Monastery, without commendation according to the Rule [RB 61.13], or by disturbing your congregation by any cunning or violence. We confirm as reasonable and laudable the decision which was made in the controversy between you and the monks of Molesme by our brother the Archbishop of Lyon, then vicar of the Apostolic See, along with the bishops of his province and some other good men on the orders of our predecessor, Urban II of apostolic memory. You, therefore, our best

---

and, while in captivity, on 13 April signed the Concordat of Worms. See J. Gilchrist, "Pascal II," *New Catholic Encyclopedia*, 10:915–16.

[98] The "Roman Privilege," EP 14.

beloved and most longed-for sons in Christ, should remember that you have given up your portion in the broad way of the world and also any portion in the less austere ways of the laxer monastery. And we charge you to be always the more worthy of this grace by taking care to have the fear and love of God in your hearts so that, as you are so far set free from the tumults and cares of the world, so too you should aspire all the more to please God with all the strength of mind and heart. If in the future any archbishop or bishop, emperor or king, prince or duke, count or viscount, judge or any other person, cleric or lay, shall attempt to set aside our written decree, and if he does not make amends with appropriate satisfaction after the second or third warning, let him be deprived of the power and honor of his rank, and let him know that because of his wrongdoing he stands convicted before the judgment of God. Let him be cut off from the holy Body and Blood of our God and Lord Jesus Christ, and let him lie under strict vengeance at the Last Judgment. But may the peace of our Lord Jesus Christ be with all those who deal righteously with those serving in that same place, that here they may receive the fruit of good works, and when they come before the strict judge, may they receive the reward of eternal peace.

Following this authorization and confirmation of their church and way of life by the Apostolic See, the abbot and his brothers, not unmindful of the promises and the vows which they had made to follow the Rule of Saint Benedict, in complete freedom of spirit began to arrange their new way of life in the manner prescribed in the Rule [EP 15.1-2], which they had been able to do less freely before because of the envious and malicious persecution of neighboring monks. They first decreed that they would observe the traditions of the Rule in the manner and order of divine services: they eliminated and entirely rejected all supplementary psalms, prayers, and litanies, which had been arbitrarily added by less discerning fathers. For they perceived by wise consideration that because of the frailty of human nature these made for the ruination, rather than the sanctification, of monks, because they were being performed tepidly and negligently not only by those who were halfhearted but even by those who were conscientious in all things. So having the

Rule before their eyes, and sifting each chapter by careful examination, they decreed whatever seemed to them to break the Rule to be entirely outside their way of life. They rejected tunics and fur coats, linsey-woolsey and linen shirts—which some have foolishly substituted for linsey-woolsey—undergarments and hoods, combs and coverlets [RB 55], soft mattresses and a variety of dishes in refectory, as well as fats and other such things [RB 39; EP 15.4-14] which were contrary to the purity of the Rule.[99] So strongly did the fire of divine love and the desire for holy poverty burn within them that they quailed at neither the coarseness of fabrics nor the chill of winter; rather, they made do with the simplest garments the Rule prescribes: the tunics and cowls which until that time had been unusual for monks; and to practice silence and manual labor; and carefully, to the best of their ability, to manifest in their demeanor gravity, modesty, and humility, conforming all their actions to the paths of the holy Rule. They rejoiced in exaltation of spirit that in this way they were casting off the old man and putting on the new [Eph 4:22-24; Col 3:9-10].[100] And because neither in the Rule nor in the life of their Father Benedict did they read that their teacher possessed churches, altars or offerings, burial fees or serfs, or the tithes of other men, bakeries, mills or villages; nor that women entered the monastery, nor that the dead were buried there[101]—except his sister[102]—they forbade all this, saying, "The blessed Benedict taught that a monk should make himself

---

[99] There are numerous references to food, clothing, and the like in Cistercian legislation; see Cap 11–14; and Inst 4, 10, 14, 15, 24, 34, 58, 65, 67, 83, 85. In the Acts of the Synods of Aachen in 816–17, Benedict of Aniane had listed the clothing allowed monks and specifically permitted "fat" in the monastic diet. See Kassius Hallinger et al., *Corpus consuetudinum monasticarum I: Initia Consuetudinis Benedicti. Constitutiones saeculi octavi et noni* (Siegburg, 1963). See also Annette Grabowsky and Clemens Radl, "The Second Benedict: A Review of Recent Scholarship," in *Benedict of Aniane: The Emperor's Monk*, trans. Allen Cabaniss, CS 220 (Kalamazoo, MI: Cistercian Publications, 2008), 10–15.

[100] See EM 2.14 and 4.6. *Le Grande Exorde*, 38n16, notes that the profession ceremony for a new monk in EO 102.41-43 and Annex 15, also incorporates the Pauline allusion to the "new man."

[101] Gregory, Dial 2.33. See also Cap 17; Inst 7.

[102] On the burial of Benedict's sister Scholastica, see Gregory, Dial 2.34.

a stranger to all worldly affairs [RB 4.20], and this clearly testifies that these things ought not to enter into the actions or the hearts of monks, who, as the etymology of their name implies, ought to be distanced from them by fleeing." They also asserted that the holy fathers—who were instruments of the Holy Spirit and whose statutes it is a sacrilege to transgress—had divided tithes into four parts: one part for the bishop, one for the priest, a third for providing hospitality to all who came to the church or for widows or paupers who had no sustenance from elsewhere, and a fourth for the upkeep of the church. And because among these calculations they did not find a monk who, holding his own lands, lived by the labor of himself and his beasts, they refused unjustly to appropriate tithes belonging by right to others. Notice the soldiers of Christ spurned worldly riches and gave back everything that they knew they would not be able to keep without pangs of conscience, placing themselves under voluntary poverty for the sake of the poor man, Christ. They now began to discuss by what ability, craft, or exertion they should provide for their own livelihood and that of the guests, rich and poor, who came to them and whom the Rule bids them receive as Christ [RB 53.1]. After this discussion they decided that, with the permission of the bishop, they would receive lay brothers[103] and would treat them in life and death as themselves, except for the status of choir monks; and they decided to employ hired servants, for they realized that without their help they would not be able to keep the Rule in its fullness day and night, and they took over lands far from human habitation for their own use, with fields, woods, and waters to be worked by mills and fish ponds, and the upkeep of horses and cattle[104] and various other

[103] *Conversi* (sing. *conversus*, "convert") is a name widely used first for adult vocations and then, as monasticism became clericalized, for lay brothers; see above preface. See Bernard of Clairvaux, Sent 1.26 (SBOp 6/2:16; CF 55:129). For background, see Giles Constable, "'Famuli' and 'Conversi' at Cluny: A Note on Statute 24 of Peter the Venerable," *Revue Bénédictine* 83 (1973): 326–50; Knowles, *The Monastic Order in England*, 2nd ed. (Cambridge: Cambridge University Press, 1963), 214–16, 654–61; and James S. Donnelly, *The Decline of the Medieval Cistercian, Lay Brotherhood* (New York: Fordham University Press, 1949).

[104] Cap 15; Inst 5.

things that are useful for human needs. They also decided, when they had established granges anywhere to carry out farming, the lay brothers should work them and not the monks, who, according to the Rule, ought to live within their cloister [RB 66.6]. Because these holy men knew that their holy Father Benedict, whose statutes they desired to follow in all ways, had built his monasteries, not in cities, towns, or villages, but in places far from the haunts of men,[105] they promised to do the same. And just as he had arranged each monastery with twelve monks and a father, they agreed that this is what they would do,[106] if the Lord by his grace deigned to increase and multiply their congregation in merit and in number.

Now [EP 17.2] the man of God, Alberic, by the grace of God the first abbot of the monastery at Cîteaux, in the tenth year of his abbacy went home to the Lord glorious in faith and in virtue, to be blessed, deservedly, in eternal life. It was especially by his hard work and energy that the brothers had made the move to this place. For his involvement he had patiently endured not only great blame but, as we said above, even blows and imprisonment. For nine and a half years, under the tutelage of the Holy Spirit, he had taught regular discipline in the school of Christ,[107] that those in high places should behave not haughtily but with fear [Rom 11.20]. His holy body was buried before the doors of the chapel of his church, as he had commendably chosen; and there he and his successors rest, to rise as glorious on the great day of the general resurrection as it had been worn out in this life of holy poverty and laborious discipline.

---

[105] Cap 9.3; Inst 1.2.

[106] Inst 12.

[107] The "school of Christ": see RB Prol. 45; and Bernard of Clairvaux, Ep 385.1 (SBOp 8:351; James, Ep 423, p. 491); and the index.

CHAPTER TWENTY-ONE

*About the Promotion of Blessed Stephen, Second Abbot*
*of Cîteaux, and What Kind of Decrees He Added When the*
*Order Was Still New, How the Order Grew and Multiplied under*
*Him, and How His Life Shone with Virtues*[108]

After the death of their first abbot, the church at Cîteaux, still poor
and small, met to hold the election for an abbot, without partiality
with respect to persons [Rom 2:11; RB 2.20]. By the intervening
grace of the Holy Spirit they elected a good man named Stephen, an Englishman [EP 17.3], who had come with them from
Molesme.[109] He was a man of outstanding holiness, adorned with
the grace of all virtues, a lover of the wilderness and very zealous
for holy poverty. This blessed man had, in his youth, left his own
country and kinsmen as a pilgrim to the tomb of the holy apostles.
On that journey he did not occupy himself with idle tales, as is
usually done, but with his companion he chanted divine praises
at leisure, saying the entire Psalter daily.[110] When he had fulfilled
his vow of pilgrimage, he left the city and went on to Gaul. He
reached the monastery of Molesme, and there he received the holy
habit of monastic life.[111] Later, when there was talk in that house

---

[108] In those manuscripts containing the lacuna (EM 1.14–20, see the introduction),
the text resumes at the beginning of this chapter with "After the death of . . . ."

[109] Stephen Harding was educated at Sherborne in Dorset and died in 1134.
His *Vita* and the works ascribed to him are found in PL 166:1361–1510. See J.-B.
Van Damme, *The Three Founders of Cîteaux*, CS 176 (Kalamazoo, MI: Cistercian
Publications, 1998); H. E. J. Cowdrey, "*Quidam frater Stephanus nomine, anglicus
natione*: The English Background of Stephen Harding," in *Revue Bénédictine* 101,
nos. 3/4 (1991): 322–40; and *The New Monastery*, 57–77; and Martha Newman,
"Stephen Harding and the Creation of the Cistercian Community," *Revue Béné-
dictine* 107 (1997): 307–29.

[110] For an account of this pilgrimage see H. E. J. Cowdrey, "Peter, Monk of
Molesme and Prior of Jully," in *Cross Cultural Convergences in the Crusader Period:
Essays Presented to Aryeh Grabois on His Sixty-Fifth Birthday*, ed. Michael Goodich,
Sophia Menache, and Sylvia Schein (New York: Peter Lang, 1995), 59–73.

[111] Herbert of Clairvaux, LM 2.24 (PL 185:1333–34).

of changes in observance, he was first among the instigators and worked very zealously to organize all things so that the Order of Cîteaux should be established. He was later, by God's design, installed as its father and distinguished teacher. Now, as we have said, all this was done by the gift of the Lord, and as a faithful and wise steward [Matt 24:45], Stephen began to handle affairs with the most devoted attention of his mind. For his Order was newly founded and still in a state of uncertainty on many points, and its statutes had not yet been worked out into perfect and unalloyed poverty, so he sought how he might better advance, perfect, and strengthen it by such government as would bring the most fruit to the Lord Jesus [John 15:2]. He called the brothers together and consulted with them [RB 3.1-2], and he as well as the brothers forbade the duke of that region, or any other prince, to hold court at any time at that church, as they had previously been doing at major solemnities. Then, lest there remain in the house of God, where they wanted to serve God devoutly day and night, anything that would reek of pride and superfluity or in any way corrupt poverty—the custodian of virtues which they by the grace of God had freely chosen—they determined to keep no crosses of gold or silver but painted wooden ones; no candelabra except one of iron; thuribles only of copper or iron; chasubles only of wool or linen, without silk, gold, or silver threads; albs and amices also of linen without silk, gold, or silver brocade. Palls, copes, dalmatics, and tunicles they entirely eliminated but retained chalices of silver, not of gold, and, if possible, gilded, a communion straw also of silver and, if possible, gilded. They kept stoles and maniples of silk but without gold or silver thread. They decreed that altar cloths be made of linen and be plain, without embroidery, and that cruets for use at the altar should contain no gold or silver [EP 17.4-8]. By these and similar holy statutes well pleasing to God, the servants of God strengthened their new Order. And from those statutes which they had first put into use, they made others which utterly cut off whatever was contrary to true humility, as well as other customs, better and more redolent of holy poverty. Thus they turned wicked delight into the straight way of conscience and the bitterness of vanity and pride into a plain way [Luke 3:5], so that, as the prophet says, in this way even fools could not err [Isa 35:8]. How great were the fruits of continence yielded by those in the Order of Cîteaux when tilled by the hoe of discipline; if they had been placed elsewhere, where the rigor of discipline was less exacting, they would easily have been brought to ruin by the unnatural stirrings of pleasure and fleshly desire. Therefore, let it never be supposed that our holy Order was invented by men, but truly it was handed down to us by the Holy Spirit; for the negligence of the human heart is prone to evil from its youth [Gen 8:21] and is always soiling the purity of holy observance. But the Holy Spirit never ceases to repair it at opportune times through his humble servants, so that no flesh may glory before God [1 Cor 1:29], and so that the voice of blasphemers who trust in their own efforts and cleverness—the ones who say "it is our mighty hand and not the Lord that has done all this" [Deut 32:27]—will be far removed from all monks.

Once the venerable Abbot Stephen and his brothers day by day advanced more and more in virtue and proved by their happy experience how good a bargain they had made [Prov 31:18] in giving away earth and the transient things of time to receive heaven, which is eternal and divine, there was one thing that marred their exultation of spirit and caused them no little grief: that seldom in those days did anyone come to them to follow their way of life. These holy men ached to hand on the treasury of virtues which they had received from heaven to some successors, but almost all those who saw or heard of the unusual and almost unheard of rigor of their life hastened less to join them than to put them out of their minds and out of their presence; for they had little hope that they would persevere. But the mercy of Almighty God, who had deigned to inspire his servants to this spiritual warfare, continued to enlarge and perfect it to the great profit of many, as the following will show [EP 16.3-5].

When they had come almost to the brink of despair because they had almost no successors, they cried out to God with the most earnest prayers, asking that the Lord might deign to pour out his mercy upon them [EP 17.10]. The Lord heard their prayers, as we believe, by the merits and prayers of the blessed Mother of God, the Virgin Mary, to whose holy name our Order is especially dedicated, as well as by the prayers of our most holy Father Benedict, whose Rule the aforesaid brothers had promised to keep in its entirety. And the Lord stirred the spirit of a young man [Dan 13:45] whose name was Bernard. He was a young nobleman, sensitive and well-educated, who was so intensely aflame with the fire of godly love that he left the world with its many delights and riches, and its ecclesiastical preferments, and set himself with a devout spirit to imitate the very strict way of life of the Cistercians as firstfruits to the Lord [Exod 23:19; Deut 26:10; Prov 3:9; et al.]. O, how wonderful is God in his works, how swiftly runs his word [Ps 147:15], how easy he shows things to be when he wills them, even those which are impossible to human beings [Luke 18:27]. While not only those who were noble and wealthy but those in middling circumstances and even the poor declined to enter the Order at seeing its austerity, this sensitive and delicate young man went about like someone emerging from a wine cellar, drunk with the wine of the grace of God which gladdens the heart of man [Ps 103:15], ardently and zealously preaching the message of the vocation which he had heard as a soft whisper [1 Kgs 19:12] in the secret ear of his heart, intent on passing it on to others; as Scripture says, "Let him that hears say: Come" [Rev 22:17]. So it happened that, once he had allied with himself his brothers, his relations and friends, and other noblemen who were well-educated and influential in the world, thirty of them eagerly entered the house of the novices in the church at Cîteaux and began to struggle in the spirit of fortitude against the lust of the flesh and the temptation of evil spirits. Not by words but by deeds they persuaded other men that the rigor of the Order to which they had fled was nothing other than the easy yoke and light burden of the Lord [cf. Matt 11:30; EP 17.11]. Stirred by their example, a countless multitude of men of all estates and conditions—the nobility, the poor, and those in-between—filled that stable of Christ and were wrapped in the swaddling clothes of his innocence. The brothers who had suffered discouragement and despair at having no successors wondered and rejoiced.[112] As if by rivulets from a pond teeming with rational fish

---

[112] William of Saint Thierry, Vita Bern 1.3.18 (PL 185:237).

demonstrating their purity by the fins of good intentions and the scales of holy works, they flowed out to populate monasteries in all parts of the Western world.

CHAPTER TWENTY-TWO

*How Abbot Stephen Knew of the Expansion of His Order by a Revelation of the Lord through a Departed Brother Who Appeared to Him While He Was Keeping Vigil*

This unexpected grace of divine visitation the Lord deigned in advance to show his humble little servant, Abbot Dom Stephen, by a highly gracious revelation a short time before it happened. As we have shown above, they were afflicted with heavy sorrow because they had scarcely any successors. Now it happened that one of them had run the course of his present life and, like a retainer after long service, he was close to entering into the joy of his Lord [Matt 25:21] and to receiving in death the reward [Phil 3:14] of his labors. When his end was very near, the venerable abbot, deeply affected by discouragement at the lack of successors, dared to take a course of action which would have been called presumptuous had his good intentions not excused him. For we believe it to be true that "whatever men do should be judged by their intentions,"[113] and in the eyes of the Lord the uprightness of his intention and the pressure of harsh necessity took away the blemish of presumption. When, as we have related, the brother was awaiting the last moment of his life, the holy abbot came to him and said, "You see, dearest brother, in what discouragement and despondency we are caught up because in one way or another we have set out along the straight and narrow way [Matt 7:14] that our most blessed Father Benedict placed before us in the Rule [RB 5.11; EM Prol.; 1.9;

---

[113] J. Werner, *Lateinische Sprichwörter und Sinnsprüche des Mittelalters* (Heidelberg, 1912), 81.165.

1.12; 6.10], but whether or not our way of life pleases God is not clear to us, especially since we are judged by all the monks in the vicinity as inventors of new things and instigators of scandalous schism. More than anything, however, the paucity of our numbers pierces my heart with the bitterest dart of grief, for every day the inroads of death deplete our numbers, and I am very much afraid that the monastic life we have begun anew will end with us, for up until now the Lord has never deigned to join to us industrious men adaptable to holy poverty through whom we would be able to pass on the organizing principles of our undertaking to posterity. Therefore, in the name of our Lord Jesus Christ [Col 3:17], for the sake of whose love we have entered upon the straight and narrow way [Matt 7:14] which in the Gospel he sets before us to follow, and in virtue of your obedience, I command you to come back to us sometime and somehow after your death, however our Lord shall by his grace decree, and let us know for certain what God in his mercy wills about our state."

To him the sick man replied, "Lord father, I will readily do what you command, if, by the aid of your prayers, I find myself in a position to carry out your order." He said this and after a short while he happily went up from this vale of tears to the mountain of joy, to the mount of eternal bliss. A few days went by after this, and the venerable abbot was at work with a group of brothers. As is the custom, he had given the signal for a break [EO 75.14] and was sitting a little way off from the others with his head covered with his hood, intent on meditation and prayer. And behold, that dead brother suddenly stood before him, flooded with a great glory of light, so much that he seemed to be suspended in the air rather than standing on the earth. Asked how he found himself and how it had been with him, he answered, "Well, best of fathers. All is very well with me, and all will be well with you. Through your teaching and your care, by enduring the hard labor of our new life with patience and humility, I have deserved to enter into unending joy, into that peace which passes understanding [Phil 4:7]. And now I have returned as you commanded me, father, to tell you and the brothers of the grace and mercy of our Lord Jesus Christ toward you. Because you commanded that I give you information about your state, you may know and hold as certain, casting away any scruple of doubt, how holy and pleasing to God is your life and monastic demeanor. In the future you will be able to put away this sorrow at not having any successors, which is eating away at your heart, and emerge into joy and exaltation of spirit. For the children of your barrenness shall say in your ears, 'This place is too narrow for us; give us space that we may live' [Isa 49:20]. Look, even now, at this very moment, the Lord is doing great things for you [Ps 125:3], sending you many persons, among them many noble and well-educated men [EP 17.11], who will fill this house so full that, teeming and spilling out like a swarm of bees, they will fly away from here and penetrate into many parts of the world. From the seed which the Lord has blessed [Isa 65:23] and which he has gathered together by his grace in this place, the sheaves [Ps 125:5-7] of many holy souls, gathered from all parts of the world, will be harvested in celestial granaries."

At hearing this, the holy abbot was filled with joy and exaltation and he gave thanks from the very depths of his heart to the loving-kindness of God, proving by happy experience how true is the testimony of Scripture that the Lord will not forsake those who put their trust in him [Ps 9:11]. The heavenly messenger then prepared to withdraw, but, marvelous to say, he did not presume to do so without the blessing of his spiritual father. He said therefore to the abbot, "Lord father, it is time for me to return to him who sent me [Tobit 12:20], and so I ask you to dismiss me strengthened by your blessing." Amazed and afraid at this the abbot replied, "Whatever are you saying? You have passed from corruption to incorruption, from vanities to verities, from darkness to light, from death to life. And you ask a blessing of me who am still groaning miserably under all this? It seems to be against all the integrity of law and reason. I ought instead to be asking a blessing of you, and here and now I beg you to bless me." But the brother said to him, "That would not be fitting, father. The Lord has granted you the power of benediction in having set you in the lofty position of dignity and spiritual instruction, but it is appropriate for me, as your disciple, who by your saving instruction has escaped the defilements of the world, to receive a blessing from you. And I will not go without obtaining it." The abbot was filled with wonder and admiration and did not dare go on resisting, so he raised his hand and blessed him. And so, as he went up, that holy soul, shedding the visible form he had taken on, returned to the invisible mysteries.

To another of the brothers about to go the way of all flesh, there appeared in a vision an innumerable multitude of men, washing their robes in an extremely clear fountain [Rev 22:14] near the oratory of the church, and in this vision he was told that the fountain [John 3:23] was called Ennon.[114] When he told the abbot about it, that splendid man understood immediately that God was signifying by this his divine consolation, and, greatly relieved, he gave thanks to God for what he had promised, though later still more when the promise was fulfilled.[115] For fourteen uninterrupted years the Lord had tested the patience and faith of his servants by various tribulations and great poverty and had found them faithful. Only in the fifteenth year from the foundation of the monastery at Cîteaux did the sun rising from the east visit them [Luke 1:78] by sending them in that year the aforementioned men. In those days, the community increased in meadows, vineyards, fields, and mills, but nor did it decrease in religious observance [EP 17.9].

## CHAPTER TWENTY-THREE

*How the Blessed Abbot Stephen Understood a Certain Secret of a Novice by the Spirit of Prophecy*[116]

Bernard, that child of the Lord [Ps 28:1], later to become the first abbot of the church at Clairvaux, when he was still a novice at

---

[114] *Exordium Magnum Cisterciense oder Bericht vom Anfang des Zisterzienserordens*, trans. Heinz Piesik, 2 vols. (Langwaden: Bernardus-Verlag, Kloster Langwaden, 2000), 1.497n180, refers the reader to Bede, *In Regnum Librum XXX quaestiones* 27.17ff.; CCSL 119:317–18.

[115] William of Saint Thierry, Vita Bern 1.3.18 (PL 185:236–37).

[116] Taken entirely from Herbert of Clairvaux, LM 2.23 (PL 185:1332) or in some manuscripts, 45. See Grießer, EM, 82n3.

Cîteaux used to say silently each day the seven penitential psalms [i.e., Ps 5; 30; 36; 49; 100; 128; 141] for the soul of his mother. One day, although he had begun to say these psalms after Compline, he left some out, whether through forgetfulness or sleepiness I do not know. He went to bed and refreshed his limbs in quiet slumber without fully completing what he had undertaken for the peace of his mother's soul. The abbot, aware of his negligence by the Spirit, came to him the next day and said, "Brother Bernard, where, I ask you, did you leave off your psalms yesterday after Compline or to whom did you entrust them?" When the young man heard this, he blushed—for he was shy and timid—and began to mull this over, marveling within himself, and said, "Lord God, how was this promise made known, of which I alone was aware?" He understood that he had been caught out by a spiritual man and threw himself at his feet, confessing his negligence and asking pardon. This was readily granted, and thereafter he took care in every way to fulfill both private and public observances carefully, and he did not lightly fail to carry out what he decided on reasonable grounds to do.

CHAPTER TWENTY-FOUR

*How Greatly the Kindness of the Good Lord Provided for His Poor Abbot Stephen after a Bloodletting*

One day Abbot Stephen, the poor man of Christ, was weak from bloodletting.[117] The cellarer of the house, upon whom fell the care of the poor and sick according to the Rule [RB 31.9; EO 76.33], had nothing on hand with which to prepare a meal which would in some way be more appetizing for his poor sick abbot. Because he loved his abbot with genuine charity, the cellarer wanted to find some

---

[117] Bloodletting was a common treatment in the Middle Ages and is addressed in Cistercian legislation: Cap 12.5; Inst 14.4, 45. See also Nancy G. Siraisi, *Medieval and Early Renaissance Medicine* (Chicago: University of Chicago Press, 1990), 115–17, 136–41.

way by which the charity which was burning within him could be expressed outwardly, and imagine, a huge bird flew down, bearing in its claws a fish as big as itself, and before the wondering gaze of all the brothers it dropped the fish and flew away, leaving enough food for the cellarer to provide sufficiently for the abbot in his great need.

## CHAPTER TWENTY-FIVE

### *How the Lord Relieved Him and His Brothers in Their Need*

Another time, the most holy festival of Pentecost came and on that holiest of days scarcely enough bread could be found in the house to meet the needs of the brothers. Then, however, the brothers rejoiced exceedingly, for they trusted that inasmuch as they were poor for his sake, the Lord would sustain them. They began to sing the solemn Mass with great devotion and delight in their hearts and, lo, the Mass was not yet over when they suddenly received, with considerable thanksgiving, a sizeable gift from an unexpected source, someone prompted by the grace of God. In these and similar ways the man of God judged that, as Scripture truly says, "They that fear the Lord shall lack nothing" [Ps 33:10]. The abbot wondered greatly at the great mercy of the Lord toward him and his brothers, and increased more and more in their holy observance, and gloried in the discomforts of blessed poverty as in all kinds of riches.

## CHAPTER TWENTY-SIX

### *With What Purity and Devotion the Venerable Father Stephen Celebrated the Holy Vigils of the Divine Office*

Moreover, he was not a deaf hearer of the holy Rule when it teaches that, when we stand to sing the psalms, our minds should be in harmony with our voices [RB 19.7], as what we record below shows. It was his custom when he went into church after the reading at supper [RB 42.3; EO 81] to hold the door of the church with his hand and press it quite firmly with his fingers, as a sign, just as people customarily make a sign or a knot to impress quite clearly on the memory something they do not want forgotten. He did this frequently, and one of the brothers with whom he was on familiar terms asked him why he did it. The holy father replied, "Throughout the day I am compelled to entertain thoughts about matters of business for the welfare of the house, and I tell them to remain on the threshold and not to presume to follow me; tomorrow I will give them my first attention." When the brother heard this he was greatly edified, understanding how greatly the holy father transcended the negligence common in the lives of others.

## CHAPTER TWENTY-SEVEN

### *About His Sincere Humility*

He was a true shepherd, not a hireling [John 10:12], and his humility was so great that he hated all proud display; he was marked out only by his staff of office which he was accustomed to carry in processions on feast days. Even to this day it is kept in the sacristy at Cîteaux out of reverence for so great a father and held in great veneration. It seems little different from the ordinary supports that the old and sick are accustomed to lean upon. He was the father in holy religion of our most blessed Father Bernard. So perfect a teacher deserved to have the most perfect disciple, and to this day by their teaching and examples [RB 2.11-12] innumerable captives have been snatched from the king of pride, that is, the devil, and incorporated into Christ the Lord, the true king of humility [RB Prol. 3].

## CHAPTER TWENTY-EIGHT

*How the Holy Abbot Stephen Sent a Certain Brother*
*to a Nearby Market Town to Buy What the Brothers Needed*
*When the Monastery at Cîteaux Had Reached Its Lowest Ebb*
*in Poverty, yet Gave Him No Money,*
*Knowing by the Spirit of Prophecy That All Would Go Well*
*with Him*[118]

Once when the house of Cîteaux was in dire straits of poverty, the venerable abbot Stephen called one of his brothers and spoke to him by the spirit of God, saying, "Dearest brother, you see how hard-pressed we are by need and that our brothers will be risking cold, hunger, and other hardships unless something is done quickly. So go to the fair at Vézelay, which is nearby, and purchase three carts and for each three strong draught horses, which we badly need to carry our burdens. Load these carts with bread, food, and other things that are needed and return to us bringing them with you in joy and prosperity." The brother answered him and said, "I am ready to do what you command, Lord Father, if you will give me the amount by which all this may be procured." The venerable abbot answered him, resolutely presuming in his poverty on God's mercy [Jdt 9:17], "Brother, you know very well that although I have sought anxiously and carefully to find something to provide for the needs of the brothers, only three pennies could be found in the whole house. Take those, if you want, and whatever else is lacking our Lord Jesus Christ will provide. Now go in safety, for the Lord will send his angel with you and make your journey prosperous [Ps 67:20]."

The brother set out and when he arrived at Vézelay he received hospitality from a certain God-fearing and faithful man. When this man realized the reason for the monk's journey and the brother's destitution, he went to the man next door to urge him to bequeath his goods to the poor [1 Cor 13:3; RB 58.24], for he was very rich,

---

[118] Entirely from Herbert of Clairvaux, LM 2.24 (PL 185:1332–33) with a few words added.

hopelessly ill, and near death. When he had told the sick man about the penury of the monks of Cîteaux—who were already famous in that district for their holiness—he called the brother into his house, and he received from the dying man a sum of money that enabled him to purchase everything the abbot had commanded him. So taking the three carts with their nine horses the brother loaded and equipped them with all the things he knew the brothers would find useful, and so he who came out empty returned to them well laden and joyful, just as his abbot had prophesied. When he drew near Cîteaux he sent a messenger on to tell the abbot about his approach and his success. When the venerable father heard it, he praised the Lord greatly and, calling the brothers together, he said, "God, the merciful Lord God, has bestowed his mercy freely and generously [Neh 9:31]. Indeed, admirably, indeed, graciously have you dealt with us, O Lord, our procurator and our shepherd; you have opened your hand and filled our penury with your blessings [Ps 144:16]." Then they formed a procession and went out as far as the gate to meet the returning brother; the abbot headed it, clad in sacred vestments, with his pastoral staff, and servers preceded him with a cross and holy water. So with solemnity and great thanksgiving they welcomed these alms, not as a gift from men but as a blessing from the Lord, from heaven, and as mercy from God their Savior [Ps 23:5]. That prudent and spiritual man, so we are given to understand, wanted, by receiving these gifts so ceremoniously, to point out to his sons—those present and those to come—that they should keep the grace of the miracle in continual meditation, and so learn to trust in the mercy of God in all their needs with a holy confidence, for God never forsakes those who hope in him [Jdt 13:17] and is always the most loving and kindest of consolers and helpers to his poor in all their circumstances and tribulation [Ps 9:10]. From that day forward and ever afterward, just as the spiritual largess of the Lord had always abounded in that monastery, so too they had no lack of temporal goods, while according to the constitutions of the Order they conformed to moderation in all things.[119]

---

[119] One manuscript adds another story about Stephen Harding taken from Hélinand of Froidmont, *Chronicle* 47, year 1107 (PL 212:1004); see Grießer, EM, 86n1.

CHAPTER TWENTY-NINE

*How Monasteries of the Cistercian Order Were Founded*
*in Several Dioceses; about the Institution*
*of the General Chapter and about the Privilege*
*for the Confirmation of the Statutes Which*
*the Lord Abbot Stephen Obtained with His Fellow Abbots*
*from the Apostolic See*

After this, by the generous grace of God, the number of persons in the church at Cîteaux increased and the mother who had hitherto mourned in sadness because she was barren began to rejoice in many children [Ps 112:9]. That vine of the Lord of hosts began to send out shoots far and wide.[120] There were cities of refuge [Josh 21:36], founded in various places and regions, so that those who had poured out the blood of souls might flee to them. There they might deserve to come to eternal redemption and perpetual absolution through the death of that High Priest [Heb 9:12] who by his own blood entered once into the sanctuary for his exiles.

In those days the abbeys which that church founded in various dioceses grew by the great and potent blessing of the Lord so much that within eight years, from the time of the foundation of La Ferté—which was the first daughter house of Cîteaux and even then by its beautiful name prefigured the firmness and stability of the Order—twelve monasteries had been founded and built by those who were originally sent out from Cîteaux and by others who were raised up by them [EP 18.2]. It was a pleasant enough sight, and in this activity they stood out as imitators of the most blessed Father Benedict, whose life and statutes they desired with all their hearts to emulate, for it is written of that father that he built twelve monasteries which handed down the precepts of his Rule to be observed. So in the renewal of this way of life according to

---

[120] Bernard of Clairvaux liked to speak about working "in the vineyard of the Lord"; see, for example, Div 15.1 (SBOp 6/1:140).

that Rule they established twelve monasteries[121] which passed on the cup of salvation to the whole world, like the twelve apostles of Christ, drunk with the grace of the Holy Spirit [Acts 10:45].

In fact, before the Cistercian abbeys began to flourish [CC Prol. 2], the most reverend father Stephen, inspired by the Holy Spirit and in council with his brothers, set out to write down a decree which was called the *Charter of Charity*. In it we are taught how the communities of our Order, dispersed throughout various parts of the world and divided by various languages, have been bound by the cord of marvelous charity and the manifestation of mutual respect and have become one church, one way of life, even one body in Christ [Eph 4:4]. He decided to call this decree the *Charter of Charity* because by its statutes all monetary exactions were rejected and only what belongs to charity and the salvation of souls [CC Prol. 4] was maintained in all things human and divine. Among those things which the blessed man and his brothers had with marvelous foresight decreed for the preservation of peace and charity and to keep the discipline of the holy Order from censure, this was especially found worthy of acceptance: that all the abbots of the Order were to meet once a year at Cîteaux and hold a General Chapter at which they should discuss very carefully the whole ordering of their life and the unbroken peace which was very deliberately to be kept among themselves [CC 7.2]. To this end, their mode of life was quite often examined and consolidated by the authority of the Holy Scriptures so that it could not easily grow tepid but would be able to thrive over the space of many years. It is for this reason that from then until now the reverend fathers of the Cistercian Order visit their motherhouse once a year to hold a General Chapter, and by the anointing of the Holy Spirit they formulate statutes, a full description of which is contained in the *Book of Determinations*.[122] So, from diverse elements they confected an

---

[121] Gregory, Dial 2.3; 2.13.

[122] It is not clear what the Latin *libro diffinitionem* refers to. Grießer, EM, 87n1, notes that there are references elsewhere to a small book that briefly defined the statutes of the General Chapter of 1204 and was printed "so that everyone should have the teaching of the chapter as soon as possible." He, however, believes that Conrad is probably not referring to such a volume. *Le Grande Exorde*, 52n8, cites Bernard Lucet, *La codification cistercienne de 1201 et son évolution ultérior* (Rome,

antidote for the health of souls and endeavored to discern what was necessary throughout the whole brotherhood of our congregation.

The holy father Stephen, deeming he could not act in such a matter without consulting the authority of the Apostolic See, in accordance with the example of his predecessor in monastic life and with the accord of his fellow abbots and brothers in religion, sent to the Lord Callistus in Rome, then pontiff of the Apostolic See, petitioning that what he, with his fellow abbots and brothers, had established for the strengthening of discipline of the monastic order might be ratified in perpetuity by apostolic authority.[123] The pope kindly received their petition and promulgated this decree for the confirmation of the Order.[124]

## CHAPTER THIRTY

### *The Decree of Pope Callistus*[125]

Callistus, bishop, servant of the servants of God, to his beloved son in Christ, Stephen, venerable abbot of the monastery of Cîteaux, and to his brothers, greetings and apostolic blessing:

We perceive that by the will of the Lord we have been raised up to hold authority in the Apostolic See, and so we ought by the authority of our office to encourage that which best

---

1964); and Bernard Lucet, *Les codifications cisterciennes de 1237 et de 1257* (Rome, 1977). See the description of MS Arsenal 785 in Chrysogonus Waddell, ed., *Twelfth-Century Statutes* 81.

[123] Pope Callistus II (1119–24), formerly archbishop of Vienne, knew Cîteaux well. He had supported the establishment of Bonnevaux in the face of Benedictine opposition. See Louis J. Lekai, *The Cistercians* 19.

[124] The textual questions in regard to the CC are probably the most contentious among Cistercian founding documents; for a concise synopsis of the scholarship and a new hypothesis about the CC, see Waddell, *Narrative and Legislative Texts*, 261–73.

[125] The decree is dated 23 December 1119. See Grießer, EM, 87n2; and Bouton and Van Damme, *Les plus anciens textes de Cîteaux* (Achel: Saint-Remy, 1974), 104. This date is accepted by *Le Grande Exorde*, 53n1.

serves the increase of religious observance and what is properly established for the salvation of souls. Therefore, dearly beloved sons in Christ, due charity urges us to give our assent to your petition, and as your father in religion we rejoice in your work which you have begun for the love of God and confirm it with our hand. By the assent and common deliberations of the abbot and brothers of your monasteries, and of the bishops in whose dioceses these monasteries are contained, you have established statutes concerning the observance of the Rule of Saint Benedict and other matters which seem necessary to your Order and locale, and you ask that these, which are for the greater peace of the monasteries and monastic observance, be confirmed by the Apostolic See. We rejoice in your progress in the Lord, and confirm your statutes and constitution by our apostolic authority, and we decree that this shall remain so forever, and in every way we expressly forbid any abbot to receive any of your monks without a recommendation made according to the Rule [RB 61.13]. We also forbid anyone to presume to receive as residents either your lay brothers or professed monks. If any ecclesiastical or secular person dares in any way to have the temerity to set aside your constitution and our confirmation, by the authority of the blessed apostles Peter and Paul, and by our authority, let the sword of excommunication be turned against him as a disturber of the peace and quiet of monastic life until he makes satisfaction. To whoever keeps this: may the blessing of Almighty God and the holy apostles be on him. Amen.

CHAPTER THIRTY-ONE

*How, by the Spirit,*
*the Blessed Father Stephen Was Aware of the Unworthiness*
*of His Successor and about Stephen's Precious Death*[126]

Although the blessed father Stephen had vigorously administered the office entrusted to him according to the true rule of humility of our Lord Jesus Christ [RB 31.17], he became so afflicted by old age that his eyes were darkened and he could not see. He entrusted pastoral care to God alone and desired to be free to taste holy contemplation. His successor was a man unworthy of respect by the name of Guy, who, although impressive in his external gifts, may be likened to a whitened sepulcher, for he was polluted inside with the rot of vices [Matt 23:27]. At the outset of his term of office, while Guy was receiving the profession of the brothers according to custom, Stephen, the servant of God, saw an unclean spirit coming to Guy, entering his mouth. Scarcely had one month passed and—take note—by a revelation of the Lord his impurity was revealed and the upstart plant, which the heavenly Father had not planted [Matt 15:13], was quickly uprooted from the paradise of God.

It was at that critical time that the old man, worn out by his praiseworthy labors, was led forth into the joy of his Lord [Matt 25:21]. And having been taken up from the lowest place of poverty, which in this world Stephen had chosen, following the counsel of the Savior, he reclined at the banquet of the supreme Father of the family [Matt 20:1]. The brothers gathered from the other abbeys of the Order—which by that time had increased in number to twenty—that they might, with devout homage and prayers, accompany their faithful friend and ever-humble father as he went home. As the death agony set in, the brothers were already beginning to speak among themselves, praising the great merits of the man, saying he could be sure of going to God because he had borne

---

[126] The first paragraph is taken from Herbert of Clairvaux, LM 2.24 (PL 185:1334).

such fruit in the Church of God during his lifetime. Overhearing this, the abbot recovered as much as he could and rebuked them as if with the voice of the Spirit, saying, "Be silent, brothers, be silent. What is this that you are saying? Truly I tell you that I go as fearfully and anxiously to God as if I had never done any good at all. If any good was in me, or if any fruit has come by means of my little efforts working with the grace of God, I fear and tremble exceedingly that I may have impeded that grace by being unworthy and not humble enough." So protected by this shield of utter humility which resounded in his mouth and resided in his heart, he put aside this mortal man and passed over, powerfully repelling all the darts, however fiery, however sulfurous, of the wicked adversary, and he ascended to the gates of paradise to be crowned. The remains of his holy body were buried reverently near the remains of his predecessor, so that they who in this life were one in spirit and one in faith [Eph 4:4-5] might not be separated in the blessedness of eternal glory.[127]

## Chapter Thirty-Two

### On the Life and Excellent Conduct of the Most Reverend Fastrad, Abbot of Cîteaux[128]

What a certain observant monk has written about the life of the holy Fastrad, beloved of God, abbot of Cîteaux, which is full of edification and suitable for instruction and is based on the true testimony of a monk of Clairvaux who deserved the friendship of such a man, I have inserted into my narrative, along with admirable

---

[127] Stephen Harding was buried next to Alberic under an altar in the cloister of Cîteaux. Both bodies were hidden and subsequently lost during the religious suppression of 1791. See Archdale A. King, *Cîteaux and Her Elder Daughters* (London: Burns & Oates, 1954), 21.

[128] Blessed Fastrad was the founding abbot of Cambron (1148–57), third abbot of Clairvaux (1157–61), and finally eighth abbot of Cîteaux (1161–63).

stories about other seniors of Clairvaux I found in the same little book,[129] so that what was scattered here and there, and mixed up with other stories, could better enlighten and better profit anyone reading it, once the whole had been edited into some order and joined together with similar pieces. This, then, is what he wrote:

Fastrad, of venerable and holy memory, the former abbot of Cîteaux, was a man of outstanding sanctity. He was nobly born but more noble by the refinement of his conduct. He was no mean student of the liberal arts but dedicated himself with ardent desire to the Sacred Scriptures,[130] so that once he had grown in age and wisdom he had them incessantly before his eyes and in his hands and would not sit down to a meal without them. He did this not only in his own house but even as he was going around to the various schools. It was while he was abbot of Cambron that, after the death of Dom Robert of blessed memory who had succeeded the blessed Bernard, he was elected to rule Clairvaux.[131] He pretended he could not go to that election although he was summoned by name, fearing that what he dreaded might actually happen. Nevertheless, before the messengers from Clairvaux could reach [Cambron] to summon him, he heard gossip already going around that they had elected him unanimously. Troubled and anxious at this rumor, he took flight and went to the monastery of Val Saint-Pierre, a house of the Carthusian Order, and hid there for some days.[132] There, as he was continuing in prayer day and night, he fell into an ecstasy [Acts 11:5; Pss 30:23; 67:23; 115:11]. And there appeared to him in great glory the child-bearing Virgin, the Lady of Angels, bearing in her arms the King of Glory, her little Jesus. When he saw her, he fell at her feet and besought her to have mercy upon him. The Blessed

---

[129] This chapter is taken from Herbert of Clairvaux, LM 22.25 (PL 185:464–66).

[130] The liberal arts refers to the traditional learning of the schools—the trivium (grammar, logic, rhetoric) and quadrivium (geometry, astronomy, arithmetic, music)—and is here being contrasted with the sacred learning of monasteries. See Jean Leclercq, *The Love of Learning and the Desire for God,* which raised modern awareness of a distinctive "monastic theology."

[131] Robert, previously abbot of Les Dunes, succeeded Bernard and served as abbot of Clairvaux from 1153 to 1157.

[132] Val-Saint-Pierre, founded in 1140, was in the diocese of Laon.

Virgin answered him and said, "Why are you upset, dear man?" And placing in his arms the noble bundle she carried, as she had once done with Simeon, she said, "Receive my Son and take care of him for me" [Luke 2:21-25]. Once the vision had disappeared from his eyes, he came to himself and understood that this was a message from the Lord and that what was really being committed to his providence were the sons of God and members of Christ. Forewarned by so happy a vision, he dared resist no longer, for fear he should seem to resist the will of God.

How discerning, how careful, and how kind a shepherd he showed himself to be once he had accepted the administration of this outstanding community is not within my poor power to express. He excelled others in his position of responsibility, just as he outdid them in the example of his monastic observance and the merit of holiness: chaste, dutiful, humble, meek, and modest beyond all others whom I remember seeing in those days. As Severus said of blessed Martin: it is not necessary to praise his frugality, for when he was still in the world he lived so frugally that he was thought to be not a scholar but a monk.[133] As he confidentially related to one of his closest friends, two years before his conversion, when he was scarcely of age, he took up fasting to the extent of never wanting more than bread and water. He would never consent to eat meat, even when he was sick and near death. By what sober living and, indeed, by what rigid fasting he kept his body under control once he became a monk, I refrain from saying, because, truth to tell, he was even more vigorous on this score. I noted enough along this line during the many years I served at his table. When he had subdued in himself the vices of the flesh without mercy, he seemed to have less pity than he ought for the miseries which are natural to the flesh. In the outward bearing and vesture that his position of dignity required, how humble and temperate he showed himself to be, can be easily shown by what I am about to say.

One day the brother vestiarian placed on his bed a cowl or a tunic, I don't know which; it was a little better than the ordinary

---

[133] Suplicius Severus, *Vita beati Martini* 2.7 (SCh 133:256–57).

and he wanted him to put it on. The father rebuked him in my hearing, saying, "My dear brother, what is this you want to do, cutting me off from the society of our brothers and disgracing me with a better quality habit? Because I bear the title abbot, am I not allowed to be a monk? Surely I have not been made the minister and servant of others so I can eat more splendid meals and wear grander clothes? If you love me, if you seek my peace, if you do not scorn to obey my commands, I pray and command you not to carry this any further. Since I am less than all and unworthy before God, it is a great thing for me to be allowed the honor of having the same food and clothing as everyone else. For in taking on myself the guidance of souls there is one thing I always feared—and fear—above all else: that because of the demands of administration I should forsake the life of poverty which I have professed and lose the reward of a monk." In this way he—beloved of God and men [Sir 45:1] and endowed excellently with the gifts of grace—taught those under him not simply by word and example but inspired in them a wonderful devotion even by the very great grace of his bearing. The grace of the Spirit, the Comforter, so shone in his angelic face that scarcely any of the faithful could take in enough of his longed-for appearance, especially those who knew the purity of his soul and his singular gentleness, which could be discerned in the outward man as if it had been stamped there by the seal of God himself.

When the church at Cîteaux, which is the mother of us all [CCP 19.4 (120)], was without a pastor, the abbots and monks taking part in the election were attracted by the fragrance of his virtues and by common consent they elected this venerable man, adorned as he was with the marks of the virtues, as father of the monastery of Cîteaux and of the entire Order.[134] We believe that his governance would have brought forth great fruit, had not the exigencies of our sins taken him so quickly away. Because we were not worthy to have the benefit of his very holy life any longer, it was cut off like a thread that is still being woven [Isa 38:12]. Yet even though he was taken away in a short time, he accomplished much, for his

---

[134] This occurred in 1161.

soul pleased God [Wis 4:13-14], and he deserved the company of angels. When his happy passing over was still in the future, one of the seniors at Clairvaux, a certain Peter of Toulouse of blessed memory, of whom I will have more to say later [EM 3.15], received this revelation. He had a vision at night. In the clouds of heaven [Dan 7:13] the Son of God was coming down from heaven with a great throng of his saints, seated on a throne of glory suspended in the air; and the splendor radiating from him enlightened the world. At the right hand of his majesty appeared a very glorious tomb, suspended in the air; its workmanship was a great wonder which delighted the eyes that beheld it. There stood by the door of the basilica at Clairvaux an innumerable multitude of both sexes with faces uplifted, gazing intently at the King of glory, our Lord Jesus Christ, and at the tomb. The aforesaid monk, Peter, approached the crowd and began to ask them about the tomb that appeared beside the Lord: whose it was and what it meant. One of them answered him: "You should know that the tomb you are asking about is that of a certain holy man who is soon to be taken from the earth, at whose passing there will be great desolation far and wide in these parts, but whose death will be precious in the sight of the Lord [Ps 115:15] and prestigious in the sight of men." When the vision had passed, the senior who saw it, in thinking about it, began to be troubled and downcast. The next day, when I saw him, his face clouded with the marks of his grieving soul, I quizzed him about what was causing his grief. After I had asked for a while, he told me about the vision he had seen, and I—knowing that he had often been provided with great grace and honored by great consolations from the Lord—concluded and believed that the message this man, so holy and so perfect, had seen could not help but come to pass. After some twenty days, suddenly the very sorrowful rumor of the unexpected death of that most holy abbot reached our ears, and we did not believe that a sadder event had happened for many days past in those parts or in the entire Cistercian Order.

And indeed his death, in the way foretold in that revelation, was—as we confidently expected—precious in the sight of the Lord, celebrated and prestigious in the sight of men. While he was attending the Lord Pope Alexander at Paris on the business of the monastery and the entire Order, he was taken ill, took to his bed, and within fifteen days made a holy end.[135] All the dignitaries of the Roman Curia stood round at his death, and the Lord Pope himself anointed him with his own hands and strengthened him with his apostolic blessing, consoled him with a great sense of tenderness while he was dying, and rejoiced at his death. Not only was the pope present, but Louis, the most pious king of the Franks,[136] was also there with all his court, and he mourned this most holy man with great sorrow, as if he had been a very dear father, and shed many tears over him. His holy body was taken back to Cîteaux and interred with the devotion. It is undeniable that the happy end of this very holy father and the magnificence of his funeral rites were perceptibly commemorated in the splendor of the very costly monument placed in the sight of the Lord.

I will mention briefly another vision about the same holy father. I am rather uncertain who saw it, but I am sure I have had it recounted to me many times by many people. They tell how there was a certain man in the country of England who was very religious and highly virtuous. On the very day when blessed Bernard, abbot of Clairvaux, left this world, this man, though he was in England, saw by the Spirit a great angel sent down from heaven take from the earth a soul of great merit and bear it with him back to the stars amid great rejoicing. Afterward, on the day when he of whom we were speaking—blessed Fastrad—went forth from the body, this same man on that very day saw the same angel descend to the earth and take a soul up from it and raise it to the heights of heaven. This vision seemed to be very great and glorious, but compared to the

---

[135] Alexander III (1159–81) was an influential, reform-minded pope and the first canon lawyer to become pope. As Rolando Bandinelli, a teacher of canon law, he wrote commentaries on the *Decretum*. Many of his decisions as Pope Alexander became part of the *Liber extra*, the collection of decisions and decretals which in 1234 was issued to supplement Gratian's *Decretum*. He convened the Third Lateran Council (1179) and canonized Bernard of Clairvaux in 1174. During his reign, he was challenged by three imperial antipopes: Victor IV, Paschal III, and Callistus III. See note below in EM 5.17, where Conrad refers to this schism.

[136] Louis VII (1137–80), the first husband of Eleanor of Aquitaine, leader of the ill-fated Second Crusade, and father of Philip II Augustus (1180–1223).

previous one it fell somewhat short. These things about the way of life of the most blessed father and his precious death I have set out in a succinct manner; I do not intend to trace the entire course of his life and work, which would be too great for my littleness to attempt, but I want to hand on in writing what I myself and a few others with me have known, lest it be lost.

CHAPTER THIRTY-THREE

*About the Wonderful Conversion of Dom Alexander,*
*Abbot of Cîteaux of Blessed Memory*[137]

In Cologne, which is the chief city in the second part of Germany, there was a certain master named Alexander, a very famous canon and professor in that town. It happened that the servant of God, blessed Bernard, abbot of Clairvaux, went into Germany at the order of the holy Pope Eugene to preach the crusade to Jerusalem to the Emperor Conrad and the people of that land.[138] There, he gleamed with innumerable signs and virtues, and the emperor, seeing the mighty marvels that the Lord showed through him, was pierced to the heart and received from Bernard's hands the sign of the cross for the journey to Jerusalem. An infinite multitude of men made no delay in doing the same; burning with the raging fire of an incredible faith they tore bits and pieces of clothing off the servant of God. Because of this he was obliged frequently to get new clothes, and on all sides those who had not managed to get crosses made from his garments were considered unfortunate.

---

[137] Herbert of Clairvaux, LM 2.22 (PL 185:1331–32); see also Geoffrey of Auxerre, Vita Bern 4.8.48 (PL 185.348); and Vita Bern 6.1 (PL 185:373–74). Alexander became a monk in 1146, abbot of Grandselve in 1149, and abbot of Cîteaux in 1168. He died in 1178. See Grießer, EM, 93n1.

[138] Eugene III (1145–53) was a Cistercian of Tre Fontane near Rome and the recipient of Bernard's *Five Books on Consideration*. On Bernard's preaching of the Second Crusade in 1146, see Williams, *Saint Bernard of Clairvaux*, 269–76.

Many noble and wise men among them gave themselves to the Lord by his hand, and these he took back to Clairvaux, and, having become monks, they one after another bore great fruit in the Church of God. Among these the venerable man Alexander, whom I mentioned above, stood out.

In the time of his youth he was swollen with the pride of secular learning, adorned with riches, and loaded with transitory honors. Nothing was less in his mind than conversion to the monastic life. But God, who catches the wise in their craftiness [Job 5:13; 1 Cor 3:19], brought it about in a marvelous way, as the following shows. When the most blessed Father Bernard urged him to conversion, he—brimming with secular learning and possessions—replied that at present there was nothing he thought of, or wanted, less than taking the monastic habit [EO 102.13]. But that very night, when he had given his limbs up to sleep, the man of God appeared to him in a vision, raising him from the pallet, on which he seemed to be lying gravely ill, and restoring his health. Then Bernard took off the habit in which he was dressed and wrapped it around Alexander. After he had shaken it indignantly from his shoulders once and then a second time, Alexander was forced the third time to keep it because it was tightly wrapped around his neck and body. Then the holy father passed to him the staff which he held in his hand, denoting the grace of a future prelacy, and disappeared. When Alexander woke up he was not in any way swayed by this vision and persisted in his hardness of heart. That same day the most blessed abbot was reclining at table and was offered the fish called perch to eat. Seeing it, the man of God raised his eyes to heaven and prayed over the fish for quite a long time; then he blessed it and sent some as a treat to the aforesaid Alexander. As Alexander began to eat it, at the first mouthful he happily deserved to experience within himself how great was the power of the prayer of the servant of God. Suddenly he was pierced to the heart and changed into another man, and he began copiously to shed tears over the fish.[139] He marveled, not knowing what was happening and why

---

[139] For Bernard on sorrow for sins, see Conv 11.23 (SBOp 4:95–96; CF 25:58) and Sent 2.128 (SBOp 6/2:48; CF 55:166–67).

he was weeping. Finally, he remembered the vision he had seen the previous night, and he understood that the free mercy of the Lord had forewarned him. So he gave thanks from the depths of his heart for the heavenly vocation and went at once to the servant of God. Bernard received him kindly, and he became a monk of Clairvaux. He was later made abbot of Grandselve, and he grew so much in holiness of life that after that he was made abbot of the monastery of Cîteaux and father general of the entire Order. In this trustworthy record I have set down all that I have heard from the servant of God, Alexander himself.

## CHAPTER THIRTY-FOUR

*About a Revelation Which the Blessed Monk Christian Deserved to See, Concerning Abbot Raynard and the Community of Cîteaux*[140]

The venerable man Raynard, former abbot of Cîteaux,[141] hearing the reputation of the blessed monk Christian, desired to see and speak with so holy a man. So he wrote to the lord abbot of l'Aumône, in whose care was that servant of God, Christian, and

---

[140] The life of Christian is recorded in letters of Ulrich, abbot of L'Aumône in the diocese of Chartres, to the abbot of Cîteaux about revelations of various monks. The letters were edited by M. Coens, "La vie de Christian de l'Aumône," *Analecta Bollandiana* 52 (1934): 5–20; and the complete text was published by Jean Leclercq, "Le texte complet de la Vie de Christian de l'Aumône," *Analecta Bollandiana* 71 (1953): 21–52. Grießer, EM, 94n1, states that Conrad used Hélinand of Froidmont's *Chronicle* (PL 212:1063–65).

[141] Blessed Raynard (Rainald or Rainhard) de Bar was the son of Milo, count of Bar-sur-Seine and the fifth abbot of Cîteaux (1134–51). He succeeded Guy (Guigo) after the latter was deposed and by the end of his abbacy the Cistercian Order had become one of the dominant forces in Christendom. See Knowles, *Monastic Order*, 246–52; and Lekai, *The Cistercians*, 48. Waddell (*Narrative and Legislative Texts*, 167–75) considers him the likely author of the *Capitula*, though the authorship remains controversial.

asked him with great respect to send the monk over to him. The abbot summoned one of the brothers whom he knew to be up to the task and placed the servant of God into his care, so that he might take Christian to the lord of Cîteaux as he had been instructed. So one day they set out, and when it was time according to their calculations they said the canonical hour of Sext together. The monk who was going with the man of God drew apart from him, so that they might say the hour of Our Lady privately, for permission had not yet been given for the public recitation of the hours of the Blessed Virgin.[142] The man of God, as he went on alone, was suddenly rapt in an ecstasy of mind, however, and tears streamed from his eyes. With his face turned up toward heaven he swayed to and fro so much that he could scarcely stay on the horse he was riding. When the other monk noticed this, he was very much afraid that the horse would falter, but out of reverence for God he dared not go nearer but waited patiently to see what would happen. After a moment the senior monk came to himself, and his traveling companion approached him respectfully and began asking humbly whether he had seen anything to the honor of God and the edification of his neighbor which he would deign to tell him. The servant of the Lord said with a cheerful expression, "My dear brother, let me ask you, whereabouts is the house of Cîteaux located?" And although he had neither seen Cîteaux nor even once walked along the way by which they would get there, he stretched out his hand to that part of the horizon in which Cîteaux was situated, and said, "Surely it is that way." The monk marveled and said, "Even so, holy Father." Then, bursting with jubilation of heart and mouth, he said: "O blessed brothers who dwell at Cîteaux; how blessed and holy is that community which strives to serve the Lord sincerely and devoutly day and night." And turning to the monk he said, "Just now, when you saw that I was, as it were, out of my mind, I was carried away in spirit to Cîteaux and saw

---

[142] Cistercians were permitted to recite the Office of the Virgin while traveling outside the monastery. See Statuta 1157.1 (Canivez 1:60); 1186.5 (Canivez 1:102); 1191.75 (Canivez 1:144–45). See also 1157.2 (Waddell, *Twelfth-Century Statutes*, 67).

the community of monks standing in their proper order in choir, surrounded by great brightness, singing praises to God with utter devotion. But above that community I saw another community of holy angels, standing in the same order, who radiated an even greater brilliance of light and seemed to rejoice at the devotion of the brothers. Moreover, in that higher choir I saw the lord abbot standing, as if he were in his own stall, and surrounded by glory he was emitting rays of great light."[143] When the brother asked what it meant that he saw the lord abbot shining with a brightness equal to that of the holy angels, the senior monk replied, "You ought to know that in this mortal and corruptible life, however much one advances, one cannot possibly be clad with a glory of brightness equal to that of the holy angels." Hearing these things, that brother was greatly edified and knew without doubt that the lord abbot of Cîteaux had great merit before God.

## CHAPTER THIRTY-FIVE

*About the Vision Which Converted Dom John,*
*Monk of Cîteaux and Later Bishop of Valence*[144]

Bishop John[145] was a man of venerable life who was elevated from the Order of Cîteaux to the church of Valence, which he ruled

[143] Grießer, EM, 95 (see note on line 28), notes that the Paris manuscript adds: "the senior described his height, appearance, and behavior, so that the brother was sure this was the abbot of Cîteaux, and he knew for certain that he was to be taken up from the many who knew him."

[144] Except for the last three sentences, this chapter is taken from Herbert of Clairvaux, LM 143, which is not contained in the PL (Grießer, EM, 96n1). *Le Grande Exorde* (62nn2–15) notes, following Grießer, that references to John are found in Hélinand of Froidmont, *Chronicle* 48, year 1120 (PL 212:1019C); and in Geoffrey of Auxerre, Sermon 17 on the Apocalypse (*Geoffredo di Auxerre: Super Apocalypsin*, ed. Ferrucio Gastaldelli [Rome: Edizione di Storia e Letteratura, 1970], 203–6; CF 42:170–71). See Grießer and *Le Grande Exorde* for additional bibliography.

[145] John was elected abbot of Bonnevaux in 1119 and became bishop of Valence in 1141. He died 21 March 1146.

with great energy. When he was still in the world, he resolved in his mind to leave the vanity of the world and take the religious habit, serving the Lord in the Order and house of Cîteaux. Although he had made this saving resolution, he put it off through negligence, and little by little the fervor of his good intention began to cool in his mind. Meanwhile, he set out to pray at the shrine of Saint James.[146] When he returned home from this pilgrimage, there appeared to him in a vision that very night the Lord Jesus Christ with his blessed apostles Peter and James. Blessed Peter had a very beautiful book which he held open before the Lord, in which the name of the same clerk was written. The Lord said to Peter, "Erase that name out of my book, for he has gone back on his promise." But blessed James came up to the Lord and said, "I pray you, spare him, Lord, for he is a pilgrim of mine and he is even now hurrying to put himself right." In fear and trembling, the aforementioned clerk reaffirmed his promise, and the Lord said, "And how can I be sure of this?" Blessed James replied, "Lord, I will be his surety." Then the clerk woke up, and while he was still wondering about it all, he fell asleep again and saw the same vision. When Blessed Peter held the aforesaid book open before the Lord, in the place where the name of the clerk had been written there appeared this inscription: "We will make for you chains of gold inlaid [Song 1:10] with silver."[147] The vision passed and he woke from sleep. Stirred by the grace of God, he single-mindedly cut off all that remained to him of the vanities of the world and hastened to the house of Cîteaux, where he was tested and, once found faithful, received the monastic habit.[148] In that house he advanced in religious observance

[146] That is, he undertook a pilgrimage to Santiago de Compestela in northern Spain.

[147] Chrysogonus Waddell ("The Exegetical Challenge of Early Cistercian Hagiography," *Cistercian Studies Quarterly* [1986]: 195–212) discusses the symbolism behind Song 1:10: gold was understood to represent the spiritual understanding of Scripture; and silver, the gift of eloquence to impart wisdom to the faithful. Waddell traces this from Origin, Ambrose, and Gregory the Great by way of Bede's *Commentary on the Song of Songs* (207).

[148] The liturgy for receiving the monastic habit is found in EO, appendix, 15.374 (*Le Grande Exorde*, 62n12).

and wisdom and was afterward made abbot of Bonnevaux. From there he was appointed bishop of the town of Valence, which he ruled vigorously for several years, bearing with many adversities in defense of righteousness.

Now I beg you all to attend to this if you have made a resolution to do any good thing and have neglected to carry through with it. There are those who think themselves not culpable if they do not carry through on some good thing they have resolved, but not vowed, to do, even though blessed Gregory clearly teaches that "if anyone following a lesser good promises a greater good, he has already invalidated the lesser good, and if he does not carry out what he promised, although in the eyes of men he seems to stand in the lesser good, yet in the eyes of the all-seeing God, who will come to judge not only the works but also the thoughts and intentions of the heart, he has already fallen from the greater good."[149] This servant of God of whom we have spoken was known to have made no vows, of course, but what he had simply resolved he did not carry out through negligence. The ever-subtle Examiner of hearts had seen this and meant to cut him out of the book of life if he did not bring the good he had conceived in his heart to a good effect.

We have brought together in this faithful account some traits that give an idea of the virtues of the most reverend fathers of the monastery of Cîteaux; these are only the ones that have come to our attention, but we know with absolute certainty that this holy house shone with these perfect men, accomplished in all religious observance, and we confess that our meager investigations have been insufficient to discover all their merits.

---

[149] Gregory the Great, *Regula pastoralis* 3.29 (SCh 382:456–57). On the greater and lesser goods, see note above at EM 1.15.

Book Two

# Bernard of Clairvaux and the Early Abbots of Clairvaux

CHAPTER ONE

*About the Virtues and Miracles
of Our Most Blessed Father Bernard, First Abbot of Clairvaux,
and How a Departed Brother Appeared to Him
during High Mass*

After the outpouring of divine grace which we recorded above,
the vineyard of the Lord of Hosts[1]—that is to say, the church of
Cîteaux—began to send out [Ps 79:12] shoots. With houses already
founded at La Ferté and Pontigny, in the year of our Lord 1114,
at a third place, the house of Clairvaux was founded in the name
of the Holy and Undivided Trinity, and Dom Stephen of blessed
memory, abbot of Cîteaux, made our most blessed Father Bernard
its first abbot. His admirable way of life, his singular holiness, and
the special privileges of his signs and virtues have been set out fully
in the book of his life[2] [Rev 3:5], but even so I think it fitting to
record here some of the things which have been omitted there to
commemorate so great a man and to edify readers, lest in this little
book which I am hammering out about men of virtue, we might
seem to pass over in silence the very splendid pillar on which our
whole Order rests.

It happened once at Clairvaux, while the conventual Mass was
being celebrated in the presence of this venerable father,[3] that after
reading the gospel there was, through negligence, no water for
washing the priest's hands. The community stood there, facing east,
for a while.[4] While the holy father was standing in his stall at the
altar step, a certain monk who had died a few days earlier appeared
and, standing opposite him, began to shake his head as if in reproof.
The servant of God saw and recognized him and asked why he

---

[1] Bernard of Clairvaux, Div 15.1 (SBOp 6/1:140). See also EM 1.29.

[2] William of Saint Therry *et al.*, Vita Bern, citing Rev 3:5.

[3] From this sentence to the end is taken from Herbert of Clairvaux, LM 2.11
(PL 185:1322).

[4] Facing the altar. See EO 56.25.

was shaking his head at him. To him he replied, "If only you knew how great and what kind of companions you might have in heaven, surely you would guard yourself against all negligence." The saint heard this appreciatively and replied, "Do you truly think that all the brothers who are in this monastery shall be saved?" "Indeed," he replied, "they will be saved. And not only these, but all who live lives of humility and obedience in our Order shall be saved." The good father, remembering a certain brother whom he had often had to correct for negligence and hardness of heart and over whom he had fretted a great deal, asked about him, saying, "Do you know anything for sure about the salvation of that brother?" He replied, "The mercy of God will not fail him." When the man of God heard this he was overjoyed and, with his brothers, kept more eagerly to the hard path [Ps 16:4], by the word of the Lord's lips, being the more certain of the hope in his heart of eternal reward.

CHAPTER TWO

*About the Soul of a Departed Brother*
*Whom One of the Senior Monks Saw Struggling with Demons,*
*and How He Was Set Free from Pain by the Prayers*
*of the Brothers*[5]

A lay brother at Clairvaux died. When the brothers met for the Office of Commendation, as was the custom [EO 94.2], a certain senior monk, a man of outstanding religious observance, heard crowds of devils walking about in the hundreds and with a great din shouting aloud and saying, "What a good thing, what a good thing. At all events we have got one soul from this wretched valley to share our lot." When, in the stillness of the night, the senior

---

[5] See Herbert of Clairvaux, LM 1.33; and Brian Patrick McGuire, *Difficult Saint*, 165.

monk who had heard this lay down to sleep,[6] the departed brother appeared to him with a sad appearance and mournful face, and said to him, "What you heard yesterday was the devils cheering over my punishment. Come and see into what terrible torment I have been cast by the just judgment of Almighty God." And he led him to a pit, very wide and hideously deep, and said to him, "Look, time and again I am being tossed into this pit by the devils [Ps 52:24; Ps 68:16]; so great is their cruelty that if there were a choice I would rather be thrown down here a hundred times by men than once by those devils."

When morning came, the aforesaid senior monk reported what he had heard and seen to the blessed Father Bernard, and although he understood it in spirit, Bernard groaned and said, "I know the devils would never presume to do such a thing unless there was a weighty cause." Then he went to the brothers in chapter [EO 70.28] and laid before all of them the calamity of the departed brother, and he called on the conscience of each one, warning them to walk more carefully in the way of holy observance, affirming that the malice of the devils is great toward all Christians but especially toward those who profess the monastic way of life. Then he exhorted them to come to the aid of the soul of the brother in distress quite deliberately by psalms and prayers and to turn aside the Lord's anger by celebrating Masses, on the chance that the loving Father [RB Prol. 1], pelted with their prayers, might deign to cast down the tyrannous pride of the devils by the sacrifice of so special a Victim and set the brother's soul free from their wickedness. The brothers did this with intense devotion and, after a few days had passed, the departed brother appeared again to the same senior monk with a smiling face and indicated that his state had improved. When the senior asked him how he was, he replied, "Thank God, I am well." Asked how he had been set free, he said, "Come and see" [John 1:46]. And at once he led him into the oratory of that place where at each altar priests stood with their servers celebrating the sacrifice of the Saving Victim with the

---

[6] Horace, *Satires* 2.2.80–81. Grießer, EM, 99n2, notes that while Conrad took this from Herbert of Clairvaux, LM 1.33, the phrase was by Conrad's day a *topos*.

utmost devotion [2 Macc 3:32; EO 98.39]. "Look," he said, "here are the weapons of God's grace by which I have been delivered. Here is the might of God's mercy which endures invincible. Here is that unique Victim who takes away the sin of the whole world [John 1:29]. Truly, I tell you that nothing can resist these weapons of God's grace, this might of God's mercy, this Saving Victim, save only an impenitent heart." On waking, the old man rejoiced exceedingly at the liberation of the brother's soul, and he told the rest of the brothers about the vision, increasing their devotion in offering the sacrifice of the Saving Victim by their greater certainty of its efficacy in releasing this brother.

CHAPTER THREE

*How at Vigils Saint Bernard Saw Angels Standing Next to Each Monk, Writing Down What They Were Chanting*[7]

The holy father was once attending Vigils with his accustomed purity and devotion [RB 20.2], which was known only by God and himself. While the slow modulation of the psalmody was prolonging Vigils, the Lord Abbot opened his eyes and, looking around, saw an angel standing beside each monk, diligently recording on pieces of parchment, like a notary, what each monk was chanting, omitting not the slightest syllable uttered in negligence. But they were writing in different ways. Some were writing in gold, others in silver, several in black, and some in water, and a few did not write anything at all. The Spirit who was revealing this inspired him to understand in his heart the different kinds of writing. Those who wrote in gold

---

[7] An account of this story is contained in John of Clairvaux, *Liber visionum et miraculorum* (Troyes, Bib. mun., MS 946, f. 134v); see McGuire, *Difficult Saint*, 159 and 165. Norman Russell, trans. (*Lives of the Desert Fathers*, CS 34 [Kalamazoo, MI: Cistercian Publications, 1981], 138n3), notes the similarity between this story and that of Piammon in *Historia monachorum* 25.2.

signified the very fervent zeal of those monks for the Lord's service and the complete attention of their hearts to what they were chanting. Those who wrote in silver registered less fervor but still a pure devotion in chanting the psalms. Those who wrote in black noted down an ongoing goodwill in psalmody but not much devotion. But those who wrote in water designated those who were oppressed by sleep or laziness, distracted by idle thoughts, or made the sounds but whose heart was far away and not in harmony with their voice [RB 19.5-7]. How wonderful is the leniency of God! Just as no evil goes unpunished, so no good, however small and however negligently performed, will be unrewarded. The rest of them—who were writing nothing—were reproving the woeful hardness of heart of those forgetful of their profession and unmindful of the fear of God, who were either indulging themselves in a deadly sleep by a sinking will or were in fact awake with their mouths closed, occupied with vain and wicked thoughts, not out of weakness but because they chose to be. These monks, when measured against the teaching of the law, have no fear of appearing empty-handed in the sight of the Lord.[8] When the holy father saw this, he remembered those statements about how "ministering spirits were sent to minister to those who are heirs of salvation" [Heb 1:14], and the fervor of the proficient ones gladdened him, but his fatherly affection grieved at the deficiencies of the tepid.

## CHAPTER FOUR

### *How Bernard Saw Holy Angels Urging the Brothers to Chant the Hymn* Te Deum Laudamus *More Fervently*[9]

Solemn Vigils were once being celebrated and the man of God was present with the other brothers. While they were singing the hymn

---

[8] Exod 23:15; 34:20. See Bernard on the "sight of the Lord" in Div 25.1 (SBOp 6/1:187–88).

[9] *Te Deum laudamus.*

"We praise you, O God,"[10] he saw holy angels radiating great brightness, their faces aglow with attentiveness, passing now here, now there, through each choir, urging the singers on, joining with them, and standing back as if applauding, so that they sang that divine hymn all the way through with devotion and succeeded in accomplishing it in all its modes. The holy man learned from this that the hymn was indeed divine and well known to the holy angels, who seemed to give great attention to the task of having the brothers sing to the honor of God with fervent devotion. One of the spiritual brothers was even allowed to see a flame of great radiance burst from the lips of the cantor and rise up on high as the hymn was being intoned.

## CHAPTER FIVE

### *On the Magnificent Word by Which, While He Preached, He Gave Hope of Pardon to the Fearful and Despairing*[11]

Once when the blessed Bernard was preaching the word of God to the brothers, he vehemently denounced vices and incited in their minds a terror of the tremendous judgment of God. He sensed in spirit that some of those sitting there were gravely disturbed in conscience and on the point of falling into the pit of despair. Then, entirely inflamed with the spirit of brotherly love and to the amazement of all who were there, he burst out with these words: "My brothers, why are your consciences bothering you? Is the enormity and number of the offenses you detect there making you forget the inexhaustible depths of the mercies of God? In truth I tell you that if that son of perdition, Judas [John 17:12], who sold and betrayed the Lord, were sitting here in this school of Christ [RB Prol. 45] and had been incorporated into this way of life, even he could obtain forgiveness through penance." At hearing such a magnificent word

---

[10] Sung at Vigils on Sundays and solemn feasts; see RB 11.8.

[11] The source of this story may be John of Clairvaux, *Liber visionum et miraculorum* (Troyes, Bib. mun., MS 946, f. 3v). See Brian Patrick McGuire, "A Lost Clairvaux *Exemplum* Collection Found," 43.

of consolation, not only those who had been faint of heart [Ps 54:9] and on the brink of despair, but all those who were present glorified the Lord and took heart in the hope of divine grace.

CHAPTER SIX

*About a Monk Who Could Not Summon up Faith*
*in the Sacrament of the Altar,*
*and How the Holy Father Ordered Him to Receive Communion*
*by Virtue of His Own Faith*[12]

One of the holy father's monks had reached such great inner poverty by the deceits of the devils and by the simpleness of his own understanding that he said that the bread and the wine mixed with water which are placed upon the altar could not be changed into the substance [*transsubstantiari*] of the true Body and Blood of our Lord Jesus Christ. He despised the life-giving sacrament so much on this account that he would not take it when it was offered to him [EO 66]. The brothers noticed that he did not receive the sacrament of the altar, and they referred the matter privately to their seniors [RB 23.2]. When asked the cause, he did not deny it but said he could never summon up faith in the sacrament. When he did not acquiesce to those instructing and warning him and did not believe the testimony of the Scripture which they advanced, the matter was referred to the venerable abbot. When, having been summoned, the monk came and the holy abbot refuted his lack of faith according to the wisdom given him [2 Pet 3:15], he replied, "I cannot be persuaded by any of these assertions to believe that the bread and wine which are placed upon the altar are truly the Body and Blood of Christ, and because of this I know that I shall go to hell." At hearing this the man of God displayed a marvelous

---

[12] McGuire (*Difficult Saint*, 165) notes a close similarity between this story and other Communion stories found in Herbert of Torres's *Liber Visionum et Miraculorum*.

authority, just as he always did when he found himself in difficult situations, and said, "What? A monk of mine go to hell? Certainly not! If you have no faith of your own, I order you by virtue of your obedience to receive Communion on my faith."

How good that father was, how truly wise that physician,[13] who knew how to minister to the temptations of weakness by the anointing of the grace that taught him all things [1 John 2:27]. He did not say, "Get out, heretic; go, be damned; be lost, be damned!" Instead he said confidently, "Go, receive Communion on my faith," believing without a doubt that his little son, whom he had brought to birth in the pangs of holy desire until Christ should be formed in him [Gal 4:19], would not be a stranger to the foundation of his faith, just as he could never be outside the very bowels of his charity. And so, constrained by the virtue of obedience, but inwardly without faith (as it seemed to him), the monk went up to the altar and received Communion. And by the virtue of holy obedience and the merits of the holy father, he was immediately enlightened and received faith in the sacraments, which he preserved unabated until the day of his death.

## Chapter Seven

### About a Spiritual Monk
### Who Saw the Image of the Crucified Embracing
### the Holy Father in Prayer[14]

Dom Menard, the former abbot of Mores[15]—which is a monastery not far from Clairvaux—was a religious man. He told his friends

---

[13] Matt 9:12; Luke 4:23; RB 27.2. See also Bernard of Clairvaux, Par 6 (SBOp 6/2:293; CF 55:81); and Sent 3.97 (SBOp 6/2:155–59; CF 55:313–19).

[14] Herbert of Clairvaux, LM 2.19 (PL 185:1328). Cistercian crosses were not to be made from silver or gold; see EP 17.6; Cap 26; and Inst 20.

[15] Mores was a daughter house of Clairvaux in the Diocese of Langres. Menard was the second abbot and died in 1168. See Grießer, EM, 102n1; Janauschek 135; *Gallia Christiana* 4:842.

about a marvelous thing as if it happened to someone else, but we think that it was his own experience. This is what he said:

> I knew a certain monk, who once came upon the blessed Abbot Bernard praying alone in the church. He was prostrate before the altar, and a cross with the Crucified on it appeared on the floor in front of him. The most blessed man adored and kissed it with deepest devotion. Then it seemed as if that Majesty, detaching his arms from each side of the cross, embraced the servant of God and drew him to himself. When the monk had watched this for a while, he became astounded with great wonder and was as if outside himself. But at length he withdrew silently for fear he might offend the holy father by seeming to pry into his secret, no doubt understanding and knowing that in all his prayer and way of life the holy man indeed surpassed other men.

## Chapter Eight

### *About a Monk Whom the Holy Father Refused to Heal Completely from Epilepsy, but Cured in Part*[16]

One day, the holy father went out to visit his brothers as they were harvesting in the fields. But because he was ill and could not go on foot, he rode on a small donkey. Now a certain monk was walking with him and leading the animal when, during the journey, the falling sickness from which he used to suffer seized him suddenly and he began to writhe badly in an epileptic fit. When the holy man saw this, he had compassion on him and prayed to the Lord for him, asking that the suffering might not seize him any more when he was unprepared. From that time on until the day of his death—and he lived for another twenty years—there was granted him what he had previously lacked, and what almost never happens to other epileptics. Whenever he was going to fall because of

---

[16] Herbert of Clairvaux, LM 2.20 (PL 185:1328–29).

this sickness, he had a premonition of the suffering a little before it, so that he was able to lie down on his bed and be on his guard against sudden fits. If the holy father had requested this gift for him from the Lord, we believe, he could have received a complete cure, if he had thought that would advance the salvation of his soul. But because that monk's habits were difficult to put up with and he was thoroughly hard-hearted, a rod of correction and staff of consolation always seemed necessary to his salvation [Ps 22:4], so this was mercifully granted him, that the danger of a sudden fall was avoided by the premonition, but the stimulus of the health-giving illness remained.

CHAPTER NINE

*About a Dying Brother,*
*Whom the Holy Father Ordered to Postpone His Death*
*Lest the Brothers' Sleep Be Broken*[17]

One of the brothers of Clairvaux was on his deathbed when blessed Bernard came in after Compline to visit him. Seeing the man was near death and almost ready to depart, he said to him, "Dearest brother, you know how exhausted our community is from working and that in a little while they will have to get up again for Vigils [EO 96.7]. If you pass away in the meantime, they will have to interrupt their sleep. It would be very disturbing, and the lengthy Vigils would be celebrated with less solemnity. Therefore, that it may go well with you and that you may live eternally in the land of the living [Isa 38:11] into which you are now entering to possess [Deut 11:10], I order you in the name of our Lord Jesus Christ to wait for us until it is time for the Divine Office." The sick man replied, "My lord, willingly shall I do what you ask, if only you will support my intention with your prayers." The holy abbot went

---

[17] Herbert of Clairvaux, LM 1.13 (PL 185:1291).

away silently to the dormitory and the other, who had practically drawn his last breath, did not die before the set time. But as soon as the signal for Vigils began to be sounded, the board was rapped[18] and he departed. This happened with many other monks besides that brother; they prolonged their departure at the behest and will of the most blessed father.

CHAPTER TEN

*How the Man of God Predicted That His Brother, Dom Guy, Would Not Die at Clairvaux Because of His Sin[19]*

When the man of the Lord heard that one of his spiritual sons, a good and religious man whom he had sent into Normandy,[20] was laboring there under hopeless sickness, he decided to send for the man and have him brought to him so that the devoted brother might die in his own nest [Job 29:18] and not be deprived of the grave he had desired. But one of Bernard's own blood brothers, whose name was Guy tried to block this plan.[21] Now I believe this was because he was one of the procurators at Clairvaux and wanted to spare the expense and the labor. When he stubbornly insisted on having his own way, blessed Bernard said to him, "Do you care more for money and animals than for your brothers? Because you do not want our brother to rest with us in this valley, neither shall

---

[18] A wooden board was struck to announce a death or impending death; EO 94.2.

[19] Herbert of Clairvaux, LM 2.11 (PL 185:1323–24).

[20] There is no record of a Norman foundation by Bernard (*Le Grande Exorde*, 81n10).

[21] Guy (Guido) was Bernard's eldest brother. See William of Saint Thierry, Vita Bern 1.3.10; 1.9.45; 1.13.64 (PL 185:232–33, 253, 262–63); Geoffrey of Auxerre, Vita Bern 5.3.18 (PL 185:362); Geoffrey of Auxerre, *Fragmenta* 53, *Analecta Bollandiana* 50 (1932): 117; and Williams, 73–74. Guy is reputed to have died on the night of the Feast of All Saints (1 November) in 1141 or 1142, having returned to Pontigny after founding the abbey of La Prée.

you rest in it." And so it was. Guy was a good and religious man, but so that the saying of the holy man might be fulfilled he did not die at Clairvaux; instead, he took to his bed at Pontigny, laid low by sickness, and, by the will of the Lord, he ended his life and had his gravesite there.

CHAPTER ELEVEN

*How the Venerable Father Spent Three Years*
*in the Regions of Italy but Still Visited Clairvaux*
*in Spirit Three Times*[22]

The venerable Father Bernard once spent three years in the city of Rome and various parts of Italy, settling the schism of Peter Leone.[23] In that undertaking the Lord Christ clearly honored his servant magnificently [cf. Wis 10:10]. At length he returned to Clairvaux, and after saying a prayer he immediately went to the brothers' chapter [EO 88.22-24ff.]. He was exhausted by the long journey and could not speak for long, but he gave a sermon which was short but full of consolation, saying, "Blessed be God, who has restored to me my dearest brothers and to you your father, such as he is. My little sons, although I may seem to have been far away from you for three years, do not think that I have been absent all the time. Know that during this interval I have returned three times, visiting this house and walking through the workshops. I was always exhilarated, always consoled at seeing your unanimity and persistence in carrying out the directives of our way of life."

There are innumerable other things which the servant of God said and did, in which he clearly showed that by the grace of

---

[22] Herbert of Clairvaux, LM 2.14 (PL 185:1324); and Vita Bern fragmenta 7.6.13-14 (PL 185:463–64).

[23] On the antipope, Peter Leone (Pierleoni), see P. Savage, "Anacletus II," *New Catholic Encyclopedia*, 2nd ed., 1:370–71; and Williams, 114–54.

prophecy he was present in many places in spirit when he seemed to be absent in body and that by the revelation of the Lord he knew many things that were hidden and even far off, which were thought to be concealed from him. Dom Gerard, former abbot of Longpont,[24] made this clear to us when, as one of the oldest senior monks at Clairvaux, he set about carefully examining the words and deeds of the holy father. From the same source, we heard that the saint of God was once preaching the word of God in some chapter of monks when two of the brothers who were present saw him and the chair in which he was sitting suspended in the air about a foot above the ground.

CHAPTER TWELVE

*When He Had Been away from Clairvaux for a Long Time,*
*He Returned in Spirit and Entered into the Cells of the Novices*
*and Consoled One Who Was Grieving*[25]

This faithful and wise steward of the Lord's goods [Luke 12:42] was once absent for a long time—as usual on Church business, either making peace, healing schism, or confuting heresy, very often by order of the pope who urged him to go although he was most unwilling. When he had settled the business on which he had gone away, he returned to the monastery and, as soon as opportunity arose, he went to the novices' room so that the new and tender little sons who had been a long time without the sweetness of his holy exhortations might be more lavishly refreshed from the breasts of his consolation [Isa 66:11]. Whenever the holy father went away he sowed the seed of the word of God [Matt 13; Mark 4] over all

[24] Gerard was the fourth abbot of Longpont and died in 1161.
[25] Compare Geoffrey of Auxerre, *Sermon on the Anniversary of the Death of Saint Bernard* 3 (PL 185:575); and the same author's *Fragmenta* 50, *Analecta Bollandiana* 50 (1932): 116. Also see Grießer, EM, 105n2.

the waters and scarcely ever did he return without a rich spiritual harvest, filling the probationers' room with a multitude of novices. At one time their number reached nearly one hundred, so that at the hours of the Divine Office the choir was full of novices and, except for a few senior monks who maintained discipline, the monks had to stand outside. So, as we have said, after he had gone into the novices' room and cheered them by his pleasing and edifying talk and had recalled them to a more fervent observation of their holy undertaking, he called one of them to him and said, "Dearest son, what is this sadness which is so perniciously eating away at the depths of your heart?"[26] To the novice, ashamed and scarcely daring to speak, he—meek and humble of heart [Matt 11:29], aware of how to show himself to be a shepherd and not the hireling of the flock [John 10:11-12]—said, "I know, dearest son, I know what has been happening to you, and with the fatherly affection of loving kindness I am suffering right along with you. In the course of my long absence I have been compelled to do without the deeply longed-for company of my brothers although I very earnestly desired to be physically with them, but it has been granted me by the Lord's grace to do in the spirit what physically I could not do. I have returned in spirit, going through each of the workshops, diligently exploring how the brothers are behaving themselves, even the novices' room. There I found them all exulting in the fear of God and girding themselves for the labor of penance. I sighed at seeing only you pining in deep distress. Although I wanted to draw you to me to comfort you, you turned away from me and averted your face, weeping so bitterly that our cowl was drenched with your tears." Saying this and giving salutary advice, the holy father put to flight the sorrow gripping him and recalled him who had just been nearly overwhelmed by sadness to the freedom of spiritual joy.

Truly God is wonderful in his saints [Ps 67:36]; truly God is ineffable and ineffable are all his works. I do not know which to admire more in our most blessed father: that he deserved to receive so much and such extraordinary grace from the Lord not once but

---

[26] The novice is Geoffrey of Auxerre.

many times, or that having received such excellent grace he did not keep it to himself by the witness of his conscience but revealed it to not a few of his friends—something he scarcely seemed able to do without peril. He even made it public in the community, as we have related above, and showed what had happened to him before all the brothers because his mind was so firmly fixed in the fear of God that he was never afraid of being struck by the spirit of vanity. It is even found in the deeds of the blessed man that when he was absent in the flesh he appeared in spirit, along with a crowd of monks, to a certain novice who was gravely ill at Clairvaux. He foretold that in five days he would die. At sunset on the fifth day he came to visit the dying man again and ordered him to trust and not to fear but to hold a straight course [RB 73.4] toward our Lord Jesus Christ and to offer to him the humble greetings of his family at Clairvaux. At the sound of his voice the novice assented by bowing his head as best he could and moving his lips, and closing his eyes at that very moment he fell asleep in the Lord.[27]

CHAPTER THIRTEEN

*About the Miraculous Conversion of Many Clerks*
*When the Holy Man Preached the Word of God*
*in the Schools of Paris*[28]

On another occasion, Bernard, the man of the Lord, had occasion to go to Paris. As was customary he went into the schools at the invitation of the clerks.[29] Laying before them the form of true philosophy, he warned them earnestly about despising the world and embracing

---

[27] Geoffrey of Auxerre, Vita Bern 4.2.8 (PL 185:325–26).
[28] Herbert of Clairvaux, LM 2.17 (PL 185:1326–27). Geoffrey of Auxerre writes in his *Fragmenta* 49 (*Analecta Bollandiana* 50 [1932]: 115) that he was among these clerks (Grießer, EM, 106n3). Clerks refer to clerics, i.e., students.
[29] For additional context, see Bernard of Clairvaux, Conv (SBOp 4:69–116; CF 25:31–79).

voluntary poverty for the Lord Christ.[30] When he had finished his sermon he left, saddened that not one of them was converted and that this should happen despite his prayers and contrary to what usually happened to him. Arriving at the house of a certain archdeacon who had extended hospitality to him, he withdrew into the chapel set up there. Once he had begun to pray vehemently in the Spirit, he broke into tears of the deepest compunction, until the groans and sobs, which he could not hold back, could be heard outside. At hearing this, the aforesaid archdeacon began to ask his friends what might be the cause of such sorrow. One of them replied, a religious man named Rainald,[31] the former abbot of Foigny, who was well aware of the secrets of the man of God and from whom I learned what I am relating. He said to the archdeacon, "This wonderful man is entirely aflame with the fire of love and entirely absorbed in God. He desires nothing in the world but to be able to lead the erring into the way of truth and gain their souls for Christ. And because he just now sowed the word of life [John 6:69] in the schools and did not receive the fruit of the conversion of the clerks by his words, he thinks that God is angry with him, and in his preaching today he did not sense his presence. Hence this storm of groans; hence this flood of tears. I hope very much indeed that today's lack of fruit will be outweighed by tomorrow's great and rich harvest." In the morning the famous preacher went again to the schools, and at the Lord's command he sailed the ship of his thoughts into the deep and let down the net of holy doctrine for a catch [Luke 5:4]. At the end of the sermon several of the clerks gave themselves to the Lord by his hands. Immediately, as if they were sailors rescued from the perils of the world, he put them in hired carriages so as not to delay in bringing them to the safety of Clairvaux.[32] With this great company he went out of the

---

[30] See Bernard of Clairvaux on voluntary poverty: Ep 1.4 (SBOp 7:4; James, Ep 1, p.4); 345.1 (SBOp 8:287; James, Ep 388.1, pp. 458–59); and 462.2 (SBOp 8:439–40; not in James); also Bernard, Tpl 9 (SBOp 3:222; CF 19:143). See also Grießer, EM, 107n1.

[31] Rainald became the first abbot of Foigny in 1121 and died at Clairvaux in 1131. See Bernard of Clairvaux, Ep 72–74, 413 (SBOp 7:175–81; SBOp 8:396; James, Ep 75–77, pp. 103–7; Ep 444, pp. 509–10).

[32] See Bernard of Clairvaux, Conv (SBOp 4:69–116; CF 25:31–79).

city as far as the town of Saint Denis, where they stayed the night.[33] By midmorning, however, when the brothers thought they would go directly on their way with him, he said, "We must return at once to Paris for some are still there who are ours. We ought to draw them out from there and join them to the Lord's sheep so that there may be one flock and one shepherd [John 10:16]." Just as he was beginning to enter the city, he saw in the distance three clerks running toward him, and he said to his companions, "The Lord has been favorable to us and now we can go on with our journey. Here are the clerks for whose sake we have come." They came up to him when they realized he was there and rejoiced with great joy [Luke 24:52; John 20:20], and said, "Most blessed father, how much we have longed for you to come. We had intended to come with you, but we thought we could not follow you once you had gone." Bernard answered this by saying, "I knew this, dearly beloved, and therefore I hurried to come with bread for you who are fleeing. Let us travel on together at once, and by the grace of God I will be the guide for your journey." They joined the others who, you remember, were following the holy man, and under the discipline of his instruction they strove in spiritual warfare all the days of their life.[34]

## CHAPTER FOURTEEN

### *About Those Novices Whom Bernard Blessed and Clothed in the Monastic Habit, and in the Spirit Foretold That They Would All Become Abbots*[35]

Certain novices, after being blessed by the holy father, put off the old man with his deeds and put on the new man, created for God

---

[33] The Benedictine abbey of Saint Denis was reformed in Bernard's day under the famous Abbot Suger. On Bernard's relationship with Suger, see Williams, 222–27.

[34] RB 2.20. On the image of monastic "spiritual warfare" and militaristic images of the monastic life, see note 1 to EM Verse Prol.

[35] McGuire (*Difficult Saint*, 166) thinks that the story in this chapter may have originated in Sweden and come to Conrad by an oral source.

in righteousness and true holiness [Eph 4:24; Col 3:9].The blessed man spoke about them in the Spirit of God and foretold that they would all receive spiritual grace and be elected to the title and office of abbot. In good time his prophetic word was in each case fulfilled. Only one of them, Peter by name, whom Bernard had sent to the monastery of Nydala in Sweden,[36] was not invested with this position until many years after the holy abbot's death because he was a very simple man and was considered somewhat unsuitable for such a high office until well into his old age, nearly into his decrepitude.What happened? Could he possibly evade the almighty power of the Holy Spirit, whether hiding at the extreme bounds of the world or bearing the limitations of the weight of years? Could he not carry out what the Spirit had so long ago foretold by the mouth of his prophet Bernard? Finally, after this long space of time, when it had almost been forgotten, the thing which the very reverend father had foretold of this man of dove-like simplicity came to pass.The brothers of Nydala on the island called Gotland were deprived of their abbot.[37] According to the general custom of the Order they came back to the mother house, so that by the oversight and care of the father abbot their house might be provided with a worthy head [CCP 4]. By the will of the Lord, without whose nod no leaf falls from a tree or sparrow to the ground [Matt 10:29-31], the father abbot and the others involved in the election were pleased to confer this responsibility on the aforesaid old man. They trusted as confidently in the goodness of God and the merits of the most holy father as Peter was diffident and humble about his own inadequacy. When this was accomplished and the word that the saint had once foretold was called to mind and divulged everywhere, everyone who heard it marveled. They said that the promotion of so old and simple a

---

[36] Nydala (*Domus Novae-Vallis*), a daughter house of Clairvaux, was founded in 1145 in the Diocese of Linköping, Sweden. Janauschek, 74. See James France, *The Cistercians in Scandinavia*, CS 131 (Kalamazoo, MI: Cistercian Publications, 1992), 29–31.

[37] The abbey, called Gudvala (Gutnalia or Guthualia), was founded in 1164 and was the only daughter house of Nydala. Janauschek, 152. See Lekai, *Cistercians*, 42; France, *Cistercians in Scandinavia*, 41.

man had been foreseen by divine dispensation and that not one word or one syllable spoken in the spirit of prophesy by the man of God had been in vain [Matt 5:18].

CHAPTER FIFTEEN

*About the Robber Who Was Bound with Cords*
*and Already Had the Rope around His Neck, Ready for Death,*
*and How Bernard Put His Own Habit on Him*
*and Made Him a Lay Brother at Clairvaux*[38]

It happened one time that the servant of God was going to see Count Theobald[39] on business. As he drew near the town where Theobald then was, he saw on the road a large crowd of men who were, at the count's order, taking a nefarious and infamous robber away to punishment. When he saw this, the ever-gentle father laid his hand on the ropes that bound the wretch and said to his executioners, "Leave this assassin to me, for I want to hang him with my own hands." The count, having heard that the man of God was coming, had immediately hurried to meet him, for he always loved and honored him with a wonderful affection. When he saw in his hand the rope by which he was dragging the robber after him, he was extremely horrified and cried out, "Hey, venerable father, what is this you want to do? Have you called back from the gates of hell [Ps 88:49] this brigand, a thousand times condemned? Surely you cannot mean to save him, for he is already completely made into a devil. His rehabilitation is entirely hopeless and he will never be able to do any good except by dying. Let it go, lord father, let this man of perdition go to perdition [John 17:12], for the lives of many have been endangered by his pestilential

---

[38] This chapter, except for the last sentence, is taken from Herbert of Clairvaux, LM 2.15 (PL 185:1324–25).

[39] Theobald, count of Champagne, 1125–52. See Williams, 190–204; and Bernard of Clairvaux, Epp 37–40 (SBOp 7:94–99; James, Epp 39–46, pp. 71–76).

life." The holy father answered him, saying, "I know, best of men, I know that this robber is thoroughly wicked and deserves full well the bitterness of every kind of torment. Do not think that I want in this way to release a sinner from punishment; instead, I intend to hand him over to the torturers [Matt 18:34] and to apply an appropriate punishment which will be all the more deserved because it is more divine. You have condemned him to quick death and momentary suffering, but I will inflict on him a daily crucifixion and a long, drawn-out death. You have caught a thief and would have him stay on the gibbet for one or several days; I will leave him nailed to the cross [Matt 27:38; Mark 15:27; Luke 23:33] for many years to live and hang continually in punishment." When that most Christian prince heard this he was silent, and he did not dare to contradict the words of the saint. Immediately, that most kindly father took off his tunic and put it on his captive and after cutting his hair he added him to the flock of the Lord [John 10:16], making of the wolf a lamb [John 10:12], of the robber a lay brother.[40] He came with him to Clairvaux, where he was then made obedient even unto death [Phil 2:8], and he was called Constantius, expressing by this beautiful name the constancy of his intention. Unless I am mistaken, he lived in the Order thirty or more years before he went home to the Lord who had mercifully deigned to deliver him by the merits of our most blessed father from the double death of both body and soul.

## Chapter Sixteen

### About the Wonderful Devotion with Which Bernard Was Received by the People of Italy When He Went to That Region[41]

Dom Rainald, whom we mentioned earlier [EM 2.13], told us that when the servant of God, Bernard, went to Milan to heal the

---

[40] See Augustine, *Sermon* 295; PL 38:1351; and *Sermon* 317; PL 38:1436 (*Le Grand Exorde*, 282n13).

[41] The entire chapter is taken from Herbert of Clairvaux, LM 2.18 (PL 185:1327–28).

schism of Peter Leone he was received with such universal acclaim that the whole city ran out one league to meet him.[42] In fact, many of them went on with him for four or five miles. They were so pleased with him that, although they had never seen Bernard before, when he entered the city they wanted to coerce him to become archbishop by unanimous consent rather than election. When he refused, they were quite prepared to take him by force had he not evaded them by fleeing secretly. When he was seated in a very large house there, such a crowd of people surrounded him that no one could get in. Meanwhile, a certain citizen of that town, honorable in dress and countenance, longed to approach the man of God by any means, but he could find no way to him. So he crawled on his hands and knees through the midst of the crowd and climbed over the shoulders of those who were seated until he arrived at the one he wanted. After seizing Bernard's feet, he began to embrace and kiss them with astounding devotion. When the aforesaid Rainald, who was sitting nearby, saw this, he got up to move the man away, knowing that the holy man found this kind of veneration and groveling distasteful. But the man turned to him and said, "Let be, I beg you, let me see and touch this man who is near God and who is truly an apostolic man. For I tell you and swear by the Christian faith that I saw him among the apostles of Christ." When the monk heard this, he marveled and wanted to know more. He wanted to ask him about the vision but modestly did not presume to do so because of the people standing around. Nevertheless, he believed very firmly that this had been a great revelation because the man loved the servant of God so intensely because of it.

[42] This journey took place in June 1135; Williams, 134–46.

CHAPTER SEVENTEEN

*About the Magnificent Reply
by Which the Man of God Refuted the Cleverness
of a Certain Heretic in Gascony*[43]

At the time when the legate of the Lord Pope and some other bishops went to the Toulouse area to refute the Manichaeans' heresy, they took with them Bernard, the saint of the Lord.[44] The brothers prepared a mount for him, one a little better than usual, which would suffice for so long a journey. Once he had arrived in that region with the band of bishops, a certain Henry,[45] once a black monk but now a vile apostate[46] and the ringleader of the heretics, panicked when he realized by his appearance that a servant of God had come, knowing that he was unable to resist the wisdom and Spirit which spoke through him [Acts 6:10]. He snuck away in hasty flight, and during that time very little was seen of him.

There the Lord glorified his servant in the sight of the whole people and the princes of the land and wrought great signs and wonders daily among the people [Acts 6:8] by Bernard's hands. It is hard to believe how enormous a crowd followed the apostolic man every day—some seeking his learning, others a cure, and all a blessing from him. One day while a countless crowd of people was there and he was warning them at length about keeping the Catholic faith and avoiding the company of heretics, there happened to be present one of those heretics who seemed to be

---

[43] The entire chapter is taken from Herbert of Clairvaux, LM 2.16 (PL 185:1325–26).

[44] The year 1145; see Williams, 340–45. On Bernard and the Cathars, see Beverly Mayne Kienzle, *Cistercians, Heresy and Crusade in Occitania: Preaching in the Lord's Vineyard, 1145–1229* (York: York Medieval Press, 2001), 90–108.

[45] About Henry and his follower Peter Brusi, see Bernard of Clairvaux, Epp 241–42 (SBOp 8:125–29; James, Epp 317–18, pp. 387–91); and Geoffrey of Auxerre, Vita Bern 3.6.16-19 (PL 185:312–14).

[46] The EM refers often to apostates or apostate monks: see EM 2.22; 3.15; 4.9, 16, and Index.

more powerful and more prudent than the rest. With an embittered glance he noticed the veneration which the people were showering upon the servant of God and set about finding something to do that would somehow cloud his shining reputation and besmirch his good name. When the man of God had said all he thought necessary for the moment, he got on his horse to go. And what happened? The aforesaid heretic, like a coiled serpent with head raised to strike, came up to the man of God and, shouting in front of everyone, said, "Lord Abbot, let me tell you that the pack horse of our master, who seems to you so wicked, is not as proud-necked and sleek as this high stepper of yours."

After the gentle and patient man heard this, he answered him at once with a tranquil face and mind, saying, "I won't argue with what you say, friend. Indeed you should know that this animal you taunt me about is a brute beast and one of those which nature has made to face downward and be obedient to their stomach. If he eats at pleasure and gets fat, that is not an offense against justice nor is God offended, because the beast is only following his nature. Wherefore, your master and I will not in God's judgment be examined over the crests of animals, but each of us will be judged by his own neck. Now then, if you please, take a look at my neck and see if it is fatter than the neck of your master. If it is, you can perhaps justly reproach me." Having said this he threw back his hood and bared his head to the shoulders to show his neck which was long and slender; although the flesh was wasted and thin, yet by the gift of heaven it was beautiful and white like the neck of a swan. When all those who were present saw this they rejoiced with great rejoicing and blessed the Lord, who had put into the mouth of his servant a reply so ready and fit to confound and stop the mouth that speaks wicked things [Ps 62:12].

CHAPTER EIGHTEEN

*About a Blind Man in That Region*
*Who Received His Sight through the Dust of the Earth*
*Where the Footprints of the Holy Man Were Shown to Him*

While the most reverend father was still staying in that region, traveling like one of the apostles through cities and towns preaching the Gospel, curing all who were sick [Matt 9:35], confounding the thoroughly wicked ravings of heretics by convincing and refuting them, it happened that a certain blind man in that neighborhood learned of the virtues and miracles which were daily multiplied by the hand of the man of God. Animated by the hope of recovering his health, he decided to go to the servant of God to see if perchance the darkness of his blindness might be wiped away and sweet light restored by the blessing of that heavenly grace which was being freely given through him to wretched men. So he made haste and inquired carefully where he might meet the saint of God. He heard that Bernard was attending some huge assembly along with a great crowd and sowing the word of life [John 6:69]. When he got there, stumbling and gasping for breath from running, he was met by the depressing rumor that the man of the Lord had already left and gone on to another place. What was he to do? The desire to receive healing urged him to run farther, but the incredibly deep darkness that covered his eyes made this course of action time-consuming and difficult. Just when he was becoming convinced in his mind of failure and drooping with grief, suddenly he was inspired by divine grace. Holding with all his heart to his hope in the merits of the blessed man, he said to those standing by, "I beg you by the mercy of God, lead me to that place in which you know with complete certainty that the man of God stood or sat." By the goodwill of those present he was taken to the place at once, and when he got there he flung his whole body down on the ground in wonderful devotion and veneration, kissing the very dust in which the holy footprints of the man of God remained, and by the merits of his servant he implored the Lord's mercy ever more earnestly. When he had done this for quite a long time, he rubbed that very dust in his eyes, full of faith, and suddenly he received the light of his eyes by the mercy of God, who deigned to declare by this grace the holiness of his servant Bernard even when he was absent. What was done not only bolstered the faith of orthodox Catholics but also increased the confusion and shame of the vainglorious heretics.

Who can worthily describe how grounded in humility, how submissive in fear, how trembling in caution this blessed man was—and all this amid the glory and honor in which he was held by peoples, tribes, and tongues wherever the business of the Church caused him to go? To say nothing of the peoples of other areas, certainly the people of Gascony, who received through him the light of the purity of the Catholic faith and whom the holy father brought back from the jaws of the most putrid heresy as if from the belly of hell by the word of his preaching and by his wonderful signs and miracles, and who venerated him with such fervent devotion that he once gave in to their repeated demands and sat down in a chair to give himself up to their will. So great was the throng of people coming to him to obtain his blessing and to kiss his holy hands that his very thin and delicate flesh could not bear the pressure and force of so many kisses, and his hands and arms swelled up like those of fighters. Whereas others received a blessing for themselves through the virtue which went out from him, he, fairly weak and almost crushed, suffered serious bodily harm.[47] Blessed be God in all things, who in these recent days has deigned to raise up in the Cistercian Order a man of such perfect observance and consummate justice, through whom the monastic way of life flourished anew in the ancient vigor of holy religion, and the Church of God, by the apostolic grace bestowed on him, has received the many benefits of divine mercy.

[47] Bernard practiced such harsh asceticism that it seems to have affected his physical health. See Vita Bern 1.8.39–41 (PL 185:250–51); Ep 345.2 (SBOp 8:287–88; James, Ep 388.2, pp. 458–59); and McGuire, *Difficult Saint*, 24–25.

CHAPTER NINETEEN

*About a Dead Man Whom Blessed Bernard Raised to Life*[48]

At the time when the Saracens were occupying the land of Jerusalem, blessed Bernard, whose soul the sword of Christian desolation pierced with a special sharpness, went about everywhere urging crowds of the faithful, not only by words, but also by signs and wonders, to take up the fight to avenge the injury to the Savior. Now he happened to come into Germany, and one day he was leaving Freiburg, an important town in Burgundy, with Henry, a noble and still a young man. Preceded and followed by a great crowd, they were going to a house of his where they were to spend the following night. Having taken the sign of the cross Henry had vowed to go not on horseback but on foot until he had gathered the funds needed for his proposed pilgrimage. Nevertheless, the holy abbot directed him to mount his horse and accompany him. So he mounted a horse and soon rode along after him. Seeing this and envying it, a certain son of Belial,[49] a man who served Henry and who loved all kinds of depravity and was skeptical of any good, began viciously to blaspheme the servant of God and to hurl curses at his lord, such as: "Go on then! Follow the devil and the devil take both of you!" Alongside them were two poor little women carrying between them a third whose feet and limbs were withered and useless. They wanted to ask the man of God to relieve the adversity of the sick woman and the anguish of her bearers by the remedy of the cure they hoped for. Realizing this, Henry took pity on them and said, "Lift the sick woman over the neck of my horse and you go on ahead to ask help of the servant

---

[48] Grießer (EM, 113–14) comments at length on this chapter, which seems to have been inserted later, as it does not appear in several manuscripts and never in the earliest. It is also included in Caesarius of Heisterbach, *Dialogus miraculorum* 1.16 (Strange 1:22–24; S-Bland 1:23–25). Compare Tubach 593, 1355, 3598.

[49] "Son of Belial" is an Old Testament expression (2 Sam 16:7; 20:1) that came to imply a good-for-nothing person. Compare Deut 13:13; Judg 19:22. *Le Grande Exorde*, 83n6.

of God." But the aforesaid servant was affronted and irritated at his lord's work of piety, and he complained endlessly with bitter invective, as if he were taking the wretched woman to a wizard or a sorcerer who would drive her crazy with magic. Henry said to him, "No, I am sending her to be restored to health by the man of God's blessing and I promise you on my unswerving hope of salvation, that if he does not cure her, I will give you the horse I am riding on." The servant accepted this statement with gratitude and gratification, for he entirely distrusted Bernard's power of good deeds and smiled and sniggered equally because he doubted the cure and because he was also already reveling at getting the horse. In fact, when the woman was brought to the saint of the Lord and had obtained his hoped-for blessing, she immediately got up, cured of what was wrong with her and no longer needing to be carried as she had been.

Seeing this, the servant was stupefied and, in the grip of the evil spirit he carried in his heart, he hurried for a while to get ahead so that, face-to-face with the man of God he might shriek against Bernard all the vile, wicked things breathed into him by Satan. But the judgment of the Lord soon came down upon him: he fell on his back, broke his neck, and breathed his last. Henry was stricken with sorrow at this sudden and lamentable death, and he broke the mournful news about this to the abbot, begging him to go back—for he had got a little ahead—and see this sad sight. And he said, "This happened to him on your account, because he had no fear of blaspheming and slandering you." "Alas," said Saint Bernard, "the Lord does not will that anyone should die because of me." So he went back and gave himself up to prayer, in which alone he trusted in all difficulties. He prayed over him in silence for the length of an Our Father. Then he ordered the bystanders to lift the dead man up. When he was upright, but still dead, his head, unsupported by his neck, wobbled hideously back and forth. "Hold it!" Bernard said. "Hold his head firmly!" Finally Bernard traced over the break with his spittle—whose medicinal unction he very often used—and made the sign of the cross, saying, "In the name of the Lord, get up!" and "In the name of the Father, and of the Son, and of the Holy Spirit, may God restore your spirit to you!" [Acts 3:6]. Then the servant did in fact receive his spirit again and was made a living soul, or rather, he was restored to life. All those who had witnessed and seen so manifest a miracle as the raising of the dead marveled and rejoiced and shouted their praises to heaven. Asked by the saint of God how he was going to live, what he was going to do with the rest of his days, he said, "My Lord, I will live in whatever way you prescribe and do whatever you command, whatever you wish." Asked by those present if he had really been dead, he said, "I was dead, and I had received the sentence of damnation, and if the holy abbot had not made haste to help me I should irrevocably have been led down to hell." With the encouragement of those who were present, he took the cross and set out for Jerusalem with the rest.

On the same journey Henry himself dedicated himself to God and blessed Bernard and afterward became a monk at Clairvaux. He thought that this miracle he had seen with the trustworthy testimony of his own eyes was very well known to the writers of the life of the holy father, and he was depressed to find out later that it had been passed over in silence, and he narrated everything he had seen to the glory of God and of his saint so that all generations to come forever might hear and understand how venerated he had been and how the Most High had glorified him.

CHAPTER TWENTY

*About the Death of the Most Blessed Abbot Bernard*
*and the Miracles That Happened after His Death*

When he had happily reached the full term of his days at Clairvaux, the venerable Father Bernard, beloved of God and men [Sir 45:1], rested in peace, full of days but still more full of virtue. At his passing many bishops, abbots, and other religious men gathered together. They celebrated his funeral rites for two days, and so great a multitude of men gathered that scarcely any reverence was paid to the bishops, none at all to the monks. The grace of healing [1 Cor 12:9] which dwelt within him in life did not depart at his death. Once the holy body had been laid out in public, appropriately dressed in priestly garments, with his face showing and his hands also uncovered [EO 94.33], a certain brother who had for a long time suffered the grave sickness of epilepsy humbly and reverently approached the father as though he were still alive. He began to beg and tearfully pray that he have pity upon him. And the loving father, placed in the midst of his sons, could not disregard so grave a calamity in one of them. As if he had said, "My son, I sleep but my heart is awake" [Song 5:2], immediately what was asked was granted by the grace of God. From that time on the brother recovered fully, and this happy experience showed that the holy abbot yet lived after death.

The next day when that most precious treasure was to be buried, a boy came from a nearby village. He had a shriveled arm and a contracted hand, owing to the dryness of the sinews. Those who were present had compassion on his age and disability and invited him, after the ninth hour[50] of prayer [Acts 3:1], to touch the body of the saint with more confidence than his innocent age presumed by itself to dare. When the shriveled arm was laid on the arm of the saint, and the contracted hand on the blessed hand, suddenly the force of nature flowed again; the arm was restored, and he stretched and bent the fingers of his hand. He was perfectly restored to health before the eyes of the crowd that was standing around for the holy funeral rites. So great was the acclamation of all those present at this cure, loudly praising God, that the brothers' discipline could scarcely be maintained.[51] As night fell, another man, entirely disabled in body, was brought in; he stretched out before the coffin and in front of those who were singing the psalms he stood erect and was led to the altar.[52]

---

[50] None.
[51] Grießer (EM, 116n4) attributes this portion to a particular manuscript of Geoffrey of Auxerre.
[52] See Grießer, EM, 117n1. See EO 94.46 on the brothers singing psalms.

The Lord Abbot of Cîteaux, who had come with many abbots of the Order to the obsequies for the man of God, considering the insistent demands of this great crowd of people, and conjecturing the future in light of the present experience, began to be very much afraid that if increasing miracles were to draw an intolerable crowd of people their unruliness might endanger the discipline of the Order and that the fervor of holy observance might grow tepid in that place. So after deliberating about this he reverently and by virtue of obedience forbade the saint from working any more miracles. And since the Apostle said of our Lord Jesus Christ that he was made obedient to the Father even unto death [Phil 2:8], and since, following his example, our lawgiver Saint Benedict in his Rule proposes obedience unto death to us, the holy and truly humble soul of our father was obedient to a mortal man even after the death of the flesh. The signs which had already begun to shine forth ceased, and from that day forward he performed no public miracles, even though to this day he cannot let down any of the faithful, and especially the brothers of his Order, who cry to him out of their various needs. For it was clear that the abbot of Cîteaux was averse only to those signs which threatened the discipline of the Order by attracting crowds of people.

After the passing of this blessed man, many years went by, and there was a certain matron in the Italian territories whom an evil spirit seized and began to vex grievously. Her relatives and friends were extremely upset by so doleful a case, and by earnest reflection they tried to think what could be done to cure her. There was in that district a certain monastery of the Cistercian Order. And as hope flickering in anguished minds is usually given credence, they had an idea which grew only out of their faith, and they decided by common consent to take the possessed woman to that house to seek help. This they did. They put the wretched woman at the gate while they sent some of their company to let the abbot and the brothers know about this great affliction and ask them to do something about it. The abbot, along with some of the senior brothers whom he knew to be spiritual men, went out to the sufferer, taking with him the abbatial cross and holy relics. Although the evil spirit was confronted with the cross of the Lord and the holy tokens of the saints, it was unmoved. The abbot recalled that they had for veneration the relics of the hair and beard of Saint Bernard, which, if I am not mistaken, he had received that year as a blessing in going to Clairvaux to Chapter and which he continually carried about with him for his own protection. Saying nothing, he silently put his hand under his scapular and as soon as he withdrew the relics he goaded the demon with them. The fiend, catching a glimpse of them, began kicking the sufferer's footstool and spitting and involuntarily manifesting by the indecent movements of its entire body what it was suffering inwardly. And it broke into speech, saying, "Ah, petty abbot, what are you trying to do? What evil thing are you contriving against me under your clothes? Your attempt is in vain, your labor is useless! Keep your little Bernard, for you're not going to get anywhere." Then the abbot said, "By the grace of the Lord and the merits of this most holy man you will leave *now*." The demon replied, "What? Does it escape you that he has been forbidden to work signs? Knowing this I rest securely in this my home." Hearing these words, the abbot and the brothers who were with him were extremely amazed that the wicked spirit so quickly appropriated that interdict as a shield in its own defense.

We have touched briefly on the virtues of the blessed Abbot Bernard, asking the mercy of God that our dearest father may keep us from all evil by his merits and prayers and grant that we not be deprived of a share in life eternal after we have gathered the heads of the grain of divine grace in the footsteps of so great a patron.

## Chapter Twenty-One

### About Dom Robert, Second Abbot of Clairvaux, and about the Novice Who by His Exhortations and Prayers Was Confirmed in a Holy Promise through a Great Miracle

Dom Robert[53] succeeded the most blessed Father Bernard in the governance of the monastery of Clairvaux. He had been abbot

---

[53] Robert of Bruges entered monastic life in 1131 and served as abbot of Les Dunes (1138–53) and then of Clairvaux (1153–57), where he died.

of Les Dunes,[54] and the Lord deigned to reveal his prelacy to him some six or seven years before this promotion occurred. For some years earlier two of the brothers of the monastery of Clairvaux were discussing the blessed deeds of their beloved Abbot Bernard, and one said to the other, "Do you know how long our father has left to live among us?" The other replied that he did not, and the first one said, "I know that he will live for six or seven years, and that Dom Robert, who is today abbot of Les Dunes, should succeed him in governing this monastery."[55] When, by the gift of God, this came to pass, this observant abbot exercised his pastoral charge with a considerable humility, as he judged himself to be much inferior in merit to his predecessor. The more he thought of the eminence of the virtues of him who had preceded him, the more he despised in himself whatever good he was able to do. So it happened that, though he provided an example of great religious observance, yet in his eyes he disparaged his own life by comparison.

During the time of this venerable abbot there was at Clairvaux a certain observant monk who saw a glorious vision, which the Lord deigned to show for the consolation of his humble family at Clairvaux.[56] The brother who deserved to see this vision was uncertain whether he was asleep or fully awake when he saw it, but he was inclined to think that he had been keeping vigil and was rapt into ecstasy. On the Monday of Easter week, then, when he was at Vigils in the choir at Clairvaux, the hand of the Lord came upon him [Ezek 1:3]. And lo, there appeared to him rising in the air in the middle of choir a resplendent and glorious right hand which blessed the family of the Lord who were confessing his name in psalms and hymns and spiritual songs [Col 3:16] and twice with an elongated movement made over them the life-giving sign of the cross. The Spirit spoke in the heart of the brother to disclose the

---

[54] Les Dunes (*Dunae*), an abbey in what was then the Diocese of Thérouanne, founded as a Benedictine house in 1107, became Cistercian in 1138. Janauschek, CXXVLL (pp. 51–52); Cottineaux, 1:1008. DHGE 14:1039–44.

[55] Geoffrey of Auxerre, Vita Bern 5.3.17; PL 185:361.

[56] From this point to the end of the paragraph, Herbert of Clairvaux, LM 2.3 (PL 185:1314–15).

mystery he had seen, saying, "This is the mighty arm of the Lord [Isa 40:10]; this is the right hand of the Almighty."

On that same day there was converted to monastic life there a very noble man, Andrew by name, archdeacon of Verdun, who had come there to pray, nor had he then any intention of converting.[57] But once he had entered the brothers' chapter to ask the help of their prayers [EO 70, 78–80] and seen that well-ordered holy multitude and their, as it were, angelic way of life, he was sharply pierced to the heart; the Spirit of the Lord suddenly stirred within him, and he was changed into another man. He was so eager to leave the world that he did not even stay long enough to say good-bye to his friends or to dispose of his house and his goods, but he left everything straightaway, breaking with it all rather than disposing of it, so that he might the sooner cleave to Christ. And making the meaning of the double sign of the cross clear, another clerk, called Geoffrey, a man of more humble birth but in no way his inferior in right conduct and generous behavior, gave himself at the same time with Andrew. They entered together, and persevering in the Order together they fought the good fight, and when the struggle had ended they became partakers of eternal blessing. Yet the aforesaid Andrew had many temptations to bear during his novitiate, but the heavenly right hand which had given him the blessing preserved him unhurt through them all. For he was, as it were, the tenderest little woodworm [2 Sam 23:8 (Vulgate: 2 Kgs 23:8)], soft and overly delicate, and therefore the triumph of the right hand of the Lord was more glorious in him for his being a fairly weak vessel but able to do all things in his strength. Although he found it hard to unlearn the soft ways of his original way of life and began at the outset to think the labor too arduous, he thought of Lot, who went out of Sodom and was not able to save his soul on the mountains [Gen 19:19], and it seemed to him that he should fall back on an Order with a laxer observance. Andrew often mentioned this to Robert, his spiritual father, who by his salutary advice held him back for a while from taking such

---

[57] Beginning with this sentence, and to the end of the chapter, Herbert of Clairvaux, LM 2.4 (PL 185:1315–16).

a step, until at last one day, overwhelmed by timidity of spirit and the tempest [Ps 54:9] within his soul, he declared to him that he was no longer able to carry on. The abbot, with prayers and kind words, persuaded him to persevere and remain patient for three more days. Having barely extracted this promise, he went into the brothers' chapter to ask the community to pray to God for him.

This conscientious father turned his whole mind toward the Lord and prayed very devoutly that the Lord in his mercy would deign to preserve the lamb whom the devil was trying to snatch away. On that same day, when the novice came to the table, he found set out a serving of peas, which was a kind of vegetable above all others he usually so disliked that they made him sick. When he saw the vegetable which he hated so much he became flustered and in spite of his hunger was scarcely able to compel his reluctant stomach to eat any of it. O Righteous God, how rich you are in mercy [Eph 2:4], bearing with the tender and fastidious, so that in all things the counsel of your good pleasure may be fulfilled and your holy name glorified. When the aforesaid novice very gingerly began to taste the food he loathed, he sensed in it such a wonderful succulence that its flavor outweighed even the taste of meat and fish. When this dawned on him he seized a nearby spoon, pulled the dish closer, and, forgetting restraint, quickly cleaned the dish and devoured the dish of vegetables down to the bottom. While he was eating, he kept putting his fingers into his mouth, thinking he could come across bits of the fat in which he thought the vegetables had been cooked. When the meal was over, he went quickly to the abbot and anxiously inquired whether he had ordered the vegetables to be cooked specially in lard or some other rich fat especially on his account. He said he had not and summoned those who had prepared it. They protested that in truth nothing had been put into them except salt and water. When the novice heard this, he joyfully recognized a miracle of divine visitation on his behalf, and, continually thanking God, he could not thereafter be deflected from his intended way of life. By the great gift of God, on the second and third days, and many times afterward, he found this tastiness in his food, and so he learned by Mistress Experience that the Lord has power, when he wills, to comfort his servants by

conferring the grace of the same tastiness on vegetables and roots
as on meat and fish. And he often said thereafter that he enjoyed a
stew of peas in vegetable oil much more than he had ever enjoyed
fowl or game.

CHAPTER TWENTY-TWO

*About a Senior Monk*
*Who Foresaw in the Spirit the Apostasy of a Certain Monk*
*and Foretold It to Dom Robert*

Now I have told you about the happy example of these two athletes of Christ to encourage the tender and pampered, lest they
turn away from conversion of life, for the hand of the Lord is not
ineffective in holding, strengthening, and confirming those in the
holy Order who have been rather delicately raised. But now we
are going to add the very sad example of another two who turned
back after they had received the monastic habit and followed Satan.
I do this lest anyone incorporated into the holy Order think he is
immediately assured safety, even though he is obliged first to put his
hands to strenuous things [Prov 31:19], for unless he has struggled
acceptably, he simply will not attain the crown set before him [2
Tim 2:5]. One of the senior monks at Clairvaux, William by name,[58]
well-on in religion and in age—whom even Dom Robert, the
abbot, highly venerated for his holiness—was lying in the infirmary,
stricken with a bodily illness. One night after Lauds, while the rest
of the patients were asleep, he, because he was extremely fervent,
was keeping watch on his own and praying in bed, as was his
custom. And there appeared quite clearly before his eyes a demon
entering the door of the infirmary in the dress and appearance of

---

[58] Herbert of Clairvaux, LM 1.4 (PL 185:1284–85), except for the final sentence in the chapter. See EM 3.16 for another reference to a senior monk called
William.

a harlot. It crossed in front of William and wandered around as if it were looking for someone. In the middle of the room there was a lamp burning [RB 22.4], which shone brightly enough to make visible its wanton movements and lascivious gestures. The phantom harlot went about everywhere, looking around and examining every single bed, searching each to see who was asleep and who was awake. If by chance it recognized anyone as its own, it would investigate more carefully; if anyone resisted its flattery and seductions, it would pass on quickly; here and there it would pause and then hurry on again, sometimes gently putting its hand to the mouth of the sleeper as if it wanted to leave nothing untouched or unexamined. What it was causing inwardly by its suggestions, by the permission of the Lord, was revealed visibly to the eyes of this spiritual man for our admonition. At last, running into the one it was looking for, it came to a stop by his bed. It was a young monk who had recently taken the habit. Then, moving the covering with its wanton hand from his head, it gently tapped the sleeper and said in a clear voice, "Foolish man, what are you doing here? Get up at once and follow me, and tell your friend to come with you too. I will be waiting for you outside at the gate." Having said this, the relentless monster left quickly and went out by the same door it had entered. The young man, now aroused, sat up in bed, rubbing his forehead with his hands, looking around here and there to find out who had disturbed him. When he saw no one, he lay down again and fell asleep, but not in the Lord.

When morning came, the man of God who had seen all this confided what had happened to the abbot; this was Dom Robert of holy memory. As a good shepherd [John 10:11], he was indeed worried that he might lose one of the sheep entrusted to him [RB 27.5]; so he met with the young man in private about his thoughts, warned him quite earnestly, instructed him cautiously, and from him received the reply that he had not been bothered by any unclean thoughts at all and had been drawn by an utterly steadfast will to persevere in what he had set out to do. But iniquity lies to itself [Ps 26:12]. With the demon in possession of his heart, access to confession was being blocked for fear saving pardon might be let in through the gate of penance. When the abbot told the aforementioned man of God about the young man's reply, he responded, "Wait a while and what I have said will be proved true by events."

What more need I say? Not many days had passed and the young man was shaken by the passion of lust; unmindful of the terrible judgment of God [RB 7.64], he broke the bonds of profession; having returned to his worldly vomit [Prov 26:11], he became a vile apostate and so was snatched up by the seduction of the deceitful phantom. His companion, who had entered the novitiate and received the sacred habit with him, but in vain, was enjoined to leave with him. He had been transferred to another house, but when he heard that his friend had thrown off the yoke of the Order, then and there he broke the bonds of profession and did not hesitate to become an apostate with him. It is obvious from this that the spirit of fornication,[59] which—according to the prophet—blows on coals in the furnace [Isa 54:16], had kindled in their hearts a virulent delight in the pleasures of the flesh, and by its delights seduced both of them. May the omnipotent and merciful God keep far from his frail servants the inextricable bonds of evil which, according to the opinion of blessed Job, tangle the sinews of the testicles [Job 40:12].

## CHAPTER TWENTY-THREE

### *About a Delightful Vision Which Dom Robert Saw at the Death of a Spiritual Brother*

At length it pleased the Lord to put an end to the labors of one of the spiritual sons of the very reverend father Robert so that he might rest and sleep in peace [Ps 4:9]. He had run with unflagging zeal the steep and arduous way that leads to eternal life [Matt

---

[59] Here, "fornication" almost certainly refers to masturbation; see McGuire, "Structure and Consciousness," 84–85; and Bernard of Clairvaux, Sent 3.53 (SBOp 6/2:95; CF 55:230); and the note below, EM 2.31, where fornication is used quite literally.

7:14; RB 5.11]. When the hour had come for him to be called from the arena of this world and invited to the heavenly reward [Phil 3:14], the lord abbot, like the rest of the brothers, had gone quietly to bed.[60] Deep sleep from the Lord overtook him [1 Sam 26:12], and in his sleep he saw two very attractive young men, shining strikingly in appearance and apparel. They were scattering, as it were, lilies and roses, violets and other kinds of flowers in such rich profusion over the floor of the choir of Clairvaux that the floor seemed to be entirely decorated, adorned, and embellished with variegated colors. He wondered at seeing this and, fervent for the simple ways of the Order, he said to them, "My good fellows, what do you think you're doing, strewing the floor with flowers and introducing this novelty into our monastery this way, contrary to the custom of our Order?" But they said to him, "Do not be amazed or annoyed with us for discharging our duty, for we are celebrating in this new way because soon there will be in this choir a new celebration of the feast of a new saint, in whose solemnity the angels shall rejoice and a hymn shall be sung unto the Lord [Ps 64:2] in Zion."[61] They were speaking with him and they were overwhelming with admiration the mind of the listening, watching [abbot], when the sudden knocking of the board of the dead [EO 94.2] roused him from sleep, summoning him by the usual signal to officiate outwardly, according to the dignity of his office, at the festival which he knew inwardly in his spirit was about to be celebrated. He made haste with the rest of the brothers and came to [the dying brother], and he commended his soul with great devotion [EO 94.1-37], believing and trusting with complete certainty that this was the new saint whom the holy angels had been taking up to his rest in celebrating a new feast and a new joy.

Lord, how blessed, and truly blessed, are those whom you choose and take to yourself [Ps 64:5]! Here in this life they so purge all dross of sin within them by their burning love of penitence that in

---

[60] From here to the end of the paragraph, Herbert of Clairvaux, LM 1.8 (PL 185:1285–86).

[61] This passage was used as the Introit of the Mass on the feast of Saint Agatha and solemnities of the Virgin Mary and the saints (*Le Grande Exorde*, 92n5).

that life to which they pass by the death of this present life, in that life, in which the Lord washes away the filth of the daughters of Zion by the awesome spirit of judgment and the spirit of fervor [Isa 4:4], they need no purgation, but at once without the hindrance of any fault they attain the rest of the blessed.

Dom Robert of blessed memory, second abbot of Clairvaux, was led into the joy of his Lord [RB 2.39; cf. Matt 25:14–30] after he had faithfully, prudently, and humbly spent the talent entrusted to him in gaining souls. Even though he was not equal in merit to his most holy predecessor, he was nevertheless joined with him in bliss, so that in heaven he rejoiced along with him, whose worthy successor in his monastic community on earth he had deserved to be. The remains of his body were placed in the burial chamber which had been built in the wall of the cloister at Clairvaux, by the door of the church, and there also rested those other perfect and God-pleasing monks,[62] about whom we are going to say more in what follows.

## Chapter Twenty-Four

### *About Pons, Fifth Abbot of Clairvaux, and Later Bishop of Clermont*

In charge of the monastery of Clairvaux, third in place, was the blessed Fastrad, to be mentioned with all reverence, of whom we made mention above.[63] After he had been taken up there was chosen as the fourth abbot and pastor to guide the monastery at Clairvaux Dom Geoffrey, formerly secretary to our father Saint Bernard and very much beloved by him—who in fact penned the last three books of his *Life* in honeyed speech.[64] After his retirement some years later

---

[62] *Monumenta s. Claraevallensis abbatiae* 5 (PL 185:1558–59).

[63] Fastrad was abbot of Clairvaux from 1157–61; see above, EM 1.32.

[64] This Geoffrey of Auxerre (c. 1120–after 1188), once a student of Abelard, became Bernard's secretary after he joined the Cistercians and was probably responsible for bringing together Bernard's letters. He became abbot of Igny in

he was succeeded by the venerable Pons,[65] abbot of Grandselve.[66] Pons was raised to the dignity of that office on the merits of his religious observance and prudence, by the common election of the abbots and the brothers of Clairvaux [CC 11.4]. This servant of God was as yet a monk at Grandselve, which is one of the daughter houses of Clairvaux in the region of Toulouse, where there had been from the beginning many men of outstanding and great merit. He had worked hard to crucify himself to the world in every way and the world to him [Gal 6:14], to dry up the vices of the flesh and the heart, and to long for the heavenly homeland with the sighs of prayers and holy desire; to seek out eagerly those of the senior monks whom he recognized as outstanding in things spiritual and in religious observance to be his friends and associates—to the end that, strengthened by their example and exhortation, he might daily be renewed in the spirit of his mind [Eph 4:23] and might daily and steadily mount up to the knowledge of the true philosophy. Among others he attached himself especially to one who was the master of novices in that house, a man of outstanding holiness and grounded in all the purity of the virtues. Like an old man after long service, he began to think about the rest of eternal happiness, too weary of everything that is of the world and the flesh, and to long with the very marrow of his heart for the most blessed presence of our Lord Christ, having a hotly burning desire to be dissolved and to be with Christ, which is better by far [Phil 1:23]. While he was caught up in the throes of this spiritual desire and saying daily in his prayers, "When shall I come and appear before the face of God" [Ps 41:3]? the most holy day of the Lord's Supper came around. On that day the community always came solemnly to the Lord's

---

1159 and then abbot of Clairvaux from 1161/2 to 1163. He subsequently served as abbot at both Fossa Nova and Hautecombe before returning to Clairvaux, where he died. Geoffrey is credited with compiling books 3–5 of the Vita Bern (PL 185:301–68).

[65] Herbert of Clairvaux, LM 3.1 (PL 185:1353–55) from here until the last sentence of the chapter. Pons was abbot of Grandselve (1158–65), of Clairvaux (1165–70), and bishop of Clermont (1170 until his death in 1189).

[66] Grandselve was a Benedictine abbey in the Diocese of Toulouse; it became a daughter house of Clairvaux in 1145. Janauschek, 81; Cottineau 1:1330.

table, as is the custom, to share in the life-giving sacrament [EO 21.1-2]. When the hour of the holy sacrifice arrived, the brothers went up to the altar in order of seniority to receive Holy Communion [RB 63.4]. He went up with them, eager to partake of the divine gift. He received Holy Communion and while he still had the eucharistic Host in his mouth, his soul was melted within him [Song 5:6] by the inexpressible sweetness of divine love [RB Prol. 49], and his soul was moved with the impatience of holy desire, and he placed his finger against his throat to delay swallowing while pouring out this prayer to the Lord: "Lord Jesus Christ, son of the living God, Savior of the human race: for us sinners you deigned to take from the womb of the immaculate and inviolate Virgin Mary this most pure and most innocent flesh [Matt 15:27], which I am not worthy to receive. If this petition from your insignificant little servant does not offend you, I beg and entreat the indulgence of your loving goodness that you will never again allow earthly bread or any other earthly substance to pass through my throat, through which I must now swallow this heavenly bread, this bread of life."[67] As he said this, with all speed and devotion he took the saving Host which he held in his mouth, into his soul rather than into his body. Immediately, just as if the Lord were replying to him, "Let it be done to you as you ask" [Matt 15:28], at that very hour and in that very place, the powers of his body suddenly began to leave him, and on the third day, which was Holy Saturday, he fell asleep in the Lord, to be made eternally replete before his face, which he had sought with such signs and prayers and on which the angels long to gaze [1 Pet 1:12]. How blessed the man who thus achieved his desire; how happy that prayer which deserved so speedy a reply to its request. Moreover, the aforementioned Dom Pons, then still a monk of that monastery, loved him especially [2 Sam 1:26]; he devotedly and attentively ministered to him when he was sick and dying, and he inquired earnestly whether he was gravely weighed down by afflictions of the body. He replied that in truth he was placid and tranquil and had no feeling of affliction, except in his

---

[67] The passage concerns reverence for the sacrament, not the Virgin.

throat, where he had placed his finger; there, he said, he suffered just a bit. Because this same Dom Pons was touched by such amazing devotion at the man dying so happily, he approached him and with great contrition of heart asked him for the innermost prayer of his heart, that, if he was able to do so with God's consent, he might return to him after death and attest to what had been going on around him. Having agreed to this, the dead man after a few days appeared to that aforesaid brother in his sleep, shining with a great brightness and glowing like crystal or very clear glass in his whole body. He said to him, "I make known to you, dearest brother, that by the mercy of the Lord I have been received into great bliss. Indeed, this body in which you see me has been given to me until the day of the general resurrection, when I shall receive again my own body which is now being eaten by worms and is returning to dust, a body more wonderful and shining with a glory beyond compare. Meanwhile, I rest very easily in this body, for through it everything accommodates itself to me and is so crystal clear that I discern very clearly through every single member and all of its parts as if with my eye; indeed, the whole body is entirely as if it were a single eye [cf. Rev 4:6-8]." But on one foot of that very pure and translucent body there appeared the darkness of some sort of stain; about this he spoke with a bit of sadness on his face, saying, "That stain you see I contracted by my negligence, for I used to go listlessly to daily work, and I did not follow the company of the brothers with the fervor I should have had when they went out to manual labor" [EO 75.1-13]. This and many other amazing things that holy soul made known to the aforesaid monk, and at length he left him, leaving him greatly edified and consoled. Pay attention, I say, those of you who not only go listlessly to work but are even in the habit of staying away from common labor for some frivolous reason, for it is certain that all the institutes of the Order are holy and pleasing to God and cannot be neglected without grave peril to the soul.

## CHAPTER TWENTY-FIVE

*About a Dying Brother*
*Who Made Known to Abbot Dom Pons*
*the Glory of Eternal Blessedness*
*Which Had Been Prepared and Shown to Him in Advance*

The servant of the Lord Pons, who deserved to see the aforesaid vision for the consolation of us in the Cistercian Order who bear the burden of days and age [Matt 20:12], after some time had passed was elevated to the governance of his church because of his growing merits; and he enhanced this position with his habits of worthy dignity and exercised his pastoral charge with due authority but without losing the innocence and gentleness of a sheep.[68] It happened that, during his days of his abbacy, the Lord, by some hidden dispensation of his awesome judgment, let loose upon that house so virulent an epidemic that in less than two months between forty and fifty brothers were carried off from their midst. Almost all accepted this passing away with a great longing of devotion, as if they had already foreseen in heavenly vision that after the miseries of this life they would share at once in eternal bliss. And many of them deserved to receive this preview and foresaw that this heavenly grace would be conferred on them. That we may trust these words as being true, let us cite a few examples from many.

There was there a monk of very long and proven observance who died in the aforesaid epidemic. And when he was approaching his last hour, the board was sounded after Compline, and the brothers gathered around to support him at his passing [EO 94.2]. As the monks all around him were singing the litany and psalms, he was so strengthened by the Lord that he sang aloud along with them as best he could [EO 94.13, app. 17]. When the psalmody was ended, Dom Pons, the abbot, gave the signal to dismiss the community, and

---

[68] The rest of the chapter comes from Herbert of Clairvaux, LM 3.5-6 (PL 185:1356–57).

he looked at the sick man who had been singing and thought that in a little while his spirit would pass. The brother noticed this; he signaled to the abbot with an outstretched arm to make the brothers stay there a little longer, for he knew to the last jot when he would depart. The abbot, realizing that this very zealous monk would not break silence after Compline even at the point of death out of respect for the censure of the regular discipline [RB 42], could not contain himself for joy and himself broke the silence. And beginning with the usual formula, "Let us bless the Lord," he said, "Dearly beloved brother, I see that the Lord is with you and so I pray you to indicate to us if something has been revealed to you about the blessed hope which you await, so that we too may be strengthened to hope in the Lord and to share equally in your joy."[69] Then the sick man replied, "My lord father, I shall reply briefly to what you ask, for you should know that I have seen that of which it is not lawful to speak [2 Cor 12:4]. Nevertheless, there is just one thing I can say: that if I alone surpassed the merits of all human beings, I should not consider myself in the least worthy to obtain the glory of that eternal bliss which has been prepared and foreshown to me now at my departure." And when he had said this he fell asleep in the Lord.

## Chapter Twenty-Six

### About a Timid Brother
### Who Was Magnificently Stirred to Repentance
### by the Abbot, Dom Pons[70]

In the same monastery there was at the time a brother of exemplary observance, whose name was Bernard. In the first stage of his conversion, whenever he pondered the enormity of his sins and

---

[69] It was customary, before speaking to someone, to say *Benedicite* ("Let us bless"), to which the other person replied *Dominus*, "the Lord" (*Le Grande Exorde*, 97n12, provides references to *Règle de s. Benoît*, SCh 182:697; and to EO, 572).

[70] Except for the final paragraph, this chapter is taken from Herbert of Clairvaux, LM 3.8 (PL 185:1358–60).

the justice of the stern judge, he was moved by such terror that he sank very near to despair. Becoming aware of this, the venerable abbot Pons tried to persuade him by many examples and admonitions that anyone, however guilty, who confesses and repents would never be refused pardon. But he could not satisfy him in this way, so he added, "I designate myself as surety for your salvation, and let my soul be demanded for yours [RB 2.37-38], provided you persevere obediently in this way of life." Marvelously strengthened by this promise, the brother overcame almost entirely the spirit of diffidence with which he had been struggling. He rejoiced in the Lord with trembling [Ps 2:11], and thereafter he used to sing of both mercy and judgment [Ps 100:1]. Although he was of noble birth, he thought no abundance better than to be poor for Christ and to serve his poor.

He was appointed infirmarian to the poor in the hospice. There, he looked after them with the greatest care, serving them not as if they were strangers and beggars but as if they were the Lord and the members of his body [1 Cor 12:12-27]. If he noticed among them a patient infested with ulcers and worms, he cared for him, applying every act of piety by washing, cleaning, and cherishing him, as a mother would an ailing son. While the servant of God was doing this and similar things, he contracted the sickness I mentioned above and went to the Lord. When he saw that his companions were being taken away daily, he too desired with a great desire likewise to be dissolved and to be with Christ [Phil 1:23]. The good Lord, who is always present to the contrite hearts and troubled spirits of his servants [Ps 50:19], decided to fulfill his desire. Having caught a slight fever, he began to get somewhat worse and took to his bed. When the lord abbot came in to visit him he was surprised that so very zealous a man should be kept in bed for such a minor illness. So he said to him, jokingly, "Bernard, my brother, don't be afraid. You're not going to die now; you're still going to be eating our beans and lentils with us." The monk replied, "I am not afraid, father. I am not afraid, but I trust in the Lord [Ps 10:2] that I shall not now be disappointed of my hope [Ps 77:30; see RB 58.21]." What more shall I say? After four or five days, the little spark grew into great fire, and the fever he had thought short-lived turned deadly. Then the abbot regretted his own judgment and realized that the brother's opinion which he had made about himself had been accurate. As the hour of his departure was approaching, the brother was anointed with holy oil. When the anointing was finished, he was suddenly taken in spirit and lay rapt in contemplation for a long time, unconscious and unmoving, so that he almost seemed to be dead. In this interval, heaven was being opened to him, and he deserved to look upon the glory of God with unveiled face; and therefore he could say, "I have seen the Lord face-to-face and my soul is preserved" [Gen 32:30].

While lying for many hours as if lifeless, he searched out the secrets of heaven, not out of presumption but led by grace. At length he came to himself and the joy on his face showed well enough where he had been. The good father Pons came to him and asked him how he was, and he replied, "Lord father, I am well, by the mercy of God. And now, dearly beloved father, I set you free from your obligation, and I thank you with all my heart for your concern for me, a sinner. A man who has stood surety is legally absolved when the outcome of the promise has already been attained."

But the abbot had forgotten what he had undertaken earlier when he made himself responsible for the soul of his brother and wondered what he was talking about. So the brother reminded him quite expressly and said, "Have you forgotten how you once made yourself responsible for my salvation? It is from that solemn pledge that I absolve you, for by the mercy of our Lord Jesus Christ I am now certain of my salvation." Then the abbot began to probe with careful questions to discover how he could know this. But when the brother declined to say anything at all about it, the abbot saw he was getting nowhere with requests and ordered him in the name of the Lord and by virtue of his obedience to describe—for the edification and consolation of many [1 Cor 14:3]—what he had seen. When the sick brother heard this, he uttered this solemn statement: "Because the virtue of obedience forbids me to be silent about the truth, I am going to tell you something you may believe or may doubt. But to make my testimony credible, know that when I have reached its end, I shall also come to the end of my life. Know by your love for me that, wretched and unworthy as I am, I was in the presence of our Lord and Savior Jesus Christ and I have seen him face-to-face [Gen 32:30]. I have not, however, seen him in his divine nature but rather in the most blessed form of the human nature which he deigned to assume for us, and by his ever gracious indulgence I received the remission of my sins, and I have the hope of eternal happiness by his grace laid up in my bosom [Job 19:27]. From his most sacred lips I have heard that all those who persevere unto death in obedience in this way of life will receive from him eternal salvation. I have seen our brothers who have passed out of this world resting in great bliss and among them I foresaw my place, to which by the mercy of God I am now going." When he had said this he was silent and immediately gave up his blessed soul.

Let us gird ourselves for penitence, brothers, and with this penitence let us come before the face of the Lord in confession and contrition of heart, so that hereafter we may deserve to see the face of God in jubilation of heart and exultation of spirit [Ps 94:2]. Truly, by the testimony of the Lord, the kingdom of heaven suffers violence and the violent take it by storm [Matt 11:12]. Think about that great sinner who, in the first stage of his monastic vocation, carefully considering—as well he should!—the number and enormity of his offenses, almost fell into despair; then illuminated by divine grace, he set himself against himself, endeavoring with tears and the sorrow of repentance and by his devout service to the sick to offer to God daily the sacrifice of a contrite heart and a humble spirit [Ps 50:19]. And therefore, for the consolation of all who are truly penitent, he was permitted in this frail mortal body to see that Face—which he was utterly terrified of seeing angry and had tried in every way to placate—not only placated but indeed forgiving his sins by a wholly gracious leniency and inviting him to contemplate the glory of eternal bliss. The kingdom of heaven is given, not to the sleepy and the listless or those hiding their sins or pinning their hopes on their many years in holy religion, but to those who have stayed awake and willingly exerted themselves in keeping the commandments of God day and night. Therefore, Dom Pons of holy memory—abbot of Grandselve, whose holiness and monastic observance may be judged by such perfect and religious disciples as we have been describing, for as it is written: "He who is holy, let him be holy still" [Rev 22:11], and "He who is found to be faithful in a few things will be set by the Lord over many" [Matt 25:21]—was, by divine choice and human election, made father and shepherd of the monastery of Clairvaux and all the daughter houses of Clairvaux. There, with vigilant solicitude he watched over the flock of the Lord, and in his term of office sought not his own gain but that of the Lord; and lest the lamp lit by the grace of the Holy Spirit be hidden under a bushel [Matt 5:15], at the call of the Lord and by the choice of all the clergy and people, he was raised to the bishopric of Clermont. Promoted to the honor of the episcopacy, he did not lose the humility of a monk but within himself showed how the two graces could be marvelously combined. In him the dignity of the high priest gave place to the more praiseworthy purity of monastic humility, and the vigor of monastic observance bolstered his authority as bishop. So by word and example he nourished and instructed the people to whom he had been given as bishop, and among the prelates of his day he appeared outstanding. And when at last the course of his life had been praiseworthily run, he received the reward of his labor from the Lord and rested in peace.

CHAPTER TWENTY-SEVEN

*About Blessed Gerard, Sixth Abbot of Clairvaux*

After Dom Pons, the fifth abbot at Clairvaux after Saint Bernard, had been elevated to the episcopacy, blessed Gerard, abbot of Fossa Nova,[71] replaced him as the sixth abbot at that place. A man

---

[71] Fossa Nova, in the Diocese of Terracina, was founded from Monte Cassino in the eighth or ninth century and affiliated with the Cistercians as a daughter house of Hautecombe in 1135. Janauschek, XC (pp. 37–38); Cottineau 1:1200; DHGE 17:1208–12.

praiseworthy in the purity of monastic life and the integrity of his habits,[72] he reached the perfect number of six in his life as well as in his death. This venerable father, pleasing to God and beloved of man [Sir 45:1], was adorned with such grace that the whole company of that brotherhood saw in him a fresh flower of paradise, and they venerated him with marvelous affection. For, someone whom God so flooded with grace had to be loved by everyone. Christ, the author and giver of all virtues, in whom are hidden not only all the treasures of wisdom and understanding [Col 2:3] but those of piety and grace as well, so filled his servant with the nectar of spiritual grace that not only did he believe in him and serve him faithfully but he was also not afraid to endure a harsh and horrible death for his sake. For, if tribulation tests the quality of such a man's faith and confirms that he who perseveres in it has perfect charity, then it is clear that this blessed man was perfect in both. Like a good and faithful servant [Matt 25:21] he took care in tribulation to preserve his faith unfeigned and to practice charity with a pure heart and good conscience [1 Tim 1:5], so much so that he loved even the enemy who cruelly thirsted for his blood. He prized more the life of the soul than that of the body and shrank less from the death of the flesh than the detriment of faith; he preferred to suffer for justice rather than to betray the Order by a deceptive silence which would have disgraced the Order and endangered souls. The story of how, after a praiseworthy life conspicuous in religious observance, he achieved the palm of martyrdom, we will therefore disclose as briefly as we can.

There was a certain monk, noble by birth but degenerate in behavior, who wandered around everywhere, contrary to the pattern and right behavior of the Order, frequenting the courts of princes and impudently interfering in secular business and showing himself in his entire way of life to be a gyrovague rather than a cloistered

---

[72] Blessed Gerard was a monk of Igny, abbot of Fossa Nova, and abbot of Clairvaux from 1170 to 1175. He was murdered while making a visitation at Igny and became a martyr of the Cistercian Order (see below, EM 2.28). According to tradition, he died on 10 October or 7 December. See Piesik, *Exordium Magnum Cisterciense* 1:503n293. Lenssen, *Hagiologium Cisterciense*, 1:111–12.

monk [RB 1.10-11]. Dom Gerard, abbot of Clairvaux, out of concern for the Order and a zeal for justice, ordered him to be arrested, seized his horses and all that he had, and handed him over to the venerable Dom Peter, abbot of Igny,[73] so that, bound to the strictures of the Rule in his house and denied all license to wander about, he might do penance, however unwillingly. The good shepherd [John 10:11] did this with the laudable intention of correcting fraternal faults, but the spiteful man was so moved by sinister suspicions that he murmured this had been done with less than good intentions, and so what ought to have made him better, in fact, made him worse. In fact, prey within his entire mind to a devilish spirit, he breathed out a venom of heinous bitterness and, like the cruelest wild beasts, thirsted for the blood of the dutiful father.

Meanwhile, it happened that Dom Gerard, the abbot of Clairvaux, was traveling in the regions of Germany to visit monasteries which Clairvaux had founded in those regions [CC 5]. Among other places he happened to come to Trier, the metropolitan city of the Belgians, once a very important city and called the second Rome; now only by the desolation of its ruins does it show what it used to be. On the outskirts of the city there is a famous monastery, which is called by the name Saint Matthias because the entire body of the most holy apostle rests there.[74] Helena Augusta, the mother of Constantine the Great, had moved it there from Judea and re-interred it there with honor. It added to the authority conferred on the place that the bodies of Eucharius, Valerius, and Maternus, three disciples of the blessed apostle Peter, located in the crypt of this same church were appropriately honored by the faithful. These saints, sent out by the aforesaid apostle, were the first to preach the word of salvation [Acts 13:26] and the victory of the cross to the people of Germany, in what were in those days the three most

---

[73] Peter Monoculus; see below EM 2.32. Igny was a daughter house of Clairvaux in the Diocese of Reims (Janauschek, 14; Cottineau 1:1443).

[74] On the translation of Saint Matthias, see BHL 5697ff.; and *Acta SS* Feb 3:441, 451; on the Benedictine abbey of Saint Matthias, which still exists, see Cottineau 2:3211.

important cities in Germany—Trier, Tongres,[75] and Cologne—and their episcopacies added significantly to their luster.[76]

Coming to the city of Trier, Abbot Gerard requested hospitality at the monastery of Saint Matthias, where he was very hospitably received by the abbot and the brothers. But he was lodging there not so much for physical convenience as for spiritual enlightenment, and rising in the dead of night, he went in search of the chapel; he went down into the crypt and prostrated himself in body and mind before the shrines of the aforesaid confessors of Christ to entreat with heartfelt prayers divine help for himself and his own by their intercession. When this protracted prayer earned the grace of devotion, an infused grace expanded his mind, making his expanded mind capable of understanding heavenly secrets. Suddenly he saw these confessors of the Lord standing near him, gleaming with heavenly grace. One of them, Eucharius, addressed him in these words: "Brother, do not be afraid or trouble your heart at our appearance. We are those who, sent by the apostle Peter, first preached the gospel of Christ in these regions. I am Eucharius, and these are my brothers Maternus and Valerius, whose shrines you just visited to beseech aid. On this account, we also, rejoicing together in your faith and devotion, come to you through the will of God to give you advice about the things disturbing your heart.[77] Your will and your heart's intention is to lay down the office of abbot and be freed from the caustic uproar of business so you can begin to be at leisure for yourself and God alone. But you should know that your will does not accord with God's will. Therefore, I urge and admonish you not lightly to abandon the rank of honor you have attained by the gift of God's grace but to be steadfast

[75] Tongres, Tongeren, in modern Belgium.

[76] Eucharius became the first bishop of Trier in the late third century. Maternus was bishop of Cologne *c.* 313. On the legend, well-established by the Middle Ages, that Eucharius (a bishop), Valerius (a deacon), and Maternus (a subdeacon) were sent to Gaul by Saint Peter, see Gabriel Meier, "Eucharius," *Catholic Encyclopedia* (New York: Encyclopedia Press, 1913), 5:594–95. See also, *Gesta Trevorum*; MGH SS 8:111–74.

[77] *Soli Deo et tibi vacare.* A parallel with Aelred of Rievaulx, *The Mirror of Charity* 1.8 (CCCM 1:22–23; CF 17:100–101), is noted in *Le Grand Exorde*, 103n22.

and to act manfully [Ps 30:25]. Because the day is near when you will be visited by the Lord and you will attain for your labors the unfading crown of glorious victory [1 Pet 5:4]." Having said this they vanished, leaving the abbot who had seen and heard this torn equally between stupor and amazement. Meanwhile, he hastened to continue the journey he had begun. He visited the houses for which he had come to those regions; by his cheerful presence and his teaching he left the brothers more fervent in the praise of God and the observances of the holy Order, all the while turning over in his mind the sweetness and the impact of the aforesaid vision and the words he had heard, pondering in attentive meditation, that is, that before long he would be visited by the Lord. As he began to think more and more lovingly about the saints who had appeared to him, he very much wondered about the soul of blessed Maternus, where it had been and what kind of life it had lived during the forty days when his body had lain in the tomb, before he was restored to life by the staff of the apostle. He began to regret that he had failed to ask this while, during the aforesaid glorious vision, he had had the chance of asking. When he had completed the business for which he had come, he returned to Trier, but this time he did not stay at Saint Matthias.

A certain powerful and rich man of that city had got him to promise when he was there earlier to deign to bless his house with his presence when he returned. So he stayed in that house, but before he went to bed, he privately spoke with and instructed his lay brother to have two horses ready before dawn and to go alone with him to Saint Matthias. He got them ready and, after saying morning prayer at the appointed time, the devout abbot visited the bodies of the saints. There, while he was attentively and tearfully praying, he deserved by God's gift to see the saints, just as he had done previously. But this time Saint Eucharius, looking at the abbot and holding out his hand toward Saint Maternus, said, "Look, here is my brother Maternus; ask him whatever you wish." When the abbot hesitated, not daring to reply out of reverence and at the glory of their faces, blessed Maternus spoke thusly to him: "My dearest brother, you are afraid to come right out and ask what you long to know, for it seems presumptuous to want to scrutinize the deep abyss of the judgments of God entirely hidden from human senses. But because you are asking out of piety more than curiosity, I will explain to you as much as you can understand about this hidden secret. You are wondering and turning intently over in your mind where my soul was and what kind of life it lived during the forty days when my body lay in the tomb, and you long to know this out of a burning sense of piety. Know then, that I lay in the womb of the earth, just as an infant lives enclosed in its mother's womb, and in my body I slept the sleep of death, but my soul was alive to God, and I was already then held in his almighty presence: just as I would be in the sight of men after I had been resuscitated." Strengthened by this twofold vision and the assurances of the saints then, Dom Gerard, abbot of Clairvaux, strove day after day to show himself a good servant of Christ, for he was quite sure that the end of his life was near at hand because he knew that it was foretold by the heavenly visitation, which could not be wrong. Nor did he wish it to be.

## CHAPTER TWENTY-EIGHT

### *How Dom Gerard, the Abbot of Pious Memory, Was Crowned with Martyrdom out of Zeal for Righteousness and for the Order*

Now in the same year in which he had seen the blessed vision, and very near the time when the holy abbot merited being made a sacrifice of Christ and a follower of the immaculate lamb [1 Pet 1:19], pouring out his blood for righteousness in the same way that Christ did for the whole Church, the abbot proposed to make a second visitation of his houses according to the statutes of the Order,[78] and he decided to go, among other places, to Igny. The brothers, however, were suspicious of that rabid beast, the pseudo-monk who

[78] SCC 3.5; CC 5; CCP 2.

had been confined by the lord abbot in that house to do penance, as we recounted above. They warned the lord abbot to be careful, lest the light of Israel be put out [2 Sam 21:17], something they very greatly dreaded. But the abbot, fearless of death, commended himself wholly to the divine will; he said he could not shrink from what it was his duty to do because of the threat of death. He was already prepared for the journey and ready to set out when a certain spiritual brother came and asked to speak to him privately. Once this was granted, he began to beg him with tears and sighs not to go on the journey he proposed, saying that it had been revealed to him that if he were to go to Igny he would suffer a cruel death. The man of God replied to him, "Dear brother, thank you for your concern about me, but I want you to know that I set no greater store by my soul than by myself, that is to say, by my temporal life, and no imaginary fears about death are going to prevent me [Acts 20:24] from doing this, my duty, which I, however unworthy, am bound to perform. I cannot omit it because I am terrified by some frightful imaginary death. Who knows whether my Lord is trying me? Who, after all, does not know that God is almighty, and if he wills he can very easily turn aside this death which you say threatens me and which I can say with a sure conscience that I do not deserve? Yet if he does not will this, we unprofitable servants [Luke 17:10] must comply with his will in all things. May his will therefore be done for us and in us."

Thus he spoke, and commending all the brothers to the grace of God, he set out in a spirit of great fortitude on the journey he had planned and arrived at Igny. There he was received, as he deserved, with great reverence and rejoicing by the abbot, Dom Peter of blessed memory, and by all the brothers, and he showed himself pleasant and friendly toward all of them. When he had spoken to each of them both in public and in private about the salvation of their souls and the observance of the Order, he commanded that the man of whom I spoke should be brought to him, even though he was no monk but soon to be a detestable parricide. When he arrived, the holy father, so soon to be a sacrifice for Christ, began to warn and entreat him in the gentlest terms to bear patiently all that he was being made to do for the salvation of his soul; he affirmed that he had not the least rancor against him and was prepared to embrace him as his very beloved son if he could but discern signs of amendment in holy humility and patience. But by now he had become one spirit with the devil, who was a murderer from the beginning [John 8:44]; he had long since conceived in his mind the heinous crime of parricide and was looking for some way to accomplish it. So, like a very cunning serpent [Gen 3:1] he pretended that he was without malice, listening humbly and with downcast head to what the other was saying and uttering with his mouth words of gentleness and peace which he did not hold in his heart.[79] The brothers were overjoyed and—from the false garb of humility this troublemaker had put on so that his wickedness might not be noticed—hoped that he was bringing forth fruit worthy of repentance [Luke 3:8]. Nothing was further from their minds than how soon and in how horrible a way he was to commit his crime and entrap himself in the snare of eternal death and damnation. The next day, when the brothers met for the Night Office, the abbot was excused—as it was the custom for those who arrive after a journey to skip Lauds so that in the quietness of the night they might shake off their fatigue—yet so fervent was he in spirit that he stood attentively in divine praise for the entire length of Vigils. It was as if he foreknew by the spirit of prophecy what was coming upon him and was preparing himself for his approaching agony. What more is there to say? At the end of Lauds, to which, according to the custom of the Order, they added the Office of Prime [EO 69.25; 69.74], the lord abbot left the choir and went up to the dormitory, planning to come back down to wash his hands to be ready more promptly at the end of the Office to celebrate the holy mysteries. That execrable man,[80] no monk but the unspeakable parricide, wickedly noticed this and followed him, foreseeing that this might be a good place to perpetrate his heinous crime. And so he hid himself in the darkness like a lion lurking in

---

[79] *Et pacis . . . in pectore*: compare Rupert of Deutz, *Commentaria in evangelium sancti Iohannis* 13; CCCM 9:715, 134 (*Le Grande Exorde*, 106n14).

[80] Archdale King (*Cîteaux and Her Elder Daughters*, 254) claims the monk's name was Hugh de Basoches.

ambush for its prey [Ps 16:12].The man of the Lord, coming back and going down the steps into the cloister, came to the place of ambush. And suddenly, that son of perdition [John 17:12; 2 Thess 2:3] leapt out and attacked him, thrusting the sharp point of a long, broad knife into his entrails, cruelly cutting, slicing, and stabbing, until he reached his spine. But like the true Lamb of God [John 1:29, 36], our Lord Jesus Christ, who was silent not just before his shearers but before those who pierced his sacred hands and feet and did not open his mouth [Acts 8:32], this true imitator of Christ, this true sacrifice, uttered no shout at the man who mangled and dug out his entrails, nor hardly even a small cry of pain [Ps 21:17; Isa 53:7; John 1:29].Then, when he felt the resistance of his rib cage [and realized] he could not run the body clean through as he had wanted, that murderer—abhorred of God and loathed of men—added still more hideous to already hideous torments by turning the detestable dagger in the wound again and again to make sure by every means that the holy father would not escape his hands alive.The mild shepherd shuddered at such accursed persistence and said to him in a gentle voice, "I beg you, brother, stop! Stay your hand now [1 Chr 21:15], for there is no way I can live any longer."At this plea the wicked man took hasty flight and, become the prey of demons, he carried with him the avenging conscience of so great a crime.The venerable abbot marshaled his strength and went down by the steps which went down into the church, sliced through by this horrible wound, but when he came to the last step, having lost so much blood, he felt his strength fail him and lay there as if dead. Prompted by God, the sacristan was coming through the church and stumbled over him as he lay there, but in the darkness he could not make out who it was or why he was lying there.Terrified, indeed, and shaken to the core, he lit a candle, and with the help of the light he recognized the holy father. Immediately, he burst out in lamentations and groaned, "Oh no! Oh no!" which brought all the brothers to that tragic spectacle. Then Dom Peter, the abbot, arrived, and when he saw the martyr of Christ lying in his own blood, he poured out the inward sorrow of his heart with many tears and sighs.The mourning brothers bore him in their hands to the infirmary.There he lay quiet for a little while, recalling in spirit the unbounded power of almighty God; he began to give enormous thanks that he had been allowed to endure in the present a death so harsh that would absolve him from the sharper punishments for his sins and negligences in the place of purgation after death. If we remember rightly, he lived on for three days, fortified during that time by the sacraments of the Church [EO 93], and he longed with devout prayers and holy desires for the future life of blessedness. With the deepest affection of his heart, he especially commended to divine grace his sons at Clairvaux. He pardoned his assailant from his heart and earnestly begged all those who were present that, if by chance he were caught, he would suffer no evil from anyone. And so his holy soul was set free from the flesh, and we believe that he entered supernal heaven more readily for having chosen to be so greatly purged in the furnace of tribulation [Prov 17:3; Isa 48:10; Dan 3:17] here on the pathway of tribulation and by the extremity of a hideous death. His holy body was placed on a litter and transported the entire way to Clairvaux amid the chanting of divine psalms and hymns and with the abbot, Dom Peter, attending with great reverence. There this same abbot deserved to be assured of the glory of the martyr by a sublime and manifest revelation, and I think it would not be out of place to refer to it here, in order to commend the memory of so great a martyr to later generations.

## CHAPTER TWENTY-NINE

*How Dom Peter the Abbot Deserved to Be Assured by a Revelation of the Glorification of Christ's Martyr, Gerard*

When the community of Clairvaux solemnly celebrated the Mass for the commendation of that blessed soul, as is the custom [EO 95 and 97], the aforesaid abbot, Dom Peter, was standing at the holy altar to offer up the Saving Victim with his usual devotion. Though he assumed a cheerful countenance for the onlookers, he

was, however, sad and grieved at the undeserved death of the good
father, most of all because it had been in his own house, that is, Igny,
that the Lord had permitted so heinous a crime to be perpetrated.
He was growing agitated at various thoughts, thinking that this
had happened because of his sins, when suddenly he saw the most
blessed Bernard in visible form, standing to the right of the altar,
and on the left Dom Gerard, whose death he was mourning, both
of them shining with the glory of inestimable brightness. He was
astonished by the vision, and while he stood there, flabbergasted,
blessed Bernard said to him, "I pray you, tell me why you mourn
so much at the death of someone who has been changed through
transitory death into the everlasting state of blissful life by a death
so precious in the sight of the Lord [Ps 115:15]." He stretched out
his hand to Gerard, the martyr of Christ, who was standing at the
left side of the altar, and said, "This is my brother, whose funeral
rites you have performed; insofar as he is seen in the sight of men
to have come to a cruel and unworthy end, so much the more has
he deserved to receive the reward of his calling, having been raised
to a greater glory by the Lord among the band of victorious and
purple-clothed martyrs." After this was said, the joyful vision was
taken up from the sight of the beholder. Such joy and certitude
about the glorification of his beloved friend was in the heart of
him who had deserved to see and hear this that he thought no
more of weeping for him as one dead but put away all clouds of
sorrow and doubt, judging that he had an utterly faithful intercessor before the almighty and merciful God. We heard about this
revelation from Dom Gerard of pious memory, formerly prior of
Clairvaux, afterward abbot of Eberbach, who, as those acquainted
with him knew, was a man of great truth, purity, and innocence.[81]
We have heard it said of him by the senior monks of Clairvaux that
when he put his hands between those of the most blessed Bernard,
since it was through him that he gave himself to the Order and
the house of Clairvaux, those who were present heard the same
venerable father, speaking by the Spirit of God, give testimony to

---

[81] Gerard was the third abbot of Eberbach (1171–77); Conrad refers to him
again in EM 6.10. See Grießer, EM, 135n2.

his innocence, saying, "Behold, an Israelite indeed, in whom there is no guile" [John 1:47]. In the celebration of the funeral rites joy mingled with sorrow, and the spiritual sons of such a father did not so much mourn his temporal death as rejoice in the glorious victory by which he had triumphed over the enemy, dying bravely for righteousness. His holy body was buried reverently in a tomb raised above the paving stones outside the doors of the chapel at Clairvaux in the little chamber which had once been built to receive the holy bodies of the confessors Bernard and Malachy.[82]

So the fame of his precious death, and how, in this cruel death, he innocently suffered for justice and zeal for the Order, spread abroad everywhere and reached the ears of the supreme pontiff, Pope Alexander of blessed memory.[83] He had loved Gerard with a special fondness out of reverence for his sanctity, and he was grieved with a deep feeling of piety at his so undeserved death. He excommunicated the perpetrator of so great an outrage and condemned him to be banished from the society of all the faithful. Some years went by after this, and the cruel killer who had committed this crime was led to repent. He went to the pope, falling at his feet to beg for mercy. When the apostolic lord asked him who he was and what evil he had committed, he said, "I am the one who killed Gerard, abbot of Clairvaux." When the lord pope heard him name the abbot whom he had once loved and realized the perpetrator of Gerard's death was before him, he was utterly horrified and violently disturbed, and, lacking discretion, he kicked him with his foot, saying, "Get out, son of perdition!" [John 17:12]. Hearing this, the wretch abruptly got up and left. The cardinals who were present came forward and deferentially suggested to the lord pope that even the most heinous man should not be dismissed without mercy, that the Lord Jesus had prayed on the cross for those who

---

[82] *Monumenta s. Claraevallensis abbatiae* 5 (PL 185:1557D) places the grave in the great cloister, under the first arch by the door of the church. For more on Malachy, see Bernard of Clairvaux, Epp 341, 356–57, 374 (SBOp 8:282–83, 300–302, 335–37; James, Epp 383–86, pp. 452–57); and Ep 545 (SBOp 8:512–13; not in James); V Mal (SBOp 3:297–378; CF 10:15–93).

[83] Alexander III, pope from 1159 to 1181. See above, EM 1.32.

crucified him [Luke 23:34], and that it did not become his apostolic state to leave to those who followed an example so harsh that
it might lead to despair. The pope, moved by these words, hastily
ordered the parricide to be called back, for he had repulsed him,
not to make him despair, but to impress more deeply upon his
heart the horror and enormity of his crime and in doing so to
urge him to endure something harsh for the forgiveness of his sin.
But O how terrible God is in his counsels concerning the sons of
men [Ps 65:5], for no one can correct someone he brushes aside.
Although, at the pope's order, the servants sought everywhere for
that wretched sinner, he could be found neither in the consistory,
nor in the palace, nor anywhere in the entire city. And what became
of him or how he met his end is unknown to this day.

## Chapter Thirty

### About Dom Henry of Pious Memory, Seventh Abbot of Clairvaux, Afterward Cardinal Bishop of Alba

After blessed Gerard, sixth abbot of Clairvaux, had been glorified
with the palm of martyrdom, Dom Henry, abbot of Hautecombe,
was elected as seventh spiritual father of the congregation at Clairvaux[84] in the desire of having the rest of the seventh age which is
the Sabbath of the people of God [Heb 4:9], of which the Spirit
says, "They shall rest from their labors" [Rev 14:13]. This venerable
father was of noble birth but far more noble in the generosity of

---

[84] Henry of Marcy (Henry of Clairvaux), born *c.* 1135, was abbot of Hautecombe in Savoy from 1160 to 1176 and of Clairvaux from 1176 to 1179 and
was made cardinal bishop of Albano in 1179. He was active in Church affairs,
notably in campaigns against the Waldensians. See Beverly Kienzle, *Cistercians,
Heresy and Crusade*, 4–5, 109–34. He died in 1189. Henry's letters and *Tractatus
de peregrinante civitate dei* are in PL 204:215–402. See also, Lenssen, *Hagiologium
Cisterciense*, 1.259–60.

his virtues; from the first years of his young manhood he put his hand to vigorous deeds in the sanctuary of the Lord [Prov 31:19], preferring the sweet yoke of the Lord and his light burden [Matt 11:30] to being called a son of Belial, that is, without the yoke. He sought rather to be humiliated with gentleness for the Lord Christ than to divide the spoil with the proud [Prov 16:19] and so to fall under the domination of him who is king over all the children of pride [Job 41:25; RB 2.2-3, 7]. He passed the days of his youth in such purity and innocence that he gained the gray hairs of wisdom in his tender years, and when he had barely reached the threshold of man's estate, he was made a mediator between God and men more for the merits of his religious observance and prudence than for his age and deserved to attain both the title vicar of the Son of God and the office of father and shepherd. Once he had received the privilege of this honor, or rather the weight of its responsibility, he administered it with such faithfulness and ready devotion that the inward Judge—the discerner of the thoughts and intentions of the heart [Heb 4:12] who seals in his hands all men that each may know his works [Job 37:7]—found him faithful over a few things and decided therefore to raise him up to a greater gift of grace. Certainly more mature in age and well versed in the habits of virtue when he was made abbot of Clairvaux, he did not in the slightest neglect in himself the rigor of discipline by which he urged others to the paths of righteousness. As much as the dignity of his office would permit, he bound himself to the common life and even worked with his hands, sweating it out sometimes with the rest of the brothers. The good Lord deigned to show by this, his servant, how salutary is the counsel which the wise man gave to those who are raised in dignity, when he said, "The more you humble yourself in all things the greater you become" [Sir 3:20], how acceptable it is to God if a superior, out of fear for him, does not despise disciplining his flesh with hard and menial labor. He wanted at the same time to rebuke him in a wonderful and merciful way because of a certain negligence he had committed while working very hard at manual labor but which he did not think serious.

It had happened once that at harvest time the venerable abbot was present at the hay harvest in the fields of a grange situated across the river Aube near the monastery of Clairvaux,[85] and he was working energetically with his brothers. And while he was doing the work with considerable zeal, a certain brother came hurrying out to say that one of the ailing lay brothers had grown worse and was near death and that he on this account desired the grace of unction. The abbot, knowing that the others were encouraged by his presence and spurred on to work harder, could not bear to tear himself away from the work, so he sent one of the senior monks as his substitute to give the sick man the solemn office of unction [EO 93.1-23]. When that had been accomplished, the brother ended his life in peace, fortified by the rite of the sacraments of the Church against the powers of the air.[86] One day after this, after Compline had been said, while it was still light, the brothers had lain down on their beds, but the lord abbot was still lying awake on his bed. While he was lying there, a monk who had departed this life just before the aforesaid brother, visibly appeared and spoke to him like this: "Lord father, you should know that as soon as the brother who has just died put off the garment of the flesh, he was presented before the throne of glory to our Lord Jesus Christ by the holy angels. There was a very close examination of his life, and at length the discussion turned to the actions of those who had been around him at the very last. The ever-gracious judge asked him if everything had been done for him, that is, according to the ritual, as is supposed to be done for a dying brother, and he replied that the rites for him had been fully done, except for one: since the abbot had insisted on going on with manual labor, he had neglected to anoint him himself but had sent a substitute. So the Lord called me, as I was standing before his tremendous majesty with the rest, and said to me, 'Go and tell the abbot from me, that

---

[85] See Grießer, EM, 137n4; and Piesik, *Exordium Magnum Cisterciense*, 1:504n315, for notes on this grange. Arbois de Jubainville, Henri d. *Etude sur l'état intérieur des abbayes cisterciennes, et principalement de Clairvaux, aux XIIe et XIIIe siècles* (Paris, 1858), 311.

[86] "The powers of the air": an expression used by Jerome, Ambrose, Augustine, and others to indicate demons who live in the air (*Le Grande Exorde*, 111n11). Bernard also used the phrase in Sent 3.33 and 3.92 (SBOp 6/2:86, 147; CF 55:219, 299); Div 14.1 (SBOp 6/1:45); and Div 53.2 (SBOp 6/1:278).

for this negligence he is to offer up the seven penitential psalms every day for the rest of his life.'"[87]

The celestial messenger, having with these words proclaimed openly what he had heard inwardly, returned to the Lord who sent him, from whom, despite outward appearances, he had inwardly departed not at all. The abbot, however, turning over in his mind with fear and amazement the many things he had heard, gave thanks from the bottom of his heart, proving that he knew now from his own experience that the statement made about the Lord by the Apostle, "He cares for you" [1 Pet 5:7], was founded on irrefutable truth. The abbot accepted the penance enjoined upon him by the highest of all abbots with thoroughly humble obedience and took very great care to observe it carefully. So much so, in fact, that later, when he was made cardinal bishop of Alba, he was known to say to his friends that if he was so hard-pressed that he had to make a choice between omitting Mass or these psalms on Easter Day or Christmas, he would choose to omit the Mass. "Blessed is God in his gifts and holy in all his mercies,"[88] who in these latter days [2 Pet 3:3] consoles his humble servants by revelations so clear and evident that, drawn by them from things visible to the invisible, we may indeed set our foot more surely in the faith, knowing most certainly that he alone and uniquely is God of realms visible and invisible alike [Col 1:16], who in his incomprehensible majesty causes there to be of both one single homeland.[89]

---

[87] Psalms 6, 31, 37, 50, 102, 129, and 142 (in the Vulgate enumeration).

[88] Used for table grace; see *Le Grande Exorde*, 112n20.

[89] *Soli polique patriam / unam facit rem publicam*: from the Easter hymn *Chorus novae Ierusalem*; see Chrysogonus Waddell, ed., *The Twelfth-Century Cistercian Hymnal*, Cistercian Liturgy Series, 1/2:145.

CHAPTER THIRTY-ONE

*About a Lay Brother Who Escaped the Sentence of Damnation*
*by the Grace of God and the Prayers of the Venerable Abbot Henry*

There was at Clairvaux a certain lay brother who had been converted for some time, though he had not been nourished under the
very chaste discipline of Clairvaux; in fact, he had been transferred
there from another house for an extremely serious offense which
he had committed in his previous house. By a dismaying hardness
of heart he concealed this offense in the very bottom of his very
bad conscience, without confession or repentance, even at the very
point of death. Almighty God, who holds all things in his power
and will [Esth 13:9], freely and mercifully deigned to snatch him
away from the pit of the eternal damnation already hanging over
his head. He was weighed down by an extremely grave sickness,
and when he felt death drawing nigh and was illuminated by that
divine grace which sometimes spares miserable and unworthy
sinners, he had every intention—a confessor having been summoned—of confessing his sins. But an envious mob of evil spirits,
who are always (so far as they can manage) extremely opposed to
the grace of God, were afraid that through the saving antidote of
confession they would lose a sinner whom for a long time they
assumed they were going to be able to trap in their snares. They
rushed upon him with such malicious force that he lost the power
of speech, remaining mute for quite a long time, and seemed about
to draw his last breath. But the good Lord knows both how to spare
suppliants and how to cast down the proud,[90] as he once managed
to do in the silence of the middle of the night [Wis 18:14] looking through the pillar of cloud and of fire at the army of Pharaoh
[Exod 13:22; 14:24]. So now again in the silence of the middle of
the night, through the intercession of blessed Bernard and the saints
who rest at Clairvaux, so we believe, the holy Lord rebuked the
tyrannical arrogance of the demons and put them to flight. He then

---

[90] Virgil, *Aeneid* 6.853.

freed his sinner and, having returned the power of speech to him, moved him to the sacrament of confession. The brother infirmarians, watching over him solicitously, were already expecting nothing but death when suddenly, at the stroke of midnight, he opened his eyes, and, speaking clearly, he told his brothers that he wanted to make his confession. To the venerable abbot Dom Henry, hastily summoned, he made his confession, speaking to him in bitterness of soul, saying, "I am a foul sinner and I, the most reprobate of all, confess to God and to you, father, that in my former monastery [EO 110.9; 111.18], which is called Esrom, located in Denmark, I fathered a son by fornication, and I have never before confessed this sin or done penance for it.[91] Just now while I could not speak, evil spirits snatched away my wretched soul to hellish places, and I saw the suffering to which I will be delivered when I go forth from the body.

"There, to crown my damnation, I met my son, already long-since dead, and he censured and reproached my wickednesses with these words: 'Woe, detestable sinner, alas, vile betrayer of chastity and religion, would you had never been born [Job 3:3-16], would you had never grown up; would you had passed from the womb to the tomb as if you had never existed, for it is on account of your evil deeds that I have deserved these miseries.' When I saw and heard this I was deeply disturbed and anguished, both that my punishment should be visited upon my son and that my own damnation now looms over me."

When Dom Henry the abbot, that discerning and prudent shepherd, heard this he became agitated [1 Kgs 3:26] at such tribulation and anguish in a sinner who was in mortal danger during his final agony. Moving close to the man, therefore, he began with salutary words to quicken the hope of pardon by all sorts of urgent arguments of piety, consoling and persuading him with useful admonitions to stir him up to the hope for the pardon for his soul, lest he despair of the inexpressible mercy of the all-powerful Redeemer.

---

[91] Esrom: a daughter house of Clairvaux in the Diocese of Roskilde in Denmark. See McGuire, *Cistercians in Denmark*, 2, 84–87, passim; Janauschek, 136; Cottineau 1:1072.

But he shouted with full devotion of faith and said to him, "Lord, I believe [Mark 9:23] that even if I were mired in the depths of hell, your mercy is able to free me from there." The abbot enjoined a penance and gave him absolution; he left the sick man and went back to the dormitory. Scarcely an hour passed and the abbot was summoned again by the anxious sick man, and he returned to him without delay. The sick man said to him, "I beg you, lord father, have mercy upon me and pray for me, a miserable sinner, because soon after I talked with you, I was taken back to the place of punishment, where also it was made known to me that because of the confession I made by God's mercy, and because of the penance I received, by the grace of God I am about to be set free from the pit of eternal damnation, but I am going to atone with suffering in purgatory for my wickedness and all the sins I have committed even to the last farthing [Matt 5:26]. Yet because, in fact, I did not make a full confession, and without a full confession I cannot be saved, by the great largess of God I have been permitted to make it a second time, so that the poison that still gnaws at my conscience may quickly be spewed out by the salutary purge of confession. Therefore, I confess to God and to you, father, that I presumed to receive a tunic from a certain brother without permission and have until this day lived without confessing or doing penance for this sin of having property and being disobedient [RB 33.5-6]." The observant and dutiful father Henry wondered greatly at such an abundance of divine goodness upon so great a sinner, and as the good shepherd of the lost sheep who rejoices when he has found it [Luke 15:3-7; John 10:11], he gave him absolution and enjoined a penance a second time, and with the most tender affection of piety he commended him to the grace of God. By the prayers of the abbot, the soul of the sick man was quieted, and he manifested his improved state by his serene expression. He fell silent again, and after a brief interval he rested in peace.

"Who shall lay anything to the charge of God's elect? If God justifies, who will condemn" [Rom 8:33-34]? The Almighty alone both can and may make from the common mass of humanity one vessel for dishonor, another vessel for honor [Rom 9:21]; nor can anyone ask him "why do you do this?" His judgments are true, and they are justified in themselves [Ps 18:10] from age to age, and he will have mercy upon whom he will have mercy, upon them that fear him [Ps 102:17], beyond the understanding of men or angels. For in his commentary on the gospel passage where the Lord says, "No one can come to me unless the Father who sent me has drawn him" [John 6:44], Augustine, aware of the secrets of heaven, said, "Do not wish to discuss or to make judgment about whom the almighty Father draws or does not draw, if you do not want to be in error."[92] Those who deserve to be saved by a special dispensation of grace are exceedingly blessed, like this man we have described, who turned back from misery, and exceedingly unhappy are those who, as in the example of such a man, only pretend to confess their sins until at the point of death, daring with extremely rash imprudence to presume that they will obtain such grace at their last gasp, even though the Lord says by the psalmist, "I will not gather together their libations of blood" [Ps 15:4] for few of those who have persisted in the blood of sinners receive this grace. But the privilege of the few is not made the common law,[93] and those who presume thus proudly on the mercy of God and through their own negligence squander the time of grace which is within their grasp, when the time of grace has passed and the horror and eternal darkness of death has snuffed out the light of his life, will find themselves trapped in that wretched time like a fish on a hook or a bird in a snare [Eccl 9:12]. Then they will perceive the tremendous majesty of almighty God—which they despise now, when he generously turns a blind eye to the sins of men for the sake of [inducing] penitence—to be something which punishes their sins with suffering by an utterly just and severe judgment that will never end.[94]

[92] See Augustine, *Tractatus in Iohannem* 26.2 (PL 35:1607), trans. John W. Relting, *St. Augustine: Tractates on the Gospel of John, 11–27*, Fathers of the Church 79 (Washington, DC: Fathers of the Church, 1988), 260–61.

[93] Gratian, *Decreti secunda pars* C.25 q.1, c.16, *Corpus iuris canonici*, ed. E. Friedberg (Leipzig: Bernard Tauchnitz, 1879), 1012, using Jerome, *Commentariorum in Jonam prophetam* 1.7 (PL 25:1126).

[94] Paraphrased from an antiphon used during the Ash Wednesday liturgy (*Le Grande Exorde*, 116n25).

The most reverend father Henry, abbot of Clairvaux, while he was daily making progress in the increase of virtue and his reputation for shining holiness was being talked about everywhere, was elevated to be cardinal bishop of Alba by the choice and election of the supreme pontiff and with the advice and agreement of his brother cardinals. Once he attained this dignity, he adapted to the pontifical state in such a way that he never forgot his first profession and his humility.[95] Outwardly, he displayed the authority proper to the priestly office, but inwardly he offered up the mourning of a monk in the spirit of contrition and a humble heart [Ps 50:19], hastening to please him who beholds what is within. When he was made bishop he did not hand over his Clairvaux and forget it but instead loved it with a heartfelt love, intent with an ever-faithful devotion on working for its honor and advantage wherever he could, whether at the Curia or elsewhere. When the days of his life were happily completed, he was buried at Clairvaux in a place he had chosen for himself and selected in advance with great longing. This place, between the shrines of the holy confessors of Christ, Bernard and Malachy,[96] he chose for his burial place so that, by clinging to them on the day of the general resurrection, whatever merit he himself lacked he might gain from the companionship of these great saints.

CHAPTER THIRTY-TWO

*About the Venerable Man Dom Peter,*
*the Eighth Abbot of Clairvaux*

After the mother of us all, the holy Roman Church which holds the fullness of power, admitted Dom Henry, formerly abbot of Clairvaux, to a share of its pastoral responsibility, the abbots and the

---

[95] *Nequaquam immemor existeret*: from the antiphon on the *Magnificat* at first Vespers of the feast of the Assumption (*Le Grande Exorde*, 116n27).

[96] *Monumenta s. Claraevallensis abbatiae* 3 (PL 185:1553B).

brothers of Clairvaux looked strenuously about to see whom they should put in his place. And very soon there wafted from nearby the very sweet fragrance of the virtues of Dom Peter, abbot of Igny,[97] whom we mentioned above; among his contemporaries he had obtained the special grace of being proclaimed holy and good, and he was elected from among thousands [Song 5;10]. A worthy successor of a worthy man, him they elected unanimously as the eighth abbot of Clairvaux. Worthy, I say, was he who ascended to a higher place in that temple of the Lord which is built of living stones [1 Pet 2:5], becoming on account of reverence for his humility that servant of whom Ezekiel said that by the eight steps of the principle virtues he would ascend to the eight days of eternal bliss [Ezek 40:34]. This servant of God, although he had been considered perfect and holy in the judgment of all before he took charge of the church of Clairvaux, yet as if his past way of life had been of no value, began to exert himself in a new struggle, endeavoring in all ways to give to his own voice the voice of virtue [Ps 67:34], that is, not to destroy by his deeds what he taught by his lips; to demonstrate all that was holy and just by his deeds more than his words [RB 2.12]; and continually to keep before his eyes the footprints of the fathers who preceded him, especially those of our most holy Father Bernard, whose unworthy deputy he considered himself. Although he abounded in the other virtues, he was so adorned with the grace of gentleness that the outward signs of dress, demeanor, countenance, and speech all clearly disclosed the holy humility profoundly rooted in his heart. At length, he committed almost all the temporal administration of the house to the cellarer and procurator and proposed to leave himself free for God alone [1 Tim 1:17] and to attend to the salvation of souls.[98] Whenever he

---

[97] Peter Monoculus, monk and then prior of Igny, was abbot of Valroy from 1164 to 1169, abbot of Igny from 1169 to 1179, and abbot of Clairvaux from 1179 to 1186. According to Grießer (EM, 141n6), he was a blood relative of Philip II Augustus, king of France (1180–1223). Peter's letters are in PL 201:1393–1404; other documents concerning his life are in *Acta SS*, Oct 13:53–90. See Lenssen, *Hagiologium Cisterciense* 1:254–57.

[98] Gregory, Dial 1.1.8; SCh 260:22–23.

could be unoccupied, he sat alone in silence in the parlor,[99] with his face turned toward the ground, so that if any of the junior monks or sick brothers were being tried by a multitude of temptations or weighed down by any other problems, they might be free to approach him. With healing counsel and sweet words of edification, he would strengthen them to bear well the struggle they had taken on for Christ's sake. On the other hand, how strict a chastener of his own body he was is evident enough in this: that never did he wear two tunics and cowls at once, but either one tunic and two cowls or two tunics and one cowl, even in the sharpest cold, and very rarely did he wear house shoes.[100] He put so much effort into frugality and temperance that he even used the common dishes very sparingly, demonstrating that he sought more to sustain his frail body than to indulge it by titillating his palate. Always in his heart and frequently in his speech he held himself to be unworthy and inadequate to rule so great a monastery, lacking the ability and the discernment needed by someone whom abbots and brothers in all parts of the world should look up to.

Once he is reputed to have said to the king of the Franks, who was his kinsman, "You see, my lord king, how puny a little man I am to have undertaken the governance of so important a house. I have absolutely no presence and am weak in mind and reason, and I seriously worry that through my imprudence and inadequacy the state of Clairvaux, which has until now remained inviolate, may fall to ruin." The king, absolutely delighted by his humility, replied, "Why, lord father, do you depress yourself with such timorousness that you want to give up the care of the souls which, at God's bidding, you have undertaken to govern? Do not do this, I beg you, but according to the grace bestowed on you by the Lord, do not neglect to exercise vigilantly the care of the Lord's flock. You

---

[99] *Auditorium*: the passage, or slype, in which short practical communication was permitted during times of silence and may have been the area in which monks experiencing spiritual difficulties were allowed to speak with the abbot. Brian Patrick McGuire believes that Conrad may have had experience at Clairvaux of Dom Peter waiting for brothers to discuss such problems. See "Structure and Consciousness," 81–82, especially n. 96. See note below in EM 4.12.

[100] EO 74.19n157.

be the abbot inside in those matters which pertain to the honor of God and the salvation of souls, and I will be the abbot outside in everything that touches on the interests of your house, guarding your possessions and keeping them free of all exactions. And anybody at all who in any way presumes to disturb you by his ill will shall find he has the king to reckon with."

That the conduct in holy observance of this man was extremely pure and well pleasing to God was shown clearly by that glorious revelation which we wrote about above, in which he was found worthy to see and hear the glorification of Christ's martyr Gerard, former abbot of Clairvaux, not only with his spiritual, but even with his physical eyes and ears. Indeed, how copiously the rich sweetness of heavenly grace was poured out upon him and how not ineffective he was as an intercessor for criminals and sinners is clearly shown by the marvelous and memorable deathbed conversion of the knight and wretchedly wicked sinner Baldwin. We will set down how this happened—not to hold out hope of impunity to wrongdoers, but to honor God and console penitents, just as that same most reverend abbot himself told it in detail to a certain brother who had quizzed him repeatedly. Not to put credence in his words would be to denigrate all religion. The aforesaid brother committed what he had heard to writing, and what we say now we express in his own words.[101]

---

[101] "The aforesaid brother" is Herbert of Clairvaux, who wrote the LM around 1178–81.

CHAPTER THIRTY-THREE

*How Almighty God Granted the Fruit of Repentance*
*to a Certain Very Wicked Sinner*
*by the Merits and Prayers of the Venerable Abbot Peter*[102]

A certain knight named Baldwin, lord of the castle called Guise, which is situated in the territory of Reims, was a warlike man well-trained in arms. He had abandoned all fear of God and daily perpetrated many evils by pillage, arson, murder, and other similar works of the devil. The only good thing about him seemed to be that he sincerely loved the most holy Peter—then abbot at Igny, later at Clairvaux—as well as the whole monastery of Igny, honoring him magnificently and trusting greatly in his merits. Nor was this in vain, as the outcome was to show, that there might be fulfilled the passage of the gospel where the Lord says, "Anyone who receives a just man in the name of a just man shall receive a just man's reward" [Matt 10:41].

Now when he was still at the height of his powers, he was struck down by a deadly sickness and approached the end of his life. As fast as he could, he sent a messenger to ask and entreat the aforesaid abbot to deign to come to him. Coming quickly, Peter found this man almost at his end and totally deprived of speech. But by the prayer of the holy abbot and the lavish liberality of our Lord Christ, the ability to speak and the will to make his confession was granted the sick man. Once he had confessed many things with contrition of heart, he wanted to leave the world and take the habit of religion right away. But his wife loved the body of her husband more than his soul and delayed this by withholding her agreement; but

---

[102] Everything from this point until the note below at "sign of his reconciliation" is taken from Herbert of Clairvaux, LM 2.27 (PL 185:1335–37). The same story is told by Thomas of Radilio in his *Life of Peter* 2.26-34 (*Acta SS*, Oct. 13:74–75). Virtually nothing is known of Baldwin of Guise, who seems not to have been a lord of Guise, located in the Thiérache in northeast France, but he typifies the rapacious lords repeatedly condemned by the Church; see n. 2–39 by Jacques Berlioz in *Le Grande Exorde de Cîteaux*, 119.

at last she despaired of his recovery and gave her consent.[103] He greatly rejoiced at obtaining leave to carry out his conversion and had himself taken to the monastery of Igny, where—if he lived—he would become a monk. But death came quickly, and his soul was released from his body, groaning with the bitterest contrition and violently ruing that he had passed the time of repentance without repenting. After he died, many revelations about him were disclosed to the abbot and the seniors of that place. Of these I have chosen to write down only a few because it would take a long time to set them all down.

The night he died he appeared in a vision to a certain observant monk; he seemed to be trying to raise himself from the bed in which he was lying, oppressed by grave sickness. The monk tried to help him, but he said, "There is no need to tire yourself on my account, brother. Saint Benedict, under whose wings I, unworthy though I am, have taken refuge, is my strongest helper. It was he who sent me to our lord, Abbot Peter, that I might be made a monk by him." That same night the venerable abbot, who was concerned and extremely worried about his soul and his repentance, began to turn over in his mind how he could help the dead man, weighed down by so heavy a burden of sins. While he was thinking about it, suddenly there stood before him someone whose face he did not recognize but whom he believed to be an angel of the Lord. Answering his thoughts, he said, "He is in great need of help." There was no doubt that the angel was speaking of the dead man, and immediately after he had said these words he was taken up from his sight. The holy abbot received this as a divine reply and was completely dissolved with the oil of piety and brotherly compassion and at once turned to prayer and went around to the altars of the saints and from the depths of his being implored their prayers for the salvation of the departed. After he had been doing

---

[103] The dispensation from a vow of marriage in order to take monastic vows was an issue addressed by Gratian and the later Decretist tradition. Canon lawyers upheld the legitimacy of such an action but required the consent of one's spouse; see James A. Brundage, *Law, Sex, and Christian Society in Medieval Europe* (Chicago: University of Chicago Press, 1987), 242–43, 296 (citing Gratian).

this with a burning affection of piety for rather a long time, sleep began to overtake him, grieved and exhausted as he was by the infirmity of human frailty. His eyelids were drooping slightly, and he seemed to be neither fully asleep nor fully awake when suddenly Satan appeared to him, threatening and raging against him with a fearsome countenance, saying, "What? You would take Baldwin from me?" When he had said this he leaped on him in a furious rage, pummeling and holding him violently down. Peter woke up at once and found all his limbs so stiff that he could not move. But "the word of God is not bound" [2 Tim 2:9]. So he said to that insatiable murderer, "I adjure you, unclean spirit, by the blood of Jesus Christ, the Son of God, who deigned to endure the cross for us miserable sinners, and by his glorious mother the Virgin Mary, that you not dare to harm this soul that has confessed and repented." When he had said this, the devil, by divine power, let go of him and fled. He understood through his own deliverance what he should do for the liberation of the dead man, so he persisted in his prayers and interceded with ever more and more renewed constancy. In that hour he was filled with so much grace of devotion and he conceived in his mind so great a confidence in the mercy of God that never in his life was he to lose it. He believed without any doubt that his prayers and those of his brothers for the departed man would be heard by God. In the morning when he presided at the brothers' chapter, he solicitously bade them and intently admonished them to pour forth devout prayers in common for the soul of the sinner who had fled to them in his final moment of need; he ordered many and daily prayers, and he took care that for thirty days [Deut 34:8] the sacrifice of our redemption should be offered for his soul [EO 98.37-38; 98.45-57]. For the whole of those thirty days hardly a day passed without the dead man appearing to remind the abbot, whether he was asleep or—which is more to be wondered at—whether he was awake, bending his knees before him and joining his hands, seeming to beg in this way that he not cease praying for him.

Now it happened at that time that a certain abbot of the order of black monks, whom the knight, when still alive in the flesh, had once gravely injured, turned up seeking hospitality at the house of Igny. The most reverend abbot Peter rejoiced very much that the Lord had presented him with this opportunity of helping the sinner's soul, and he led the aforesaid abbot to the dead man's grave and implored him for the love of Christ to pardon him for all the injuries he had committed against him at the devil's prompting. At once and without delay, for the sake of God's honor and the sake of relieving the brother's misery, he did what he was asked. And that same night the dead man appeared to Dom Peter the abbot, full of gratitude, showing him his body purged of leprosy, a disease by which he let him know he had been contaminated for a long time. On his face, however, there appeared the scar of a huge wound completely healed, and its restored health showed that the offense he had committed against the abbot had been blotted out. After this—because the Lord willed to show that the prayer of the holy abbot Peter and his brothers for the penitent soul had been heard in his presence—on the holy day of Good Friday, about the time the Office of None had just begun (that very hour when the Lord Jesus Christ deigned to endure the torture of the cross and to taste death for sinners), while this venerable abbot, dressed in priestly garments, was sitting by the altar, there appeared to him two young men with glowing faces and shining silken garments who led the dead Baldwin up to the altar, one on his left and the other on his right. They came into the abbot's presence and turning to him said, "Here is the lord Baldwin. When he died his clothing was black, but now it appears white and beautiful, as if made of costly cloth." When the holy abbot saw this he rejoiced greatly, understanding, of course, that the black robes were a sign of penance and his being brought to the altar a sure sign of his reconciliation.[104] But to remove any lingering doubt about that reconciliation from the heart of the servant of God, he who used to appear often begging for the help of his prayers, no longer appeared to the abbot or to anyone else. By this he let it be known that by the great mercy of God he had been received into the number of the penitent and was being refashioned into the likeness of God in the places of purgation.

---

[104] To this point the text follows Herbert of Clairvaux.

Who, I ask, is able to judge the bowels of the divine goodness and the mercy shown upon us wretched sinners? Our mother, the Church Catholic, believes most firmly that the Lord Jesus poured out his wholly innocent blood in his passion and death for sinners and the godless, but to whom this sacrament pertains and to whom it does not is entirely uncertain. We are rightly forbidden to pass judgment on even the most heinous sinner, for we can only judge what he is today, and we have no means at all of knowing what he will be tomorrow. For this is true not only of those who by the grace of God pass from sins and vices to the remedy of penitence but also—something to be deplored in a flood of tears—of those who, by the terrible judgment of God, slip from virtues and good works into vices. So let someone who stands [firm] see to it in fear and trembling that he not fall [1 Cor 10:12], and let someone who has fallen take care by every possible means to get up again. For wherever the timber of human nature falls at the death of the flesh, there it will lie [Eccl 11:3], whether to the south or to the north, that is, either with Christ, who is true life, in eternal blessedness, or with the devil, who is true death, in the everlasting misery of damnation.

Ponder then, O reader, how dear and acceptable to God was the blessed Abbot Peter, by whose merits and prayers he saved a sinner who, because of the number and enormity of his sins, seemed to have almost no hope of being rescued from the deep pit of death. If then, even before he undertook the governance of Clairvaux he was distinguished by being perfect and afterward deserved to become the pastor and rector of that religious house at which, as Bernard once said in a sermon, God has year after year gathered the endowment of the best and most precious souls,[105] shall we not conclude that he has increased in merits? Surely he did increase, for he piled atop his earlier monastic observance the later holiness of his many increasing virtues, so censuring in himself the restless occupations of Martha that by the pursuit of holy contemplation he embraced the calmness of Mary [Luke 10:38-42] with all the affection of his mind. In this way he taught those in his charge to

---

[105] Bernard of Clairvaux, Ded 3 (SBOp 5:381; SBS 2:403).

follow the straight and narrow way [Matt 7:14], so that he might demonstrate that the law which he imposed on others was lived out first in his own holy way of life.[106] Having commendably reached the end of his days, he paid the universal debt. Closing his eyes in mortal death, he who had for a little while sown in tears [Ps 125:5] reaped eternally the sweetest sheaves of his labors in the joy of life immortal. His venerable body was buried with full honor in the little chapel where, as we said above [EM 2.28], the martyr of Christ, Gerard, was in a tomb raised above the pavement. There with his blessed companion he rests and sleeps in peace [Ps 4:9], awaiting the day and the glory of the general resurrection which will then be joyously granted to the saints.

## CHAPTER THIRTY-FOUR

### A Review of the Foregoing

From among the virtues and praiseworthy lives of our most reverend fathers blessed Alberic and blessed Stephen, the first and second abbots of the monastery of Cîteaux, and no less those of the most blessed Bernard, first abbot of Clairvaux, and of their successors—we have from the broad and flowery field (not without some utility, I think) plucked, as it were, and assembled the most fragrant nosegays for our brothers who study and want to profit from them, asking the mercy of almighty God, that he may deign to raise up, not only at Cîteaux and Clairvaux, but throughout our

---

[106] Regarding Cistercian interpretations of Mary and Martha, see Ælred of Rievaulx, Sermon 19 (CCCM 2a:147–54; CF 58:263–74); and Bernard of Clairvaux, Asspt 2.9 (SBOp 5:237–38; SBS 3:234–35); Ep 459 (SBOp 8:437; James, Ep 395, p. 468); Sent (SBOp 6/2:13; CF 55:123–24). On the exegetical tradition on Mary and Martha, see Gerhart B. Ladner, *The Idea of Reform* (Cambridge, MA: Harvard University Press, 1959), 330–40; G. R. Evans, *The Thought of Gregory the Great* (Cambridge: Cambridge University Press, 1986), 105–11; and Giles Constable, *Three Studies*, 3–141; also below, EM 4.33.

Order, fathers who will emulate their religious observance and perfection so that all of us in the Cistercian Order who have resolved to bear the burden and heat of the day [Matt 20:12]—which our founders bore with indefatigable zeal and handed down to us to bear—may not only become acquainted with the sacred endeavors of the earlier fathers by reading [about them] but also, illuminated by the examples of present-day fathers and strengthened by their teachings, deserve to be received into the sheepfolds of the Lord, where, as we enter and exit, we may discover the pastures of life [John 10:9].

Let no one think that we have written about the holy way of life of the abbots of Cîteaux and Clairvaux as if in other houses of our Order—particularly in those recognized as being, along with Cîteaux and Clairvaux, chief within our Order: La Ferté, Pontigny, and Morimond[107]—other fathers did not also shine by their outstanding lives and monastic observance. We know very well that in various monasteries of our Order there are fathers flourishing with the grace of diverse virtues, by whose merits and prayers even today the vigor of discipline and the fervor of holy religion—with God's help—is preserved throughout our entire congregation. But we believe that what we know personally about the fathers of the principal houses of our Order will suffice as examples; their holiness is believed, without prejudice, to be more excellent than that of the rest, and one hopes that their authority will more easily enkindle reverence and love of holy religion in the soul of the reader.

[107] For additional context of the place of La Ferté, Pontigny, and Morimond in early Cistercian expansion, see Newman, *Boundaries of Charity*, 142–55.

# Book Three

# The Monks of Clairvaux

CHAPTER ONE

*About Dom Gerard,*
*Brother of Saint Bernard and Cellarer at Clairvaux*

We are now going to write about some of the senior brothers who were outstanding at Clairvaux under our most blessed Father Bernard. They were truly observant men, distinguished by their contempt for the world, fervent in zeal for our way of life, gleaming like the stars of heaven with diverse gifts of grace [1 Cor 12:31], and keeping watch in holy contemplation without flagging in spirit. With the insistency of a praiseworthy devotion, they endeavored to adorn the name and habit of a monk by holy behavior and the best conduct, that they might truly be what they were said to be.

Not without reason we place first among them Dom Gerard, the former cellarer at Clairvaux, as the firstborn who is, as the law prescribes [Exod 13:12], to be the firstfruit offered to the Lord. He was the blood brother of our holy Father Bernard and very greatly loved by him. As difficult as he found it at the beginning to assent to conversion of life,[1] that much more steadfast and sincere was he afterward in keeping all of his conduct in accordance with his altered way of life. When the Lord's servant Bernard, as a young man like a very tender little worm in the wood [2 Sam 23:8; Vulg.] until the Holy Spirit turned him from living delicately to putting his hand to strong things [Prov 31:19], received the grace of conversion and vowed to follow it, he, inflamed by the same Spirit, gathered up from various quarters companions in his new way of life. Whereas the rest of his brothers gave their assent to his saving admonitions, Gerard found his advice harder to take. He was a knight skilled in arms, robust with the strength of youth, great prudence, and such loving-kindness that he was loved by everyone, but at the bottom of his heart he had deeply rooted a love of the world and its vanities. When Gerard obstinately refused his brother's

[1] William of Saint Thierry, Vita Bern 1.3.11-12 (PL 185:233–34).

advice, Bernard, already burning with faith and the zeal of brotherly love, and somewhat exasperated, said to him, "I know very well that only hardship will make you understand." At that moment there appeared to him a lance transfixing his brother's side, a presage of the future, and at once he placed his finger on the place in his side where he had seen the lance, saying, "The day is coming, and coming soon, when a lance will pierce your side, and a way will be made into your heart for the counsels of your salvation which you now reject. You will be afraid then, but you will not die." As he spoke, so it was. Only a few days later Gerard was surrounded by his enemies and captured, and, as his brother had foreseen, he was wounded by a lance in that very place in his side it had been predicted. Pulling out the lance and terrified of impending death, he cried out, "I am a monk, a monk of Cîteaux." Nevertheless, he was taken prisoner and locked up in custody. Against all hope, he soon recovered from his wound, but he did not change the vow he had made. Although his brother tried to get him released, he could not manage it. Gerard began to be more and more worried and upset at having made, and now was being held back from keeping, a vow which he had made to the Lord and which, when he had been free and intoxicated with love of the world, he had scorned to make or to fulfill. Bernard, although he was not allowed to talk with him, went close to the prison and shouted, "Gerard, my brother, I want you to know that we are going to set out soon and enter the monastery. Since you cannot escape, however, you will have to be a monk here, knowing that what you will but cannot do shall be counted as if done." Gerard was locked up in prison for some time, bound with chains, and he discovered how hard it is to kick against the goad of the grace of God [Acts 26:14]; he learned, I tell you, how full of misfortunes and bitterness is the gall-filled charm of the love of this world.

At length, after he had been sufficiently and salutarily chastised by the Lord for his obstinacy, one night he heard a voice saying to him in his sleep, "Tomorrow you will be set free." That same day, toward evening, his fetters were divinely broken, the door of his prison opened of its own accord, and Gerard walked out a free man, passing through the midst of those who had taken him prisoner and locked him in prison. By the great mercy of God set free from a double captivity, of body and of soul, he could say the words, "Thy rod and thy staff have comforted me, O Lord" [Ps 22:4]. He came to Cîteaux with his brothers and the others who had taken the oath of this spiritual crusade, there more humbly and devoutly to make good the vow he had vowed to the Lord, knowing that it was only by divine grace and will in a manifest miracle that he had been given the means of fulfilling his vow. Later when the very reverend Father Stephen, abbot of Cîteaux, sent blessed Bernard and his brothers with other observant men to begin the monastery at Clairvaux, Dom Gerard was made cellarer of that house. How he discharged the office assigned to him with ability, prudence, and humility we can better explain by using the actual words of venerable Bernard than our own. After Gerard's death, the venerable abbot preached with the most loving sorrow about his virtues to the assembled brothers, and among other things he said:[2]

> You know, my sons, how well-founded is my grief, how grieved I am by my sorrow. You are well aware how faithful was the companion who has left me on the way in which I was walking [Ps 141:4], how careful he was of his charge, how never tardy in work, how gentle in his ways. Who was so especially necessary to me as he? By whom was I so well loved? He was my brother by blood but still more my brother in religion. Share my misfortune, I pray, you who know all this. I was weak in body and he sustained me, timid at heart and he strengthened me, slothful and negligent and he urged me on, improvident and forgetful and he reminded me of my duty. Gerard, why have you been torn from me? Whither have you been snatched out of my hands, you who were of one mind with me [Ps 54:14], a man after my own heart [Acts 13:22]? We loved one another in life, how can we be separated in death? It is a very bitter separation, one which nothing but death could have brought about. While you lived, when did you ever desert me? This sundering that death has wrought is a thing to be shuddered at. Who would not have

---

[2] The following is from Bernard of Clairvaux, SC 26.4-12; (SBOp 1:172–79; CF 7:61–72).

spared the sweet bond of love between us, except death, the enemy of all that is gracious?

In every need that arises I look for Gerard as I used to do, and he is not there. Alas, unhappy man that I am, I groan then like a man wretched without help [Ps 87:5]. In perplexing matters, whom shall I consult; in adversity, in whom shall I trust? Who will bear my burdens? Who will put perils to flight? Was not the eye of my brother Gerard wont to direct my steps everywhere? Gerard, your breast knew my cares better than I did, bore them more and felt them more acutely. Your tongue was so winning and persuasive that you could free me from the burden of any worldly business and restore me to my beloved silence. The Lord had given him a learned tongue so that he knew when and how to speak [Isa 50:4]. By the grace given him from above he gave such satisfaction by the prudence of his answers, both to those in the monastery and to strangers, that no one who had conferred with Gerard had much reason to talk with me. He even went to meet visitors lest they unexpectedly break in on my leisure. If he could not satisfy someone he brought him to me; the rest he sent away. O man of industry, faithful friend! He took pleasure in a friend but never shirked the demands of charity. Whoever went away from him empty-handed? A rich man would carry away advice, a poor man substantial help. And he, who burdened himself with many cares in order to free me from them, did not seek anything for himself [1 Cor 13:5]. The most humble of men, he hoped that my leisure would bear more fruit than his own would have done.

But there were times when he asked to be released from his office and that it be given over to someone else, as if anyone better could be found. But where could I find another like him? Nor did he detain anyone in the line of duty from any preference, as often happens, but from the impulse of charity alone. He used to labor more than all the rest and receive less than any, so that often while he handed out the necessary food and clothing to others he himself was in many ways more in need of them. Thank you, my brother, for all the fruit of my studies, if under God there has been any. If I have made any progress I owe it to you. You involved yourself in the cares of the monastery and, thanks to you, I could sit at leisure, or rather I could occupy myself more devoutly with the Divine Offices or concentrate more usefully on instructing my sons. Why should I not be at peace within, knowing that you—my right hand, the light of my eyes [Ps 37:11], my heart, my tongue—were busy without?

But why do I say Gerard was busy without, as if he had no experience of the inner life and spiritual gifts? Those who knew him knew that his words were scented with the Holy Spirit. His close friends knew that his habits and endeavors were warmed by the fire of the Spirit, not savoring of the flesh. Who was stricter than he in maintaining discipline? Who more rigorous in disciplining his body? Who more absorbed in contemplation, more penetrating in discourse? How often in discussion with him have I learned what I did not know, and I who had come to instruct have gone away better instructed. With me this is no wonder, but eminent and learned men have told me that the same thing happened when they were with him. Though he was not highly learned, he had an innate sense that enabled him to perceive many truths, and he also had the illumination of the Spirit. Nor was he accomplished solely in great things, but he was great in small things too. What was there, for example, that eluded his expertise in building, farming, gardening, drainage, and in the other arts and labors of country people? He could easily direct masons, smiths, farmers, gardeners, shoemakers, and even weavers. In the judgment of all he was wiser than any, but in his own eyes alone he was not wise. Would that many, less wise, were as little touched by the curse that says, "Woe to you that are wise in your own eyes" [Isa 5:21]? All this I am saying to those who knew him and who have experienced and learned still more about him.

I pass over many things because he is my brother and my flesh. Yet one thing I add with complete assurance: he was useful to me in all things and beyond all men—useful in small things and in great, in private affairs and public, in the monastery and outside. It was with good reason that I was wholly devoted to him who was everything to me. He left to me the honor and title of being the provider, but he did all the work. I was called abbot but he was the one who, in fact, bore all the responsibility. Rightly did my spirit rest on him, and by his means I could rejoice in the Lord, preach more freely, and pray safer from all interruption. Because of you, my brother, my mind was calmer, my rest more peaceful, my discourse more efficacious, my prayer richer, my reading more frequent and my affection more fervent. Alas, you have been taken up and all these things with you. With you there has passed away all my joy and gladness. Already cares are breaking in on me, anxieties are knocking, from all sides troubles are pressing in on me [Dan 13:22]; with you gone, they all fall on me, and alone I groan under the burden. I must lay it down or be crushed by it since you have withdrawn your shoulders. Who will grant me death quickly after you? I do not wish to have died in your place, nor to deprive you of glory, but as long as I live on after you, I labor and grieve. Flow forth, flow forth, tears wanting since yesterday to flow. Flow, for he who would have hindered your course is gone. I admit that I am not without dread of future punishment and I shudder at death for me and mine. Gerard was mine, all mine. Was he not mine: my brother by blood, my son by profession, my father in the care he took of me, my companion in the Spirit, my intimate in affection? He has left me. I feel it; I am wounded, and grievously so. Forgive me, my sons, or rather, if you are my sons, lament in the grief of your father. I grieve for you, my dearest Gerard, not because your state is to be grieved over, but because you have been taken away. And so perhaps it is rather I who should be grieved over, for I drink the cup of bitterness. O death, where is your victory? O death, where is your sting [1 Cor 15:55]?

Gerard does not fear you, shadowy phantoms! Gerard passes through your jaws to his homeland, not only safely, but also with joy and praise. I grieve, first of all, then, for my own trouble and for the loss this house has sustained. I grieve, secondly, for the needs of the poor, to whom Gerard was a father. I grieve, certainly and above all, for our Order and our way of life which derived no little strength, Gerard, from your zeal, your counsel, and your example. I grieve, finally, not over you, but because of you. It is this that wounds me so deeply: that I loved you with all my heart.

CHAPTER TWO

*About the Praiseworthy Abstinence of Dom Gerard, the Cellarer*

This is the testimony that the most reverend Father Bernard gave to the life and conduct of his beloved brother Gerard, and we have strung together several excerpts from his long sermon to show the virtues of so great a man. We know that false adulation was entirely foreign to the words and expressions of such a father as ours, nor was he influenced by the affection of kinship, for he was resolved not to give one word of praise beyond what was really due. Even so, if his testimony was true, or rather because it was true [John 21:24], it makes very clear how perfect in the virtues was the Lord's servant, Gerard. By God's great gift, true religious observance was in no way hindered by external administration, which had turned so many from the highway of claustral discipline and plunged them into the marketplace of worldly behavior. Who, moreover, could satisfy a statement of such praise, worthily to be admired: that laboring more than others he received less than anyone; that he was kept in his office by no peevish desire but solely by the consideration of charity—a thing most rare in our times? Or that when he ministered to the needs of the rest, he himself was in want among plenty? To prove how unswerving was his observance of discipline and how strict he was in chastising the body, we will set down one from his praiseworthy deeds as an example, so that those who are fervent in religious observance and take care to look to the virtues of the holy fathers for their own profit may have something which they ought to imitate, and those who are remiss and weak may have something to make them ashamed of themselves.

Gerard, the servant of the Lord, used to go round the granges in his official capacity;[3] he was content with the common table and the food of the brothers, and he drank water as they did; he would not easily allow himself to be given anything beyond the communal fare. It happened once that he was ill while traveling

---

[3] *Statuta* (1134) 68 (Canivez 1:29; Waddell, *Twelfth-Century Statutes*, 556).

to a grange. The lay brother who had the duty of going with him knew this and went to the prior to tell him that the cellarer was ill; he said he was afraid that if Gerard drank the water at the grange as he usually did his sickness would get worse.[4] By the order of the prior, a small vessel filled with wine was placed near the cellarer without his knowledge. When he sat down with the brothers at the table he received a sign made by the prior, as is the custom, that because of his sickness he alone could take some wine. But how could someone who was so very fervent in striving for poverty and the common life agree to this—that while all the rest were drinking water, he alone should take pleasure in a goblet of wine? Now there was a jug full of water placed in the middle of the table for the brothers to help themselves. For a little while, therefore, he thought about what he ought to do; then he got up. He picked up the small vessel of wine and poured the wine in the sight of them all into the jug that held water, making a sign that they were all to drink communally. He chose to expose his body to sickness rather than have on his conscience the stain of even so small a lapse from abstinence. The brothers, equally exhilarated and edified by such a religious act, drank that water with more delight than if he had set the rarest of wines before them. Let those who read about the life and conduct of this best of cellarers see how the allurements of the flesh should be condemned, for he did not take a goblet of wine for the cure or restoration of his bodily health when it seemed that his sickness might give occasion for scandal.

## Chapter Three

### *About the Precious Death of the Venerable Man, Gerard*

When the holy Father Bernard went to Italy for a third time at the behest of the Lord Pope Innocent to settle the schism of Peter Leone and was being noticed everywhere by his signs and miracles,

---

[4] *Le Grande Exorde*, 131n8, notes that this passage mirrors the *Usus conversorum* 15.

he took with him everywhere Dom Gerard, his cellarer, as his most faithful helper and most prudent counselor. Now it happened that while they were at Viterbo, this Dom Gerard had to go to bed, laid low by his very grave state of health, and the abbot became very upset and worried about him.[5] When clear signs of imminent death appeared, Bernard, the servant of the Lord, took it badly that this should happen to the companion—and what a companion!—of his journey, and he was not prepared to leave him in a foreign land and fail to restore him to those who had committed Gerard to him, for Gerard was loved by all because he was extremely worthy of love.[6] Bernard turned to the Lord with tears and groans: "Lord," he said, "wait, wait until we return home. Take him then, when I have returned him to those who love him, if you will, and I will not complain." How could the good and merciful Lord ignore the humility of his servant when he was asking for such a suitable thing in such contrition of heart, when he used to hear him so often, so readily, and so kindly in the cause of others?

Contrary to the expectations of everyone, then, Gerard came back to life from the gates of death and quickly regained his strength. Having completed their business and restored the peace of the holy Roman Church, entirely stamping out the madness connected with Leone, they returned to their own country to the praise of the whole world, carrying sheaves of peace with them.[7] Not many days had passed when, as if the Lord had answered the prayers and faithful desire of his servant Bernard, Gerard suddenly began again to lose his bodily strength, and little by little he drew near his end. He who had patiently borne the office enjoined upon him like Martha, now embraced with his entire soul the stillness of Mary [Luke 10:38-42]. He sensed with utter certainty that he was going to pass over from the labor of earthly cares to the rest of eternal blessedness, there to begin to have the leisure to taste and see how gracious is the Lord [Ps 33:9]. In order to show that

---

[5] Bernard was in Viterbo in 1137; Gerard died at Clairvaux in 1138. See Williams, 122–33.

[6] Bernard of Clairvaux, SC 26.14 (SBOp 1:180–81; CF 7:73).

[7] Bernard of Clairvaux, SC 26.14 (SBOp 1:181; CF 7:73).

there had been nothing of carnal or worldly desire in his work, he raised his eyes to heaven and said, "O God, you know that insofar as I was able, I have always sought quiet to take thought for myself and to be at leisure for you. But I have been kept busy by your love, the will of my brothers, my zeal for obedience, and above all the love of him who is both my abbot and my blood brother." About the middle of the night he passed away from mortal misery; his face became marvelously happy, and to the amazement of all present he broke out with a voice of exultation into the words of David: "O praise the Lord of heaven, praise him in the height" [Ps 148:1]. Already for that blessed man dawn was breaking in the middle of the night, and the darkest night was becoming as clear as the day, for his night was enlightened by the joy of the eternal light which is Christ the Lord [Ps 138:11-12]. How should it not be that darkness was turned into light when the man who was singing died and sang while he was dying? He went out toward you, O death, our enemy, into joy, even though you are the mother of sorrow; you give rise to glory, though you are glory's opponent; you give entrance to heaven, though you are the gate of hell, the pit of perdition, you become the means to salvation.[8]

Those brothers who were present were astonished at this latest miracle and ran quickly to tell his beloved brother Saint Bernard how the man was exulting in death and taunting death. He hastened to him, although weak and infirm, and as he listened, Gerard finished the last verse of the psalm he was singing and, looking up to heaven, said in a clear voice, "Father, into your hands I commend my spirit" [Luke 23:46]. He repeated these words and groaned often, "Father, father." Then he turned with a glad countenance to him who was his holy abbot and his brother and said, "How great a condescension it is that God is the father of humankind; how great a glory it is that human beings are the sons and heirs of God, for if they are sons they are also heirs" [Rom 8:17; Gal 4:7]. In this way, the flesh of that holy soul was dissolved with jubilation and the exultation of spiritual joy and, with the flesh left behind, he was

---

[8] Compare Bernard of Clairvaux, SC 26.11 (SBOp 1:178; CF 7:70).

able to seek his home among the stars and to join with the singing of angelic choirs all the more because the troop of wicked spirits could find nothing in him. The holy abbot, his brother, celebrated his funeral rites and performed the last Offices with loving affection and devotion of heart, but when others wept he wept not. He disciplined his outbreaks of weeping with great constancy of faith, lest anyone think that he was weeping at Gerard's death, when in fact he had no doubt that he has passed by his death into eternal life and everlasting glory.

## CHAPTER FOUR

### *About the Very Reverend Father Dom Humbert, a Former Prior of Clairvaux*

After the monastery of Clairvaux had been founded by the grace and mercy of our Lord Jesus Christ, its very fragrant reputation for holiness became the odor of life for many [2 Cor 2:16]. Among those whom the secret counsel of the divine bounty called from many parts of the world were many men in religious Orders who seemed to be perfect in religious observances where they already were, but having heard that the Lord had magnified his mercy [Luke 1:58] so specially and outstandingly in that house and in that very holy abbot, they wanted with a very fervent devotion of spirit to ally themselves as new recruits with a group of such holiness, even though they had already given themselves to the labors of long-standing warfare. Among these men the first and most outstanding were Humbert, the first abbot of the monastery of Igny;[9] Rainald; Peter, called "of Toulouse"; William; and Gerard of Farfa.[10] They did not all come from the same place, but, living in different regions

---

[9] Igny, founded from Clairvaux in 1127–28, in the Diocese of Reims. Janauschek 29 (p. 14); Cottineau 1:1443; DHGE 25:749–53.

[10] All of these men are mentioned later in this book: Humbert, EM 3.5, 6; Rainald, EM 3.13; Peter, EM 3.15; William, EM 3.16; and Gerard of Farfa, EM 3.17.

with a wide distance between them, they had given themselves over to learning obedience to God from their childhood, and, abounding in the grace of all the virtues, they seemed to have little need of being instructed by the example of other, as it were, more perfect men. But they had learned from abundant and reliable information about the sweet honey of holiness which put our holy Father Bernard far above all others in those days, like a cedar high on Mount Zion [Sir 24:17]. Truly gentle and lowly of heart, they did not turn a deaf ear to the word of Revelation—"him that is holy, let him be holy still" [Rev 22:11]—but they counted what had gone before as nothing, stretching out toward what was to come. They placed themselves of their own free will in all humility under such a great spiritual father and teacher. Because of his respect for their goodness, blessed Bernard always lovingly embraced them by the same affection of charity.

Now we will recount the very pure and truly monastic way of life of the very reverend Father Humbert, and then we shall say something about the others in their turn, as the Lord allows.

The servant of God Humbert was placed from boyhood in the sanctuary of the Lord, and for twenty years he fought for the Lord strenuously in monastic life.[11] Then seized with the desire for a more perfect and holier way of life, he betook himself to Clairvaux just after the house was founded. There, he shone with such great gifts of virtue and was so graced by gentleness and charity that, as if he were one of the number of celestial seraphim, by his own outstandingly fervent way of life, he vehemently enkindled the entire community to the love of God. The blessed abbot of this congregation, holy and blessed by God with special privileges, a man so upright in virtue that he had no need to beg for increase in religious observance from men, was humbly taught by the anointing of the Holy Spirit to follow the humble rather than the proud [1 John 2:27]. So he set himself to follow Humbert the servant of God as an example of perfection, admiring his virtues, considering

---

[11] After being professed for twenty years in the Benedictine monastery of La Chaise Dieu (*Casa Dei*), Humbert entered Clairvaux in 1117. He was the first abbot of Igny (1126–38) and died at Clairvaux in 1148.

his great and sublime merits, reflecting on this example of holiness, this pattern of religious observance, this mirror of monastic purity, to value his own behavior as nothing in comparison with Humbert's holy fervor, to chastise himself day and night as if trying less hard than he, knowing for certain that all men fail by looking at the weaker and that they increase in virtue by contemplating the more perfect; as much as possible he was consummate in virtue, because of his praiseworthy concern for holy humility. So blessed Bernard said this in a certain sermon:"My brothers, would that we sinners had the humility about our sins that the saints have about their virtues."[12]

The venerable Humbert was later sent, therefore, to build up the monastery of Igny, and he was made first abbot of that house by blessed Bernard. He bore this very impatiently, because he considered that this had taken away from him the possibility of practicing poverty, humility, and obedience, which he loved. At last, not being able to bear the soft-eyed Leah in place of the holy quiet and contemplation of the beautiful Rachel, that is, the tumult and worry of worldly business that he had to carry, he asked and obtained from Saint Bernard leave to lay down the burden of pastoral care and return to Clairvaux.[13] He replaced the yoke of subjection and obedience on his noble neck, because no neck is noble unless it can bend, and carried it unwearied to the very end of his life as the yoke of the Lord which is easy and whose burden is light [Matt 11:30]. Although as he grew old the vigor of his body failed as his members weakened and he was beset by various adverse and inconvenient ills, his soul was vigorous and fervent for the work of God. So much so that this decrepit old man bore patiently and even sought out [RB 37] with alacrity the hard labor of the Order which robust young men can scarcely tolerate. Not only would he never

---

[12] This is not Bernard but Guerric of Igny, Pur 1 (SCh 166:308; CF 8:100).
[13] Compare Bernard of Clairvaux, Ep 141 (SBOp 7:338–39; James, Ep 150, pp. 218–19). Rachel and Leah, wives of Jacob (Gen 29:6–35), were long associated with the contemplative and active lives. *Le Grande Exorde*, 366n6, cites Augustine, *Contra Faustum* 22.46; and Gregory the Great, Mor 6.37 (CCSL 143:325–32) as prominent examples. Conrad also uses the image in EM 6.1.

ask for the remissions and merciful indulgences which are granted out of compassion to the old, but he would never willingly agree to accept them. After spending some thirty years at Clairvaux, he crowned his happy contest with a joyful death; he was not taken away but taken up into the new life of glorious triumph in soul and body. At his passing, blessed Bernard was deeply disturbed and told the assembled brothers in a sermon what he knew of the excellence of his way of life.

CHAPTER FIVE

*Bernard's Sermon at the Death of Humbert of Pious Memory*[14]

1. Humbert, the servant of the Lord, the devoted servant, the faithful slave, is dead. You have seen how last night he breathed his last between my hands like one of the worms of the earth. Death wore him down for these three days, and he was devoured by its jaws that it might be sated with the blood for which it thirsted. Alas, death has done what it could; the flesh died and is buried in the heart of the earth [Matt 12:40]. It has separated us from our dear friend, our prudent councilor, our strong helper. Not me and not you has this insatiable murderer spared, least of all me. O bitter death, is this how you separate us? O cruel beast, keenest bitterness, terror and dread of the sons of Adam! You have killed and you have taken possession. Of what? Only the flesh, for there is nothing you can do to the soul. Humbert has gone to his Creator whom he so ardently longed for and followed so firmly all the days of his life. Even the body, which you now seem to have, will be taken from you when you, the final enemy, shall be destroyed and swallowed up in victory [1 Cor 15:26, 54]. At some point you will give up his body, you will surely give up that body which yesterday at the

---

[14] Bernard of Clairvaux, Humb (SBOp 5:440–47; SBS 3:61–72); Bernard of Clairvaux, *Sermons for Year's End*, trans. Irene Edmonds, CF 54 (Collegeville, MN: Cistercian Publications, forthcoming).

sign of your coming became so much slime and excrement and sordid filth, and there will be joyful rejoicing and praise [Isa 35:2], for then you will be caught in your own snare. He will come; he will come, the only-begotten of the Father, with great power and majesty, to seek Humbert and to make that same dead body which now rots in the dust like unto his glorious body [Phil 3:21]. What about you then? Clearly what is written in the prophet Jeremiah: in the last day you will be outwitted, and while Humbert is alive for all eternity, you will die in perpetuity [Jer 17:11]. The sea-beast vomited out the prophet Jonah whom he had swallowed [Jon 2:11]; you will give up Humbert whom you seem to have folded entirely into your great maw.

2. What is more, my brothers, the servant of God preached to you a long and a great sermon by all the ways of holiness he exhibited. Long, for it reached the full length of the way; great, for it reached into the fullness of life. I need say no more if you have remembered his sermon well, if you have it clearly imprinted on your hearts. Fifty years and more he lived in the service of the One for whom to rule is to serve; from his childhood he was at home in the sanctuary of God.[15] For thirty years, almost from the beginning of this monastery, he led the monastic life along with us, not only without grumbling, but also with grace. His memory will be a blessing to us and to generations still to come [Sir 45:1; Ps 70:18]. He passed through life, and this way of life, as a stranger and sojourner [Gen 23:4], accepting as little as he could of this world's goods because he knew that he was not of this world [John 17:14]. Here he had no lasting city [Heb 13:14], just as his fathers had none, but he pressed forward to the palm of his heavenly vocation [Phil 3:14]. The world had nothing it could by right claim in him or of him, because the world did not content him nor he the world. He took as little as he could for sustenance and would have

---

[15] On serving and bearing with the Lord, see Bernard of Clairvaux, Epp 111.1, 377.1 (SBOp 7:283–84; SBOp 8:340–41; James, Epp 113.1, 404.1; pp. 170, 475); QH 7.3-4 (SBOp 4:414–15; CF 25:153–54). The theme "to serve is to reign" has been prominent in liturgical, theological, and homiletic works since at least the seventh century. For extensive bibliography, see Pascal Collomb, *Le Grande Exorde*, 137–38n19.

taken less had he not been compelled by obedience. Having food and clothing, with these he was content, wanting what was necessary [1 Tim 6:8], not wanting superfluity—though he quite often complained that necessity was in fact superfluity. A few days ago, if I remember rightly, when we were talking together, he spoke of himself as the charity case of the monastery, a useless fellow being fed in the house of God. He was indeed gentle and humble of heart [Matt 11:29], and although all the other virtues abounded in him, he had especially obtained the grace of gentleness. He showed himself loving and kind to everyone, and so he was greatly loved.

3. You all know full well how circumspect he was in all his words and speech [Exod 6:12], for you have all known him very well and have seen his conduct for a long time and heard his words. Who ever heard from his mouth any syllable of fault finding, any word of mockery, any phrase of self-vaunting, any hint of envy? Who ever heard him judging others or going along with someone else passing judgment? Who ever heard a vain word from him? Indeed who, making such remarks, did not quail at being overheard by him? He guarded his ways carefully so that he might not offend in his tongue [Ps 38:2], knowing that he who does not offend in word is a perfect man [Jas 3:2]. Far from you, Humbert, was the dire warning of the gospel: "Woe to you who laugh now, for you shall weep" [Luke 6:25]. Did any of you ever find him laughing, even with those who were laughing? By the indwelling of grace, his countenance was serene and not oppressive, but if you remember, he would not allow himself to laugh outright. Moreover, with how much zeal he applied himself to the Office by day and night we not only saw but stood in awe of up to the day of his death. When he had to bear the failings of old age, he was troubled beyond what is usual by the many and great infirmities of old age, which many of you know all too well, the lack of energy and the tremors; yet as it is said, his soul was victor over years and knew not how to give way to infirmity. In cold and heat, climbing mountains, descending into valleys, he participated in all the labors of young men, to the wonder and amazement of everyone. If sometimes I kept him away from community because of the press of business or to ask his advice, he would be sad and downcast until he could

return to your company. Very rarely was he ever found away from the solemn Vigils, at which he would sometimes arrive early, and until he was compelled to do so by the infirmity of death [1 Cor 1:9], he was very rarely absent from the rest of the choir Offices, except from necessity.

4. In the refectory he scarcely touched the communal food, and if by chance someone else served him something else, he would either not take it or take it with such discomfort that the rest of us were also quite often discomforted over it. He would have chosen always to drink water if I had not opposed him with all my strength. Wine, when he was made to drink it, was wine in color rather than in taste, for he added a great deal of water to it. He would scarcely ever go to the infirmary, even when he was compelled to do so by obedience; once he got there, he could scarcely be kept there. I confess that in this matter his lack of obedience was a burden to me. Do I praise him? In this I do not praise him [1 Cor 11:22], because, as you know, he continued to be obstinate about it. I believe that when he did agree to this, it was because he knew he was causing trouble, not because of the needs of his body. How good was he at offering advice? He was always clear and discerning, as I know best since I have most often leaned on his bosom. But not only did I know it—you all knew it. Who was there beset by many and great temptations who did not hear from his lips the root of each temptation and the remedy to cure it? He would go so carefully through all the corners of a troubled conscience that those who confided in him believed that he saw everything and destroyed it all.

5. And how great was his charity? He had so put on bowels of loving-kindness that he excused everyone and interceded for everyone [Col 3:12], not thinking about gaining favor with those on whose behalf he spoke, approving not the persons but their needs [Acts 10:34]. He was humble of heart [Matt 11:29], gentle of speech, strenuous at work, fervent in charity, faithful in what he did, prudent and circumspect in his advice. He was well balanced above all men whom I saw in those days, and he remained just the same at every time and every hour. He put his footprints in the paths of the Lord Jesus and did not withdraw his foot until he had finished the course of the journey. Jesus was poor, so he was poor.

Jesus lived in hardship, and he lived in many hardships. Jesus was crucified, and he, having been bound to many great crosses, bore the wounds of Jesus on his body, making up those things which the sufferings of Christ lacked, even in his own body [Col 1:24]. Jesus rose, and he shall rise. Jesus ascended into heaven, and he believed that he would ascend; surely he shall ascend when the king of glory descends for our sake, just as he first ascended that he might make his power known [Ps 105:8], when he descends through the clouds with no less glory than he ascended through the clouds. As once the angels foretold, this same Jesus who is taken up from you into heaven shall come in like manner as you have seen him go into heaven [Acts 1:11]. Praise no man during his life, Scripture says, for it is not safe to praise until after death [Sir 11:30]. I tried hard to do this with Humbert, and while he was alive I did not open my mouth like this, for fear I might incur a reputation for adulation or he blame me for vanity. Now there is no fear of either, for I do not see him and he, perhaps, does not hear me. But if he does hear me, he will not be swayed by the words of men, for he abides firmly and gladly in the word of God. The enemy has no advantage over him [Ps 88:23], and he who suggests vanity cannot approach to harm him.

6. Look, dearest father, before you now is that font of purity for which you used to long with such ardor of soul. Look, you are drowned in that abyss of divine loving-kindness, the memory of whose abundant sweetness you used to praise aloud so devoutly [Ps 144:7]. Was there ever a more devoted preacher of divine loving-kindness, a more enthusiastic promoter of human purity, or a greater lover of both? Of whom else could it be said that whenever he spoke five words, in them true purity resounded, in them was heard the love of God? I do not grieve over you, for God has granted the desire of your soul; I grieve rather for myself, that I have lost a faithful adviser, a great helper, a single-minded man, a man after my own heart [1 Sam 13:14; 2 Sam 1:26; Ps 20:3]. "All these ills have fallen upon me" [Gen 42:36]. "Your anger passes over me, Lord Jesus, and your terrors disturb me" [Ps 87:17]. "You have put away from me my friend and companion; you have taken those I know away from misery" [Ps 87:19] and left me in misery.

You have removed from me my brother in the flesh, my brother in the Spirit, wise both in your affairs and, by your light, in those of the world. One after another, you have taken away those who helped me carry my burden, that great burden which you have imposed on me. One remained to me, nearly the only one of those so needful to me, Humbert, a dearer friend for being one of long standing, and you have taken him away, because he was yours. I am left alone to be buffeted. I die with each of them "and your waves pass over me" [Ps 87:8]. Would that when you scourge me, you would kill me at once and not deliver a wretched man to so many and such great deaths. In very truth, I am not going against the decrees of the Holy One. But "let Him who has made a beginning wear me away, and let this be my consolation, that when He afflicts me with sorrow He does not spare me" [Job 6:9-10]. "I have prepared myself for afflictions" [Ps 37:18], if perhaps the loving Father will change afflictions into benefits. So my words are filled, not with complaint, but with grief. I do not weep for Humbert, nor is he someone to be wept over, for he has been called to the table of God [Luke 16:21], but I weep for myself and for you, for this house, and for the rest of the brothers, who all used to await counsel from his lips. Thus Our Savior, while carrying his cross like a robber his noose, turned to the women who had followed him from Galilee and whom he saw wailing for him, and said, "Daughters of Jerusalem, weep not for me but for yourselves and for your children" [Luke 23:28]! Those things that concern me will have an end [Luke 22:37]. Those things you see being prepared for me are temporal; those you do not see are eternal. If things are temporal, they are transitory; if they are transitory, then they are mortal, and the one indication that things are transitory and mortal is that they can be seen. Those things which we beheld in Humbert's death were temporal, but now he has gained joy and gladness [Isa 35:10] in perpetual eternity.

7. We should not mourn for someone for whom there is no mourning or sorrow [Rev 21:4]. And nor should we complain for ourselves, from whom he has been taken. Let us rather give thanks that he was granted to us for so long. Indeed, ten years have passed, I think, that he lived with us and for us alone. And this is my fear:

that he may have been taken away because we were not worthy of his companionship [Song 4:10]. Yet who knows whether he has been taken away in order to protect us by his intercession with the Father? Would that it be so. If, while he was with us, he had such great charity that he would have given everything related to physical needs to me rather than to himself, how much more freely will he give grace and love to me now that he abides in that abiding Charity? Perchance now that he knows the truth about me and my way of life more fully, he will not be as forgiving as he used to be but, as I fear, indignant. Yet even if it is because of our sins that God took him away, let him pray that we may be mercifully pardoned, lest we receive punishment upon punishment.

8. For the rest, brothers, I tell you that if you follow in his footsteps, you will not lightly fall into vain thoughts and idle words, jest and slander, in which you lose so much of your life and your time. "Time goes by and cannot be recalled,"[16] and while you believe you are avoiding this slight punishment, you are in fact incurring greater. Know this: that after this life everything which has been neglected here will be required of you a hundredfold in the place of purgation, down to the very last fragment [Matt 5:26]. I myself know how hard it is for a dissolute man to embrace discipline [Ps 2:12], for a garrulous man to endure silence, for someone used to wandering about to stay in one place, but it will be much, much harder to endure that future torment. And this man who was just buried here, as I know, overcame all these temptations, but he fought with great determination and he won. And just as it was a hard fight for him then to endure temptation, it would be even harder for him now to go back to those weaknesses, because good habits became second nature to him. Exercise yourself in this teaching, brothers, and pay attention to this model [Phil 3:17] which you have heard and seen in Humbert, the servant of God, so that you may arrive before Him before Whom he has arrived, Our Lord Jesus Christ, who is God blessed forever [Rom 9:5]. Amen.

---

[16] Horace, *Epistles* 1.18.71.

CHAPTER SIX

*A Summary of the Virtues of the Old Man Humbert,*
*Taken from the Foregoing Sermon*

Reflect, reader, how in one little document the perfect virtue of this man has been beautifully set before your eyes, so that from these sentences you can say that this blessed one was "a man who having become a monk was vigilant to be a monk in his actions."[17] He worked out that what he was in habit and in name, he might by unremitting application become in very truth, counting it unworthy to glory in the empty name of monk without the work of virtue. He knew well that virtue is a step on the way to glory, and he would have no part in the vain grace and deceitful beauty that does not give rise to it [Prov 31:30]. Therefore, most blessed Father Humbert,[18] far from you be that ironic elegy which someone composed in fun after the death of someone who during his lifetime took pride in the empty name of monk without working at virtue:

> If dark clothes, a shaven head, and an ample cowl
> make anyone just, then this man was just.[19]

O how great is the distance between light and darkness; how great is the void [Luke 16:26] between sons of wrath and sons of grace; how different the sentences that true monks and false monks receive when going forth from here. Humbert was not of the number of foolish virgins who received their lamps but with a negligence to be abhorred forgot to take oil with them [Matt 25:1-10]; he was of the number of the wise. Someone, not a fawning flatterer but a

---

[17] The origin of this saying has not been found.

[18] From here through "the fountain of justice sprang up, to gain eternal life" is from Bernard of Clairvaux, Humb (SBOp 5:440–47; SBS 3:61–72).

[19] See H. Walther, *Initia carminum ac versuum medii aevi posteriori Latinorum* (Göttingen, 1959), Nbr. 18063. See Grießer, EM 161n3; and Piesik, *Exordium Magnum Cisterciense,* 1:506n366. Cf. Ælred of Rievaulx, Sermon 8 (CCCM 2A:65–69; CF 58:147–54); and Bernard of Clairvaux, Apo 6.12, 10.26 (SBOp 3:91–93, 102; CF 1:46–49, 61–62).

genuine admirer of him, said of him that he was the most composed man he had ever seen in his lifetime, continuing one and the same at all times and seasons. In a lovely statement he delineated him, although in other words, as the poet describes the wise man: "true to himself, polished and well rounded,"[20] which is to be one and the same in all times and seasons.

One should know, moreover, that this blessed man held the office of prior under Saint Bernard at Clairvaux, by whose doctrine and by the example of whose virtues the whole of Clairvaux, like a garden of delights, like a paradise of the Lord [Rev 2:7], was irrigated and a fountain of justice spilled over in each and every one for gaining eternal life. Because Humbert's memory will truly be a blessing for all generations [Sir 45:1; Luke 2:48] of brothers who shall serve the Lord at Clairvaux, the venerable body of the right reverend Father Humbert was buried in the monument in which, as we said above [EM 2.23], Dom Robert, the second abbot of Clairvaux, was placed, which is beneath the arch of the wall of the cloister near the chapter house.[21] There, the casket which holds his sacred bones bears his name, so that hereafter brothers, sitting in the cloister and from their reading knowing about his very fervent strivings in religious life—strivings so wonderful that the most blessed Bernard did not hesitate to pass on the record of them in literary form—and at the same time having before their eyes the tomb of his sacred ashes, may be warmed in spirit, flee forgetfulness [RB 7.10], put torpor and negligence far from themselves, and realize full well that they will gain the crown promised to monks [RB 7.10] only by the arduous rigors of claustral discipline.

---

[20] Horace, *Satires* 2.7.86.
[21] *Monumenta s. Claraevallensis abbatiae* (PL 185:1559).

CHAPTER SEVEN

*About Dom Odo, Former Subprior of Clairvaux*

There was, among the seniors at Clairvaux, one, Odo by name,[22] who energetically fulfilled the office of subprior in that house for many years. He was truly a man poor in spirit and humble of heart [Matt 5:3; 11:29], who from almost the first years of the house, while he was in the novitiate, had taken care of the arduous demands, not only of voluntary poverty, but also of the dire necessities by which the house was quite often straitened because of its dearth of goods, and he did this so briskly that he was observed at the time to be more fervent in the praises of God when he lacked material help in some way. He had such a graciousness of manner, and he treated the community of brothers—which, going and returning with them [EO 75.4-52], he industriously led to and from work whenever the prior was busy—with such endearing gentleness, that even today that holy congregation speaks of his overflowing gentleness [Ps 144:7] with thanksgiving. When the body of that faithful shepherd Saint Bernard was becoming increasingly feeble and he was drawing ever nearer to laying down this corruptible life and entering into blessed incorruptibility, Almighty God, who never despises the prayers of the humble, granted blessed Odo his heart's desire: that he might die before the holy father, lest, after the golden age which flourished so joyfully under so great a father, he might, with weeping eyes, be compelled to see the age of iron[23] that was to follow. That this was to happen the Lord deigned to show beforehand by a clear vision to one of the brothers. A certain brother saw in a vision of the night [Dan 7:7] that that most blessed man Bernard was preparing to go up to Jerusalem and was even entering its precincts. The venerable Odo, deferentially coming

---

[22] Grießer (EM, 162n3) notes that Odo is mentioned in S. Lenssen, *Hagiologium Cisterciense* (Tilburg, Holland: B.M. de Villa Regnia, 1948), 1:216. See also Piesik, *Exordium Magnum Cisterciense*, 1:506n371.

[23] Ovid, *Met.* 1.87-162.

up to him, said that he ought to precede him. What was shown in this vision came true, and the aforementioned man of God was found worthy to enter the heavenly Jerusalem [Heb 12:22], which is the true vision of peace, as an ambassador for the holy father who followed him a little later.[24] After this vision, the servant of God, Odo, was touched with bodily sickness and came to his end. Blessed Bernard arrived to visit him and, seeing that he was fearful and anxious, like someone who had lived less than perfectly and so was thinking of the uncertain judgment that awaited him, said to him, "Why are you fearful; why are you troubled, blessed soul? From the days of your youth you have shown yourself to be a devoted servant of Christ by many and great labors, so why do you dread dying? Go forth, go forth untroubled, for I tell you in very truth that you will go by a straight course [RB 73.4] to your Creator and you will appear holy before him." Strengthened by the loving father's consolation, the humble Odo approached his end with a more peaceful countenance. And after a short while he put aside the old man, overcame death, and truly laid hold on life.

The holy father confirmed the words he had spoken about him by his pious humility at his obsequies. While the holy body was still lying uncovered on the floor before it was taken away to be washed [EO 94.17-21], he came up with reverence to the holy feet of him who was worthy of God and kissed them, showing clearly to all how worthy of honor was he who had fulfilled the Rule, which they all professed, and kept it without guile and delighted in the way of the commandments of God as in all manner of riches [Ps 118:14]. The remains of his blessed body were buried in the tomb in which we have said Humbert of blessed memory was interred;[25] there they laid him, out of reverence for his holiness, and there he rests in a happy respite, awaiting our Lord and Savior Jesus Christ, who shall change the body of his humiliation into the likeness of

---

[24] The image of Jerusalem as a "vision of peace" refers to the hymn *Urbs Ierusalem beata, dicta pacis visio*, which is sung for the dedication of a church and dates to at least the eighth century; see *Le Grande Exorde*, 144n8, which cites *Analecta hymnica medii aevi* 51 (1908) no. 102, and U. Chevalier, *Repertorium hymnologicum*, 6 vols. (Louvain, 1892–1922), 20933.

[25] See above, EM 3.6; and *Monumenta s. Claraevallensis abbatiae* (PL 185:1560).

the body of glory [Phil 3:21]. As the psalmist says, speaking to the Lord, surely "the seat of iniquity does not stick to you, who fashion labor by law" [Ps 93:20]? Could we not say this in fact, for to the elect of God what is all the affliction, the sorrow, and the anguish of these present times but an appearance of labor? The tribulations which they have now are momentary and light [2 Cor 1:4], but they work an immense weight of glory for them in the height of eternal life [2 Cor 4:17], to which the venerable Odo's soul has now arrived in spirit and to which we hope with assurance that he will also come hereafter in his body.

## CHAPTER EIGHT

### *About Blessed Guerric,*
### *a Former Monk of Clairvaux, and Later Abbot of Igny*

Dom Guerric of holy memory, a former abbot of Igny,[26] while still a monk at Clairvaux under the discipline of blessed Bernard, had been suckled on holy doctrine at the breasts of kings [Isa 60:16] and proven by his life and conduct that he was not a degenerate son of such a father. He had so learned to ascend to the height of virtues that he could glory secretly in having, by the great mercy of God, preserved before him the title and witness of a conscience without stain. Those who had the privilege of knowing the inner secrets of so great a man testify that by the working of grace he preserved the immaculate robe of innocence intact to the end of his life.[27] The Lord himself deigned to demonstrate by marvelous and irrefutable signs how holy and pure was his life and conduct

---

[26] Guerric entered Clairvaux *c.* 1125 and was abbot of Igny from 1138 to 1157. For further information on him, see the introduction by John Morson and Hilary Costello in CF 8:vii–lxi.

[27] The "immaculate robe of innocence" is an allusion to the white garment received at baptism.

and how especially pure was that incense of holy devotion which he burned daily to God upon the altar of his heart.

It happened once that he was appointed to read a lesson at Vigils. And when he came out of his stall and was coming to the steps of the sanctuary to bow, as is the custom [EO 68.48], another spiritual monk was watching him who was in the habit of being a curious observer of his holy strivings in the Lord, not consumed by a plague of jealousy or hatred, but so that he might be stirred by his example to do better. As Guerric was bowing with devotion before the steps of the sanctuary, an angel of the Lord came down from heaven and, with the aforementioned spiritual brother looking on, clothed him in a very splendid and very white robe and, leading him respectfully down the middle of the choir to the lectern, mounted the reading desk and stood next to him while he read through the whole lesson, very reverently acting as his assistant. When the reading was over, the angel led him back to the middle of choir as far as the sanctuary step, and when Guerric had made the reverence that is usually made at the step after a reading [EO 68.53], the angel of the Lord took back the robe and was taken up into heaven from the eyes of the onlooker. The brother, to whom it was given by the special favor of God to witness this unseen gift of the loving-kindness of God, confessed that he was greatly edified by this glorious vision. He understood that this man, about whom he had seen such wonders, was truly a servant of God who in the chastity and innocence of his life resembled angelic purity, like Benjamin, the best-beloved of the Lord [Gen 43–44; Jer 6:1], who stayed all day long in his chamber in holy contemplation.[28]

At a later date Guerric was made abbot of Igny, and the energy with which he fulfilled the office [RB 31.17] committed to him is beyond our poor words. The soundness and richness of his teaching is reflected in those extremely lucid, wise, and indeed spiritual sermons which he used to preach to the brothers in chapter on major festivals [EO 67.5] and were taken down by the cantor of

---

[28] On the connection of Benjamin (son of Rachel) with contemplation, see Constable, *Three Studies*, 9–10, 35–36, 96.

his church.[29] The heavenly Architect, whose custom it is to polish with blows and chiseling[30] the vessels of mercy to distinguish them from vessels of wrath [Rom 9:22–23], allowed his servant to labor under continual and serious illness. He bore these discomforts very patiently, knowing that he would one day receive from the hands of the great King a glorious crown in proportion to how earnestly he had exerted himself in the throes of the present struggle. Yet he was saddened and deeply embarrassed to be continually away from the community of the brothers and lying in the infirmary because of his illness, unable to give his brothers a good example in daily labor to put before them as a word of holy preaching. Whatever he lacked in bodily practices, he made up for by the total affection of his sincere piety and his burning devotion to God.

In one of his sermons he laments his feebleness and weakness in these terms:[31]

> My friends come to see me and I have nothing to put before them [Luke 11:6]. "I am not a doctor and in my house there is no bread." From the beginning I used to say, "Do not make me a superior" [Isa 3:7], for someone who is not able to do some good ought not to command.[32] And how can someone do good who is not a doctor and has no bread in his house, that is, one who has not the knowledge of how to cure people and has no doctrine with which to feed them? I told you this, and alas, you did not listen to me; you made me a superior. Since I could not avoid the danger, as my only recourse I sought a remedy and heeded this advice of the wise man on the subject: "they have made you their leader; be among them as one of them" [Sir 32:1].

---

[29] A reference to Guerric's well-known sermons, contained in SCh 166 and 202 and translated in CF 8 and 32.

[30] From the hymn *Urbs Ierusalem beata*; see n. 24 above at EM 3.7.

[31] Guerric, Rog 1.2 (SCh 202:260–63; CF 32:98–100). Rogation Days are the three days before Ascension Day.

[32] Compare RB 64.8. Piesik, *Exordium Magnum Cisterciense* 1:506–7n379, provides citations (*praesum*) on *praesse/prodesse* (to command). They include Augustine, *City of God* 19.19; Gregory the Great, *Regula pastoralis* 2.6 (see *Pastoral Care*, trans. Henry Davis, 66–67); RB 64.6; Ælred of Rievaulx, *Oratio pastoralis* 6 and 8 (CCCM 1:760, 761; CF 2:112, 115); and Bernard of Clairvaux, Ep 86 (SBOp 7:223–24; James, Ep 88, pp. 127–28); and Abb 6 (SBOp 5:292–93).

But woe is me, even that is no longer possible for me. As my inexperience made me incapable of being set over others, so my weakness makes me unable to be among others. And as I am not mentally up to ministering the word, so because of my physical weakness, I cannot provide a beneficial example. Since I am fit neither to lead my brothers nor to be among them, what is left for me unless I choose the lowest and also the safest place, which is to be subject to them all? This I can do. I can subject myself to all; nothing prevents me from thinking myself lowest, in fact it is only right for me to be under all in spirit, since in office I am required to be above you all. Lord God, you advise me to be under all, and yet you have set me over all. You I expect, you I entreat, to make me both humble and useful in the service enjoined on me. Humble, by feeling honestly about myself; useful, by speaking rightly about you. Inspire the one in my heart; grant the other to my mouth. You have said, "Open your mouth wide and I will fill it" [Ps 80:11]; give me therefore right speech and clear utterance that your family may all be filled with blessings.

## CHAPTER NINE

### *How Dom Guerric Was Very Much Exercised in Conscience at his Death*

Consider, reader, the sincerity of conscience of this holy man, who frankly claimed that he could with ease—something which is granted by divine generosity to very few and only the most perfect—esteem himself as less than all others although by his office he was set over them. When Guerric, the faithful servant of the Lord [Luke 12:42], had with great fidelity distributed to his fellow servants the Lord's means of subsistence apportioned to him, he was preparing, full of days and virtues, to pass from this world to his Father. He was stricken with illness, and as the afflictions of the illness grew rapidly worse, his end was in sight. Then he looked closely into every corner of his heart to discover if by any chance there was any fault which he had not amended that might anger the stern Judge and give the malign spirits cause to accuse him. He remembered a little book of sermons he had written, and at the same time recalled that the fathers had decreed that no one should write a book without permission of the General Chapter.[33] Groaning grievously within himself, he said to the assembled brothers, "My brothers, in working for your benefit and in acceding to your requests, I have incurred the grave sin of disobedience, which, by the witness of the prophet Samuel, is like the sin of idolatry [1 Sam 15:23]. The little book of sermons which I dictated at your request, I presumed to publish with great temerity and without the permission of the General Chapter. Bring the book here at once and burn it, lest for the fault of disobedience I be handed over to be consumed in the flames of hell." In fact, by the providence of God [Jdt 11:16], other copies of the book had already been made. God arranged something better for us, so that his holy Church, and especially the Order of Cîteaux, should not be deprived of the grace of such learning. The beauty of style fills this book with such marvelous proportion, and the humility of Christian simplicity is so resplendent in it, that those who read it find it delightful and not in the least wearisome. Furthermore, the word of the Lord which is found in these sermons so strongly moves, touches, and enkindles the reader [Ps 118:140], that he would be very hard of heart who would not be moved by reading them to strive for better things.

So this righteous and God-fearing servant of the Lord, having by rigorous examination corrected that fault which was gnawing on his conscience, now longed the more eagerly and impatiently for heaven. He sought with prayers and desires the most blessed and joyful presence of Our Lord Jesus Christ, and we prayerfully believe that when he left the misery of this mortal life, he amply deserved to enjoy it.

---

[33] Inst (1134) 58; Canivez, 1:26; Waddell, *Narrative and Legislative Texts*, 481, number 60.

CHAPTER TEN

## About Dom Robert, Monk of Clairvaux, Nephew of Saint Bernard, Later Abbot of Noirlac

Dom Robert, former abbot of Noirlac,[34] was a relative of Saint Bernard. As a young man he had taken up at Cîteaux the sweet yoke of the Lord and his light burden [Matt 11:30]. Later, when the most reverend man of God, Bernard, was made abbot of Clairvaux, Robert was formed in heavenly discipline under him in that monastery. Although the good father taught him how to repel the stirrings of the flesh by holy prayers and how to overcome the petulant and uneasy urges of youth by manual labor, vigils, and fasting, the delicate young man lost heart and grew weary of unremitting religious exercises, and, behind his back, he listened with less patience to the word of his adviser. Meanwhile, the brothers at Cluny heard that Robert had joined the Cistercian Order and were indignant. They asserted vehemently that he simply could not do this under the law because as a child he had been promised to their monastery by his parents. In support of their claim, they pointed out the land which they remembered his parents had given with him to the monastery of Cluny. Although they were too much in awe of the authority of Saint Bernard to dare to reclaim the young man openly, they tried a more cunning way.[35]

A certain prior was dispatched by the grand prior of that great house to see if he could get around the young man by flattery and persuasion, so that he would of his own free will renounce the Cistercian Order and leave the monastery of Clairvaux to transfer to Cluny. This above-mentioned prior came to Clairvaux, and they believed that he was as good within as his affected appearance in

---

[34] *Domus Dei* (House of God, Maison-Dieu), better known as Noirlac (*Niger lacus*), was a daughter house of Clairvaux founded in 1136. Robert was its first abbot. Janauschek, 43. Cottineau 2:2049.

[35] Oblation is provided for in RB 59. The Cistercians, like most twelfth-century reform orders, did not receive child oblates, and the practice was also becoming less common at older Benedictine houses. See Newman, *Boundaries of Charity*, 23–24.

habit and mien led them to suppose. But, alas, "there is no more good faith; men seek to deceive one another."[36] Woe to the sinner who walks the earth two ways at once, whose double-heart sunders his conscience [Sir 2:14]. Even among monks, we are ashamed to say, these thorns of slander and duplicity are found to grow [see RB 13.12]. The prior of whom we are speaking approached the masters of the brothers and asked their permission to talk to Brother Robert, saying he had come on purpose to visit and strengthen him. Who could say no to such a man? Who would not have believed that Christ's new young recruit would be built up in virtue by the edifying words of such a wise old man and be strengthened in resisting vice? But alas, "the wolf's mind lurked under the fleece of the sheep" [Matt 7:15], and the very man who was thought to be urging him on in virtue persuaded the yet raw knight to desert his post and throw away his arms, to turn himself over to the cruel enemy by his own will, not so much free as wretched.[37] What more is there to say? He urged and persuaded the delicate young man to flee the austerities of Clairvaux and accept the statutes of Cluny, gentler and kinder to the flesh than to the spirit. And the little lamb followed the wolf without realizing that he was being led into the pit of apostasy.

The venerable Father Bernard took this very much to heart, but he hid his feelings, not wanting to seem to the offenders to be looking for retaliation.[38] But after he had hidden his feelings for a while, he decided to write to ask the brother to return. At his dictation, Dom William, later first abbot of the monastery of Rievaulx,[39] took down the letter, writing it on parchment. They were sitting together under the open sky. They had gone out of the monastery

---

[36] Virgil, *Aeneid* 4.373.

[37] For more on "the wolf's mind lay under the fleece of the sheep," see J. Werner, *Lateinische Sprichwörter und Sinnsprüche des Mittelalters* (Heidelberg, 1912), 69, 38; and H. Walther, *Proverbia sententiaeque Latinitatis Medii ac Recentioris Aevi*, vol. 3 (Göttingen, 1965), n. 21158.

[38] The rest of this chapter, except for the final sentence, follows William of Saint Thierry, Vita Bern 1.11.50 (PL 185:255–56).

[39] William was Bernard's secretary at Clairvaux and later abbot of Rievaulx (1132–45). See Bennett D. Hill, *English Cistercian Monasteries and Their Patrons in the Twelfth Century* (Urbana: University of Illinois Press, 1968), 119–20.

enclosure to take the dictation in greater privacy. Suddenly without any warning there was a cloudburst. William, who, as we explained, was writing, wanted to cover the page but the holy father said to him, "This is God's work; write on and have no fear." So he wrote the letter in the rain, and it never got wet. While it rained all around them, the virtue of charity protected that exposed page and kept dry the man dictating the letter as well as the piece of parchment. Because this letter was preserved by so great a miracle, it was thought right by the brothers that it should be placed first in the collection of his letters. Here is the text of the letter.

## Chapter Eleven

### *A Letter from Saint Bernard to His Nephew, Very Gently Urging His Return*[40]

1. My dearest son Robert, I have waited long enough, perhaps too long, to see if the goodness of God would deign to visit both your soul in his own person and my soul through yours, moving you to salutary compunction and me to joy in your deliverance. But since I find I am still disappointed of my hope, I can no longer hide my grief, restrain my anxiety, dissemble my sorrow. And so, against the order of law, I, the one who has been hurt, have to recall him who hurt me; the one who has been scorned has to seek out the one who despised him; I who have been injured have to placate him who struck the blow. I have to entreat him who should be entreating me. Sorrow does not count the cost, is not ashamed, does not concern itself with calculations, is not afraid of rejection, respects no rules, is not content with justice, overrides ways and means, cares only that it has what it grieves to have, and lacks that

---

[40] See Bernard of Clairvaux, Ep 1 (SBOp 7:1–11; James, Ep 1, pp. 1–10). The text of the letter, as recorded in the EM, differs in many places with the generally accepted version of Bernard's original.

which it grieves to be without. But, you will say, I have not hurt or scorned anyone; I am the one who has been scorned and hurt in so many ways that I could only fly from my tormentor. Whom have I hurt in flying from being hurt? Is it not better to yield to a persecutor than to resist him? Better to avoid him who strikes you than to hit back? That is true; I agree. I am writing not to argue with you but to remove the grounds of disagreement. I do not deny this. I overlook what has happened, and I do not ask how or why it came about. I am not attributing blame, looking into causes, or remembering injuries. For to flee from persecution is the fault not of the persecuted but of the persecutor. I am speaking only of that which lies closest to my heart. How wretched I am in not having you with me, not seeing you, having to live without you. I am lamenting not that you went away but that you did not return. I blame not your going away but your not coming back. Only come and there will be peace; return and there will be satisfaction. Come back, come back, I say, and I will sing with joy: "He who was dead is alive again; he who was lost is found" [Luke 15:24].

2. No doubt it was my fault that you went away. I was severe with a sensitive boy; I dealt with a stripling in a way that was inhumane. I remember that it was this that you used to hold against me in your complaints, and you still do. Both then and now, as I said, for when I am away from you, you do not cease to complain about me. This will not be held against you. Perhaps I could excuse myself and say that the passions of youth have to be curbed in this way, and that at first the strict way of discipline is bound to be harsh to an untried youth; as Scripture says, "Smite thy son with a rod and thou shall deliver his soul from hell" [Prov 23:14; RB 2.29], and "Those whom the Lord loves, he disciplines" [Heb 12:6], and, again, the wounds of a friend are better than the deceitful kisses of an enemy [Prov 27:6]. But let us say it was my fault that you left, lest in arguing about who is to blame we put off emending what is blameworthy. But you will certainly start to be guilty now if you do not spare me when I am sorry and forgive me when I acknowledge it—for though I lacked discernment in all kinds of ways, I was certainly not malicious in my treatment of you. If you are afraid that I will treat you unwisely in the future, you must understand that I am not

the man I was, and I do not think you are what you used to be. You have changed and you will find I have changed too; you can safely embrace me now as a friend whom you used to fear as a master. Either you left because of my fault, which is what you think and I do not deny, or by your own fault, which is what many believe but I do not affirm, or you left because of your own fault and mine, which I think is more likely, but from now on if you do not come back, you alone will be to blame. Would you be free from blame in this matter? Then return. If you acknowledge your part in this, I forgive you, and you must forgive me when I acknowledge my share in it. If you acknowledge your fault and do not admit it, you are being too easy with yourself, and you would be too hard on me if you do not forgive me when I am ready to make satisfaction.

3. If you refuse to return now, you must find something else to be a sop to your conscience, for what you said before about fearing my rigor will not do any more. You should not fear that I will be fearsome in the future when you are with me, for even while you are not with me I cast myself at your feet with all my heart [RB 53.7], with the love of my affection. I humble myself before you; I promise you my love; what, then, can you fear? Come boldly where humility calls you and love draws you on. With so many previous assurances, come without fear. You fled from me when I was fierce; return to me now that I am gentle. I frightened you away by my severity; let me draw you back by my meekness. See, my son, how I long to lead you no longer in fear, in the spirit of a slave, but in the spirit of adoption by which you may cry, "Abba, Father" [Rom 8:15; RB 2.3], and not be confounded. You have been the cause of much grief to me, but I shall lead you with encouragement, not threats, by beseeching, not by threatening. Others might try other ways. And indeed anyone else would insist that you are guilty and try to inspire you with fear, point to your vows and point out the judgment, charge you with disobedience, be angry at your apostasy. You have left the rough habit for soft clothes, vegetables for delicacies, in short, poverty for riches.[41] But I know your heart:

---

[41] On the richness of Cluniac life, see Bernard of Clairvaux, Apo 9.19-20 (SBOp 3:96–98; CF 1:54–56).

you can be swayed more easily by love than forced by fear. What need is there to urge you on when you are not recalcitrant, make you more fearful when you are already afraid, confound you more when you are already ashamed enough? For you are schooled by your reason, your own conscience is your rod, your natural shyness is your law and discipline. Does it seem strange to anyone that a shy, simple, and timid lad should dare to carry out his decision to desert both his vows and this place, against the wishes and commands of his superior and his brothers? He may equally marvel that the holiness of David was stolen from him [2 Sam 11], the wisdom of Solomon deceived [1 Kgs 11], the strength of Samson overthrown [Judg 16]. What marvel if he who could cheat the first man and cast him out when he was in the paradise of happiness should also deceive the tender youth in a place of horrors and vast loneliness [Deut 32:10; EP 3; EM 1.13]? This happened to him, not by the false lure of beauty like the elders in Babylon [Dan 13], nor by love of money and honor like Gehazi [2 Kgs 5:20-27], nor by ambition like Julian the Apostate;[42] rather, he was deceived by sanctity, misled by religious observance, betrayed by the authority of age. How did this come about?

4. First, a great prior, sent by the prince of all priors, who was in his outward appearance a lamb but inwardly a ravenous wolf [Matt 7:15]. The shepherds were deceived and thought him genuine, and they admitted him alone into the sheepfold. The little sheep did not fly from the wolf because he thought him to be a sheep. What happened then? He drew the sheep to him, allured, flattered, and preached a new gospel that was contrary to the Gospel [Gal 1:7]. He praised feasting, condemned fasting; he said voluntary poverty was wretched and called fasts, vigils, silence, and manual labor foolishness. On the other hand, he called laziness contemplation, and he commended gluttony, chattering, curiosity, and any intemperance

---

[42] Flavius Claudius Julianus (332–63) was proclaimed Augustus in 360. In his early years he received a Christian education, but as Augustus he declared a policy of religious toleration in the empire and professed his own belief in paganism. See "Julian the Apostate," in *Late Antiquity: A Guide to the Post-classical World*, ed. G. W. Bowersock, et al. (Cambridge, MA: Belknap Press, 1999), 529–30.

as being discernment. "When," he said, "did God ever delight in our sufferings? Where does Scripture teach us to kill ourselves? What sort of religion is it to dig in the earth, cut down forests, cart dung? Does not Truth say, 'I will have mercy and not sacrifice' [Hos 6:6; Matt 9:13; Matt 12:7], and, 'I desire not the death of a sinner,' and so on [Ezek 33:11]; and 'Blessed are the merciful,' and so on [Matt 5:7]? Why did God create food if we are not supposed to eat it? Why did he give us bodies if we are not to keep them alive? Finally, if a man hates himself, to whom will he be good [Sir 14:5; Eph 5:29]? What wise and sane man ever hated his own flesh?"

5. With these sorts of allegations a credulous boy was talked round and he followed his seducer. He led him to Cluny, where he was trimmed, shaved, and washed. He was taken out of his rough, old, soiled habit and given a fine new clean one. And so he was received into the community. And with what honor, triumph, and respect! He was favored above all his contemporaries; this sinner in the desires of his heart was praised [Ps 9:3] like a victor returning from battle. This youth was set in a high position, placed in no mediocre state, in charge of many who were his seniors. All the brothers favored, flattered, and congratulated him, exulting like victors over their prey when they divided the spoil [Isa 9:3]. O good Jesus, what a lot was done to bring about the ruin of one poor little soul. Who is so hard of heart as not to be softened by it? Who is there whose soul, however spiritual, would not be troubled by this? Among so many vanities, who is there who could recognize the truth and maintain humility?

6. Meanwhile, they sent representatives to Rome. The apostolic authority was talked round, so that the pope could not refuse his assent; it was suggested to him that the youth had been offered there as an oblate while still an infant. No one was there to refute this, and no contradiction was expected. Judgment was given in the absence of the judged. Those who had done the wrong were upheld; those who had suffered lost their case; the prisoner was set free without making satisfaction. This cruel privilege was confirmed by a too indulgent sentence of absolution. By this the doubtful and fluctuating young man was confirmed in an ill-advised and dubious stability. The tenor of the letters, the summary of the judgment, the

meaning of the whole case, was that they could keep what they had stolen, and those who have lost it must keep quiet. And so a soul for whom Christ died is lost to please Cluny. So he makes profession when he is professed, is bound before he has been loosed; he promises what will not be kept, and since the first contract has been broken, the second transgression is doubled, and sin is added to sin [Rom 7:13].

7. But he is coming, he is coming, who reverses wrong judgments, who overthrows unlawful contracts, "who executes justice for those who suffer wrong" [Ps 145:7], who "judges the poor with justice, and reproves with equity for the meek of the earth" [Isa 11:4]. He will surely come who has warned us by the prophet in the psalm, "When I choose the time, I will judge justices" [Ps 74:3]. What will he do about unjust judgments, who judges even justices? It will come, I say; the day of judgment will come, when purity of heart will avail more than cunning words, a good conscience more than a full purse, for this Judge cannot be deceived by words or turned aside by gifts. To your judgment seat, Lord Jesus, I appeal. I commit my judgment to you. I leave my cause to you [Acts 25:10-11], "Lord God of Hosts, who judges justly and tries the reins and the hearts" [Jer 11:20], whose eyes cannot deceive or be deceived; you see who seeks you and who it is who seeks himself [Phil 2:21]. You know how I was always afflicted when Robert was tempted in his heart, how I beat upon your loving ears for his sake, how I burned, suffered, and was afflicted in his scandals, troubles, and worries [2 Cor 11:29]. I now fear that it has all been in vain. For I think, insofar as I can judge, that such an impetuous and proud young man would not find such medicine any help to his body or such temptations of glory to help his mind. So be my arbitrator, Lord Jesus, and "let my judgment come from your countenance, for your eyes behold what is right" [Ps 16:2].

8. Let them see and let them judge which vow ought to have greater force, the one a father makes for his son, or the one the son for himself, especially when the son vows something better. Let your servant and our lawgiver, Saint Benedict, say which is the more proper, that which is done on behalf of a child who knows nothing, or what he does for himself when he knows his own mind

and can judge, when he is old enough to speak for himself [John 9:21]. But there is actually no doubt that he was only promised to Cluny, that there was no formal oblation. The petition prescribed by the Rule was not made by his parents [RB 59.1-2, 8], nor was his hand bound with the altar cloth and the offering made before witnesses. They show you the land which they say was given with and for him. But if they received him with the land, how have they not kept him as well as the land? Or perhaps they valued the land more than the fruit, the earth more than the soul? If he had been offered to the monastery, what business had he to be out in the world? Why was a nursling of God exposed to the devil? Why was this sheep of God put in the way of the attacks of the wolf? You yourself testify, Robert, that you entered our Order from the world and not from Cluny. You sought, you asked, you knocked [Matt 7:7-8]; but against your will your admission was postponed for two more years because of your tender age. When that time had passed patiently, without pretense, at last with many prayers and, if you remember, with tears, you asked for the mercy you had waited for so long, and you obtained the admission you desired so much [EO 102.3]. After this you were tested in all patience for a year in accordance with the Rule [RB 58], conducting yourself perseveringly and without complaint, and after that year you of your own free will made your profession and then for the first time put off secular clothes and received the habit of religion.

9. You foolish boy. Who has bewitched you into breaking the vows which you made with your lips [Ps 65:13-14]? Will you not be justified or condemned out of your own mouth [Luke 19:22; Matt 12:37]? Why be anxious about the vow your parents made and neglect your own when you will be judged about the keeping of the vow you made with your own mouth and not that of your parents? They deceive you in vain who point to an apostolic absolution, when your conscience is bound by the sentence of God. "No one," I say, "who puts his hand to the plough and turns back is fit for the kingdom of God" [Luke 9:62]. Do those who say to you, "Well done" [Ps 39:16], really persuade you that you have not looked back? "My son, if sinners entice you, do not listen to them" [Prov 1:10] and do not believe every spirit [1 John 4:1].

"Have many friends, but let one in a thousand be your councilor" [Sir 6:6]. Pull yourself together; reject flattery; shut your ears to praise; look into your own heart, for you know yourself best of all. Listen to your inclinations; examine your intentions; look at the facts. Let your conscience tell you why you left your Order, your brothers, this place, and me, who am kindred to you in blood and more kindred in spirit. If you left in order to lead a harder, higher, and more perfect life, you are safe; you have not looked back, but rather you can glory with the Apostle, saying, "I forget what is behind, and intent on what lies ahead I press on to the palm of glory" [Phil 3:13-14]. But if it is otherwise, do not think highly of yourself but fear [Rom 11:20], lest—and you must pardon my saying this—whatever way you permit yourself indulgence, in food, unnecessary clothes, idle talk, vain and curious traveling, beyond what you promised when you were with us, in this you are certainly looking back, prevaricating, apostatizing.

10. I do not say this, my son, to put you to shame, but I warn you as my dearest son, for if you have many instructors in Christ, you have not many fathers [1 Cor 4:14-15]. If I may say so, I begot you in religion, by word and by example. I fed you with milk when as a child that was all you could take [1 Cor 3:2], and I would have given you bread if you had waited and grown up. But alas, how soon and how early were you weaned. But now I am afraid that what I cherished with kindness, strengthened with encouragement, and confirmed with prayers is wasting away, fading, and perishing. I weep, not for my lost labor, but for the lost state of my unhappy offspring. Are you content that someone should glory in you who has not labored for you? I am in the same case as the harlot who came to Solomon, whose child was taken secretly by another who had overlain and killed her own [1 Kgs 3:20]. You were taken from my side, snatched out of my womb. My heart cannot forget you, for part of it has been taken away, and what is left cannot but suffer.

11. But for what advantage of yours, what necessity, have our friends the Cluniacs done this to us? Their hands are full of blood [Isa 1:15]; their sword has pierced my soul [Luke 2:35]; "their teeth are spears and arrows, and their tongue a sharp sword" [Ps 56:5].

If I have in any way offended any of them, and I am not aware that I have, they have paid me back in full. I would be surprised to hear that I have not suffered more than my share, if they have received anything like as much suffering as I have. It is not bone of my bone, flesh of my flesh [Gen 2:23] they have taken but the joy out of my heart [Lam 5:15], the fruit of my spirit [Gal 5:22], the crown of my hopes, and, if I may say so, they have divided my soul from me.[43] Why have they done so? Perhaps they were sorry for you, worried that a blind man was leading the blind, and that you would perish with me [Luke 6:39], so they took you under their leadership. Unwelcome charity, hard necessity. They cared so much for your good that they struck at mine. Could you not be saved unless I was hurt? Would that they might save you without me and that I might die so that you might live. How can this be? Does salvation mean soft raiment and good food rather than sober fare and moderate clothing? If saints are made by warm and comfortable furs, fine and precious cloth, long sleeves and ample hoods, soft covers and woolen shirts, why do I delay to follow you? But these are comforters for those who are weak, not the arms of soldiers. Look, "those who wear soft raiment are in kings' houses" [Matt 11:8]. Wine and white bread, honey and bodily comforts fight for the body, not the spirit. The soul is not fattened out of frying pans. In Egypt many monks served God for a long time without fish [Num 11:5]. Pepper, ginger, cumin, sage, and the other many spices please the palate but inflame lust. Will you put your trust in such things? Can you safely spend your youth among them? For a man whose life is sober and prudent, salt with hunger is savor enough. If we eat before we are hungry, we have to concoct I know not what flavors to arouse our taste and stimulate our appetites.

12. But you ask me, what can I do if I cannot live otherwise? All right. I know you are delicate, and now you are accustomed to this and could not support a harder way of life. But what if you are able to make yourself do so? You ask me, how? Rise up, gird yourself, stop being lazy, show strength, do something with your

---

[43] Horace, *Odes* 1.3.8.

hands, work in some way, and you will find you need to eat only to satisfy your hunger, not to tempt your appetite. Much that you could not eat when you were idle you will be able to take after work. Laziness makes you fastidious, work makes you hungry, and it is wonderful to find how work will bring back the taste to that which idleness has rendered insipid. Vegetables, beans, roots, bread, and water are poor fare to a lazy man, but they seem very good to someone who works hard. Perhaps now you have stopped wearing our habit since you dread it as too cold in winter and too hot in summer. Have you ever read, "The snow will fall upon him who is afraid of the frost" [Job 6:16]? You are afraid of our vigils, fasts, and manual labor, but these are light compared with the fires of damnation. If you remember the outer darkness [Matt 8:12; 22:13] you will not be afraid of the solitary desert. If you remember that you must give account of every idle word [Matt 12:36], silence will not displease you. Hold before your eyes eternal weeping and gnashing of teeth, and the difference between a mat and a bed is smaller. If we spend the night well in the psalmody and watching, which the Rule prescribes [RB 8], no bed will be too hard for us to sleep on. If we work as hard during the day as we promised to do, hard indeed will be the food we cannot eat.

13. Arise, soldier of Christ [2 Tim 2:3], "shake off the dust" [Isa 52:2], and return to the battle from which you fled; you will fight more valiantly after your flight and conquer more gloriously. Christ has many soldiers who have set out very bravely, stood firm, and conquered, but few who have fled from their way of life and then turned back and flung themselves back into danger, who have fought again the enemy from whom they fled.

That which is rare is the more precious, so I am glad that you can be so much more glorious for being rare. But if you are still full of fears, why should you be afraid when there is no reason to fear, yet unafraid where there is every reason to fear [Ps 13:5]? Do you suppose that because you have fled from the battle line, you have escaped out of the hand of the enemy? Your enemy will follow you in flight more readily than when you fight back; he is more bold to attack you from behind than face-to-face. Can you sleep resting on your arms in the mornings when at that hour Christ rose from the dead?[44] Do you not know that unarmed you have more to fear and are less terrible to your foes? An armed multitude surrounds the house and you go on sleeping? Already they are scaling the walls, swarming over the barriers, pouring in the back door [Dan 13:26]. Will you be safer alone or with others, naked in bed or armed in the camp? Get up and arm yourself, and go back to your comrades whom you deserted by running away. Let the fear that drove you from them bring you back. Feeble soldier, do you shun the weight and harshness of arms? When an enemy approaches and darts begin to fly, a shield does not seem too heavy; the helmet and corselet are not noticed [cf. Gen 27:3]. When anyone comes suddenly from the darkness into the sunlight, from ease to labor, to begin with everything seems hard. But when you have got out of your ways you will soon get used to these ways; use makes things easier, and you find that you can easily do what previously seemed impossible. Even very brave soldiers tremble when they first hear the bugle summon them to battle, but when battle is joined, hope of victory and fear of defeat inspires them with courage. What have you to fear, surrounded by a band of brothers of one heart and mind, when there are angels on your side, when Christ leads into battle encouraging his friends with the words, "Fear not, I have overcome the world" [John 16:33]? "If Christ be for us who can be against us" [Rom 8:31]? When you are certain of victory, you can fight with confidence. It is indeed safe to fight with Christ and for Christ. Neither wounds, falls, nor bruises, not even a thousand deaths, if that were possible, can defraud us of victory if we do not run away. The only reason for losing the victory is flight. We are defeated by flight, not by remaining. Blessed are you if you die in the battle, for you will be crowned. Woe to you if you desert in battle, for you lose both victory and crown. May you be saved from this, beloved son, for at the last judgment you will incur a greater damnation if you have read this letter of mine and done nothing about it.

---

[44] Bernard of Clairvaux, Apo 9.22 (SBOp 3:99–100; CF 1:58).

CHAPTER TWELVE

*The Dangers of Leaving the Cistercian Order for Another*

When that brother received and read this letter, he soon recognized the character of his loving abbot and kinsman and reflected on how he had dipped his quill in the profoundest depths of charity. At the same time, he thought over how different were the activities of the place in which he was now living and those of the place that he had so unadvisedly left. He was filled with compunction, he reconsidered, and, although belatedly, he rued his error, or rather the error into which he had been led. Filled with the spirit of holy liberty, he left in good order that place to which he had come in disorder and went back to Clairvaux; there he placed himself once more under the discipline of the blessed Father Bernard and so increased in virtue that he was later made abbot of Noirlac. We should learn by this example that no one who makes his profession in the Order of Cîteaux can change to another Order without grave peril to his soul. Moreover, and we say this frankly because it is true, anyone who, cravenly overwhelmed, loses the greater good that he had, also loses the lesser good, because by having chosen the greater, he made the lesser unlawful for himself.[45] He will, moreover, carry the foul brand of apostasy with eternal confusion unless he comes to a better mind. So that our assertion may be trusted and any doubts removed—for in the mouth of two witnesses every statement stands [Deut 19:15]—we are going to add another example to support it.

There was a certain man acting as abbot of a daughter house of Clairvaux in the territories of Italy. Although otherwise a good monk, he had been deposed from his office as superior for some fault. He bore this demotion with less patience than he ought and, prodded by blind grief, left the Cistercian Order and joined the Cluniacs. There for some time in the simplicity of his heart

---

[45] Cf. EM 1.15 and 1.33, which also discuss changes in vocational status. See also Bernard of Clairvaux, Pre 44–53 (SBOp 3:283–88; CF 1:138–44) on returning to the black monks after having been a Cistercian.

he served the Lord according to the customs of that place. But almighty God, who alone sees into the simplicity of the heart, remembered his past labors, those wrought in the Cistercian Order, and he deigned to reveal to him that, although he now seemed in the eyes of men to have a lesser good yet he could never save his soul there, for in the eyes of God he had fallen away from a greater good, so that anything less good would be of no avail for him. The old man was positively admonished by this warning and showed himself not unmindful of the divine grace that had so mercifully recalled him from his error. He immediately withdrew his foot from the precipice of prevarication and returned to Clairvaux; there he did penance for his fault and, having thereafter lived his life in a holy monastic way, consummated it in a good end.

## Chapter Thirteen

### *How the Monk Rainald, of Blessed Memory, Saw Blessed Mary Visiting the Monks Who Were Reaping*

In the monastery of Clairvaux there was a monk, observant and worthy of remembrance, called Rainald, a man of simple goodness who feared God and kept his innocence from infancy to old age. About this, the senior monk who, as we already mentioned [EM 2.32], passed down to us in writing many reminiscences about the observant persons of our Order, especially the seniors, both monks and lay brothers, of Clairvaux, wrote this (and I insert it here with as much faith as he had in writing it).[46]

The Lord's man, Rainald, passed the first thirty years of his life in the world, yet he did not live a worldly life; always intent on doing good works, he took great care to glorify God by bearing him in

---

[46] What follows is from Herbert of Clairvaux, LM 1.1 (PL 185:1273–76). See also Caesarius of Heisterbach, *Dialogus miraculorum* 1.17 (Strange 1:24–25; S-Bland 1:25–26); and Piesik, *Exordium Magnum Cistercienser*, 1:508n402, for references to a monk called Rainald.

his body [1 Cor 6:20]. Among other good deeds he did with his whole heart, he dedicated the integrity of his body to God, and by the aid of his grace he passed his entire life, from his mother's womb to the grave, unsullied by the stirrings of the flesh, untouched by the stirrings of lust and the pollutions of the body.[47] Having taken the monastic habit in the monastery of Saint Amand,[48] he lived an exemplary life there for more than twenty years, giving everyone no small proof of his holiness. But then, set on fire with zeal for greater perfection, he transferred to Clairvaux, already turned in that direction by many revelations from God.

I will not bore the reader now with an account of all the hardships and afflictions the blessed man endured from the brothers of that Order who were envious of his propitious actions and wanted to turn him from his intention. Having been received at Clairvaux, he girded himself manfully for a new conflict, and although he was a veteran in this warfare he presented himself to us as a courageous new recruit, mortifying himself all day long in labors, in work, in watchings, in fastings [2 Cor 6:5], and in the other exercises of the holy discipline. He prayed continually and his prayer was accompanied by a marvelous outpouring of tears.

One day after he had gone out with the rest of the brothers to harvest grain, he drew a little apart from the rest of the reapers and began to look at them with great delight of mind, marveling that so many wise, so many noble and delicately reared men there should submit to hardship and toil for the love of Christ and at how they bore the burning heat of the sun with as much readiness as if they were picking fruit in a garden of delights or savoring the food set out for a sumptuous banquet. Raising his eyes and his hands toward heaven, he thanked God that he had permitted him, although unworthy and sinful, to join such a holy company.

While he was turning this and similar things over in his mind, he was seized by a joy he could hardly contain, for suddenly he

---

[47] From the fourth response in the Vigils for Saint Agnes (21 January), according to *Le Grande Exorde*, 161n4.

[48] Saint Amand was a Benedictine house in the Diocese of Tournai (until 1148 Noyon-Tournai). Cottineau 2:2581.

saw three venerable women with shining faces, dressed in white raiment. One of them, who came first, stood out from the others by her brighter clothing, fairer face, and more gracious bearing. They came down the nearby hillside and went toward the gathering of brothers harvesting produce on the hillside. When the brother saw this he was astonished and beside himself with wonder; he cried out, "Lord God, who are these beautiful and reverend women who, against the custom of other women, are going toward the community?"[49] As he was saying this, a grey-bearded elderly man dressed in pure white appeared at his side and said to him, "The greatest who goes before the others is Mary, the Virgin Mother of Jesus Christ. The two who follow her are Saint Elizabeth and Saint Mary Magdalene."

When he heard the Mother of the Lord named, his stomach turned over out of devotion to the name of her whom he deeply loved, and wanting to know more, he again asked, "Where is she going, my Lord? Where is our Lady going?" To which the man replied, "She is going to visit the reapers." When he had said this the person who had spoken suddenly vanished. At this sight the saint was even more amazed. He turned his eyes to the holy Mother of God and her companions, watching them with astounded awe. The three ladies slowed down and approached the company one after the other. When they reached them, they began to walk separately from one another so that they could mingle better with the monks and lay brothers. When they had done this they disappeared from his watching eye and went back to heaven whence they had come. The man of God stood stock-still and could not move from the place until the vision had ended. By his enviable monastic observance and his continual growth in virtue he showed how much he had profited by this visitation and how much he grew in love for the Lord and for the most blessed Bearer of God.

He often received many other visions from God, but he preferred to keep quiet and not speak about them, for fear of the vice of vainglory. For eight years he kept hidden the vision I have recounted, and it was only a short time before his death—forty

---

[49] *Instituta Generalis capituli*, 7; Waddell, *Narrative*, 32.

days if I remember correctly—that, asked and, in fact, pressed by me, although unworthy, he made it known under this circumstance. One day when we had both been talking intimately about the salvation of our souls, I dared to ask him to tell me about his own experiences, for I knew that he was a good and holy man often visited by the Lord, and I had confidence because I loved him and sensed that he loved me. So I begged him, for the love of Christ and out of compassion, to tell me about some of his spiritual favors, whichever of them he thought would most edify me, for the greater glory of God. He gave in to my request and told me the vision I narrated above. But how can I convey the feeling with which he told it to me? God alone knows with what fear and trembling [Phil 2:12], with what tears and sighs he told me about it. Groans and sobs from the bottom of his heart frequently choked his voice as if he were still seeing the vision.

Fourteen days after this conversation, the Queen of heaven, the Lady of the angels, appeared to him again in a vision, cutting out and making ready white and precious garments in which he was soon to be clad. When the blessed Virgin had completed them, she folded them up and started to carry them away with her. When he saw this Rainald followed her and called after her, "My most longed-for Lady, when am I to wear the garments that you have deigned to prepare for me?" And the most holy Bearer of God answered him, saying, "You will receive them when you come to join me." O joyous vision; O sure promise! It was indeed quickly to be fulfilled. In the morning this servant of God came to pay me a visit in the infirmary, for I had been ill and near death. The sickness had been so extremely grave [1 Kgs 17:17] that the doctors had despaired of me, and the day before I had received the anointing of the sick because they believed that I was going to die any minute. When Rainald came to see me, he took pity on me, greatly affected by loving-kindness, and in order to console me a little, he recounted to me the vision he had had during the night, convinced and assuring me that it was not about him but about me. For he was very humble in heart and could not suppose that his virtues merited such favors. But I replied at once, "Dearest father, do not, I beg you, try to give a wrong impression of the blessing you have been given. These garments which are being made ready for you in heaven will not be given to anyone else. By the mercy of God they will be kept safe and whole for you. But beseech your gentle visitor, by her merciful loving-kindness, to prepare for me also some raiment. For she is powerful, kind, and gracious to all those who call upon her [Rom 10:12]."

What more is there to say? I who was thought to be near to death was called back to bear the tribulations of this life whether I would or no, while he, who seemed well and whole, did not live more than twenty-five days. Having finished his course, he came joyfully to the end of his life and laid aside the corruptible garment of the flesh, and without any doubt he received the stole of immortality from the most blessed Mother of God, whom he devoutly served, just as she had promised.

Nor should we pass over this in silence: on the sixth day before his falling asleep, while he was praying alone in the church after Compline, that man of God suddenly heard two knocks on the board for the departed. At the sound he immediately rose and went to the infirmary, thinking that one of the brothers who was ill must be dying [EO 94.2]. Having made sure that none of the sick were near their end, it came into his mind that the signal had been meant for himself and that the knocks on the clapper indicated his imminent passing. At the thought of death, he suddenly shuddered and was seized by trembling and hair-raising, and immediately he began to run a fever. As his fever worsened, he shortly reached his end. While he lay in bed he repeated ceaselessly in his heart and mouth the salutation of the blessed Virgin Mother, as he had often done over the years, and he breathed his last saying the words of this sweet little prayer. As it happened, a certain lay brother, a man of good repute and monastic observance, went home to the Lord that same day. So their funerals were celebrated together and they were buried in the same tomb. As this was happening, a certain spiritual man was shown a vision of two glorious temples being built at Clairvaux, one in the monks' infirmary, the other in that of the lay brothers', but the first was by far more glorious and beautiful than the other. There is no doubt that the twin construction of these temples and the twin knocks on the board signaled the death of these two religious, both of them dear in the sight of the Lord [Ps 115:15]. The difference in the two temples indicated the difference in their merits, for although both were holy, one, we believe, was more holy than the other before God from whom each had received from the store of mercy as much as grace, our mother, deigned to bestow.[50]

## CHAPTER FOURTEEN

### *How a Monk Heard the Board of the Dead as a Sign of His Own Death*[51]

In the same month when the aforesaid servant of God went home to the Lord, something quite similar happened there. There was a sacristan in the abbey named Gerard, an able man of good habits and a sound religious. He followed the counsel of the prophet and had borne the yoke of the Lord from his youth [Lam 3:27-28] and had outdone himself, for although he was delicate and frail, he had put his hand to great things [Prov 31:19]. Suckled at the breasts of kings [Isa 60:16] and happily formed by chaste discipline, he grew and increased continually in virtue. And, as his friends bear

---

[50] Here we have rendered *mater gratia* as "grace, our mother." Grießer (EM, 179n2) notes that Conrad added this final sentence to Herbert's LM version and that the phrase occurs in Richard of Saint Victor's *In cantica canticorum explicatio* 6 (PL 196:422A): "Our mother is the grace of the Spirit, which regenerates us spiritually and whose abode is the human mind in which that same grace has been received." Other twelfth-century uses of the phrase include Bernard of Clairvaux, Div 37.3 and 56.1 (SBOp 5:223 and 6/1:285); Guerric of Igny, Nat 5.5 (SCh 166:234; CF 8:66); and Pur 3.2 (SCh 167:344; CF 8:115); and William of Saint Thierry, *The Mirror of Charity* 2.21, ed. Jean Déchanet, *Le Miroir de la foi*, SCh 301 (Paris: Éditions du Cerf, 1982), 84; trans. Thomas X. Davis, CF 15 (Kalamazoo: Cistercian Publications, 1979), 19–20. Conrad also uses *mater gratia* in EM 1.16; 3.18; and 4.17 (Grießer, EM, 194n7 and 242n5).

[51] This chapter is taken verbatim from Herbert of Clairvaux, LM 1.2 (PL 185:1276).

witness, by the great grace of God he had never experienced defilement of the flesh. When the time came that he should pass out of this world to God, on that day as he stayed behind in church after Compline, as was his custom, suddenly there was sound in his ears as if someone were knocking repeatedly on the board of the dying. When he heard it, he thought some brother in the infirmary was passing away. When after a bit, he realized very clearly that no human being had made that sound, he recalled the prophetic board which the man of God, Rainald, had heard as a signal of his approaching death—for the story had spread among the brothers [John 21:23] and caused great amazement and astonishment. Then, as soon as he remembered it, it came into his heart [Acts 7:23] that this was a sign that his own death was not far off. At the thought of death, his hair stood on end [Job 4:15] and fear and trembling came upon him [Ps 54:6]. Soon a deadly fever came over him, and within ten days later he died and passed happily from this world.

One thing about his pious devotion we cannot pass over in silence, for it was a kind of miracle that happened if not by him at least to him and made us very glad. When he was drawing his last breath and no longer had the strength of talk, for three or four hours before, he clasped his hands and held them out steadily against a cross, as if they were held there by a cord. When every other part of his body was thrashing about in pain, yet he never separated his hands and never drew them back, but, as we've said, held them steadily against the cross [EO 94.14]. What he had done all his life, he continued to do in his death.

## CHAPTER FIFTEEN

### About the Servant of God Peter, Who Used to See the Lord Jesus Christ on the Altar during Mass

Among those in the blessed house of Clairvaux who arrived at spiritual strength and learned from the examples, the exhortations, and the prayers of our most holy Father Saint Bernard to climb

the height of virtue was an old man from Toulouse named Peter.[52]
He was a man of great purity and deep devotion. From boyhood
his only desire and endeavor had been that he might be crucified
to the world and the world to him [Gal 6:14]. In his youth, before
he submitted himself to the Cistercian Order, he lived in solitude,
continually mortifying the old man by fasting, prayer, and all kinds
of work, offering to God daily upon the altar of his heart the sacrifice of a humble and contrite heart [Ps 50:19]. He lived solely on
wild herbs and bread soaked in warm water, and there he fought
for Christ for a long time and with God's protection bravely won
many battles against the temptations of malign spirits. Later, praise
for the holiness of the most blessed abbot Bernard and of his monastery at Clairvaux reached him, and in a great fervor of spiritual
desire he went to that place so he could live more safely in such
an association of the just, as it were in the tabernacle of the Lord.
In security and hidden from rain and storm under the direction of
the aforesaid father, he obtained whatever was lacking in himself in
his quest for perfection. Indeed he served the Lord Christ faithfully
there for many years and persevered to the end of his life.

While he was still a young man, the Lord deigned to appear to
him in a vision, sitting high upon a throne with his host of saints
around him. It seemed to Peter that he was being taken before the
Lord for judgment. When he was brought before that tremendous
Majesty, he fell, pale and trembling, at the feet of him who sits upon
the throne and besought him to have mercy on him. The Lord
said to him, "What do you want me to do for you" [Luke 18:41]?
And Peter replied, "Lord, that I may be saved." Then the Lord said
to him, "Go and consecrate yourself immediately to my service,
persevere in it to the end, and you will be saved as you ask." The
servant of God Peter saw this promise as an utterly sure pledge of
eternal salvation, and he cut himself off entirely from the world
and gave himself over completely to the divine service. He girded
his loins with courage and strengthened his arms [Prov 31:17] to
fight against the spiritual wickedness that assailed him bitterly for

---

[52] Herbert of Clairvaux, LM 1.3 (PL 185:1277–80). Cf. LM 2.5 (PL 185:1316).

many days and years. Most of all he had to put up with the pangs of the spirit of fornication, which continually stirred in him the stings of temptation, both waking and sleeping.[53] He was so deeply disturbed by this in himself that he chastised his flesh incredibly with labor and hardship [2 Cor 6:5], vigils and fasting, and many other excruciating forms of penance. At length he became so upset about it that he decided to castrate himself, for he could find no other remedy for the temptation.

Nor can we fail to mention that the ancient enemy often appeared to him many times and in various forms. Once he had appeared to him in choir at Clairvaux in human form, with flashing eyes and fierce face, huge in stature and hideously deformed. He wore a hairy, very black cowl, and its sleeves were cut short, scarcely reaching to his elbows, and the rest of his arms were bare. Wicked apostate that he was, he came and stood before the man of God, looking down at him with a haughty gaze and showing how angry it made him to have his temptations so stubbornly resisted. The man of God was astounded at the sight and was like a bound man, unable to move. At length, by the inspiration of God, he defended himself by the sign of the cross; the monster disappeared without doing him any harm, except to increase the fire of his temptations. A few days later he appeared to him again, in the same place, taking the form of a monstrous beast which seemed to be part fierce lion and part rapacious eagle. This ferocious monster stood opposite the highly courageous athlete soldier of Christ, threatening him and making savage grimaces as if he were about to devour him alive. But divine power prevented it from touching him, and then at the invocation of the name of Christ the phantom monstrosity disappeared. When he had gone, the man of God felt the force of his passion so much increased that he clearly recognized the monster of which Isaiah speaks, which breathes on the coals in the fire [Isa 54:16]. He knew that the violence of this temptation was beyond the measure of his endurance, so he decided to castrate himself there and then, preferring the judgment of God to the inferno of

---

[53] "Spirit of fornication" (*spiritum fornicationis*) probably refers to masturbation; see McGuire, "Structure and Consciousness," 84–85. See also above, EM 2.22.

lust. He was only waiting until he could find a sharp knife or other instrument suitable for the purpose.

Truly the merciful and mighty Lord, the helper in due time of those in tribulation [Ps 9:10], who alone sees the struggle and the sorrow [Ps 9:35], would not leave his servant in such peril, but along with the temptation he provided a way for him to bear it [1 Cor 10:13]. While Peter was asleep, an angel of the Lord appeared to him in the form of a young man who said he was an experienced doctor and had come to castrate him and heal him of his passions. Peter accepted this gratefully and willingly exposed himself as he lay there. He felt the knife cut him and bore patiently the cutting and the sharp pain. When he woke up he thought he had really and truly been castrated. But then he found that his physical member was still there; he knew that it was the temptation that had been cut away at its roots by the gracious kindness of God, so that he might be troubled by it no more, and he gave thanks, as was right, and resolved to run more joyfully in the way of God's commandments [Ps 118:32] since he had experienced his goodness so generously in his temptations.

From that time the stirrings of passion were eradicated in him, and the Lord began to visit on him the blessings of sweetness and fill his soul with so much light so that he could repeat this saying: "According to the multitude of the sorrows of my heart thy comforts have refreshed my soul" [Ps 93:19]. From then until the end of his life the Lord stilled the wild beasts who live among the reeds [Ps 67:31] and rebuked the assaults of the flesh in him, and the Spirit of consolation rested upon him. The Lord magnified him in his mercy [Luke 1:58] and crowned him with joy and exultation and filled him with all the good he desired. After he had for so long drunk the bitter wine of salvation, he deigned to inebriate him with the nectar of the sweetest contemplation.

Among other gifts he received from God the special grace of devotion in prayer, especially at the consecration of the Body and Blood of the Lord. The brothers who assisted at his Masses wondered that he wept so much at that moment. The Lord revealed to him many and great heavenly secrets and visited him with innumerable consolations, when he was awake and when he was asleep, and very often when he was in ecstasy. If all this were to be set down in writing, a great number of books would be filled, but it is already a long and burdensome business for me to set down what has been told me about this blessed man. So I shall restrict myself to the one event that I learned from his own mouth, for I dare not in conscience omit it. I will tell it because on the basis of it the others can easily be inferred or believed by those listening carefully. I am afraid, very much afraid, that our Divine Master would be offended if by my silence I allowed to be forgotten the glorious and wonderful thing that the saint confided to me and to no one else, or only to a few, all the rest of whom are today, I think, no longer living. I hope my account will give glory to God and increase faith and devotion in many souls.

So then, while this blessed man was standing at the altar, offering the life-giving sacrifice of our redemption at the altar, at the moment he was holding the most holy Body of the Lord elevated over the chalice [EO 53.102-4], he saw under the appearance of a child the one whom the prophets called the most beautiful of the sons of men [Ps 44:3], our dear Savior Jesus Christ, true God and true man, gentle and humble of heart [Matt 11:29], who always shows himself to the little ones [Matt 11:25] and hides himself from the wise and haughty of heart. Once he saw this, he closed his eyes, overcome by the awe he felt for his majesty, not daring to look at him. But he still saw him as clearly with his eyes shut and with them open. If he turned to one side with his eyelids closed, he still saw him as if he were in front of him; he saw him sometimes in front of him, sometimes over his hand, sometimes over his arm, as if he had eyes in his forehead or in the back of his head by which to see him in a marvelous and ineffable manner. And it was not just once or twice that the man of God received this grace but so frequently that Christ often appeared to him every day for four or five months. And if sometimes he seemed to delay a while, so familiar was this man with God and so great was his trust in his goodness that he would prolong the holy sacrifice and not complete it until he had been deemed worthy to receive the usual blessing by having returned to him the joy of God's salvation [Ps 50:14].

Now as I have already said, I have taken pains to narrate this simply and sincerely, as it was told to me by the one who received the grace to behold it. It was because I had sought to stay very close to him because of his holiness and had hung on his consolation and his words, that I managed, by dint of much pleading and a certain violence of love, to draw from him the account of this vision, and many others, on the condition that I not presume to share them with anyone until his death. That was easily done, for he was nearly at the end then. After a holy life, he went to his fathers, and he now rests with them in the peace of the Lord at Clairvaux, where he had dutifully lived the monastic life and where he had always ardently longed to die.

## CHAPTER SIXTEEN

### *About the Venerable William,*
### *Who Was Corrected for His Fault by an Angel of the Lord*
### *and Given a Penance*[54]

There was at the time at Clairvaux a certain venerable monk named William, as advanced in religious observance as he was in age [EM 2.22]. He had served the Lord in the monastic state for fifty years, assiduously crucifying the desires of the flesh [Gal 5:24] so that for a long time his life was a martyrdom. Before he entered the Order of Cîteaux he had lived for a long time in the monastery of Saint Aubin at Angers,[55] where by his devout way of life he showed himself to be a model of virtue and was thought to be a pattern of holiness by the brothers there. He was held in great respect and was as much loved by the abbot as by the entire community. The abbey owned a certain piece of land that was more solitary and seemed better suited to a quiet religious life, so he obtained leave of the abbot to live there with a few of the brothers. For many years he lived there enclosed in a narrow cell, so that he could practice

---

[54] Herbert of Clairvaux, LM 1.4 (PL 185:1280–84).
[55] Saint Aubin is a Benedictine house in Angers; Cottineau 1:101.

greater asceticism without upsetting the weaker brothers by the sight of an austerity greater than their own. He redoubled his prayers and fasts day and night, utterly refusing not only meat but also the better fare that had by custom been served to the brothers at their first monastery; indeed, he supported his frail body on very little food, often abstaining even from Lenten fare, and drinking water. It was not without much pain that he reached this state of abstinence, but when he had fasted a long time, by groans and prayers and by the grace of God, he dislodged the natural pleasures of the stomach, the delights of the gullet, and other vices.

One day, one of the seniors of the monastery had come to see him, and because he was a frail old man and seemed tired by the journey, William instructed that a small serving of meat be given to him. The old man replied that he would not taste the bowl of meat unless William, who had ordered it to be served for the sake of charity, would eat it with him. Persuaded by his affection for his visitor and, as he later confessed, somewhat wanting to eat, William agreed to do so. When the meal was over he saw his friend and guest off to return to the monastery. As soon as he had gone, that brother came to himself and he began to sigh deeply from the bottom of his heart and seriously to bemoan that he had, on so light a pretext, broken the resolution which he had kept faithfully for so long.

He had scarcely begun to think about all this when someone knocked on the window of his cell. When he had opened to him, he was struck speechless by what he saw. It was a person of very dignified face and bearing, splendid beyond human measure, in every aspect unlike anyone William had ever seen. His clothing was white and glorious, his hair white as fleece or as snow [Rev 1:14]. His face, shining with matchless beauty, indicated it was an angel rather than a human being. Moreover, his words were gentle and gracious, full of heavenly wisdom. Everything about him seemed to be superhuman. He entered barefooted and said he was a stranger who had come from a far country to visit him. After greeting William courteously, he then began to talk with him as a friend and kinsman about the subject of his thoughts as if he already knew and was able to judge them. He said, "You are right to groan and weep for the excess you committed under the pretext of charity by breaking the practice of abstinence which you have kept for so long. Charity is not good if it destroys charity, and the good deed that wounds the conscience by pleasing the body is damnable. Listen to this example which I will give you.[56]

"There was in the territory of Spain a nun who was a recluse and lived only on bread and water, and occasionally on a few half-cooked vegetables; by her chaste and sober way of life she manfully resisted the naggings of the flesh. One day, at the tempting of the devil, the desire to eat meat assailed her. For a time she resisted this temptation courageously, but when she could no longer endure the ever-more urgent suggestions of the enemy, she gave in to his illicit persuasions. So she ordered that a plate of meat be prepared, and when it was set before her on the table, but before she dared to taste it, she entreated God, prostrate in prayer and with tearful voice, that if he foresaw that anything there would endanger the salvation of her soul, he would not let her eat. Rising from prayer, she went to the table, said the blessing, and lifted the cover off the plate of meat. But in place of the meat she had been offered, she found three squalling, featherless little crows in the middle of the plate.[57] At this sight the nun was extremely surprised and summoned the sister who helped her and asked her about it. She called God to witness that she had not served three plucked birds but three pieces of cooked meat. The cell of the recluse was situated near a wide, swift-flowing river which burst from the stony mountains and rushed along its steep course turbulently down to the plain. Thanking God and rejoicing that he had answered her prayer, this handmaid of God, now finding eating the meat she had

---

[56] See Berlioz, *Le Grand Exorde*, 171–72nn26–40, for extensive bibliography on the varied imagery of the following story, most notably Caesarius of Heisterbach, *Dialogus miraculorum* 4.82-85 and 7.16 (Strange 1:249–51; 2:20; S-Bland 1:284–87, 476).

[57] This anecdote is found in a fourteenth-century manuscript from the Augustinian house of Waldhausen (Upper Austria). In that version a monk named Gwilhalus is visited by an angel who tells him the story about the Spanish nun and the crows; see J. A. Herbert, *Catalogue of Romances in the Department of Manuscripts in the British Museum*, vol. 3 (London, 1910), 593–94, no. 131.

just been wanting downright repulsive, ordered that the birds of dark and evil enticements, and the bowl they were in, be thrown into that river. Once thrown into the torrent, they could not get free of each other; the plate floated on the current until it was caught in an eddy near the cell where a hollow formed by large rocks held a pool of water. There they are still, whirling around in circles, and to this day, as proof of this great miracle, they can be seen in the basin, floating on the water."

As the stranger finished telling this and other similar stories, Brother William was moved by his very helpful conversation to a great state of repentance. He fell to the floor on his face, weeping for his guilt and asking pardon for his fault. He received from his guest a penance and not only absolution for his sins but great consolation. Being bold now to speak freely he began to inquire who he was and where he came from. The stranger replied, "It is not for you to know who I am or to discover where I am from or where I am going" [John 3:8]. "At least, my lord, you will stay here today," said the hermit, "and we will be glad to serve you." "I do not want anything," replied the stranger. "I need neither your food nor clothing nor domicile. I have everything in abundance, and to eat I have bread of which you know not [John 4:32]. Your salvation is my only concern. Do not be concerned about anything else yourself." And with these words he went away so quickly that he seemed to have vanished rather than departed. The saint immediately called together the brothers who served him and told them to run after him and by repeated entreaties make him accept his hospitality. They went without delay, but although they searched everywhere, they could find no trace of him. The man of God was thoroughly convinced that it was an angel who had come to discover the secrets of his heart and to heal by his kind and consoling words the heartache he was feeling over his indulgence. This visitation had made such a mark on the old man that when he told me about it twenty years later he could not hold back his tears.

As time went by, the celebrated name of blessed Bernard and his reputation for virtue, not to mention the outstanding religious life at his monastery, were being talked of everywhere. When this reached William his spirit would not rest until he could put himself under the beneficial direction of the great abbot in order to become ever more fervent and holy. He was received with kindness by the blessed abbot and joined the monks of Clairvaux as he wanted, and there the grace of the virtues so radiated from him that he seemed quite amazingly holy, even to the well-advanced monks. The Lord often sent him great consolations by his Spirit and—as we know ourselves—revealed to him the mysteries of heaven. But he was afraid of succumbing to the plague of vainglory and spoke very little of these favors and only to a very few. One day Prime was being sung in choir and he was standing in his place in choir, joining in with those reciting the psalms, offering in joyful praise to the Lord the calves of his lips [Hos 14:3].[58] While he was watching and chanting, he saw Saint Malachy, who had been a bishop in Ireland and whose body rests in the church at Clairvaux, appear.[59] He was sitting on a throne by the altar, a ring on his finger, a crozier in his hand, a miter on his head, and vested in the rest of the pontifical garments, as if he was going to celebrate a full pontifical Mass at the end of the Office. It was the anniversary of the burial of that great and blessed bishop and also All Souls Day. With him appeared blessed Bernard, the very beneficial pastor and protector of this monastery. He also was resplendent in precious white vestments and wore a miter, though it was less elaborate. The reason for that was that he was there as the father of the family in his own house, doing honor and deferring to a distinguished guest. He very happily left to his dear friend the honor of offering the Holy Sacrifice, since it was on that day that the saintly bishop had been taken up into heaven and first honored by the sound of celestial hymns. The blessed Father Bernard himself was the server, and he fulfilled this duty at the altar with attention and care. The blessed bishop leaned upon his pastoral staff and kept his eyes continually fixed on the choir; but Saint Bernard watched sometimes the bishop,

---

[58] Alt. "fruit of his lips."

[59] Malachy was archbishop of Armagh and died in Clairvaux on 2 November 1148. He was buried there in the chapel of the Virgin. See Lenssen, *Hagiologium Cisterciense* 1:76. *The Life and Death of Saint Malachy the Irishman*, CF 10:97–121, contains a translation of Bernard's sermons, epitaph, and hymn to Malachy.

sometimes the community, and sometimes the altar, as if he was taking care of them all. The servant of God saw this vision clearly, awake and with his eyes open, during the space of one psalm being sung by the community at that hour. When the psalm ended the vision ended, but the tender devotion in his heart at seeing it did not fade with the vision.

On another day, blessed Bernard again appeared to him, clothed from head to foot in glory. When he saw him, William fell at his feet and made a request of him [cf. Matt 20:20]. The saint said, "What do you want me to do" [Luke 18:41]? And he replied, "My lord father, if I have found favor in your sight, tell me, I pray, if I am going to be saved." The saint answered him, "Surely you are aware that in this you have asked me no little thing? Today when I came out of Paradise, I saw outside the gates many thousands of men tormented with the same fear as you, not knowing if they would be counted worthy of love or of hatred [Eccl 9:1]." Once having said this, he answered the question that had been put to him, but what his definite reply was we do not know, because William was afraid of the plague of vainglory and would not tell us, for he was a cautious man and serious in what he said, and he was careful not to say anything that could be turned to his praise. But from the assurance of his words and the joy in his face it was easy to tell that he had been given a favorable reply to his question. This is the same William that we wrote about earlier [EM 2.22] when I described how he saw a lewd spirit in the form of a prostitute run through the infirmary seeking something and who after that ominous vision told Dom Robert, abbot of Clairvaux, about the apostasy of the two young brothers. Their wicked flight a short while afterward fully confirmed the truth of his prediction.[60]

About this man of God we know many other things which would excite the devotion of the reader, but we pass them over in silence so as not to bore the reader and in order to get on with the narrative. This blessed and holy man had lived faithfully, and so he died happily and full of days and virtues and went to the Lord

---

[60] From here to "and went to the Lord" is almost verbatim from Herbert.

whom he had desired and sought with all his heart, and he was buried in the most holy house of Clairvaux.

CHAPTER SEVENTEEN

*About Gerard of Farfa, a Very Holy Monk*[61]

Gerard of Farfa, beloved of God and men, whose memory is blessed [Sir 45:1], was especially honored by Saint Bernard for his great purity of heart and holiness of life, and he was especially loved and admired by all the brothers for the virtues that made him a perfect monk. When he was still a monk at Farfa, which is a noble abbey in Tuscany,[62] he received a vision from the Lord: he saw himself being carried in spirit to Clairvaux and there being given the task of going around the various workshops with two basins, pouring water over the hands of each of the brothers as they washed them. Events later taught that this meant he was to be the one who would wash away the faults of the brothers of Clairvaux by the tears that flowed daily, well-nigh unceasingly, from his eyes, as from two ewers. Once he accepted this gracious vision as a presage of the future, it kindled in his heart a vehement flame of holy desire, and he could not rest in spirit until he had joined the company of the poor men of Christ, whom he knew he had been sent by God to serve. He increased in every virtue, but it was the gift of holy compunction that specifically filled his heart so that his eyes, like those of a dove, were hardly ever closed; rather, they were like twin fountains, especially when tears dampened his face during the celebration of the Holy Mystery. Everyone wondered at this grace which made him specially dear to God and to men, and his face seemed to them as the face of an angel [Acts 6:15] standing

---

[61] Herbert of Clairvaux, LM 2.29 (PL 185:1338–40), see also EM 3.4. According to Piesik (*Exordium Magnum Cistercienser*, 1:508n421), Gerard is known only through the EM and the *Liber sepulcrorum* 5 (PL 185:1560).

[62] Farfa was a Benedictine house in the Diocese of Sabina. Cottineau 1:1107.

in their midst, and they said, "This is indeed a 'lover of the brothers and of the people of Israel; this is he who prays greatly for the people and for our entire' fellowship [2 Macc 15:14]." There was no doubt that in secret God favored him with great consolations, but he kept quiet about them for he was humble and shy, and no one dared ask him about it because of their respect for his goodness.

Now there was a novice called Julian, a priest of honest life who had come to Clairvaux from the canons regular. One day in choir he saw an unclean spirit wandering wantonly about in the likeness of a goat. When it came to him, it stood in front of him and with its gaping mouth began to insinuate disgusting things, wagging its head and grinding its teeth. Then it left him and went and stood by the man of God, Gerard, and began to jeer at him with similar lewd gestures. By him, however, it was mocked in return, and, deflated, it soon disappeared and vanished like smoke and the novice saw no more of it. As soon as he managed to get permission to speak, the novice quizzed him on whether he had seen anything in choir at that time. When the senior realized that the novice knew what he thought he alone had seen, the old man admitted that he had seen the goat mocking them both with his lascivious movements. When the novice heard this he marveled greatly, realizing that the old monk often had revelations of this kind but that he kept them secret between God and his conscience.

Although the man of God was now nearly ninety years old, and although his body had become very frail, neither old age nor debility could make him give up any of his regular practices, but he seemed to grow younger each day in the fervor of an indefatigable spirit, so that he could hardly be forced to stay in the infirmary, even by serious illness, or hardly be kept away from the work of harvesting. One night as he lay on a bed in a quite private part of the dormitory suffering from a very grave illness, it happened that the lamp which was burned there went out. Seeing this, the brother who was looking after him at the time got up and went to light it again. But when he discovered that all the workshops were shut, he came back without a light, locked the door, and sadly went back to bed and fell asleep. In the middle of the night the saintly man wanted to get up for personal needs, and the brother arose, worried that there was no light. But when he looked into the nearby hearth, where there had been no fire for eight days, he saw there some glowing coals. No sooner had he lit the lamp from them and looked back down at the hearth than the coals were not to be seen and he could find there no trace of heat.

During his final illness, from which he died, he was lying down, already approaching his end, when Saint Bernard appeared to him, with angelic face, dressed in white robes, but in the same physical condition and appearance that he had had before he died. Seeing the saint coming toward him leaning on a stick to support his aged but august limbs, Gerard signaled as best he could to those looking after him that they should get up for the approaching saint and quickly make ready a place for him to sit [RB 63.16]. The brothers were astonished and asked what saint the old man was talking about. But he could not reply because of his pain. Later he got back the power of speech and when the monks again asked him about it, he confessed that he had seen Saint Bernard, who had consoled him with kind words, and that he had blessed him and all the community, saying, "This is my house, which I built. May the Lord protect it forever and throughout all ages." Strengthened by the blessing of his most holy father, the man of God Gerard paid his debt to death, happy to be satisfied in the fountain of life from which he had so greatly desired to drink.

Sometime later he appeared to a lay brother named Lawrence in a vision. He was full of joy, surrounded by light, and fittingly clothed in glorious robes. He indicated to him that by the grace of God he would one day enjoy everlasting joy and glory. The brother begged him insistently to bless him and pray for him, and he did bless him, saying, "I do not cease to pray for you or for this whole community now. But I have one small complaint to make: the brother infirmarians over-hastily picked me up, still living and breathing, and carried me out of the sickroom as if I were already quite dead." Several years after his death, once the new church and cloister which had been begun with the permission and blessing of blessed Bernard had been completed, Gerard's sacred bones were taken up, with the honor and reverence their sanctity deserved, from the place where they had first been buried and placed in the tomb in which, as we said earlier, the venerable fathers Abbot Robert, Prior Humbert, and Subprior Odo had been laid.[63]

CHAPTER EIGHTEEN

*About a Marvelous Grace Which God Bestowed upon a Perfect Monk*[64]

A young gentleman raised in German lands was going to Paris with his master to study. On their way they passed by Clairvaux, and the master, seeing the community and their way of life, was immediately moved by I know not what impulse from God to ask and obtain leave to be received into monastic life. He urged the young man to stay with him, but he refused absolutely. He shrank from the company and the conversation of Cistercian monks, and he had often asked God never to give him the will to join that Order. Neither the request of his master, nor the prayers and exhortations of the brothers could overcome his stiff-necked opposition [Acts 7:51]. How wonderful is God, though, above the schemes of men [Ps 65:5], and how irrevocable are the secrets of his eternal design. Who can adequately admire how he mercifully changes the minds of his elect and smiles at their feeble efforts and turns their rebellious wills into the way of his goodness which he has determined for them and in them, in time, place, and manner, from all eternity?

On that same night while the young man was turning the advice of the brothers over in his mind, he heard a divine voice saying to him, "If you leave this place and go to Paris and stay there until Pentecost, you will die; you will surely die." The young man was greatly taken aback at the voice, but it did not soften the hardness of his heart. The next night when he fell asleep he seemed to be plunged into the slime of a deep pit [Ps 68:3]. As he was lying

---

[63] Conrad added this last paragraph.
[64] Herbert of Clairvaux, LM 2.9 (PL 185:1318–21).

there in despair, suddenly there appeared to him at the edge of the pit the blessed evangelist John in the garb and appearance of Saint Bernard, who was then still physically alive, and with him was another saint who looked very much like the good monk Gerard, who was the porter at Clairvaux. Trembling and anxious when he saw them, the young man asked them rather insistently to have mercy on him. Blessed John replied, "You have scorned accepting the good advice given you, so what do you expect us to do?" He promised to do whatever they wanted, if only he could escape the danger that threatened him. Saint John then said, "Will you become a monk at Clairvaux?" And the young man replied, "Yes, my lord, I will do so very willingly." When he made this sincere promise, they drew him out of the deep well and let him go away freely.

In the morning he asked to be introduced at once to Saint Bernard, for, although he had never before seen him, he soon, with total certainty, figured out by his dress and appearance who it had been who rescued him that past night on the condition that he become a monk. Very much impressed by all that had happened and pierced by compunction, he put himself immediately into the hands of the abbot, who received him with kindness, and soon everyone was marveling at such gravity and mature wisdom in one so young. The aforesaid master, however, quite soon abandoned his good resolve and tried to turn away the young man too, but he was not able to move the young novice who was so established in the love of Christ. This delicate and very raw youth, although he was only fourteen years old, put his hand to hard things [Prov 31:19], and to the joy of angels and men he bore the sweet yoke of Christ [Matt 11:30] and like a lamb was harnessed to the plough of the way of life he had accepted. From the beginning of his conversion, by the help of God, he had the strength of a horse but always kept the gentleness of a lamb. From his early years he shone with such outstanding gifts that all the brothers rejoiced in the exemplary fervency of his way of life and earnestly tried to fashion themselves according to the holy devotion and humility which appeared in him.

A certain spiritual and observant monk of that monastery told me he had once seen a vision of this sort: one day he was watching the young man sing the invitatory in front of the altar step and saw the image of Christ which was above the altar detach itself from the cross as if pleased by the young man's singing.[65] Christ came toward him with outstretched arms, tenderly embraced him, holding him close and kissing him. Having seen it, the brother understood by it that the young man's soul was holy and pleasing to God and had been specially permitted access to an intimate relationship. The well-beloved of the Lord remained all day long in close union with him, enjoying his blessed presence in the soothing delights of contemplation.

The Lord deigned to show through the aforesaid vision how replete with love and grace his servant was. Devout and fervent in all the exercises of the holy Order, this monk ever-more earnestly implored the mercy of God through continuous application to holy compunction. One night there appeared to him in his sleep an angel of the Lord [Matt 1:20] who led him into a chamber full of light. There he saw the Lord Jesus Christ hanging on the cross and his blessed Mother, the Virgin Mary [John 19:25], with John the Evangelist, standing beneath the cross. Once he had entered, he sensed a fragrance of sweetness, as if he had stepped into a spice shop filled with all kinds of powdered unguents.[66] When he saw that the Lord of Glory had deigned to set before his eyes the signs of his cross and passion, he prostrated himself flat on his face, adoring him and from the very bottom of his heart begging for his blessing. He obtained what he asked, but then he awoke and clear signs convinced him that what he had seen had not been an illusion. The same fragrance of heavenly sweetness which he had breathed in when asleep, once awakened from sleep he sensed permeating his spirit with a sweet and wonderful unction. Nor was this momentary, but for the next three days he continued to be renewed and illuminated by that heavenly blessing.

Another night when he was intently at prayer, he deserved to hear, with his bodily ears, angelic voices in sweet clear harmony resounding in the air. The voices were so high that no human

---

[65] *Le Grand Exorde*, 179n18, notes a connection to EO 68.18.

[66] Bernard of Clairvaux, Sent 3.123 (SBOp 6/2:233; CF 55:428).

voice could possibly reach that pitch. For some time he enjoyed the sweetness of this heavenly music, then its loveliness faded from his ears, but in his heart there remained the immense joy of the devotion to which it had given rise and often later the memory of that rich sweetness [Ps 144:7] would come back to him and fill him with joy. Like the patriarch Abraham he came to share the secrets of heaven, and he did not stop growing and increasing until he became very great [Gen 26:13]. But by far the best of it was that however much he accumulated divine favors the more humble he showed himself, not only before God, but also before his brothers, not presuming to have anything out of the ordinary or singular in his monastic life, but living the ordinary common life, though with a singular and singularly pure devotion. But since the Lord gives grace to the humble [Jas 4:6; 1 Pet 5:5], he magnified his servant still more by allowing him to see with his bodily eyes him to whom the heaven of heavens and their armies, the seraphim and cherubim, sing praises and on whom the angels long to gaze [1 Pet 1:12], Our Lord Jesus Christ in his blessed humanity.

After the blessed man of whom I have been speaking had been giving himself with his brothers to fasting and prayer during Lent, like Ruth the Moabite [Ruth 2:14] soaking his morsel of bread each day in the sour wine of compunction, the all-holy day of the Lord's resurrection began to dawn. While the brothers were celebrating the solemn Vigil of Easter with all the solemnity that great day demands, he opened his expanded heart to deep meditation and began to consider the passion and resurrection of the Lord so attentively that he broke down in tears from his burning love and devotion. And after the second lesson had been read, and the response, "The angel of the Lord," was being sung by the community,[67] the Lord Jesus Christ—who had kindled this fire of devotion in his heart—appeared to him who was weeping and watching and stood in front of him in the middle of the choir and stretched out his hands as if to show them to him. In each blessed palm there very clearly appeared the place of the nails [John

---

[67] *Le Grand Exorde*, 181n39, notes that this phrase occurs in the second responsory on the Vigil of the Resurrection.

20:25], and from them blood was oozing as if from recent wounds. At seeing the Lord, the brother rejoiced with exceeding great joy [John 20:20], but he was so astonished and beside himself that for a while he did not know what to do. He wanted to throw himself down in the midst of the choir and kiss the feet of the Savior, but embarrassment and conventual reverence held him back, for fear he should be thought to be out of his senses. For he did not know whether the Lord was appearing to him alone or to the others as well. He wept profusely, and his heart melted within him at the boundless sweetness of the love of him upon whom he gazed. The vision lasted until they chanted the words in the responsory, "I am risen, come and see," which by custom is sung very slowly. Who can explain how much he profited by this vision and how completely all the movements and affections of his soul were re-created and renewed and inflamed by the love of Him whom he had seen? He alone, and the Giver of such grace, knew how joyfully he passed the next days with his Beloved, like the bride crying out in his heart, though not with his voice, "I have found him whom my soul loves" [Song 3:4], and with the patriarch Jacob, "I have seen the Lord face-to-face and my life is preserved" [Gen 32:30]. He took care, by guarding humility to extend the foot of confidence further, for according to divine promise, "every place where you set your foot will be yours" [Deut 11:24] and will deserve to be enriched by still more excellent gifts.

As I have said, he saw with his blessed eyes the dearest humanity of Christ our Lord, and by an awesome condescension of God's grace, he was even allowed to contemplate the eternal mystery of the undivided Trinity, as far as that is possible for men still mortal. It happened on the holy day of Pentecost, while the community was celebrating Vigils in choir with eager earnestness and singing the divine hymn *Te Deum laudamus*, the song of praise preceding the reading of the holy gospel [RB 11.8]. At the words "Holy, holy, holy, Lord God of Hosts," by which the one God in three persons is declared and worshiped, the whole community made a profound bow, as is the custom [EO 68.70]. The aforesaid servant of God bowed with the rest and—not presuming to scrutinize or break into the secrets of the faith, but fearful and trembling with wonder—meditated in simplicity of heart on how profound and incomprehensible is this hidden mystery of that Majesty, whom to know is life and life eternal [John 17:3], to enjoy is wisdom without error, to please is happiness beyond compare, to be conformed to whom is to recover the likeness to God which we lost in Adam,[68] whom to serve is to reign,[69] without whose grace all nations are as nothing before him [Isa 40:17], and in the life to come will be the peace that passes understanding [Phil 4:7] in joy with all the saints which is without interruption or ending. The brother straightened up from his bow, and the eyes of his understanding were suddenly opened, and, as if he was entirely caught up out of himself, he saw a glorious and marvelous vision of God the Trinity which he understood to be more marvelous, worthy, and excellent than all the visitations he had ever been granted by God. O happy soul, in whom the fire of divine love had so entirely burnt up the dross of sin and the rust of negligence that he was allowed already in this corruptible life to taste and to savor of the joy and bliss that the Lord keeps as a reward for his elect. And no less happy was the most blessed Father Bernard at seeing his disciples reach such perfection at Clairvaux under his guidance.

By such visitations from the Lord the monk was encouraged and strengthened, and in daily laments he sighed and longed to put off the corruptible weight of this life and see the face of the Lord whom he had glimpsed through a glass darkly [1 Cor 13:12] and become one spirit with him by contemplating him in his purity. He was asked, for the honor of God and to edify his neighbors, to disclose the ways in which he had been visited by the Lord, but he was reluctant to assent for fear this might not be pleasing to the Lord. Yet he gave in to repeated requests, and with fearfulness and profound humility he revealed all that we have reported and some other things. We know many admirable things about him, but I am going to omit them in the interest of brevity and moving

[68] For Bernard of Clairvaux on the soul returning to a likeness of God, which he calls a "reforming of the soul to the Word," see SC 83 (SBOp 2:298–302; CF 40:180–87).

[69] For information on "to serve is to reign," see note above in EM 3.5.

on to other things. He always refused to tell us what it was he was allowed to see in his vision of God the Holy Trinity. He said he would never presume to speak about it, unless he knew clearly that God willed him to do so. Even what he did choose to tell us was told only on condition that it should not be revealed to anyone before his death. And that is a promise I have scrupulously kept.

For twenty-six years he lived in sincere devotion in the Cistercian Order, which in his youth he had so much abhorred, until he was forty years old, when he was released from the flesh by a happy death. He was so perfected within a brief period that it was said he was fulfilled over a long time [Wis 4:13], for his soul was pleasing to God. Of him we could say with the fear and exultation of the psalmist, "I will sing of your mercy and judgment, O Lord" [Ps 100:1], and "It is neither from the east nor from the west, nor from the desert mountains that our help comes; for God is a just judge," and "he casts down and he raises up" [Ps 74:7-8].

The master of the young man, whom we mentioned earlier, wanted to do strong things [Prov 31:19] and undertook the good works of monastic life, but he was led not by grace but by presumption, and like the seed that fell on the rock he sprang up at once, but in time of temptation he withered away [Luke 8:6]. On the other hand, the young man whose faith and holiness we have been describing was drawn by grace, our mother, despite his distaste and his reluctance.[70] And the motherly care of God was not content simply with inserting him into the community of the servants of God but, once he had overcome his spiritual negligence, deigned to count him among the small number of the perfect who reach the peak of virtue and contemplation. Just as he is "blessed whom you choose and bring near to dwell in your courts" [Ps 64:5], O Lord, no less shall "those who forsake you be put to shame and those who turn away from you be written in the earth" [Jer 17:13].

---

[70] "Grace, our mother" are Conrad's words, not Herbert's; see n. 50 above at the end of EM 3.13.

CHAPTER NINETEEN

*How Saint Bernard Converted the Highborn Man Arnulf,
and the Virtues Which He Exemplified*[71]

When the most reverend Father Bernard traveled to the province
of Flanders once, he cast the net of the word of God [Luke 5:4;
cf. Matt 4:18; Mark 1:16] in every direction to catch souls, and he
drew many noble and learned men out of the waves of the world
to the shore of conversion; and among these was a certain illustrious man who was wealthy and very pampered, Arnulf of Majorca,
who secretly put himself into Bernard's hands. They both agreed,
because of certain worldly difficulties, to keep quiet about it up
to the very last day when he would leave his land and his relations
[Gen 12:1]. For he was the head of his family, responsible for many
sons and brothers, and so entangled in wealth that he could not
break away without causing scandal and recrimination unless he
first wisely and prudently set his house in order.

In the meantime, however, while all these things were covered
by silence [Wis 18:14] and these secret negotiations were known
only to these two people in the world, the word of the Lord came
to a certain peasant cowherd while he was hitching his cows to
the plough, saying, "Go and tell Arnulf of Majorca that he is to
take you with him when he goes to Clairvaux to become a monk,
which he will do very soon, and become a monk with him." He
heard a voice but saw no man [Acts 9:7]. After the voice finished,
the peasant began to ask God very earnestly to repeat this message,
if indeed the tidings had come from the Lord. The same message
came again in the same words. When he had received the oracle
a second time, the peasant went to the aforementioned man and
said, "My lord, I want to talk to you" [see 2 Kgs 9:5]. After Arnulf

---

[71] Herbert of Clairvaux, LM 1.11 (PL 185:1287–90). The conclusion of this
version is noticeably different from an older version found in Vita Bern 7.22 (PL
185:437C–D). Piesik, *Exordium Magnum Cisterciense*, 1:509n435, refers the reader
to the *Hagiologium Cisterciense* 2.21.

had led him aside, he fell on his knees, saying, "I beg you in the name of our Lord Jesus Christ, take me with you when you go to Clairvaux, and you shall save my soul with yourself. And if you want to know, it was our good and merciful Lord who deigned to reveal your secret intention to me for the sake of my salvation." At hearing these words, the noble lord marveled and rejoiced greatly. He received the man and kept him with him; they were companions on the journey and in the novitiate, and I am sure that they share the same eternal reward. When Arnulf had completed all the business that had delayed him, he went to Clairvaux and was as submissive in humility as he had been sublime in the affluence of worldly goods, and from his fortune he bestowed great gifts on Clairvaux and not a few other monasteries. Blessed Bernard was delighted at his conversion and said this about him to the brothers in chapter: "In the conversion of Brother Arnulf, Christ is no less to be admired and glorified as in his raising of Lazarus when he had been dead four days. For Arnulf was enclosed in the tomb of his great riches and though he seemed to be living, he was dead."

With groans and many tears, Arnulf confessed all the sins he had contracted in the world, and when blessed Bernard saw the bitter contrition in his heart and his freely given willingness to do good works, the only penance he gave him was to say three times the Our Father and to continue in the Order till his death. When he heard this, Arnulf was upset and said, "Father most blessed, please don't make fun of me." "In what way am I making fun of you?" he said. "For me to fast for seven or ten years in sackcloth and ashes would not be sufficient penance, and all you tell me to do is say the Our Father three times and persevere in the Order?" To which the saint replied, "Do you know better than me what you should do for your salvation? Does it seem to you a small thing to remain in the Order and persevere until death?" Arnulf replied, "May such wicked presumption be far from me. But for the love of God I beg you, do not spare me in this life; spare me instead in the one to come. Impose some penance now so that at the death of the flesh I may attain rest without punishment." The blessed father then said to him, "Do as I have said, and I assure you that as soon as the burden of the flesh has been laid aside, your soul will be taken up into God without suffering." He received this reply as if it had come from God and was greatly comforted. From then on, neither the violence of temptation nor the distress of sickness could turn him from the course he had chosen and in which he was entirely intent on God. He was very careful and exacting about all the observances of the Order and about guarding his heart; in fact, I never knew anyone so concerned to purify his conscience. Everyone, especially those who heard his confessions, marveled at the insistence, or rather the importunity, with which he came daily to them, giving them no rest and taking none himself. With tears and groans he would confess not only idle words or gestures, on the rare occasions when one escaped him, but even the vain or idle thoughts which most other men, except the few who are perfect, are wont to regard as of little concern; he would mention them very scrupulously as if censuring a crime. Scripture tells us truly that "whom the Lord loves he chastises and the son whom he cherishes he whips" [Prov 3:12; Heb 12:6]. Merciful fatherly correction was never lacking to this venerable man, cutting away the vices of his flesh and increasing and multiplying the virtues of his soul. For many years right up to his death he was tested by continuous and difficult illnesses. He bore them all with patience and even glorified in them as in great riches.

It happened once that he was so enfeebled and weakened with suffering that he could bow only with great pain, but he would not omit this and bowed deeply and reverently every time "Glory be to the Father" was sung during Vespers in the church. Standing beside him in the back of the choir was an equally holy monk. An angel of the Lord appeared in the form of a very handsome young monk in a cowl white as snow, but Arnulf did not see him. When he bowed at the Gloria after the psalm, as was the custom, the angel of the Lord stood before him and stretched out his hands to support his head. When the monk next to Arnulf saw this and realized from the brightness of his face and clothing that it was an angel, he was overjoyed and went up to him to take hold of him and embrace him. But when he wanted to hold out his hands to touch him, the angel suddenly was not there but suddenly appeared again in another place. Catching sight of him, the monk ran after him and tried again to hold him, but with the angel vanishing and quickly reappearing elsewhere, he was frustrated in his attempt. After this had happened several times, the angel vanished completely, letting the monk see him but not lay hold of him.

Arnulf, the athlete of the Lord, was subject at times to stomach pains and a fatigue so severe [1 Kgs 17:17] that, with his breath nearly failing, he sometimes seemed close to death. When he had lain silent and unconscious in this way for some time, he was thought to be dying, and he was anointed with the unction of the sick. But he revived a little, and when he was able to speak he broke out into praise and thanksgiving, saying, "All you have said is true, Lord Jesus." He repeated this often and those present were amazed; they asked him how he was and why he was saying this. To these questions the sick man made the same reply: "All that God has said is true." Some of them said that the intensity of his pain had turned his brain and he was delirious. But to these he retorted, "That is not so, brothers, I speak with a sane mind and a peaceful spirit because all that the Lord Jesus has said is true." So they said to him, "We know that is so too, but why do you keep insisting on it now?" He replied, "The Lord says in the gospel that if anyone renounces the love of parents and riches of the world for his love, he will receive a hundredfold in this world and eternal life in the future [Matt 19:29; Mark 10:30]. I am now experiencing the meaning of this saying, and I am receiving now in this life my hundredfold. I love the harsh intensity of this pain, so pleasing to me for the assurance of mercy it will bring me that I would not exchange it for all the worldly goods I left behind. And if I, an unworthy sinner, am made so happy even in the midst of sufferings, how much joy and delight must the saints and the perfect rejoice and dance in their consolations? Indeed, the spiritual happiness which exists only in hope exceeds by a hundred and a thousand times the secular joy which exists now. If anyone leaving the world behind and coming to monastic conversion does not deserve to receive this hundredfold, it clearly means that he has not perfectly given up everything, but by an act of self-will—which is a bad characteristic—he has kept something back." Everyone marveled to hear such words from the mouth of a man who was a layman and not a clerk. They knew that the Holy Spirit, who had allowed his body to undergo such violent sufferings, had gently anointed his soul with a sacred unction which, when it touched the man, taught him all he needed to know [1 John 2:27]. This holy man received from the Lord's hand double for all his sins, and like gold tried in the furnace [Wis 3:6], after the long crucifixion of martyrdom, he fell very peacefully asleep in the Lord. And we can be sure that as he left his body he went straight to God without any more punishment, as Saint Bernard had promised.[72]

I ask you, did this poor man of Christ lack anything at the time of trial? For as the prophet says, he trusted in the Lord [Isa 40:31] and subdued the flesh by the power of the Spirit, not considering what was possible for the flesh, but what was enjoined by the Rule and the Order. Like a seal upon his heart [Song 8:6] he placed the brief word [Rom 9:28] he had received from the holy father that he should serve the Order because of all his sins. His constancy and penitence rebukes our tepidity and negligence. We have undertaken to repent of our sins in the same Order, but we do it tepidly and negligently; we are not embarrassed to be excused from Vigils for some trivial illness and go to the infirmary. But the servant of God would not go to the infirmary except for mortal illness, and what is more, he continued to serve God at Vigils when he had been suffering a serious illness. "Time flies and cannot be recalled";[73] it is precious and we are wasting it. We no longer accept with patience the sufferings that the Lord sends us in the present, so we must expect the hundredfold in the future. If anyone makes excuses of the weakness of his nature, let him remember that it is written that those who fear God lack nothing [Ps 33:10; RB 2.36], and that the prophet, once young and then old, never saw the righteous forsaken [Ps 36:25]. "Who has hoped in the Lord and been confounded, or who has been faithful to his commandments and been deserted" [Sir 2:11-12]? This is clear from the testimony of Scripture but also from the example of the aforesaid fathers, and to confound our lukewarmness and strengthen our weakness in the contest, I will add two more miracles.

---

[72] Up to this point, the chapter is from Herbert's LM.
[73] Horace, *Epistles* 1.18.71.

CHAPTER TWENTY

*About a Monk Who Had a Bad Headache,*
*and How He Was Cured by the Power of Christ's Sacrament*[74]

There was a certain brother called Peter, afterward abbot of Clairvaux,[75] who in his youth tried daily by practicing the observances of the sacred Order to offer himself as a living victim, holy and pleasing to God [Rom 12:1]. But all who will live godly in Christ Jesus will suffer persecution [2 Tim 3:12], and God, who makes all things work together for good for his elect, allowed him to experience violent headaches. The brave soldier of Christ bore this suffering patiently and was careful always to give thanks in his suffering and to restrain the viper of self-will from complaining. Like the prophet, he preferred that rottenness should enter into his bones, that he might deserve to rest in the day of trouble [Hab 3:16], but he was deeply worried that the ardor of his spirit could not overcome the weakness of his body and let him do what he desired.

One Sunday while he was at Vigils he felt his sickness more harshly than ever, and because of his headache, he thought of leaving choir and going to lie down. But at once he thought again, by God's inspiration, that he would be able to stay until Prime because on that day he was going to receive the pure and most precious Body and Blood of Christ in the holy mysteries [EO 66]. Once Prime had ended, though the pain did not lessen, he did not leave the community but resolved to put up with it until after the high Mass at which he could receive Holy Communion. He went to the altar step to receive Communion and on bended knee humbly asked forgiveness, according to the custom [EO 58.2], when suddenly it seemed as if a great lump of lead rolled off his forehead and fell on the floor. He very distinctly heard it fall and shatter, but he could see nothing and was extremely dumbfounded by this strange event. But how wonderful is the kindness of our Savior! The

---

[74] Herbert of Clairvaux, LM 2.26 (PL 185:1335).
[75] Peter Monoculus was abbot from 1179 to 1186; see note above at EM 2.32.

brother had been suffering terrible pain, but he had disregarded it out of reverence for the sacrament, and as soon as he received the sacrament devoutly and in faith, he was cured of his sickness and so perfectly cured that he never suffered from that debility again. He did not show himself ungrateful for the gift of God but made great progress in holy religion and was eventually given the office of pastoral care; first at Igny and later at Clairvaux he received the same title of abbot [RB 2.11-12]. He always led those under him to Christ by the way of true humility, and he was a sweet fragrance to God in every place [2 Cor 2:15].

CHAPTER TWENTY-ONE

*About a Brother*
*to Whom the Blessed Virgin Mary Gave Heavenly Food*
*in a Vision*[76]

There was at Clairvaux a certain monk, a man of goodwill but delicate and sickly in body, and on that account he was always fussy about the quality of what he ate and superstitious about collecting medicines for himself. The kind Lord, who mercifully corrects the erring, willed to lead him back into the way of truth, and in order to make him understand the saving admonition of the Apostle that we cast all our care upon him, for he cares for us [1 Pet 5:7], deigned to visit this monk who erred out of simplicity. In a night vision [Dan 7:7] the brother saw the whole company of the brothers hurrying to church as if to celebrate the Divine Office of Lauds. At the door of the church stood the Mother of mercy, the dear Virgin Mary, as humble as she is sublime; she held a bowl of precious food, and as each brother went into church, with her own hand she graciously gave a spoonful to each of them, and

---

[76] Herbert of Clairvaux, LM 3.14 (PL 185:1366).

each was refreshed by tasting such a sweet elixir.[77] When the brother saw this, he was very glad because he thought that there would be nothing to hinder him taking some of that heavenly food. When he came up to the hand of that dearest giver of good things, the mild Virgin, by a merciful pretense, repulsed him very gently, saying, "Surely you have no need of my medicine. Aren't you a wise doctor who can take care of yourself? Go, then, go and use your own medicines if you need them, for these others who have cast all their care upon my son, their Lord [Ps 54:23], are now especially in my care." When he heard this, the brother blushed and asked pardon; he promised to stop worrying about himself and commit his whole life to her care and to God's. Then she who is the refuge of all Christians, but especially the protectress of her servants the Cistercian brothers, accepted his repentance very graciously and forgave him and gave him as medicine some of the saving pittance. As soon as he tasted that heavenly remedy, the brother recovered from his delicacy and debility and gave up eating special food and medicine and took the common fare. Soon by the help of God his looks and his strength increased and he recovered health of body as he recovered health of soul.[78]

Where are those brothers now who seem to follow the school of Hippocrates rather than the school of Christ,[79] who focus their attention on the health of their dying flesh all summer by searching for, or collecting, vile and wild herbs or roots and are no less concerned all winter with drying, crushing, pounding, and mixing the same herbs into potions which have not the effect of medicine but rather increase that most dangerous of medicines, their own self-will? Let them learn from these examples to trust in the Lord rather than in Galen,[80] to hope more in the Queen of heaven than

---

[77] The EM contains several references to Mary as the "Mother of mercy" (*mater misericordiae*). See EM 3.27, 31; 4.13; 5.5, 9, 15, 16.

[78] The text is from Herbert to this point.

[79] A reference to Hippocrates, the ancient Greek physician and contemporary of Socrates (fifth century BCE).

[80] Galen (*c.* 129–*c.* 199 CE) was a physician and philosopher from the eastern Roman Empire who became court physician in Rome. His writings became the basis for much of medieval medical knowledge. Bernard of Clairvaux, SC

in the herbs of the earth. For at the last tremendous judgment, the just Judge will judge them not by their complexion but by their profession. Then, when it is too late, they will be sorry that they spent their lives uselessly caring for their bodies rather than cherishing their souls.

CHAPTER TWENTY-TWO

*About the Venerable Old Man Achard,*
*Former Novice Master at Clairvaux*[81]

A certain old man called Achard, a man of noble birth but nobler still in monastic observance, was given charge of the novices at Clairvaux.[82] He had the rare talent of edifying and consoling by his words, and in the flush of his youth he had been sent by the blessed Bernard to found and organize a number of monasteries, which he had done with great devotion. Now this veteran of meritorious service, this elderly man was assigned the office of instructing newcomers. He did this with firmness and used his long experience to strengthen the inexperienced novices in his care by his daily teaching against that threefold cord that is so hard to overcome [Eccl 4:12]: the world, the flesh, and the devil. He told them about the events of the past and of the present to keep them vigilant and on guard against their own vices. Here we will recount one of the stories which we heard from his own mouth.

When this same Achard was still a novice, the venerable abbot Bernard came into the novitiate, as was his custom, to give the

---

30.10 (SBOp 1:216–17; CF 7:121), also contrasts the school of Christ and that of Hippocrates and Galen.

[81] Herbert of Clairvaux, LM 1.5 (PL 185:1285). See also Vita Bern 7 (PL 185:453–55).

[82] Archard was from a noble family and entered Clairvaux in 1124. He became novice master around 1140 and died at some time after 1170. See Piesik, *Exordium Magnum Cisterciense*, 1:509n442.

novices some words of encouragement. When he had finished speaking, he took the aforesaid Achard aside with two of the other novices and in a prophetic spirit forewarned them, saying, "One of the novices [and he named him] is going to sneak away furtively before daybreak. Watch and hold yourselves ready, and do not let him get away with what he plans to steal from us. That wretch is leaving us because he is not one of us, but take his booty from him because that belongs to us." Those who heard these words were astonished, but they kept quiet and waited to see how the prediction would be fulfilled. In the middle of the night two of them saw that the fugitive was deeply asleep in bed, and they too fell asleep, for the spirit of deceit had made their eyes heavy [Mark 14:40]. But Achard, very sure that the word of his superior would come true, tried courageously to fight off the sleep weighing him down. Sometimes he rubbed his forehead or pulled his hair and his beard; sometimes he washed his head and his hands or walked about to rouse himself. By these means he managed to keep awake in spite of being tired. It was nearly time for the signal for Vigils to be rung when two gigantic Ethiopians dressed in black cloaks came quite visibly through the door of the dormitory.[83] The one who was first carried a roast chicken on a spit. Wrapped around the chicken on the same spit was a huge adder, affixed by head and tail. With this delicacy they approached the bed of the faithless novice, and the two black men put the smoking viands under his sleeping nose. At once he awoke and the demons vanished. What the devils did in this horrible scene showed the kind of temptation they had put into his heart. When this wretched man had wakened from his sleep—not the sleep of contemplation, like Jacob [Gen

---

[83] In both the ancient and medieval worlds black was considered the color of the devil. Thus, here and elsewhere "Ethiopians" should be taken as synonymous with the blackness of the devil and not as a racial comment. For precedents of devils as Ethiopians, see Tubach, 1912, 1913, 3108 (Saint Gregory sees Ethiopians, Saint Brendan prays to end a brother's apparitions of an Ethiopian, and Saint Macarius sees an Ethiopian in a vision). In addition, Tubach, 3096 (lust portrayed as an Ethiopian); 3703 (in which a perjurer is carried off by an Ethiopian); and *Vita S. Antony* 6, in *Athanasius: The Life of Saint Antony and the Letter to Marcellinus*, trans. Robert C. Gregg (New York: Paulist Press, 1980), 34–35.

28:16], but the sleep of deception, like a vile apostate—he got up quickly, took a bundle of clothes, and followed his seducers. When he reached the doors of the cupboard in the cloister where the books were kept, he looked for some means of breaking the lock so that he could take the books. But the aforesaid Achard very quickly woke up his companions and by signs and motions indicated to them that the desertion which had been foretold was happening. All three pursued the fugitive, and they caught up with him as he was pushing back the bolt of the door. When he saw them coming, he tried by great leaps to escape and raced through the door into the orchard, but they caught him at the enclosure wall and took him back. When day came and he showed no sign of repentance for his misdeeds and was unwilling to own up to them, since he seemed to be given over to his debased mind [Rom 1:28], they finally released him and let him go to his own place [Acts 1:25]. The same day the devil entered into him and he lost his reason; he remained mad to the end of his life.

As a venerable old man Achard also told us that at the beginning of his monastic life he put up with many battles with and attacks from demons, and he saw many appearances of them. Quite often when he was reciting psalms and praying in the church, lanterns in great number, like candles and lamps, would light up around him, which would immediately disappear like a trifle at the invocation of the name of Christ. One day the devil appeared and challenged him to a physical struggle, like gladiators in the arena. The devil beat him down with blows and wounded him, but Achard gave as good as he got. And in the end he overthrew him. He broke his skull and spilled out his brains; then he dragged him by his hair, and part of the flesh and bone of the crushed head remained in his hand and gave out a smell more horrible than anyone can imagine. Achard threw this hideous scrap away from him with horror and suddenly the stinking monstrosity disappeared. But for a whole year his hand reeked constantly of the stench so much that he could not put it to his mouth or his nose without feeling his heart lurch.

When this servant of God went to stay awhile in German lands to help build a monastery called The Cloister in the Diocese of

Trier,[84] he was fortunate enough to see and talk with a saint, a truly holy man, a solitary of heroic virtue. For the name of Christ, he had been wandering naked for a long time over mountains and through forests in those parts, without refuge or clothing, eating wild herbs and roots to maintain life in his moribund body. He bore the burning heat of summer and the bitter cold of winter with patience so incredible that one day when he was shivering even more than usual in the midwinter chill and a heavy snowfall, the servant of God, having nothing to protect himself from the snow and cold, lay down naked on the ground. The thick snow covered him entirely until it was impossible to see any sign of a body underneath it, except for a little opening near his mouth that the warmth of his breath made through the snow covering him up. Achard used to tell his novices about the wonderful virtues of this holy man and about his patience, which far surpassed the ordinary scope of human weakness. By such stories he would wonderfully strengthen the first attempts of the new recruits and enkindle in them no small love of the virtues.

## Chapter Twenty-Three

### *About Dom Geoffrey, a Monk of Clairvaux Who Later Became Bishop of Sorra*[85]

Dom Geoffrey, of holy memory, was first a monk at Clairvaux and later became bishop of the church of Sorra on Sardinia. Before he

---

[84] Grießer (EM, 202n3) posits that what Conrad refers to as "a monastery called The Cloister" was the monastery of Himmerod, built between 1134 and 1138. The solitary in question was probably a man called Gosselin; see Herbert of Clairvaux, LM 1.6 (PL 185:455–59).

[85] Herbert of Clairvaux, LM 3.9 (PL 185:1360). Geoffrey of Melna was consecrated bishop of Sorra (Sassari) on Sardinia in 1171 and died at Clairvaux in 1178. Compare Willi, *Päpste, Kardinäle und Bischöfe aus dem Cistercienser-Orden* (Breganz, 1912), 48; and *Monumenta s. Claraevallensis abbatiae* (PL 185:1556–57) where it says he was infirmarian at Clairvaux.

was promoted to the episcopate, he was in choir one day with his brothers, actively offering to the Lord the homage of his lips, when he deserved to see with his blessed eyes the following vision—as we had it straight from him. He saw a glorious and splendid procession come to the north end of the church, as if from the cemetery; it went across the front of the sanctuary and went straight to the infirmary. First in the procession he noticed were the acolytes, then the subdeacons, then the deacons and priests; they walked seven by seven, one after another according to the dignity of their rank. The acolytes were wearing albs and each held a candle in his hand, but the candles seemed to be of fire rather than of wax. The subdeacons wore rich tunics; and the deacons, splendid dalmatics; and the priests had on wonderfully wrought silken chasubles. Each one of them carried in his hand the articles distinctive of his ministry. Behind them came a great crowd of persons garbed in white, likewise walking in order and with reverence. At the end followed the glorious God-bearer, the Virgin Mary, and the apostles Saint Peter and Saint John attended her, one on her right and one on her left. The most loving Theotokos radiated such beauty and brightness of face and garment that the whole basilica glowed with the light coming from her. As Geoffrey was watching, the Spirit who had shown all this to Geoffrey said within his heart, "This is the Queen of Heaven, the Lady of the Angels." After the procession had wound its way solemnly past the sanctuary step and gone out of the church by the door which led to the infirmary, as we said before, the monk saw it no more. Now there was then in the infirmary a venerable old priest, holy in monastic life, named Tescelin; he had been ill a long time and, like a submissive son, he had borne with great patience his heavenly Father's corrections. Just then he was in his death throes and before long he exchanged the bitter life of earth for the joys of eternity. The man of God Geoffrey, who witnessed this scene, was absolutely certain that the procession meant the passing of this holy man and his procession into bliss.

How great are the good things that "God has laid up for those who love him; the eye of man hath not seen, nor his ear heard, nor his heart understood" [1 Cor 2:9]. For if one God-fearing soul, as it goes forth from the body, is met with such a welcoming procession, how much more joy, do we think, will the soul feel in arriving in the heavenly homeland, where it will rejoice forever in the glorious vision of its Creator?

## CHAPTER TWENTY-FOUR

### *More Visions of the Same Servant of God, Geoffrey*[86]

At another time the same servant of God was standing with the other brothers at the Office when he clearly perceived an unclean spirit in the form of a monkey crossing the middle of the choir. This ridiculous brute came and stood in front of him, scornfully staring and sneering at him, flaring its nostrils and all the while making rude gestures. After a while it left him and went out of choir to be seen no more. Later, this same blessed man fell ill and suffered a great deal of pain in his throat. His weakness increased daily, and then the illness became chronic and the doctors nearly gave up on him. What most distressed Geoffrey was that the illness constricted his windpipe and prevented him from singing and chanting the psalms. He turned to blessed Bernard and entreated him day and night that he be deemed worthy of receiving the grace of being able to sing again. The good father, moved by his prayers and tears, appeared to him in a vision and, touching the sick place with his hand and blessing it, he made the sign of the cross on it. When the man of God awoke, he found himself wonderfully cured and able to sing, and never afterward was he troubled by that malady.

At another time, a certain spiritual monk whom Geoffrey loved very dearly in Christ fell gravely ill. The illness was so extremely serious [cf. 1 Kgs 17:17] that he was thought to be dying. So the aforesaid man, ravaged by grief, began fervently to send up a stream of tearful prayers for the recovery of his friend. He stood in the breach before the Lord [Ps 105:23], and while he was interced-

---

[86] Herbert of Clairvaux, LM 3.10 (PL 185:1360–61).

ing and weeping, someone appeared to him in a vision and said, "The brother on whose behalf you are so afflicted will be restored to health, but another whom you love equally in the spirit will be going in his place." And so it was. When the monk who had seemed so near to death was getting better, there died a venerable and saintly old man called Rainald of Cluny, whom Geoffrey also loved in Christ with deep affection. Moreover, when his mother died, he was extremely solicitous for her welfare, and daily water went forth from his eyes [Ps 118:136] on her behalf, for he had an abundant gift of tears. He pestered the Lord earnestly to deign to reveal to him if she was still in punishment or if she had entered into her rest. At last, as he wearied heaven with his prayers he heard a voice saying, "Why do you keep asking about something you have no right to know? Be content to pray for your mother, and she will be saved."

## Chapter Twenty-Five

*How It Was Revealed to Geoffrey That He Would Become a Bishop, and about His Holy Death at Clairvaux*[87]

One day when the man of God Geoffrey was deep in prayer, a person of venerable bearing appeared to him by a vision and put a golden ring on his finger, as a sign of the pontifical dignity to which he was soon going to be raised. The same year, as we said,[88] he was raised to the bishopric of the church of Sorra. He actively governed that church for the span of seven years and as bishop he led an unsullied life, crowned his ministry with honor, and left to his successors an example of holiness. Toward the end of his life, and only God knew it was the end, he left Sardinia to revisit Clairvaux,

---

[87] Herbert of Clairvaux, LM 3.10 (PL 185:1361–63).

[88] The year would be 1171. Because this passage is copied, the "we" refers to Herbert of Clairvaux, not to Conrad, the author of the EM.

of which he was a son, for he had long and intensely desired to be buried there. When he saw the abbey from afar, he raised his eyes to heaven and sighed, asking the Lord with all his heart [Ps 72:7; RB 7.51] that if he was going to die before three years had passed he would not allow him leave this house. For he always visited his former monastery every three years and was afraid he might die somewhere else and so be deprived of the burial he so much desired. He entered that beloved monastery and stayed there some time in good health to the joy of the monks who were all glad to have him as their guest. But then he was stricken with an acute sickness which daily grew worse and as it worsened brought him to the brink of death. At the very hour he was anointed with holy oil and prepared by the viaticum of Christ's sacrament, almost at the very moment, to the amazement of all he slept in the Lord. He passed over during the night of the feast of the dedication of the church of Clairvaux.[89] The venerable abbot of the monastery knew well his purity of conscience, and when he closed the eyes of his lifeless body, he said with much faith, "My dear and reverend father, may almighty God give me the grace to join you soon." When he conducted the Office of Commendation, he was so overcome that he could not restrain his breaking tears; everyone was moved, even the hardest of heart.

When the holy priest had first fallen ill, the approach of his death was revealed to a monk in the house. A few days later when this brother was at the Divine Office of Vigils, he saw in spirit a bed decked with a soft cushion and covered with sheets white as snow; it was readied for the bishop and was a symbol of the rest of eternal happiness into which he was soon to enter. On the night on which he died, this aforesaid monk woke up when the bell rang for solemn Vigils of the dedication. He began to think about the departed bishop whose body was already laid out in the church [EO 94.26ff.], and he heard a voice in his ears speaking to him about the departed servant of God and saying [Luke 1:44], "At the first signal

---

[89] The date is 13 October 1178 and refers to the second dedication of the church, when the relics of Saint Bernard were placed in the church. See Grießer, EM, 205n3, and *Le Grande Exorde*, 196n8.

for the Office all the saints of heaven will receive him into their company." The monk experienced great joy when he heard this. He got up and went into choir and stood with the others to chant the psalms, thinking the whole time about the holy bishop being raised to glory. While they were celebrating Lauds, he looked up and saw more candles than can be counted, miraculously alight, on the walls of the church surrounding the body of the late prelate. In looking at the light of this spiritual brilliance with his physical eyes, he was deeply moved and gave thanks to God for what he had seen and heard, and he cried in the joy of his heart, "'Lord, God of Hosts, happy are all those who hope in you' [Ps 83:13]. Indeed, 'happy is the man whom you have chosen and taken for your service; he shall dwell in your courts' [Ps 64:5]. I believe and I am confident that he is already worthy to be counted among your saints and chosen ones, for while he was in this world he walked in the way of humility and endeavored faithfully to keep your commandments."[90] Two months after Geoffrey was buried, the same brother was in choir, keeping watch and singing psalms, when suddenly he fell into an ecstasy. The blessed bishop appeared to him dressed in priestly vestments and preparing to celebrate Mass. So the monk helped him vest and turned back the edge of the chasuble on his arms. At that moment the choir was chanting, "I will go unto the altar of God, even unto the God of my joy and gladness" [Ps 42:4].[91]

After that brief account of the life and death of this holy man, may I add here another miracle which ought to be more widely known and which this same servant of God assured me he had joyfully witnessed? The good bishop had decided to raze and rebuild the old basilica, which was falling into ruin. When they demolished the altar in front of him, he found an old rusty box containing relics of the saints. Among the relics they found a Host, as well preserved, whole, white, and uncorrupted as it had been when it was first put there. But there was no one in the country who could remember

---

[90] *Le Grande Exorde*, 197nn15–16, notes that Ps 83:13 and Ps 64:5 were used, respectively, in the second and first nocturns of Vigils on the Feast of the Dedication.

[91] Ps 42:4. *Le Grande Exorde*, 197n19, notes that this psalm was used in the first nocturn of Vigils on the Feast of the Dedication and also as an antiphon.

seeing either the building of the church or the consecration of the altar.[92] Seeing such a miracle, all those present were overjoyed and confirmed in their faith, and they glorified God, knowing full well that this was the most holy Body of the Lord of which it is written, "I will not suffer my holy one to see corruption" [Ps 15:10]. The blessed bishop died in the year of our Lord 1178, on the third ides [eleventh] of November. He was buried with fitting honor next to the venerable Geoffrey, former bishop of Langres,[93] who had held the office of prior at Clairvaux under Saint Bernard and who had carried out an honorable ministry with a very edifying and religious life when he was later raised higher to episcopal dignity.

## CHAPTER TWENTY-SIX

### *About Baldwin, Monk of Clairvaux, Later Bishop of Pisa*[94]

Among the offshoots sprouted in a profusion of heavenly grace and sent out from the vines of the Lord of Hosts,[95] that is, the church of Clairvaux, to be transplanted over many waters, that is, among people in many different regions, and elevated to the honor of holding episcopates, Baldwin especially shone out and was the glory of his native soil.[96] He followed the teaching of his most

---

[92] For other stories of the miraculous properties of the Host, see Peter the Venerable, *De miraculis libri duo* 1.1, ed. Dyonisia Bouthillier, CCCM 83 (Turnhout: Brepols, 1988), 7–8; and Caesarius of Heisterbach, *Dialogus miraculorum* 9.8 and 9.16 (Strange, 2:172–73, 178; S-Bland 2:114–15, 121). See also Tubach, 2662, for stories related to *Dialogus* 9.8.

[93] *Monumenta s. Claraevallensis abbatiae* (PL 185:1557).

[94] Baldwin was made a cardinal by Innocent II in 1130 and was archbishop of Pisa from 1137 to 1145.

[95] Bernard of Clairvaux, Div 15 (SBOp 3:140) also uses the image of the monastery as vineyard.

[96] The image of a plant-like growth of the Order is used by William of Saint Thierry, Vita Bern 1.4.19 (PL 185:237C), and has roots in the Bible: see Ps 79:12 and Isa 16:8. For more on Baldwin, see Bernard of Clairvaux, Ep 144.4, 245,

reverend Father Bernard, and, despising the glories and pleasures of this world, he died to the world at Clairvaux and began to live for the Lord Christ. There, he counted himself happy to prefer the true riches of voluntary poverty to the enticements of fickle wealth. Learning, like the Apostle, to be a fool to become truly wise [1 Cor 3:18], he despised the false goods of the world which make a man thirsty but do not satisfy him and embraced with all his heart and mind those goods which in eternal blessedness will gain an immense weight of glory [2 Cor 4:17]. He set himself to imitate the most perfect monks and tried to ascend from the lower stages of the life of penitence, where he wept for his sins, to the higher peaks [Josh 15:19] of perfection, where he longed with unutterable groans [Rom 8:26] for the joys of heaven. As someone already deserving to live not for himself alone but to lead many others by word and example to salvation, he was called by God to be elected archbishop of the church of Pisa, the capital of Tuscany. Once he acceded to the eminence of this important position, Baldwin displayed such great wisdom, exercised his office with such great energy and freedom of spirit, and still manifested such gentleness and humility, as is proper to a monk, that not just the Cistercian Order but all the Christians of Italy rejoiced and thanked God that in their times he had given to the Church this gleaming pillar and unshakeable support. But because, regrettably, in human affairs no happiness is perfect, the devil stirred up a bloody and disastrous war between Pisa and Lucca,[97] which, fanned and drawn out by the rivalry of the two sides, lasted for some years even after his death, and even then they could scarcely be brought to make peace and be reconciled. The reasons for this war are of no interest to us; we need only say that this war was hurtful and painful to the soul of such a prelate, as was made clear in a divine revelation.

---

505 (SBOp 7:346; SBOp 8:136–37, 462–64; James, Ep 146.4, 321, 115, pp. 215, 395–96, 172–74), and Ep 542 (SBOp 8:509; not in James).

[97] A reference to the prolonged period of war between Pisa and Lucca, 1008–1144. The causes were a combination of economic rivalry and imperial/papal politics, see U. Benigni, "Lucca" and "Pisa," *The Catholic Encyclopedia* (New York: Encyclopedia Press, 1913), 9:405–6, 12:110–12.

Shortly after the blessed archbishop's death, there lived on the island of Sardinia a priest of honest habits[98] who had charge of a parish there. His church had been built outside the village and far from all human habitation. One day while he was celebrating Mass there and was about to give Communion, he discovered the sacred Host broken in half on the corporal, although when he consecrated it, it had been whole and entire. This sight troubled him, and he felt uneasy about it; he finished the celebration with fear and wonder. After the service, he dismissed the others and stayed there alone. He was sad at what he had seen, and he went outside and stood along the east end of the church with his back against the wall of the temple and his face turned toward the east. He stayed there for a while, reflecting nervously and anxiously about the strange thing that had happened. Suddenly, a shiver ran through all his limbs and his hair stood up on end [Job 4:15]; some external force—I know not what—seized him and held him in place with such force that he could not move. With his eyes wide open, he saw a throng of innumerable hosts of soldiers on horseback and on foot coming swiftly toward him. Among them he could see people of every age, sex, and condition, a great many of whom he had known during their earthly life.[99] One of them who was once known and dear to him came up to him, stopped, and began to speak familiarly with him. The priest asked him who the endless crowds were and what they were doing; the other said, "These are the souls of those who have put off their mortal flesh, and they are all being punished according to their sins by wandering far and wide over all the world. Some will be delivered sooner, some later, but the punishment of some will remain forever unpardonable."

As he said this, the priest looked back and saw the aforementioned bishop go by, his head bent down as if he were bearing the sentence assigned to him by the just Judge with great patience and

---

[98] From here until the last paragraph, the text is from Herbert of Clairvaux, LM 3.31 (PL 185:1375–76).

[99] For more on the army of the dead, see Jean-Claude Schmitt, *Ghosts in the Middle Ages: The Living and the Dead in Medieval Society* (Chicago: University of Chicago Press, 1998), 93–133.

(with the prophet) saying to the devil with the power to insult him for a while, "Do not be too quick to rejoice at my downfall, my enemy. I will arise. While I sojourn in the darkness, the Lord will give me light" [Mic 7:8]. At this sight the priest was very much astonished, and in a transport of admiration he cried out, saying, "Alas for me, miserable sinner. What is this I'm seeing? Is not this Lord Baldwin, former archbishop of Pisa and monk of Clairvaux?" And the man talking with him said, "Indeed, it is he." "But," said the priest, "how can such a holy monk, such a perfect bishop be punished? Someone we were hoping was already rejoicing with the angels in heaven?" The other replied, "You may know for certain and have not the slightest doubt that this man here is indeed a saint and a prelate worthy of heaven and that his reputation before God will be great. But since the already long war between the Pisans and Luccans was further drawn out because of him, he cannot rest until they have made peace." Some moments later, the same priest saw a column of dazzling radiance, the light of which seemed to shine more brightly than the sun. It stretched from earth to heaven and along it was a soul guided by angels struggling toward the stars. When the priest inquired whose soul that was, the other replied, "It is the soul of Constantine, formerly judge and lord of Torres.[100] For nine years since his death at this very hour his soul has been continually exposed to the winds, the rain, and the frost under the gutter of his house in expiation for his sins. But because he was merciful and generous to the poor and passed right judgment on those—even the bad—who suffered wrongs and left his body shriven and penitent, the Lord has had mercy upon him. Tomorrow he will deserve to be delivered from all ills, put in possession of all good, and enter into eternal bliss."

The priest saw and heard all this and many other secrets about the next life. For one thing, he learned that he was to die during that year, and his death proved the truth of that prediction. By this, Almighty God willed to make known to him how dear to him

---

[100] For bibliography on Constantine I of Lacon (1082–1127), see J.-M. Poisson, *Le Grand Exorde*, 201n27. Constantine was the father of Gonario (see EM 3.29), who was himself judge in Torres from 1116–53.

was the soul of the venerable Bishop Baldwin and that, albeit holy and albeit righteous, it was encrusted with the slight rust of guilt and unable to enter into the kingdom of all purity or to enjoy the full noonday light in which the Spouse dwells [Song 1:6]; only after grace had taken away every stain and peace had been made between the two peoples would he be able to hear the Spouse say to him, "Thou art all fair, my love, thou art all fair, and there is no spot in thee. Come from Lebanon, come and be thou crowned" [Song 4:7-8]. But what are we to make of the miraculous division of the Host? What, if not that such revelations, made by the will and permission of our Lord, serve as warnings and calls to correction to those about to die, most of all, to religious persons?

## CHAPTER TWENTY-SEVEN

### *About Dom Eskil, Archbishop of Denmark, and Later a Monk at Clairvaux*[101]

Eskil was a remarkable man, whose name has to be pronounced with respect. He was archbishop of Denmark and legate of the Apostolic See to the northern islands and afterward a humble monk of the Cistercian Order, professed at Clairvaux.[102] In his childhood, before he was twelve years old, he was sent to Saxony by his parents to study in the then-flourishing monastery church of Hildesheim, where clerks of various countries gathered. He had been living there only a short time when he fell seriously ill. As he wasted away from his lengthy infirmity, he was eventually given

---

[101] Herbert of Clairvaux, LM 98, but this chapter is not in the PL; see Grießer, EM, 210n1.

[102] Eskil, bishop of Röskilde in 1134, became archbishop of Lund in 1138. He entered Clairvaux in 1179 and died there in 1181. Compare Brian Patrick McGuire, *Cistercians in Denmark*, 63–74; and James France, *The Cistercians in Scandinavia*, CS 131, 32–42, 63–69. See also Bernard of Clairvaux, Ep 390 (SBOp 8:358–59; James, Ep 424, pp. 493–94).

up on by the doctors and anointed with consecrated oil. Priests and other faithful people were pressing around his bed for the ceremony when he suddenly seemed in his death throes; he lost the use of his limbs and his senses and was considered nearly dead by everyone. While he lay there without any feeling in his body, he was transported in the Spirit to a house whose interior seemed to be a burning furnace. He went closer out of curiosity and a whirlwind of fire caught him unaware and dragged him despite his efforts into the midst of the flaming inferno. As he immediately began to burn, he thought that nothing was left to him but death and fire eternal, when, by the mercy of God, he saw on one side an opening that looked like a narrow corridor leading from door to door. It seemed to be free of flames, so, seeing it, invigorated by the hope of making his escape, he attempted to crawl as well as he could toward this place of refreshment. He arrived at the door and in fear and trembling ran out and fled as fast as he could from the devouring flames. Soon he found himself in a grand royal palace, and when he went in he came face-to-face with the Queen of heaven, the Lady of the angels.[103]

Her face and her clothing shone with incomparable brightness, and she sat upon the throne of glory. Breathless and terrified, he came up to her and begged her urgently to have mercy on him. She gave him a scornful glance and reproached him for having dared to appear in her presence; she told him to go away at once and get back into the tormenting fire. But among those attending the Mother of mercy were three venerable men: one of them was the bishop of the city, another the dean, and a third discharged I know not what position in that church. The young man spied and recognized the men and begged them tearfully to deign to intercede for him with the most gracious Lady. They did so very earnestly and the most merciful Lady, as if pretending, replied, "How dare you pray to me for this conceited boy who is not worthy to appear

---

[103] *Le Grande Exorde*, 202nn8, 9, 12, notes that "place of refreshment" is a phrase used in the Mass (see EM 3.28 and 5.19), and that "Queen of heaven," "Lady of the angels," and "Mother of mercy" (below) occur in the antiphons *Ave Regina caelorum, Ave Domina angelorum,* and *Salve Regina.*

before me? He is a misguided and wayward boy and he has never once honored me by a Hail Mary." They urged her to overlook with her usual generosity the slights and heedlessness of youth [Ps 24:7], provided he promise to amend. The terrified young man approached her again, entreating her and saying: "Have mercy upon me, most gentle Lady. Have mercy on me [Ps 50:3], humankind's merciful Lady. Do not close up the limitless bowels of your mercy to such a wretch as me, for I am prepared to serve and honor you above all others, after God, now and always. If my father knew of this deep distress in which I find myself, he would willingly give a great deal of gold to deliver me."

When she heard him asserting such things in a quivering voice, the most blessed Virgin, the true Mother of mercy, looked at him with a serene face and said, "So now you think you can offer me a worthy price for your safety? Well, if you can pay me an appropriate price, you will indeed please me." These words cheered the boy no end, and he approached her and said more confidently, "Yes, yes, most clement Lady, I will redeem myself totally and very willingly do whatever Your Graciousness tells me to do. Only take pity on me and do not send me back into that agonizing fire." The Queen of the virgins replied, "I want you to give me five measures of grain of five different kinds, one of each kind." The boy readily agreed to this contract and cried out eagerly, "Dearest Lady, what you have required is very dear to me, very pleasant. I promise to put into your granary 'good measure, pressed down, well shaken, and running over' [Luke 6:38]." Once he had solemnly and in good faith made this promise, and the abovementioned intercessors had attested to it, the boy was allowed to return to the land of the living.

When he came to himself, he immediately opened his eyes, recovered the power of speech, and sat up on his bed. Soon he began to sing, bursting with joy and saying with great gladness, "Blessed be God, I am delivered; I will not burn. Thank you, most holy Virgin, Mother of God, for you have delivered me from the furnace, and I shall burn no more." Everyone present who saw the young man recalled from the gates of death, speaking this way and raving for joy, was thoroughly amazed and inquired of him the cause of his rejoicing. But for a long time all he would say was, "God be praised; I am not going to burn. I am not going to burn." After he had repeated these words for some time, he turned to those present and told them what he had seen and heard. One of them, a good and learned man, saw that he was not certain of the meaning of the vision and took pains to draw him aside and explain it to him. He said, "Understand first of all that you will have a great name and be elected to high rank in the Church. When by God's help that happens, you must build five monasteries of different Orders in honor of God and the holy Virgin Mother. In each, in order to fulfill the measure you were given, there must be at least twelve persons continually serving in divine worship." After hearing this, Eskil kept silent and awaited with much interest the result of these events. During the vision it had been pointed out to him that the three venerable men who had interceded for him—who were then still alive—were going to die that year. Their death soon followed and proved the reality of the revelation.[104]

As time passed, the young man grew in age and wisdom; he became an able man and by the Lord's providence he was raised up to govern the church at Lund, the capital of Denmark. As soon as he was raised to the high dignity which had been foretold of him, he knew that the time had come to carry out his vow to the Queen of heaven and founded five monasteries of different Orders,[105] which were symbolized by the five measures of grain she had talked about. When a favorable occasion presented itself, he went to the far-off country of France, which he knew was the fountainhead of religious life, and took pains to invite not just five but still more communities professed to spiritual activities. Among them, he acquired two communities from the Cistercian Order, one from Cîteaux itself and another from Clairvaux.[106] He settled them

---

[104] Grießer (EM, 212n1) notes that Udo, bishop of Hildesheim, died in 1114 and posits that this could be one of the deaths to which Conrad refers.

[105] Here and elsewhere, Conrad's Latin, *regina caeli*, alludes to the formal reference of the Virgin as patroness of Cistercian churches. See *Institutes* 18; Waddell, *Narrative and Legislative Texts* 463; Canivez 1:17, *Statuta* (1134) 18.

[106] There is debate over whether Eskil did indeed found five monasteries and over what is meant by "founded" in each case. The most likely five to which Conrad refers are Næstved, a Benedictine house in south Zealand (*c*.1135); Herrisvad,

in the best sites on his lands and cherished them as the choicest vines, which would produce wine of special sanctity. So he could pay his ransom well and give his dearest Deliverer a measure full and abundant, as he had promised, he was not content to found just five monasteries, but with his own goods and the gifts of others he founded many more.

He also worked to uproot completely the pagan superstition with which a large part of the country was sullied and to form his people in the saving discipline of the Christian religion. He smote the proud and the scornful with an avenging blade and, armed with a zeal for righteousness, he set out to destroy everything that was noxious and superstitious and strove to introduce all the things that would help to save the souls of his people, and he did it so well that with hindsight we think no other occupant of that see could have produced better fruit in God's Church than he. The Lord, in whose love and honor he did all these things, made his voice a voice of power [Ps 67:34], and those whom the archbishop put under anathema he punished with a miserable death. For instance, on Maundy Thursday he publicly excommunicated a rich and powerful man for adultery, and on the most holy night of Easter this man was cruelly suffocated by a demon along with his adulterous partner and the two children born of their adulterous union. They were thrown into hell to be punished eternally.

He held Saint Bernard, the highly revered abbot of Clairvaux, in especial esteem, and although he was far away, he honored him with unequaled affection.[107] Not content to see him in his sons—even after founding a new monastery and, as we said earlier, obtaining from him the group of monks he wanted for the holy congregation—a desire to see him for himself so burned within him that this man who had unrivaled authority, both spiritual and temporal, in the northern islands left all his duties and exposed himself to the

---

a daughter house of Cîteaux in Skåne (1144); Esrom, a daughter of Clairvaux in Zealand (1150/51); Vitskøl in northern Jutland (1158); and Løgum in southern Jutland (*c*.1170/71). Each of these is, however, problematic in its own way; see Brian Patrick McGuire, *The Cistercians in Denmark*, 38–60, 105.

[107] From Geoffrey of Auxerre, Vita Bern 4.4.25 (PL 185:335).

perils of a long and tiring journey. So this humble man, yet great in every way, traveled to Clairvaux, drawn not by curiosity for hearing wise things but out of zeal for the faith and fervent devotion. It is hard to describe how much he wept and how much tenderness he showed not only toward the one whom he specially admired but also toward the least brothers in the monastery. Eventually, as he was leaving France to go home, he wanted to take back some bread blessed by the servant of God. In order to keep it for so long, he ordered, using common sense, that the bread be baked twice in an oven, as sailors do. But the holy abbot reproached him in a friendly way for his lack of faith. "So you do not think my blessing will preserve the bread without a second baking?" he said. And he refused to bless it and brought him some ordinary bread, blessed it, and said, "Take this with you and do not worry that it will go bad." Eskil took it and returned to his diocese after a long journey by land and sea, and he rejoiced to find his lack of faith put to shame by the fulfillment of the saint's promise.

Shortly after his return, the grievous news of the death of that blessed man, his special friend, reached his ears. He had the news in a letter from Dom Geoffrey, a monk of Clairvaux who for some time was Saint Bernard's secretary.[108] His "heart grew warm within" him "and as [he] meditated the fire burned" [Ps 38:4]; he understood how vain, transitory, and blind are all the things that can delay a man in his course toward the blessedness of his heavenly country. So he commended the church he had led so well to God and to the princes of the country, and he left parents and kinsmen, acquaintances and friends, bade farewell to his homeland forever, and came as a refugee, a noble exile, to Clairvaux. He visited the burial place of the blessed man, once his intimate friend, and there decided to live and die near his holy tomb. There, a little later, he received, by God's grace, the habit of holy religion. He put his trust in the departed abbot, as he did while he was alive, for he never doubted that though Bernard was dead in the body, he was

---

[108] This letter is in Codex Parisinus B.N. 7561, along with another from Geoffrey to Eskil which is edited in MGH SS 26:117ff. See Grießer, EM, 213n2, for further bibliography.

still truly alive. The less he attended inwardly to the affairs of the Church and the world, the more conscientiously he tended the holy practices of monastic life. He gave himself daily, indeed almost continually, to the exercises of devotion and prayer, offering to God for his past sins the myrrh of a humble and contrite heart [Ps 50:19] and earnestly imploring with the incense of holy compunction the grace of supernal blessing.

One day, while he was watching and praying alone in the oratory, there appeared to him one of his blood brothers who had long before been killed in battle. Cut down by the sword, he had died so quickly that he had not received the viaticum. While he was alive this brother had for no good reason offended the archbishop and had made no effort to make it up with him before his death. When he appeared before Eskil he bowed deeply, with head bowed, as if asking pardon for his offense and begging for prayers. He stood thus before him for a time without saying anything at all, expressing by his humble attitude his misfortune and his need. The archbishop said not a word to him, for he was torn between fear and wonder, troubled in mind and not quite in control of himself. He could see nothing but the head, neck, and shoulders of the dead man; the rest of his body seemed to be on fire, so that the shapes of his other members could not be distinguished for the flames that completely surrounded him. When he had shown himself in this miserable way for a few minutes, he disappeared from sight, leaving his brother's soul shattered by grief. The next day he asked in the monks' chapter for many Masses and prayers for the dead man.

## Chapter Twenty-Eight

### *The Happy Deaths of Two Pilgrims at the Tomb of the Lord; They Were Uncles of Dom Eskil*[109]

Since we have mentioned the brother of this great bishop, I do not consider it out of place to record the death—precious in the sight of the Lord [Ps 115:6]—of two of his uncles who were greatly blessed by God. We hope to inflame no small love for Christ in devout minds by letting them read about the great and wonderful mercy of our Redeemer toward the most heinous sinners [Ps 115:15]. So then, the two brothers were born of an illustrious family in Denmark, and they were the most distinguished in the land after the royal family. One of them, Eskil by name, a soldier proud of his physical prowess, had a fierce and terrible temper, shed a great deal of blood, and daily committed numberless outrages. The other, named Sven, was outstanding in the holiness of his life and bishop of Viborg.[110] He lived an exemplary life, and the nobility of his birth showed in the remarkable gentility of his conduct and virtue. He loved the soul of his brother dearly in Christ but abhorred his acts of tyranny, and he often went to him secretly and took him to task for his crimes. But all his warnings were of little avail. One day when they were talking together, the venerable prelate advised Eskil to take the cross and set off for Jerusalem. He replied that it was absolutely impossible to do this unless he who was giving this counsel would go with him. Gratified at hearing this, his faithful and sincere friend agreed to do what he asked, thus choosing to explore for himself the great pain and peril of the journey rather than risk failing to deliver the soul of his brother from the jaws of the lion [Amos 3:12]. They took the cross and set out together for Jerusalem. As soon as they arrived safely, they venerated with

<hr/>

[109] Herbert of Clairvaux, LM 97 (or 98), which is not in PL 185; see Grießer, EM, 214n2.

[110] Bishop Sven died on 30 March 1150 in the River Jordan (Grießer, EM, 215n1).

a great sense of piety the glorious tomb of the Lord and the living wood of the holy cross upon which had hung the Savior of the world. Then as they went around very devoutly visiting and venerating and worshiping at the other holy places, they arrived at the place not far from Jerusalem which the locals call Pater Noster, because they say it was there that Our Lord Jesus Christ taught his disciples how to pray and gave them the Lord's Prayer. There, they found a church of meager appearance.[111] When the aforesaid pilgrims became aware that this was the place at which the font of prayer springing up to life eternal first burst forth from the mouth of God's Son to become the living water flooding the hearts of the faithful and filling the whole world with blessings [John 4:14], they entered the chapel and imbibed from the font of the Savior [Isa 12:3] the spirit of piety and trust; then they let flow from pure hearts prayers to the Lord, asking him to forgive their sins and deliver them from all evil. Divine clemency was not unmoved by their prayers, as what happened next showed.

They soon went on to the River Jordan, and they drank from and bathed in the holy waters. There, one of them, to wit, the great sinner Eskil, counting on the mercy of God, poured out his soul in prayer to the Lord and cried out, "Almighty and forgiving God, be merciful to me a sinner, and do not despise the soul of your servant, which you have delivered from the depths of evil and, after the shipwrecks of my many offenses, have mercifully brought into the port of penitence. Now Lord God, I greatly mistrust my frailty and my deeply rooted habit of sinning; I am very much afraid that if I return to my own land the enticements of material goods and the alluring opportunities for sin will draw me back into my old ways. Most kind Father, rich in mercy toward those who call upon you [Ps 85:5; Ps 144:18], if it seems good in your eyes and if you think it will advance the salvation of my soul, I beg you by your

---

[111] The place called Pater Noster is on the Mount of Olives. The "meager appearance" of the church dates the story to before its rebuilding by the crusaders (*c.* 1160), to which the story refers below. For slightly later accounts, see Theoderich, *Guide to the Holy Land* (*c.* 1172), 2nd ed., trans. Aubrey Stewart (New York: Italica Press, 1986), 43–44; and Joannes Phocas, *The Pilgrimage* (*c.* 1185), trans. Aubrey Stewart (London: Palestine Pilgrims' Text Society, 1896), 17.

ever-indulgent generosity to take me out of the bonds of this body now, after I have fulfilled the vow of pilgrimage, and command that I be taken from the filth of sins into the place of refreshment."[112] Once he had finished praying he knew immediately that his life was nearing its end and that Christ would not be slow to fulfill his desire. He received the sacraments and said farewell at the same time to his brother and the others who were present, and, professing his faith, without delay he gave up his soul to God.

O how incomparable is the mercifulness of God our Savior! In this sinner do you not see a living image of the prodigal son [Luke 15:12ff.] who spent his patrimony on harlots in vanity and luxury; whom his merciful father already saw afar off and to whom he, moved with tender compassion, soon restored the robe of innocence? He hastened so quickly to absolve the miserable wretch of the guilt pressing on his conscience that in fatherly love he indulged the sinner almost faster than the sinner was aware of being indulged. What else could it mean, that this thoroughly reprehensible sinner prayed like this on the threshold of penitence and so quickly obtained the answer to his request, if not that divine mercy flooded over him, removing the miserable rags of corruption and investing him in the glorious robe of immortality? He gave him the ring of divine love and put new shoes on his feet, that is, gave his affections the first purity which they had lost, and commanded all heaven to make holiday to celebrate the homecoming of the son that was lost.

When the venerable bishop saw the soul of his brother, for whose salvation he had been so concerned, go promptly and happily to God, he, too, longed to leave the earth and he prayed that he might die, crying, "Thank you, Lord Jesus Christ, for seeing my tears and hearing the prayers in which I have so often entreated you to receive the penitence of my brother. Now I beg you, most merciful Son of God, do not leave me long separated from him. Command that I be received with him into your peace that we may leave together and together, by your grace, may enter into your mercy." O the mercy of our Lord Jesus Christ, ever to be loved and

[112] For "place of refreshment," see above, EM 3.27, and below, 5.19.

embraced! Scarcely had he uttered this prayer which he poured out with the flaming ardor of faith than he heard the Savior's call. His strength suddenly left him, and he knew that he had reached the end of this transitory life. He used what little time remained to him to arrange his affairs, and he told his helpers to be sure to take his body, along with that of his brother, to the Church of the Pater Noster, which was mentioned earlier and for which God had inspired in him a special and holy love, and there to inter them. He then put into the hands of providence the people committed to his care, said farewell to those who were present, blessed them, and went gladly home to God. There is no doubt that God performed a great miracle in crowning the desires of the two companion pilgrims; once they had fulfilled the vow of pilgrimage they also ended their exile on earth; both left the world at the same place and on the same day, and they were buried together in the tomb they had chosen. This chapel I am talking about, although previously small and dilapidated, was torn down and, thanks to the alms the two brothers had left for the purpose, rebuilt in greater and more beautiful form, and in it their bodies rest in an honorable tomb to this day.

Eskil of blessed memory, the former archbishop of Denmark, was a close kinsman of these blessed pilgrims; he shared not only their noble birth but also their faith and devotion, and spurred by their example, he resolved to live as a pilgrim and as a pilgrim to die for the Lord Christ [Matt 19:29]. Laying down his lofty estate, in which he had been singularly illustrious in his country, he took the Cistercian habit and generously gave his great wealth to help the poor of Christ. He lived as a pauper and confrère in the midst of these poor men, and having spent his life in the most edifying possible observance, he was buried in the sanctuary of the church in front of the altar of the blessed Virgin Mother.[113] His memory, like those of other pious men who, drawn by the odor of the virtue of our blessed Father Saint Bernard and by the holiness of the Cistercian Order, will be a benediction [Sir 45:1] at Clairvaux

---

[113] *Monumenta s. Claraevallensis abbatiae* (PL 185:1555C).

from generation to generation. They preferred the shame of the Crucified to the riches of Egypt and left the false honors of the world to escape eternal punishments.[114]

CHAPTER TWENTY-NINE

*About the Noble Prince Gonario Who Became a Monk at Clairvaux*[115]

Gonario, a most noble prince, formerly judge and governor of the tetrarchy of Sardinia, went to pray at the tomb of Saint Martin of Tours. On his way home he called at Clairvaux, where Saint Bernard received him with loving-kindness and gave him considerable advice for the salvation of his soul. Gonario did not convert to monastic life, although he even had the privilege of seeing Bernard give sight to a blind man. As he was leaving, the Lord's man said, "I have prayed earnestly to the Lord for your conversion and as yet have not deserved to be heard. I am letting you go now, for I cannot keep you against your will. But you should realize that you are going to come back here from Sardinia." Gonario went home, but the parting words of the man of God worried him and the Spirit kept nudging his mind all the time, hinting that the prediction such a prophet had made about him could not be altogether in vain. A little while later, when he heard that the blessed had passed from this world to the Father [John 13:1], he was very much upset and deeply regretted he had not become a monk when he told him to. Soon he blazed with the fire that the Lord kindles in the hearts of his chosen ones

---

[114] "Riches of Egypt" is a common image with roots in Heb 11:26. See EM 4.26. See also Piesik, *Exordium Magnum Cisterciense*, 1:511n461, for several citations, including Bernard of Clairvaux, Sent 1.30 (SBOp 6/2:17–18; CF 55:130–31).

[115] Herbert of Clairvaux, LM 2.13 (PL 185:1324, 185:463A). In 1178, by which time Herbert was writing, Gonario was still alive. For additional information on Gonario, see above, EM 3.26; Poisson, *Le Grand Exorde*, 210n1; and Piesik, *Exordium Magnum Cisterciense*, 1:511n462.

and wills should burn [Luke 12:49], and he brooked no delay but put his eldest son at the head of his domain. At this point he himself was forty years old, with all his strength of body and spirit intact, so he left his island and abandoned the glory of the world and entered Clairvaux, poor and humble, and there he lived under the discipline of the Order to an advanced old age. He persevered until his death in the Lord's battles and rejoiced to have exchanged his earthly kingdom for the kingdom of heaven. He was buried with great respect near the door of the oratory at Clairvaux, on the north side. There, he lies with the poor ones of Christ, whose company he preferred to the pomp and riches of his lands, waiting for the revelation of the glorious liberty of the servants of God [Rom 8:21], for whom to serve is to reign [EM 3.5; EM 3.18].

## CHAPTER THIRTY

### *How the Venerable Abbot Simon Left His Abbey and Made His Profession at Clairvaux*[116]

The venerable Simon, former abbot of Chézy-sur-Marne, a not unknown monastery of the Order of black monks, loved blessed Bernard dearly and in everything seemed to depend on his advice and his decision. He had a great desire to lay down his pastoral charge and become a monk at Clairvaux.[117] But the holy Father Bernard knew the man's merits and his gifts and realized that he was very well matched and indispensable to his monastery, and as long as he lived in the flesh, he was never willing to approve his petition.

---

[116] Herbert of Clairvaux, LM 2.12 (PL 185:1324 and 185:461).

[117] Chézy Abbey is in the Diocese of Soissons. Cottineau, 1:767. On Simon of Chézy, see Bernard of Clairvaux, Epp 250.3, 263, 293 (SBOp 8:146, 172, 210–11; James, Epp 326.3, 336, 358, pp. 402, 416, 434); Peter of Celle, Letter 38 (PL 202:450–52); and Nicholas of Clairvaux, Letters 19 and 20 (PL 196:1617–18). According to Piesik (*Exordium Magnum Cisterciense*, 1.511n466), Simon died on 27 July 1163.

One day this abbot said to him, "Lord and Father, I am old and weak now; I get very tired and am beset by illness and feel myself becoming more and more feeble. If I am far away from Clairvaux when I die my sorrow will be inconsolable and without remedy. So you must let me come at once as I wish, for hastening death lets me delay no longer." The man of God said to him, "Stay where you are and do not fear; I assure you that you will die at Clairvaux." The man trusted the saint's words and stayed peacefully at his post for some years. After the death of the blessed man, now that there was no opposition and he could no longer bear the pricking of his desire, he laid down his office and went to Clairvaux. There, by the grace of God he lived on miraculously for seven more years, and in spite of his age and infirmity he gave us all a great example of fervor and devotion till he died.

## CHAPTER THIRTY-ONE

### *About One of the Senior Monks Who Saw Blessed Mary Presiding in the Monks' Chapter*[118]

Among the seniors at Clairvaux there was a devout and holy monk. One day, as we heard from his own lips, he saw in a vision the most blessed Virgin Mother presiding in chapter with resplendent appearance and dress. In chapter she assumed the place of the abbot and exercised his office. She had on her knee the blessed fruit of her womb [Luke 1:42], the Child who was born for us, and all the brothers were sitting in their assigned places around her. The senior who saw this was overcome with wonder and completely overjoyed at seeing that glorious Child, the most beautiful among the sons of men [Ps 44:3], and his holy Mother, but he could not keep his eyes fixed on their faces, for he was blinded by the brightness of

---

[118] Herbert of Clairvaux, LM 49 in some manuscripts, but not in the text of the PL.

their light. When the chapter was over and the monks were about to leave, the resplendent Virgin turned to the senior monk on her right and graciously gave him the kiss of peace; she held out the blessed fruit of her womb for him to see and embrace. Then she turned and did the same to the monk on her left, likewise kissing him and holding out Jesus, the joy of her heart, for him to contemplate. All the monks present, having exchanged the kiss of peace with the seniors, were filled with joy and praise at the presence of this great queen bearing in her arms the Savior of the world. The chapter was over and the vision vanished from the sight of the onlooker. But it left behind such an increase of piety in the old man who had seen it that the chapter house became for him a sanctuary of God and a gate of heaven. Whenever he passed that way he would bow toward the place he had seen the Mother of mercy with her adorable Son.

## Chapter Thirty-Two

### *About a Brother to Whom Our Lord Jesus Christ Appeared with Saint John the Evangelist*[119]

There was an observant and God-fearing brother [Acts 10:2] who burned with the desire for perfection and gave himself to holy meditations day and night. He felt a special affection for the most blessed John the Evangelist. He had him always in his thoughts and fed upon his writings. He applied himself to collecting from his works short passages which he stored away and used like pomegranate seeds to refresh the bed of his conscience with the scent of virtues against the stench of vices. On the Vigil of All Saints, while the community was celebrating Mass, he stood in his place in church, and with the pestle of watchful care he was grinding in the mortar of his heart the incense of sacred devotion in celebration of this great feast. As is the custom, the epistle for the day was

---

[119] Herbert of Clairvaux, LM 2.10 (PL 185:1321–22).

read from the Apocalypse, and he enjoyed the marvelous sweetness of the words. But when they came to the last verse, "Worthy is the Lamb that was slain to receive power and honor," and so on [Rev 5:12], his soul was entirely melted by the fire of divine love and pervaded with an outpouring of such happiness that he could scarcely contain himself for boundless joy. Quite beside himself in jubilation, he saw Christ with the eyes of the heart, as if he were present, and he embraced him with arms aglow with faith and devotion. For the rest of the Mass he stood there like that, as if filled to overflowing with heavenly food. When Mass was over he fell into a divine sleep [1 Sam 26:12], which was light but sweet with divine grace. The Lord Jesus Christ, who had flooded him with the joy described above, graciously revealed his presence to the sleeper with his beloved disciple John at his side. In the brother's hearing, he spoke with the apostle and said, "Long ago I showed you this vision of the Lamb not for yourself alone, who know my power and have experienced my love, but especially for others, so that they may love me as you do and at last know my glory, so they may have confidence in me." At these words the monk awoke; he was full of great joy [Matt 2:10] because of the grace of visitation and consolations and graces vouchsafed him and also because the Lord had given him clear proof of the truth of the Apocalypse, and especially for that, because he had been grieved at hearing that heretics undervalued this book and claimed that it was not the work of Saint John the apostle.

Some fifteen years later, this same brother, having become extremely concerned about his sins, sought in confession and daily examination of heart to appear before the face of the Lord. The Lord Jesus Christ appeared to him again with his disciple John. It was he who, in the brother's hearing, spoke first: "If anyone wants to obtain of God full pardon for his sins, he must weep continually and chastise himself in penitence." To which our Lord replied: "Whoever will come to me must desire this ardently." Later, on the day of the feast of the Nativity of Saint John,[120] he again saw in a

---

[120] John the Baptist, 24 June.

vision the Lord Jesus Christ with his glorious Mother going into a great palace which was none other than paradise. The door remained open after they had gone in. He was surprised and curious to know why the door was not closed when he heard these words: "This is the door of life, which is shut no more after Christ and his Mother entered it, and until the day of judgment it will remain open to all the faithful." Hearing this, he trembled and said to himself, "Then the door of paradise is open to me too. Yes, I will go into the marvelous tabernacle of God, even into the house of God [Ps 41:5]." He took a few steps to go in, and all his senses were at once filled with such happiness and sweetness that the thought of the mercy and justice of God alone [Ps 70:16] totally absorbed his senses. When he awoke from the enjoyment of these ineffable pleasures, he thought he was still among the delights of God's paradise. But soon he felt again the weight of this corruptible life and understood that the great happiness which had been given him as a foretaste to arouse his desires was not for his immediate enjoyment. These visions and revelations of this sort released that brother from the bed of laziness, torpor, and negligence and vehemently enkindled in him the flame of divine charity, and like Issachar whom Jacob compared to a lively goat [Gen 49:14-15], he put his shoulder unremittingly to the task of bearing the weight of penitence, and at last he deserved to possess the rest that he had foreseen.

CHAPTER THIRTY-THREE

*About a Brother Who at the Death of Another of the Brothers Saw the Lord Jesus Christ Come down from Heaven*[121]

There was in the brotherhood of Clairvaux a spiritually minded monk, strong in good conduct. In accordance with the word in the Apocalypse, "those whom I love I chasten" [Rev 3:19], the

---

[121] Herbert of Clairvaux, LM 2.6 (PL 185:1316–18).

Lord allowed him to suffer a very serious illness to purify him of the dross of sins [Isa 1:25]. But by the will of God, before he came to the critical day,[122] he went, by God's grace, into an ecstasy, and for the space of half the night he was beside himself, seeing and hearing many things which we do not propose to recount now. On this same night there died a young religious, a wonderfully gentle and patient monk, who had for many years suffered a cruel daily martyrdom from an incurable illness. As he was dying and drawing his last breath, he frequently groaned and cried out from the sharpness of the pain. When the sick monk we mentioned heard his cries, he said to himself, "'These lamentations will soon be turned into songs' [Ps 29:12], and this extremity of suffering will soon give place to eternal joy [Prov 14:13]." As he was thinking this and similar thoughts, it was as if someone invisible came and stood for a long time by his bed. At the dying brother's every groan he experienced a marvelous and never-before-experienced fragrance and taste in his nostrils and mouth. He was experiencing in his senses some kind of heavenly virtue, and it penetrated delicately to the depths of his being. When he was regenerated by this marvelous unction and somehow entirely renewed, suddenly he saw the heavens open and through this opening he looked, as it were, into the third heaven [2 Cor 12:2]. At that moment he heard a voice from on high, crying, "Let all the earth be quiet [Hab 2:20] and all evil flee; the Christ comes." At this hour there appeared to him the Lord Jesus Christ, the consoler of the poor and humble, coming down from heaven and filling the whole house with his blessing. The brother who was granted this revelation was so imbued with joy and grace that he believed himself to be in heaven, and in the joy of his heart he cried out, "O Lord our God, surely this is that life eternal that you promised us. Now, if it is permitted, let me also see with my eyes and possess forever what I am experiencing with my senses, and my joy will be full and perfect." Now the moment of the death of the young monk was at hand, and the board was sounded. The brothers came together to commend to the Lord his

---

[122] Regarding the phrase "the critical day" (the day of his death; *ad diem creticum*), see Grießer, EM, 221n7, who reports that the usage is found in Isidore.

soul [EO 94.2], which was soon to be delivered from the body of this death [Rom 7:24]. His groans and pain ended and gave place to the rest of eternal happiness. And we believe and are quite sure that our Lord Jesus Christ who had deigned to visit his servant upon earth also led him into paradise. As his body was being put into the grave, another brother of good observance told me that he himself saw a sort of bier rise from the tomb and go up in the air. The other sick monk by the mercy of God was restored to health and gave thanks to God that he had been privileged, for his own consolation, to see and hear all this at the death of his brother. The sweetness of the blessing which, like hidden manna [Rev 2:17], he had experienced as an extraordinary scent or uncommonly sweet taste remained with him for many years, not all the time, but very often and very fully, just as the kind and gentle Spirit who blows whenever and wherever he wills [John 3:8] chose to give it to his poor servant. He experienced it not only in sleep or in ecstasies, when his senses were beside themselves or suspended, as sometimes happens during serious illness, but also sensed that grace of divine sweetness when he was awake and active, praying, chanting psalms, or reading or doing something else. Lord, in your mercy, how freely and richly you give to all, both great and small, who call upon you and seek you [Ps 144:18]! You hide the ineffable taste of eternal delights from the great and wise and reveal them to your little ones [Luke 10:21] who regard the things of the world as dung [Phil 3:8], so that one day they may be rewarded in your sweetness.

## Chapter Thirty-Four

### How the Man of God Boso
### Heard the Angels Singing at the Death of Another Brother[123]

We think it unfitting to pass over in silence the venerable Boso, a man equally distinguished by birth and conduct. He was one of

---

[123] Herbert, LM 1.30 (PL 185:1303).

the first sons that the most blessed Bernard fathered in Christ [1 Cor 4:15] by the Gospel, and by his noble religious observance he showed that he had been suckled at the breasts of kings [Isa 60:16] and been formed from his early years in the rudiments of our chaste discipline. He was a patient man, a son of peace, so kind and gentle with everyone that not one of us ever saw him troubled or angry. In adversity and prosperity alike his spirit remained tranquil and his faith unmoved. When he became so old and frail that he could scarcely walk even with a stick, he would never rest or give in to his body but tried still to carry out various hard labors. While we were once talking privately with this venerable brother and exchanging stories about the pious and enviable death of some of the brothers which we had often seen, he declared to me that at the demise of a certain observant brother, he heard choirs of blessed spirits singing sweet melodies in the air and taking away the soul of the departed with joy to the rest of eternal blessedness. The higher they ascended the more muted their voices became, and when at last they entered heaven he could no longer hear them. When this blessed old man himself was called by God and gave up his spirit as if falling asleep in peace [Ps 4:9], he glowed with such serenity and his face by some wonderful alteration shone with such glory that at that moment we had no doubt whatever that the blessed spirits of the Lord were present or that he had gazed upon the face of our God. To this the devotion of all those present bears witness. We had never seen a face so transformed with light in anyone dying or dead. We all gave thanks to God and quickly carried out the funeral rites, for by this wondrous sign we were sure that he was in glory.

# Book Four

# More on the Monks of Clairvaux

CHAPTER ONE

## *About the Monk Alquirin of Holy Memory,*
## *Whom the Lord Jesus Visited as He Was Dying*[1]

There lived in the community of Clairvaux a monk named Alquirin whose monastic profession and way of life were in complete accord. He was a religious and spiritual man, restrained in his eating, humble in his clothing, and rigorous in chastising his body. He was so circumspect and temperate in matters concerning the body that he refused all pleasure and vanity and even used necessities very sparingly, although an opportunity often prompted him to exceed the established limit. He was skilled in the art of medicine, and although nobles and great men of that region were always asking his help and drawing him, unwilling and reticent, toward many places, yet he was always more solicitous of the poor and needy [Ps 40:2] and would go to any lengths to cure them. Not only did he treat their sicknesses and wounds, but he tended with his own hands the putrid flesh and ulcerated limbs of the suffering with such care that one would have thought he was caring for the wounds of Christ. And this really was so. He did everything for Christ, and Christ received everything he did as being done for him, so that at the end he could say to him what was said of those who do works of mercy: "I was sick and you visited me" [Matt 25:36]. Thus the Lord often visited his servant with secret consolations and urged him on in his ministry of healing in a marvelous way. Once, then, he had a vision of this sort at Clairvaux.

First of all, Alquirin heard a voice saying from heaven, "Look! Christ is coming [Matt 25:6]! Get up and run out to meet the Savior."[2] As everyone rushed out to see him, Alquirin also ran out and stood by the door of the cloister, through which he hoped he would arrive. When the Lord came in, he went up and worshiped

---

[1] Herbert of Clairvaux, LM 3.15 (PL 185:1366–68).
[2] Invitatory verse at Vigils on the first Sunday of Advent in the Cistercian Antiphonary; see *Le Grande Exorde*, 219n10.

him, begging to receive the blessing and mercy from the God of his salvation [Ps 23:5].[3] Having done this, he gazed more attentively at the Lord and felt his sufferings with a deep sense of piety. Christ seemed to him to be suffering and weak, transfixed with nails and pierced with a spear, as if he had just been taken down from the cross and blood was flowing freely from recent wounds. The Lord was pressing white linen cloths like corporals to his wounds and then, when they were soaked in blood, letting them fall to the ground. Gathering them up with great veneration and kissing them with much devotion, this brother kept them hidden in his breast as if they were a pledge of the redemption of his soul.

Alquirin was frequently strengthened by visions like this from the Lord and continued to do good to everyone, especially pilgrims and the ailing poor. He was so stern in doing his penance and he chastened his flesh so strictly, as is apparent from this, that while he was lavishing the work of caring lovingly on everyone else, he excepted only himself from such care. Even when he was in bad health and physically frail, he would never agree to take any medicine for his body but committed himself wholly to God, for he cares for us [1 Pet 5:7]. He knew for certain that the soul is strengthened by infirmities in the body [2 Cor 12:9] and that a monk who is so anxious to hold onto the little consolations of the flesh that he cannot taste and see how gracious the Lord is [Ps 33:9] cannot receive spiritual consolations from the Lord.

Having spent his life in this praiseworthy manner, when the time came for him to receive eternal mercy for his labors and his works of holy piety, he fell ill and neared his end. The venerable Abbot Pons, whom we mentioned earlier,[4] came to visit him and asked him how he was and what he was doing. He replied, "I am well, dearest Father; all is very well with me because I am going to my Lord." Pons asked him, "But are you not suffering in body, and do you not fear the anguish of death?" Alquirin replied, "I look upon

---

[3] An allusion to the sixth response from the Vigils of Palm Sunday in the Cistercian Antiphonary; *Le Grande Exorde*, 219n11.

[4] EM 2.24, 25, 26. The clause was added by Conrad. Pons was abbot of Clairvaux from 1165 to 1170.

it all with tranquility and joy, because I have received beforehand from the Lord the blessings of a sweetness [Ps 20:4] that has taken all sorrow from my heart and nearly all pain from my body." Then the abbot asked him, "I beg you, my dear brother, for the love of God and for our edification, tell us anything that God has revealed to you." To which he replied, "Just now, before you came in, the Lord Jesus appeared to me, miserable and unworthy though I am, and he looked at me with a kind and serene expression and showed me the marks of his most blessed passion, saying, 'Look, your sins are taken away from before my face. Come confidently, then, come and see, and kiss my wounds which you have loved so much and tended so often.' I was so strengthened by this promise that now I am not afraid to die, because of the hope laid up in my heart [Job 19:27]. And know that tomorrow night, which is the Vigil of the blessed Martin, I will be passing over when, at the very hour the work of God is being celebrated in church." He died on the very night at the very hour he had foretold, and we are very sure that he now rests from his labors [Rev 14:13], and like a dove whiter than snow, he dwells in the cleft of the rock [Song 2:14; Jer 48:28], that is, he embraces and adores the most holy wounds of our Lord Christ, who is God over all, blessed throughout the ages. Amen.

## CHAPTER TWO

### *About a Brother with a Wondrous Gift of Compunction, Whom the Lord Consoled Magnificently*[5]

There was in the same monastery a brother who had greatly offended God by his sins and went about all day long gloomy, anxious, and trembling [Ps 37:7], refusing to stop weeping and lamenting, for he knew with certainty that a confession of the mouth without contrition of heart will not deserve pardon before the judgment of

---

[5] Herbert of Clairvaux, LM 3.16–18 (PL 185:1368–69).

God. Although the tome of the fear of God, in which are written lamentations and woe [Ezek 2:9], had long given him heartburn in the stomach of his conscience, at length by God's grace the parchment of the love of God, on which is written a song, became in the devotion of his heart like a sweet honey [Ezek 3:3]. He began already to have a foretaste of the firstfruits of his labor and to learn by experience that God does not despise the sacrifice of a humble heart and a contrite spirit [Ps 50:19].

While he was still in the great bitterness we spoke about earlier, on a certain night he had a vision of the Lord Jesus Christ dressed, as it were, in priestly vestments, celebrating Mass. Each time he turned to face the people during the rite of the sacrifice, taking the chalice from the altar in his hands, he showed it to all those who were present. And in this chalice was nothing other than the many tears that Mary Magdalene shed as, weeping and repenting, she washed his feet [Luke 7:38] in the house of Simon.[6] When the aforesaid brother, standing at the feet of the Lord, saw this he said to him, with hesitation, "I ask you, Lord, why do you show us this chalice and the tears that are in it?" And the Lord replied, "So that everyone may see how pleasing to me contrition of heart and grief of penitence are; as an example of penitence I have saved the tears of the sinner who, weeping and repenting, washed my feet." The more the brother learned how acceptable the tears of repentance are to the divine majesty, the more he was stirred and inflamed in his spirit to seek nothing in reading, chanting the psalms, and meditating other than to train his soul in weeping and to awaken in himself the grace of compunction. For he knew that the kingdom of heaven suffers violence and the violent take it by storm.[7] Yet the Lord added still more to console his servant who was so

---

[6] Tubach, 927, recalls a story in which Christ himself celebrates a Mass with a chalice of Mary Magdalene's tears; see Tubach, 4719. For devotion to Saint Mary Magdalene as the penitent sinner, see *The Prayers and Meditations of Saint Anselm*, trans. Benedicta Ward (New York: Penguin Books, 1979), 201–6.

[7] Bernard of Clairvaux also used this image from Matt 11:12. See Ded 5.2 (SBOp 5:389; SBS 2:418); Div 25.2 (SBOp 6/1:188); and SC 27.11 (SBOp 1:190; CF 7:84).

constantly tormented for his sins in the skillet of discipline.[8] In a night vision the brother saw that he was in an incredibly deep lake, turbulent and perilous. Although he had no hope of escaping it, suddenly the Lord Jesus Christ was there, a helper in due time, walking barefoot upon the waters [Ps 9:10; Matt 14:25]. He came to him and lifted him out of the waters and carried him in his arms to a lovely flower-strewn meadow. When the brother realized the great grace he had received, he fell at the feet of the Lord Jesus; transported with immense joy and with an insatiable desire of devotion he held the dear feet of the Savior and covered them with kisses. When he awoke, he thought deeply about the meaning of the vision; he interpreted the lake as the depths of sin in which he had been immersed, the arms of grace which had so gently lifted him as forgiveness, and the flowery field into which he had been carried as the freshness of eternal rest. And for this reason with his whole being he turned toward the Lord as if his previous labors had been petty, and he pressed forward in fasts, vigils, and continual prayer, beseeching the Lord with tears and unspeakable groans [Rom 8:26], that just as the breadth of his mercy had been shown to him in advance in the vision, so by the action of grace he might deserve to experience it in reality, and he asked him for other signs of divine goodness.

Truly the Lord distributes and moderates all virtues, and he determined that the brother who was unremittingly burdened with sorrow and daily ate the bread of affliction [Ps 126:2] should be consoled. One night the brother, filled with the longings we have described, went to Vigils. During the psalmody and prayers he was suddenly taken up in an ecstasy of the mind [Acts 10:10], and he saw a hand which lightly and gently in the twinkling of an eye [1 Cor 15:52] brought a razor close to his head, and without his feeling it the hand shaved his beard, his neck, and his pate, showing by this sign the goodness of divine indulgence to this man of sighs and tears. A few hairs were left on his forehead, I think to signify

---

[8] For more on the various senses of the word "discipline," see Henri de Lubac, *Medieval Exegesis*, vol. 1, trans. Mark Sebanc (Grand Rapids: Eerdmans, 1998), 15–24.

the daily negligences that are inevitable in this life. Enlightened by these and other consolations, the brother learned to relax in the hope of forgiveness, to thank God for the benefits he received, and to sigh for still greater. O how happy is the humility of the penitent! How blessed the hope of those who repent perfectly of their sins! How powerful they are before the All-powerful! How easily they defeat the invincible! How quickly they turn the tremendous Judge into an utterly tender Father! Their purity in eternity will be the greater insofar as they have plunged the more deeply into the Jordan [2 Kgs 5:14] to wash away the leprosy of their sins.

CHAPTER THREE

*About a Monk Who Experienced a Sweet Taste in the Eucharist*[9]

A certain brother who was fervent and careful in the observances of holy religion came one Sunday morning, according to the customs of the Order [EO 66.2], to receive the Body and Blood of Christ. It seemed to him that for the rest of the day he held in his mouth a very sweet taste like honey. On the following Sunday he again received the Eucharist and experienced a similar grace for three days. On the third Sunday, after he had yet again received the divine sustenance, he was allowed to experience the privilege of that sweetness for an entire week. From then on, he experienced the sweetness of the bread of life [John 6:35] many times, sometimes quite rarely, sometimes quite frequently, as the Holy Spirit, the giver of grace, deigned to give it to his poor servant.

It happened one day, however, that he rebuked one of his friends for his fault with immoderate and unjustified invective, and he did not take the trouble before going to receive the sacrament of the

---

[9] Herbert of Clairvaux, LM 1.22 (PL 185:1298–99), except for the final paragraph, which is Conrad's. See also Caesarius of Heisterbach, *Dialogus miraculorum* 9.39 (Strange 2:195; S-Bland 2:142); and Tubach, 2599, who notes related stories in *Dialogus miraculorum* 7.49 and 9.46; as well as other sources.

altar to heal his brother's wounded conscience with an apology. So it came about that, having presumed to receive the sacrament of peace without having made peace with his brother [Matt 5:23-24], he was appalled to find his mouth filled with an acrid bitterness beyond that of gall and wormwood [Isa 38:17] instead of with the honey of spiritual sweetness which he had grown used to receiving and being refreshed by. He immediately remembered his accusations and did penance and humbly made amends for his sin of correcting more with invective than discernment. And afterward he was careful to observe the word of the Apostle, "You who are spiritual, give instruction in a spirit of gentleness" [Gal 6:1]. Pay heed to this story, I beg, any of you who are zealous for our Order, any who burn with zeal for justice. Pay heed, I say, and learn to be more careful that a quite proper correction not become a weapon of fury and a cup of correction intended to help a brother not become through lack of discretion the ruination of both oneself and others. For when correction is given in anger, it tears apart the one who gives it, vexes those it was meant to help, and only makes them find excuses to hide any sins in the future [Ps 140:4].

## Chapter Four

### *About a Monk Who Withstood the Assaults of Many Demons and Deserved to See the Lord Jesus*[10]

In order to rebuke laziness and stir up our devotion, let us mention one of the soldiers of Christ in our midst who sweated under the yoke of monastic discipline from adolescence to an advanced old age in the monastery at Clairvaux. He countered so many and such fierce assaults of the demons that, had the Spirit not helped his infirmity, flesh and blood [Matt 16:17] could not have borne the malice of such ghostly shades. He served the Lord with all holiness and righteousness and preserved from his mother's womb an undefiled

---

[10] Herbert of Clairvaux, LM 1.19 (PL 185:1294–96).

body and soul by God's great gift. And to him as a witness to his double purity, the Lord deigned to reveal many heavenly mysteries. Once when Vigils had been especially long and he was praying alone in some private place, suddenly the hair on his skin stood up [Job 4:15], and he began to be terrified more than usual by a fear of the night. And a crowd of demons rushed in gangs through the door and, piling on top of one another, filled the room, making such an uproar that they distracted him from his prayer. As soon as he became aware of them, he quickly armed himself with the sign of the cross, began praying with frequent prostrations, reciting over and over again the salutation of the blessed Virgin, and so quickly routed the crowds of demons from his place of prayer. The next night when he was again praying in that same place of prayer, again the infernal powers rushed on him with all their fury, pounding like a battering ram against the stone wall of the room with such violent blows that the whole building shook. When the man of God raised his eyes to the large open window in the wall, he saw in it a demon standing with wings like a griffin or a vulture, threatening him with menacing gestures as if it was about to strike and devour him. At seeing it, he recognized this fiendish trick, and calling upon the name of the Savior, he countered it with the sign of the cross and put the apparition to flight.

Many times he suffered this kind of attack, but as an untiring wrestler he did not cease to face the evil spirits and battle against them [Eph 6:12], giving neither quarter nor treaty. He received from the Lord a special grace granted to few human beings: in full daylight he could see, with his bodily eyes, crowds of demons going here and there in the air, in such swarms that he could not count them. They used to appear in many forms, but they used one form, or rather deformity, quite frequently: in the general outlines of their monstrous bodies, they seemed to be human beings, gigantic in stature, Ethiopians in color, as agile as snakes, as fierce as lions, having great swollen heads, protruding stomachs, bodies thickset and hunched, with lanky, skinny necks and very long arms and legs.[11] When any of them paused in the air, his limbs could be

---

[11] Such descriptions of demons have a long history; see note in EM 3.22.

seen clearly. But when they were darting hither and yon, nothing of them could be made out except ghostly shadows and whirling clusters. It was on clear days when the sun was shining at full strength that he could see these visions most clearly and frequently.

Blessed Augustine, the great Doctor of the Church, once appeared in a vision to this venerable man and led him through countless places of punishment and even to the threshold of the pit of Gehenna. He looked into it from above with trembling limbs and pounding heart, and he saw with intolerable panic the burning pit of hell, full of horrible sounds and the groans of the wretches who in that devouring fire live forever an accursed life that is the most bitter death, a death the worst of all deaths, for it can never die.[12] He drew back and was led from the lake of horror and darkness into the regions of joy and bliss, where the saint showed him the thrones of light and the blessed mansions of souls, where after the death of their bodies they live in the incorruptible life of Christ's peace, which surpasses all understanding [Phil 4:7]. They rest in the greatest happiness, awaiting the regeneration of their bodies. Then Saint Augustine said to the monk, "Look, you have seen the ultimate end of evil and of good.[13] Choose what is good in your eyes! If you decide to hold to the way of righteousness which is fully described in my books, you will receive your portion with these saints in the land of the living [Ps 141:6]; but if you choose to go after your own lusts, you will be numbered [Isa 65:12] with those you have seen in this terrible state, who were thrown into that pit of oblivion by the justice of God." When the vision was over and the man came to himself, he trembled all over and was deeply horrified, terrified by a double fear: that he would lose the glory of the elect and that he would incur the punishment of the reprobate. From then onward he began to love more dearly the most blessed doctor Augustine and to read his works more frequently.

---

[12] See Augustine, *De catechizandis rudibus* 25.47 (CCSL 46:170), translated in *Christianity in Late Antiquity: A Reader*, ed. Bart D. Ehrman and A. S. Jacobs (New York: Oxford University Press, 2004), 119.

[13] Augustine, *City of God* 9.4.

Once it happened that he fell ill at Noirlac, an abbey of the Cistercian Order in the province of Bourges.[14] At the time, another brother, a man of good monastic observance, was deathly ill. He had already been laid on the floor when he breathed his last, as it happened, while the infirmarians were absent. The aforementioned brother, who was lying there very ill on his bed, by a revelation from the Lord, very clearly saw with his bodily eyes the soul of the brother going forth slowly from his body like a trail of smoke rising from a censer. When it had entirely come out, it drew itself into a ball and stood over the corpse, suspended in the air about four or five cubits up.[15] It appeared like a cloud, transparent but visible, and diffused to about the measure of a bushel. It remained there motionless until, fortified by the prayers of the brothers and the commendation of the priests, it deserved to receive a guide for its dangerous and uncharted journey. When the brother saw this, he yelled as loudly as he could for the infirmarians, who ran in and sounded the board of the dead, calling the brothers together for the last rites. Once the community had gathered, and with cross and holy water the sacramental prayers of commendation were begun [EO 94.4-59], the soul went forth, as if already confident, into the air, and the cloud which he had seen evaporated.

Another time, this man of God was present on Sunday at the divine service in a certain parish church. As the offerings were presented and the bread and the water mixed with wine were placed on the holy table, the Lord Jesus suddenly appeared to him, standing above the altar in the form of a very tiny infant, beautiful beyond the sons of men [Ps 44:3], and he saw him so clearly and so long that the vision continued almost until the end of the holy sacrifice.[16] Now the priest of that place, who was celebrating Mass,

---

[14] Also known as *Domus Dei* and *Niger lacus*, Noirlac was founded in 1136 as a daughter house of Clairvaux. Cf. EM 3.10 about Robert, abbot of Noirlac.

[15] A cubit is the distance between the tip of the middle finger and the elbow, roughly sixteen to twenty inches; the spirit in the passage was thus six to ten feet above the brother's body.

[16] There is a precedent for this story in fourth-century monastic texts. See *The Desert Fathers: Sayings of the Early Christian Monks*, trans. Benedicta Ward (New York: Penguin Books, 2003), 186–87.

was a man of dishonest life and profligate. Just as long as this priest had his back to the altar, whether receiving the offerings of the faithful or preaching a sermon to the people, as is the custom on a feast day, the holy child stood in front of the chalice. But whenever the priest turned to face the sacrament, the holy child shrank away and hid from him behind the chalice, as if abhorring the breath of an impure priest. When the brother saw this, he was pierced by compunction and wept so copiously that his flood of tears impeded the acuity of his eyes from seeing clearly our dearest Redeemer. When the revelation was over, he glorified God who had deigned to show this to him. And so he knew that a lack of merit certainly does not create an infraction in the sacrifice of the Mass, because the efficacy of the sacrament depends not on the virtue of the celebrant but on the institution and grace of the Savior.[17]

CHAPTER FIVE

*How the Lord Jesus Christ Appeared to an Old Monk*
*as He Was Keeping Vigil on Good Friday*[18]

There was a monk of the same monastery, advanced equally in age and in religious observance, who was once sitting in the cloister on Good Friday holding a book in front of him. The Lord Jesus Christ appeared to him with his hands and feet stretched on the cross as if he was being crucified at that very moment. This most happy vision, although very brief and barely momentary, was so clear and telling for the monk that he could never afterward avert from his heart the devout remembrance of what he had seen. For just as one who adds oil to a flaming fire makes the whole thing

---

[17] For Mass celebrated by another sinful priest, see Caesarius of Heisterbach, *Dialogus miraculorum* 2.5 (Strange 1:64–67; S-Bland 1:70–73). See also, Augustine, *On Baptism, against the Donatists* 4.12-19 in *A Select Library of the Nicene and Post-Nicene Fathers*, First Series, vol. 14 (Grand Rapids: Eerdmans, [1887] 1989), 455.

[18] Herbert of Clairvaux LM 1.23 (PL 185:1299).

flare up, so the grace of this revelation set ablaze the inmost heart of this old man [Ps 83:6], long accustomed to a holy monastic life, so it burned still more ardently and perfectly. He kept it burning in his heart and went from virtue to virtue [Ps 83:8] in our Order for some forty years, if I am not mistaken. Then he laid aside the weight of corruptible flesh and he deserved to see, no longer in the weakness of the flesh as before, but in the glory of his majesty, the God of gods in Zion [Ps 83:8].

## Chapter Six

### *How the Merciful Lord Warned and Converted a Certain Clerk*[19]

How ineffable is God and how unutterable are his works! Who can fitly utter how wonderful he is in his saints [Ps 67:36] and how, by marvelous and diverse ways, he calls those whom he has foreknown and predestined from all eternity to be conformed to the image of his Son [Rom 8:29]? By the power of virtue he draws even those who seem to be completely absorbed by their sins in a mass of perdition into the brightness of the kingdom of his dear Son [Col 1:13]. Within this number there was a young clerk, rich and noble and given over to the downward trend of this world, whom he mercifully snatched from the maw of pleasure by paternal chastisement and taught not to put his hopes in uncertain riches or to follow the lustful desires of youth but to come to the true riches of eternal life by the hard labors of penance.

This pleasure-loving young man refused to accept that festal days were instituted for the clergy by the holy fathers so they might be still and know that the Lord is indeed their God [Ps 45:11], not so they might spend their time at chess or dicing or some other diabolical nonsense.[20] He frequently used to squander the day with

---

[19] Herbert of Clairvaux, LM 1.12 (PL 185:1290–91).

[20] See Bernard of Clairvaux, Tpl 4.7 (SBOp 3:220; CF 19:139). On the connection of chess with gambling, see H. J. R. Murray, *A History of Chess* (Oxford:

his contemporaries and associates in various games and spectacles. One day, when a number of them were meeting at some house for merrymaking, to waste the day, as usual, in watching theatrical displays and entertainments, this aforesaid young man joined them to pasture his flocks [Song 1:7] on this spectacle of wasted effort. Among them were some gamblers throwing dice, and in order to see better he lay down flat on a table sitting there. And suddenly it was as if an invisible hand was holding a whip above him and beating him for a long time, raining blows on his head, his shoulders, and his entire back. He lay still, not knowing what to do or where to turn. He wanted to cry out and complain about the agony and pain of it, but for shame he did not dare in front of so many people, lest they should think him mad; so he bore the pain of the blows without saying a word. When he came to himself and had, as it were, imminent death still in view, he accused himself in the sight of the Lord and groaned in the bitterness of his soul [Job 10:1], crying, "Oh, my Lord God, now my sins have found me out and I am dying. I will go to hell in sorrow, lacking the fruit of penance [Matt 3:8; Luke 3:8]. Father of mercies, my Lord God, if you will but look upon the affliction and anguish of this sinner and mercifully allow me, unworthy though I am, to escape this present danger, I promise, I vow, I pledge that I will not be ungrateful for your benefits but will give up all the despicable things of this world to become your servant forever." This and similar things he said in his heart to the Lord, and he seemed to hear a voice saying to him, "If you will go to Clairvaux and enter monastic life, you will be saved in both your soul and your body." Relieved by the voice and knowing he was being visited by the Lord, he immediately replied, "I give myself to serve God and the monastery of Clairvaux." As he was turning this over in his mind, the beating ceased and his pain vanished. He recognized the mercy that had been shown to him and did not find pleasure in flesh and blood [Gal 1:16], and if he had had a means of transportation at hand he would have brooked

---

Oxford University Press, 1913), 652. *Le Grande Exorde*, 228n3, also refers to J.-M. Mehl, *Les Jeux au royaume de France du XIIIe au début du XVIe siècle* (Paris: Fayard, 1990), 320–73.

not a moment's delay in fulfilling his vow. He did not yield to the impulse to go home and consult his parents and friends, to dispose of his house and savings, pay his debts, deal with his fields and property. He broke rather than renounced all these bonds, counting them all as dung for Christ's sake [Phil 3:8], and he procured a horse that very day and rode away the next morning at sunrise, leaving the world as if fleeing the face of a lion, to attain solitude. He came with a very fervent desire to the solitude of Clairvaux, which was formerly called the valley of wormwood, and, having explained to the brothers the manner and way of his conversion,[21] was received with great rejoicing and love, for they thought that because of these signs his life and conduct would be pleasing to the Lord. Having been received and tested, and, by God's gift, found faithful, he put off the old man with his works and put on the new man which is created in accordance with God in righteousness and true holiness [Col 3:10]. Until the end of his life he gave himself with such generosity to the hard work of the Cistercian Order that it was perfectly apparent to all those who saw his most holy way of life that that first call to monastic conversion had truly come from him who rebukes and chastises [Rev 3:19] those he loves and like a loving father scourges all the sons whom he receives [Heb 12:6].

## CHAPTER SEVEN

### *How Blessed Bernard Often Appeared to a Novice*[22]

There was a brother in the order of canons regular who was eager to make progress spiritually and who strove for the better gifts [1 Cor 12:31]. With great desire he desired [Luke 22:15] to put himself

---

[21] The Latin here contains a play on the name of Clairvaux, *Claraevallis* (clear valley), and the *vallis absinthialis* (valley of wormwood, absinth); see note above in EM Prol. See also William of Saint Thierry's reference to the "valley of wormwood" in Vita Bern 1.5.25 (PL 185:241D).

[22] Herbert of Clairvaux, LM 2.21 (PL 185:1329–31).

under the direction of blessed Bernard and join the community at Clairvaux, but he was unable to do so during the lifetime of the holy father. The news of the precious death [Ps 115:15] of the great abbot upset him very much and he called himself an unworthy wretch because he had not put his desires into action sooner. A few days later the venerable father appeared to him in a vision, girded like someone who works hard laboring in a very broad field covered with countless sheaves of wheat. A great many of these he had gathered into a large heap, and he was doggedly attempting to gather in any stray ears, which were still more numerous, and stack them up. When the canon saw this, he understood at once that the great heap was a symbol of the multitude of brothers whom the great preacher had gathered to the Lord Christ while he lived in the flesh and that the innumerable remainder was the ones he would now lead to the grace of salvation by his example and merits. He was very glad at this and did not despair of being one of the latter. He went to Clairvaux as quickly as he could and begged them to admit him to the novices' quarters.[23]

While he was still a novice there, he thought about the memory of the holy man ceaselessly and tirelessly, and on a certain Sunday near the end of Vigils, when he was tired and afflicted in many ways, he fell asleep. And the very reverend father whom he loved so much appeared to him, speaking kindly and advising him to direct his thoughts continuously to God with a daily outpouring of tears. If he did this, he could confidently count on divine mercy and the visitation. When he had said this he went back to his tomb, which is situated in front of the altar of the Blessed Virgin Mother. The brother had seen all this so clearly that he did not know if he was asleep or awake. When he had opened his eyes and was thinking with pleasant recall about the advice of his loving father, suddenly Bernard appeared to him, now fully awake, and presented himself to be seen with his physical eyes. Bernard was standing so closely beside him that he could easily take him by the hand and looked hard at him, as if trying to discover whether the brother was asleep

---

[23] The Latin for novices' quarters is *probatorium*. See RB 58.1–5 for an example of novices' quarters and the novitiate as a time of probation.

or awake, like those who are charged during Vigils with waking up drowsy brothers. The novice, stupefied and amazed, gazed at him, and at once the visitor vanished and, marvelous to relate, seemed to sink almost palpably into his very being. From that time on, the novice burned more ardently with love for God and that blessed man, and daily in his new life he increased in joy and exultation of spirit.

Finally, the following night, while the brother was again at Vigils, he experienced the grace of a divine visitation greater than any he had ever before known, and he attributed this happiness to the merits of the saint whom he loved. For many days afterward, whenever he recalled this abundant sweetness [Ps 144:7], he would shed gentle and loving tears which he seemed incapable of restraining by day or night. After he had completed the year of his probation, he received the holy habit with great devotion, and he preserved the garment of innocence with which he was invested not so much externally as internally by unabated prayer and solicitude. He set himself to follow in the footsteps of the venerable father whom he singularly loved, studying him unwaveringly. He completed his life in faithful perseverance, and, we are sure, he is united in heaven with the one whose companionship on earth he desired ardently and sought vigilantly.

## CHAPTER EIGHT

### *About a Monk to Whom the Lord Jesus Christ Appeared Twice*[24]

In the same monastery there was another novice brother who set out to seek the Lord with his whole heart. It was his custom to pray often with his hands joined or stretched out when he could do so without inconvenience. Now one night at the beginning of Vigils he was in choir and he closed his eyes and stretched out his

---

[24] Herbert of Clairvaux, LM 2.8 (PL 185:1318).

hands toward God, when suddenly the Lord Jesus Christ was there beside him, speaking to him and saying, "Stretch out your hands to me." At hearing these words the brother opened his eyes and was greatly astonished, not easily able to discern whether he had been asleep or awake when he heard the words. From hearing this he increased in fervor and devotion and was always thereafter careful to maintain this same way of praying. A little while later, when he had been professed as a monk, he was standing in a corner of the church [RB 52:4], praying secretly with mind intent and hands joined together, as was his custom, and suddenly he was in the Spirit. The Lord Jesus Christ stood before him, and opening and stretching out his hands, he took his hands between his own, as if admitting him to profession.[25] Afterward, when the man came to himself, he rejoiced with a very great joy. He understood by this happy experience that God was present everywhere, as our holy legislator Benedict taught [RB 19.1], and especially when we are at the work of God, whether at prayers or chanting psalms.

## CHAPTER NINE

*How Brother Ansulph Saw the Lord Jesus Hanging on the Cross*[26]

A man of great devotion and gifted with great grace, Ansulph by name, when he was a novice at Clairvaux, saw appearing to him in a vision the Lord Jesus Christ hanging on the cross. It seemed to him that on either side of the Lord were the two other novices who were in the novitiate with him, and he fell down in adoration and

[25] See RB 58. This traditional gesture made by abbot and postulant at the time of profession was similar to the gestures made during an oath of fealty.

[26] Herbert of Clairvaux, LM 2.2 (PL 185:1314). For other stories that involve visions of the crucified Christ, see Caesarius of Heisterbach, *Dialogus Miraculorum* 8.10, 17, 18, 20, *Die Fragmente der Libri VIII miraculorum des Caesarius von Heisterbach*, ed. A. Meister (Rome, 1901), no. 2.4, pp. 71–72; and Tubach, 998, 1179, 1235.

in humblest prayer begged the Lord to have mercy upon him and his companions. The good Lord, moved by mercy, looked on him kindly and blessed him and, with him, one of the aforesaid novices. Observing that the other had not been given the same benediction, the novice who was seeing this was moved with brotherly love and began to entreat the Lord that he not be excluded from the generosity of God's blessing. The Lord replied that he would never be blessed but rather belonged to the number of the damned. At these words the novice awoke, glad that he and his companion had been allowed to receive the blessing of the Lord but wondering what would happen to the one against whom he had heard such a grievous sentence. Three days later the third neophyte broke away from this band of three and lived up to his unhappy name—for he was called Malgerus[27]—by leaving the Order and returning to the vomit of secular life [2 Pet 2:22] and so became a vile apostate. The remaining two, who had been confirmed by the Lord's blessing, by his mercy possessed the blessing as their inheritance and were numbered among the elect and persevered in their just and pious resolution to the end of their lives.

## Chapter Ten

### *About a Brother Who Kissed the Hand of the Lord When He Blessed Him in a Vision*[28]

There was a certain brother of that same monastery who entered monastic life with the great desire of seeking the Lord. He continually ruminated with delight on the memory of our dear Savior, the Lord Jesus Christ, and one day saw him appear to him in a vision.

---

[27] The name Malgerus contains the Latin prefix *mal*, which conveys the image of evil, as in English "malignant" or "malevolent," and the verb stem *gero*, "to act, to do."

[28] Herbert of Clairvaux, LM 2.5 (PL 185:1316).

Anxious about his salvation, he emphatically begged the divine Master to give him the blessing that brings salvation, saying, "I beseech you, Lord; bless me, that I may be saved." The good Lord, who had deigned to appear to his poor servant to do this very thing, to give him some droplet of sweet consolation, raised his holy right hand and blessed him. At once it seemed to the brother having the vision that he was entirely filled with ineffable joy, and with holy audacity he seized the most blessed hand which was blessing him, kissed it with enormous devotion, and cried, "Thank you, Lord Jesus Christ, Son of the Living God,[29] for giving me your blessing so that I shall be saved."

## CHAPTER ELEVEN

*About a Brother Who Saw Blessed Mary Magdalene in a Vision*[30]

Another devout and religious brother was permitted to see in the Spirit the blessed Mary Magdalene; she was standing by the altar with shining raiment and countenance. The brother was filled with great joy when he saw her. Reflecting on this, he then hoped and prayed and longed in his soul to see likewise the most blessed Bearer of God, the Virgin Mary, whom he served very devoutly day and night. And a voice came to him in that vision, saying, "Understand that you are not yet worthy to see the most sublime and immaculate virgin Bearer of God. So work hard, grow, and prosper, so that one day you may yet deserve to see her."

---

[29] These are the traditional words of the Jesus Prayer.
[30] Herbert of Clairvaux, LM 2.7 (PL 185:1318).

CHAPTER TWELVE

*About the Great Progress Made by a Certain Lay Monk*[31]

The Lord says by the prophet: "Let not the wise man glory in his wisdom, nor the rich man in his riches, but let him who glories glory in this, that he understands and knows that I am the Lord" [Jer 9:23-24]. The ones who were imbued with the lessons of heavenly philosophy under our blessed Father Bernard in Clairvaux perfectly imitated this formula of divine knowledge, not only the many who were literate and learned in the mysteries of the sacred law, but even many laymen and those who were illiterate. They may have attained minimally the substance of human learning through which one climbs to the heights of perfection; nevertheless, they had the illuminating grace and the life-giving Spirit[32] who taught them a knowledge incomparably more effective than that of the world. One of these was a lay monk, learned not in the letter but in the Spirit. He was fervent in the work of God and not slow to desire the better gifts [1 Cor 12:31], he learned under the tutelage of the Holy Spirit not to seek to know high matters but to humble himself in all things, he considered great and lofty the pursuits of holy religion which he assiduously observed with humility in the habits of his fellow brothers, and he despised his own virtues which were not at all shabby in comparison to theirs. So in the excellence of holy humility he surpassed those to whom he was perhaps not inferior in the other virtues, and, what is very rare among human beings, he saw in himself only faults and in the others only good

---

[31] A lay monk, nobly born but unschooled, was distinguished from a lay brother (*conversus*) by the fact that, even though he was not ordained a priest, the lay monk was a member of the chapter and thus part of the main monastic community. Most of the lay brothers did manual labor at the monastery or worked on the granges. General Chapter in 1188, *Statute* 10, required that "uneducated noblemen coming to the monastic shall become monks, not lay brothers" (Waddell, *Statuta*, 151). See James France, *Separate but Equal: Cistercian Lay Brothers 1120–1350* (Collegeville: Cistercian, 2012).

[32] *Le Grande Exorde*, 234n4, notes that this is from the Nicene Creed which is sung at Mass on Sundays and major feasts.

qualities, and this not in a spirit of jealousy but as a fair-minded observer.

It happened, however, that one night he was preoccupied with these thoughts at the brothers' solemn Vigils. Overcome by deadly inattention and sleepiness, he seized on all the usual weapons, which perhaps he did not know were ineffective in putting the enemy to flight. He began to reflect on his sins and to examine severely his daily negligences. He accused himself before the eyes of the Supreme Majesty of being a wretch, guilty, and a sinner, and in consequence, as was his custom, he magnified and praised the life and observance of his brothers. In his heart of hearts he singled out one of them who seemed to him to surpass all the rest in his humility, charity, patience, self-control, and other spiritual gifts, and next to him he could only think of himself as dust and ashes [Gen 18:27]. At the end of these thoughts, he could not bear the ardor of the holy humility he had conceived in these reflections, and at daybreak, although he was hardly able to wait for the time when he was allowed to speak according to the Rule, he made a sign to draw the most reverend Father Bernard into the parlor.[33] He asked permission to speak and sorrowfully poured out the grief of his heart. When Bernard asked him what this was all about, he said, "Alas, I am a wretched sinner bereft of all good. Tonight I counted thirty virtues in that brother of ours who excels in all of them, and I cannot find the least trace of them in my poor self. I pray you, lord father, intercede for me to the Lord that by your holy merits and prayers I may be made worthy to carry through the actions of the virtues which I have so far, because of my sins, been unable to do." Listening to the profound humility of his disciple, whom he knew to be an outstanding religious even though the brother clearly was happily ignorant of it, the spiritual master rejoiced with exceeding great joy [Matt 2:10]. He longed and hoped that all those committed to him might make such progress in the virtues, yet somehow, in pondering their own infirmities, might remain

---

[33] *Le Grande Exorde*, 235n10, suggests this could have been a sign given to go to the *auditorium*, a room set aside specifically for this purpose; see EO, n. 2. See also note above in EM 2.32.

unaware of making progress. How highly he esteemed such humility is evident in this, that he often mentioned and praised this brother in the sermons which he gave to the brothers in chapter,[34] and he affirmed that all the virtues this true monk had named to him could not be compared to his own humility. For he closed his eyes to the negligences and imperfections of those around him and saw only what was edifying in their lives and habits, so that in his own eyes his life, compared to theirs, seemed despicable.

## Chapter Thirteen

*About a Lay Brother,*
*Whose Devotion Saint Bernard Knew through the Spirit*

It was the custom, if I remember correctly, that on the most sacred solemnity of the Assumption of the most inviolate and immaculate Virgin Mary, Bearer of God, the brothers at the granges of Clairvaux would hasten to the abbey out of respect for the day. On one of these granges which was quite nearby there was a certain lay brother who was devout and God-fearing. He was too simple to master the greatest demands of religious life, but he was full of piety and goodwill and venerated and loved the dearest Mother of God, Our Lady, very sincerely. When the master of the grange made arrangements about who should go to the abbey and who should stay behind to take care of the house, among those to stay was this brother, who was in charge of the sheep. He took this decision very ill as he had been hoping and longing to be present for the hymns and holy canticles which he knew would be very devoutly sung by the community in honor of the Queen of Heaven.[35] But he did not dare to object and with utmost obedience prepared to

---

[34] Bernard of Clairvaux, Div 3 (SBOp 5:215–16).

[35] *Le Grande Exorde*, 236nn4, 5, points out that the last two sentences reflect the *Usus conversorum* 2-3.

follow orders. So it happened that this holy devotion which filled his thoughts, and which he was afraid of losing if he submitted to the distraction of the earthly task he had been given under obedience, by his prompt and willing obedience sparked like fire and burned more and more in his heart.

On the night of the sacred feast, while he was carefully watching his flock rest in the fields, he heard—despite the distance, so silent was the night—the sound of the bell that calls the brothers to Vigils. His heart warmed [Ps 38:4] at hearing it and burned like fire as he thought about the assembly of that holy multitude, and about their great zeal and devotion, and about how they were in community offering up odes of celestial harmony to the most holy Mother of mercy, and about how each one privately was asking the protection of this same blessed Virgin with prayers and sighs.[36] Rising and wanting to take part in these loving ceremonies in his own small way, he stood there with his eyes and his heart fixed on the part of the horizon where the monastery was situated. As devoutly as he could, he said the prayers which the lay brothers say in place of Lauds,[37] and then he searched the little cupboard of his heart diligently to find some prayers and praises that he might offer to the holy *Theotocon*,[38] Our Lady, as a way to compensate for the lengthy and protracted vigils performed by the brothers, and discovered he knew none other than the salutation of the holy Lady which he had somehow learned.[39] And so he repeated this word, as it were, brief and complete [Rom 9:28], in which there is a plenitude of devotion, and he lifted up his eyes to heaven praying prayers, sighing sighs, and adding salutation to salutation tirelessly for the rest of the night and part of the morning.[40] By the help of divine grace, which kindled such fervor in the heart of this poor

---

[36] Regarding the "holy multitude" see *Le Grande Exorde*, 236n8. The main chapel at Clairvaux had 128 choir stalls, 34 places for the infirm, and 328 places for lay brothers: a total of 490 places.

[37] *Usus conversorum* 1.

[38] "God-bearer": EM uses the Greek, *Theotocon*, as below in EM 4.32.

[39] The Latin here is *Dominae nostrae offerret . . . salutationem piae Dominae*, that is, the scriptural first half of the modern *Ave Maria* prayer.

[40] In effect, this is an example of using the *Ave* as a form of perpetual prayer.

servant, the monotony—which is usually the mother of contempt, the step-mother of devotion—in an amazing and opposite way instead put an end to boredom and dispelled weariness. These most agreeable words, sweeter than honey, offered from a simple heart and repeated often quickly gained for him the favor and grace of the Queen of heaven for him as he prayed and sighed.

Finally, the Lord deigned to reveal through the Spirit to our most reverend abbot, blessed Bernard, that his sighs were not in vain and that he did not implore the Mother of mercy in vain. When the divine hymns had been completed and the sacred mysteries in honor of the most high Mother of God, the Virgin Mary, very devoutly celebrated by each of the priests, the holy abbot, in the assembly of the brothers, preached a sermon in honor of importance of this solemnity [EO 67.3-7], a sermon aglow with the grace of the Holy Spirit, and did it in these terms: "My dearest brothers, we need have no doubt that you have offered this night a pleasing and acceptable sacrifice of your devotion to the Lord Jesus Christ, truly our king, and to the glorious Virgin Mother, our special patroness, and you ought therefore to be utterly sure that there is laid up for you an eternal reward from the Lord and our most gracious guardian.[41] But I want you to know that one of our humblest and simplest lay brothers, whom obedience forced to celebrate the joys of this great feast tonight out of doors in the mountains and woods, offered a service of morning worship to our Lady so pleasing, so devoted, so festive, that the contemplation of none of you, however exalted, or your intensive devotion could be preferred to his devotion, which was offered not in the lofty sublimity of contemplation but in the humble submission of holy simplicity."[42] Everyone marveled at hearing this, but it caused joy and great edification, especially among the lay brothers, whose obedience often kept them at work on feast days as well as ferias.

---

[41] For other references to Mary as guardian, see Bernard of Clairvaux, Csi 2.22 (SBOp 3:429; CF 37:76—though here the term is not used in relation to Mary), and SC 75.1 (SBOp 2:247–48; CF 40:98).

[42] About this sermon, Grießer, EM, 239n1, cites Jean Leclercq, "Etudes sur Saint Bernard et le texte de ses écrits," *Analecta Sacri Ordinis Cisterciensis* 9 (1953): 50–54.

They knew with great certainty that enclosure and the walls of the church were no guarantee of sanctity for those who do not fear the Lord and that no temporal work enjoined by obedience need ever prevent them from lifting up pure hands to the Lord and serving him with a pure conscience.

## CHAPTER FOURTEEN

### *About a Vision*
### *in Which a Certain Brother Sees the Death of Another Brother*[43]

A certain brother of worthy and holy observance, to whom the Lord deigned to reveal his secrets, had a vision one day. It seemed that he was in the infirmary at Clairvaux, and he saw there some venerable persons cutting out and preparing garments of silk and precious cloth. He was astonished at this novel activity,[44] and he heard a voice saying to him, "These garments that you are wondering at are being prepared for one of the daughters of the abbot of Clairvaux who is soon going to celebrate her wedding. Because she has less beauty in her than becomes her parentage, she needs precious and beautifully scented and ornamented clothes to please her eternal Spouse, for not only can no stain of sin but no wrinkle of negligence, which is not covered by the indulgence of his most gracious love, can in any way enter his most pure marriage chamber."[45] At that moment the board of the dead sounded and there died a certain brother [EO 94.2] who had lived an innocent and gentle life but had been somewhat negligent and remiss in his duties. So it was necessary that what he could not achieve himself by the grace of perfect adornment should be supplied for him by the copious splendor of his brothers' prayers.

---

[43] Herbert of Clairvaux, LM 1.9 (PL 185:1286).

[44] See *Exordium Cistercii* 25; Waddell, *Narrative and Legislative Texts*, 413.

[45] Herbert/Conrad's use of spousal imagery (*aeterno sponso*), especially with "stain" (*macula*) and "marriage chamber" (*thalamum*), is a deliberate allusion to the Song of Songs; *Le Grande Exorde*, 238n2.

CHAPTER FIFTEEN

*About a Lay Monk*
*Who Learned to Say Mass in His Sleep*[46]

The Holy Spirit who dispenses the grace of heaven "coming down from the Father of lights in every good and perfect gift" [Jas 1:17] gives to each of the faithful as he chooses. And he deigned to confer upon a certain uneducated lay monk a special and wonderful gift of his grace. This blessed man, Walter by name, had no less faith and devotion than did the lettered and the learned; he was in charge of clothing for a long time at Clairvaux and handed out garments to the brothers with great sweetness and charity, not according to preference of persons [Rom 2:11], but according to the needs of the brothers. He was beloved and accepted by God and man for the purity and innocence of his life. One day when he was resting on his bed, a certain reverend person appeared to him in his sleep and ordered him to go to church at once and devoutly chant Mass to the divine majesty. Not a little astonished at such a novel command, he hesitated out of modesty, thinking of the humbleness of his own person, but out of respect, constrained by authority, he did not dare to resist and hastened to obey. Having set about the unfamiliar task and vested in the garments of priesthood, in his sleep he celebrated a Mass of the Holy Spirit with great devotion. When he woke up he found that he knew the words of that Mass by heart, even though, being unlettered, he had not known earlier, and for many years he kept them in his memory, and in his prayers and meditations he strove to ruminate about them sweetly because he happily remembered that he did not learn this from human teaching but by divine inspiration.

---

[46] Herbert of Clairvaux, LM 1.32 (PL 185:1304).

CHAPTER SIXTEEN

*About the Great Patience of a Certain Lay Brother*
*in His Sickness*[47]

There was a certain lay brother, who had left Clairvaux three times
out of levity and three times been received back again [RB 29.3].
At last he was moved by the salutary advice and holy prayers of
blessed Bernard, the abbot, and began to abhor from the very bottom of his heart his triple fall into apostasy. He sought earnestly for
some penance or satisfaction that he could offer the Lord for such a
great offense. By the inspiration of God he decided and understood
that there is nothing more efficacious for obtaining the forgiveness
of sins and the grace of virtues, nor anything more acceptable in
the sight of the Lord, than the sacrifice of a contrite heart and a
humbled spirit [Ps 50:19], and that the kingdom of heaven can only
be taken by force, and he set himself to bend the formidable severity
of divine justice by his unutterable groans [Rom 8:26]. He took up
the arms of piety and set himself against himself, and first of all he
tried to observe all the rules of the Order as well as he could and
without negligence and above all to wash away his former sins by
daily prayers and lamentations. By his salutary example, he taught
those who stood fast how not to fall [1 Cor 10:12] and those who
had fallen how to get up again.

By the will of the Lord, who applies stronger remedies to stronger sins so that in his ineffable tenderness he may turn a vessel of
wrath into a vessel of honor [2 Tim 2:20], decay entered into the
bones [Hab 3:16] of this aforesaid brother, his leg became hideously
ulcerated with a cancerous abscess, and the anguish of this illness
increased every day until the flesh on either side of the ulcer was
eaten away to the bare bone and the wound was teeming with
worms. For many years he was chained to his couch and humbly
suffered the chastisement of divine blows, and he suffered nearly

---

[47] Herbert of Clairvaux, LM 1.17 (PL 185:1292–93).

as many deaths as the hours he lived. His suffering soul endured grief and anguish at the sight of the decay of his body and those who served him were revolted by the horrible stench that came continually from his wasting ulcer. But in God's sight they were all generously rewarded for their labor and patience. This same infirm brother always gave thanks in his pain and affliction, believing in his heart and confessing with his mouth that he had received far less than he deserved. He was being refined out of the dross of his sins, as the wise man said: "Take the dross from the silver and a most pure vessel will emerge" [Prov 25:4]. When at length he emerged from the furnace of his purgation, his blessed soul was clean and shining, like silver tried by the fire [Ps 11:7], and he was taken with the other vessels of mercy into the palace of the most high King.

But even before he was taken out of the dregs of muck and the pit of misery [Ps 39:3] he was allowed in this life, for the consolation of all who truly repent, to taste beforehand the fruit of his labors and patience and to know the ineffable sweetness to which he would be admitted in that life without end. After he had tasted this sweetness, he shouted his joy in songs of heavenly praise as if intoxicated on the new wine of heaven, and, with his countenance aglow, this unlettered man who had never learned to sing or to read was singing the sweetest hymns and melodies of the songs of Zion [Ps 136:3]. "At hearing his voice a multitude [of brothers] came together" [Acts 2:6] to see what great miracle had happened to this man, weighed down by such great miseries and calamities, at the very moment of death singing and rising triumphant over death, saying, "'O death, where is your victory' [1 Cor 15:55]? Look, I am a great sinner, a very poor sort of man. Because I have patiently borne in my body the marks of the Lord Jesus [Gal 6:17] for the glory of his name, I fear you not, ghostly shade, mother of sorrows, killer of joy, destroyer of life; instead I despise you, for I know that you will be cast down and finally swallowed up in the victory [1 Cor 15:54] of the cross of my Lord Jesus Christ." So our precentor intoned the Alleluia which echoes in the streets of the heavenly Jerusalem, somehow anticipating by this prophetic miracle what his body was going to become while as yet he was in this corruptible body. Rejoicing and giving praise [Isa 35:2] in a voice of exaltation and confession [Ps 41:5] he breathed out his spirit. At his happy death, blessed Bernard greatly rejoiced and preached a very stirring sermon about him to the brothers in chapter,[48] commending in him his fruit of repentance [Matt 3:8; Luke 3:8] and holding up to them all the example of his patience.

CHAPTER SEVENTEEN

*How a Lay Brother Received Knowledge of Divine Scripture*[49]

The infirmarians at Clairvaux were wont to refer with joy and admiration to the religious life of a certain lay brother to whom the Lord granted a wonderful grace and worthy memorial before he died. Indeed when grace, our mother,[50] set out to reward the merits of his good life and he was bedridden with a lingering ailment, as the illness got worse, the obvious signs of death announced that the dissolution of his body was near [2 Tim 4:6]. And the Holy Spirit who breathes where and when and how it will [John 3:8] wrought a new and stupendous miracle, illuminating his understanding and opening his mouth. This rustic fellow who had never learned letters began to speak in eloquent Latin, explaining wonderfully some teachings of Holy Scripture and saying nothing that did not agree with sound doctrine. The lay brothers who did not know Latin were amazed at the novelty of this and fetched some of the monks to hear him, and in a dazzling discourse the sick brother also expounded the mysteries of the Scriptures to them. What is more, he sang sweet canticles about the mysteries of holy Church with such a well-modulated voice, which they had never before heard, that all who heard it were astonished at the unheard-of miracle and touched by the exquisite chant.

[48] This sermon no longer exists; see note above in EM 4.13.
[49] Herbert of Clairvaux, LM 1.16 (PL 185:1292); Grießer (EM, 242n4) notes that the brother is called Geoffrey in *Fragmenta* 36, ed. R. Lechat, *Analecta Bollandiana* 50 (1932): 108.
[50] On the expression "grace, our mother" see note above at the end of EM 3.13.

What did Almighty and Merciful God wish to make known to mortals by this unusual grace bestowed on a simple rustic man, if not that in the eternal bliss of his kingdom, according to the word of the Apostle, there will be neither Jew nor Greek, barbarian or Scythian, slave or free [Gal 3:28; Col 3:11], educated or uneducated, but as the prophet says, all will be taught of God [John 6:45], and all from the greatest right down to the least will know me, says the Lord? Would that restless men follow this example, that is to say, those who travel over sea and land in order to be filled with the chaff of letters and swollen with the image of knowledge, in order to be called rabbis and masters [Matt 23:7-8] by men, in order to boast that they are lawyers and canonists, dialecticians and sophists, in order to serve greed and ambition out of a pious enterprise. Would that they might perceive, I say, and understand with the ear of the heart that, just as this rustic and unlettered man who strove to walk in the fear of the Lord had bestowed on him at his death the height of divine learning and acquired a clear knowledge of heavenly mysteries, so they, on the other hand, at their deaths will still be foolish and stupid, spewing out the knowledge they have devoured without fear of the Lord, and God will draw it all out of their bellies. We are saying this not that we condemn generally those who want an education but so that we may teach every man first to lay a foundation of the fear of God in the trench of humility, because, according to an accurate definition, fear of the Lord is the beginning of wisdom [Ps 110:10; Prov 1:7; Sir 1:16]. After that let everyone build up as much knowledge as he wants, because no knowledge ever inflates [1 Cor 8:1] where divine and fraternal charity alike do the building. So this new theologian, of whom we have been speaking, began in the fear of God, and at the end of this present life he deserved to take hold of perfect wisdom. For a while he delighted his listeners with the variety of his holy teachings and the gentle beauty of his songs, and at length, in the midst of this confession, he crossed from this world to the Father [John 13:1] to be plunged, in a joyous plunge, into the depths of eternal light. As I believe, he received the firstfruits of this eternal light for this alone: that we might recognize in the fragrance of the ointments [Song 1:3] with which he had been anointed that the more avidly one runs the course, the more open is the font of true wisdom for the gentle and the humble alone.

## Chapter Eighteen

### *About a Lay Brother, a Cowherd,*
### *Who in a Vision Saw the Lord Jesus Helping Him Herd His Cows*[51]

A certain lay brother held the office of cowherd on one of Clairvaux's granges; he was a man of purity and great simplicity who promptly and devoutly did everything enjoined on him by his masters and who bore the labors of each day with utmost patience, looking to the rewards of heaven. One day in a dream he saw the Lord Jesus Christ beside him, and in this truly wonderful sight he was holding a goad in his most gentle hand, and with it he was prodding the cows along on the other side of the harness beam. When he awoke [Gen 28:16] and thought about the gentleness, kindness, and sweetness of his very devoted helper, there surged in his heart a vehement desire, and he hoped and yearned to see face-to-face [Gen 32:30] the One whom in his vision he deserved to have as such a companionable coworker. As he was yearning vehemently to be dissolved and be with Christ [Phil 1:23], the good Lord who walks with the meek and speaks with the simple [Prov 3:32] did not delay to answer the desire of his poor one. Soon the brother was stricken with sickness and took to his bed, and on the seventh day he ended his labor and sorrow in death and happily took hold of eternal life and rest everlasting, which is Christ the Lord. When he was dying, the right reverend abbot, blessed Bernard, came to visit him, to say good-bye to his son who was going home, for he knew his conscience to be pure and simple and he wanted to defend him with his blessing against the attacks of spiritual wickedness as he

---

[51] Herbert of Clairvaux, LM 1.15 (PL 185:1291–92).

went forth. Once he learned about the vision we described from the sick man, he rejoiced greatly. When the lay brother died Bernard declared confidently that he had walked with God [Gen 17:1] and that God had indeed worked with him, and in this manner he passed over to the Lord. The Almighty who is so merciful, who had been a most worthy companion and helper in labors, could not desert his servant in his final agony.

## Chapter Nineteen

*About the Great Humility of a Certain Lay Brother*[52]

One of the lay brothers at Clairvaux was a man of innocent life and honorable monastic conversion. When he eventually fell gravely ill, he came quickly to his end. Blessed Bernard came to visit him, however, and to comfort him said, "My son, be assured that you are going to pass from death to life, from temporal labor to everlasting rest." And with great confidence the sick man exclaimed, "Am I not going to my Lord and my maker? Indeed, I trust, and by the mercy of my Lord Jesus Christ I am so bold as to presume that I shall soon see the good things of the Lord in the land of the living [Ps 26:13]." The blessed father, who was a wise physician [RB 27.2] and a concerned shepherd, fearing that such a firm reply from a peasant came from rashness of presumption rather than from purity of conscience, said, "Brother, guard your heart, guard your heart! What are you saying? Where can you have picked up such presumption? Were you not just a poor miserable sort of fellow who, having nothing or almost nothing in the world, fled to us more out of necessity than out of the fear of God, begging for admission with many prayers? For the sake of God we took you in, destitute, and gave you food and clothing and the common goods, just the same as those men among us who are well educated and

---

[52] Herbert of Clairvaux, LM 1.29 (PL 185:1301–3).

nobly born, and made you as one of them. What return have you made to the Lord for all these things? And now look, your ingratitude is not satisfied with having received so much from the hand of the Lord; now you dare to claim as your heritage his kingdom, which no king or prince has been able to obtain with treasures of gold and silver."

With a calm face and a serene soul the brother replied, "You have scolded rightly, dearest father, quite rightly, and all you say is true. Nevertheless, if you will allow, my lord and father, I will reveal to you in a few words how it is that I, poor and miserable, could say this, not out of presumption, but, as I am sure, out of devotion. If the message you have so often preached to us is true, 'the kingdom of heaven is gained not by noble blood or the riches of the earth but only by the virtue of obedience,' I have thought of this one phrase as a summary of the Gospel,[53] and I have placed it as a seal upon my heart [Song 8:6] by diligent meditation and upon my arm by painstaking practice. If you wish, ask all my superiors and peers, the brothers whom I have obeyed according to your orders, ask them if I have ever disobeyed one of them or if I have ever grieved any of them by a word, a sign, or, to the best of my ability, in any other way. If I have tried to obey everybody in Christ and to serve and to love them all by the grace of God, why should anyone hinder me from having confidence in his mercy?" The blessed father rejoiced with great joy [Matt 2:10] at hearing such a reply from the mouth of an unlettered man, and he said, "My dearest son, 'you are truly blessed, because flesh and blood have not revealed this wisdom to you, but the Heavenly Father' has taught you [Matt 16:17], and 'he has set you on the straight path to life' and led you directly to the homeland [Ps 65:9]. Go forth therefore with confidence, for the gate of life is opened to you." After the brother died and his funeral had been celebrated, the venerable father, with his usual eloquence and devotion, preached a moving sermon to the chapter

---

[53] Bernard of Clairvaux often used the phrase "shortened word" (*verbum abbreviatum*; Rom 9:28): see Ep 235.1 (SBOp 8:108; James, Ep 202, p. 271); Dil 21 (SBOp 3:136; CF 13:113); and SC 12.1, 59.9, 79.2 (SBOp 1:67, 140, 273; CF 4:78, 31:128, 40:138). See *Le Grande Exorde*, 245n9.

about this man's consummate conversion[54] and how by his example stirred all of them to a love of obedience. He had been profoundly affected by the brother's reply, and he offered more praise for the great strength of his obedience and the purity of his mind than if he had seen him gleaming with marvels and prophetic signs.

CHAPTER TWENTY

*About a Lay Brother and How, after He Died,*
*the Lord Deigned to Show through a Glorious Revelation*
*How Perfect Was His Life*
*and What Blessed Felicity He Attained in Death*[55]

There lived in the same monastery another lay brother who was a good religious and extremely gentle. He had learned to be meek and humble of heart [Matt 11:29] in the school of divine grace. The other brothers bore witness that, whatever affront was offered to him, he was never angry or even impatient. Under the inspiration of God, he had resolved in his own mind that whenever any of his brothers accused him of a fault, justly or unjustly, he would pray for them and say for each of them at least one Our Father. Many of the brothers at Clairvaux followed his example and to this day still keep this as a rule. If the devotion and humility of this blessed man was agreeable to God and pleasing to man, what, I ask, will those who take the opposite pathway to the Lord do on the terrible day of judgment? Whenever they are accused by someone, they get angry, burst into words of impatience, and do not hide their rancor against those who accuse them, but instead, impelled by resentment and not by any kind of charity, they blame them in turn with all the exaggeration of the fault possible.

---

[54] This sermon no longer exists, see note above for EM 4.13.
[55] Herbert of Clairvaux, LM 1.7 (PL 185:1285; 185:459–61).

The aforementioned man of God once had to travel through a wooded pass when he was away on business for the church. He fell into the hands of robbers who stripped him [Luke 10:30] and took his horse and his scanty luggage, leaving him with nothing but his charity. Indeed, he had not carried his charity carelessly outside in his rucksack but wisely attached it to his heart within by the bonds of unfaltering patience, so he had no need to fear the violence of the brigands. With his charity intact, the servant of God could lose nothing, for in comparison with his charity he counted what he had lost as nothing. After the robbers had left and gone on a little way, he fell on his knees in prayer [Matt 5:44], begging the Lord to forgive their impiety. One of them, by divine permission, turned back and followed the brother from a distance, curious to see what he would do. And seeing him deep in prolonged prayer, he hurried back to his companions, beating his breast and saying, "Alas, we will be damned. We are all going to die because we have mistreated a holy man, a brother from the holy monastery"—for he realized the lay brother was from Clairvaux—"since we left him he has not stopped praying with tears and sighs [RB 4.57], and he is even asking God to help his enemies." This news moved them to repent, and they went back and found the brother still kneeling, hard at prayer. They returned all they had violently stolen from him, humbly sought his pardon, and left in peace. The brother, at seeing this, praised the great action of the grace of the Savior Christ and was filled with exceeding great joy [Matt 2:10], not that his goods had been restored, but that the robbers had repented. This good man persevered to the end in his holy course and at length the Lord called him to be joined with his fathers [2 Kgs 22:20; 2 Chr 34:28; 1 Macc 2:69] and taste now and forever the good things of the Lord in the land of the living [Ps 26:13].

Here is a vision that showed his glorification on the very day of his death. In a monastery far from Clairvaux, there lived an observant monk, a man held in high esteem, and all of his monastic brothers especially loved and respected him [RB 72.10] for his holiness. On the same day that that aforesaid brother died at Clairvaux, this monk was himself near his end. When he seemed to be at the point of death, he went into an ecstasy and lay without the use of his limbs and stayed like that from morning until the ninth hour. Only shallow breathing showed that he was not yet dead. After being rapt in ecstasy from morning, as we've said, until the ninth hour, he came to himself and his tongue was loosed and he spoke. Those around were amazed and asked him what had caused his abrupt departure and return. He told them, "Today while I was suspended in the Spirit above my physical senses, I suddenly found myself entering into a paradise of marvelous delights, into a place so glorious and bright that the human senses cannot understand the extent, the beauty, and the charm of it. There appeared a great variety of precious jars in that place, splendid ornaments with all kinds of decorations, placed as if for the reception of some very great emperor or king. Multitudes of saints, shining with tremendous light, were already there and others were coming from every direction, as if hurrying to see a brilliant spectacle and gathering as if for a solemn feast. There, I heard sweet celestial music and echoes of thanksgiving and the voice of praise [Isa 51:3]. Charmed by what I saw and heard, I asked the angel who was leading me what the cause of this joy and celebration was. He said, 'It is a new celebration for the new saint who is arriving today from the house of Clairvaux and solemnly entering into this delightful rest.' When he had said this he sent me away without delay to return to humankind, although I was very reluctant. I begged not to be sent away from such bliss to return to this life but he said to me, 'You must return to your brothers and tell them what you have seen. After that you will soon come back here and you will take your part in the eternal joy.' This is why I have been sent, to tell you what I have seen, so that you may continue and persevere in good works in the assurance that your labor will not go without reward." When he had said this he bade them farewell and slept in the Lord. The whole community of the monastery mourned him with great mourning [1 Macc 2:70] because he had been a very holy and also a very useful man. Everyone had been edified by his example, and everyone loved to ask for his advice. They carefully took note of the day and the hour of his death and learned from Clairvaux that the brother in question had died on the same day that the vision had taken place.

We can easily estimate the holy and exemplary life of this lay brother from this miraculous revelation. When one of the brothers related the story, with great admiration, in blessed Bernard's presence, he replied, "Does this surprise you, brothers? I am more surprised at the incredulity and hardness of your hearts [Mark 16:14], that you should not yet quite believe and seem not to have ever paid attention to this word of truth which cries from heaven, 'Blessed are the dead who die in the Lord, for they rest from their labors, says the Spirit' [Rev 14:13]. To me it is clearer than day and more certain than the life I live that all who persevere in the purity of this Order, practicing humility and obedience, will be immediately stripped of all misery and clothed in the glory of immortality as soon as they will have shed their flesh." The brothers were greatly encouraged at hearing from the mouth of so great a father this witness to the purity of our Order and to the glorification of a brother who had taken such care to maintain the purity of the Order with all his strength. Praising the graciousness of the Lord, they set themselves never to fall away from the path of this strict way of life, so that they too could be made sharers of the glorification[56] which is promised to those who walk the straight and narrow path for the sake of Christ [Matt 7:14]. If only, when we hear and read this in the present day, when love has grown cold [Matt 24:12] and lukewarmness and negligence have begun to infiltrate everything, if only we might be warmed again to imitate the vigor of the fervor and devotion of the holy fathers, lest by chance we, who have made the beginnings of a conversion similar to theirs, may so neglect the purity of our holy Order that at the end we will be excluded from the repose of the highest blessedness and sent to the place of eternal horror where there is no order [Job 10:22].

---

[56] The Cistercian emphasis on gaining the reward of salvation is often mentioned in secondary sources; see R. W. Southern, *Western Church and Society in the Middle Ages* (New York: Penguin, 1970), 250–53. So too is their emphasis on doing so within community; see Newman, *Boundaries of Charity*, 21–23; and Constable, *Reformation of the Twelfth Century*, 134–39. See also EM 1.13; 5.19; and 6.10, which further reinforce the rigor of the Cistercian quest for salvation.

CHAPTER TWENTY-ONE

*About a Brother Whom Saint Bernard Warns in a Vision
Not to Give Way to Temptation*[57]

After the passing of the most reverend Father Bernard, there lived
at Clairvaux a brother who, at the beginning of his monastic life
when he was still a new knight, was assailed by frequent temptations
of the enemy. He manfully deflected the frequent lances of temptation with the shield of patience, but above all he experienced the
unclean spirit of fornication so badly that he could scarcely defend
himself by the arms of compunction and prayer against the fantasies
of the wretched flesh which the evil one tried constantly to raise
in his heart,[58] and, fried in this skillet, he went around in agony
all day long [Ps 37:7; Ps 41:10]. The anguish of this very burdensome conflict increased daily, and the brother was not sure he had
enough patience to continue enduring the onslaughts of this dire
passion. So he decided he would yield to the tempter, take off the
religious habit, and go back to the world. He was already looking
for a chance to do this when blessed Bernard, who had recently
died, appeared to him in a vision, chiding his silliness and scolding
him for the wicked plan he had dreamed up and was trying to put
into effect. After the brother explained that he had resisted for a
long time and could no longer bear the anguish of the temptation,
the saint said to him, "You must realize that many battles lie ahead
for you. But you should act manfully [Ps 26:14] and be unwilling
to quit, because the Lord will come to you as a helper in due time
[Ps 9:10] to rescue you. I promise you this: if you persevere in the
Order to the end you will be saved. And if even perhaps on the
last day anyone attempts to harm you, I will answer for you and
lay down my soul for yours" [John 13:37].

    What a faithful friend and strong helper was our dear father,
who even after the death of the body proved himself still faithful

---

[57] Herbert of Clairvaux, LM 1.31 (PL 185:1303–4).
[58] Perhaps masturbation or wet dreams; see above, EM 2.22; 3.15.

in the blessed life by deigning to visit a little sheep with one foot in the pit of apostasy; he cherished him with sweet consolation, strengthened him with encouragement, and by the grace of God he led him back from the brink of destruction to the pathway of life! The brother was so encouraged by such a promise from such a father that he strengthened his feeble spirit for the struggle of the contest and banished vacillation from his heart. He remained true to his calling despite the wiles of the evil spirit and the violence of his attacks. As Bernard had foretold he endured many hard contests, but by the grace of God he deserved to snatch the triumph of victory, and at the end of his life, after persevering in the holy Order, showing the finest manner of life, he happily attained eternal salvation according to the solemn promise of his father beloved by God.

## Chapter Twenty-Two

### *Concerning a Brother to Whom Saint Malachy and Blessed Bernard Appeared, Chastising Him for a Fault*[59]

Another of the brothers at the same monastery was so corrupted by diabolical influence that he had made plans to apostatize from God and make a pact with hell by returning to the world. And in the night he had a vision of Blessed Bernard and Saint Malachy, the most reverend patrons of that place, walking around in the dormitory and pausing by and blessing each of the brothers as they slept on their beds. When, in the course of their visit, they came to see this brother in his bed, they neither looked at him kindly nor blessed him as they did the others. Instead, they stood in front of him, as if in indignation. Blessed Malachy said to Saint Bernard, "This wicked and restless man thinks nothing good in his mind, has no hesitation in meditating evil in his heart, and has already

---

[59] Herbert of Clairvaux, LM 1.28 (PL 185:1301).

assented in his perverse will to yield to the diabolical suggestion of returning to the vomit of the world as fast as he can" [2 Pet 2:22]. Hearing this, blessed Bernard addressed him: "So you want to run away from my monastery? And just where will you flee from the sight of the Lord, you wretch [Ps 138:7]? Believe me, it does you no good to have such thoughts. I know, indeed I know, that 'only vexation will make you understand' [Isa 28:19]. You who have neglected to correct yourself out of a fear of God will try to flee no farther once you've been punished by the lashes you deserve." After he said this, Bernard began to pound him with repeated blows of the staff he was holding and added, "Look, the wages you deserve! Now get up and run away if you can!" Upon waking, however, the brother found himself so completely bruised and battered from that beating that he was taken to the infirmary and kept in bed. Trembling and frightened, he begged the brothers who were helping him to ask the prior to come to him right away. Once the prior arrived, he confessed with great contrition of heart the malicious plan he had conceived in his mind and intended to carry out[60] and also the punishment he had received. The prior reproved him for his laziness and slackness as he deserved and gave him a penance for the guilty state of his instability. When the brother recovered fully he had no more thoughts about running away. He had healthfully learned that it was hard for him to kick against the goad [Acts 9:5; 26:14], and he set out with fear and trembling to cooperate with the action of grace that was so mercifully working for his salvation.

---

[60] *Le Grand Exorde*, 251n10, notes that the expression about "the malicious plan he had conceived in his mind and intended to carry out" can be found in Jerome, *Commentarii in Ezechielem* 6.18 (CCSL 75).

CHAPTER TWENTY-THREE

*About a Lay Brother Who Deserved to See Holy Angels at His Death*[61]

A lay brother in the aforesaid monastery was once sick. He was a true religious and praiseworthy in his monastic life, who had run along the straight and narrow way that leads to God [RB 58.8] with unfaltering step in the simplicity of his heart, as was clear at his death.[62] When he had 'fought the good fight and finished the course' [2 Tim 4:7] and arrived at the final end, he saw with his eyes open [Acts 9:8] holy angels hover around his bed. As he saw them he became excited in a wonderful way, as if already triumphing over death, and he said to the brothers standing around, "Do you not see that the angels of God have already come? Sound the board [EO 94.2] right away, for they are waiting here for my departure." Scarcely had he finished saying this when he gave up his happy soul in a precious death. There is no doubt that the blessed spirits whom he had been privileged to see in advance took his soul straight into the joys of eternal blessedness.

CHAPTER TWENTY-FOUR

*How a Lay Brother Was Punished by God for Washing His Socks without Permission*[63]

For the edification of those making progress we have already given some details about the exemplary conduct, religious observance,

---

[61] Herbert, LM 1.14 (PL 185:1291). Grießer (EM, 250n4 notes that the lay brother in this story is called Geoffrey in the *Fragmenta*; see above, EM 4.17.

[62] See note above at EM 1.9 on "the straight and narrow way."

[63] See also a story about Bernard of Clairvaux's great humility, shown by the act of cleaning his own shoes, in Caesarius of Heisterbach, *Dialogus miraculorum* 4.7 (Strange 1:179–80; S-Bland 1:202–3).

and precious death of our holy fathers [Ps 115:15]; now, as a pre-caution for the indolent, we are going to recount the negligence of a brother and how God punished him for his negligence. If these examples of virtue encourage those who aspire to do still better, the negligent should also find in the terrifying vengeance of divine censure a motive for fearing to transgress not just the greatest but even the least institutes of the holy Order.

On one of the granges of Clairvaux, a lay brother presumed to wash his socks without the permission of the master. He went alone to the side of a little stream which ran beside the grange, and, entirely concerned with the work he had begun, he, alas, gave little thought to how gravely they transgress who presume to violate the purity of the holy Order even in little ways. While he was doing his ill-advised job without the knowledge of his master, he heard a voice call out, as if one person were speaking to another, "Hit him, hit him!" And at once the lay brother felt two very hard blows, one on his head and another on his feet. Pale and trembling, he ran to the grange and told the brothers in a faltering voice what he had done, heard, and suffered. He was immediately taken to the abbey, and there, with as much humility as he could muster, he declared both his fault and the punishment for the fault. He said that the two blows he had mysteriously received little by little had spread inside him, one from his head, the other from his feet, and that, in any case, he was going to die when the blows met in his heart. And the outcome of the matter proved this to be true. A few days later the brother died, making a good confession, and we devoutly believe that he went to God more pure because his death was such a terrible one and canceled his sin.

Why is it, do we think, that the just Judge [Ps 7:12], the Lord of Hosts who judges the earth with equity [Ps 9:9], seems so often to level quite different sentences for very similar faults, when it is certain that the wisdom of God, which orders all things with sweetness and prudence [Wis 8:1], cannot err or seem to err? O, how many are there today who wear the religious habit and let themselves be called monks, who in accordance with the Rule and the Order have renounced all private property, and yet, following the example of Ananias and Sapphira [Acts 5:1-11], with rash presumption do not hesitate to hold property? Even though a single word from the mouth of the apostle Peter punished that pair with a terrible death, no misfortune touches these people; on the contrary, they seem to pass their days happily. May they not suddenly find themselves in hell [Job 21:13]! In the very Order of Cîteaux, which by the grace of God is pure and free from the huge vice of private property, there were and, even after that brother received a sentence of death for what seemed a minor fault, there are still some who easily allow themselves exceptions without respect for the holy Order and then sign or say, "What is wrong?" or "Is it so important?" They take no heed of what and how important it is according to Scripture, where it is written, "He who despises little things, little by little will fall" [Sir 19:1]. Nevertheless, Almighty God does not always punish them immediately, not because washing something without permission or doing something else without a senior's assent is now no longer as grave a fault meriting punishment as it was those times when God chose to strike down such people as an example to posterity, but because he is good and merciful [Sir 2:13] and deigns with his ever-blessed patience to urge us to seek the saving remedy of confession and penance. If there are any, God forbid, who think they can commit these little faults without grave danger to their souls, and who neglect to remedy their transgressions by the worthy fruits of confession and penance, they can be certain that they cannot stay at this level of negligence, but little by little as they become less careful, the increasing bilge water of negligence will without doubt plunge the ship of their consciences into the depths unless God helps them. Wherefore, let all of us who are professed in this most illustrious Order have the zeal to observe faithfully not only the major but even the least of all its institutes, lest perchance—may it never happen—the fervor of the Order should grow cold and pass away in our times, and we, if we are found guilty before the just Judge of such great sacrilege, shall with the impious receive his strict sentence: not to see the glory of God.

CHAPTER TWENTY-FIVE

*About a Monk Who Presumed to Sleep without His Socks,
and How He Was Prohibited from Becoming an Abbot
through a Divine Revelation*[64]

We have come to realize in the preceding accounts how a deliberate transgression is punished severely, but less, I think, than one committed through contempt. So now I will recount a similar story that happened not at Clairvaux but at another house of the Cistercian Order, which also shows how the transgression of the least of our Order's mandates is not a small thing with God. And by this double example, as by a caring hand, may our souls be stirred out of indolence and put on guard.

The abbacy of a certain house in the Cistercian Order was vacant. The father abbot was summoned so the monks of that house could hold the election in his presence and with his advice and, in accordance with the rules [CC 11], elect a suitable person to serve as father and pastor of their souls. When the time for the election was at hand and the father abbot had learned the vote and wishes of each member from public and private discussions [RB 64.1], he realized that the greater part had settled unanimously on someone who was then absent but expected very soon to return. That person was the great cellarer of the house. On the night of the election, however, the father abbot heard, by divine revelation, a voice saying, "Take care, lest you install as abbot that monk who dared to sleep without socks." Greatly troubled by these words, the venerable abbot only knew in his surprise that the Lord was trying to tell him something. The person mentioned above, whom he thought suitable for the dignity of such an office, had arrived the previous evening to take part in the election. In the morning

---

[64] See RB 22.5-6 on monks sleeping already dressed and ready to rise. McGuire ("A Lost Clairvaux *Exemplum* Collection Found," 45) posits that this story was almost surely taken from John of Clairvaux's *Liber visionum et miraculorum* (Troyes MS 946, f. 153v).

he made the sign to the father abbot that he wanted to make his confession and took him into the chapter house [EO 70.87-96]. There, he humbly confessed that on his journey he had presumed to pull off his socks because of the intense heat and to sleep without wearing them. After that, the seniors and the more mature monks were assembled in council with the father abbot to discuss the election, and they all unanimously began to cast their vote for the man whom the confidential divine revelation had judged ineligible for such an honor. So the father abbot told them secretly about the divine order given him and advised them to elect someone else, saying that he could not go against his conscience and disobey the Lord's command.

CHAPTER TWENTY-SIX

*About the Wonderful Fervor of Dom John,
a Former Prior of Clairvaux*[65]

I think it appropriate to recall in these pages for the edification of posterity the sweet memory of John, a former prior of Clairvaux, a virtuous man whom circumstances have taken from us. He was set on fire by the warmth of the house of Father Rechab [1 Chr 2:55], whose name means "to go up," that is, by the fervor for heavenly discipline which the holy Father Bernard passed on to him, and he disposed his heart to ascend [Ps 83:6]. He set himself with unabated constancy to observe the boundaries laid out by the tradition of the fathers and without exception carefully refrained from drinking of the wine of sensual pleasures and worldly pomp, which he abhorred like deadly poison. This is just that what is demanded by the miserable indigence of our time, when lukewarmness and negligence are

---

[65] Prior John of Clairvaux was the compiler of the *Liber miraculorum*, used by Conrad in the preceding chapter; see *Chronicon Claraevallense* (PL 185:1249C). See Grießer, EM, 253n1, for additional bibliography.

so prevalent that everyone thinks himself a model of fervor, if not found to be slack and negligent. This energetic man held the office of prior at Clairvaux for many years, and he carried out this part of his responsibilities with such energy of spirit and endurance of body that he seemed to have placed as a seal upon his heart [Song 8:6] this rule of conduct which the blessed Father Benedict laid down for the prior of the monastery when he said, "The more he is set above the rest, the more he should be concerned to observe the precepts of the Rule" [RB 65.17]. He was always prompt and energetic at divine service and gave himself no relief by day or night. He particularly devoted himself with full attention of mind to the sweet psalmody that is celebrated in that holy community with great deliberation and vocal concentration, to the extent that everyone admired him, but there were few who could imitate him. The Lord had given him a marvelous talent for his pious exercise; he had a deep and strong voice, and he was careful to use it faithfully in the service of him who had given it. He knew that the streams of grace must return to their source if they are to flow out abundantly. So when he stood in the midst of the young men playing on the timbrels [Ps 67:26], he was superior to the others because of the dignity of his office but also more eminent because of his holy fervor, singing psalms with all his heart as if he were seeking to outdo the princes, that is, the angelic spirits who mingle with the choir, ready to offer in the sight of divine Majesty the devotion of those chanting psalms as the odor of very fragrant incense.[66] For him, it was a great privation when hoarseness or another infirmity prevented him from taking part in the holy service of psalmody with less than his usual vigor. That happened very rarely, for along with his other gifts he had received a healthy and suitably robust body, always able to carry out whatever good work [2 Tim 2:21] his soul desired. Who can sufficiently admire and worthily express his inner constancy in the service of God and his courage in bear-

---

[66] See Bernard of Clairvaux, Csi 5.7-8 (SBOp 3:471–73; CF 37:146–49) on the orders of the angels, which include angels, archangels, virtues, powers, principalities, dominions, thrones, cherubim, and seraphim. See also Bernard, SC 19 (SBOp 1:108–13; CF 4:140–44). The EM also refers to the order of angels in EM 6.2.

ing the daily fatigue of the very long daily period of holy Vigils? How manfully he fought off sloth, laziness, and sleepiness, and how severely he reproached himself when by the frailty of human nature they sometimes caught up with him! He thought up a devout device for keeping himself on watch constantly. Above the stall in which he stood he put an ingenious mechanism, so that if by chance he grew tired by the length of Vigils and began to nod off, his head would fall against a hammer which would come down and its blow would immediately return him to vigilance.

He often went out to do manual labor when he happened not to be otherwise occupied and there showed himself not dilatory at the task, and by his word and example he encouraged the flagging [RB 48.9] to keep at their work. Especially during haying and harvest time, when the blessed martyrs of Clairvaux were being baked all day as if in an oven, he persisted at the job so tenaciously that he reckoned he was washing away all the negligences he had committed at other times [RB 49.3] by the sweat of those punishing days. To remind himself that he was a pilgrim and a stranger on this earth [1 Pet 2:11] and that here he had no abiding city but looked for the city that is to come [Heb 13:14], he used as little as possible of the things of the world. He sanctified his body with the ornament of temperance and soberness and perfected the virtues of the soul by mortifying the flesh. All his apparel showed this same modesty and humility; he sought out and embraced old and tattered clothes and fled like the plague from stuff that was expensive, soft, and fine. Not to mention other things, he would allow no feathers to be put in the pillow on his bed, on which he rested his exhausted head after the labors of the day and vigils of the night but instead stuffed it with hay and straw, certainly not deaf to that maxim one reads in *Lives of the Fathers*—which is spurned by many as being overly harsh—that "too much rest for the body is an abomination."[67]

How blessed was the scorn and low opinion this holy man had of himself because of his sincere humility, and how preferable it is to the arrogance of a certain abbot whose pathetic pretensions

---

[67] For this saying: *Le Grande Exorde*, 257n16.

we know about from a reliable source. He governed a certain Cistercian monastery in Saxony and never deigned to use fabric made from the wool produced in the country, but each year he had precious fabrics delivered from Flanders to satisfy his panderings to luxury and vanity. At his death, when the monks divided his clothing among themselves, the prior of the house kept one of his tunics. When he put it on one night for a solemn feast, out of reverence, so to speak, he cried out terribly, as if he were being burned by glowing strips of red-hot metal, and threw the accursed garment as far away as possible. Once discarded, it gave out sparks like a fire in a brazier. Terrified by this miracle, everyone else who had taken part of this abominable spoil went hastily to find it. They tossed them into a heap and from it on all sides came sparks of fire as from a burning furnace. This repulsive sight went on until the neighboring abbots had been summoned to see for themselves this remarkable judgment of God.

Quite unlike this was the humble John, quite unlike. He preferred the abasement of Christ's humility to all the pomp of the Egyptians [Heb 11:26; EM 3.28]. He did not seek expensive clothes but showed contempt for them; yet by the coarseness of his habit he did not crave worldly renown but longed and prayed that one day he might be clothed in glory like the angels.

CHAPTER TWENTY-SEVEN

*With What Great Constancy the Venerable Prior John*
*Spurned the Luxuries of the Flesh*

John's patience and inner constancy remained unaltered in all the exercises and pious labor of the religious life. Although he sweated in the daily struggle, he would not easily allow himself the relief of any kind of material comfort and would agree to skip the brothers' Vigils or go to the infirmary only as a last resort. It happened once that he was suddenly taken ill at holy Vigils and could not chant the psalms with his usual zeal. As he felt the disease getting worse and worse and spreading throughout his body and even though his own thoughts urged him to leave choir, he remained, thinking sadly that the poor state of his health was going to force him to go into the infirmary, something he had always tried to avoid. After Vigils was over, he went to a more private spot, and when he believed he was alone, he talked to himself, saying, "What now, poor John, what are you going to do now? Are you really sick? Are you really so stricken with some little inconvenience as to go to the infirmary—the place where they tenderheartedly revive bodies that are beaten by the rod of God? Where they terribly weaken the consciences of those fooling themselves they are being beaten? Great! You will get into a bed fitted out with a soft mattress. Out of regard for the office which you hold unworthily, they will prepare for your flesh, destined for death and decay, all the best things in the cellar and the most delicate things in the pantries, and then because of your example, the more negligent brothers will seek easy comfort for their bodies. Ought you to interrupt the course of your penitence with this self-indulgent infirmity? Why do you not instead rely on the mercy of God, who is powerful and who can temper your illness so that your body will be kept in trim and yet not taken away from the work of penitence which is the seed of eternal blessedness?"

God allowed a monk to be near the place where the man of the Lord was talking to himself like this. Separated from him by a single wall, he heard clearly the whispers of John's pious murmurs, and he soon ran to tell the right reverend Abbot Gerard, whom I mentioned above [EM 2.27, 28], what he had heard the prior say. Summoned by him, John was obliged to go to the infirmary, compelled by obedience, although the seriousness of his illness alone seemed to necessitate this.

His energy; his discernment; his prudence in the exercise of his office; his goodness, tenderness, and charity toward his brothers; his firmness and authority when justice demanded—my paltry ability is not equal to describing. Accordingly, John bore the ways of the delicate and tender, but new and wrongly acquired customs contrary to the form of the Order and smacking more of the flesh than the spirit and known to sprout easily through the negligence of prelates and the subversion of religious observance, he never allowed to sneak in while he was prior of Clairvaux. He certainly knew that, just as those prelates are blessed who preserve the traditions of the fathers intact through the vigor of discipline, so too those are absolutely worthless who allow their religious observance to become tepid and their Order to perish through negligence and inattention. For, once observance has been put aside, it cannot be reformed without great trouble and distress for both subjects and superiors. John's watchfulness was extreme, not only in great matters, but also in lesser ones, as they occurred. For instance, the venerable Abbot Gerard had given leave for one of the senior monks, entirely decrepit and almost toothless, to eat the infirmary bread in the brothers' refectory. The prior could not contain himself. His impatience came not out of the invidious vice of jealousy but out of his zeal for the religious life and the observance of the Order. He said, therefore, "Were there never before now old and sick men in this holy house? Did they ever usurp things that we now presume to allow ourselves? Did they not accept special privileges and physical dispensations out of obedience to the person ordering them rather than taking them of their own will, and did any lenience granted them in any way ever contradict to the customs of the Order? Indeed, we know that many of them rose so high in spirituality and were so freed from the cares of the body that even in decrepit old age they thought themselves very unhappy if they were found to be inferior to the rest in fasting and vigils. They refused even the small dispensations the superiors offered them. Our holy predecessors began courageously with ardor of spirit and ended with still more ardor of spirit. God forbid that we need fear, and greatly fear, that we may be beginning in the spirit and ending feebly in the flesh [Gal 3:3]. If there is among us any senior monk whose life of labor and enfeebled limbs do not allow him to be in the ranks of the community, it would be better to let him gain release and go to the infirmary for the care of his ailments than to let him stay in community among those who are fasting and sustaining nature with rough food, and demand the luxuries of the ill. I am sure that each will receive a due reward for his labors

[1 Cor 3:8], that he who sows little reaps little [2 Cor 9:6], and that the judge who threatened terrifyingly to carry lamps to the most hidden places in Jerusalem [Zeph 1:12] will examine very closely the circumstances and the need that would take anyone out of the burden and heat of the day [Matt 20:12; EP Prol.], above all, when that one is engaged in the vineyard of the Lord of Hosts."

John, this veteran of God's grace, laudably reached the end of his life with unflagging zeal for holy fervor and radiance of monastic conduct and, afflicted by illness, took to his bed to be received by the supreme Father of the family and receive his penny for the day [Matt 20:2] and that good measure, pressed down and running over [Luke 6:38], which he had gained by his many labors and extraordinary watchings and also by his courageous fidelity in the service of God. Two holy men came to visit him—Eskil, former archbishop of Denmark [EM 3.27], and Alan, former bishop of Auxerre.[68] Seeing that in his extremely grave illness this fervent man had not departed one bit from his usual austerity, not even to the extent of accepting the relief of a softer habit, one more appropriate to his suffering and feebleness, they were moved with fervent compassion and ordered that more supple and commodious garments be brought, things they considered much more appropriate to such a person and to his weakened state, and entreated him to wear them for some relief. This brave athlete of the Lord looked very severely at the garments they put in front of him and said, "Will I be any more blessed under this soft, dainty stuff than under something thick and coarse? What will be the good of my having tried so hard to persevere in humility since the first years of my conversion if I am to lose it at the point of death? Be quite sure of this: while there is breath in my body, I will not draw back from the lowliness by which I chose to be of no account in the house of my God [Ps 83:11], nor will I give my enemies occasion to criticize me when I speak with them at the gate [Ps 126:5]. But when, at God's summons, I lay aside this moribund and already

---

[68] Alan of Auxerre, a monk of Clairvaux who became bishop of Auxerre in 1152 and fifteen years later retired to Clairvaux, where he died in 1185. He composed the second book of the *Vita Prima Bernardi*.

dying shell, you may dress and decorate this putrid sack of flesh as you will, for I confess it does not matter to me what happens to my body once the spirit has gone out of it." And strengthened by such firmness of faith and virtue, the man of the Lord, John, put off the material world of corruptible flesh and deserved to see the good things of the Lord in the land of the living [Ps 26:13]. His body, buried with suitable honor, rests in peace alongside the holy bones of the brothers of the old abbey whom he had enthusiastically imitated in patience and humility.[69]

## Chapter Twenty-Eight

### *About the Venerable Man Dom Gerard, Monk of Clairvaux and Later Abbot*[70]

Our great Father Bernard, like a powerful "eagle with great wings" and abundant feathers, great in merits, sublime on the wings of holy contemplation, adorned with all virtues, planted the "pith of the cedar tree" [Ezek 17:3]—that is, the perfection of religious life— which he had undertaken on the heights of Lebanon—that is, the height of divine grace—in the solitude of the valley of wormwood, into the saving bitterness of penitence which soon turned it into the Valley of Light, Clairvaux.[71] Soon that monastic life began to be transplanted over many waters—that is, turning the fractious and arrogant wills of many nations, for they are like violent dark green whirlpools—toward the veneration of true piety.

---

[69] For the location of his tomb, see *Monumenta s. Claraevallensis abbatiae* 6 (PL 185:1559).

[70] Probably Gerard, second abbot of Alvastra in Sweden. Alvastra was in the Diocese of Linkoping and was the location of Saint Bridget's visions. See James France, *The Cistercians in Scandinavia*, CS 131 (Kalamazoo, MI: Cistercian Publications, 1992), 27–42; and Grießer, EM, 258n5. The manuscript tradition of the EM is very confusing in regard to how this chapter is numbered; for details see Grießer, EM, 260 at line 28 in the critical apparatus.

[71] Conrad again employs valley imagery to describe Clairvaux (*vallis absinthialis . . . Claramvallem*); see above in EM 4.6 and Prol.

The venerable abbot wanted to produce some fruit among the peoples of the north too, and at the request of a religious woman, the queen of Sweden,[72] he sent a group of monks to those parts. The monks and lay brothers who were selected to train these rude and untamed people in the ways of religious life and discipline were overcome with grief. They begged Bernard not to send them out into such distant and barbarous regions where they would be far from the presence of such a father. The holy abbot replied, "What are you doing, dearest brothers? Why do you afflict my soul with unreasonable tears and prayers? Am I to follow my own will in this matter and not that of God to whom we all owe obedience?"

Near him lay the vestments, holy vessels, and other things needed for carrying out the Divine Office, which the brothers being sent were supposed to take with them. Wishing to assure them that his comments had come from the Lord [Gen 24:50], he took the basin meant for the water that is poured over the hands of the priest, and putting his finger on the bottom of it, he said, "Here is a sign that it is the Spirit of the Lord who is sending you" [see Luke 2:12]. And the hardness and inflexibility of the metal took a soft impression of his finger, and still today one can clearly make out the size of his blessed finger, for the metal was dented on the outside just as it buckled on the inside. As proof of this great miracle, the basin is kept with great reverence in the sacristy of the monastery which the venerable father sent them to found. The aforesaid brothers, seeing clear evidence of divine grace, rejoiced and held back the goad of destructive tears, and although they could not but go with some horror of spirit to the extremely remote nations shrouded in the most wintry of northern climates, they nevertheless knew with a trusting confidence that they went with the grace of God and with the intervention of the favor and the prayers of their holy father.

There was among them a young man with a naturally happy disposition and dove-like simplicity. He was called Gerard and came from Utrecht in the province of Second Germany.[73] More

[72] Ulfhild (*c.* 1100–1148), consort of King Sverker I (1134–55).

[73] The Latin place name is *Traiectum*. As Grießer notes, this could be either Maastricht (*Traiectum ad Mosam*) or Utrecht (*Traiectum ad Rhenum*).

worried than his companions, he said to the man of God, with tears in his eyes, "Most blessed father, I am a most unhappy young man, for I left my father's house and spurned everything that I might have loved and wanted in this world, and out of love for the religious life I came to you as to my father, hoping to rejoice in your sweetest presence and be formed by your teaching and example, to be helped by your merits and prayers and to find in the retreat of this holy community a place of safety against the storms of passions and the heat of youthful yearnings. And what I long for with all my being is to await the last day [John 6:39-40] near the blessed remains of our brothers resting in this cemetery. And now look, today you are sending me far away from you [Gen 4:14]; I will lose the companionship of this holy community, and what is more, I shall be deprived of the tomb I desired. For that, above all, I am desperately sorrowful and my heart is troubled within me [Ps 54:5]." Moved by compassion for the young man, the blessed man took pains to comfort the grief-stricken soul of his son with gentle words, and in the spirit of prophesy he foresaw and foretold what was to happen half a century later. "My dearest son," he said, "go where the Holy Spirit deigns to send you, and work as an energetic laborer in the field of the Lord. I promise you, in the name of the Lord, and I guarantee you that you will die as you desired at Clairvaux, and together we will await the glorious coming of the celestial Bridegroom." With great joy the young brother regarded this solemn promise from the pious father as a pledge of the realization of his desire, knowing that the man whose miracles and prophetic signs gave clear evidence that he was the repository of truth and divine wisdom could neither deceive nor be deceived.

So he went, and he carried out energetically the duties of cellarer and prior in the house that he and his brothers were sent to found, and then by divine grace he was elected abbot in title and responsibility. He accepted this eminent position only with reluctance, preferring to work out his salvation in an obscure position rather than run the risk of high office, but he decorated the office he undertook with the luster of a very observant monastic life. Because there were not many priests in that country, few of the people embraced the monastic life, but from German and English lands God sent to his faithful servant educated and discerning men who made monastic discipline flourish in that kingdom and bear fruit among people who had only heard of monks but had never before seen one.

As lord abbot he freed himself for spiritual duties by turning over the temporal administration of the house and all its affairs to the cellarer Abraham, whose prudence he knew well. He set himself most of all to gaining souls. He was active and vigilant in the service of God and busied himself with work when he was not doing anything else and also with reading; he sought physical sustenance from the common store and strove to be a model of piety and regularity for his brothers. He had a marvelous gift of gentleness and patience. For example, he once reproved a monk for a fault, and the man, possessed by a demon, came down the steps of the dormitory and struck him hard with his fist, which caused him no little suffering. Far from expelling the wicked man or punishing him for his grave fault [RB 25], on the contrary, he took him aside and begged his pardon and asked him, for the love of God, to set aside the resentment he felt against him.

## CHAPTER TWENTY-NINE

### *About a Monk Who Had an Invisible Bloodletting by a Great Miracle of God's Grace*

Among the first sons of the aforesaid house whom the Lord called to conversion from that land, there was a certain monk of wonderful simplicity and innocence who, like another Paul the Simple, followed the way of humility and obedience without complaint [Phil 2:15], behaving like a very meek lamb among his brothers.[74]

---

[74] Paul the Simple was a disciple of Antony the Great, well-known for his asceticism and obedience. See Russell, *The Lives of the Desert Fathers*, CS 34, 114–15, 137n1, 155; and Ward, *The Sayings of the Desert Fathers* CS 59, 8n31, 205–7.

He brought forth honey from the rock and oil from the hardest stone [Deut 32:13]; in short, he brought forth from a barbarous and stiff-necked people [Ps 113:1; Bar 2:30; Acts 7:51] the flower of gentleness and humility. Indeed he showed himself very obedient in everything, and if by chance he asked for something necessary, but which seemed less than necessary to the person in charge, he bore the refusal of his request patiently. Yet there was one thing which he could not calmly put up with being refused. In fact, by the grace of God his impatience was turned into virtue's merit because of his innate simplicity. Now it happened once that he was vehemently afflicted with a very severe headache and had no hope of being able to bear the stabs of pain in any way other than by letting some blood through an incision in his temporal artery. So he went to the abbot and explained to him the calamity he was suffering [Job 6:2] and humbly asked that he might order him to undergo the one remedy he hoped for in his need. The abbot refused, afraid it would be dangerous, so the monk went away silently in great sadness and weariness of mind, and entering the church in the simplicity of his heart, he gave himself to prayer before one of the altars, and with many tears and sighs breaking from the depth of his heart, he began to cry out to the Lord like this: "Lord, my God, you know that out of love for you I have renounced the world and all worldly things and that out of love for you I have also so bound myself by the strictest bonds of obedience that I cannot move either hand or foot without the order of a superior. And my abbot, who fills your sacred place, whom I must obey as if he were you and who ought to help me in all that I need but who is not sympathetic to this great calamity of mine, which he is not suffering [Job 6:2], has by the authority of obedience blocked off from my wretched self the remedy through which I could, I hoped, easily escape. So my Lord God, you who neither despise the groans of the contrite nor spurn the feelings of those who grieve nor pass lightly over the needs of the poor but rather see to the very root of misery: have pity on my pitifulness, dear Lord, help me in this tight corner, console the sorrowful, and grant the help that I dare not look for from man, lest I become disobedient. May I deserve to receive from your abundant generosity."

How greatly does God value devout and humble conversation; how swiftly does the pure and simple prayer pierce heaven [Heb 4:14]. How unbreakable is the truth of that testimony which rests upon the word the wise man speaks about God, that his communication is with the simple [Prov 3:32]. For no sooner had he finished the words of dove-like simplicity than this loving plaint sent from a contrite heart sounded in the ears of the Lord God of Hosts. And the inexhaustible compassion of divine love and mercy was moved toward this needy and poor soul [Ps 40:2], and the tremendous majesty so hastened to set his miserable servant free from his misery that, if one may dare to say so, he was more stirred by his compassion than was the poor fellow by his passion. At the same hour and in the same place there was an invisible bloodletting from the very vein he wanted, and he caught the spurting blood with his hands and clothing and ran swiftly and breathlessly to the meeting place, rejoicing and exalting with fear, for what he could not obtain from man he had been granted by the maker of men and the consoler of the humble.

Moreover, Abbot Gerard of pious memory did not attribute to his own actions any progress in virtue or advancement in religion, either in himself or in his subordinates, but attributed all to the glory of the Lord and to the merits of his most holy Father Bernard. If some necessity of business obliged him to go out from the monastery, he showed so much discipline and self-control in his dealings with the worldly that both the king and the princes of that land respected him as a true man of God, making much of his advice and hearing him willingly [Mark 6:20]. The duke of that land, a brave and powerful man, had such reverence for the blessed man that he deferred to him and counted his sovereignty and rank such a small thing next to the abbot's heavenly sanctity that he would sometimes say to his associates, "Any time I think the Abbot Gerard is watching me, I tremble with fear, as if the most hidden secrets of my heart were clear to his eyes."

When, after his fortieth year as a prelate, Gerard grew old and had reached frail old age, and his body was racked with various infirmities, the brothers with whom he had lived for so long began to beg him to choose the location of his tomb among them, with whom he had so long lived in community. But the man of the Lord replied, "I beg you, do not speak about that, my sons. It is proper by any measure that I die at Clairvaux, and then, according to the promise of my beloved father, I will sleep and rest there in peace [Ps 4:9] with the saints who lie there." The monks insisted, saying, "Father, how are we going to get you to Clairvaux when you are so bowed down and weakened by the infirmities and the hindrances of your great age that we're convinced there is scarcely enough breath in your body to get you to the closest boundary of Denmark?" He replied with much confidence, "The word of God that I heard from the mouth of that most reverent man is powerful and strong, living and effective [Heb 4:12], and it has penetrated deep into my heart. It is for me a gauge or a pledge of the hope for my heart, and it tells me that I can make the journey, but take care to do quickly what I tell you." They placed him in a litter between two horses, and truly by a great miracle he came from the edge of the world to Clairvaux, having crossed immense spaces of land and escaped all kinds of perils on the sea and rivers. There, after a short while in the infirmary, he gave up his spirit with a good confession. He was buried where he had wanted to be, near the tomb of the Dom Benedict of blessed memory, who had loved him like a friend during his life. When news of his death reached the king of Sweden, he sighed and said, "The soil of my kingdom was not worthy to offer a tomb to the sacred bones of such a venerable man."

CHAPTER THIRTY

*Concerning a Vision*
*through Which a Novice at Clairvaux Was Delivered from*
*a Temptation*

A clerk of the Order of canons regular wanted a more austere and holy form of life, and he came devoutly to Clairvaux where he was received. In the early days of his training, he worked earnestly to make the sweet flowers of religious virtues grow in his soul.[75] But he had barely forgotten the pleasant sweetness of his previous life, and the austerity of his new one seemed to him more bitter every day. From deep within him tempests of various temptations soon began rising, as those who pass from another Order into the Cistercian Order often experience more than do seculars who come from the world. Images of the customs they followed for so long remain in the eyes of their hearts, and the wily enemy persuades them that those customs were reasonable and good. On the other hand, their minds flee and abhor the observances of Cîteaux that they are now required to learn as being rougher and less agreeable. This indecisive and irresolute little lamb was already thinking of retracing his steps in shameful apostasy, but divine mercy saw fit to remove his error and confirm him in his good purpose.

There appeared to the novice in a vision of the night [Dan 7:13] the Lord of majesty, King of kings and Lord of lords [Rev 19:16], Christ Jesus, Son of God, coming on the clouds of heaven to judge the earth in equity [Acts 17:31] and render to each according to his works [Matt 16:27]. Then truly, with the entire race of humankind uncertain with fear and much trembling at this examination, all the Orders which are in the Church of God gathered together, one by one in separate groups, very worried about the observances and rites of their Rule and Order, for fear the most severe Judge with his most subtle scrutiny might perhaps discover something done amiss by them. If only those who profess the Rule of Saint Augustine had paid attention to what the sentences they read daily in his Rule, rather than seeming to live as seculars, indeed, not just seeming to be seculars but taking pride in it. And then there were those who professed the habit and form of religious life through the Rule of Saint Benedict: their way of life was wholly secular; maintaining a faith in this world they are known to have lied to God by their tonsure [RB 1.7]. In the meantime, the aforementioned novice saw one illustrious Order of many members set apart from the others, and a young man resplendent with celestial

---

[75] "In the early days of his training" (*primordia tirocinii*) is an example of the military imagery sometimes used in monastic texts. See EM Prol, n4.

glory stood in its midst as if he were the leader and patron of this divine army. When this holy group had moved forward to come before the Lord, the aforesaid young man came forward quickly, and they all followed him with no lack of confidence that they would receive mercy. The other Orders drew back out of respect for those who were coming and bowed as they passed, and they seemed to be praising them for the privilege of their happiness. Then the Lord Jesus Christ, the splendor of the Father's glory,[76] terrible in his almighty majesty yet tender as a little worm of the wood [2 Sam 23:8] in his goodness and kindness, received the young leader with the kiss of peace and shed his divine light on him and all his monastic family. The novice who was watching this began to wonder which congregation it was that was so favored and received from the Lord more honor than all the rest. Someone told him it was the Order of Cîteaux and that the splendid young man was the great Saint Bernard, first abbot of Clairvaux. As soon as he had heard this, returning to himself as from an ecstasy, he said to himself, "Have I not become a novice in this Order and in the great monastery of Clairvaux? Why then do I rest in idleness like a wretch and not hurry to join this illustrious company and so at last have a share in the eternal blessedness?" Saying these things he began with all his strength to quicken his pace, but something was in his way and stopped his advance. It was like a twisted and knotted tree whose branches twined around his feet and lower legs so that he labored in vain and could not move a step. Whence he became incredibly angry at being held back from so great a good by such a paltry impediment, and struggling to free himself he awoke. When he reflected prudently on his vision now that he was awake and sober, he manfully turned the resentment he had conceived in his sleep against the snares of temptation which had held him in their grip. And so, with great strictness, he banished from his heart those images of his former customs that had previously seemed delightful and after which he had gone whoring and did not let them control him anymore. He now embraced

---

[76] "The splendor of the Father's glory" appears to originate in the Ambrosian chant for Vigils and Lauds; *Le Grande Exorde,* 267n12.

with all longing of his mind the holy institutes of Cîteaux, which are the mirror of justice but which he had denigrated in his mind while under the influence of the evil spirits. Thus, running on the straight and narrow way, not, as it were, aimlessly [1 Cor 9:26], he obtained eternal beatitude.[77]

## Chapter Thirty-One

### *How Demons Wished to Do Harm to a Certain Lay Brother, but Were Not Able to Do So*[78]

Among the shepherds at Clairvaux there was a lay brother who was a good and observant man and carried out his duties with zeal and gentleness in the fear of God. The jealous enemy of all good was extremely upset by his devotion and the simplicity of his monastic way of life. He attempted to wield some of his wickedness against him, but with the assistance of God all the efforts of his malice came to nothing. One night the brother was at the sheepfold, watching and keeping the night watch over his flock [Luke 2:8], and suddenly there was a violent storm, winds howling and rushing, thunder rolling all around in a terrifying manner, with frequent flashes of lightning in the clouds spreading fear and terror in human minds. This brother jumped up in terror, made many signs of the cross, called upon the name of God, and commended himself earnestly to all the saints. While he stood there praying, he began to hear the clamor and shouting, as it were, of a great army coming at a quick march toward him, and the closer they came, the more clearly their voices resonated. There was not only the din of men and the cry of trumpets, but on top of this the roaring of monsters and savage animals and great outcries could be heard. This multitude arrived

---

[77] Concerning the phrase "straight and narrow way," see note above at EM 1.9.
[78] Herbert of Clairvaux, LM 137 in some codices, but it is not in the PL; see Grießer, EM, 264n3.

with a deafening hubbub by the sheepfold, as if they were going to tear the sheep limb from limb and devour them, but the brother redoubled his prayers and repelled the attackers with divine power. The band could not break into the enclosure, but the battle lines divided and they passed quickly by without causing any harm. Nevertheless, two enormous giants, blacker than soot, turned off and came toward the praying brother. After they had stood right in front of him for a bit, one of them said to the other, "It is truly the devil that leads us on and has brought us here. Did I not tell you that we would not be able to cross this good place?" With these words, they fled quickly as if they had wings, and once they had moved on a little, all the inhabitants of darkness that had accompanied them also disappeared. The very brother who saw this vision vouched for its truth to me. His way of life was such that we would think it outrageous to doubt his word. Certainly there are powerful enemies who are forbidden to oppose the goodness of the just, unless God allows it for some purpose.

## Chapter Thirty-Two

### How the Lord and His Glorious Mother Appeared to a Brother[79]

In the house of Fontmorigny[80] lived a certain lay brother, named Robert, who, having been sent from Clairvaux, never forgot the discipline and observances he had learned there, but, in fact, he gave an example of virtue and devotion in all his conduct to the brothers of the place. Among other pious endeavors which he diligently offered to the Lord, he especially honored the Virgin Mary, the most blessed Bearer of God. He also ruminated in frequent and sweet meditation on the memory of blessed Bernard, also his

---

[79] Herbert of Clairvaux, LM 2.40 (PL 185:1349–50).

[80] In Latin *Fons-Morigniaci*. Fontmorigny, founded 1148, was a daughter house of Clairvaux in the Diocese of Bourges. Janauschek, 115; Cottineau 1:1192.

special patron. Having finished the course of this present life, he deserved to see in advance the certainty of his own salvation and also the day of his death in a prognostic vision.

Five days before his falling asleep he saw in a vision the Lord Jesus Christ and his most blessed Mother with Saint Bernard the abbot, standing in some garden of delights; the vastness of its beauty and magnificence no human language can describe. The same brother who saw this stood among them and humbly asked for the refuge of divine mercy. Then the most conscientious Mother said to her son, "Lord and son, what are you going to do for this poor one of yours?" And the Lord said to her, "Whatever you please, Mother." The protector of the weak and consoler of the humble replied, "I want you to bring him into your rest," to which he said, "It shall be as you ask." Then the most blessed Virgin asked, "And when will this happen?" And the Lord replied, "He will come and be saved in five days." After this vision ended the lay brother told others what he had seen and heard. They were all very astonished and curiously awaited the day named. The event proved the truth of the prediction. The sickness from which he suffered grew worse, and on the fifth day, as the Lord had promised, Robert left his body and went into the eternal rest and peace that passes all understanding [Phil 4:7] and was taken up, as the most blessed virgin Bearer of God had deigned to obtain for him through her most caring prayers. Happy, therefore, are all those who trust in her and devote themselves to her service, because the most generous Benefactor will give back to them a good measure, compressed, shaken together, and running over [Luke 6:38]. The brothers of the monastery were greatly edified by the happy death of this man of God, and they imitated the discipline of Clairvaux that they had seen in him. They also devoted themselves with much zeal to the veneration of the holy *Theotocon* [EM 4.13], Our Lady, knowing that no work undertaken for her glory is ever lost to them.

CHAPTER THIRTY-THREE

*About a Monk Who Was Told, "Your Sins Are Forgiven"*[81]

Among the athletes of Christ who did spiritual battle in the arena
of Clairvaux, there was the valiant contender Everard, who had
been a notable soldier in the world.[82] He had renounced the pomp
of the world and exchanged service in a useless army for that in a
more fruitful one. He joined the Knights of the Temple, and was so
distinguished by his fidelity that he was made Grand Master of the
Order. In this office he used the vigor of his body and powers of
soul with which the Lord had endowed him, not against his fellow
citizens, but against the enemy, and he was careful to use his vigor
not for the applause of the world but for the rewards of heaven.
Nevertheless, since that army did not know the rest of Mary and
was totally occupied in the labors of Martha [Luke 10:38-42], at
which it is impossible not to raise at least some dust of dereliction,
he took the oath to a more sacred army and went to Clairvaux,
where, just as he had ennobled his first military service by his second, he now surpassed the second by the third.[83] After this he no
longer labored to develop the strength of his body but set himself to
subdue it by fasting, vigils, and many labors and to test his love by
the mortification of his own will and the voluntary poverty which
alone forms the true militia of Christian observance. Given entirely
to prayer and remorse, he earnestly and with daily tears asked for
the mercy of the Lord Christ for his earlier mistakes. After doing all
this for a while, he became, according to the prophet, a man seeing

---

[81] Herbert of Clairvaux, LM 120 (or 121) in some codices; not in the PL; see
Grießer, EM, 266n2.

[82] Everard, the Master of the Temple, was in Clairvaux for some period. According to Herbert of Clairvaux he was there for twenty-one years, but Grießer,
EM, 266–67n3, provides extensive bibliography to show that this was almost
certainly not the case. It appears that Everard was in the Holy Land with Louis VII
in 1147 and that he witnessed a charter of King Baldwin III of Jerusalem in 1154.

[83] Regarding the spiritual interpretation of Mary and Martha, see note above,
EM 2.33.

his poverty by the rod of the Lord's indignation [Lam 3:1]. At last, the good Lord willed to mix the wild herbs of his bitter penitence with the unleavened bread that is the grace of consolation [Exod 12:8], without which the Lamb of eternal life cannot be eaten. He deigned in this way to show his generosity to his remorseful and self-disciplined servant. Once, when he was at prayer, coming before the face of the Lord in confession and imploring for his sins [Ps 94:2], he was suddenly rapt in an ecstasy of the mind [Ps 30:23; Acts 11:5], and he saw the Lord Jesus Christ saying to him in a voice full of kindness, "Your sins are forgiven" [see Luke 7:47–48]. Soon coming out of his ecstasy and returned to himself, he felt enormous consolation. He thanked God and learned anew to serve the Lord in fear and rejoice in him with trembling [Ps 2:11; RB 19.3]. And in a very edifying way he lived to an advanced age, and full of days he went to his fathers and received eternal life from God as the reward of his labors.

This venerable man told us about a memorable miracle that happened shortly before this. He had heard about it from his brothers in arms who were very honorable men and who had witnessed it and investigated it quite carefully. In German lands a brave soldier of illustrious birth breathed his last at the end of this present life. He had lain dead for some time and the hour of his burial was at hand when suddenly the dead man came to life; he began to breath, pulled off the pall, opened his eyes, and sat up on his funeral couch, to the amazement of those present. The tears and lamentations of the mourners abruptly ceased, and they quizzed the resuscitated dead man on what had caused such a strange thing. In the presence of his wife and brother, who had been going to inherit his estate, he said the following to them: "When I closed my eyes in death I was led without delay to the tribunal of the sovereign Judge to be examined. Weighed on the scale of justice, I was found to be too light for salvation. The sentence of my damnation, which I deserved, was about to be pronounced when, thanks to the intercession of the saints who were present, I was allowed to come back among you to implore of your charity the remedy needed to remove the two chief obstacles to my salvation: considerable unpaid debts and an illegitimate marriage contract."

Then he turned to his wife and said, "My dear spouse, you knew that we were linked by a line of affinity when we were joined in an illicit marriage, and we have both thereby been placed in danger of eternal death.[84] Acknowledge that, for there is only one remedy: if you leave the pomp of the world and take Christ as your spouse by monastic profession, you will obtain pardon for me and glory for yourself." She gratefully agreed to this proposal and promised to do it without delay. Then he gathered together all his creditors and told his brother to pay each of them any just claims. Among them was a Jew who came up to demand the sum of three hundred gold pieces. The knight regarded him with a fierce face and flashing eyes and said, to the astonishment of those present, "You have nothing to claim either in heaven or on earth, or from any creature of God. But it is not for me to judge you before the time." Then he ordered that he be paid along with the others.[85] When he had finished saying this and many similar things, he laid his head down again and gave up his spirit.

## Chapter Thirty-Four

### About an Observant Lay Brother of Clairvaux Named Lawrence[86]

There was in Clairvaux an observant lay brother, Lawrence by name, whom we mentioned earlier while writing about the venerable

---

[84] Canon law texts of the day (particularly Gratian) did not tend to view a long-standing marriage based on such a deceit as one that should be dissolved outright. Rather, Gratian (and some Decretists) would generally have held that a dispensation should be granted depending on circumstances. See James A. Brundage, *Law, Sex, and Christian Society* (Chicago: University of Chicago Press, 1987), 243, 288–89.

[85] Bernard wrote specifically that Jews should not be persecuted or killed. See Epp 363.6-8 and 365 (SBOp 8:316–317, 320–22; James, Ep 391.6, pp. 462–63; Ep 393, pp. 465–66). See Paul Lockey, "Conflicting Cistercian Attitudes toward the Jews," *Truth as Gift: Studies in Medieval Cistercian History in Honor of John R. Sommerfeldt*, CS 204 (Kalamazoo, MI: Cistercian Publications, 2004), 355–76.

[86] Herbert of Clairvaux, LM 2.30 (PL 185:1340–42).

man Dom Gerard of Farfa [EM 3.17]. This man was truly spiritual and devout in his whole monastic way of life, persevering always with such remarkable tenacity in prayer and contrition that, during the many years he was in charge of the precious relics of the holy confessors Malachy and Bernard, guarding them day and night in the sacristy, he was almost never to be found elsewhere but there, applying himself to prayer and wetting the floor with his tears. It was only with great effort that he had, by the grace of God, arrived at such a high degree of purity and devotion, for at the beginning of his monastic life he had been vexed by many temptations and had had daily battles against the poisonous suggestions of malign spirits.

One night after Lauds, when he found himself alone in a room, an unclean spirit circled all around him, bellowing and sniveling. He made the sign of the cross on his forehead and asked who he might be. The double-dealing evildoer [Prov 14:25], to strike fear into the brother's yet inexperienced and tender mind, replied, "I am he who tempted Job and covered him with boils." At these words the brother, who was still new to monastic life, was greatly affrighted and fled the sight of the malignant spirit. He never saw it again.

After the passing of blessed Bernard, this brother was sent by the venerable prior of Clairvaux, Dom Philip,[87] to Roger, king of Sicily, on some business of the monastery. When he reached Rome, he heard that the king had very recently died.[88] Bewildered, he did not know what to do next. He remembered his holy Father Bernard, for whom he had frequently come and gone with success on various items of business. Turning with a groan and many tears to prayer, he invoked the same saint of God, saying, "'My father, my father, the chariot of Israel and its horseman' [2 Kgs 13:14], why have you abandoned me? Woe is me, holy father, what am I to say or do, poor and miserable as I am, bereft of any advice or help? While you were alive I went without fear under your orders into various lands and peoples, and I was received everywhere on

[87] Philip was Clairvaux's prior at the time of Bernard's death. He had taken holy orders from the Antipope Anacletus (King, *Cîteaux and Her Elder Daughters*, 247) and became abbot of Eleemosyna in 1156. See Grießer, EM, 269n1.

[88] Roger II, king of Sicily (1094–1154) died on 26 February 1154.

account of your grace. When I carried your greetings and letters, kings, bishops, and all the world received them as blessings sent from heaven; the most distinguished people were honored to be distinguished by your words of greeting. Now you are gone, and my credit has gone with you. No one will stretch out a hand to help a poor, helpless stranger. And what is more, the king who loved you with a sincere affection is dead, and his son reigns in his place, a child who perhaps never knew you.[89] If I go so far to find him and get a bad reception, my grief will be inconsolable at returning unsuccessful after the exhaustion of such a very long and laborious journey, I who during your lifetime returned to Clairvaux laden with all sorts of goods. Yet if I go straight back and without trying to accomplish the business, I am much afraid of being accused of laziness and poor judgment. Come and help me, I pray you, and give me the advice I need, and do not despise the groans of your wretched little servant." That same night the most blessed father appeared to him and lavishly consoled him, saying, "My brother, why do you despair of God's mercy and my help? For when or where did you sense that my assistance had failed you in your needs? Or do you perhaps think me less powerful now, when I have been led into the full power of God [Ps 70:16], than I once was while I lived in the flesh? Go forward with assurance because everything will come out fine, and you will know by this sign that I have sent you." While the saint was saying this and much besides, the soul of the brother dissolved in the ardor of his love, an immense joy filled his heart, and tears of devotion burst from his eyes. When he awoke, he found his eyes and cheeks were wet, as was the pillow on which his head had been resting, and he realized that they had been drenched by his flood of tears. Early the next morning he took to the road, and at the entrance to the town he met a group of merchants who were going to Sicily for trade. When they learned he was from Clairvaux, they were glad to take him into their company, and each day they gave him whatever he needed. When he was presented to the king of Sicily, he gained great prestige in his

---

[89] According to Grießer (EM, 269n4), Roger was succeeded by his son William I (1154–66), who was not a child but a young man at the time.

eyes. Not only did he bring the matter on which he had been sent to Roger to a happy conclusion, but the king opened his treasures and for the repose of the soul of his father he gave the same brother, with great devotion, a considerable sum toward the construction of a new abbey church at Clairvaux.[90]

On his return to Rome, the aforesaid brother was received so warmly that cardinals and many other Romans loaded him with gifts, to the point that he left the city with ten buffaloes bearing their gifts and hauled them to Clairvaux to the great astonishment of everyone. God protected him, and the merits of his holy father were his safeguard. Who would not be surprised that a feeble old man with the help of two boys could, safely and soundly, drive such enormous and redoubtable beasts, two or three times heavier and stronger than oxen, over so long a distance, over such dangerous places, at the risk of being surprised by robbers and bandits, especially if one remembers that no one in all the West had seen this kind of animal above the Alps?[91] They were able to avoid meeting with evildoers or violence, even for one day, and traveled unharmed, with God protecting his faithful servant through the prayers of Saint Bernard. It did happen one day that he was attempting to pass through a town where brigands were holding sway and where no one could avoid their hands unharmed unless he prevailed by sheer strength. At sunrise he got up, and as he left the field where he had passed the night with his buffaloes, he prayed intently to God and Saint Bernard to deliver him from this imminent danger. Then two men appeared in the distance and seemed to be coming toward him, each carrying a lighted candle in his hand. They came gradually closer, and when they had almost reached him, they suddenly disappeared from sight; this gave the servant of God great confidence that he would escape. Scarcely had he entered

---

[90] Piesik (*Exordium Magnum Cisterciense*, 2.411n115) notes that the first abbey church at Clairvaux was begun in 1115. A second, called "Clairvaux II," was begun in 1135 farther up the valley and finished around 1150 (Vita Bern 1.13.62; PL 185:261), while "Clairvaux III" was consecrated in 1174.

[91] Buffalo are said to have been brought to Italy by the Longobards after the fall of the Western empire.

this nest of demons when he was suddenly stopped and robbers surrounded him on all sides. But God watched over him, and at that very moment some honest men came by. When they learned that he was from Clairvaux, they freed him from the hands of his assailants and made them let him go on his way with all his goods. When he finally arrived at Clairvaux, to the amazement of everyone, he led in this novel kind of beast, which was propagated by repeated breeding and spread from there into many areas. The aged brother returned to his spiritual exercises and with full enthusiasm put his aged shoulders to the holy discipline he had learned from Saint Bernard. The merits and prayers of the holy abbot gave him a pious confidence that he would be protected from eternal harm and enjoy everlasting joy, since his protection had deigned to preserve him from the many perils of his journey and had mercifully brought him safe and sound to his Clairvaux.

## Chapter Thirty-Five

### *The Story of a Certain Spiritual Monk of Clairvaux*[92]

An observant and spiritual monk from the community of Clairvaux lived for a long time in one of that monastery's houses in Denmark. He returned one day to his motherhouse, and to edify his brothers he told them about a pleasant miracle worthy of credence which had recently occurred within the borders of Saxony. There was in that country a monastery of the Order of Cîteaux in which lived a monk of excellent religious observance and admirable humility. He served Christ the Lord in simplicity of heart, fervent and zealous about all the observances of the holy Order, despising himself and humbling himself on every occasion, particularly giving himself to silence and the work of peace, so that wherever he found himself, he was either praying or reading. He sought in his reading the

---

[92] Herbert of Clairvaux, LM 2.33 (PL 185:1344).

fruit less of learning than of devotion and delighted in it as in all manner of riches [Ps 118:14].

As the hour approached for him to leave this world, he was seriously ill and had already been anointed with the unction of the sick when he asked the infirmarians to wash his body and dress him in the clothing in which he would be buried. The brothers objected to this novelty and put off doing it, but he persisted in his request, and out of regard for his holiness they gave in at last to his wishes. After they had done all this, he said to those standing around him, "Go about your work, for I am not going to die just yet; it will be tomorrow after the servers have had their meal [EO 77] that the Lord will call me." All the brothers waited for this prediction of the man of God to be fulfilled, and the following day, at the very hour he had predicted, the sound of the board [EO 94.2] called them quickly to come to recite the office of commendation. They did this with such devotion that they anticipated with certainty that the dead man would soon enter into eternal life. That brother was drawing his last breath when he was illuminated by divine grace, his face was gladdened, and he said to those around him, "Look, the beloved disciple of the Lord, Saint John the Evangelist, is coming to us." For a little while he was silent, then he said, "And now look, the blessed Virgin Mary, the Bearer of God, is coming." At last, after a brief interval, beaming with still more abundant grace, he suddenly added in a clear voice, "Oh goodness, brothers, here is our Lord Jesus Christ with a legion of holy angels and saints." Then, after he had said this, suddenly ravished with jubilation and exaltation of heart, he began to intone the antiphon, *Subvenite sancti Dei*, "Help him, come to his aid, angels of the Lord."[93] He sang until he gave up his soul to God. The brothers were full of wonder at the sight of this man who thrilled with joy even in death and died singing, and they took up the antiphon from his lips and finished it with great fervor and in heavenly tones.

---

[93] *Le Grande Exorde*, 276n13, notes that this echoes EO 94.15, Annex 18, pp. 380–82. The passage that the monk was singing is from the Cistercian antiphon for the burial of a monk. He is, in effect, beginning the liturgy for his own funeral.

Therefore, the senior monk mentioned above faithfully made these things known to the brothers of Clairvaux and vehemently enkindled their souls with contempt for the world, disdain for themselves, and love for God. Would that everyone who reads or hears of these actions become imitators of them, knowing most certainly that the more one has been despised in this world, seeking silence, quiet, and humility, the more glorious and sublime he will appear in the future with God.

* * * * *

And so, thus far it has sufficed for us to discuss the bright luminaries of Clairvaux and especially the clearest sun, which, rising in that same distinguished valley, has illuminated the whole world with the rays of his clarity.[94] We have tried in these pages to pluck a few of the flowers of that incredibly vast and flowering meadow to enkindle in us through their radiant beauty the fervor of holy devotion so that we might learn with complete mental vigilance to refresh ourselves in the luscious perception of their beautiful rose color, to reject this world with every kind of vanity and sensual pleasure, and to strive eagerly for the fatherland of eternal light, as we read in the book of true theology which contains lamentations, canticles, and woe [Ezek 2:9]. But who today is capable of such things? What is left for us to do but eat the bread of sorrow [Ps 126:2] in the bitterness of compunction, so that our tears will be our bread day and night [Ps 41:4], so that we will sigh from the very core of our heart to those of whom we have spoken, in the hope that those at the heavenly banquet will be moved with compassion and let some crumbs from their abundant feast fall to the poor little dogs under their table [Matt 15:26-27], that they may be sustained and not abandon the way of penance?

Just as we learned from the aforementioned fathers how generous God's mercy is toward his saints and how loving is his oversight of his chosen [Wis 4:15], those who preserve the mandates of life without pretense, in the same way we will show in the following examples with what goodness he pardons sinners and yet with what

---

[94] See note in EM 4.6 regarding Conrad's use of the valley metaphor.

severity he punishes transgressors, so that we, prepared for every good work [Titus 3:1], may embrace his mercy to the point that if by chance we discover that we are more negligent on the way of God's commandments [Ps 118:32], with a trembling mind we will remember the punishment aimed at those who carry out the work of God negligently [Jer 48:10].

Book Five

# Devotions and Dangers
# in Monastic Life

CHAPTER ONE

*A Warning from Dom Gerard, Abbot of Clairvaux,*
*against Swearing and about the Danger There Is*
*for Those Who Swear*[1]

Dom Gerard of blessed memory, formerly abbot of Clairvaux, whose precious death in the sight of the Lord [Ps 115:15] we described earlier [EM 2.27 and 28], sometimes used to warn the brothers against the habit of swearing, and to give emphasis to his words he took pains to tell this story of something terrible that happened recently to someone given to swearing. He said he had learned about it from the venerable bishop of Cahors, and his chaplain, a very trustworthy man, confirmed that he had himself been there.[2]

There was in that region a worldly man, keen on gambling, who every time he made a bad throw of the dice lost his temper and swore any oath that in his fury came to his lips. One day when he had lost almost everything, another wretched gambler went up to him, indignantly pushed him aside and said, "Give up, you fool, give up! Let me play for you; you don't know how to play or to swear." And when he too, also a son of perdition [John 17:12], also lost, he was suddenly seized with a diabolical rage and began to curse, one by one, every part of the body of our Lord Jesus Christ, both within and without, deliberately leaving not a single one out. He spat out

[1] Herbert of Clairvaux, LM 123–24 (or 124–25); these chapters are not contained in the PL. There is a great deal of material about swearing and blaspheming in various kinds of pastoral literature. See Caesarius of Heisterbach, *Dialogus miraculorum* 4.21, 52; 8.42; 9.48; 10.17; 11.51 (Strange 1:192, 218–19; 2:114, 202–4, 230–31, 306–7; S-Bland 1:217–18, 248–49; 2:41–42, 151–53, 187, 279); and Tubach, 672–685, 773, 1749, 1753, 2239, 2267, 5106. Compare Lev 19:12; Matt 5:33-37; Matt 23:16-23; Heb 6:13; Heb 7:20-22; and Jas 5:12. See also E.D. Craun, "*Inordinata locutio*: Blasphemy in Pastoral Literature, 1200–1500," *Traditio* 39 (1983): 135–62.

[2] Grießer, EM, 273n4, identifies him as probably bishop Gerard IV Hector (1159–99).

all the strange oaths and horrible blasphemies that he received in his heart and on his lips from the devil, his instructor and indeed his destructor. When he had devoured all the limbs of our Lord, God and man, with his furious and blasphemous mouth, he put the seal on his damnation by cursing with a hideous audacity the most holy limbs of his unspotted Mother, one by one, as if he was tearing every one of her sacred limbs with his poisonous teeth. All those present who were in their right mind covered their ears in the face of these blasphemies and reproaches [Ps 43:17] and beat their breasts. Scarcely had the sacrilegious swearer finished all his curses when suddenly the well-deserved divine vengeance of God struck him down with an invisible and burning force, making him a horrible example of offended majesty. The blasphemer fell to the ground, thinking he had received a blow from a sword, and groaned hideously, exclaiming, "Alas, alas, you wretch, who are you, who has killed me?" After he had rolled on the ground trembling in agony for a long time, at last, at the instigation of the devil, to whom he had been delivered [1 Tim 1:20], he vomited out his abominable soul to be burned to a crisp in hellfire. When they came to wash his naked body, they found a recent terrible gaping wound in his back as if a large ax had been driven in so hard that his inner organs, his heart, his liver, and his entrails, were all visible. The other gamblers were terrified by this sight, because the zeal of the Lord of Hosts [Isa 37:32] had punished the impious and blasphemous gambler with such a heavy chastisement.

The rumor spread quickly, and trembling neighbors were drawn from all sides to see that sight, and a mourner from among his friends hastened to him. While he was on his way, there appeared to him a certain dead man whom he had known while alive, and he said to him, "Do you recognize me? I am the dead man you used to know. I know where you are going, but you're wearing yourself out in vain. The one you think you shall find alive has already been swallowed up by death. But there is one thing that I do not want to conceal from you: Our Lord Jesus Christ suffers many outrages and injuries from his servants and patiently waits as a patient rewarder [Sir 5:4]. But he does not easily put up with injuries and abuse against his immaculate Mother, and either he takes vengeance at once or, if perchance he delays punishment until later, he strikes more harshly than against other evildoers." With these admonitions the dead man who'd been speaking disappeared. And indeed, his friend was already dead when he arrived at that place, just as the dead speaker had warned, and reporting what he had heard added terror to terror and miracle to miracle.

The aforesaid venerable Abbot Gerard affirmed that near the same town of Cahors there had been another impudent and execrable swearer of oaths. When he presumed to swear with his most foul mouth by the holy and most intimate parts of the blessed and unspotted Virgin Mary, Bearer of God, he was soon given over to the foul spirit and vexed and distorted by such long and very cruel torments that his eyes turned up and his whole face swelled enormously and his burning tongue protruded far out of his mouth. After he had been racked a long time by horrible torment, he gave his miserable soul up to the demons, and even after his death he did not draw in the unbridled tongue he had stuck out. By these and other examples, Dom Gerard, the abbot of Clairvaux, used to warn his brothers against swearing oaths because, although the custom of swearing is dangerous for everyone, for monks and all religious even a little bit of swearing can most certainly not be undertaken without great peril.

## CHAPTER TWO

### *About the Danger of Property*[3]

Dom Abraham of pious memory was formerly abbot of La Prée, one of the daughter houses of Clairvaux.[4] By the grace of our Lord Jesus Christ he remained chaste until the end of his unspotted life,

---

[3] Herbert of Clairvaux, LM 2.36 (PL 185:1345) and 2.34 (PL 185:1344). See Gregory, *Dial* 4.57.8-17. Berlioz (*Le Grand Exorde*, 281n2–9) discusses how Paris, BN lat. 15912, fol. 76r-v, may be the source for this chapter.

[4] La Prée is in the Diocese of Brittany: Janauschek, 86; Cottineau 2:2358.

along with the fruits of good works without which chastity loses all its value before God. This very holy man had the gift of great gentleness; he bore the yoke of Christ [Matt 11:30] from his youth with unflagging zeal all the days of his life. When he was still young in age and new to monastic life, without permission he hid under his mattress a piece of new cloth which he meant to use to mend his clothes [see RB 55.16-19]. When, after a little while, he needed it, he turned his mattress over to look for it but found nothing. His conscience reproached him about his fault and, stunned, he went as quickly as possible privately to confess his furtive little theft and obtain pardon. How great is the power of confession! No less great is the great loving-kindness of the Redeemer in somehow giving us in this sacrament of confession the greatest hope of human salvation! Just as neither the enormity of the offenses nor the number of wicked deeds can prevent grace from doing its work and raising the sincere and humble penitent from the depths of the abyss to the heights of heaven, so it is no less true that the lightest sins, if hidden, can throw one from the summit of perfection to the lowest point of miserable undoing. So this aforementioned young monk, who had prudently realized that this very tiny sin could not be cleansed without the remedy of confession, found himself shortly afterward alone in the kitchen doing dishes [EO 108.21]. Suddenly, as if someone wanted to give him a cloth to dry with, the little piece of material which Satan had used to tempt him to soil his soul with the vice of possessiveness fell through the air into his hands. He recognized it very clearly, and looking all around, he saw no one in the house, up or down. So it was obvious to him that an unclean spirit had stolen it but after he had made his confession could no longer keep it from him. He gave thanks to God with heartfelt joy mixed with fear and understood how dangerous it is to keep anything, however slight, when one has professed pure and perfect poverty. Even a certain nun, they say, had to face the accusations of the devils at her death for having kept in her bed a little thread of silk without permission.

There was another monk of the Cistercian Order who became ill. He had come to his final moments and had already lost the ability to speak when he saw a demon in the form of a monkey sitting on the perch where he had hung his scapular.[5] The scapular was old and ragged and the brother had recently mended it with a small patch without asking permission. The impure spirit was holding it, constantly kissing it, even licking it with his tongue and patting it with his hand. When the dying man saw this, and since he could not speak, he groaned and pointed at the monkey with his finger and babbled as best he could with malformed words to get rid of this dreadful mocker. The brothers standing around him marveled and for a long time were demanding to understand what he wanted to say and what he meant, when suddenly by the mercy of God his voice came back to him, and he said, "Do you not see the hideous demon sitting on our scapular and licking with his dirty tongue that patch which I recently dared to put on without permission?[6] Chase the monster away, and cut out that piece of cloth or else at my death this malicious and wicked mocker will laugh at me." They all looked attentively, but they could not see the evil demon. But they carried away the scapular and very soon the wicked accuser took himself away. The sick brother received a penance for his fault and again lost his speech, and a short time later he died in good confession.

We who profess the pure and unspotted observance of the holy Cistercian Order and have renounced the world and everything in it, especially ourselves, must be extremely careful in every way not to give, receive, or keep without permission the least thing, however small we consider it, so that it may not hurt our conscience [RB 33.2]. For if we give our cruel enemies material for lying accusations when Israel goes out of Egypt [Ps 113:1], that is, when the soul leaves its body, they will pursue us with reproaches and implacable jeers, and by the just judgment of God they will execute upon us a vengeance that will be all the worse because in

---

[5] In Caesarius of Heisterbach, *Dialogus miraculorum* 12.5 (Strange 2:318; S-Bland 2:293), the devil appears as an ape; compare Tubach, 1532. The so-called perch (*in pertica*) was a common feature of Cistercian dormitories, EO 72.24n149.

[6] *Le Grande Exorde*, 282n13: the use of the plural possessive "our scapular" was done in accordance with RB 33.6, which states that no one should presume to call anything his own, itself a reference to Acts 4:32.

this life we could have easily avoided it. Then, when it is too late, we will regret not having had the fear of God always before our eyes as our Rule prescribes [RB 7.10].

## CHAPTER THREE

### *About How Dangerous It Is for a Monk to Die without His Habit, That Is, without His Cowl*[7]

A Roman of very noble birth and a monk of holy observance, Dom Jordan of Fossa Nova,[8] a daughter house of Clairvaux, told us about a most remarkable miracle which the Lord allowed to happen in Italy at a monastery of the Cistercian Order for our warning and correction. There was a monk who, after having run in the way of monastic discipline with devotion and humility to the end that the Lord had appointed for him, was taken ill unto death. And when he was already near his end and was burning with a high fever, the infirmarians without discernment—or rather not considering sufficiently the sacramental meaning of the monastic habit—took off his cowl to relieve his fever and replaced it with the scapular. Because of their negligence he stayed like that until he breathed his last. And indeed, before the body was commended to the earth, to the amazement of all, he who was dead suddenly came back to life and began to speak: "When I had closed my physical eyes and, having lost the use of my bodily senses, opened the eyes of my soul, I was soon received with kindness by the holy angels and conducted to the gates of paradise in the clothing in which I had died, that is, without my cowl. My guides tried to

---

[7] Herbert of Clairvaux, LM 2.35 (PL 185:1345). Berlioz (*Le Grand Exorde*, 283n1) describes how the dead were literally wrapped in a shroud, sometimes with additional straps wound around the body. In the case of a monk this covered his cowl. See Berlioz for bibliography.

[8] Fossa Nova is in the Diocese of Terracina. Janauschek, 37; Cottineau 1:1200.

lead me into the place of eternal bliss, but the angelic spirits who guard the entrances looked at me closely, and, seeing a monk not dressed as a monk, they at once closed the door to exclude me, saying, 'Surely someone without a cowl cannot be received into the company and repose of monks.' Repelled, I stayed outside trembling and afraid, fearing above all to hear and to suffer the sentence of damnation. However, my guides interceded for me, saying that apart from this, I had been well-proven and devoted in the observances of the monastic order. But the others replied immediately that according to the eternal law, to which there are no exceptions, no monk is admitted through those gates without the proper monastic habit, that is, the cowl. I became more and more anxious and trembled violently for fear I would be forever excluded from the eternal happiness of the elect. Suddenly I heard the holy guardians say that the good Judge, our Lord Jesus Christ, had given the judgment that I should return to the human condition so that having done penance for my negligence and having put my cowl back on, I might enter the gates of paradise without obstacle." At hearing this, the brothers gave many thanks with joy and wonder to God who alone does wonderful things [Ps 135:4]. And soon the same brother who had come back to life, having accepted a penance and put on the cowl, passed over in peace to confirm what they had said [Matt 22:11].

It is true that the monastic habit, which is in the form of a cross, has a very mysterious meaning if the life of the monk conforms to it. This meaning, as we read in the *Lives of the Fathers*, was shown to one of the saints who just as he once saw the grace of the Holy Spirit come down over the sacrament of baptism, so also he saw it descend on the monastic habit when it was being blessed.[9]

---

[9] *Vitae patrum lib. vi libellus* 1.9 (PL 73:994). On the importance of the monk's habit in connection with baptism and profession, see *Le Grande Exorde*, 284n10, who refers the reader to EO 102.40, and Appendix 15, p. 374.

CHAPTER FOUR

*About a Lay Brother Who Forgot a Grave Sin*[10]

At one time there was a fatal epidemic in the house of Grandselve under the venerable Father Pons, who was later abbot of Clairvaux [see EM 2.24]. An observant lay brother named Stephen became sick, and, drawn by his desire to die, he would scarcely agree to eat anything. He prayed with continual vows and tears that he might deserve to be led from this vale of tears, the prison of his harsh exile of the sons of Adam. And so it happened; the Lord granted him his heart's desire [Ps 20:3]. When his infirmarian, who had ministered to him carefully, saw that he was dying with so much devotion and peace of heart, he himself was greatly inflamed with a desire for death and said to him, "Dearest brother, because I see that you are going to be delivered from the miseries of this life soon and are going to enter happily into the joy of our Lord, I beg that when you come into the presence of our most sweet Lord Jesus Christ you would obtain for me from his goodness the favor of following you quickly." The dying man replied that he would not postpone his help as far as it was allowed. A few days after his death, he appeared to his infirmarian in a vision and said to him, "I myself have been received in peace by the Lord; I see the goodness of the Lord in the land of the living [Ps 26:13], which incomparably surpasses all the delights of flesh and blood. And now I have returned as I promised to help you, not in the way you rashly asked, but rather in a way that I know will be better for you. Therefore, remember that when you were still in the world, you committed such an offense, from which you have not deserved to be absolved through contrition of heart and confession of the mouth. Therefore, confess it at once and do penance, for if this stain is not removed by confession before death, after death it will remain insoluble." Waking up, the brother remembered that grave fault which he had committed twelve years earlier but which he had blotted completely out of

---

[10] Herbert of Clairvaux, LM 3.7 (PL 185:1357–58).

his memory by a lethal forgetfulness. He hastened to be set free by confession and satisfaction, and thanking God, he realized clearly that one does not ask for the prayers of the saints in vain, and one does not underestimate the sacrament of confession without which one remains guilty even of faults one is not aware of.

CHAPTER FIVE

*About the Danger for Someone Who Was Ashamed
to Confess His Sins*

Since we have already heard how the Lord in his mercy removed the ignorance and forgetfulness of the aforesaid brother and procured for him the saving remedy of confession, I am now going to show how great will be the condemnation of those who are unmindful of the great judgment of God toward those who forget the grave sins they have committed. They are blinded by their vain and useless shame about which Scripture says, "There is a shame that leads into sin" [Sir 4:25], and they either gloss over or blush in confessing and trust in the good works which they may perhaps have done in the course of their life, but they deceive themselves, for as it is written, "He who offends in one point loses many good things" [Eccl 9:18] and is made guilty of all [Jas 2:10].

Dom Arnold,[11] abbot of Beaulieu,[12] a faithful and observant man, told me about a glorious miracle that he said had been told to him by a holy man who was a certain prior of the monastery of Le Chalard[13] and who had been present when it happened. There

---

[11] What follows is from Herbert of Clairvaux LM 121, which is not in the PL.

[12] This abbey was either Belloc (Beaulieu-en-Rouergue) in the Diocese of Rodez, or Beaulieu-en-Bassigny in the Diocese of Langres. Grießer (EM, 278n6) notes that its identity cannot be confirmed because an incomplete list of abbots' names does not include that of Arnold.

[13] Le Chalard is an Augustinian priory in the Diocese of Limoges. A similar story is told in the life of Saint Godfrey, the first prior who died in 1125. See Grießer, EM, 278n7.

was in the area of Limoges a matron whose way of life showed very great piety, and although she was held by the chains of marriage, she still gave herself up to fasting, prayer, almsgiving, and other good works and so seemed to lead a life according to rule in the dress of the world. But in her youth this lady had committed a great offense which had covered her with confusion and of which she was so ashamed that she had never wanted to confess it. Whenever she confessed to her priest she made a veiled reference to that crime, saying at the end of her confession, "For all my sins, whether I have mentioned them or not, I hold myself guilty before God and you." And when she had said these enigmatic words in this way at the end of her confession she sighed greatly and broke down in tears. She did this often over many years, and at last her priest, who was a wise and understanding man, discerning some hidden sin in the heart of his penitent, set to work to get her to acknowledge it. When he achieved nothing by this solicitude, he advised her to go to the prior of the nearby monastery of Chalais and to open her conscience fully to this very holy man. She actually went to him and made her confession to him, but he could not get her to say anything beyond what she usually said to her priest.

As it happened, this unhappy woman fell ill and died little confessed. Sometime after she died, she had still not been buried; the interment was delayed because her daughter, who lived some way off, had been summoned to her mother's funeral. Arriving as quickly as she could, the daughter was so shaken with sobs that she made everyone who saw her weep. Scarcely had she reached her mother's side when, by the power and mercy of God, the woman who had died returned to life and her soul joyfully came back into the body from which it had been so sadly separated. As if she were waking out of a deep sleep, she said to her weeping, mourning daughter, "My daughter, do not fear. Dry your eyes of tears, for by the mercy of God I am brought back to life. Undo the winding cloths that hinder me so that I can get up." The bands were cut hastily and the woman raised her head and sat up. At her request, a priest was quickly summoned and as everyone else withdrew, she confessed to him, unburdening her soul of the deadly poison that had been infecting it. Afterward people came from all parts to see such a miracle, and this woman gave witness that it was true, attesting before the crowd the inestimable grace that God had shown toward her. She recounted in detail what had happened to her and how she had been set free through the merciful intervention of the Bearer of God and Virgin Mary.

"Miserable sinner that I am," she said, "while I was living in the world I seemed upright because of the good works I did and the pious way of life I led, but in the eyes of the omnipotent God I lay in the ruins of death because I was not afraid of daring to disobey his commandments. For the Lord has established through his holy Church that it is impossible to be saved without confession. And I, wretch that I am, although I often went to confession, I never dared to reveal a grave sin I committed in my youth because of extreme shame. This made all the good works I had done pointless and fruitless. Yet during almost every day since, I have confessed the lapse I had committed against God to the blessed Virgin Mary, repenting, weeping, and full of sorrow at her altar or her image or anywhere I could, lest I endure a sentence of eternal damnation because of that sin I committed. But when I paid the debt to death, I immediately found myself snatched up, surrounded, and closed in by hellish spirits. They held me with every kind of cruelty, hit me, and turned me around and committed other outrages, drawing me among them in order to throw me forever into eternal punishment. All the while I recalled my alms, my fasts, my vigils, my prayers, and all the other good works that I had toiled over for a long time, and I wondered that I should be condemned without pity to the tortures of hell as if I had committed many sins. But I sought in vain for light from my works. The wicked sin that I had buried at the bottom of my conscience rose like a horrible smoke, obscuring my gaze, wrapping me in darkness, and I could not see any rays of that true and eternal brightness which must light upon all the good we do. Unhappy woman that I am, I understood then, when it was too late, that these were the wages for my obstinacy and hardness of heart. And I was forced not simply to know but to know through my own experience how dangerous it is for us miserable mortals to disobey the precepts of the Creator and sovereign Master of all things.

"So I was deprived of all help and succor, and then I remembered as I thought about it, that I had often confessed to the most blessed Bearer of God, with groans, tears, and sobs, the wicked sin for which I was suffering the just sentence of damnation. This gave me a ray of hope, and I turned toward the Mother of mercy and the sole refuge of those who are in distress, and I tried by my prayers, vows, and signs rather than by my words to urge her not to abandon me in this extremity of distress.[14] I had no sooner invoked the consoler and protector of all those who have recourse to her than I saw her coming like the morning star [Sir 40:6] or the sun at midday. She filled the demons who surrounded me with terror, reproaching them for having dared to attack her little servant, and ordering them at the same time to let go of their prey until the Lord should decide what fate he had in store for me. The wicked demons obeyed at once, and the Mother of mercy approached the blessed fruit of her womb, our Lord Jesus Christ, worshiped him, and said, 'My Lord Son, I beseech you of your goodness not to give over to the beasts [Ps 73:19] this soul who has often deplored her transgression before my image.' And the Lord replied to her, 'Dearest Mother, do you not know that it is not possible to be saved without confession?' 'Lord,' she answered, 'all things are possible with you [Mark 14:36]. Do not, I beseech you, upset the countenance of this poor little sinner who has trusted in me and who has sought to please you with many good and just works although she has not done them in a suitable way.' The Lord then said, 'It is not right for me to refuse anything you ask of me, but since after this life it is not possible to confess or do penance, I have decided that her soul should be returned to her body and that what she did badly, but even worse kept to herself, she should confess humbly and for it do penance, and then returning immediately she may finally, in the proper order, obtain mercy.' So by the order of the Lord and by the loving care of our most pious Lady, a good angel was sent to me to snatch me from the expectations of the evil spirits and restore me to my own body, as you can witness. Now I have made

---

[14] For more on the practice of calling on the help of the Virgin at the time of judgment, see Berlioz, *Le Grande Exorde de Cîteaux*, 288nn27–32.

my confession, and it is time for me to go, never to return, but for all eternity to praise the goodness of the Lord and always sing of the mercy of him who has gone before me and been with me and because of whom I, wretch that I am, have been preserved from the dread judgment." After she said this, she laid her head on the bier and breathed forth her spirit, fortified by the sign of the holy cross.

May anyone, having been pierced by the blow of eternal death through any mortal sin, who reads and hears this example, be moved toward the healing remedy of confession and penitence, knowing that no one can obtain pardon from the Lord who refuses to humiliate himself in front of his representative, that is, a prelate or a priest. And if, through a groundless presumption, there is anyone tempted to build good works without a foundation of confession, or if because of his good works he is counting on a confession made at the end of his life—let him know, as we have just described, that he is dreaming with great foolishness about such things, because the higher he has flown without the wings of confession, the deeper will be his downfall, and because the more arrogantly a deathbed confession is presumed, the less likely it is to be accepted. Moreover, it is clear that the divine Goodness is not carelessly generous with its special favors; they are for the few, not the throng. Let us conclude from this that, while we have time and are in this body [RB Prol. 43], it is better to come before the face of the Lord by confessing our sins openly than by continuing in wicked obstinacy and on the day of the general resurrection to endure shame and unending dishonor before angels and men. And worse yet, to fall under the blow of this horrible malediction that strikes the impious and those who neglect penitence. "Depart, accursed one, into everlasting fire, prepared for the devil and his angels" [Matt 25:41].

CHAPTER SIX

*How the Lord Corrected Leniently a Devout Monk*
*Who Fell Asleep, and How He Severely Corrected Another*
*Who Was Lazy out of Tepidity and Negligence*

There was in the aforementioned monastery of Grandselve [EM 5.4] a monk who was very spiritual and endowed with grace, but he was inclined to sleepiness, and although he fought faithfully against it and struggled, as was his duty, to offer the Lord the devoted service of psalmody [RB 18.24], despite all his efforts he could not overcome his natural frailty in this matter. One day when he was in his place in choir and seemed to be singing the psalms in the sort of dazed way caused by sleepiness, a venerable person whose countenance he did not recognize stood before him. To rouse him in his sluggishness, he seized the clothing on his breast as if he was going to carry him out of the church. When he was seized in this way, the monk opened his eyes and seeing him said, "Lord, who are you and where are you taking me?" The other replied, "And why are you sleeping like this?" as if to say, "Have you left your bed and gone into choir just to make yourself the laughing stock of your enemies by dozing and nodding your head? Should you not rather be chanting psalms eagerly in praise of the Lord your creator in the sight of the angels [RB 19.5]?" After saying this he let him go and disappeared at once. The brother who had had the good fortune to be so mercifully reproved by the Lord for his sleepiness shook off the torpor of negligence and sleep in the fear of God, and thenceforward he was more careful and prompt in staying awake and chanting the psalms.[15]

In the same monastery there was another monk, named Bernard.[16] He appeared very robust, having a youthful and vigorous body, yet he performed less diligently than the rest, showing

---

[15] Up to this point, Herbert of Clairvaux, LM 3.3 (PL 185:1356).

[16] The text is now Herbert of Clairvaux, LM 3.4 (PL 185:1356), until Conrad's exhortation begins with "So this lazy and negligent brother."

himself lazy in manual labor and sleepy at Vigils. So he was a not inconsiderable nuisance even to his fellows and was known for his indolence everywhere, but especially in church, where he was even more lackadaisical. One night when he was dozing at Vigils, the community's precentor lost all patience with such laziness and woke him up more roughly than usual. Bernard got up in a surly frame of mind and stormed back to the dormitory. As he passed the latrine, a troop of demons hiding at the opening shouted at him in a loud, terrifying din, screaming, "Seize him, seize him." Utterly terrified at hearing them, he quickly fled at a fast pace back into the church. When he reached his stall, trembling and out of breath, he fainted and lay motionless and senseless a long time, as if he were dead. The brothers lifted him up and carried him to the infirmary, and when he had recovered a bit from his terror and come to his senses, they asked him what had happened. He admitted to them how he had been punished for his stubbornness and laziness. Moreover, a certain novice who had been in the chapel at the time assured him that he too had heard the noise and clamor of the demons.

So this lazy and negligent brother, chastised with the saving prod of divine correction, realized that laziness, sleepiness, apathy, and other bad habits of this kind are like the dung which oxen drop behind them, that is, which men strong in the fear of God hate and detest. Indeed, the idle and useless are forever being pelted with this dung by filthy demons, to their extreme confusion. Look at how great a difference there is between the negligence caused by weakness—against which a vigorous mind, being tinged with the filth that comes from sleepiness, struggles each day, as if washing itself in melted snow [Job 9:30], to acquit itself faithfully in the service of God to keep itself from becoming insolent or proud—and that detestable inertia that refuses spiritual arms and prefers to give up to the enemy without a struggle. Sleeping and snoring deeply in choir as well as in bed, it does not offer the resistance of an active mind to the malignant spirits making fun of them and saying, "Stoop down so we can crawl in over you" [Isa 51:23]. The difference between the two reasons for failure is well-expressed by this pair of examples I have related, because the good angel by a gentle rebuke made that athlete of Christ whom we mentioned above more concerned for himself as he struggled through grace but succumbed from infirmity. The crowd of evil spirits, by pursuing that other monk whose indolence and folly we disclosed, however, took possession of his mind with terrors and evil shouts and rendered him nearly senseless. Let us take our example from the good ones, choosing to do spiritual battle valiantly with men of virtue, but let us be compassionate of heart for the tepidity of the lazy and useless, so that, nevertheless, we may strive in every way to flee their negligence, either on account of the expectation of divine retribution or on account of fear of the fire of Gehenna [RB 5.3].

On this subject the elders at Clairvaux used to tell of our most blessed Father Bernard that once while he was at nighttime Vigils he saw an angel of the Lord passing from one side of choir to the other with a censer of heavenly incense. The hearts of those he found awake, chanting psalms and giving themselves to prayer, he refreshed with the intensely sweet aromatic odors of the Spirit, banishing weariness and rousing their devotion. But those whom he found sleeping, idle, and useless he passed over with scorn, no doubt deciding that they did not deserve the indulgence of such a wonderful gift.

The venerable father Dom Richard, former abbot of Savigny,[17] told us that in one of the Savigniac houses there was a holy and observant abbot who had been favored with a very remarkable grace—one granted, I think, to very few. This largess of divine goodness was granted him as a reward for his great devotion, for he not only was dead to the desires of the flesh but had eliminated from his heart all thoughts of them. He gave himself to vigils, prayer, and psalmody with a devotion and purity beyond compare, and heaven rewarded him by letting him smell delicious perfumes and ineffable sweetness surpassing the odors of cinnamon, incense, balm, and any other aromatics. In his mouth he also sensed the infusion of a sweetness like heavenly manna which reminded him of all that

---

[17] Herbert of Clairvaux, LM 1.33 (PL 185:1304). Abbot Richard resigned in 1158 as abbot of Savigny, in Normandy. See *Gallia Christiana* 11:546; and Grießer, EM, 283n1.

was most tasty and agreeable to the palate [Wis 16:20]. This celestial food was under his tongue like a living fountain, spreading from there into the interior of his body, flooding both and penetrating and filling him with such wonderful sweetness that he could cry out with Scripture: "How sweet are your words in my heart; they are sweeter than honey in my mouth" [Pss 18:11; 99:5; 118:103]. Happy the soul that deserves to taste and see how sweet the Lord is [Ps 33:9], not only in himself, but even in the flesh that will decay.

There can be absolutely no doubt that such an excellent gift, working in the one who receives it, powerfully extinguishes carnal desires, enkindles spiritual thoughts, and melts the entire soul in the fire with divine love. Moreover, it betokens the flight of malicious spirits, indicates the presence of the holy angels, and reveals by an experience as happy as it is true the greatly longed-for glance of divine favor. In this way, the Lord chooses to console the humble who show themselves vigorous and devoted in his service. So too he chooses to terrify the lazy and idle who seek to ease the flesh more than is meet, and, in this way, he shows by a present judgment what the prophet declared will be made manifest in the judgment to come: the distance that exists between those who serve the Lord and those who do not serve him, those who make vows to the Lord and keep them and those who make vows to the Lord and do not keep them [Mal 3:18]. As Holy Scripture bears witness, "It will be better for those who have not made vows than for those who have made a vow and not kept it" [Eccl 5:4].

In this way, in the diverse persons mentioned above and in the quality of rewards each deserved, the Lord has willed to show in a physical and visible manner that we should know with utter certainty that this will be accomplished invisibly and spiritually for all those who are vowed to the service of God. Those who remind themselves of their profession and are not discouraged either by the effort or work or the demands of Vigils—but, on the contrary, discharge the daily course of psalmody and hymns with prompt and eager devotion—he will relieve, comfort, and console by the secret visitation of his divine goodness. But the others, who forget their obligations of their profession and are unwilling, as they say, to touch their fingertips to the hard labor of Vigils and the service of God are continually infested by the hideous connivances of various demonic illusions and passionate phantoms, trying to force them down day by day into the very dangerous pit of slackness and negligence.

CHAPTER SEVEN

*The Danger of Aspiring to Holy Orders*

Let the ambitious who long impatiently for holy orders or ecclesiastical benefices listen. Let them listen carefully to this story of an ambitious man. Let them listen, I say, and tremble with fright, and consider that small matters as well as great are to be feared, and be cautious above all about anything to do with the inheritance of the crucified Lord. For the heritage that they hasten to acquire at the outset will not in the end be blessed [Prov 20:21] by the angry Lord of majesty who was crucified in weakness.

A monk of the Cistercian Order who had always lived a very observant life was delivered by death from the temptations and sufferings of this miserable life.[18] After he had died, the sacrist of the house was sitting on his bed one night just before time for Vigils [RB 47.1; EO 114.2 and n. 245], waiting for the signal from the clock to be given, when suddenly the spirit of the departed brother appeared, clothed in a solid and palpable body. In a sorrowful voice he spoke to him: "Lord sacristan, I am the brother who just died. Please pause to consider with pious insight my reason for coming to you now. While I was still living in my body, I was, by the grace of God, quite attentive to all the observances of the Order. On one point, however, I strayed gravely. I desired the holy order of the diaconate for human reasons and, because I was not guided by the fear of God, I was very unsettled about rising to this

---

[18] Grießer (EM, 284n3) suggests that this story was taken either from John of Clairvaux's *Liber visionum et miraculorum* or from another source common to both texts; McGuire ("A Lost Clairvaux *Exemplum* Collection Found," 42) asserts that Conrad certainly borrowed this from the *Liber visionum*.

rank of honor. What is even worse, I left my body without doing a penance appropriate to this fault, because I thought it was not as grave as, I discovered after I died, it is. Our good Lord has let me appear to you so that, since I myself cannot gain any merit now, I may ask help by the prayers of my brothers, for they can still obtain the mercy of God both for themselves and for others. I beg you, then, by the love of Our Lord Jesus Christ: tell the prior of my misfortune. Ask him please to absolve me in the chapter and assign some general prayers for my deliverance to the brothers [EO 94.41–42]. And to prove to you that you are not the sport of a fantastic illusion, and to show you that what you see and hear is true, I tell you truly that the Psalter, which a few days ago the porter said in chapter was lost and has not yet been found, you will find lying in such and such a place."

The sacristan, although he was very astonished at hearing and seeing such an extraordinary thing, decided, because he was a man of mature judgment, to say nothing to anyone that day about this message. He was afraid of being laughed at as a dreamer or the butt of demonic delusions. But the next night, when he was again sitting on his bed watching, thinking about what he had seen the night before, the same dead monk again appeared to him, awake and amazed, and said, "Lord sacristan, you have not done right, you have not done right by me! I am bearing the wrath of the Lord because I have sinned against the One into whose hands it is a fearful thing to fall [Heb 10:31]! I only hope you never have to experience it! If you could only know how great are the least pains of a soul separated from its body, you surely would not behave so negligently. You would try with all your strength to provide relief. I entreat you yet again in the name of God, delay no longer, but hasten to put my request into effect. For I hope to obtain mercy from the clemency of God by the prayers of our brothers. To dispel for a second time any scruple of doubt from your heart and convince you that I really am me, whom alive in the flesh you knew a short while ago, here is the Psalter that the porter reported in chapter as lost and has not found." The sacristan took the Psalter from his hands, utterly struck dumb at such an unheard-of wonder, for it is truly God who alone does great wonders [Ps 135:4]. But wishing to know if the body he saw was solid and palpable and if he would be able to touch it as well as see it, the sacristan, since he had a stick by him, picked it up and to satisfy himself by touching him, nudged him lightly with it. But the stick did not encounter any obstacle and passed through the body as if through thin air. The next morning he told the prior and the brothers what he had seen and heard, and to prove the truth of his report he produced the Psalter he had been given. And so, we may believe, by the common prayers of the brothers and celebrations of Masses the soul of that brother was released from punishment and now by the mercy of God enjoys the fellowship of eternal bliss.

But why is it that in our day Almighty God makes known to us things about the state of our souls of which we were ignorant until now? Is it to show us, by open revelations and visions, some portion of the life of the soul beyond the death of the flesh, the world to come now already beginning to appear? Is it also because the present age, according to the words of Pope Saint Gregory, is coming to an end and we are coming closer to the next age?[19]

Woe to those who still, despite all the signs breaking so manifestly in upon us now to show the redoubtable judgments of God, consider religious piety as, according to the Apostle, "running after sordid gain" [1 Tim 3:8; 6:5] and do not blush to intrude themselves into holy orders and ecclesiastical benefices by any means, legal or illegal. Although the Apostle says that no one should take this honor upon himself "but only those who are called by God as was Aaron" [Heb 5:4], yet many do not blush to sell the most honorable positions in the Church with a proud eye and insatiable heart [Ps 100:5], using prayers, money, and flattery for the purpose, not so that they can exert themselves in vigils, fasting, and prayers for the salvation of souls, but so that they can fill their bellies and their throats, satisfy their vanity, their love of pleasure, and their pride of life. If they do not repent and do penance, the damnation of such men will be harsher and more insupportable than that of all others because they have not feared to receive holy orders un-

---

[19] Gregory, *Homiliae in Hiezechihelim Prophetam*, 2.4.12 (CCSL 142:267–68; SCh 360:208–9).

worthily and to usurp the divine offices of the ministers of Christ for carnal motives.

But what are we to do? Or more to the point, what torrents of tears must we shed at seeing the whole race of Adam's offspring infected with this leprosy of ambition to such a point that even those who show themselves to be more observant, more holy and perfect, are the ones who blush the least at being dominated by this vice of weak souls. "We are truly noble creatures," as blessed Bernard says in one of his sermons,[20] made in the image of God [Gen 1:26]; so we all aspire to the heights, seek great things, and tend to raise ourselves up. And this appetite to rise would not be a vice if only those who wish to rise did not transgress the law fixed by the most High. But because of intervening sin, our intention is crooked, our reason blind, our will weak. And because of our imperfection we need to pierce our heart by compunction, to open it in confession, to humble ourselves by works of penance, and to be always on our guard lest we make ourselves instruments of iniquity [Rom 6:13]; that is to say, we must never allow our neighbor or our superiors to discover in us the sickness of ambition and the symptoms of vain adulation, or obsequious respect, or a flattering and deceptive sweetness.[21]

## Chapter Eight

### *About the Dangers of Disobedience*

As the Apostle says of our Lord and Savior, he was made obedient to his Father even unto death [Phil 2:8; RB 7.34], and our most holy legislator Benedict enjoins obedience even in impossible things [RB 68]. The Lord himself commends this when he says to prelates in his Church, "Whoever hears you, hears me; and he who despises

---

[20] Bernard of Clairvaux, Div 40.3 (SBOp 6/1:236), also implied in Asc 4.3 (SBOp 5:139–40; SBS 2:255–56).

[21] Bernard of Clairvaux, Div 32.3 (SBOp 6/1:219–20).

you despises me" [Luke 10:16; RB 5.6; 5.15]. It is very distressing that those who profess holy religion, and obedience before all and above all [RB 36.1], sometimes dare to carry pride and disobedience so far that they cannot be either bent by prayers or menaced by threats or by any other means to reduce the heat of this insanity. So I think it is necessary to give an example of disobedience by which those whose souls are full of gall and whose pride rots their hearts like an ulcer, who have no fear or respect either for God or man [Luke 18:2], when they hear how "God [who] resists the proud" [Jas 4:6] by a terrible judgment may learn how it is far better to be humbled and obey with the gentle than to divide the spoils of arrogance and rebellion with the proud [Prov 16:19].

There was a lay brother at Clairvaux who became disobedient to his prior, with a proud mind despising what he was ordered to do. Neither the fear of God nor the gentle admonitions of his brothers could induce him to obey his orders.[22] By arrogant and insolent responses, moreover, he repeatedly insisted that he was never going to do these things. As the sun was going down toward its setting, marking the end of the day, he lay down on his bed to go to sleep, full of rancor and bitterness and unworried about persevering in his obstinacy, forgetting the word of the Apostle, "Let not the sun go down on your anger" [Eph 4:26; RB 4.73]. And in the early silence of the night, not yet able to sleep and still satisfying his pride by thinking up wicked plans, two evil spirits, blacker than coal and crueler than dragons, were suddenly standing beside his bed. One said to the other, as if asking a question, "What sort of man is this who lies here?" And the other replied, "Some lay brother." And the other, who had spoken first, responded angrily, "Not at all; he is a disobedient man." "Well, if he is disobedient," said the other immediately, "let us drag him out of the door." No sooner said than done. They seized the wretch, threw him roughly out of bed, gagged his mouth so he could not cry out, and dragged the cantankerous and disobedient fellow out of the dormitory and out of the society of the obedient brothers. They carried him through

---

[22] On the procedure for admonishing brothers, see RB 23 and 24, and above, EM 2.2.

the air outside the walls of the monastery[23] and began to play with him in a horrible way, throwing him from one to the other like men playing ball, throwing and catching it. After they had amused themselves for a long time, they put him down and suddenly vanished. But oh, unspeakable malice of diabolic wickedness! After a bit they came back and began their game again. Suddenly the signal sounded for Divine Office, and at its ringing they fled, terrified as if a crack of thunder from heaven had broken over them. As for the unhappy lay brother, who was no longer proud and rebellious but terrified and trembling like a poor fawn, they had thrown him into a nearby marsh. He dragged himself out of the boggy marsh when he could and sat, filthy and stinking, under a tree. As he sat there, weighed down with sorrow and anguish, fearing that he would soon see the spectral forms of the demons coming back, a venerable person was suddenly standing before him, saying, "Be of good courage and do not be afraid because the malicious servants of darkness, the avengers of pride and rebellion, will not dare to harm you anymore. This has happened to you by the just judgment of God because you were not afraid of being arrogantly rebellious to your superior." When morning came and the lay brother did not appear among the other brothers, they searched for him in various workplaces but did not find him. They all suspected that he had crept back to the vomit of the world [2 Pet 2:22].

Now the site of the monastery was such that the kitchen workers had to go outside the gates to draw clean water. So the brothers who were then serving in the kitchen went out at dawn. Seeing the lay brother sitting under a tree looking as if he had lost his senses, they ran back to tell the prior and the brothers what they had seen. And the prior, taking some of the brothers with him, went out to him, and seeing him hunched over so pitiably, he asked him why he was sitting there and what evil had befallen him. At this word, the unfortunate man bared his teeth like a dog about to bite, and looking with threatening eyes at the brothers trying to approach him, he said, "You saw me being mistreated all night by demons

---

[23] Bernard of Clairvaux, Sent 3.31 (SBOp 6/2:85; CF 55:217).

and not one of you took the trouble to come to my aid." As soon as he said this the brothers understood that he had undergone chastisement for his disobedience and contumacy. By the order of the prior he was taken to the infirmary where for a long time he lay, still in the same demented state, and he learned from what he had suffered to be no longer disobedient and contumacious [Heb 5:8]; as the Scripture says, affliction gives understanding only to those who listen [Isa 28:19].

Just as rebellion and pride are evils without equal, the proud, the arrogant, and the rebellious will be punished, damned, and tortured without parallel. May their sentence be far from all of us who have resolved to love God with humble and sincere charity and who for his sake obey and submit to his representatives, our superiors.

## Chapter Nine

### *More on the Danger of Disobedience*

There are some who very carefully and quite properly avoid this kind of flagrant and clearly mortal rebellion but are less attentive to the little things they are ordered to do, and easily exceed the limits of obedience. Although they attempt to wash away their stains of disobedience by confession and penitence, it is presumption rather than true contrition of heart that makes them do so. So I have no hesitation in recording here an example of disobedience to strike terror into those who find sweetness in the bread of lies [Prov 20:17], that is to say, in following their own will contrary to the orders of their superior. May this account recall them to themselves lest this stolen bread with which they love to feed themselves turn into bitter poison in the stomach of their conscience. Unable to digest the richness of the disobedience they have devoured with delight, they would retch and God would make them choke on it.

In the province called Germany-across-the-Rhine, referred to more generally as Saxony, near the town of Paderborn, which the emperor Charlemagne founded and where he built a palace, there is a monastery of nuns called Arolsen.[24] Dedicated to the very holy apostles, the sons of Zebedee, it has long become celebrated for its strict observances and very exacting discipline.[25] For a time the conduct of the monastery was in the hands of someone of very upright life called Peter,[26] who belonged to the Order of canons regular, because the monastery had been established according to the Rule of Saint Augustine. This man meditated tirelessly on God's law and devoutly fulfilled it. He had remarkable charity, profound humility, and exemplary chastity. As a faithful companion and friend of the Bridegroom, he watched with utmost care over the purity of the brides of the Lord who were entrusted to his care. He manfully cast out all petty thieves, the corrupters of integrity who might sully the bedchamber of the heavenly Bridegroom. To these good habits he added, as it were, a pearl beyond price [Matt 13:46], by which I mean his devotion to the Mother of God, whom he venerated and loved with unequaled affection. With heartfelt affection he would often offer in her honor the singular sacrifice and the saving Host that takes away the sins of the world, choosing her as his advocate in every need and imploring her intercession with tears and unceasing prayers. He had even developed this praiseworthy custom: each time he heard the honey-sweet name of the blessed Virgin Mother mentioned, if it was not possible for him to prostrate, he bowed his head with respect and bent his knees a little and offered the angelic salutation to the Mother of mercy as devoutly as he could.[27] When this athlete had fought the good fight and come to the end of his life, the time came for him to experience the truth of this heavenly and prophetic word, "Blessed are the dead who die in the Lord" [Rev 14:13]. He was gravely ill and seized by a burning fever, and

---

[24] Arolsen was a convent of Augustinian nuns; see Grießer, EM, 289n1.

[25] I.e., Saints James and John, sons of Zebedee; see Matt 4:21; Mark 1:19.

[26] Grießer (EM, 289n2) provides bibliography for Peter (d. 1158), whose *vita* has been published by the Bollandists: *Catalogus Codicum Hagiographicorum Bibliothecae Regiae Bruxellensis* 2:106–20. *Le Grande Exorde*, 299n5, notes that the phrase *vir vitae venerabilis* was much-used by Gregory, Dial 1.6, 9, 10; 2.Prol.; 3.6, 14, 16, 20, 21; 4.27, 33, 36, 58.

[27] He is saying the *Ave Maria*; compare EM 3.31; 5.5, 27.

as all the emerging signs pointed to his imminent death, he began more earnestly to entreat the help of Our Lady, his special patron, frequently repeating her salutation with which he was so familiar and begging her fervently to come to his aid at the moment of death to protect him against the wickedly cruel attacks of malicious spirits.

A few days before his death he summoned the prioress of the monastery, an observant and highly prudent virgin called Gisela,[28] and also some of the older sisters, and he said to them, "I am now going the way of all flesh.[29] I have tried to serve the Lord in my small way as purely as possible. But since no one knows if he is worthy of love or hate [Eccl 9:1], I tremble with an uncertainty, full of fear, about the sentence that the strict Judge will pass upon me. But I am letting you know that tomorrow at about the sixth hour, the blessed Virgin Mary, Bearer of God, Queen of heaven, and Lady of the world, is going to visit her poor little servant, and I hope, believe, and trust that she will deign to take him out of this world's exile and carry him with her into the bright home of the celestial homeland. That which I can in no way expect because of my own merits I trustingly count on obtaining by her very holy merits. Now, put everything in the house in order at once, arrange and adorn the seats, and at the time I said tell all the sisters to come here with incense and candles. When I begin this verse of the sequence of the Assumption of the Blessed Virgin, 'Thee, O Queen of Heaven,'[30] let all the sisters sing together in voices full of fervor and devotion, and let them sing this sequence straight through from that verse to the end with joy of heart and voice." The prioress and sisters who were present immediately believed his words, being sure of his holiness and innocence.

But a lay brother called Theodoric, who was at the head of the bed where the man of God lay, refused to believe what he said and

---

[28] Grießer (EM, 289n4) notes that the prioress Gisela is mentioned in the Life of Peter.

[29] *Le Grande Exorde*, 300n11, discusses precedents for the phrase "going the way of all flesh." He includes numerous references, biblical (Josh 23:14; 1 Kgs 2:2) and traditional (including Peter the Venerable and William of Tyre). See also EM 5.21.

[30] *Te Caeli Regina*, a sequence hymn; G. M. Dreves, *Analecta Hymnica* 53:180; see Grießer, EM, 290n2.

muttered in his heart thus: "How fickle and weak women are to believe words like these so readily. Here is a man at the point of death who has lost his senses and is speaking nonsense, and these sisters take as much notice of his orders as if he were a sane and sensible person and imagine that they must carry them out." While the brother was thinking all this, the holy priest suddenly raised his head with an effort and directing his eyes to the side where the lay brother was standing, he said, "Brother Theodoric, are you there?" "Yes, I am here, my lord," he replied. "Come here," said the sick man and, when he came forward, "put your hand in mine." The lay brother was surprised and more sure still that the holy man was out of his mind, but not daring to contradict the words of the holy man he gave him his hand. The man of God took it and clasped his fingers firmly between his own and said, "Just as truly as I am holding your hand in my hand and clasping your fingers in my fingers at this moment, what I have said by the power of God's grace is true. What you are thinking at the bottom of your heart you must know is false; I am not delirious, I am in my right mind, and I know what I am saying." This divine and prophetic correction of the only doubter present dispelled all clouds of doubt from the spirits of the other witnesses. They all rejoiced at the great favor heaven had bestowed on their spiritual father.

When the next day dawned and the sun climbed to its height and the hour the man of God had foretold grew near, the community of sisters and lay brothers all assembled waiting for the most holy Queen of heaven, sure that her coming would prove the truth of the prophecy by an unmistakable wonder. At about the hour appointed, those around felt themselves filled with such reverence of mind that they could not doubt that at that moment some divine force was present. The blessed priest, his face wonderfully shining and his eyes raised to heaven, stretched out his hands and began to intone the verse, "Thee, O Queen of heaven, your children celebrate with pious hearts."[31] And who can estimate the compunction and piety with which the sisters chanted this sequence? During this time

---

[31] *Te, Caeli Regina, haec plebicula piis concelebrat mentibus.*

the servant of God, although in agony, was rapt in ecstasy, and by revelation he understood many of the heavenly mysteries and many things concerning the state of the community, which he later told to the prioress and senior sisters. But while all eyes were fixed on him, suddenly his face clouded over and he frowned; he showed clear marks of distress and great anxiety. At last, crying out in a voice of woeful lamentation, he uttered these words: "Why, my most sweet and merciful Lady, why do you leave your poor little servant in the dregs of this mortal life, having deigned to console him, however unworthy, by your gracious visitation? You have granted me at the moment of death your very sweet presence, begged for by so many vows, asked for by my tears and prayers. And now you are going back up to the homeland of eternal life, toward the joys of paradise, and you will not allow this unhappy one to go with you." And as he repeated over and over again, "O my good mistress, O my most pious Lady, my most merciful Lady, do not leave me. I want to go with you. I want to go with you," he brought everyone to laments and tears to the eyes of all.

Suddenly coming to himself after resting a few moments because of the extreme weakness of his poor body, he sent everyone away, keeping with him the prioress and a few of the senior nuns. He said, "I need to gather some strength. Give me some drops of liquid to wet my dry tongue so that I can more easily tell you what I have to say." The prioress herself at once brought him a small vessel containing a little wine, but scarcely had she reached the threshold of the house in which the man of God was lying, and although he could not see or by any other physical sense perceive what she had brought, he stopped her, saying, "No, no, Lady Prioress, don't bring us wine, not wine. Wine betrays secrets and makes wise men traitors [Sir 27:17; 19:2; RB 40.7]." At hearing that she had been detected by a true spirit of prophecy, she was seized with such trembling that she could scarcely turn back. Restored somewhat by a few drops of water, the sick man felt strong enough to speak. "Oh," he exclaimed, "how great and considerable is the sin of disobedience! Wretch that I am, if only I had understood this sooner and better than I have, I would not have had to experience the chastisement which has been inflicted on me today. If only I could effectively impress on your minds how important it is! It is because of a sin of disobedience that my dearest Lady has now left me in this vale of tears[32] and judged me unworthy to go under her protection through the spirits of the air to the secret places of heaven. Now I want to tell you about my disobedience! At one time many priests of this diocese made a mistake in their calculations and with their parishioners celebrated the fast of the ember days in the month of September at the wrong time.[33] I myself fell into this error by not paying close enough attention to the canonical rules. At the next synod those who had celebrated the fast at the right time denounced this transgression, and then it was prescribed in the name of obedience that whoever knew himself to be guilty of this failing should acknowledge his guilt and ask pardon. The others whose consciences accused them obeyed humbly, preferring to risk their reputation rather than their conscience. But I, wretch that I am, had less regard for truth than for my rank and my reputation, for I was a prelate in the Church and was thought to be very observant. I could not bring myself to sacrifice my self-respect, and I was ashamed to make public reparation. That was my sin, this fault of disobedience, and because of it this day I have been deprived of the happiness of accompanying the Lady of the all that is, the Mother of mercy. This is why I have been recalled from the brink of eternal life and glory to the pains of this mortal life."

The prioress then asked him if he could not wash out the stain of this sin in the saving bath of confession and penance, but he replied that he had done so, not once, but many times. "Alas for me," she

---

[32] "Vale of tears" is a common expression with roots in Ps 83:7; and *in hac lacrimarum valle* occurs the antiphon *Salve Regina*. See *Le Grande Exorde*, 302n29.

[33] Literally, "the four-season fast." Ember Days are four series of fast days: the Wednesdays, Fridays, and Saturdays after 13 December, Ash Wednesday, Pentecost Sunday, and 14 September. This scheme does not appear to have been finalized until the Roman Synod in 1078 under Gregory VII, and so the custom could well have varied in Peter's time. See R. E. McNanny, ed., "Ember Days," *New Catholic Encyclopedia*, 5:186–87; and Berlioz, *Le Grand Exorde Cîteaux*, 302n30. The science of measuring time in the effort to construct a reliable liturgical calendar was known as *computus*. For background on this, see Wallis, *Bede: The Reckoning of Time*, xv–lxiii and 425–26.

cried, overcome with wonder, "alas for me, my lord father, poor sinner that I am. What can we say about the sacrament of confession, if you are refused pardon for a sin that you have acknowledged, not once, but many times? Can anyone else then hope for the pardon of faults through confession?" Then the dying man made this memorable reply: "You should know that it is the intention and the contrition of the one who confesses and does penance that determines the intention of the judge and God's remission of the debt. But because I, miserable man that I am, failed to assess my sin by its true character and I did not confess it with contrition and heartfelt compunction, as I should have done, therefore I have still not been forgiven." He said this with profound sadness and the hearts of the sisters who were present experienced feelings of terror and also burned with no small desire to practice obedience with great fidelity. The sick man lived three days longer if I am not mistaken, weeping more bitterly for his sin for knowing the severity of divine judgments of God by such clear experience. As he was dying, he foretold that a great epidemic would befall that house, and this happened soon after his death. Having lived out his days in peace and rich in good works, he was united with his fathers. Nevertheless, he was deprived by his disobedience of the joyful and glorious assumption by which he would have been raised with the blessed Bearer of God and a crowd of holy angels had his fault not intervened. May all of us who have professed obedience learn from his example so salutary a fear that we never slip toward this vice, or if we do fall because of human frailty, let us hasten to purify ourselves by the remedy of a worthy penance.

## Chapter Ten

### The Dangers of Conspiracy

In that province which is called First Germany, whose capital is Mainz, in the territory of which the capital is Worms, the city of the Vangions, there is a community of the Cistercian Order in the line of Clairvaux which is called Schönau in German, and in the Latin *Pulchra-Insula*, "Beautiful Island."[34] In this monastery in the time of Abbot Geoffrey of holy memory there came about by the instigation of the devil an event that caused a very great scandal. In earlier times, a custom quite contrary to the usages of the Order had crept into the abbey by negligence, or rather by the imprudent permission of the superiors: each year new boots were given to the lay brothers as well as to the monks.[35] Dom Geoffrey was an active and energetic man, called from another house by the choice of God and man to exercise in this monastery the first rank of honor, which he had obtained not through money or the prerogative of flesh and blood but by the merit of his life and the distinction of his prudence. He saw that the lay brothers enjoyed this excessive luxury, and, spurred by praiseworthy zeal, he thought it right to correct this unseemly presumption. Privately in his council and publicly in the brothers' chapter [EO 111.4 and n. 239] he began candidly to deplore this innovation, exhorting, asking, and finally ordering that this breach of custom, which diverged from the right line of the constitutions of the Order, be abandoned if it was possible without the scandal of dissension. But the sludge of harsh worldly presumption so gummed up the minds of the brothers with the sticky glue of obstinacy that they could not be detached from it without scandal. The abbot was a prudent man, and in accordance with the teaching of blessed Gregory, "he preferred to let scandal arise rather than abandon the truth."[36]

[34] Schönau, in the Diocese of Worms, was founded in 1145 as a daughter house of Eberbach in the Clairvaux filiation. See Janauschek, 81; Cottineau 2:2982. On the rebellion of the lay brothers that took place around 1168, see Donnelly, *The Decline of the Medieval Cistercian Laybrotherhood*, 22–37, 73, 75, 76.

[35] RB 55. Tubach, 1464d, records a story in which a dead Cistercian appears to tell his brothers he is in torment because he had kept old shoes, contrary to the rule. *Le Grande Exorde*, 304n4, directs the reader to consult *Usus conversorum* 19 and Statute 1195.31 (Canivez 1:186). *Laybrother Statutes*, 1195:30 (Waddell, *Narrative and Legislative Texts*, 327).

[36] Gregory the Great, *Homiliae in Hiezechihelim Prophetam* 1.7.5 (CCSL 142:85; SCh 327:240–41).

At first the lay brothers began to murmur, whispering in corners; then little by little, as the conspiracy spread, with an unbridled madness they planned open revolt. The instigator of all this evil and author of this conspiracy was a certain lay brother to whom was committed the care of the brothers' dormitory and their footwear. Full of a devilish spirit, he thought, as the prophet says, "Silence shall be cast out" [Amos 8:3]; he talked to some alone, to others in groups, stirring them up and exhorting them not to relinquish this custom, this brand of discord, this torch that inflamed their pride no matter what the prayers or threats against them. O how amazing, rather, how lamentable is the demented spirit of the pride that ensnares those it has once deceived! They undertake arduous and extremely hard labors which they would consider intolerable if they were made to do them for God yet do not hesitate to regard as light and easy when puffed up with rebellion and pride. At the first report of these murmurs, the lord abbot ordered, by virtue of obedience, that any of them who broke silence before the meal should fast for an entire day on bread and water and that if some-one committed the fault afterward he should fast the following day.[37] The brother whom I mentioned above, a pervert rather than a convert, pretended to conform to this order as if it came from heaven, not for love of virtue, but to increase hatred against the superior.[38] Since he broke the silence daily by fomenting sedition, almost every single day he fasted on bread and water, seeking by this means to inflame the brothers' souls to hatred against the abbot who imposed such a harsh and inhuman injunction.

Meanwhile, the holy celebration of Advent Sunday drew near and the storm of controversy increased; spread and strengthened by secret intrigues it thundered on all sides and threatened to erupt into a very grave public scandal. The aforesaid pseudo-convert had

[37] On penances and especially fasts of bread and water, see *Instituta generalis capituli*, LXVI, LXIII, LXII: *De gravioribus culpis* (Versions A-D) (Waddell, *Narrative and Legislative Texts*, 484–86) and LXVII, LXV: *De levioribus culpis* (Versions A-B) (Waddell, *Narrative and Legislative Texts*, 486–87); in Canivez 1152.11 (Canivez 1:46); 1154.22 (Canivez 1:58); 1157.13, 14, 40, 54, 58, 59, 61 (Canivez 1:61, 64–67).

[38] The Latin contains a play on the words *conversus* and *perversus*, which is also found in Bernard of Clairvaux, Ep 2.7 (SBOp 7:18; James, Ep 2.7, p. 15).

conceived a very devious plan, the execution of which he urged by a very wicked insistence. It was this: on Christmas Eve, when the lay brothers from the granges were gathered in the monastery, they would all by common consent go up to the monks' dormitory during work time and take the boots from each bed and cut them up one by one with their knives and tear them to pieces with their hands. Although this prodigious and infamous project, conceived with such malice, was not unknown to the venerable abbot, he pretended otherwise; as it is written, "The wise man keeps silent in the evil day" [Amos 5:13]. The more human counsel and help failed him in this extreme situation, the more he decided to rely instead on the tender mercy of divine goodness. He then prescribed special prayers for the monks and exhorted each of them to implore the mercy of the Lord as hard as he could to deign by his goodness to change to something better the insolently carnal dispositions of those brothers. The great solemnity of Christmas was meanwhile near. A few days before the feast, the abbot held the lay brothers' chapter; here the chief author of unrest, a servant of Satan, was accused by some of his conspirators of an abstinence which lacked discernment and of entirely shaving off his beard with a razor, which the wretched man had done with the intention of stirring scandal and accusations that would be made by his accomplices, not for love of discipline or out of fraternal charity, but only with a view toward satisfying their wicked plans.[39] The lord abbot gently asked the rebel the reason for his conduct, and from his haughty and disdainful reply the abbot knew he was consumed with malice. Burning with a holy zeal for justice, Geoffrey addressed these prophetic words to him in front of everyone: "My brother, I have tried to use salutary warnings to combat your stubbornness and to try to free you from the snares in which the devil holds you at his mercy. But pride has so blinded the eye of your heart that it is like a beam I could not dare by my poor powers to cast out [Matt

---

[39] The lay brothers are described as bearded in EP 15.10. For the symbolism of beards in the monastic life, see Giles Constable, introduction to *Apologia de Barbis*, in *Apologiae Dvae*, CCCM 62 (Turnhout, Belgium: Brepols, 1985), 123–30; and *Reformation of the Twelfth Century*, 194–96.

7:3-5; Luke 6:41-42]. Since I see that you are so far removed from good sense that you scorn rather than heed my warnings, I tell you solemnly in the presence of everyone sitting here that if you do not immediately and without delay come to your senses and humbly make satisfaction, you will suffer a terrible judgment from almighty God. As Scripture says, 'The Lord will purge you in the day of his judgment' [Sir 5:9]. Again, and for the third time, I affirm to all those having sound minds that, just as the good and merciful Lord gives grace to the humble, so the same awesome God with an inflexible rod of righteousness resists the proud [Jas 4:6; 1 Pet 5:5]. You are a public enemy of peace and the institution that our holy fathers sanctioned; if you persevere in malice, within a very few days you will undergo an extremely harsh judgment. For I trust that the Lord Jesus and his glorious Virgin Mother, whose poor and useless servants we are [Luke 17:10], will not allow this house—outstanding for the bond of fraternal charity from its very foundation and conspicuous for the discipline of its laudable customs—to be corrupted by your thoroughly shameless stubbornness.'

Already the prayers of the monks who were groaning under the unhappiness of this internal disorder had reached the ears of the Lord of Hosts, and the angel of the Lord had received an order from him to pass over those who were marked on their foreheads with the cross,[40] that is to say, the sign of the humility of Christ, but to strike down without delay the miserable author of the conspiracy—on whose forehead he saw the character of the beast and the dragon [Rev 19:20] who is the king over all children of pride [Job 41:25]—and at the same time to dissipate completely all storm of scandal and smoke of pride. On the evening of the day before Christmas, the wicked man was coming down from the dormitory after Compline to meet the lay brothers' infirmarian, who seemed to be his assistant in the conspiracy and with whom he often consulted about their wicked plan, when suddenly he broke into groans and cries of pain, his face turned white, his nostrils contracted, his eyes bulged, and he gave all the sorry signs of immanent death.

---

[40] Hebrew letter *Thau*: Ezek 9:4-6.

The infirmarian was terrified and, seeing him stagger, caught him around the waist for fear he would fall abruptly to the ground. But his death was so sudden that before he reached the ground he had already given up his wretched soul while still in the hands of his deadly accomplice. Thus were the chief conspirators dismayed [Exod 15:15]; fear took the place of daring, and all those who had been involved in the schism and dissension were paralyzed. How good you are, Lord Jesus, to those who hope in you [Lam 3:25]. How sweet is your mercy in time of tribulation. It is like the dew of morning and a refreshing rain after drought [Sir 35:26]. You are King of kings and Lord of lords [Rev 19:16], and seated upon your throne of judgment you disperse all evil with a single glance. You have pacified all the other rebels by the terrible end of this sinner, and because you have found works that are dear to you in this house, you ended a long-premeditated revolt at the moment when it was about to break out.

The lay brothers assembled from all areas to their leader, on whom they had counted only the day before to give the signal for their wicked plot, and—O, Good Jesus!—they carried his dead body to the infirmary in great disarray and, beside themselves in fear and trembling, laid him down in the place where they were accustomed to put brothers who had died. Lord, you did not allow your holy solemnity, on which peace was announced on earth for the first time by the ministry of angels [Luke 2:13-14], to be troubled and dishonored by schism and discord. There was great surprise in the monastery when they sounded the board of the dead, since they had not thought anyone was near to death. Dom Theobald was present— he was then subcellarer and was later elevated to be abbot there and afterward became abbot of the mother house, Eberbach, one of the first daughter houses of Clairvaux—and he gave us all the details of the affair.[41] At that moment Theobald was reciting as fervently as he could the prayer that the lord abbot had ordered for crushing the

---

[41] Theobald was abbot at Schönau *c.* 1196–1206 and abbot of Eberbach from 1206 to 1221; Conrad, author of the EM, was his successor. Caesarius of Heisterbach, *Dialogus miraculorum* 6.4 (Strange 1:345; S-Bland 1:396–97) says that Theobald lived fifty-six years (*in quinquaginta sex annis*) in the Order.

conspiracy, which until that moment he had forgotten to say. Hearing the sound of the board, he went in haste to the infirmary. When he discovered who had died, and vehemently wondering at the judgment of God, he quickly alerted the abbot, who by chance had left the dormitory, that a brother had died and asked him straightaway to say the Office for the commendation of the soul of the departed. The abbot came quickly, and when he turned back the cloth covering the head of the body and recognized the face of the person lying there, he clasped his hands and, drawing a deep breath, from the depth of his heart he cried, "Alas, you poor man, behold, you are lying there dead, through divine justice without penance for your sin!" He said this a second and third time, groaning: "If only you had not arrogantly spurned my warnings! If only you had not excluded yourself forever from the mercy of God!"[42]

Then he considered for a time what he ought to do and decided that it would be wisest to perform the Office for the commendation of a soul at once and take the body to the church as usual, then to call all the brothers, the monks as well as the lay brothers, together early the next day to decide with them what should be done. When the community met, the lord abbot spoke thus in the hearing of all of them: "My dearest brothers, you know what perverse design was in the depraved heart and malicious will of this man when he was taken. You realize that if the just and terrible chastisement of God had not suddenly taken him out of the world he would have had no qualms about throwing this house, which had previously enjoyed great peace and concord, into confusion by a very serious scandal, along with his accomplices whom he had persuaded by his muttering and wicked counsel. Since we all know his perversity but we do not know that he confessed or did penance, I think his body ought not to be placed among the bodies of our brothers. On my part this is not a rash decision, for I can affirm in conscience that I have weighed it carefully in the balance of divine justice." When they had heard this, the lay brothers were extremely afraid and turned pale and petitioned

---

[42] *Le Grande Exorde*, 307n30, notes that this as an extraordinary example of the community following EO 94.2, that the dead are to be attended to rapidly.

humbly that they might at least be given permission to talk with the senior monks. The lord abbot indulgently granted this, and they went apart to consult. After a little while they all came back, and both monks and lay brothers prostrated themselves on the ground before the abbot and begged him earnestly not to deny mercy to the departed brother. The lay brothers promised upon oath and, calling on the divine name, swore that if the abbot would reduce the rigor of his sentence and deign to admit the brother to the common burial place, however little he deserved it, they would entirely renounce their unjust pretensions and never again ask for new boots. Some of the seniors added that except in this instance the conduct of the wretch had by all reports been very good and that they should not judge without mercy one who had, by the intervention of divine clemency, perhaps been punished on earth to prevent him from carrying out this wicked project, for which he would have deserved eternal damnation. The abbot decided to make the best of the situation, as he thought it would be a very great evil if the lay brothers, who could easily be appeased by this means, were to create a bigger scandal, which would be an error worse than the first [Matt 27:64]. He was also afraid for himself if he gave a harsher than appropriate sentence—for the measures against conspirators had not yet been promulgated by the General Chapter.[43] So he gave in to their demand, and Masses and funeral rites were celebrated as usual, and the dead brother was buried among the bodies of the brothers.

Blessed be God in all things! By his mercy and goodness he preserved this house which teetered on the brink of wicked conspiracy and was threatened with being thrown into the deep abysses of scandal by this infamous conspiracy. All the leaven of discord was buried with him, and the holy community could be happy in the fact that to this day no traces of that wily ruse have ever reappeared. Moreover, Dom Theobald, whom we mentioned above, had had an

---

[43] The sentence of the chapter to which Conrad refers was written around 1190 and is not in all codices (Canivez 1189.14, 1190.12, 1191.53). The passage's inclusion in the EM indicates that either revolts were being discussed in earlier chapters and/or that this chapter of the EM was written after 1190.

old and close friendship with the deceased, and they had promised one another that they would help each other by their prayers in life and also in death if one should die before the other. Since this lay brother had not been a bad religious before the storm of conspiracy, Dom Theobald, knowing that friendship is proved in extreme cases of necessity, and being very much afflicted by the peril of a soul he had held in such affection, resolved to pray for him for a whole year. For he believed without a doubt that although prayers for the dead do not lessen the weight of his misdeeds, they are never in vain and are always profitable, at least to the one who makes them.

After he had poured out prayers to the Lord for him for an entire year, in the course of the year the departed friend appeared to him in a vision with a mournful face that showed what a sorry sentence he had endured. Asked in what state he now was, he replied that since his death until that moment he had been paying the penalty of terrible torments for his rebellion and stubborn disobedience but that he had not yet despaired entirely of the mercy of God. Was it just a dream or was it a secret revelation? It is rash to say. Whatever it was, piety should teach us not to pass too hasty a judgment on the soul of the dead brother. Perhaps the horrible death that he suffered in time was no more than a way of showing him eternal mercy. Because truly, when mercy and justice [Ps 100:1] face each other, it is mercy that shines more clearly. It is certain that the Lord regards this house with the serene eye of his benevolence. This is shown in the church of Eberbach, where long after the question of new footwear had been raised by the malignity of the demons, it was a prickly source of such calamity and scandal that it is better to weep than to recall it in words.[44] The example it has given us should be a warning about humility and caution, so that if ever that ancient serpent [Rev 12:9], our inveterate enemy, tries to sow the weeds of discord and conspiracy in places where we are and make us go against the customs of the Order, we should fear God and flee these violators of peace and concord as we would asps and basilisks, and

---

[44] This rebellion of lay brothers occurred in 1208 or 1210; see Grießer, EM, 297n1; and Caesarius of Heisterbach, *Dialogus miraculorum* 5.29 (Strange 1:314–15; S-Bland 1:360).

along with the children of peace who by the zeal of God are trying to rip out and tear up wicked and presumptuous customs opposed to the ways of the Order, we should not hesitate manfully to put up, as it were, a defensive wall around the house of the Lord. For it must be repeated without ceasing and never be forgotten that God resists the proud and gives gifts to the humble [Jas 4:6; 1 Pet 5:5].

## CHAPTER ELEVEN

### *The Dangers of Excommunication*

It is known by everyone called Christian, by the faith that fills their minds and naturally persuades them, that the sentence of excommunication is nothing other than separation from God and the loss of eternal life. Yet because hearts made torpid by negligence are moved by examples rather than words, I think it necessary to show how this destructive sentence makes rational creatures tremble and even subjects irrational creatures no less either to death or grave calamity. The unhappy person who is struck with the arrow of anathema because of his pride ought to consider that he should tremble for himself, whereas those bereft of reason, who do not understand what it is to be proud, may be struck by the sword point of anathema through the power of the holy name.

The august emperor Louis the Pious, son of Charlemagne, was the first to endow magnificently the churches of Christ in Gaul and Germany out of the rich fiscal revenues of the imperial purse. That is why he is given the nickname "the Pious." It is said that he heard a voice telling him to do this, saying, "Louis, you have poisoned the churches." The same sovereign founded a monastery of monks in Saxon lands on the banks of the Weser, a great river, and he loaded it with honors and goods in truly imperial munificence. He decreed that it be called New Corbie to distinguish it from Corbie in Gaul.[45]

---

[45] This Corbie (or Corvey), in the Diocese of Paderborn, was founded in 822 by Benedictine monks from the older monastery Corbie-sur-la-Somme in Picardy. See DHGE 13:922–25.

During the time of the emperor Frederick of pious memory, there was an abbot of this monastery named Conrad. He gave in to the attractions of vainglory and used a gold ring in the fastidious custom of imperial prelates. This was obviously very different from the first abbot of Clairvaux who was truly poor and humble [Ps 81:3] in spirit and, as it is written about him, preferred a hoe and a rake to a ring and a tiara.[46] One day Conrad was wearing the golden ring that was very precious to him and was sitting at table and, according to court custom, took it off to wash his hands. Preoccupied with I know not what matter, serious or futile, he forgot it and left it on the table. One of the tame ravens, which were a delight of certain members of the abbot's court at that period, happened to fly past; it took the ring in its beak without anyone noticing and flew off with it to his nest, not knowing it was guilty of theft.[47] Indeed "when dinner was over, the places were removed, and everyone got up."[48] At that moment the abbot discovered his loss, and he at first accused the servers of negligence and made them look everywhere, but in vain, for no one had seen the perpetrator of the theft. Beside himself with anger and suspecting both his companions and his servants, he ordered the people of a large and very rich town situated not far from the walls of the monastery and under the authority of the abbot to publish his extremely severe sentence of excommunication against whoever had dared to besmirch himself by such a theft. The order was carried out, and for all rational creatures an oath of conscience was taken as a mark of innocence, and also creatures without reason and incapable of suffering eternal punishment because of their very creation, which is only for this world, did not escape the temporal pains of this anathema. The thief, guilty but unaware of

[46] Bernard of Clairvaux, Csi 2.9 (SBOp 3:417; CF 13:56–57); and Geoffrey of Auxerre, Vita Bern 2.4.27 (PL 185:283).

[47] For an extensive discussion, with bibliography, on traditional stories about crows stealing, being reproached, and the like, see Berlioz, *Le Grand Exorde*, 310–12nn3–15 and 314n19. In the English tradition, see the poem (originally published in 1840) "The Jackdaw of Rheims" by Thomas Ingoldsby (Richard Harris Barham), in *The Ingoldsby Legends, or Mirth and Marvel* (New York: Henry Frowde, Oxford University Press, 1910), 129–35.

[48] Virgil, *Aeneid* 1.216.

his fault, pined away little by little, eating nothing and croaking the jests and other follies of an irrational creature, by which they divert foolish people who care nothing for the fear of God. Then he lost his wing feathers, and finally the rest of his feathers fell away from his dried-out flesh in such a way that he became an object of pity and astonishment to everyone who saw him.

One day it happened that the servants of the abbot discussed in his presence the amazing change that had happened to this bird and agreed among themselves that such a thing could by no means have happened by accident; one of them said to the abbot as a joke, "My lord, I think he ought to be examined to see if he is the thief you seek and if his terrible miseries do not show that they are the consequence of the anathema that has bound him." Everyone was very taken with this, and Conrad at once ordered one of his men to climb the tree in which the raven had its nest and to search there with the greatest care among the mess of straw and bits and pieces of which it was made up. No sooner had the servant carried out the order than he found the ring, wiped it clean of dirt, and put it unstained into the hands of the abbot, to the great surprise of all around. Thus the unfortunate thief, no doubt by divine permission, suffered atrocious punishments for his theft, although he was still ignorant that he had been guilty. The lord abbot, following the counsel of prudent men, ordered that those who had published the sentence of the excommunication should annul it quickly because the stolen object had been found. From that moment, the bird, though it had been perishing little by little and languishing because of its evil doing, began to recover and regain its strength until, by a true miracle, it had entirely recovered its pristine form and the health it had lost.

It is also written in the life of our blessed Father Bernard that when he was invited to the dedication of the new church at Foigny, he found it was so filled with flies who were attracted by the dampness of the fresh limestone that no one could enter without being inconvenienced.[49] The brothers were even beginning to fear that the presence of these insects would prevent them from dedicating

---

[49] William of Saint Thierry, Vita Bern 1.11.52 (PL 185:256).

the church on the next day. They told the holy father about this, and with the sure confidence he always had in God he said, "I excommunicate them." Next morning the flies had been struck dead by this anathema and so covered the ground of the church that they had to be swept into a pile and be carried out by the shovelful.

Someone also told us about a soldier who had incurred public excommunication by his wrongdoing. When he was at table he threw bread to his dogs, but they backed away, repelled by the smell of the moldy bread, and absolutely refused to touch it. Surely any cautious and circumspect person endowed with reason and grace should be capable of avoiding evil and doing good lest he incur this terrible sentence of death and separation from God, since even beings without reason, incapable of committing sin and therefore unable to expiate it, are sometimes punished very severely by the anathema that strikes them.

## Chapter Twelve

### *About the Perils of Confessors Who Lack Discernment and in Praise of Those Who Are Discerning*[50]

How charmingly holy Scripture calls discernment the mother of virtue.[51] It is like a sacred boundary between virtues and vices which distinguishes the one from the other. Discernment's wise providence uncovers the vice that lies under the appearance of sanctity and rules; through devotion it strengthens and puts virtue in order. It does not banish the person who is weak in faith but supports him greatly with a motherly devotion. Far from alienating

---

[50] This story is taken from John of Clairvaux, *Liber visionum et miraculorum* (Troyes, Bib. mun. MS 946), though Grießer (EM, 300n1) notes that there are similar accounts elsewhere.

[51] See Bernard of Clairvaux, Circ 3.11 (SBOp 4:290–91; SBS 1:446); and RB 64.19.

with severe reproaches those sinners who come to lay bare their consciences in shamefaced confession, discernment consoles them and relieves them with tender caresses. If she sees a penitent falter under the weight of his crimes, when they seem so enormous that years of tears could not efface them, she is full of very sweet exhortations to convince him that he can easily obtain remission by the sacrifice of the humble spirit and a contrite heart [Ps 50:19]. This is not how many of the pastors of God's Church act; with an undiscerning and impetuous spirit they scatter the Lord's flock. Ignorant of the virtue of discernment and not having the treasure of a gracious tongue [Sir 6:5] with which to lick the infectious sores of sinful souls that they may be cured, they more profoundly injure those whom they ought to heal. By piling on long and hard penances without a heart of mercy, they sow the seed, as it were, of contempt and despair in the feeble. What we are saying here is not that they do wrong who impose upon sinners penances in proportion to the number and gravity of their faults but that, when he hears a penitent who is so worried not only about the sins he has committed but also about receiving a rigorous penance, the person hearing his confession sees him becoming pale, trembling, timid, and dispirited, a discrete confessor will pass it over for a while. To a soul shaken with fear he will give the milk of gentle consolation and the encouragement of pious exhortation until, once he has been settled down by the confessor's good offices, the penitent is able to take the solid food of a fruitful penitence. I want to recount an interesting and remarkable story about this which will show the reader how dangerous it is not to know how to use discernment and take account of the state of the penitent and not to know how to be weak with the weak [2 Cor 11:29], as the Apostle says, and, on the contrary, how much praise should be given to a discerning confessor who, by the oil of instructive grace, knows how to conform himself to the dispositions and strengths of all those who confess. In this way someone who is holy and prudent will be encouraged to make progress in discernment, while someone who is rigid and lacks discernment will hasten to purify his lack of discernment, as if being scrubbed by a caring hand, and will not balk at learning, by the application of careful reflection, how much he should employ loving-kindness in bringing to birth the smallest and least of the Church of God, until Christ is formed in them [Gal 4:19].

There was a knight possessed of youth, noble birth, immense riches, and great vigor and adorned with titles and because of this was swollen with a worldly pride.[52] He despised divine and human ordinances and despised both civil and natural law and everywhere spread burning and plundering, seditions and murders; he was little concerned with right and wrong, and, to describe all his wickedness briefly, he neither feared God nor respected man [Luke 18:2]. But he had a faithful wife who was devoted to all the works of Christian piety, insofar as she could with such a cruel husband. She sincerely loved her husband with a love more spiritual than carnal [Titus 2:4] and shed endless tears over his perversity and sent up persistent prayers for his conversion. Sometimes when she saw that his proud spirit was a little less bitter and his face was more serene and joyful than usual, she would reproach him for his own good and spare neither tears nor prayers to make him cease committing his many evils and please the Lord through the humiliation of confession and penance. But he rejected this best of women who desired his salvation so strongly, sometimes by a dangerous lack of concern, sometimes with violent anger. He said he could not bring himself to make such a change; his trade was arms and war, and he could never stand the scorn of his friends and neighbors who would reproach him for laziness and inactivity if he did not give his enemies two or three times the evil he had received from them. Though she was so often rejected, this good wife did not let herself be cast down or discouraged. But she brought forth her husband, as it were, from her womb by holy desire and did not cease to give him wise advice in spite of himself from time to time,

---

[52] The story that follows contains several common motifs: (1) the murder of a confessor (Tubach 3810, 4783, by a pirate and a thief); (2) a gentle confessor who may convert a penitent who has already killed others (Tubach 3810, 4783); (3) the penitent who cannot perform the assigned penance (Tubach 4713, 2243, compare 1239); and (4) the penitent who spends the night in a church fighting off temptations (Tubach 3477).

until at last, overcome by her kind persistence and softened by her wifely charity, he said, "Very well, because of your advice I will go to confession, but where shall I find a confessor to whom I can safely open my conscience and who will be kind and forbearing to me?" Seizing this utterance as a promising omen and thirsting mightily for her husband's salvation, she said joyfully, "My lord, I will find you a forbearing confessor who will deserve your trust. I only beg you not to swerve from your good and holy resolution." She then looked for a spiritual physician able to cure the many and inveterate sores of his soul, and she found a monk-priest but, alas, one who lacked the gift of discernment and knew nothing of how to discern spiritual remedies according to the character and temperament of the sick. In her simplicity, believing him to be discreet, this noble lady brought her wretched husband to him, imploring him to make a good confession, not as he would to a man, but as to the Lord Christ himself. When he had done what he could, the priest was shocked at hearing so many and such enormous crimes, and instead of pulling this soul back from the bottomless gulf of perdition by the application of sweet and consoling words, with the arrow of his indiscreet rigor he only forced him deeper into the pit by doubling his despair. "My good man," he said to him, "if your excesses had been kept within bounds, I would have been very willing to help you with my humble advice, but your trespasses are so many and so great that the sacred authority of the canons requires that examination of them be reserved not to just any priest but to the supreme pontiff himself. I therefore exhort and charge you to go quickly to the tombs of the apostles and open your conscience sincerely to the bishop who holds the seat of the holy apostles, and to carry out generously whatever penance he decides to give you."

At these words this fierce man, who had seemed so gentled and humbled, raged with fury as if he had been struck on the forehead with a violent blow from a stone, and his cruel fury returned so fiercely that the wretched man lapsed into madness. "Is this the way you repay my trust in you," he said, "when I have just humbled myself by opening my conscience to you?" The priest replied simply that for the moment he could not give him better or wiser advice. Then this son of Belial, who counted bloodshed as nothing, drew his sword and cut off the priest's head. Then he returned to his wife and told her about the unhappy outcome of his bloodstained confession. She shuddered and turned pale and nearly died of grievous heartbreak; she could only reply with groans and tears to this tale of such a terrible crime of patricide. But what can stop charity when it comes from a pure heart and a good conscience and an unfeigned faith [1 Tim 1:5]? How can charity so deeply rooted in the soul of an excellent woman give up in the face of adversity? How can it be overcome by any perversity, however great, or be broken by the hammer of human wickedness? This charity, says the wise man, is strong as death, inflexible as hell [Song 8:6]. The more harshly she was repelled, the more courageously she persevered. She did not give up until the judgment of piety achieved victory and, according to the words of the Apostle, an unbelieving husband was saved by a believing wife [1 Cor 7:14]. She was another Theodora burning with ardent desire to save a second Sisinnius,[53] a new Natalie who would, if she could, make her husband another Hadrian.[54] Nor did she allow his eyes to rest [Prov 6:4]; she reminded her husband of the terrible judgment of God and often described to him the brevity and uncertainty of human life, so that, by the help of grace, she at last obtained from him a second resolution to go to confession. Then, like a very clever bee, she began searching on every side with a very pious curiosity for someone who was not only a religious but also a discerning

[53] Theodora and Sisinnius were said to have been converted by Pope Saint Clement I. Sisinnius was a friend of the emperor Domitian (r. 81–96). The story is recorded in the apocryphal *Passion of Saint Clement* (BHL 1848); PG 2:617, Mombritius, *Vitae sanctorum*, 2 volumes (Paris, 1910), 1:22–31. See *Catholic Encyclopedia* (New York: The Encyclopedia Press, 1913–14), 4:14; and Grießer, EM, 303n2, for bibliography.

[54] A reference to Natalie and Hadrian, martyrs at Nicomedia *c.* 306 (BHL 3744). Hadrian was said to have been an officer of the imperial court who declared himself a Christian, was imprisoned, and was tortured to death. In one of several legends his wife Natalie disguised herself as a boy and bribed her way into the prison in order to comfort her husband and ask for his prayers in heaven. She is said to have died a natural death. Mombritius, *Vitae sanctorum* 1:22–31. See Donald Atwater, *The Penguin Dictionary of Saints* (Baltimore: Penguin Books, 1965), 32; and *Catholic Encyclopedia* 7:105 for bibliography.

confessor, who would be gentle with this great sinner [Gal 6:1], raise him from his ruin, and avoid suddenly breaking a bruised reed [Isa 42:3; RB 64.13] for fear that the final state of this man would be worse than the first [Matt 12:45; 2 Pet 2:20]. The judgments of the Lord are a great deep [Ps 35:7], and he calls the most wicked to life and leaves the presumptuous, who glory in their innocence, to their own devices. And by his good pleasure, she found a bishop who was outstanding in piety and also possessed of discernment; he was adept at winning souls and in every way apt for the valiant woman's plan. To him this other Naaman the Syrian, covered from head to foot with a spiritual leprosy, was led into descending into Jordan [2 Kgs 5:14; Luke 4:27], that is to say, into the humiliations of a sincere confession. And by the virtue of the sevenfold grace of the Holy Spirit he would be washed and anointed for the remission of sins and restored to the innocence of the children of Christ, that is, he was to die to sin and henceforth live to God [Rom 6:10-11]. When the fellow had made his confession and discharged the stomach of his conscience of the poison of evil humors, this pious and prudent doctor, storing away the scalpel and the cauterizing fire,[55] approached the half-dead patient with the breath of life and the anointing of sweetest consolation, saying, "Friend, your sins, by which you have offended God and wounded your soul, are grave, but however grave and numerous they may be, what are they next to the incomprehensible depth of God's goodness? They are no more than a drop in a bucket compared to the ocean. I urge you to take courage and since with the aid of grace you have already submitted yourself to the remedy of confession, do not hesitate to accept the saving drink of penitence, however bitter. We have it on divine authority that without this drink, confession avails nothing. But I will temper the potion of this penitence for you, so that by this means you can escape eternal death and not be deprived of everlasting life." He hesitated at the very mention of penitence and remained silent. "What are you thinking, my dearest brother?" the bishop said. "Can you not offer God the small sacrifice of penitence

---

[55] Bernard of Clairvaux, *Sent* 3.97 (SBOp 6/2:155–59; CF 55:313–19).

for your great sins?" The knight replied, "I cannot, and I will not, do any long and harsh penitence; but if, as you have promised, you can impose on me a moderate penance that will not exceed the limit of my strength, I will try to do what you tell me." "Well," said the bishop, "let us examine and measure your strength, so that I can enjoin something you think you can do. What then? Can you not at least do a little fasting? Will abundant alms be too much for you?" "I cannot do any of that," he replied. "I can only fast to the third hour of the day, and by my daily and ill-considered prodigality I have nearly reduced my house to utmost poverty." "If you do not think you can do that," replied the bishop, "at least agree with me that for your sins you will either visit the Holy Sepulcher as a pilgrim or at least go as a suppliant to the tombs of the holy apostles in Rome or to the body of Saint James in Galicia, so that by their intercession you may obtain mercy and forgiveness for your sins."

At these words, he who was strong in body but weak and feeble at heart and unable to control his rising indignation, replied with bitterness, "Why do you give me such useless advice? If I go away from my lands for one day, all my possessions will immediately be prey to sack, pillage, fire, and ruin. I would return to find nothing and I would become the scorn of my relatives and friends and be derided and mocked by my enemies. God forbid that I should suffer the entire loss of my honor and lands." What is an experienced doctor to do with a sick man on his hands who is beginning to perish and fail yet refuses all medicine? What, I say, was he to do for someone who drew back, not from slashing and burning, but from encouraging and soothing? It is here that holy discernment and compassion are most needed if a sick and dying sheep for whom Christ gave his life on the cross is not to be devoured by the old dragon who flatters himself, thinking that he can swallow a river of impenitents and dares to believe that he can take into his gullet a Jordan [Job 40:18] of penitents.

So the bishop remained undecided for a few moments, seeking how to deal with such a situation. Suddenly, illuminated by divine grace, he cried out with a smile, "Now, my brave knight, can you, for your sins, keep silence at least for one night?" And he, although almost at the threshold of desperation, just as Scripture warns, and not agreeing either to labor or to do anything to avoid ultimate perdition, seemed to wake from a deep sleep when he heard this. He said, "If by one night's silence all my sins will be pardoned, I will do what you advise." The bishop, trusting fully in the goodness of the Lord and fearing that through impenitence he would relapse and plunge again into all of his past crimes, replied, "Only do what I say, humble yourself before God and his representative, by accepting whatever penance and obedience I impose upon you, and if you firmly purpose not to commit mortal sin again, I will answer for your soul at the terrible day of the judgment of the just judge."

In this way a marvelous consensus was reached. It was a pact without parallel, an extraordinary interchange unheard of in this world that a debt contracted by so many years of debauchery, by crimes huge and numberless, should be paid for by one night of silence. And yet such is the force of obedience and the sublime power of charity that this daring pardon undertaken by a godly mind who wanted to save the soul of his brother could not be refused by the generous bounty of God. The sun was setting and night had fallen when this true pastor, truly deserving of the name and honor of bishop, led his penitent to the church. On the threshold of the church, he exhorted this former soldier of the devil, this new recruit of Christ, to faith, patience, and perseverance and to be on guard against the many ruses of the demon, adding that if he did not fight by the rules he would not be crowned [2 Tim 2:5]. Above all, the bishop warned him and stressed over and over that, no matter what he saw or heard, no matter what terror or horror he felt, he was not to say a word until daybreak, when the bishop would come with the cross of the Lord and by his blessing restore to him the function of speech. The unskilled new athlete[56] was thus well instructed in how he should handle himself in the spiritual contest of which so far he had no experience, and so he entered the church. The angels rejoiced over him, but the demons were enraged. He prayed for a few moments and then stood before the altar. The bishop who had accompanied him went away, warning

---

[56] Conrad uses the Greek word *agonitheta* for "new athlete."

him yet again to affirm perseverance; the doors of the church were closed very firmly, and the knight was left in the hands of God. Soon, surrounded by the fear and horror of the night, he began to become milder, to lose his proud confidence and change his beastly ferocity into gentleness as with trembling lips he invoked the mercy of God whom formerly he had haughtily scorned, and he prayed in a spirit of submission that divine goodness not abandon him in this dangerous struggle. That sinner who sinned at the beginning saw this and was enraged. He ground his teeth, and, dried up with resentment, he lamented having been cast out of his former possession by this new art of piety, and he summoned a whole troop of evil spirits to lay clever and deceptive traps.

At the beginning of the night silence, when the penitent was listening to every sound, uneasy at heart and fearing all sorts of perils, he suddenly heard a noise as if someone were opening the doors of the church. And then he saw imaginary tradesmen who were none other than demons in the guise of tradesmen well-known to him, who approached him to suggest he should buy rich cloths. They each carried fabrics of many colors, finely woven and at great price, and they spread them before him and said, as if sympathizing with him, "Lord, why do you listen to this hypocrite who is trying to deceive you and has already reduced you to this state of inaction, persuading you to stay here like a fool or a half-wit in the middle of darkness and terrors of the night among the tombs of the dead? Can you not do penance for your sins later on at a more mature age and in a more effective way, instead of laying yourself open to the scorn and mockery of your enemies like this? All your relations and friends think you have suddenly lost your reason, and they are very upset. Your enemies, on the other hand, are dancing for joy and are racing with greedy glee to grab your possessions to satisfy their greed. This is why, hearing of your misfortunes, we came to find you. If you will buy these fabrics we have brought, we will wait as long as you like for payment, but take our advice and come out of your madness and you will recover your original honor." When these very clever and malicious spirits saw that he was unmoved by their words and that they could not get him to reply, they retired in confusion to return soon with other means of tempting him.

It was nearly midnight and the soldier was remembering and reflecting attentively on what he had seen when he seemed to hear nearby the noise of horsemen advancing in a tumult and galloping toward the church where he was sitting. When they reached the church doors they leapt quickly down from their horses and began crying out in sorrowful voices, saying, "Is not our very dear companion and kinsman here?" These were the demons again, in the guise of some of his companions whom he particularly loved and who had often shared in his wicked deeds and crimes. It seemed to him that they broke open, rather than unlocked, the doors of the church and came toward him, calling him by name, speaking in voices alternately sorrowful and indignant. "Alas," they said, "alas, dearest of our friends and kinsmen! What necessity has forced you to this deplorable folly? Who can have persuaded you to this voluntary and senseless disaster? Who would believe that someone so prudent and able, so strenuous in deeds, so trained in military discipline, so very experienced in battle, could suddenly not hesitate to fall into such folly as to forget his friends and kinsmen, to neglect their honor and his own by being reduced to these extremes of unhappiness and misery, and to expose all his goods to pillage and fire? Don't you realize that your enemies, whose pride and audacity you used to smash by the force of your courage and strength, are now reveling and rejoicing at the news of your humiliation and turn of fortune? They are like conquerors already laden with spoils [Isa 9:3]. Their forces are gathered to grab everything that is justly yours and with despotic barbarity put it under their own sway. We were disturbed by their wicked plot and have come to beg you, dear friend, to renounce this absurd madness in which you are involved and quickly call together your companions in arms to go to war against your enemies. If, heaven forbid, you scorn the advice of your friends who are devoted to your interests and put off coming with us, your fields and all your goods will be ravaged without ceasing, pillaged and burnt; then it will be too late for you to repent of your stupidity. What greater folly could there be than to believe that your sins can be forgiven by only one night of silence? The pseudo-bishop thought this up, not for your good, but to say something pleasing to you to satisfy your zeal!"

In the midst of all these most subtle deceits the penitent, enlightened by divine grace, remained unmoved. He did not reply with one word to those rattling on to him, and they had to leave, furious at not gaining anything but sound and fury by all their malice. These ministers of iniquity and fabricators of deceit saw their efforts frustrated, and above all they saw that the sinner whose perdition they had previously applauded was already—in a moment, I say—returning to life by means of the virtue of obedience. Eaten up with envy and at the peak of exasperation, they planned to overcome him by cruelty and torture, to the end that he who was unmoved by flatteries might give in to fear and suffering; perhaps impatience would draw from him at least one word, and so he would lose the precious balm of salvation which he had prepared in the mortar of obedience with the pestle of patience.

Much of the night had passed and cockcrow was approaching when the wicked spirits appeared to the penitent, not under borrowed forms as before, but in their own forms, with black and deformed bodies, grim faces, menacing eyes, and breathing out fury and the poison of malice. They surrounded him on every side and challenged him with terrible voices, saying, "You are damned a thousand times, mired in crimes, stinking of sin, in a Charybdis of disgraces! What is this vain hope which is leading you on?[57] Do you think that you can ever be anything other than one of us, when you have surpassed even the demons in wickedness and evil? O how foolish, how vain, how stupid are your thoughts, to suppose that just by keeping silent for one night you can escape our hands, that you can break the yoke of our master when you already bear the mark of those who fight for the kingdom of death! If you do not want us to make our just contempt felt, if you want to escape the chastisement of those whose anger you cannot appease, leave here at once and you will be able to placate our anger if you want to, and then with our protection you can enjoy the sweetest pleasures that the world can offer you in the flower of your youth. With

---

[57] An allusion to the monster Scylla and whirlpool Charybdis (Homer, *Odyssey* 12). Charybdis became a metaphor for both vexing problems (Horace, *Odes* 1.27) and greedy individuals.

our help you will gain an ever-more glorious victory over your vanquished and routed enemies."

This they said to him. Then this strong athlete of God—who had earlier been so afraid of suffering and was now by the merit of faith and obedience firmly grounded on very firm rock which is Christ—scorned the terrors and menaces just as he had scorned the flatterers and seductions and manfully kept inviolate the silence that had been enjoined on him. The demons were thrown into such a fury by this that they flung themselves on him and rained down bitter blows, leaving him half dead and bruised and wounded but glorying in the witness of an uninjured conscience. He had overcome the nocturnal terrors of the first temptation; then, protected by the shield of divine grace, he had gained a second victory, repelling the arrow that flies by day, that is to say, prosperity; third, protected by the strong breastplate of patience, he resisted the third attack of the diabolical savagery of those who prowl in darkness. What remained except to resist the assaults of the noonday devil, who rose up in the splendor of good works that he could place himself in the man's heart more easily if he could make him glory of his virtues?[58] Already dawn had shed its shining rays, and this man, a sinner, yet a penitent, shone with his many triumphs over the diabolic evils and exalted in the grace of God. Entirely changed into another man with a great desire to receive genuine penances, he waited for the arrival of the bishop, who had promised to come at daybreak.

Indeed, such a change was clearly the work of the most high himself [Ps 76:11]. Lord, blessed is the man whom you yourself teach and to whom you instruct in your law. In the evil days when they have dug a pit of eternal perdition for the sinner [Ps 93:12-13]

---

[58] The "arrow that flies by day," "those who prowl in darkness," and "the noonday devil" are all taken from Ps 90:5-6. The "noonday devil" refers to the sin of sloth, or *acedia*. John Cassian, Inst 10 (SCh 109:382–425; English translation by Boniface Ramsey in *John Cassian: The Institutes* [New York: Newman, 2000], 217–38) warns the monk that idleness does much to cause accidie and one should remain active. See also Bernard of Clairvaux, SC 33.11 and 33.16 (SBOp 1:241–42, 244–45; CF 7:154–55, 158–59); Par 6.1 (SBOp 6/2:286–87; CF 55:71–72).

and an eternal gulf of confusion, who can lay down any charge against your elect, O Lord [Rom 8:33]? Who dares, O Lord, to close what you have opened? You, O Lord, by the power of your voice called out of the tomb him who had been dead four days, a Lazarus stinking with the outrage of his vices [John 11:39] and lying under the stone of habitual and inveterate evil. Who would dare say to you, "Why have you done this?" To you, O Lord, for the justification of sinners who are decaying like beasts in their own dung [Joel 1:17], be praise, honor, power, and glory forever and ever [1 Pet 4:11; Rev 5:13].

But the most envious Leviathan—that eye of ancient serpent who deservedly fell from the heights by his pride and yet regarded all things sublime through his desire for glory and is envious of the ones who are ascending to the sublime heights which he has lost—saw the penitent rejoicing in his victory in the grace of God, and this insatiable murderer set out to tempt him in ways that were much more perilous than those before. Knowing that the bishop would come soon, he gathered his hellish ministers and arranged a scene that would deceive even the most discerning. This ravenous wolf [Gen 49:27; Matt 7:15] had the audacity to put on the habit of the shepherd. This cruelest of tyrants by devilish art assumed the bishop's appearance, and his servants of darkness, bathed in false light, he disguised as servants of justice. This ridiculous procession set out, and the false prelate advanced wearing a magnificent stole to complete the deception. Contentment was printed on his face; his bearing and walk were so dignified that no one would ever dream he was a devil. Behind him came an array of falsities: imaginary priests got up in white, then Levites and other clerks in lower orders, each of them carrying in impure hands what seemed to be their ecclesiastical insignia, some with the sacred altar vessels, others with the vestments for the holy sacrifice, others with what looked like the books of the Divine Office.

This shape-shifting, twisted serpent, transformed into an angel of light, with his impious retinue in pretended piety, came up to the former sinner, now well-armed by the grace of God for [the warfare of] penitence, and from his lying mouth spewed out the lethal poison of deception as he said, "O Servant of God, great is your patience, invincible your faith, for you have kept inviolate the obedience proposed to you, and have set at naught the spirits of wickedness and all their wickedness and deceits. You must know that their detestable attempts to break your faith and ruin your obedience cannot be hidden from me. But I know too that by the protection of heaven they have been frustrated in their attempts." The wicked spirits who had taken on the forms of priests, deacons, and other clerks added their praises to this poisonous language, and they unrestrainedly commended the victory he had won. Some praised him for not having deigned to regard or touch the phantoms presented to his sight; others that he had preferred the fear of God to his family, friends, possessions, and everything that is in the world. All together they asserted how very patiently he had borne the atrocious beatings and how he was worthy to be placed among the ranks of the martyrs.

Then the chief, not pontiff but mastermind of the ruse, the false bishop, said, "Come, my brother, 'you have fought the good fight, you have finished your course' [2 Tim 4:7], you have kept your obedience like a valiant athlete. Now that dawn is breaking, you have permission to speak; it only remains for you to tell us in detail how you triumphed over the spirits of deceit, and we are burning to hear it." The veteran of the grace of God, however, whose ears and eyes Satan had been deceiving with such fantasies, was profoundly troubled in his mind, for the same spirits of seduction who were playing on him from without struck invisibly within through their venomous suggestions to fool him into believing their lies. But how could these very evil connivers do harm to someone whom the most merciful goodness of God had determined to save? The ancient enemy does not cease to tempt the unhappy children of men in a thousand ways, for it is only through their own rejection and confusion that they know who is among the elect.

So this man was much troubled, as we have said, anxiously and dubiously turning over in his mind whether or not he ought to speak, when, suddenly inspired by a highly secret movement of grace, he remembered that his bishop had said he would come with the cross of the Lord. He looked around inquisitively at all those false and miserable standard bearers and cleverly realized that the sign of salvation was not in their wicked hands. This was because, although Satan can fake many things by his lies and arts, he can never represent the figure on the sacred wood who had vanquished and destroyed him. Seized with terror, though he had been on the point of breaking silence by speaking, he stayed mute. For he suddenly realized that this band of ministers in white was really a legion of devilish spirits who had only faked this religious apparel to deceive him. Indeed, the former prince of light, now the prince of darkness,[59] and the rest of his apostate spirits saw that all their lying attempts were in vain and that the contrite sinner saw through their deception and scorned them like the rag of a menstruous woman [Isa 64:6].[60] They were scattered as if being hurled from the presence of divine majesty itself, which struck them like a blow on a fragile vase. They vanished like smoke, and they no longer dared to harass with their wicked traps that man who they saw was protected under the shadow of the wings of God's grace [Ps 16:8; 56:2], and they were no longer able to take him into the net of their intrigues.

When the enemies of all good had been vanquished with their leader, the bishop arrived, as he had promised with the cross of the Lord, surrounded by many clerks, not speciously but truly fortified by the insignia of true and brotherly religion. Having prayed, the bishop greeted his recluse and ordered him in the name of the Lord to speak. But he was still fearful of the terror of the night and could scarcely be persuaded to loosen his tongue in speech, for he had had so much experience of the many wiles of the demons that, in the manner of academicians, he thought everything should be doubted, and he was afraid he could no longer discern truth and falsehood.[61] When he had seen the sign of the holy cross, which he knew was the only thing that made demons tremble and put them

---

[59] *Lucifer . . . noctifer*, compare Bernard of Clairvaux, Hum 36 (SBOp 3:43; CF 13:64).

[60] "Rag of menstruous woman," see Bernard of Clairvaux, Sent 3.2 (SBOp 6/2:61; CF 55:183); and Div 7.4 (SBOp 6/1:110).

[61] The association of schools and the academy with doubt and confusion is common in the monastic tradition; see Gregory the Great, Mor 33.10 (CCSL 143B:1688–90); Bernard of Clairvaux, Ep 190.9 (SBOp 8:24–25; not in James).

to flight, he adored it by bowing his head reverently, and when asked by the bishop whether he had done the short-but-salutary penance enjoined on him, or if he could add to this more penance, he replied, "Reverend father, to obey in this matter I have run great dangers and endured terrible fights and a perilous struggle in a short space of time. But it is because of this that I give thanks to God our Savior who deigned to show me this night, miserable and unworthy though I am, what a stubborn enemy of my own salvation I have been and how foolishly I enslaved myself in the perilous company of a deadly and cruel tyrant." Such language astonished all those around, and they wanted to know what had happened. So the bishop ordered him to tell them without delay what he had seen and heard. To their general astonishment he recounted the tragedy of diabolical illusions and as indications of tyrannical cruelty, he showed the bruises on his beaten back and his swollen limbs.

Together they gave thanks to Our Lord Jesus Christ for the ineffable gift of his goodness, and the bishop, smiling with great happiness, said to him, "How does it seem to you, my brother? Are you willing to be content with only this satisfaction, or will you consent to a legitimate penance according to the laws and canons of the Church?" And completely forgetting his original weakness and strengthened by the grace of the Holy Spirit to endure any, even the hardest, labor, he replied without hesitation, "My lord father, whatever your paternity orders I will do willingly and freely, provided I can be delivered from the hateful company of these wicked demons. One has to have had a terrible experience like this to know how detestable and bitter their company is. If only unhappy mortals could be convinced of this in advance and take precautions. To this end, I am ready to make solemn and extended fasts,[62] undertake pilgrimages, and submit myself to any legitimate penance that will free me before the justice of God. For by the

---

See also Clanchy, *Abelard*, 34–40, for the context of twelfth-century schools. For pre-Christian precedents, see Piesik, *Exordium Magnum Cisterciense*, 2:415n193.

[62] "Solemn and extended fasts" is an allusion to Lent.

grace of God I have become sure that sinners can never return to life without the bitterness of penitence."

Who can adequately describe the joy of the bishop and how much thanks all those who stood around, and all his right-thinking companions and friends, gave to God when such holy, humble, and devout words escaped the lips of this sinner who only one night earlier had been so very proud and obstinate and had refused absolutely any notion of repentance? More than everybody else his wife, his admirable wife, worthy to be remembered by all good men, exalted with inexpressible joy and blessed the Lord because, through the labor and industry of her holy prayers and pious exhortations, she had succeeded in drawing her husband, to whom she had been united in temporal marriage, to the spiritual and utterly chaste marriage of the immaculate lamb [Rev 19:7]. Behold how sweet, how mellow, and how salutary are the fruits of piety which are produced by the virtue of holy discernment and, conversely, how bitter, pernicious, and deadly are the fruits produced by the vice of a wicked lack of discernment. When the priest mentioned above—who had undertaken to heal the sick but without knowing the virtue of discernment and not understanding how kind and compassionate he ought to have been toward a feeble conscience—brought death down on him, whom he should have called back to life, he had actually doubled the burden to include eternal death. But this blessed bishop, marvelously endowed with the virtue of discernment, when he saw by the insight of pious discernment that all the arguments of piety had failed, found another way to bring down a proud man in a healthy way and allow a humbled man to rise again to life.

## CHAPTER THIRTEEN

*How Dangerous It Is to Put off Confession to Another Time*

"Every good and perfect gift comes down from the father of light" [Jas 1:17], testifies James the Apostle, thus refuting the foolish philosophy of those who attribute the success of their good works freely to the quickness of their intelligence and ascribe them to their own free choice rather than submitting themselves to the righteousness of God. Who can tell how all the events and miseries to which human weakness is exposed will turn out—for the soul but also for the body—if one abandons for a moment the grace of God? Because we know that we would not pray as we should if the Spirit did not help our infirmity [Rom 8:26]. Therefore, reader, I ask your patience while I record a brief example about the necessity of sacramental confession. It shows very clearly, I think, the deplorable ruin that awaits our blindness of spirit, which has been corrupted by free will, and conversely, how powerful and effective grace is to save those who are perishing. This grace is quite able to keep us from ruin if we never forget the mercy of the Lord. As Ambrose says so well, the sin of Adam, which Christ destroyed by his death, had been necessary[63] so that the noble nature created in the image of God may know what it is in itself and what it is through grace.[64]

In a monastery of the Premonstratensian Order a certain brother was made infirmarian; to judge by appearances, he seemed to be an able religious with an honest way of life. But alas, "differing weights and differing measures, are both abominable to the Lord" [Prov 20:10]. He was weighed down with those things that the Lord abhors,[65] and "his balance was false" [Prov 11:1]. Outwardly, he presented himself as sober and a lover of poverty, but inwardly, he did not refrain his greed and was a slave to his stomach. He forgot the judgment of God to such an extent that he did not fear to make an illicit meal of the delicate morsels which had been entrusted to him for the needs of the sick. One day when he had been given over to his detestable vice with a daring that asked to be punished,

---

[63] The phrase "necessary sin of Adam" occurs in the *Exsultet*, sung on Easter night after the lighting of the paschal candle.

[64] Bernard of Clairvaux considered the human being to be a noble creature; see Div 40.3 (SBOp 6/1:236–37); Div 42.2 (SBOp 6/1:256).

[65] Prov 20:10; also Bernard of Clairvaux, Sent 3.109 (SBOp 6/2:180–86; CF 55:348–57).

suddenly he was moved to compunction for reasons I do not know and wanted to go immediately to confession. It was the holy Vigil of Pentecost and the ninth hour was near. While the abbot of the monastery was putting on the holy vestments in order to celebrate the Office of that holy day, the brother approached him and made the usual sign to him that he wanted to confess. The abbot thought he only wanted to confess daily negligences and refused, telling him to find a more convenient time, for he was about to celebrate the most holy mysteries. Rebuffed, the infirmarian went away, upset that he could not be absolved from the ignominious sin he had wanted to confess. He was afraid that this little spark of the fear of God, which had been kindled suddenly in his heart, would go out with this delay, and so not being able to support the shame that leads to glory, he fell into the greater shame that leads to sin [Sir 4:25].

Seeing him in this state of suffering and desperation, the evil spirits, those enemies of the human race, threw themselves on him like highway robbers on a defenseless being. They filled the soul of this wretched man—who had filled himself with bodily delicacies against all reason and discipline, all that is just and right—with the gall of wormwood [Jer 23:15] and the bitterness of despair. And having taken control of his mind, they very violently pushed him by persuasion to cut his throat.[66] From the hour when he had suffered rejection until Vespers, he was tormented ceaselessly by varied and pernicious thoughts inspired by the demons. At last he lost his senses and, being far from the wisdom of God, which says, "I, wisdom, dwell in counsel and am present in learned thoughts" [Prov 8:12], he resolved to imitate the deplorable folly of the traitor Judas who died hanging between heaven and earth [Matt 27:3-5], spurned by both. The brothers had already gathered for the Vespers of the most holy solemnity. His place remained empty as if he had

---

[66] For more on the suicide of monks, see *Le Grande Exorde*, 327nn2–39; and Caesarius of Heisterbach, *Dialogus miraculorum* 4.40-44 (Strange 1:209–12; S-Bland 1:237–41). For the broader context, see Alexander Murray, *Suicide in the Middle Ages*, vol. 1: *The Violent Against Themselves*, and vol. 2: *The Curse of Self Murder* (Oxford: Oxford University Press, 1998, 2000).

been detained by his duties as infirmarian; he thus withdrew himself from the company of his brothers, not realizing in his misery that the farther he was from the company of the just who praise the Lord, the more exposed he would be to the tricks and lures of malign spirits.

What happened? Overcome with sadness and despair, hating his life, the man made a foolish pact with death and an alliance with hell. On that holy night of Pentecost he plunged a knife into that throat with which he had satisfied the sin of his greed, and giving in to the most heinous of all murders, he obeyed the suggestions of the instigator who had pushed him to satisfy his cyclopean gluttony.[67] Soon the apostate spirits were dancing with fierce joy, which is all the more exuberant when they manage to secure the eternal loss of a member of a religious Order, but ignorant that their presumption would soon earn a stern rebuke from the Lord and believing that they had a sure victory, they planned to make the half-dead brother run away for fear that the brothers should find him before he died and through their good efforts bring him to the remedy of confession and penitence and so snatch their prey from the princes of Tartarus.[68] But when the infirmarian was not in his place in choir for Vespers or for Vigils, the abbot remembered that he had made a sign asking to make his confession to him and that he had been refused, and he felt a shudder run through his body. He had a vague foreboding of some misfortune, although he did not know what had happened. Full of fear, he ordered some of the monks to go to find the infirmarian. In his alarm and anxiety he regarded himself as the cause of whatever evil had befallen the brother and reproached himself before God for not having had the discernment to agree to his request, although it had been made at an inconvenient moment.

They looked for him in the infirmary and in all the places he could be expected to be found but could not find him anywhere. Then they searched with more care every nook and cranny of

---

[67] Cyclopean: a Homeric allusion, as above in EM 5.12 (Charybdis).

[68] Tartarus is the lower level of Hades in Greek mythology; it is the realm of criminals. See also EM 6.2.

the monastery and even inside the latrines of the sick. There, the ground was soaked by a sea of blood and there was the knife, the instrument of his heinous crime, covered with blood and other evidence which left no doubt as to what had happened: a crime had been committed. Pale and trembling at this sight the monks groaned and bewailed the sad fate of the unhappy man who had succumbed to the cruel malice of him who was a murderer from the beginning [John 8:44].

But where was the body that they believed dead? They searched again and went more carefully into all the farthest and most obscure corners and were amazed to find absolutely no trace of the man, dead or alive. Quickly returning, they hastened to tell the abbot and brothers the doleful details of the death of their brother. Distress and sadness darkened all their faces and their hearts were stricken, and with one voice they bewailed the fate of the brother. But the most distressed of all was he who bore the name and fulfilled the office of pastor, the one who thought that he himself had caused the loss of this unfortunate sheep.

In the meantime, the solemn day of Pentecost dawned, the brothers offered the solemn Mass with all the devotion they could on so great a feast, and they begged the mercy of almighty God to tell them what had become of the brother for whom they were mourning. Then the Lord, whose goodness always surpasses the merits and desires of those who pray to him,[69] not only answered their request but deigned to show how, by special favor, he had protected the sinner with his merciful hand [Ps 36:24]—although he deserved punishment for his fault—lest by the presumptuous malice of the devil he should be ruined and entirely lost. For the unchangeable mercy and justice of God would not permit the condemnation of someone who, in fear of judgment, wanted to find refuge under the wings of that mercy by having recourse to penitence and confession and had not been able to do so, not by his own fault, but because of the refusal of his superior. It was not right that such a solemn day, when the Holy Spirit had shed his light

---

[69] *Le Grande Exorde*, 330n28, notes that this comes from the collect for the Eleventh Sunday after Pentecost.

in the hearts of the early Church so that they might enlighten all nations, should be marred by the cruel triumph of the old enemy.

While the holy mysteries were being celebrated, one of the brothers was standing under the bell tower; he happened to raise his eyes, and he saw lying on the top of one wall a man, the lower part of whose body was hanging so far over it that it looked as if he was about to fall. Surprised, he looked more closely and called the attention of the others, and they soon recognized the sad victim of the wiles of Satan who was believed to have perished, body and soul. Supposing that it was indeed a dead body, they brought out ladders and climbed the wall, and by the mercy of him who will not allow any of his predestined to perish [Rom 8:29-30], they found that the man was breathing. After those who climbed up made known the consoling news by a cry of mingled joy and surprise, everyone rejoiced, not least the abbot who had been weeping and groaning and blaming himself for the death of one of his own. He cried out, "Glory to you, Christ, God! Glory to you, Holy Spirit, God!" and everyone repeated it. Then, by the order of the abbot, the wounded man was brought down with the greatest precaution and carefulness and taken to the infirmary. There, they could see the large and horrible wound in his neck, and they all marveled that he could still be alive. He was put to bed and left to rest for a while. The brothers came near his bed, and with their hands they tried to close the opening in his throat, afraid that the breath of life would escape with his breathing but also hoping he could in this way be made capable of speech.

By a new blessing of the Almighty, who had delivered this monk from the cruel oppression of the tyrant of hell, his breath was preserved, and at last, in spite of the feebleness of nature, he was able to confess for the glory of God. When the monks watching him with pious curiosity realized this, they understood that against all hope the Lord had given him health; they all withdrew, and thanks to this shining miracle of divine mercy the abbot was able to hear the confession of him whom he had so imprudently put off hearing the day before.

The Holy Spirit, who is called the goodness of God, would not let there be anything lacking in the perfect gift he gave to this sinner on the great day of Pentecost. Against all laws of mortal nature this brother was restored to health and therefore lived a more pure and holy life than he had, understanding by his experience that the bites of Leviathan, that old serpent [Isa 27:1], are cruel and dangerous to anyone who does not fear to soil his conscience by giving himself over secretly to bad habits. "All that is written in Scripture is," according to the Apostle, "for our learning" [Rom 15:4], and so too, it is true that the great wonders which the Lord works in his Church are also for our instruction. Let all those who have been called by the grace of God to the care of souls be on guard not to presume without grave discernment on any occasion, even of necessity, to put off someone wanting to confess to him, lest they act contrary to the saying of the Apostle, "extinguish not the spirit" [1 Thess 5:19], and lest by chance someone who would have been able to be called back to life, at such a rejection, then have a change of heart and be condemned to lose his life.

## Chapter Fourteen

### The Dangers of Discord

The Lord tells us in the gospel, "Anyone who is angry against his brother is in danger of judgment" [Matt 5:22]. And the Apostle says, "Let not the sun go down on your wrath" [Eph 4:26]. Despite this saving advice, I have to admit with sorrow that one still finds people, even among the number of religious, who quite carelessly give themselves over to rage and even engage in deplorable arguments and disagreements. Even when they long outwardly to be victorious, they have harmed themselves seriously within. In defending vile, petty external things, they lose great and precious things inside, for they are so attached to their love of temporal goods that, if these are taken from them, they are more angry than is right and they lose the incomparable treasure of true love. And so those who lead the religious life should remember that they are temples of God [1 Cor 3:16], and they should be afraid of letting the passion of their anger and discord offend the Lord of majesty abiding in them. To underline this I want to tell you about a certain priest-religious who lost the special grace which the Lord had deigned to give him because he did not keep peace with his neighbor, that peace which the citizens of heaven announced on earth at the birth of the King of heaven [Luke 2:13-14]. I will not be slow to describe, in order to warn the sluggish, how he lost the great grace especially given him by God.[70]

This priest was not one of those who wallow in shameful idleness; a person of praiseworthy life, he tried his utmost to make all his conduct be as high as his calling. Whenever he celebrated the great sacrifice in which the Son is offered to the Father as victim to take away the sins of the world, he was careful also to offer himself in the presence of the Supreme Godhead through the sacrifice of a contrite heart and a humble spirit [Ps 50:19]. He had in his parish a man who equaled him in merit by his lively faith and sincere devotion, although he was engaged in the business of a secular life. He was formed by the teaching and example of his pastor,[71] and he often came to the threshold of the church, carefully observing the celebration of Masses, and in simplicity of heart he beat against the heavens with the persistence of his prayers, speaking with the Lord during the divine sacrifice.

The Lord, wishing to make manifest the merits of these two to the honor and glory of his name, opened the eyes of the layman—both the physical and the spiritual—and with these blessed eyes he began to see Our Lord Jesus Christ standing on the altar near the sacred chalice during the sacred mysteries. The divine presence mercifully filled them both with incomparable sweetness. After the consecration—at that moment when it is usual to give the people the kiss of peace and when the priest, following the usage of some, put his lips to the sacred Host—the good Lord came to his minister and very worthily offered him the kiss of peace. O how great is

---

[70] From here, Herbert of Clairvaux, LM 1.21 (PL 185:1298).

[71] *Le Grande Exorde*, 333n7, here cites Hugh of Saint Victor, *Didascalicon* 5. See the translation by Jerome Taylor, *The Didascalicon of Hugh of St. Victor* (Columbia University Press, 1961), 120–34, 219–22.

the goodness of our Redeemer! O how great it is that piety and simplicity of heart attract him so much that he deigns to allow those who have it a foretaste in this life of the favors reserved for all the elect after death, that is to say, the sweet vision of God. This man, so privileged to be admitted to this divine mystery, kept his secret to himself alone [Isa 24:16], as the prophet says, and although he often saw him who is more beautiful than the sons of men [Ps 44:3], he said nothing about it to his priest, for he was afraid of being charged with conceit if he divulged such a godly mystery lightly and without serious reason. He was afraid he would lose that extraordinary grace which had been conferred on him by exposing himself to the vice of pride.

Now the priest had a garden full of herbs and vegetables which he cultivated and which made him happy by its fruitfulness. It happened that there was a little pig that belonged to a poor man nearby; his master's house was so poor and bare that he could not find enough there to eat, so he looked elsewhere and made secret raids on the rich garden. The priest took the devastation of his garden very ill, and having frequently warned the poor man to keep his pig at home and having often caught the pig in the act of trampling his tender plants and chased it outside the fence, raining blows upon it—all to no avail—he lost his temper and killed the pig. The poor man groaned at having lost his only possession, and he wanted to act against the priest who had sought compensation according to the law by exaggerating the damage done to his garden. The poor fellow's demand was despised and rejected with scorn since everywhere the poor man loses.[72] The priest would not be reconciled with his poor brother, yet he still dared to offer the Host of true reconciliation.

But the Lord Jesus, whom God has made our justice, our redemption, and our reconciliation [1 Cor 1:30; Rom 5:11; RM 5.11], would not deign to show himself to the priest because of the discord that stained his soul. The man of God, whom we mentioned before, stood during the holy canon of the Mass and prayed very devoutly

[72] Ovid, *Fasti* 1.218.

to him whom the angels desire to behold [1 Pet 1:12], hoping to see him as usual. He saw nothing and, frustrated of his hope, felt extremely troubled at seeing that the priest had been deprived of his former grace. It was as if he was darkened by a cloud of divine indignation. Because of modest humility he had previously made his conscience his only witness, but he could no longer be silent because of the present situation. He took the priest aside and told him what and how great a grace he had lost; secretly he suggested, warning and exhorting, that if he had fallen into any sin, he should hasten to the remedy of confession as soon as possible so that perhaps the ineffable goodness of our Redeemer might restore the gift of God to him.

The priest was very disturbed and replied that he did not think he was guilty of any great crime and that his conscience did not reproach him more than usual for his daily shortcomings. But, he added, that because he could not allow his garden to be ravaged he had killed the pig of a poor man with whom he was still not reconciled by humble satisfaction. They both saw then that the divine Lord who takes in hand the cause of the poor of this world was revenging the injury done to one of them by a punishment which although it was secret was nonetheless severe. The priest hastened to offer the poor man of the Lord a compensation appropriate to the loss he had sustained, but we do not know whether or not he recovered the sublime grace he had lost because the servant of God who received this grace with him, or perhaps more than him, was always faithful to his resolve not to reveal it unless it was absolutely necessary, and he maintained a rigorous silence about it.

This account ought to make us more watchful. But because the hardness of the human heart makes it difficult to persuade us to be on our guard, I am going to prove how great is the danger of discord by the witness of the enemy himself, an enemy who shows the truth only against his will and when forced to do so, but, nonetheless, he says words that are useful as warnings for the faithful.

The prior of a monastery of nuns wanted to sell part of the property of the monastery and put the matter to the community, and, as usually happens, each part held that their opinion was best, and it became a grave subject of discord between him and the nuns. Because the prior claimed by virtue of his authority that administration of the monastery was confided to him, he said he would deal with the matter according to his own will. The sisters thought otherwise and went away seriously scandalized. Now there lived in the monastery a laywoman who was tormented by an unclean spirit. Every day the sisters prayed ardently for her deliverance, and in order to act more effectively against the infernal spirit, they had her frequently partake of the Lord's sacrament. The next day, the prior, thinking very little of the scandal disturbing the sisters but upset with the sisters' being annoyed, went up to the altar of God to offer the peaceful Host. As usual when he had consecrated the divine gifts, he was approaching the ailing woman to give her Communion when a wicked spirit seized her, and, giving savage and horrible cries, she fell into bitter invective against the prior: "Miserable and unhappy little man, what are you doing? You breathe in only the poison of rancor and discord, and, what is more, you are guilty in the eyes of the Lord of the grave scandal which you are causing to the little ones of the Lord. Yet you dare to come, impudent and irreverent, to consecrate, touch, and eat the flesh of the Most High? Know that it would have been better for you today if you had not come into the house of the Lord than to cauterize your conscience with your foolish presumption." Only the force of exorcism and prayer and awe of the divine sacrament could make the demon be quieted while the woman it tormented received Holy Communion, and only with great difficulty could it be compelled to allow this unfortunate woman to receive the grace of the Eucharist from the man's hands, soiled by the vice of strife and dissension.

Let us realize from this story how our negligence in overcoming our sins and the ease with which we commit them gives more power to our enemies and how difficult it is to escape the very oppressive yoke of the prince of darkness. The great saint John—who was called *Eleimon* in the Greek, that is to say, "merciful,"[73] because

---

[73] Usually referred to as John the Almsgiver (d. 616). See his *Vita* 14, written by Leontius (PL 73:352); trans. E. Dawes in *Three Byzantine Saints: Contemporary Biographies of St. Daniel the Stylite, St. Theodore of Sykeon, and St. John the Almsgiver*, pp. 195–270 (London, 1948; reprint, Saint Vladimir's Seminary Press, 1977). See also EM 6.3.

of his incomparable largesse and compassion for the poor—shows us with what care must we flee from the vice of discord and how quickly we ought to renew the bonds of peace and concord. When this blessed man was the patriarch of the great city of Alexandria, a patrician of that city named Nicetas wanted to enact for the public market certain irregular laws which were neither just nor moderate; instead they looked like avarice and extortion. But the generous patriarch saw that such regulations would be to the detriment of the poor, who are so often the victims of the rich [Sir 13:23], and he courageously resisted them.[74] A lively dispute followed, and with grave dissension John and Nicetas parted ways in a vehement quarrel. But the gentle pastor had learned from his sovereign pastor, our Lord Jesus Christ, to be gentle and humble of heart [Matt 11:29]. Although his conscience assured him that he had right on his side and that he had not caused the scandal so much as the man who was blinded by irrational avarice, because of the fear of God, he hastened as the sun was already beginning to set to send to the patrician two of his most pious clerks with a message worthy to be remembered, saying, "Lord patrician, the sun is about to set" [Eph 4:26; RB 4.73]. At this word, the patrician Nicetas was moved to repentance, and he at once got up and ran to throw himself at the feet of the venerable patriarch. Thus, by imitating the gentleness of Christ, he bent from a height in humility and extinguished the spark of proud discord in the heart of his neighbor.

CHAPTER FIFTEEN

*In Praise of Patience*

O how appropriately sweet it is for me to tell here another similar account about the admirable patience of a certain brother who knew how to keep peace with someone who did not want peace

---

[74] For an earlier explication of the verse from Sirach, see Salvian, *The Governance of God* 4.4, in *The Writings of Salvian the Presbyter*, trans. Jeremiah F. O'Sullivan, Fathers of the Church 3 (New York, 1947), 97–98.

at all [Ps 119:7] and prayed for his enemy in accordance with the precept of the Lord [Matt 5:44; RB 4.72]. He was fortunate enough, by the mercy of the Lord, to draw out from the heart of his enemy all bitterness and envy, and his success was so complete that the person who had violently persecuted him for so long became his most devoted friend.

So, a rivalry between two brothers in a monastery of the Cistercian Order once sowed the seeds of discord and hatred. One of them continued in this wicked state of discord, but the other was touched by grace and recognized the evil sprouting within him. He hastened to weed it out with salutary compunction. The first, on the contrary, continued to be malevolent in public and in private, trying to irritate the soul of his brother by mockery and abusive insults. The harder he tried, the more the persecuted brother replied to these outrages and provocations with the humility that the fear of God gives. The most bitter attacks made on him by his enemy in malice, far from undermining his courage and rousing his anger, moved him to further submission, prayers, and tears.

But how great is the force of persuasion on mortals[75] when it comes in the form of the execrable pests of hatred and envy? That patient and humble brother preserved his conscience from giving room to anger [Rom 12:19], and, struck on the one cheek, he turned the other, according to the precepts of the gospel [Matt 5:39]. The perverse and puffed-up brother interpreted this wrongly as pride or scorn. And the more the other brother tried to soften his implacable persecutor, the more aroused he was to wicked fury and inflamed to persecute the innocent one still more spitefully. This went on until, twisted by bitterness like some strange vine, he had no fear of profaning what was holy, proscribing what was right, or confusing justice and injustice as long as he was able to disturb the tranquility, blot out the grace, and obscure the reputation of the one he followed with such heinous hatred.

But seeing that the strong mind of his adversary magnificently triumphed over all the wicked plots of his hatred and perversity and

---

[75]Virgil, *Aeneid* 3.56.

that his indomitable patience trampled his malice underfoot, mad with rage, this cruel wolf disguised as a sheep went to the abbot and wickedly accused his brother of a detestable crime which he had wickedly invented in order to humiliate him and, if possible, to corrupt by an abominable lie the reputation of the one who shone in the glory of innocence. So the brother was falsely accused and called to account, and following the saying that it is wrong to get yourself a bad name,[76] he protested guilelessly that he was not guilty of the fault ascribed to him, declaring himself ready to submit to any form of trial needed to prove his innocence. He knew well that the mind of man is governed from his youth up by the corruption of his heart, not only to do evil, but to suppose it in his neighbor, and so he was tormented by the thought that the accusation brought against him would give cause for scandal to the weak. He found it difficult to endure patiently being the object of the baseless suspicions of men, although he could with confidence say with Saint Paul, "I will glory in the testimony of a clear conscience" [2 Cor 1:12]. But he also cautiously wished to follow the other council of the same Apostle, "Be not overcome by evil, but overcome evil with good" [Rom 12:21]. Fearing that it might happen that his continuing grief would be turned by the spur of impatience to hatred for his enemy, he gave himself entirely to changing his sorrow into piety, imploring the mercy of the Lord and the goodness of the ever-blessed Bearer of God with earnest prayers accompanied by tears, that divine grace might both confirm him in charity and restrain the enormity of the wickedness of his enemy and by the oil of its sweetness pierce him with compunction so as to extinguish the fire of scandal.

He did not groan in vain, nor did his eyes needlessly flow with the waters of devotion, but the Lord, who consoles the humble and upholds those in tribulation, heard his voice and accomplished in him that which the most wise Solomon said: "When the Lord is pleased with the ways of a man, his enemies are converted to peace" [Prov 16:7]. Although for some time he offered to the Lord

---

[76] H. Walther, *Proverbia sententiaeque Latinitatis Medii ac Recentioris Aevi*, new series, vol. 7: A-G (Göttingen, 1985), n. 35852a1.

in simple devotion the sacrifice of a contrite heart and a humble spirit [Ps 50:19], he was being eaten away with grief at the unjust slur against his reputation and at the danger of perdition that threatened his brother who was infected with the double poison of hatred and deceit. And lo, it happened one night that he was standing in choir for solemn Vigils, filled with these thoughts, remembering his own calamity and the peril of his brother. There began to rise up from the depths of his heart a fountain of tears, truly issuing from the house of David, which cleanse the sinner of all impurity [Zech 13:1]. These tears streamed from his eyes not on behalf of the person shedding them but on behalf of the one who caused them, not that he be confounded and perish for having made a pit of shame and perdition for the man shedding them, but for vengeance against the one who was trying to confound [Sir 35:18] and lose an innocent; they did not ask that he should fall into the pit that he had made; rather, they flowed in order that the wretch might turn from his mistake and escape from the traps of the devil which held him captive to his will and recover his claim to the beatitude and glory of eternal life.

Drunk with the generous draughts of charity which cheer the heart of man [Ps 103:15]—for it is our greatest glory to love our enemies and pray for those who persecute and despise us [Matt 5:44]—he could not contain himself in the presence of the brothers, and he hurriedly found a corner to retire into. He went and prostrated himself before one of the altars and allowed his very ardent compunction to flow forth freely, and his sighs ascended to heaven as an incense of pleasant fragrance. He remembered the infinite mercy of the Lord and the unrivaled goodness of the blessed virgin Bearer of God; he called upon this Mother of mercy, who is the hope of those who suffer, and begged her, not only with words, but also with a rain of tears and unutterable groaning, to undertake his cause and to be mindful also of his misguided brother.[77] He had a holy assurance that an affair as tangled as this one would come

---

[77] *Le Grande Exorde*, 339nn16–19, discusses briefly the Cistercian context and Mary as "mother of mercy," especially noting the Cistercians' use of the *Salve Regina*.

to a happy conclusion if this tender Mother of supreme goodness would not refuse to play her role of mediator and advocate before her Son, the most merciful judge. The success that came about rewarded the simplicity of his faith. He did not cease to repeat these good words with great contrition of heart: "Gracious Lord, have mercy; Gracious lady, Bearer of God and Virgin Mary, help by your mercy an unhappy man without help or council."

His good words, murmured in heart and mouth, were favorably received by Mary, refuge and protector of all who are poor and in distress. When the virgin Mother of God, Our Lady, deigns to visit any one of her devoted servants, she herself calms their sorrow and consoles them beyond measure, as befits the generosity of the Queen of heaven, the Sovereign Lady of the world, the Mother of mercy, the Hope of the needy. As the choir sang the last verse of the psalm which the brothers were chanting in praise of God, the brother opened his eyes and saw through his tears the sublime Virgin, the Lady of the angels, the Hope of the miserable, at the right side of the altar, seeming to come toward him with the expression, the bearing, and the manner that belongs to the Mother of mercy, and she was worthy of respect and surrounded by immense light. She was followed by a splendid young man who shone like her with heavenly glory. When the brothers ended the psalm and said the Glory to the Holy Trinity and, as is the custom, all bowed out of reverence for the Supreme Majesty, the blessed Virgin also bent her most sublime head, which was as humble as it was sublime since no other creature was her equal in dignity except him whom the word of God had taken on by a unity of persons in and through her virgin womb. She stayed thus like a truly humble servant of the Lord until the brothers had finished chanting "Glory be to the Father and to the Son and to the Holy Spirit."[78]

Then she stood upright and turned to the anguished brother and strengthened him with these sweet words: "Man of God, dry the tears in your eyes, and banish from your heart the sorrow that oppresses it. Your suffering has not been lost; you have imitated the

---

[78] This is the standard conclusion for psalms in monastic Office. While it was being sung, the monks remained in a profound bow.

charity and mercy of my divine Son, who is innocence and charity itself. You have endured with equanimity of soul the violence of your enemy, not only unmoved in spirit, but with also an ardent desire for his salvation. To gain that [salvation] you have not hesitated to humble yourself in the presence of the Lord with groans and tears. Know that because of the sincere devotion of your faith, I have asked of the Lord glory for you and pardon of him who is jealous of you."

Thus initiated into the mysteries of heaven and allowed to see with his own eyes the Mother of the Lord, whom all the choirs of angels honor, the brother was no longer troubled, nor could be again, for he had seen the Mother of peace and security. He said to her confidently, "I beg you, Lady, tell me who you are, you who have spoken with so much kindness to the heart of your poor little servant? And who is this young man with you?" She replied, "I am Mary, the Mother of the Son of God, and the young man with me is John the Evangelist, to whose chaste care I was entrusted by my dearest Son when he was hanging on the cross for your salvation." "If you really are she," replied the brother, "she through whom salvation came to the human race, and she whom every creature must honor and venerate, let me ask you something: why did you bow your head like all the rest, you who are above all the angelic powers?" Our most gracious Lady replied, "You should know that all things on earth show fear and reverence at the Gloria in honor of the most holy Trinity, and all the powers of heaven are moved and stirred to praise their creator."

After these words, the blessed vision vanished from his sight, but at the same moment he smelled such a gentle sweetness of a wondrous odor that he seemed to be filled with joy, and not only the brother himself who suffered such grief and anxiety, but all who were devoutly chanting the psalms in the choir felt the influence of grace in their hearts, knowing that the scent was not of the earth but of heaven. Who can tell all the powerful works of the Lord? Who can call out all the praises of his mercies [Ps 105:1]? The ways of God truly are impenetrable [Rom 11:33], and the works of his goodness beyond understanding. The spiteful detractor and accuser of his innocent brother, who had slain both the life and honor of his neighbor with the sword of a cruel lie, deserved to be struck down by the terrible judgment which God had addressed to the children of Israel: "If you do not walk in my ways I will be against you and strike you with seven plagues for your sins" [Lev 26:23-24]. This is said again in the psalm, "Because you have preferred evil to good, God will destroy you forever" [Ps 51:5-7].

But this, which I say he deserved to hear, is not what he did hear. The patience of the innocent victim intervened, and at the humble intercession of brotherly love pleading for him, he merited instead to hear what the father of the family said in the gospel while opening the generous heart of his mercy to his prodigal son: "Let someone bring quickly the new and precious robe of compunction; let him be clothed lest he walk naked and reveal his shame. Place on his finger the golden ring [Luke 15:22] of confession so that henceforth, washed by the water of the healing shame [cf. Sir 4:25] which gives glory that leads to salvation—because in confession all is washed away;[79] let him receive the sign of innocence and put on his feet the sandals of fruitful penitence—he may walk in the way of justice and no longer hurt the feet of his affections on the stones of malice."[80] He was touched by the very sweet perfume that came from the virginal body of the unspotted and immaculate Mother of God, and along with the others who had been worthy of this grace, this perfume entered the dark anteroom of his heart which was full of hatred and jealousy. He was suddenly touched with compunction and burned with the fire that the Lord Jesus brought upon the earth [Luke 12:49], and he began to see his crime in the light of truth and his eyes were opened to his misery and wickedness. He saw that he was worthy of every torment, and at

[79] Gregory, *In librum Regum* 6.22; Bernard, Ep. 113.4 (SBOp 2:290); *Sententiae* 3.97 (SBOp 6/2:156).

[80] Berlioz, *Le Grand Exorde*, 341n29, records many references in which Bernard refers to the cleansing quality of confession: Ep 113.4 (SBOp 7:290; James, Ep 116.4, p. 176); Sent 3.97 (SBOp 6/2:156; CF 55:313–14); Div 40.2 (SBOp 6/1:235); Adv 4.6 (SBOp 4:186; SBS 1:38); Pasc 2.10 (SBOp 5:100; SBS 2:195–96); P Epi 1.4 (SBOp 4:317; SBS 2:37–39); OS 1:13 (SBOp 5:339; SBS 3:348–49); and V Nat 6.8 (SBOp 4:240); he also notes that the image goes back to Gregory the Great, *In librum primum Regnum expositionem* VI, 6.22.

the same time he recognized the innocence and holiness of the brother he had so unjustly defamed. At last, unable to bear any longer the reproaches of his conscience, he resolved to end the attacks against his brother, to confess that the story of the crime had been invented by him, and to make humble reparation to his victim in whatever way the abbot decided.

When morning came, the brothers were still asking one another in great astonishment what the sweet odor which they had smelled during the night psalms had meant. The one who knew about the mystery went to the abbot privately and laid before him with great simplicity what he had seen and heard. He assured him that the blessed Mother of God had appeared at the same moment when those chanting the Office had been enveloped in the celestial perfume. In his surprise the abbot found it difficult to believe what he was being told, since it seemed to him that such a glorious miracle surpassed the grace of the brother who had seen it. But then, in confirmation of the truth, the malicious defamer of this innocent brother arrived, pale and trembling, and he confessed, weeping and groaning, that because of hateful jealousy he had committed an infamous crime and told a tale rather than a truth and that in great contrition of heart he deplored the many ways and times he had persecuted his brother. Asked why this sudden contrition and realization of his sin had come over him, he replied that he too, despite his unworthiness, had smelled the celestial odor with the others and that the anointing of grace had penetrated into his heart in an admirable way at the same time as his hatred and malice had been replaced by a love of innocence and virtue. The abbot consulted several spiritual senior monks about what he had learned, and they all thanked the goodness of God for working so great a marvel.

The brother, who by his patience had turned his adversary's enmity into peace and trampled diabolical enmity underfoot, was very eager to go back to the place where he had seen the vision. When with deep devotion he venerated the spot on which the sacred feet of the Queen of Heaven had stood, he was happy to perceive that the sweet perfume she left behind had pervaded the stones, which confirmed again the truth of the vision. He went at once to tell the abbot, who, with respect mingled with fear, took some of the most devout of the brothers with him and went to the spot. Having tested for himself the reality of the fact by breathing in through his nose the sweet and marvelous perfume, he took counsel with his brothers, and they dug up the stones, and he ordered them to be preserved in the sacristy as evidence of so great a miracle. Thus we can literally prove, as if touching it with our hand, that "Blessed are the peacemakers, for they shall be called the children of God" [Matt 5:9]. And on the contrary, just as the beginning of this story shows, there are people, even those in religious life who seem to be among the number of the children of God, who, if they have neglected to keep the bond of peace and concord in the unity of fraternal charity, will be deprived of the fellowship of this sublime title unless they return very quickly to the tranquility of the peace without which none will see God. My brothers, let us pray to the Lord, therefore, that by the gentleness of his Holy Spirit he may extinguish in us the bitterness of discord and that he may take from our hearts resentment and the fatal animosities which we know are such a peril in the common life of religious, so that all may be of one mind toward each other [Phil 2:2] like sons of God, that we may be children of God and dwell in the house of the Lord all the days of our life [Ps 26:4].

## CHAPTER SIXTEEN

### *About the Perils of Meditating Negligently on the Psalms*[81]

Every day it is our duty to offer the Divine Office with fear and respect before the majesty of God, as the psalmist exhorts us, saying, "Serve the Lord with fear" [Ps 2:11; RB 19.3]. The weakness of the human heart from youth onward is naturally prone to weariness and negligence and easily becomes cool toward spiritual works, and this

[81] For a discussion of meditation and the psalms, see Benedicta Ward, *Bede and the Psalter* (1992, reprint, Collegeville, MN: Liturgical Press, 2005).

makes for boredom in such things as the repetition of continuous psalmody. We want to correct this evil by telling you how our Lord Jesus Christ himself corrected a certain clerk for his blasphemous negligence. This will stir up the negligent to be more attentive in this matter and to tremble for themselves when they realize the majesty of him who gave such correction.[82]

Blessed Anno, archbishop of Cologne, was founder of the monastery of Siegburg, where his holy remains await the glorious resurrection. He was a man of great sanctity and authority in the Church of God, as can be seen from reading the story of his life.[83] Whenever this venerable priest could freely remove himself from external business, he devoted himself attentively to psalmody with a certain clerk of his, whom he thought suitable for such a religious undertaking. But that clerk did this not out of free devotion but rather, I think, out of necessity, and thus he was so bored by the repetition that he used to garble the words or even omit them, so that in the Gloria he would mention only the first and third persons of the Trinity and entirely omit the second. Day after day passed and no one corrected his culpable negligence because no one noticed it; the holy bishop was entirely absorbed in the thoughts that came to his heart from the verses he was reciting alternatively. One evening the archbishop went to bed, and as he composed himself before falling asleep, he heard a man's voice quickly and negligently repeating two or three times, "Glory be to the Father and the Holy Spirit." He did not understand what he was hearing and fell asleep, and in his sleep our Lord Jesus Christ, who is more beautiful than the sons of men [Ps 44:3], appeared to him and stretched out his hand, with his thumb and little finger joined and the middle three extended. With the

---

[82] Tubach, 5379, lists a story of clerks weighed down after their deaths by the words they had swallowed while singing the psalms.

[83] *Vita sancti Annonis* 2.20 (PL 143:1557). Known for his austere way of life and associated with the establishment and reformation of monasteries, as well as with imperial/ecclesiastical politics, Bishop Anno II died in 1075. See M. F. McCarthy, "St. Anno of Cologne," in *New Catholic Encyclopedia*, 2nd ed., 1:472. Conrad's account may have been taken from John of Clairvaux, *Liber visionum et miraculorum* (Troyes, Bib. mun. MS 946, f. 181r.); see Grießer, EM, 323n4; and McGuire, "Lost Clairvaux Exemplum Collection Found," 42.

index finger of his right hand he touched the index finger of his other hand and said, "Behold, this is the Father"; then he touched the middle finger, saying, "This is the Son"; and then the ring finger, saying, "And this is the Holy Spirit." Then he added, "These three persons are one God and the universal Church honors them equally. So why do you leave unchecked the blasphemy of the clerk who every time he sings the doxology deprives me—who am the middle person in the Trinity—of the honor of the praise due to me?"

Waking from his joyful vision, the priest of God thought himself very fortunate to have been visited by such great majesty. He hastened to prove with the ear of his body the reality of what he had heard in the Spirit. After resting, he summoned the clerk as usual to say the Office with him, and the bishop decided that he would listen quite carefully to how well he did it. He was quickly convinced that in every Gloria the clerk was by culpable negligence reducing the Trinity from three persons to two by leaving out the Son. He corrected him severely, as he deserved, and threatened to chastise him more rigorously still if he did not in the future say the psalms more distinctly and devoutly.

This same blessed bishop was once taken up in spirit and, by the power of him who reveals mysteries, knew all the tribulations and calamities that would befall the Church of God to the end of the world.[84] When he came to himself he languished in mind and body for some time because of the horror of the vision he had seen. When religious men asked him anxiously to tell them what secrets he had seen for the edification of the faithful, he would only say, "Woe, woe, there is woe in all corners of the world because those who are called bishops and leaders of souls have failed to warn the people of God by their teaching and example to offer pure service to the Lord."

To go back to those who recite the psalms and other prayers without attention and piety, skipping words, or scarcely pronouncing them: they will find more warnings in a book called the *Miracles of the Most Blessed Mary, Mother of God*.[85] There, they will find

---

[84] *Vita s. Annois* 2.25 (PL 143:1565D).

[85] Grießer (EM, 324n2) gives the citation *Liber de miraculis sanctae Dei genitricis Mariae*, ed. Bernard Pez (Vienna, 1731; reprint, Thomas Frederick Crane [Ithaca:

the story of a devout virgin who each day offered the Queen of heaven, Mother of mercy, one hundred fifty angelic salutations, each with a genuflection, to equal the number of the psalms. But as this practice had become a burden and she did not do it with proper devotion, Our Lady deigned to warn this woman herself that it would be better if she tried to do less and only offered her each day fifty salutations said clearly and attentively, bending the knee at each one. By this she showed that the smallest thing that is done with care is more agreeable to God and to herself than when much more is done negligently and without devotion.

What can one say in response to those who trust in the multiplicity of their prayers and psalms and in how they draw them out and to those who take pride in racing through fifty psalms or even the entire Psalter in a very short time? Let them understand, I pray, by these examples that God weighs not quantity of material but affection of heart in the sacrifices of piety offered to him, and let them remember that something cannot be called a burnt offering unless it is entirely consumed by the flame of devotion. But if someone by the grace of God has arrived at such perfection that he can offer many words and say them devoutly, as Scripture says, there is no law against such things [1 Tim 1:9]. And insofar as he surpasses the imperfect in this life by his zeal and merits, to that degree, in sowing the good seed without boredom of mind and body, he will inherit this great weight of glory as if he were a star brighter than all the rest.

## Chapter Seventeen

### *About the Value of Devoutly Serving the Lord Daily in Vigils*

Holy David, the prophet king, illustrious among the patriarchs, whom the Lord chose rather than found to be after his own heart [Ps 88:21], was the first to organize choirs of mortals [1 Chr 16:7]

---

Cornell, 1925]), *c.* 32. See Caesarius of Heisterbach, *Die fragmente der Libri VIII miraculorum des Caesarius von Heisterbach*, ed. Aloys Meister (Rome: Herder/Spithoever, 1901), no. 3.1, pp. 128–29; and no. 3.37, pp. 164–65.

to praise the Lord, for he is good, for his mercy endures forever [Ps 105:1]. He handed over to his son, Solomon, the dispositions of the house of God and the order and alternation of the chanters, and he added, "All the things I have written have come to me by the hand of the Lord" [1 Chr 28:19]. In this is manifestly shown that whatever virtue, beauty, or grace is in the Jerusalem that is in pilgrimage on earth and which still groans under the weight of fleshly sin, all comes from the heavenly Jerusalem on high which is free [Gal 4:26] and where all are united together[86] and in whose streets sweet Alleluias [Tobit 13:22] are sung without ceasing. According to this example, the inhabitants of earth, the children of men [Ps 48:3], are constrained to render charity, chastity, and innocence and to offer praise to the Lord their Creator with attentive devotion. Although each of the faithful in the Church of God must apply himself with all his power to render this divine praise in whatever way he can, it must honestly be said that the Cistercian Order is even more bound to do this arduous task of devotion than other Orders, since the monks of the Cistercian Order get up for Vigils a little after midnight, or sometimes at midnight [RB 8.1-2; RB 11.1], and disdaining the sweetness of morning sleep they persevere in labor and hardship [2 Cor 11:27], in vigils until daybreak, appearing before the face of the Lord in prayer and praise, and saying with the psalmist, "Lord, for your sake we are afflicted all the day long" [Ps 43:22], and "Lord, because of the words of Your lips I have kept to the hard paths" [Ps 16:4]. But in order to show the value of daily vigils exactly observed in the service of Almighty God and how dangerous it is to omit them without real necessity, we will give two examples. The first is for the fervent who burn with the fire of the Holy Spirit and do not quail at the length of the holy psalmody, which is burdensome to those who think only of the flesh, but strive to praise God with a liveliness of voice and

---

[86] Ps 121:3; see also Bernard of Clairvaux, Ep 459 (SBOp 8:437; James, Ep 395, p. 468); Div 1.8 (SBOp 6/1:79); Div 19.3 (SBOp 6/1:163); Asc 3.1 (SBOp 5:131; SBS 2:240); Asc 6.5 (SBOp 5:152–53; SBS 2:272); Mich 1.5 (SBOp 5:297; SBS 3:321); Quad 2.5 (SBOp 4:363; SBS 2:81); Sept 1.3 (SBOp 4:347; SBS 2:59); and Sept 2.3 (SBOp 4:351–52; SBS 2:67).

soul and to purify their hearts, having the joy of witness given to their work and finding comfort in the grace of God. The second, on the contrary, is to warn those who are weighed down with the vice of boredom and sleepiness and have no fear of God or shame before men and who easily deprive themselves of the pleasant company of the servants of God by hurrying back to bed, neglecting to consider that they are submitting themselves to a cruel tyrant and that for this sluggishness they will be tortured after this life with hideous pains, so that, turned by this example, they will push away the torpor of their laziness.

Our Father Saint Bernard, the first abbot of Clairvaux, whose name is to be pronounced with love and devotion, spread among the peoples of all lands and languages the knowledge of monastic perfection which had been granted him by the Father of lights—from whom comes every perfect gift [Jas 1:17]—with more fullness and sincerity than to any other man of his time. He sent brothers to all points of the world to populate and with the offerings of the faithful to build monasteries of the Cistercian Order. At the behest of the venerable Albert the Elder, archbishop of Mainz, the capitol of First Germany, he founded the monastery of Eberbach, situated two leagues from the walls of that city and not far from the banks of the Rhine.[87]

Under the blessing of such an illustrious father, this house grew very powerful and developed, and soon it so rivaled the mother house in regular observance, the renown of its monks, the authority and virtue of its priests, even more than for its great riches and the number of its members,[88] that the church of Eberbach shone throughout Germany like a special mirror of religious life well lived. The perfume of sanctity which came from this abbey spread round about and even to faraway places, drawing there a great number of the faithful. The neighboring faithful and even

---

[87] Kloster Eberbach, in the Diocese of Mainz, was originally founded in 1116. It became Clairvaux's first Germanic daughter house in 1131, during Bernard's abbacy. See the introduction for more information and bibliography.

[88] Eberbach's daughter houses were Schönau (1142/45), Otterberg (1144/45), Val Dieu (1155/1180), and Arnsburg (1174/1197).

some from far-off places, attracted by the good fragrance of the virtues of this holy assembly, used to come for wise advice, prayers of intercession, and protection in danger. They generously supplied the needs of the poor of Christ from their own abundance, and moved by a feeling of devotion, these people celebrated the chief solemnities in that place. Among these latter was a knight, courageous in battle, noble by birth, and of well-known piety, named Conrad. Each year he went to Eberbach for the solemnity of the Purification of the Blessed Virgin and Mother and was present and full of fervor from the beginning to the end of the Vigils, which were especially long in honor of such a great day. Helped by the prayers of the holy monks, refreshed by the exhortations in the solemn sermon, and fortified by participating in the sacrament of the holy Mass, he went away joyfully, carrying home this blessing to all the family in his house.[89] In his humility he recognized that his was not a fruitful life because he was caught up in the work and thought of the world, but nonetheless, like a good elm tree, he offered with pleasure part of his goods to sustain the spiritual vine and its fruits.

One year it happened that domestic duties prevented him from being in such good time as usual for the solemnity of which we have spoken. It was already the depth of night when he arrived, so he went to his bed, and when he stretched his limbs on his bed, tired from the journey, he fell deeply asleep and did not hear the signal that wakened the brothers to attend divine praise. One hour later he awoke, the chanting of the monks sounded in his ears, and he got up hurriedly, ran to the church, and took his place in the southern part where guests were present at the Divine Office, and he sat down sorrowfully in front of one of the altars. Sitting and wanting to make up for his negligence, he made himself take part with ardent piety, with full attention to the chant and prayers. But he was too sleepy to pray and keep watch. Annoyed with himself, he tried, as Vigils went on and on, to overcome his heaviness by standing, then by sitting and sometimes rubbing his forehead with

---

[89] Here Conrad uses a rather archaic phrase, *lares proprios*, to convey the domestic nature of monastic life.

his hands. At the same time he considered the liveliness of voice and spirit of the monks who were singing the divine praises and scorned his own weakness, and marveling and greatly admiring them, he spoke familiarly to the Lord, asking him, "Lord God, how can these brothers bear the weariness that seems beyond the power of nature to bear, and outside the scope of human frailty? How can they give themselves over to death like this for you all the time, day and night [Ps 43:22]? For daily they fast and keep vigil; they got hardly any sleep tonight, and yet they are fulfilling their vows with total liveliness of spirit by singing your praises to you, their Creator! And I, miserable sinner that I am, for the sake of your name I cannot stand even for a little part of one night the lengthy Vigils which they are always undertaking with joy, looking to eternal rewards, always ready for new efforts without losing any of their constancy."

In the midst of these pious lamentations, a light but sweet sleep closed his eyelids. Then he saw two people of heavenly beauty and venerable appearance, dressed like monks, leaving the monks' choir and coming toward him. One of them seemed to reply to his thoughts by praising the cost of the outstanding labors and vigils of the servants of God, not in the native language of the knight, which is German, but in elegantly composed Latin verses even though he was speaking to an illiterate man: "To be able to suffer so much only the blessed can endure."[90] At these words he suddenly awoke, opened his eyes, and by a great miracle remembered the words of God that had been said to him. He thanked God, quite convinced that they contained some salutary counsel, although he could not understand them.

For the rest of the night he struggled manfully against sleep and gave himself to prayer and watching with all the devotion of which

---

[90] This line (*Talia posse pati soli meruere beati*) shows Conrad's familiarity with classical poetry. See A. Guerrau-Jalabert, *Le Grand Exorde*, 349n18. For other mention of illiterate men and the association of illiteracy with the laity, see EM 3.19; 4.12, 15–17. See also, Ernst Robert Curtius, *European Literature and the Latin Middle Ages* (New York: Pantheon Books, 1953; reprint, New York: Harper and Row, 1963), 42–45; and Clanchy, *Abelard*, 50–64.

he was capable. He waited impatiently until morning so that before he forgot it, he could find out from someone able to tell him the meaning of the oracle he had received from the goodness of God's grace. When morning came, as soon as it was possible to speak,[91] he went secretly to the prior of the place, an extremely observant religious, and told with simplicity what he had seen and heard. Then, when asked to repeat the words which he had heard from the angels, the man who was uneducated and unlettered pronounced the Latin words without any hesitation and repeated the words until the monk had learnt them by heart so that there would be no fear of them being forgotten by the wavering inconstancy of memory. And one wonder was succeeded by another. The Lord deigned to show more clearly that this man had not been shown this mystery for himself alone but rather for those whose constancy he so much admired in his pious simplicity and to show that the Lord had only told him this to assure him of their beatitude. In fact, after Conrad had communicated the words which he had heard but not understood, to someone who did understand them and could interpret their meaning, he understood the force of their meaning, but when he returned to the library of his memory he found it entirely empty, and thenceforth he could not remember a single syllable of the verse which he had received a little while before. Edified and confirmed in the grace of God by such marvels, he believed that the Lord was truly the guardian of that place, and he promised to give that church an annual payment—which he did faithfully to the end of his life. All those who trample underfoot their fear of the frailty of the flesh and banish timidity from their hearts in order to place themselves courageously and devotedly to serve God may look forward to receiving the repose of the heavenly country with as great a trust as the Lord deigned to ask of his faithful in this recent miracle; it is a pledge of the good things for which they are hoping.

[91] There are many references in the Rule to monks keeping silence, e.g., RB 6; 7.56-58; 38.5; 42; 48.5; 52.2.

The name of the prior I have mentioned deserves to be recorded; it was Meffrid.[92] He was a man of outstanding piety and enjoyed great respect from the people of that time. By his wisdom and ability he had saved his monastery and prevented its ruin during the unhappy troubles that wasted the Church for so long under the pontificate of Alexander in the midst of the horrible storm raised by the Emperor Frederick and his schismatic followers.[93] Among other gifts with which this servant of God was favored was the revelation of certain heavenly mysteries, and he was even sometimes consoled by the visits of blessed spirits; it also happened for his greater purification that he was terrified by horrible spirits. In this same house there was a young man from Strasbourg named Henry. He was endowed with a robust and vigorous body, but he had a soft spirit and a lax heart, which, alas, are vices only too commonly seen and regretted today, when many fear the discomfort of the body more than the fires of Gehenna. This young man stood out among the other brothers for his negligence and uselessness in all the observances of the Order, but he showed himself most reprehensible with respect to the execution of the Divine Office, which he neglected in every way and which he was able to do more easily than others; he would hide the hands of his natural vigor under the armpit of his extreme idleness. He used to leave the sacred Vigils often as if he were ill, and he did not blush to go back to his room to lay his miserable flesh on his bed. The venerable prior in his paternal solicitude wanted to cure this detestable negligence

[92] Eberhard was abbot of Eberbach until 1166. Meffrid was prior of the Roman monastery of Saints Vincent and Anastasia, also known as Tre Fontane; see note in EM 6.3; and Joan E. Barclay Lloyd, *SS. Vincenzo e Anastasio at Tre Fontane Near Rome: History and Architecture of a Medieval Cistercian Abbey*, CS 198 (Kalamazoo, MI: Cistercian Publications, 2005). There is also an exchange of letters between Meffrid and Hildegard of Bingen; CCCM 91A:188–201 (Epp 84–85); PL 197:259 (Epp 51–52).

[93] This refers to the eighteen-year schism that involved Emperor Frederick I Barbarossa (1152–90), Pope Alexander III (1159–81), and three antipopes. See B. M. Bolton, "Pope Alexander III," and T. E. Carson, "Frederick I Barbarosa," in *New Catholic Encyclopedia*, 1:254–47; 5:924–26; for antipopes Victor IV (1159–64), Paschal III (1164–68), and Callistus III (1168–78), see P. M. Savage, *New Catholic Encyclopedia*, 14:480–81; 10:916–17; and 2:882. See EM 6.3.

by warning and reproving him in public and private, but in vain, for he preferred the comfort of his flesh to the repose of his soul.

By a stupid reversal of values, he fed the barren that bear not [Job 24:21] and did no good for the widow.[94] As it happened, one night this lazy monk, avoiding discipline and work, left his place in choir as usual to go to Matins with the sick and thus get back to bed sooner [EO 68.27; EO 115.9]. But the Lord wanted to show the caring prior how just his anxiety was, and how pernicious was the brother's negligence, or rather his pride and scorn. As Henry left his stall stealthily and having made only a slight nod to the altar hurried to the entrance of the choir, the prior saw a black demon riding on the brother's back, urging him to the door of the infirmary, waving and snorting with laughter (to use a commonplace word); his softness rendered him worthy of such shameful treatment. When he left the infirmary a short time afterward his infernal rider sat on his shoulders and treated him like a beast, making a halter of his laziness until, ignominiously prodded by the demon of laziness, he reached his own bed which he wanted so much in his unhappiness.

O how this stupid man, truly a beast without reason, would have been more happy and wiser if he had imitated the holy devotion of this other beast, who in the simplicity of his heart said to God, "I have become as a beast before you, yet I am with you" [Ps 72:23; RB 7.50]. For he had deserved to have as his rider the one who ascends in the west [Ps 67:5] to destroy evil and establish righteousness and not the one who, for a short period of joyful pleasure, will capture him in the net of eternal misery! But nothing can correct one who neglects the fear of God. This wretch scorned the salutary advice of this best of priors who tried to tell him what he had seen, and he would not take the trouble to observe the austere discipline of the cloister but did it only in a superficial way. He followed the deadly councils of his wicked rider, left the Order, and became a vile apostate, passing his days in the false joys and corruption of the world, and finally he descended into hell.

---

[94] See Bernard of Clairvaux, Apo 16–17 (SBOp 3:95–96; CF 1:53–54); Ep 462.4 (SBOp 8:441; not in James); SC 35.3 (SBOp 1:250; CF 7:167).

The first of these examples we have given is meant to encourage the fervor of those who do not draw back from the weariness and watchings of God's service, and the second is instead meant to inspire terror and grave reflection in those feeble monks who show themselves to be delicate and incapable of hard work. These idlers who cannot suffer the least pain for God although they are strong and well will come, I am afraid, to the same kind of end as the unfortunate man we have been speaking about, and their miserable lives will degenerate like his into shameful apostasy.

CHAPTER EIGHTEEN

*How Great Are the Dangers of Serving the Lord Halfheartedly at Vigils*

More about inertia, negligence, and sleepiness during the service of God—not to mention the phantoms and illusions that the half-hearted suffer in falling asleep in choir in spite of themselves—is found more subtly and more certainly in the revelations of a certain servant of God who lived in a house of the Cistercian Order in Britain called Strata Florida.[95] The Lord endowed him with the spirit of prophecy for the instruction of the servants of the Lord. While he was still a youth, this servant of God despised the things of this world and loved the things of heaven, and he set out to observe the holy customs of his holy Order exactly. Now on the eve of Pentecost he rose at the sound of the clock to begin chanting the Morning Office of Our Lady, when suddenly his heart was filled with a new devotion such as he had never before felt and which continued throughout Vigils, increasing more and more, refreshing his heart and body equally with a wonderful swiftness.[96] When the brothers

---

[95] Strata Florida was a daughter house of Whitland Abbey (Albalanda, in the line of Clairvaux), founded in 1164, in what is now Wales. Built on the banks of the river Fflur, it was relocated in the 1180s. Januschek, 151; Cottineau 2:3095.

[96] *Le Grande Exorde*, 352n3, discusses the various settings in which an Office of the Virgin was used by the early Cistercians.

began the canticle "O all ye works of the Lord, bless ye the Lord,"[97] he saw with the eyes of his body an angel of the Lord, bright and shining, come through the window in front of him and go down the middle of the choir, holding in his hand a censer full of sweet incense. He went up to the altar and censed it as if during the Mass of a solemn feast [EO 53.59-64] then left the sanctuary and went down both sides of the choir, censing with the life-giving perfume of this spiritual incense the monks who were watching and singing. When the choir monks in their psalmody reached the verse "Let us bless the Father and the Son with the Holy Spirit," the angel of the Lord, having gone around all the others, now came to the brother who had been allowed to see this. Then indeed this brother, burning with wonderful devotion of piety, said with the prophet, "I have opened my mouth and drawn in my breath, because I longed for your commandments" [Ps 118:131], and he leaned forward to breathe in this mysterious smoke as if he were bowing devoutly to praise the Father and the Son and the Holy Spirit.[98] With two fingers, the angel of the Lord took a burning, glowing coal from the censer and threw it into the brother's mouth just as he was drawing his breath [Isa 6:6-7]. The servant of God felt the bright fire run through his body and fill it with ardor so sweet that he could say with the prophet, "The Lord has sent fire from on high into my bones" [Lam 1:13]. But soon he was unable to bear this devouring flame, both salutary and terrible, and he fell to the ground pale and ashen and was taken to the infirmary. There, he remained for three days without voice or movement, as if he were dead.

After three days and at the very hour he had gone into the ecstasy, he came to himself, so purged from the corruption of the flesh which binds the soul by the flame that had cheerfully burned him that he was able afterward to see with the eyes of the Spirit things far away as if they were near. He even knew what temptations beset the monks in his monastery, whether waking or sleeping, he understood their circumstances and causes, and he explained how they could protect themselves—all this in such a way that many of the brothers were

---

[97] The canticle *Benedicte Domino*, based on Dan 3:57-88, is recited at Vigils.
[98] The doxology at the end of the canticle *Benedicte Domino*.

stirred by his exhortations to undertake a holier life. He used to say that each night, and especially on Sundays and festivals, a huge crowd of demons would come into the choir as the brothers were singing the Office; it was their wicked task to distract the monks in all kinds of ways and to turn their minds from attending to the service of God by many and varied illusions. He saw how they would crowd around the lazy monks and those falling asleep, going from one to the other, laughing at them and applauding them. They wore on their heads awful hoods made of old rags, dirty and unclean, hiding their hideous faces behind them as if they were afraid of being recognized; they were covered inside and out with scabs and ulcers. They went from one brother to the next, looking closely to see if he was awake or asleep. If he was asleep they placed their filthy, revolting hoods over his face and called their companions to come and help them. And all the time the monk remained asleep they would stand around him, filling his imagination with fantasies and shameful dreams. But they fled as from fire those whom they found awake and attentive to the psalmody as if they could not bear even the breath coming from the mouth which was open, singing the praises of God.

Since our greatest bliss and happiness in eternal life will be to praise our Creator and Lord continually not only without effort but with infinite pleasure, before our eyes are closed in death and our tongue, created to praise the Lord, falls to dust, let us sow the good seed of the God's service, albeit with effort, so that in the time to come we may reap [Gal 6:9] a good harvest, exulting in inexpressible joy. So too, conversely, let those who are not afraid to sow the thorns and briars of tepidity and negligence in the land of their flesh dread the suffering that will chastise their transgressions at the judgment, for the same wicked spirits who advise them to be lazy will gather together their atrocious torments to punish them after having constantly incited these idlers to repose in the softness of their flesh. Therefore, if these revelations seem to be recent and therefore lacking in authority, I will give further proof from an incontestable authority, *The Lives of the Fathers*.[99] One finds

---

[99] See *Vitae Patrum* II: *Rufini Historia Monachorum* 29 (PL 21:453–54); Russell, *The Lives of the Desert Fathers*, CS 34,

it written there that when a wicked spirit said to one of the holy fathers that he was frequently present at the Vigils of the brothers with his followers, this father prayed to the Lord to show him if this was true. When he went to the assembly of the brothers, he saw demons in the form of Ethiopians running all over the church. They brought before his eyes by fantastic images everything that the brothers were thinking about while they were praying and chanting, as he found out later when they each admitted it. He realized that all the vain and dangerous thoughts and all the poisonous ideas which soil the spirit during Divine Office were suggestions of the demons. We ought therefore to pray with the psalmist in a humble and contrite heart [Dan 3:39; Ps 50:19], "Lord, do not deliver the souls of those who praise you to the wild beasts, and do not forget to the end the souls of your poor" [Ps 73:19].

## Chapter Nineteen

### *On the Dangers to Those Religious Who Live Softly in This Life*

How terrible and tremendous are the fires of purgatory, where, as the prophet says, "The Lord washes away the filth of the daughters of Zion and washes the blood of Jerusalem by the spirit of justice and the spirit of burning" [Isa 4:4], and, as another prophet says, he will avenge the blood of the children [Joel 3:21] of his people,[100] comparing it elsewhere to a refiner's fire and a fuller's soap. He will sit as a purifier of silver and purify the sons of Levi [Mal 3:2-3]. And still there are those who do not fear to pass their days in slackness, negligence, and idleness. I remember having read about this fearful judgment in a certain collection.[101]

---

153–54; compare *Verba seniorum* 43 (PL 73:765–66). See also the note on Ethiopians above, EM 3.22.

[100] See Jacques LeGoff, *The Birth of Purgatory*, trans. Arthur Goldhammer (Chicago: University of Chicago Press, 1984), 167–73, 300–310.

[101] No one has yet identified this collection.

A monk who was seriously ill was carried away in spirit shortly before his death and taken to the place of punishment and expiation—I cannot say this without trembling and horror—and he saw there a great number of souls skewered on sharp spits and burning on a great brazier, like geese being roasted. Their cruel executioners did all they could to increase their sufferings. Some, armed with bellows and similar things, blew and stirred up the fire; others caught in vessels reddened by the flames the grease that oozed from their bodies and then basted them with it. The monk watching this saw that this last torment was worse than any other. Then he was taken to a place of refreshment where a multitude of other souls were gathered,[102] resting from their work of penitence.[103] The holy angel asked him if he understood what he had seen and he answered no. Then the angel said to him, "Those whom you have seen roasting in the devouring fire belonged to your Order. They have not been guilty of mortal sins but neither have they striven to serve the Lord as Scripture warns, with fear and trembling [Ps 2:11]. They did not follow the discipline of the Order as they ought and did not apply themselves with zeal and courage to the solemn devotions of vigils and other prayers or exert themselves in the labor of psalmody. Instead, they showed themselves lazy, slack, and sleepy. Instead of keeping rest and silence, they ran here and there, curious to understand new things and seeking only to satisfy superfluous desires. In this they have violated the purity of their monastic profession. These men, after having been purified, by the most fair sentence of the just judgment of God, by the pains you have now seen, some longer and some shorter, according to the degree and measure of their guilt, have now, by the grace of God, been taken into this place of refreshment. Here, the purified souls can rest from their horrible sufferings and wait in peace until they can enter into perfect beatitude."

It is very clear that, by the dispensation of divine piety, the closer we come to the end of the world, the more revelations like this

---

[102] For "place of refreshment," see EM 3.27 and 3.28.
[103] See Bede, *Ecclesiastical History of the English People* 5.12, text and trans. B. Colgrave and R. A. B. Mynors (Oxford: Clarendon Press, 1969), 489–99.

will appear, so that, although by abundant iniquity and negligence the charity of many grows cold [Matt 24:12], the elect of God are stirred so much more to love and feel their souls inflamed by knowing that he is soon coming, he of whom it is written, "Want of all good goes before his face" [Job 41:13]. What are we to make of the grease that the aforesaid monk saw the hellish cooks carefully collecting to pour over the limbs of those from whom it dripped, unless it is that, however much they spared themselves in this life, contrary of their profession satisfying the greed of the flesh by the abundant grease of repose, so much more they will pay in the other life by the sufferings of the place of purgation? As the Lord said by the prophet about the harlot dressed in purple who made the whole earth drunk from the chalice of carnal pleasures and with the wine of worldly pomp [Rev 17:4], "multiply her torments and sufferings in proportion to her pride and the delicacies into which she plunged" [Rev 18:7].

Brothers, let us awaken at this word like a clap of thunder, and let us listen with intent minds to what the best of monks and the most reverent of fathers, our father blessed Bernard, thought of our daily and pernicious negligences. When he preached on the life and virtues of Humbert of blessed memory, the former prior of Clairvaux, and urged the brothers to imitate the purity of his way of life, he said among other things, "Concerning religious observance, brothers, I say to you that if you follow in his steps you will not fall into vain thoughts and idle words, jests, and slanders because by those things many are lost in our life and times. For 'time flies irretrievably'[104] and while you believe that you can protect yourself from some slight punishment, you are making it greater. Know this: after this life, in the place of purgation every negligence will be paid for a hundredfold to the last farthing. I myself know how hard it is for a dissolute man to lay hold of discipline, for a wordy man to endure silence, for a wanderer to stay only in one place, but it will be harder, much, much harder, to endure that future torment."[105]

---

[104] Horace, *Epistles* 1.18.71.
[105] Bernard of Clairvaux, Humb 8 (SBOp 5:447; SBS 3:71–72).

Elsewhere, the same father has warned us again to be fearful, zealous, and careful in the divine praises, not only that we may obtain the grace of our Lord and Creator, but also that we may escape the inexorable lies of evil spirits. In his forty-seventh sermon on the *Song of Songs*, this venerable father teaches when he says, "Our Rule tells us that 'nothing is to be preferred to the work of God.'[106] Father Benedict, truly blessed, calls the solemn praises we carry out each day in the oratory 'the work of God,' so it would be clear from this how intently we should do this work. So, dearest brothers, I exhort you to participate always in the divine praises correctly and vigorously. Vigorously so that you may stand before the Lord with as much zest as reverence, not sluggish, not sleepy, not yawning, not sparing your voices, not leaving words half-said or skipping them completely, not chanting softly and feebly through the nose like women, but singing out the language of the Holy Spirit with an appropriate vigor, dignity, and affection. Correctly, so that while you chant, you reflect on nothing but what you chant. Nor do I mean that only vain and useless thoughts are to be avoided; for at least that time and in that place, avoid also those things with which our brother office-holders are inevitably and frequently preoccupied for the good of the community [EO 111–120]. Nor would I even recommend that you dwell on those thoughts you have just freshly acquired as you sat in the cloister reading books, or such as you are now gathering from the Holy Spirit during my discussion in this meeting room. They are wholesome, but they will be less wholesome if you think about them during psalmody. For you will be neglecting what you owe, and at that time the Holy Spirit is not pleased to accept anything other than what you owe."[107]

Thus spoke blessed Bernard. I ask you, what should be said about the perverse and wicked thoughts we harbor at that time and in that place, if the blessed father judged that one must avoid during psalmody not only vain and idle thoughts but even the memory of those that are necessary? Here, clearly, we must admit that the incon-

---

[106] The "work of God" (*opus dei*) is a common phrase in Benedictine and Cistercian spiritual writings; see RB 22, 43, 44, 47, 50, 52, 58, and 67.

[107] Bernard of Clairvaux, SC 47.8 (SBOp 2:66; CF 31:10).

stancy of our hearts is a fact, and it is confused, as the prophet says, "like a thief is confused in the very act" [Jer 2:26], so confused that even the most perfect must say to God, weeping and groaning from their hearts, "My God, enter not into judgment with your servant, for no man living will be found just before you" [Ps 142:2]. But it is one thing to be distracted from time to time from psalmody by the infirmity of human nature, but it is quite another thing to give oneself up easily and without resistance to perverse and culpable suggestions. There is the same difference as there is between those who offend God by mortal or venial sin, and we believe that the sentence and punishment will be proportionate to the fault.

## CHAPTER TWENTY

### *The Danger for Those Who Presume to Chant the Office in a Worldly Way or for Applause*

Pay attention while I consider how this prophetic man rebuked the extreme and very miserable obstinacy of those to whom he said, "Do not spare your voices. Don't sing with interrupted and slack voices, effeminately stammering through your nose."[108] I remember the terrible thing that happened to one of those who sang like this; it was told to me by the venerable abbot of Morimond. There are those who have been very generously given by God a good voice with which to sing his praises but who use it very sparingly in his service, preferring to seek the glory of men rather than the glory of God with their instrument, and to spare their voices in the course of the daily hymns and psalms of the Office, they sing negligently, lest by chance they ruin the clarity of their voices, but when the time and opportunity for glorifying themselves and their voices arise, at once they show themselves to be strong, expert, and quite ready to sing and raise their voices on high.

---

[108] See *Instituta* LXXV (Waddell, *Narrative and Legislative Texts*, 489) and Bernard of Clairvaux, SC 47.8 (SBOp 2.66; CF 31.10).

The aforesaid abbot of Morimond said that there was in one of the monasteries of the Cistercian Order a monk who was proud of his magnificent natural voice but refused to exert himself to sing with his brothers in the communal task of the Office. But when he was assigned to sing the festal responses as a special privilege because of his remarkable voice, he sang during that solemnity rather for his own glory, joyfully but not meekly, happily but with very little devotion. On one certain festival it happened that he remained quiet, standing as if mute and dumb while the community sang the psalmody together in praise of God. But when it came to the verse of the response for which he was responsible, he sang in his usual worldly way, with a strong and sharp vocal clarity, with grace notes and vibrato, and without any of the gravity suitable to the praise of God. When it was over, in order that he and the others standing around might understand what the result of such a ridiculous performance was, there appeared to those looking on and listening a little devil in the form of a little Ethiopian boy, hideous and black, who clapped his impure hands and cried with a strange raucous tone, "Bravo, bravo, O well sung; excellently sung!"

Let anyone who has received from God the grace of a beautiful voice realize by this example how horrible it is to sing in a worldly and affected way and encourage the maliciousness of demons, when one ought to be honoring God with humility and devout rejoicing. We should strive especially to avoid chanting in a worldly manner and keep to the moderation imposed on us by our holy Order[109] and to the authority of the Rule that we have vowed ourselves to keep, the Rule which specifically teaches us, each individually and all in common, that we should chant and sing to our God with gravity, with fear and trembling, and with humility [RB 47.4]. Surely the ironic praises of that demon should cause us to blush with confusion and shame and rouse us to caution. But if the cruel mockery of the lying spirit leaves our hearts unmoved, perhaps they will be touched by the witness of the Spirit of truth rather than the whispers of the lying spirit. Therefore, we will not

---

[109] *Statutes* 1134, 73; Canivez 1:30.

keep silent about a divine revelation about the subject of worldly chant that was made known in our days to a pious virgin who was very abstinent and virtuous.[110]

The abbot of Cîteaux, who is the patriarchal father of our entire holy Order, once went to see her, and as he was speaking with her about the sweetness of eternal life, he asked this servant of God attentively if she would entreat God to reveal what had crept through negligence into the Order of Cîteaux that was most contrary to the purity of monastic life. She asked him to wait, and after presenting her prayers before the Lord, she replied, "My Lord and Father, you should know that there are three things in your Order that particularly offend the eyes of the supreme majesty: too much land; elaborate buildings; worldliness in singing."

Therefore, all those who are admitted to the holy order of clerks, and by the considered judgment of holy Church are given the function of chanting the Office and singing psalms, if they go beyond the limits of moderation, gravity, and humility, they should know that while they offer rightly, they are in no way rightly disposed, and it is necessary that they fear the condemnation of the Lord, who said by the prophet, "I loathe your solemn assemblies" [Isa 1:14], because as long as our enemies mock our Sabbaths [Lam 1:7], Almighty God will never deign to accept what our enemy sniggers at.[111]

## Chapter Twenty-One

### The Danger for Prelates Who Show a Worldly Affection for Their Families

When the Apostle speaks about those who hold on earth the place of sovereign father of the family and are placed in the Church as dispensers of the mysteries of God, he says, "It is required of stewards

---

[110] Compare Jean Leclercq, "Épitres d'Alexandre III sur les cisterciens," *Revue Bénédictine*, 64 (1954): 68–82, especially 72.

[111] Piesik (*Exordium Magnum Cisterciense*, 2:418–19n253) includes a brief discussion of chanting the Office correctly.

that they be found faithful" [1 Cor 4:2]. Alas, there are those who scarcely consider this examination and judgment! If, fearing lightly, they are called to a responsible position by divine grace, they at once glory at having been raised to the fullness of honor. And in their position they are not content merely to seek their own interests instead of those of Jesus Christ [Phil 2:21], but they also look around carefully for advantages for their kinsmen. They have no qualms in wasting and squandering on their relations the high patrimony of their crucified Lord, that is to say, the goods of the Church, which on the day of their installation they vowed to keep intact. But there is an abuse graver still. Some want to raise and train certain of their nephews so they can fulfill a high function, and they think not so much of their ability as the ties of kinship, and they designate them to be their successors without even considering that at the terrible moment of death the judgment of God sees all.

This is why we are going to recall how Almighty God, who exalts those who glorify him but punishes those who scorn him, made known for the amendment of some who are still upon the earth, the horrible torments that one such prelate suffered after death: that those who have provoked the anger of the Lord by too much attachment to their relations may, at hearing it, be terrified at the severity of the punishment and that out of fear of such frightful sufferings they would make haste to repair their fault.

There was an abbot who had in his monastery one of his nephews[112] whom he had raised from his earliest years until he had become a very exemplary monk. It happened that this same abbot was about to go the way of all flesh.[113] The brothers whom he had under his care were weeping for his loss, for he was a prudent and wise man, and they were discussing the choice of his successor, but with differing opinions. For fear the matter would degenerate into a contest, they all agreed that they would leave the decision and the choice to him who was so great a spiritual father who

---

[112] This story is found in John of Clairvaux, *Liber visionum et miraculorum* (Troyes, Bib. mun. MS 946, ff. 151r–151v). See Grießer, EM, 336n5; and McGuire, "Lost Clairvaux Exemplum Collection Found," 42.

[113] See above, n. 29, at EM 5.9.

knew best the conscience and merits of each [RB 64.1]. They all pledged themselves to vote unanimously for whomever he should choose. But alas, how hard it is for a heart that the love of God has not entirely detached from love of the world to break the bonds of tender affection with relatives. The aforesaid was at the awful moment of death, and he should have been thinking of nothing but the judgment of God [Ps 70:16] and considering only the true interests of those who had given him their filial confidence. But, seduced by an ill-considered affection, he was guided by the bonds of flesh and blood and designated his nephew to the brothers, alleging that he was a good monk, prudent and able in outside business. That was in part true, but the great punishment that followed shows that he had not been guided in the advice he had given by a pure intention, that is to say, the right ordering of the house, but that he had been thinking rather of the honor and glory of his family in the promotion of his nephew. At his death he suffered severe punishments for his fault, which the Lord deigned to show to his successor who had been promoted to the office irregularly.

There was on the property of the monastery a very fresh, cool, and pleasant wood, watered by a clear fountain of running water. The murmur of the water was sweet to hear and the surroundings, covered with grass, were refreshing and enchanting to the eyes and hearts of those who came there. During his lifetime the late abbot had often come there to refresh himself,[114] and there, because it was quite private, he could relax more freely from the many cares and fatigues of his abbacy. His successor continued this means of relaxing and frequented the place in the same way, but he, I think, was more inclined to seek the comfort of the flesh which he had observed in his predecessor than to imitate the virtues found in his way of life. On one of the days when he went up to this spot as usual he suddenly heard laments and groans in a voice that seemed to be coming from the bottom of the fountain. "Alas, alas," it repeated sadly, "how miserable I am!" Deeply terrified and alarmed, he went closer, and, listening diligently, he at once recognized by its

---

[114] Virgil, *Aeneid* 1.387-88.

quality the voice of his predecessor, the dead abbot. Then he asked, his lips trembling with fright, who it was who was complaining, and from the middle of the waters the same voice replied, saying, "I am your kinsman, the former abbot, yet now a miserable spirit, whom you succeeded in the administration of this monastery to my great confusion and unhappiness."

Asked why he was complaining, he answered, "Because I am burning." Asked again why he was burning when he had lived a religious life which seemed to deserve rewards rather than punishments, the dead man replied, "You! I am burning because of you." Then the abbot said, "Me? Tell me why and how?" The dead man replied, "Because when it was necessary to find a successor who could rule souls [RB 2.31-34], the brothers whom I so unworthily governed put all their trust in me under God and left the choice of my successor to my discretion. Alas, instead of acting out of the fear of God, I was seduced by the too natural affection that I had for you as my nephew, and acting out of the foolishness of my own self-will, I advised them to promote you to this high and dignified office. For this I am condemned by the just judgment of God to suffer torments and burn in these waves. I burn, I melt, I perish, and when I have been reduced almost to nothing I am restored to endure the same tortures again. If you want to be sure that this is no joke, have a bronze lantern brought here and plunge it slowly into the water." The abbot ordered a bronze candlestick to be brought, and it was lowered very gently into the basin of the fountain. And, marvelous to say, the hard metal melted and disappeared like wax in fire [Ps 67:3] or like a cloud before the rays of the sun [Wis 2:3]. To such a terrible sentence will God, the just judge, damn those who are not afraid to enrich their kinsmen with the goods and revenues of the churches entrusted to them and to raise them to high offices. And someone deserves to be punished this way who has listened to the voice of kinship rather than the demands of charity in naming one of his relatives to the prelature when he should have been thinking about the good of souls.

And so, for some time we have touched upon certain vices and negligences which came to mind because of the account of Dom Gerard of blessed memory, abbot of Clairvaux, who was always eager to warn his brothers assiduously about the dangers of swearing [EM 5.1]. I have taken care to put together a summary for the exhortation of readers, knowing that the souls of simple brothers, however devout, are more moved by examples than by words. For in devout minds which seek fervent compunction from spiritual reading, rather than the vain knowledge that puffs up, turning over the virtues of the saints in the memory and becoming familiar with them in thought are more likely to increase love of the good and horror of evil than reading ten thousand words in a treatise. Having absolved myself of this great debt, I will now return to our Clairvaux, which we left in order to meditate in the fields with Isaac on the marvelous works of the Lord Christ [Gen 24:63]. So now I will return to my series of narrations, composed for the edification of many, about the true religious way of life of our venerable fathers and their deaths, precious in the sight of the Lord [Ps 115:15]; I will do this as a proper conclusion. For just as a small stream flows into many channels in the midst of a dry field and revives the dried-up plants until all is irrigated, when it returns to its own riverbed it follows its course more swiftly than ever.

Book Six

# Blessed Deaths
# and a Final Summary

CHAPTER ONE

## *About the Imprudent Contemplation of a Monk of Clairvaux, and about the Dangers That Beset Contemplatives*

When the Lord told blessed Job about the old enemy of the human race known under the image of Leviathan, he said that "the sinews of his testicles are wrapped together" [Job 40:12]. By this he meant to tell us that he is powerful and cunning and to warn us that no mortal man can escape the tangled bonds of his seducing ways without the help of grace. That is why the Apostle gave this grave warning to those who profess themselves Christians and desire to press on, led by humility, to come to the highest glory whence fell proud Satan and his angels:[1] "Be careful how you walk for the days are evil" [Eph 5:15-16]. And again, "Do not be deceived by Satan, for he can transform himself into an angel of light" [2 Cor 2:11; 11:14]. But with how much care should we watch, we who desire to lead a more holy life and go into monasteries in order there to take up spiritual arms for the Lord's battles? It would be a mistake and a great error to suppose that only those who live in the world, amid the tumult of business, are exposed to the wiles of the devil and not those who live in the peace and repose of the cloister. On the contrary, our shrewd adversary sets more subtle traps for those who aspire to the higher levels of virtue and who think they are safer because they have already escaped the shipwreck of this world.[2] In order to arm all contemplatives with prudence, we recount here the very grave temptation into which a spiritual man found himself caught because, in the silence of his prayer, he lacked prudence about his contemplation. This example will no doubt make an impression on those eager readers who

---

[1] Grießer (EM, 339n2) notes that this language is from the prayer for the Third Sunday after Easter.

[2] For shipwreck imagery, see Ælred of Rievaulx, Spec car 3.35.91 (CCCM 1:149; CF 17:284–85); and Bernard of Clairvaux, Ep 111.2 (SBOp 7:284; James, Ep 113.2, p. 170); on the dangers of traps one can encounter in isolation, Sent 2.76 (SBOp 6/2:40; CF 55:157).

collect various sayings here and there and engrave them on their memories so that by using them they may focus their eye on them first in meditation and then in contemplative prayer. They must always remember this sentence: "He who studies the majesty of the Most High will be crowned by Him with glory" [Prov 25:27]. Far from encouraging them to take flight into inaccessible regions, which could be fatal to them, this example will make them abase themselves more and for the sake of the greatest good and keep themselves in fear inspired by holy humility.

There was at Clairvaux a senior of exemplary observance who had become a faithful follower of the ideal monastic life in that monastery under the guidance of our venerable father blessed Bernard, who had led many, even quite simple, souls to perfection. He was, in fact, a courageous imitator of our blessed father, and every day he gave himself with new fervor to the exercise of virtue. On account of his deep wisdom, maturity in counsel, and holiness of life he was useful, not only to himself, but also in helping others advance toward sanctity; he had been made abbot of Foigny,[3] one of the greatest daughter houses of Clairvaux and one remarkable for its observance. Placed in that honor and thinking assiduously about the weight of that honor, fearing lest, as the prophet says, he might be among those who do not understand the dangers of high office, he resolved to fulfill all his abbatial functions with the humility of a truly spiritual man. But at length he wanted to lay the weight of responsibility down from his shoulders, now bent with age, and leave the cares and perils that go with it. Preferring the rest of Rachel, which was barren, to the embraces of Leah, fruitful, it is true, but far more perilous, he returned to Clairvaux with the joy of a bird returning to its nest, following the example of his father Saint Benedict.[4] There, by daily searching his conscience, he gathered together all the movements and affections of his heart that

---

[3] Which abbot of Foigny this was is uncertain; it may have been Rainald, first abbot of Foigny, who resigned in 1131 and went back to Clairvaux. Compare above, EM 2.3.

[4] On the association of Rachel and Leah with the contemplative and active lives, see note above in EM 3.4.

had been scattered by the cares of his abbacy and, like our holy Father Benedict, he lived within himself.[5] Intent upon spiritual studies, he was entirely apart from noisy distractions of business, and all his time was occupied with prayer, reading, compunction, and holy meditation. For he was aware that there is no more effective antidote against the virulent assaults of the world and the fleshly enticements than these. Stimulated by his zeal for constant meditation and ensnared by its beauty, he then began to scrutinize divine mysteries with the subtlety of an exacting contemplation. There, he found great joy and exaltation of heart, saying to the Lord with the psalmist, "How wonderful, O Lord, are your works; therefore my soul seeks knowledge of them" [Ps 118:129]. Since, with the fruit of his good works, he had to offer assiduously the saving Victim by whom we are redeemed and reconciled to God the Father, the more he ruminated on the depth of this inscrutable mystery in sweet meditation, the more frequently would he recall the memorial of the passion and the very high humility of the Lord.

If only this man, otherwise so pious, had taken care to remain a cautious and God-fearing contemplative, especially when it came to such wondrous depths of such great mysteries, where all arguments of human reason fail and only the utterances of holy faith should be consulted! With an indiscreet curiosity, though with believing wonder, he asked himself how the bread and the wine offered on the altar are transubstantiated by the power of God into the true Body and Blood of the Lord Jesus Christ, our Redeemer. Scrutinizing this more closely than he ought, he relied proudly on the eye of profane reasoning and presumptuously attempted to submit to the temerity of reason those sacred mysteries which belong only to hidden truth. He should have remembered that blessed Bernard compared reason, when it tried to break into the realm of faith, to a burglar.[6] Moreover, blessed Gregory tells us that faith has no merit if it is mixed with human arguments.[7] This old

---

[5] Gregory, Dial 2.3.5; SCh 260:142–45; Fathers of the Church 39:62–63.
[6] Bernard of Clairvaux, Csi 5.6 (SBOp 3:471; CF 37:145).
[7] Gregory the Great, *Homiliae in Evangelia* 2.26.1 (CSSL 141:218); trans. David Hurst, *Gregory the Great: Forty Gospel Homilies*, CS 123 (Kalamazoo, MI: Cistercian

man also forgot the advice of the Wise Man, that someone who finds honey should eat it cautiously in case too much of it makes him sick [Prov 25:16]. Nor did he take account of the Apostle's advice to think of himself not more highly than he ought but with moderation [Rom 12:3]. By looking into heavenly secrets, being greedy for spiritual sweetness, and seeking to penetrate the depths inaccessible to the angelic spirits themselves, in the end he failed to show the respect due to God's majesty. He tripped on the stumbling block [Rom 9:32-33], and the Lord in his anger withdrew from his servant [Ps 26:9].

For once the good Spirit, or rather the Spirit of goodness, hid his light, the evil spirit immediately brought in the darkness of his malice, and he stirred up diverse thoughts in this wavering soul, already shaken in his reason by wicked doubts. Forgetting the obscurities of this life, he dared to gaze with an open face [2 Cor 3:18] on that which is the object of the certitude of faith, and he fell by the just judgment of almighty God from the assurance of faith into hesitation and doubt, and blinded by his presumption, he judged that what his reason could not understand was impossible. Yet, as the Apostle so elegantly defined it, "Faith is the substance of the things hoped for and the conviction of things not seen" [Heb 11:1]. "For if they are seen, where is the hope" [Rom 8:24]? In this vale of mortality, in this body of sin and death, we are told to wait patiently for those things which we cannot see until they be revealed in the homeland of everlasting clarity, where God will be all in all [Eph 4:6; Col 3:11]. Until then, our only concern should be with keeping the eyes of our hearts clear from the vice of disquieting curiosity. That is what Wisdom tells us: "A heritage that is gained hastily at first will not in the end be blessed" [Prov 20:21].

This imprudent contemplative was aware that the poison of clandestine doubt was creeping slowly into his soul, and he worried about it. He fought it with all his strength and tried to dispel the shadows produced by the malice of the devil, but he could not do

---

Publications, 1990), 201. Bernard of Clairvaux also pursues such issues; see Ep 188 (SBOp 8:9–10; James, Ep 238, pp. 315–17); and Ep 190 (SBOp 8:17–40; not in James); Par 5.1 (SBOp 6/2:282; CF 55:63); Csi 5.14 (SBOp 3:478–79; CF 37:156–57).

it—just as an unquiet will is free to throw itself into the ditch but is not equally free to get out by its own efforts and industry. This unhappy man had the rudder of faith violently wrenched from the ship of his conscience by the tempest his presumption had raised, and, prey to bad thoughts, he was like a ship given over to the fury of the waves. The lying spirits, not content with breaking the certainty of his faith, tried with all their efforts, malice, and force to throw him from the darkness of doubt into the pit of blasphemy, and, in fact, this wretch was on the point of thinking—like Berengar, the first author and upholder of this impious heresy—that the bread and wine offered at the altar were not, after the consecration, the true Body and Blood of Jesus Christ.[8] But almighty and merciful God, who had delivered this, his servant, to the angel of Satan to be tested [2 Cor 12:7] to teach him not to be presumptuous, willed that he should realize the insolent temerity of presuming to attain—while in this miserable life and sinful flesh—that supreme degree of knowledge which is part of the life of the blessed and even allowed his servant to lose something of the integrity of his faith, but he would not allow the wretch to fall onto such perilous rocks of doubt as to be thrown into heresy.

While he was wretchedly dithering and worrying this way, consumed by the agony in his spirit and the violence of the struggle, he no longer dared approach the holy mysteries which he had formerly celebrated with great devotion, and he groaned at being reduced to such horrible suffering by his own presumption. Miraculously, he saw his error and blamed himself but without being able to dissipate the cloud of his error—and, as the holy Pope Gregory wrote about blessed Mary Magdalene, he loved and he doubted at the same time.[9] The more he remembered the sincerity of his former piety, the more he deplored the blindness of his

---

[8] Berengar of Tours (*c.* 1010–88), controversial schoolman and grammarian, argued that Christ was not corporally present in the Eucharist. His position was most notably challenged by Lanfranc of Bec, but it is not clear that he was ever formally excommunicated. See Margaret Gibson, *Lanfranc of Bec* (Oxford: Clarendon Press, 1978), 63–97; and H. E. J. Cowdrey, *Lanfranc: Scholar, Monk, and Archbishop* (Oxford: Oxford University Press, 2003), 59–74.

[9] Gregory the Great, *XL Homiliarum in Evangelia lib. II.* 25.4 (PL 76:1192B).

perverse opinion. The damage done by those unhappy temptations, increasing from day to day, undermined not only his interior self but even his external self so much that the poor sufferer, lacking both mental vigor and physical strength, was often forced to seek some remedy for his condition in the infirmary.

His former spiritual sons, the brothers of Foigny, learning that their beloved one-time father had fallen under the weight of sadness and affliction, came to Clairvaux to persuade him by gentle arguments to go back with them, and they took him reverently back to Foigny. They hoped that, comforted by their love and care, he would feel his pain lessened and would at last recover peace after such agony. But as the poet says so well, "Those who cross the sea can change the heavens above them but they cannot change their souls."[10] And wisdom teaches us that "no one can correct him whom the Lord forsakes" [Eccl 7:14]. Neither change of place nor the kind exhortations of the monks could draw the sting of temptation out of the heart of this poor old man. The time of mercy had not yet come [Ps 101:14], and he felt violently the torments which were the punishment for his foolish temerity. He remained almost to the end of his life consumed in this frying pan of blasphemous doubt and tested like gold in the furnace of temptation [Prov 17:3], until at last the Lord had pity on him and he fully recovered the light of faith. Humbled, he was more resolute in his belief and careful to draw the eye of his contemplation away from the restlessness of illicit scrutiny, for he had understood by his own experience that God resists the proud [Jas 4:6; 1 Pet 5:5] and chastens their presumption.

If there is anyone in the monastery, then, who is endowed with a keen mind and has received from the Lord the better part, that is, the leisure of Mary [Luke 10:38-42; EM 2.33], and finds it his delight to read the sacred page closely, he should always remember that he is the disciple and not the master, lest he be led on by the subtlety of his own mind to search, to his own undoing, to understand the signs sealed in the faith [2 Tim 2:19] or to reason

---

[10] Horace, *Epistles* 1.11.27; see also Saint Jerome, Ep 16.2 (CSEL 54:69).

imprudently about truths that the holy fathers, despite their genius
and wisdom, and owing to the respect they had before the mysteries
of God, did not dare to discuss because of their depth.

CHAPTER TWO

*Concerning the Excellence of Faith*
*in the Sacrament of the Body and Blood of Christ,*
*and How Much Discernment Must Be Shown*
*in Contemplating It*

There is a great deal of difference between the vain researches born
of curiosity and the considerations begotten of piety, between contemplation engendered by humble devotion in simplicity of faith
and purity of conscience, and the daring, foolhardy meditations that
are the fruit of presumption. What we are going to say now should
inspire terror in those full of confidence in themselves but reassure
simple and humble souls led by the Spirit of God. Indeed, that great
and illustrious contemplative, who from the beginning caused devotion and contemplation to flourish in the most clear valley[11]—by this
I mean blessed Bernard—insists at length in his writings that care
must be taken to flee from all daring or presumptuous speculation.
And in one place he makes quite clear with how much reverence
feeble human reason should bow before the sublime beliefs of our
faith by writing, "I say clearly that I do not understand the dogma
of the Holy Trinity, but I believe in the Holy Trinity."[12] What could
be more sensible than this simplicity of faith, what more frank and
meritorious, more true to devotion? And this same faith which the

---

[11] "Clear valley" (*in clarissima valle*) is another wordplay on Clairvaux (*Clarae-*
*valles*), as above in EM Prol.

[12] While this is not a direct quotation from Bernard, similar phrases can be
found in SC 76.6 (SBOp 2:258; CF 40:115); Apo 8 (SBOp 3:88; CF 1:43–44);
and Ep 178.1 (SBOp 7:397; James, Ep 218, p. 297).

saint professes here in a few words about the mystery of the Holy Trinity, he also professed with equally unshakable firmness about the most holy sacrament of the altar; he showed this wonderfully not only in his language but also in the works he did.

It is said that when Bernard was in Italian lands the fame of his miracles and the marvelous power he had over impure spirits spread everywhere, and a woman who had been possessed for a long time by a loathsome demon was brought to him.[13] He at once ordered she be taken into the church, knowing that it would be more difficult to cure her than the others. He went up to the altar and celebrated Mass, doing everything as usual until after the consecration; then he put the Body of the Lord on the paten, and he held it over the head of the sufferer, who became horribly distorted by the fiend that was in her, and he said, "Behold your judge, hellish tyrant," and other things that are recorded in the life of the saint. So he frightened Cerberus of Tartarus,[14] who was put to flight. When ordinary prayers were powerless to cast him out, he was routed by the faith and power of the divine sacrament.[15]

On another occasion, Bernard was unable by his advice and exhortations to bring to a depth of humility and the unity of the Catholic Church the Count of Poitiers, who obstinately favored the schism of Peter Leoni and refused to submit to Pope Innocent II.[16] Saint Bernard had recourse to the power of God and trusted the solution of the matter to him when human help was hopeless. He went into a church to sacrifice the victim without spot, by whom is given to us poor mortals life, salvation, peace, and unity. Meanwhile, the count was left standing at the door of the church with all the others who were under sentence of excommunication and forbidden to enter the house of God. After the mystery of the eucharistic consecration, before giving the kiss of peace to the faithful, the man of God, not acting on human motives but guided

---

[13] Similar reports of miracles in Italy are discussed in Williams, 140–41.

[14] See note above, EM 5.13 on Tartarus.

[15] Compare Arnald of Bonneval, Vita Bern 2.3.13-14 (PL 185:276–77).

[16] The reference is to William, Count of Poitiers, a follower of antipope Anacletus II (1130–38); see note above at EM 2.11.

by heavenly inspiration, respectfully placed the heavenly manna, the most pure fruit of the Virgin's womb, on the paten. Then, to the amazement of all who were watching him with great anxiety, he took the paten holding the precious pledge of our redemption with him and went out of the church, his face aflame. In a voice not conciliatory but menacing and authoritative, he addressed these words to the count: "We have pleaded with you, and you have scorned to listen to us. Now look, the Son of the Virgin, the Son of the Most High Father, has come out to you, he who redeemed holy Church with the price of his own blood, this Church which you are not afraid to throw into as much uproar and division as you can. Here is the judge of the whole world, into whose hands your soul shall come, before whose terrible tribunal you will have to give account for the actions of your whole life. Now, resist him if you can." But the count was unable to bear looking at the tremendous and heavenly sacrament before which all the orders of angels tremble and which the abbot held in his venerable fingers.[17] And moved by Bernard's fiery language, which pierced to the bottom of his guilty conscience, he fell to the ground as if struck by a sword. His blood froze in his veins, and his mouth foamed hideously through blackened lips, and his whole body shook as if he were breathing his last. For some time he remained lying like this while everyone present wept and beat their breasts. Then the prophetic man, as if inspired, came to him and pulled him to his feet and imperiously ordered him in the name of him whom he held in his hands to get up and be reconciled at once with those bishops he had deposed from their sees, many of whom were present, and henceforth to show himself a submissive son of the holy Catholic Church and not a protector of schismatics. By the grace of God he immediately obeyed, as we know more fully from the book of Bernard's life.[18] This was beyond the hopes of all those who stood around, for they knew how obstinate the count had been about the schism. So by virtue of the immaculate sacrifice, and by the

[17] On the orders of angels, see note in EM 4.26.
[18] To this point the paragraph is from Arnold of Bonneval, Vita Bern 2.6.38 (PL 185:290).

faith of the man of God, that land was delivered from the madness of Peter Leoni. The clergy and all the people returned to the unity of the Church and praised the clemency of the Lord. How great is the devotion that faith inspires! Of it the Apostle could truly say it holds the promises of the present life and of the life to come [1 Tim 4:8]. How wonderful is the Holy Spirit in his works, who by the wonderful glue of charity unites the highest and the lowest so that the bread of the angels—the bread full of glory, splendor, and sweetness [Wis 16:20], containing in itself all pleasures, this eucharistic bread which is the Word of God himself clad in his humanity—is given as food to the poor worms of the earth. How marvelous it is that unstable matter, which in itself is only vile and perishable, when consecrated by the rites of the Church is transubstantiated into the true Body and true Blood of Christ our Lord and becomes the sweetest food by which a devout rational, but miserable, animal can receive the delightful refreshment associated with the glory of beatitude! But these sublime gifts, which ineffable bounty dispenses freely to poor mortals, can be seen only by the eyes of faith, while they remain veiled to the eyes of reason. It is presumptuous to discuss them, but to believe them is an act of piety and religion, and to know them is life and life eternal [John 17:3]. Does it not seem truly marvelous to you that this admirable saint, like the holy old man Simeon, not only recognized the hidden majesty of God in the depth of the mystery [Luke 2:28-35] but even with authority showed it to others under the accidents which are accessible to the eyes and the corporal senses? Far from seeking audaciously to understand how Christ is present in the sacramental species, he unhesitatingly believed that he held in his hands him who is the power and wisdom of God. He venerated and adored Christ with sincere faith and, filled with the force of this virtue, he terrifyingly presented God to the proud.

If only human reason could stop scrutinizing in this presumptuous way that which is sealed by faith and which we are not allowed to know in our mortal nature! Let us imitate the patriarch Jacob, who was happy in his simplicity and, knowing himself lame, did not try to hide it [Gen 32:31-32], and let us humbly admit that concerning knowledge we are like him. Let us be like Peter the apostle, who by virtue of this faith knew and crushed the duplicity of Ananias and Sapphira [Acts 5:1-10]. Let us walk firmly in matters of faith so that we may come to the fullness of knowledge. What does it matter, O curious one, if you satisfy your curiosity and know how the sovereign dispenser communicates the living gift of the divine sacrament of the altar to us? Is it not enough to have it and to prove its usefulness and efficacy and to be fully confirmed in our belief by those wonders and miracles which God has never ceased to work all through Christian history until this very day to make clear the truth of this mystery? I shall not speak of the greatest mysteries, but I who am little have spoken of the lesser marvels of God. The Lord who is so wonderful in great things [Ps 47:2] is perhaps more so still in the lesser. With what goodness, for instance, did he deign to calm the fears of that abbot who at the hour of the divine sacrifice found a spider in the already consecrated chalice with the precious Blood and, fully persuaded that death cannot prevail over life, swallowed it? And when he cut himself the same day he was shaken to see the entire spider coming out with the blood from the small cut he had given himself![19] Our loving God by another similar miracle made another priest understand that he is really present on the altar, although our senses do not discern it. When he found himself in the situation not unlike that of the abbot I have just described, this priest, armed with no less lively a faith and although he believed he was drinking death with life from the same chalice, did not hesitate at all. The next evening he felt a tickling in his foot and, scratching it, plucked out the very spider he had swallowed, whole and alive. All this seems very astonishing and unaccountable when one realizes that, while it can cause instant death to a wicked man who dares to profane the holy and wonderful mysteries, this poisonous little creature could do no harm to those into whose organs it has penetrated who are full of faith and show the respect due the sacrament of the Lord.

[19]This story may have been taken in part from John of Clairvaux, *Liber visionum et miraculorum* (Troyes, Bib. mun. MS 946, f.114r); see Grießer, EM, 345n5; and McGuire, "A Lost Clairvaux *Exemplum* Collection Found," 42.

We read in the *Acts of the Emperor Charlemagne*[20] that when that religious Augustus was hearing Mass in his usual pious manner on a solemn feast day, the deacon who had been appointed to read the gospel had not feared to befoul himself the previous night by shamelessly embracing some little trollop for whom he felt a forbidden love. Stained by this very grave offense and unafraid of the terrible judgments of God in his counsels over the sons of men [Ps 65:5], he dared to read the gospel. He would even have gone so far as to abuse the sacred privileges of his order and take into his impure hands the mystery of the divine sacrament, but divine vengeance rebuked his daring by taking him suddenly out of this world. And while his impure mouth was uttering the words of the sacred text, a spider descended by one of its threads from the rafters of the holy place and rested once, twice, and a third time on the head of this contaminated reader, and in the sight of the emperor himself, the third time it stung his filthy head. The wretch immediately fell down dead. Now I ask you, who want to understand everything: if you cannot explain by what secret ways or hidden passages this maggot could have poured its poison into hidden veins, or how, when it was introduced into the stomach, it could have slipped between the flesh and skin instead of going naturally into the bowels and come out at the extremities of the body without the least alteration, then how can you attempt to know how the bread and wine which are offered on the altar are changed into the flesh and blood of Christ? If you, as the prophet says, are worn out by running a footrace, how can you compete with a horse [Jer 12:5]? That is to say, since you find yourself enveloped in the thickest shadows of your mortal condition over this least of things, how can you dare to explore restlessly the most profound mystery of God? In the sacrament of the altar, as someone said about a martyr, "all is of God; nothing is ours."[21]

Let someone who would make progress in holiness attend to stripping himself of his vices and purifying his heart and give

---

[20] Notker of Saint Gall, *Acts of the Emperor Charlemagne*, 1.32 (MGH SS 2:746), trans. Lewis Thorpe, *Two Lives of Charlemagne* (London: Penguin Books, 1969), 130–31.

[21] The source of this quotation has not yet been identified.

himself in all ways to the study and contemplation of the mystery of the holy Scriptures. The work and exercises of the active life are suitable for imperfect beginners; the sweet rest of prayer is the portion only of humble and devoted souls. But who do you think these humble and devout persons are? These are not just anyone but those who have already been dead for a long time to wickedness, curiosity, vanity, and the love of pleasures; they are those who have climbed the heights of humility and perfection and can say to the Lord with the psalmist, "Lord, I take delight in your precepts, as in the possession of all riches" [Ps 118:14]. Let whoever is still not confirmed in this clarity of virtues—so that he walks all day in their light but has his intellect obscured by the darkness of vice although he has subtle intelligence and penetrating reason—understand that for the moment it is better for him to pray, to ruminate on the psalms, and to read sparingly, and in his reading to seek not the knowledge that puffs up but the Spirit that gives life.[22] He should aim not at becoming learned, but at being temperate; as the Apostle warns, "Be not wiser than is proper, but in moderation" [Rom 12:3]. Far from wanting to appear wiser than he is, he ought to be as wise as is proper. It does not become a monk to throw around knowledge he does not have; rather, he should keep his learning for God and himself, with a humble conscience, lest by chance the satiric poet, or rather the unclean spirit, should mock him for claiming to know what he does not know while another knows that he is ignorant.[23] As Father Augustine, that most learned of the doctors, said, "To read and to pray are equally good things when one can do both, but if one has to choose, it is better to pray than to read."[24] We are astonished that there are those who somewhat or entirely misunderstand the necessary usefulness of devotion and prayer and choose to spend whole days and nights in reading and

---

[22] *Le Grand Exorde*, 374n23, draws a connection between "the Spirit that gives life" (*spiritum vivificantem*) and the Nicene Creed recited at Mass.

[23] Persius, *Satires* 1.27.

[24] Grießer (EM, 347n3) cites a statement very close to this in Augustine, *De opere monachorum* 17 (PL 40:565), translated in *Augustine: Treatises on Various Subjects*, Fathers of the Church, 16 (New York: Fathers of the Church, 1952), 363.

speculation. It is as if they paint on thin air or throw dust in the wind; they fill themselves with knowledge while their consciences are still not purified from their vices, and with subtle meditations but without the fullness of perfection, they fly high and they are completely ruined, as I have seen in many cases. Those who act this way should greatly fear if they are trying to keep a flame in their lamps but neglecting to fill them with oil, that is to say, if they pride themselves only on the brightness of their knowledge without having the gentleness of piety and humility. God, the just judge who cast our first parents out of paradise because of their immoderate desire for knowledge [Gen 2:23], will no less reprove these foolish virgins [Matt 25:12]. Let us all take care; let each and every one take care that he earnestly offers up to the Lord our God on the altar of devotion the sacrifice of a contrite heart and a humble spirit [Ps 50:19], as much for the forgiveness of sins as for the acquisition of virtue and, not least, to avoid the unhappiness of eternal death and to come into the possession of heavenly beatitude. If anyone persevering in devotion, led by grace, makes enough progress to have securely established in his conscience the virtues of good discipline and pure religion with sincere humility, he can then in all security ask with the psalmist that knowledge be taught to him [Ps 118:66], not only the salutary learning from reading and meditation, but much more that from the anointing of him who teaches men knowledge [Ps 93:10]. As the psalmist says, it is in vain for anyone to rise before the light [Ps 126:2] of perfect humility to aspire to learning, and it is always necessary to sit down in penitence to eat the bread of sorrow, that is to say, of compunction, and then to rise up to the light of learning or contemplation, which fills the corners of the conscience with virtue and the maturity of discipline, because arrogant vanity does not have any place in learning.

CHAPTER THREE

*Concerning the Happy Death of a Monk Who Wanted*
*to Die at Clairvaux*

John the apostle and evangelist was exiled to Patmos for having given witness to the word of God, and in an inspired book
he reveals to mortals, who still sit in the darkness and shadow of
death [Ps 106:10], the secrets of heaven as far as we are capable of
understanding them. Among the heavenly revelations that he has
passed on for the consolation of all who labor on the path of God
and groan under the weight of temptation, he heard a voice from
heaven, saying, "Blessed are the dead that die in the Lord." And he
adds the reason for this beatitude: "for they rest from their labors
and their works follow them, as the Spirit said" [Rev 14:13]. Holy
men themselves who with attentive meditation consider the joyful memory of this happy death—which is a passage from work
to rest, from corruption to incorruption, from death to life, from
misery to happiness, from faith to knowledge—sigh for this in their
prayers and continuous longing, saying, "When shall I come and
appear before the face of God" [Ps 41:3]? When one of them dies
before the rest, they regard him with affectionate compassion and
congratulate him, as it is written about the blessed Abbot Bernard
who almost never buried someone without tears.[25] This is seen also
in the most illustrious patriarch of Alexandria, John, who used to
forget the dignity of his office and the authority of his person in
order to be near any of the faithful who were dying, sitting with
them and sharing in their agony with the most touching sentiments
of piety, and as their souls left their bodies he closed the eyes of the
dying with his own hands and commended their souls devoutly to
the divine mercy.[26] Then too, blessed Malachy, the Irish bishop, in
all his actions remembered his last hour so that he would be found

---

[25] Geoffrey of Auxerre, Vita Bern 3.7.21 (PL 185:315).
[26] A reference to John the Almsgiver; see note above at EM 5.14.

worthy to obtain benediction on the day of his death.[27] When he first came to Clairvaux and established links of friendship and familiarity with our holy Father Bernard, whose sanctity he revered, so great were the flames of celestial charity that united these two souls that the prelate of Ireland wanted ardently to end his days near this man of God. He went home to his country and continued to pray that he would be allowed to die at Clairvaux and to die on All Souls Day. He wanted God to give him, when dust and ashes, the grace to await the glory of the resurrection next to the ashes of the abbot who was so dear to him. He was not disappointed of his hope. The Lord gave him his heart's desire [Ps 20:3]: because of his reputation he was allowed to die in this illustrious place, because of his achievements on the day, and near the companion with whom, by his special merits, he was worthy to be associated.

The faith and devotion of this glorious prelate found an imitator in a monk of exemplary life called Balm, who deserved his name because of the fine fragrance of his virtues.[28] He was a monk of Saint Anastasius, a monastery of the Cistercian Order situated near the walls of Rome.[29] He once came to see blessed Bernard at Clairvaux on business, and when he saw the good order and mature observance in that fervent and numerous community, his heart burned within him, and in meditation the fire was kindled [Ps 38:4] that if charity—"which seeks not its own" [1 Cor 13:5]—did not lay other things upon him, he would like, above all the delights and treasures of the world, to live and die at Clairvaux. Fearing he might be deprived of his fervent desire and not wanting to go away without anything, he begged the holy abbot with very humble prayers and by the fervor of his devotion obtained the promise that at his death the full Office of the Dead would be offered for

---

[27] Bernard of Clairvaux, V Mal 16.38–39 and 31.70–5 (SBOp 3:343–45, 374–78; CF 10:52–53, 88–93).

[28] Grießer (EM, 349n1) cites Herbert of Clairvaux, LM 101, a chapter which is not included in the PL.

[29] The monastery of Saints Vincent and Anastasia, also known as Tre Fontane, was a daughter house of Clairvaux (1140); Januschek, 62; Cottineau, 2:2503. See note at EM 5.17.

him by the Clairvaux community.[30] With his request granted, he regarded himself thereafter as a monk of that house and exulted in the Holy Spirit. He went back to his own monastery and, when he heard they had died, never failed thereafter to pray the Office for any of the brothers of Clairvaux, and he added twelve Masses a year for those of whose end he was unaware. Because of his long experience, this very devout man, although he was charged with different kinds of work throughout the monastery—of which he was still a valuable and useful member and to which he was bound by obedience—always found a way of managing time for himself, despite his many occupations and without neglecting any of the common observances, and along with all the other good works that he did solely out of regard for God, each day for eight years he recited the entire psalter, thus joining in the daily discipline. The Lord was pleased with such saintly conduct, and the marvel we are going to report clearly proves it.

He was sent on business of the abbey to the lord Pope Alexander, who was then living in France. By chance he fell into the hands of some schismatics who favored the pseudo-pope Octavian.[31] They attacked him, brutally pulling him off his mule, and ordered him to be put in prison. One of the abductors mounted the mule of the servant of God to take it along with him. But the mule bucked with astounding movements and jumps, as if fighting for his master, and absolutely refused to move. He spurred the harmless beast and whipped it, but he could not overcome its resistance; it went in the opposite direction from the one he wanted, and all his efforts were in vain. The schismatics, seeing providence acting against them, were bested by this miracle and also worn out, and they decided to release the holy man. They ordered him to mount the beast then and there and leave. This time, to their general amazement, the mule behaved with great gentleness, and without any delay or the least constraint it went rapidly forward, carrying its master whom it recognized with joy.

---

[30] For details of the Cistercian use of the phrase *plenarium officium*, see *Le Grand Exorde* 377n10, which directs the reader to EO, Index 1.

[31] This refers to the schism between Pope Alexander III (1159–81) and Octavian of Monticelli, the antipope Victor IV (1159–64); see note above at EM 5.17.

The desire of this holy monk to die at Clairvaux did not diminish with time but each day it increased and lived on in his heart. And the hour was not far off, though known to God alone, who "hears the desires of the poor" [Ps 10:17], and the Lord, who works all things for the good of his elect, made things turn out so that his servant had a new occasion for going back to Clairvaux where he longed to end his days and be buried. As it happened, the monastery of Saint Anastasius, the daughter house of Clairvaux of which he was a very devoted monk, had lost its pastor and Balm was appointed by the pope and his brothers to go to the motherhouse and bring back a new abbot, chosen by the abbot of Clairvaux himself [CC 11; CCP 18]. But instead, the Lord sent him so he would pass out of the sea of this world and come to the port he had always desired and would now attain. He had been in the monastery for a few days, and, much edified by all he saw and heard in that fervent community, he was stirred to compunction and great fervor. Then, as it happened, one of the brothers died. At the sound of the board for the departed [EO 93, 94, 98], the newcomer saw the great crowd of monks and lay brothers run and gather around the body. And after he had heard them solemnly singing the commendation for his soul and the funeral chants as they carried the body out in a great and orderly procession, and saw the priests and their assistant ministers offer the sacred rite of the saving Host for the soul of the brother, and, not least, the holy vigil and psalmody they kept over the body of the dead man, Balm longed more and more to share in the precious grace for which he had been sighing unceasingly, and he prayed to heaven with many sighs for the blessing of an equally happy passing [1 Kgs 19:4]. And he cried from the bottom of his heart, "Lord, let me die the death of the just and let the end of my life be like theirs [Num 23:10]!"

The monk's funeral was celebrated with the customary solemnity, and the body was carried to the place of burial. There, according to custom, all the monks stood in a great circle around the tomb of the dead man whom they had just come to bury and of the brothers who already lay there. After singing the appropriate psalms, all the brothers, in gently modulated tones, chanted the antiphon, "Most loving Lord."[32] Meanwhile, the aforementioned servant of God, out of devotion, not out of curiosity, glanced all around and gazed with great happiness at this holy assembly, as if it were an angelic choir. He was seized with a great longing at the sight and sighed, asking God with more insistence than ever that, although the demands of obedience would not permit him to join these holy monks during his lifetime, he might at least let him be with them at his death. When the antiphon had been sung and reached the phrase "Lord, have mercy upon this sinner," everyone prostrated as usual, praying earnestly for the soul of the dead man. Balm prostrated with the others and asked for mercy in tones of tender piety. Soon, tears flowed from his eyes and streamed down his face; he was asking for rest not only for the departed but also that he himself might soon end his life in this holy house.

Soon, with divine clemency granting the desire of its little servant, he became infected at that place with a fatal fever that troubled him with various discomforts until he died, purifying him of the faults which he had committed in life and which no one on earth can avoid. And so he quickly and blissfully possessed what he desired. The following night while he was asleep, he suddenly saw heaven open above him [Ezek 1:1] and there appeared our Lord Jesus Christ, Our Lady, his most blessed Mother, Saint Bernard, and many other saints shining with glory. This happy vision filled him with such joy that he believed himself to be already among the blessed. As he got weaker, with great patience he gave thanks to God in confession of lips, contrition of heart, and devotion of holy prayer. He prayed that a portion be given him in the land of the living [Ps 141:6], and in this way he approached the end of his life, and after the tenth day he died a holy death. "Blessed is the man," says the psalmist, "who fears the Lord" [Ps 127:4], who venerates in others the good he sees and loves it. He gave himself up as much as he could to the practice of virtue and had confidence that he would obtain a full and perfect reward for his labors, for he had noticed the precious merits of his neighbors and wanted to

---

[32] *Clementissime Domine.* According to *Le Grand Exorde*, 379n25, this antiphon was added sometime before 1150; compare EO 98.8 and note 212.

join himself with the brothers whom he judged to be better than himself, whether in life or in death.

Behold, this servant of God, whose happy death we have described, had been taught by God not to take great pride in his virtues but to always be fearful [Rom 11:20] because of his imperfection. He had prayed ardently for blessed fellowship with this most holy congregation, and what the virtue of obedience denied to him when he was alive, the most holy Judge of that same obedience kindly provided to him as he was dying. This holy Judge gave him in heaven the ineffable glory for which he had earlier prayed humbly on earth, those things owed to perfect monks alone: to be associated by their sacred remains in their tombs.

## Chapter Four

### *Also about a Lay Brother Who, Burning with a Pious Desire, Prayed to the Lord That He Would Die at Clairvaux*

We know that this grace of dying at Clairvaux was not given to this one brother alone but also, by divine generosity, to not a few others. In my own day, a servant of God who burned with the same desire saw his prayers completely fulfilled. This example, of which I was a witness, is full of consolation and gives great encouragement to all those who bear the burden and heat of the day [Matt 20:12] under the discipline of Clairvaux.

At the time of the General Chapter the abbots of the Cistercian Order were hastening to Cîteaux from all the countries of the world. Despite the length and difficulty of the journey, an abbot in charge of one of the daughter houses in Spain traveled back to his motherhouse. As his companion for the journey he had a lay brother of irreproachable behavior and great piety who had often heard in his own country of the aromatic reputation of the observance and holiness that filled the house of Clairvaux; he was animated with a lively desire to visit this bright valley, to which the brightest of abbots, shining with the glory of sanctity, had given a name which shone throughout the world.[33] On the journey to the Chapter, the more closely he approached the much-desired Clairvaux, the more the lay brother was seized by a pious longing not only to see such a blessed place but to end his allotted time there in death [Mic 2:5]. When they were nearly there, and the good brother was able to see the top of the church in the distance, he was suddenly moved with such devotion that it seemed as if his heart was entirely consumed in the fire of charity. He raised his hands and eyes toward heaven and uttered to the Lord a short prayer but one full of faith and sincere emotion: "O Lord, if the prayer of the poor and the sinful is not displeasing to your Majesty, I pray you, let this holy place where rest the mortal remains of so many holy souls who are now reigning with you be also my resting place forever and ever [Ps 131:14]. It is here, O Lord, if you permit, that I want to stay, for I have chosen it." When they entered that wonderful tabernacle prepared by the hand of God [Ps 41:5; EO 98.8] rather than by men, he went to venerate the tombs of Saint Bernard, principal patron and renowned protector of that monastery, and of blessed Malachy, his illustrious companion who is buried with him, and he begged with fervor that his petition might be granted at once.

It was not long before his prayer was answered. Suddenly his strength began to fail, he was laid in a sickbed, and he prepared for the last struggle, showing as much haste and holy eagerness as if he were going to a feast. After he had revealed to the monks and lay brothers—and his abbot had confirmed by his testimony—his desire to die at Clairvaux, so promptly fulfilled by the Lord, the community was very pleased, and partaking of the joy of the dying man, they brought him into unity with the holy community with prayers and expressions of goodwill. He was anointed with sacramental oil and fortified by the Body and Blood of the Lord, and after a few days, while the abbots were gathering at Clairvaux for the Nativity of Saint Mary before the Cistercian General Chapter, it was there, if

---

[33] See note in EM Prol. regarding Conrad's use of the valley metaphor.

I am not mistaken, in the midst of so large and so holy a gathering of abbots, monks, and lay brothers, and with the assistance of their brotherly prayers, that he breathed out his spirit, as he had desired. That imposing and venerable assembly celebrated his funeral rites with solemn and devout Offices. As they returned earth to earth, they all with one voice glorified God who is wonderful in his saints [Ps 67:36] and who had shown in the person of his poor servant the power that the prayer of a truly contrite heart has before God.

Moreover, who would doubt that the abundant goodness of God sometimes grants certain men the grace to find in the merits of others what they lack in themselves? If one of these, although feeble and imperfect, has the privilege of being associated with perfect religious observance, who can doubt that all of his imperfections will be covered by their sanctity, provided that when these weak souls leave this world they show here below a sincere love of goodness and virtue and try as hard as they can to imitate the sanctity and regularity of the others; as the psalmist says, "With the holy you shall be holy and with the innocent man you will be innocent" [Ps 17:26]. Not only must it be believed that any religious community supports and protects the weak by the merits and prayers of its members still struggling strenuously in this flesh of sin [Rom 8:3] and guards their exit, but even more must it be hoped that it will achieve this by its glorious members who have merited blessed rest after the sweat of completing this holy warfare.[34] To this a perfectly observant senior among the brothers of Clairvaux who had received from the Lord the gift of seeing invisible things has borne witness, saying that the souls of dying brothers, already set free from their bodies, were helped not less but much more strongly by the devotion of those still living in the flesh, so that these souls might be enabled to evade the malicious accusations of the malign spirits coming at them with great ferocity and that they would be able to share in the true light and eternal happiness. They deploy the zeal of a most industrious charity. We say that those are blessed who persevere in the works of penitence and who at their last hour have the help of the prayers of their brothers,

---

[34] Another metaphor for spiritual warfare; see notes above on the EM Prol.

both living and dead. But we dare to say that it is a bitter and grievous thing to see the fate of those men, rightly called the most unfortunate of men, who instead of respecting the holy habit of religion which they have received dishonor it by unworthy conduct and disorderly behavior. Although they are buried with the usual obsequies, neither the living nor the dead can give them any help. Those who here have sown thorns of corruption will in eternity harvest eternal fire as the reward of their malice.

## CHAPTER FIVE

### *How the Souls of the Departed Were Seen to Celebrate the Last Rites of a Religious*

If anyone does not believe the aforementioned senior when he says that the departed assist the souls of the dying out of this life, let him not, I pray, be shocked that the holy old man said this or with me for seeming to record a falsehood. Rather, let him wait patiently, and let him know that we have made this claim on reliable testimony: not only that holy men have known this spiritually but that the omnipotent Creator has sometimes allowed it to be seen and heard by the eyes and ears of the flesh. He has done this in order to leave mortal man in no doubt that another life of happiness, or unhappiness, awaits the soul after death according to its merits. And nothing could be more convincing in this matter than the knowledge that the delicate, invisible substance of the soul, at the command of God, to whom nothing is impossible [Mark 10:27], is to be joined and, if I may say so, mingled with those still in the flesh. We learn from such things to despise deeply the present life, which we know is doomed and fleeting, and to prepare ourselves with all possible care, and by all kinds of good works, for that life which each of us approaches more nearly with every passing moment.[35]

---

[35] What follows is from Herbert of Clairvaux, LM 115, not included in PL; see Grießer, EM, 353n1.

There was in lesser Brittany a layman who, although he was engaged in worldly affairs and applied himself to the concerns of his family, was, to the best of his ability, faithful and fearful in observing the commandments of God. Among other good things he did, some in public and others in secret and known only to God, he made it a rule never to cross a cemetery, either going to or coming from the church, without offering up to the Lord a fervent prayer for the repose of the souls of the faithful resting in that place. The days of his life came to an end, and he took to his bed preparing to go out of this world. When he sensed that death was very near, in the middle of the dark of night he sent for his priest, asking him to bring him the Lord's sacrament. But the priest was lazy and, alas, cared more for the ease of his body than the salvation of a soul, and he refused to visit his parishioner; in his place he sent his deacon, Daniel, a man of exemplary life. The deacon obeyed willingly and quickly discharged his duty, and when he had given Communion to the dying man he set out for home without delay. The poor sick man, who was richer in merit before God than he was in earthly goods, had scarcely received Christ our Lord, who generously gives eternal health and wealth which do not perish, for his comfort and protection, when he died joyfully. And he who deigns to take care of the poor thought him worthy, we believe, to enter into the shining gates of paradise with the blessed spirits.[36]

As the deacon was going back, he passed the church. He had been careful to close the doors very firmly and was startled to find them open, and he wondered what was happening. At the same moment he felt himself held back by a divine force and unable to move a step, as if he were fixed to the ground. Suddenly, from the middle of the cemetery there came a resounding voice, saying, "Faithful departed, get up and leave your tombs, all you who are resting in this cemetery. Get up, so we can go into the church and pray for the soul of this dear departed man and show him our gratitude for

---

[36] Grießer (EM, 354n1) and *Le Grand Exorde* (383n9) agree that the Latin (*paradisi portas ingressus lucidas beatorum spirituum mansiones accepit*) resembles an antiphon for the feast of Saint Agnes (21 January), found in R.-J. Hesbert, *Corpus antiphonalium officii*, 6 vols. (Rome: Herder, 1963–79), 1886.

all he has done for us. Each time he passed this place he did not fail to offer a special prayer for us." At this call, the dead quickly began to get up, and as they got out of their tombs there was a noise, an extraordinary din. And in the church could be seen many candles placed around the walls, illuminating the church with plentiful light.

When all the dead were gathered in the holy place, they praised together the divine Majesty in very harmonious chants and solemnly chanted the Office for the commendation of a soul [EO 94 and Annex 17-18]. One of them recited the collects or prayers and the rest answered "Amen," as is done in the psalmody in choir. When the service was over, the same voice came again, ordering them all to return to their own graves. They left the church and dispersed to their graves with the same noise as before. Little by little the lights which had shone in the church went out, as if they were being extinguished. When it was all over, the clerk felt himself set free from the mysterious bonds that had held him. He crossed the threshold of the church and put away the sacred vessels that he carried with him, and he returned to the home of the priest who had sent him. This man judged others by himself, weighed them in the balance of his own idleness, and did not think his assistant could possibly have kept such a long vigil; so he told him, with an air of compassion, to go to bed at once and go to sleep. But the deacon replied, "Don't talk to me about sleep; get up and do your duty. The sick man is already dead and we must get on with the funeral rites." Scarcely had he said this when a messenger arrived to announce the death of the aforesaid man, asking the priest to come. So whether he would or not, without delay the priest left with his deacon, and he carried out his duty of funeral prayers for the pious man.

The deacon never showed himself ungrateful to God for having visited him with this great grace. He was moved by such a special grace and pierced by feelings of holy compunction that he renounced all he had and hoped for, said farewell to his homeland and family [Gen 12:1], and took the monastic habit at the abbey of Saint Martin in Tours.[37] There, he lived a very religious life and was

---

[37] Marmoutier, a Benedictine abbey near Tours which dates from the times of Saint Martin; Cottineau 2:1762.

always mindful of prayers for the faithful departed. He made such progress in perfection that in the end he was made prior of that church. But he told some of his closest friends in private about the aforesaid revelation he had seen, and such a marvelous and unusual thing could not be kept secret for long, and soon the abbot heard about it. Either to find out more fully the truth of the matter or perhaps to stop talk about something that seemed incredible, the abbot summoned the community, and in chapter he addressed the prior in front of the brothers and formally ordered him, under obedience, to explain in all sincerity the marvelous event he had witnessed and not to withhold the truth. Although he wanted to hold back out of modesty, the prior overcame his reluctance to speak in public and he obeyed the command given to him. For the glory of God and the edification of his neighbors, with reserve and a kind of fear, he told what he had seen. The abbot, a good and religious man, did not doubt the truth of the wonder any longer but saw it as a foretaste of the mystery of the future resurrection. He made it a rule that whenever any monk from that abbey went into the cemetery, he should say at least the Lord's Prayer for the departed who were resting there.

Now who can say that it is absurd to say that the souls of the brothers who are dead come to help dying brothers on their deathbeds and support them by their efforts in the dangers of that terrible hour? We are going to give an example which, together with the previous evidence, proves the zeal that departed souls have for helping those who remember them in this life and are conscientious in offering prayers for the mitigation of the severe sentence of the Judge. What I have already said before in this book about the blessed Geoffrey, bishop of Sorra, proves the point [EM 3.23; 3.25]. When the bishop was still a monk at Clairvaux, he saw clearly one night during Vigils, while he was praying and chanting the psalms fervently, a multitude of forms in white coming toward him from the north side of the church, that is to say, from the side of the building where the bodies of the departed brothers rest. They passed in front of the sanctuary step and went toward the door that led to the infirmary, where an old man of great virtue was at that moment in his last agony. The blessed souls of the departed brothers could only have come into the midst of the brothers to receive into their company this brother who was putting off the garments of this corruptible life and to confound the wiles of the infernal spirits and defend him against their slanderous accusations. It is permissible to believe that what we have said about the departed who help us in our last struggles applies to those who have been purified of all their faults and delivered from all punishment; it is those who have led a saintly and edifying life on earth that deserve to be helped in the perils of death by the protection of the blessed souls.

## Chapter Six

### *How a Knight Escaped the Danger of Death by the Help of the Faithful Departed*

Because the memorable miracle we have just related ought to convince us that the souls of the faithful departed requite the help that people gave them while they were alive and that they come to aid those who prayed for them devoutly, let us now look at their care for those who are in danger and see how they repay their alms and prayers by helping them in the dangers of this present life, turning from their throats the menacing swords of their enemies. All religious who give the help of their compassion and their good works to souls who are under the just sentence of God, the just Judge, can be sure of receiving the reward of their labors if they understand that even seculars who have demonstrated their devotion in this matter escape from the most extreme dangers thanks to this work of piety. Moreover, nothing is more pleasing to God than this sense of compassion, since, after all, he himself, out of his loving concern for poor humankind, left supreme beatitude and came down from heaven to earth to help the wretched. Then, too, dead souls who can do nothing for themselves receive with thankfulness the prayers of the living which, thanks to their intervention, can soften or more quickly end those just punishments which they know full well should be long and harsh in proportion to their sins.

There was a knight who was obliged by his rank to stay in worldly dress and activities,[38] but he did not live in a worldly way, and he tried to preserve himself from it by all kinds of good works. He often considered his mortality and that in his time he would die. He loved to remember before God the faithful departed with frequent prayers and all the devotion of which he was capable. He made a resolution never to go past a church without stopping there, however busy or hard-pressed he might be, and intently reciting, his face turned to the east, the Lord's Prayer for the souls of the faithful, imploring the Lord to have mercy upon the departed. One day this knight found himself surrounded by enemies who ambushed him so suddenly that he was in danger of suffering immediate death unless he saved his life by fleeing.

Fleeing by the most rapid route, he came running to the wall surrounding the cemetery. Unable to find a shorter path or one more helpful for escaping danger, he leapt, panting, over the entrance into the middle of the cemetery. Then while he was still running he suddenly remembered his pious custom, which he had done without fail for a long time; remembering this, his heart fell and he reflected anxiously on what he should do. Either he could pay his usual tribute to the dead and be in danger of his life, or he could burden his conscience with unfaithfulness to his promise before the just judgment of God, who is able to save those who trust in him from any peril into which they fall. He had to choose because the danger was imminent and he could not stop to think about it. Piety and faith overcame the fears of human weakness, and he decided at once to despise death rather than to refuse the usual help of his prayers to the faithful departed. If the Most High willed that he be cut down there by the swords of his adversaries, he had at least the consolation of knowing that he would fall upon the tombs of those for whom he had prayed. So he stopped running and stood still and calmed his turbulent thoughts, and turning his face as usual toward the east, he began to say the Lord's Prayer with

---

[38] There are similar stories in Caesarius of Heisterbach, "Die Fragmente der Libri VIII miraculorum des Caesarius von Heisterbach," ed. Aloys Meister, no. 2.49, pp. 122–23; compare Tubach 1464a.

as much sincere devotion as if it were to be his last prayer upon earth and a final farewell to the departed souls.

Just then his enemies, full of hatred, eager for vengeance, and thirsting for blood, rushed on the scene. They saw him standing respectfully, and they thought that it was fear of death that was keeping him so still; they were delighted to be able to unleash their rage and accomplish their crime impiously but with impunity, or so they believed. But just as they were about to rush the wall of the cemetery like madmen and violate the sacred asylum of the Church of God—like the first fratricide about to sacrifice their brother who stood before them with his head bowed [John 19:30] like a victim ready for the death blow—they saw the cemetery fill in an instant with a great crowd of armed men who we think, not improbably, were the dead for whom he prayed. They stood in tight array around their faithful intercessor, forming a defense so that he could finish unimpeded the prayer he had begun for them, and in a terrifying way they brandished their swords and lances against his assailants. Those murderers by intent, hateful to God, were struck with consternation and stunned at the sudden shift in the situation and the horde of armed men threatening them and hastily made their escape. Those who had intended to rejoice in the cruel murder of their fellow man suddenly found themselves reduced to think it good luck if they could seek safety in flight. The knight who was praying so devoutly saw nothing of this and had no idea what had happened. Having finished his prayer he went on the way which he had interrupted at such great risk out of piety. He thought his enemies were behind him, and when he reached safety he was astonished that he had escaped the swords of the furious enemies who had menaced him so closely.

Later on, when the cloud of enmity had been dispelled by the warmth of charity and peace had been restored, reconciliation was sincere on both sides. When they talked things over, the persecutors asked their new friend why, when he was running away from them, he had suddenly stopped at the risk of being killed and just stood there. In his turn he asked them why they had spared him when they found him at their mercy. Knowing from one another the truth of this mystery of the Lord, who alone can do such marvelous things [Ps 135:4], they magnificently praised him, and together with others to whom they spoke about this great miracle, they were on fire to pray for the faithful departed. Let us, with all who read or hear this account, not hold back from imitating their religious devotion!

How worthy of public admiration is that which happened by the power of God to Eusebius, Duke of Sicily, and which is already well-known in many regions of the world because of the written account.[39] He had for his adversary another prince who, greedy for the goods and honors of this world, trusted in the force and numbers of his soldiers. Eusebius trusted in God alone and did many good works to help the departed souls. By a great miracle of God, he was sent from heaven a great army of souls with beautifully decorated weapons and horses white as snow; they suddenly appeared and forced the enemy to surrender with all his forces. Stirred by the encouragement of these souls, who thanked him for his devotion and the prayers he had offered up for the help of the dead, Eusebius resolved to increase his pious practices for the departed and to make all the towns and churches of his estates do the same.

How sure of victory is the one who fights with the arms of religion and piety! How true is that indisputable saying: to pray for others is to work for oneself. The devout prince and the pious knight of whom we have been speaking experienced this to their benefit in extreme peril, when they were both running the risk of loss, the one of his honor the other of his life. If it is considered praiseworthy to pray for our friends and relatives who are living and can earn merit, how much more excellent shall we consider it to intercede with pious care for the souls of the faithful departed who cannot do works of righteousness by which they may acquire merit, nor do they have recourse to the remedy of penance, but

---

[39] The following story, about Eusebius of Sicily, probably originated in Cluniac circles and was picked up later by the Cistercians at Clairvaux. Conrad appears to have got it through John of Clairvaux's *Liber visionum et miraculorum*. See McGuire, "A Lost Clairvaux *Exemplum* Collection Found," 46–49. For a thorough bibliography on the issues, see *Le Grand Exorde*, 388–89nn20–23.

on the contrary, by the severity of divine judgment, they suffer the punishments due to their sins and negligences.

CHAPTER SEVEN

*Concerning a Priest Who Was Praying for the Faithful Departed Who, When He Said, "May They Rest in Peace," Heard a Great Multitude of Voices Responding, "Amen"*

Although the faithful departed can do nothing more for themselves, they are sometimes allowed by the marvelous and joyful gift of almighty God to cooperate in a certain way in works done for them and to show their thanks to those who try to help, as we learned some years ago from a very trustworthy account of some seniors of what happened many years before to a monk of holy life, and we even know that it was written down for the memory of those to come.

In the province of Germany-across-the-Rhine, which is called in the vulgar tongue Saxony, there was a monastery of the Order of Cluny built inside the walls of the city of Paderborn, dedicated to the apostles Peter and Paul.[40] And at that earlier time, when the Order of Cluny was still flourishing, a monk lived there who was full of the love of Christ and whose name fitted him exactly: he was nicknamed "Amo" or "Love."[41] When he had been raised to the dignity of the priesthood, he took care that he adorned this holy office with holy conduct, and he celebrated the divine mysteries with a devotion suitable to such a spiritual service. In order to offer this unspotted sacrifice on the altar of a contrite heart [Ps 50:19], the more devoutly as it was more secret, he used to go often to say Mass in a small chapel under the protection of Saint Alexis, which was separated from the church only by the cemetery. So he was frequently obliged to pass through it, and both going and coming he never failed to offer the

---

[40] Abdinghof Abbey in Paderborn; Cottineau 1:5.
[41] According to the necrology of Abdinghof he died on July 8, though the year is not certain; see Grießer, EM, 359n2.

hand of a fervent prayer for the faithful departed. He told himself that at the end of his days he would be among them, reduced to ashes, and this reflection as well as the thought of the pains they suffered in the other world stirred him to do all he could to mitigate the sufferings of those already there. On one of the days when he was returning from celebrating the holy sacrifice, after fulfilling the obligation he had imposed on himself on behalf of the souls of the dead, he added the verse, "May they rest in peace." And he heard a great many voices make the response very clearly, "Amen. Amen."[42] At hearing it, he trembled to think that these words came from those very souls for whom he had prayed, yet thinking how wonderful it was that they were invisible but so close to him. From then on he was all the more faithful to his pious practice since he had the happiness of knowing by this new miracle how this devotion is blessed by God and how it is good and fruitful for the faithful departed. "It is a holy and saving thought to pray for the dead, so that they may be delivered from their sins" [2 Macc 12:46].

## CHAPTER EIGHT

### *About a Young Boy Who Confessed His Sins after His Death*

O Eternal Wisdom of God which comes forth from the mouth of the Most High [Sir 24:5] and extends from one end to the other mightily and sweetly ordering all things [Wis 8:1], you who said by the prophet, "My mercy will not fail you and I will have pity on whom I will have pity" [Exod 33:19], how can human nature, so soiled with sin and vice, expect from your goodness and love more than you have already done?[43] What is sweeter and more consoling than the mercy you have shown to us poor creatures? By an admi-

---

[42] Tubach, 1465, cites a story in which the dead say responses during the Office of the Dead.

[43] The quotations from Sirach and Wisdom are used as *Magnificat* antiphons before Christmas; see *Le Grand Exorde*, 391n2.

rable interchange that only your power could establish, the dead, showing to the living their faults and negligences which they had not amended while they were still in the flesh, can come to the living and urgently ask for their prayers; on the other hand, the living can use the authority they have been given by you to help the souls already submitting to your terrible judgment and to raise them to the joys of paradise by offering the unique sacrifice and by assiduous prayers.

Behold, Lord Jesus Christ, most gentle and merciful Son of the living God, and Son of the Blessed Virgin Mary, something more sublime and sweeter flowed to us like honey from the rock when you granted to the least of your small servants, with a love as blessed as it was undeserved, the sacrament of confession, the profound and indescribable groans of a contrite heart, as well as the baptism of the most bitter tears of penitence. That which seems impossible humanly speaking you accomplished out of your immense goodness, and it must be counted as one of the most marvelous of the deeds for which you are praised. I urge everyone who reads this not to be too ready to disbelieve it and think it a fable. These things happened in our own day and many estimable members of the Cistercian Order can bear witness to it to this day.

Those who knew Dom Hugh, abbot of Bonnevaux,[44] of most holy memory, or who have heard tell of his virtues know how greatly God enriched him with supernatural gifts and favors. This holy abbot had in his service as messenger a young man who because of the energy and agility of his services was very important to the success of these errands. For this reason he was as much loved by the abbot and the other religious, who used him for external matters. But while he was still young [Isa 38:10], he suffered the frightful separation of spirit and flesh and had to pay the harsh tribute of death which does not spare age or condition.[45] Suddenly

---

[44] For Dom Hugh, see Grießer, EM, 360n1, who refers the reader to the *Chronicon Clarevallense* for the year 1183 (PL 185:1250B); Hélinand of Froidmont, *Chronicle* 49, year 1185 (PL 212:1080); and Caesarius of Heisterbach, *Dialogus miraculorum* 3.25 (Strange 1:142–43; S-Bland 1:159–61).

[45] Baldwin of Ford, *Tractate* 10 (PL 204:513B), trans. David N. Bell, *Baldwin of Ford: Spiritual Tractates*, vol. 2, CF 41 (Kalamazoo, MI: Cistercian Publications, 1986), 77.

attacked by a severe physical illness, his flourishing youth daily lost its vigor, his strength left him, and soon there was no hope of his cure. Seeing himself wither away thus, he understood by sad experience how true it is that "youth and pleasure are only vanity" [Eccl 11:10]. Despairing of the present life, he began to think about the terrible conditions of the future life, as far as the burden of his illness would allow—or, better, as the Lord inspired him. Examining himself, he found, not without fear, that he had committed many faults against God his Creator in not resisting the unregulated desires of his youth, and he wanted to make his confession as the only plank, as it were, available to those shipwrecked in the vast sea of this world. Whether he died before he could carry out this pious intention or whether he had confession we do not know, but it appears from what happened after his death as though he had not received proper assistance from those who ought to have helped in the death of such a young man who had been one of the little ones of the Lord.

One night when Dom Hugh was resting on his bed the young man, now dead, appeared to him, his face full of deep distress, his bearing showing the anguish he was suffering. He approached and knelt respectfully before the holy abbot and stretched his joined hands toward him in an attitude of supplication and begged him to hear his confession. Then with many tears and groans he humbly confessed all his sins and their circumstances; he declared many other things he had fallen into, mortal sins that brought from him such sighs and so many tears that he almost went beyond any other confession on earth in lively and sincere contrition. After his confession, the penitent continued to groan and shed tears with great contrition of heart; he begged Dom Hugh to have mercy upon him and with his holy prayers to placate the sovereign Judge who is meek to the just, terrible to sinners, but pardons those who repent. All this time the religious abbot was much impressed by such great marks of sorrow, and, moved with pity, he tried to console this unhappy young man and showed him very loving compassion. Then he awoke.

When he thought over what he had seen and heard, he felt some inward stimulus urging him to compassion for the dead boy, and so he understood that the vision had not been an illusion. But the goodness of almighty God would not let him have any shadow of doubt in his heart, and, marvelous to say, he was at once given material and convincing proof of the purely spiritual happening. When he put his hand on that part of the cover where he had seen the penitent prostrate himself, he found it was wet, as if it had really been soaked with tears. If, in this and similar miracles of divine power, someone relies on the judgment of reason, what is said begins to seem unbelievable. But when the divine power is acknowledged, they stop being astonishing. The reverend abbot did not hesitate; he was so sure of the infinite clemency of the Lord Christ and he trusted so much that he would help this poor soul that he absolved him in chapter [EO 70.38-42], and with all the brothers he celebrated Masses and offered fervent prayers for the forgiveness of his sins. The boy who had earned the punishment of eternal death by his sins could thus, we hope, satisfy the justice of God and be led by the grace of God into eternal beatitude. For charity knows no obstacle, and what is impossible with men is possible with God.

## Chapter Nine

### *How a Prioress Was Warned by a Revelation to Confess*

The Apostle, when he is speaking as he usually does about the depth of the mysteries of God [Rom 11:33], tells us that he is "making known the manifold wisdom of God to the principalities and powers of heaven" [Eph 1:21; 3:10] by the Church. The Lord also said to the blessed Job in describing his works, "Who can make the harmony of heaven to sleep" [Job 38:37]? For it is impossible for mortal nature to know the sweetness of the intimate charm of the harmony with which the manifold wisdom of God delights and enchants the blessed spiritual powers of heaven by the operation of his grace. It is this which draws holy Church from this lake of misery and mire of mud [Ps 39:3], that is, from its sins, to associate it with the holy assembly, "without a spot or wrinkle or any such thing" [Eph 5:27]. This Wisdom and Truth teach us, bearing witness that "heaven and earth will more easily pass away than that one jot or one tittle of the law of grace shall perish" [Matt 5:18], that is to say, that even the smallest opportunities—when even the last among the people of God seek the remedy of salvation—will not come too late to be effective. Let us see now how subtly this gentle Wisdom, whose ever-watchful care is the salvation of humankind and to whose eyes everything is plain and open [Heb 4:13], advised one servant of God about the state of her conscience. By this example all people of right judgment will burn more ardently with love for this divine Wisdom as they hear proclaimed more sweetly by the familiar voice of Wisdom herself "that her delights are with the children of men" [Prov 8:31].

There was a prioress in a monastery who was a virgin intensely devoted to God, and with more zeal than discernment she urged the sisters under her care to observe the discipline of the Rule as strictly as she did. Her monastic conduct was agreeable to God, but there was one stain—although she was scarcely aware of it in her conscience—that spoiled the purity of her soul. When she was a child she had committed a sin which she had neglected to confess out of the carelessness of the very young, and as time went by she forgot about it so that she had no memory of having done anything of the sort. But the loving Lord would not allow his devoted servant to be confounded by her enemies at the gate [Ps 126:5] of judgment because of a sin which she had merely forgotten, not tried to hide out of shame. And he deigned to show her when, and in what way, she had sinned.

One night when this venerable prioress was asleep, a woman who had taken care of her as a baby and formed her in virtue, insofar as her tender age allowed, appeared to her. And calling her by her name in the way she used to, she said, "Gisela, my child, what are you doing? How long will you remain in this spiritual negligence and not wash away through confession and penance the sin into which you fell when you were very little and in my care?" As soon as she disclosed the nature of the former sin, the prioress recalled what she had done long before and was covered with confusion. She asked, "Will a sin be considered so great which a weak and foolish age had committed in ignorance, with reason not having yet unfolded through experience into the full flowering of life? Is it necessary now for me to confess it and do penance?" The other replied, "Do you suppose any sin whatever is so light in weight that it should not be deleted by confession and the labor of penance? Listen closely to what I say. You should know for certain and harbor no doubt that, just as in this life you may see portraits traced on tapestries and walls showing very clear outlines of all the limbs, so too in the soul of each person, the faults, even the smallest, that have not been remedied through the grace of God by the sacrament of confession and penance leave a lasting mark, and it is easy to see what good or evil anyone has done during life."

At these words the prioress awoke. She was astonished by what she had heard and, after thinking hard about it, realized that it was not a false vision, but she remembered that she had done the thing she had heard in the vision in her childhood. Since she had come to the years of discretion and taken the religious habit, however, it had never struck her conscience because it had entirely vanished from her memory. Full of joy and gratitude at the mercy of God, she repented and confessed with complete humility and sincerity, because she knew this blessing was due only to the generosity of God's loving-kindness. Afterward she was more careful than ever to declare all her sins, past and present, as she knew for certain by this divine revelation how great the error is for those who dare to suppose that they will not be punished for what they have disregarded or forgotten.

Contained above in this volume [EM 5.4] is the story of a certain dead lay brother appearing in a vision to another lay brother who was still living and reminding him of a sin that he had committed twelve years earlier, while he was still in the world, and which had been forgotten through a lethal forgetfulness; he exhorted him to confess and do penance as soon as possible, saying that his pronouncement should be heard with fear and trembling, because a sin not forgiven before death remains even less forgivable after death.

Therefore—if that handmaiden of God had to be warned through a revelation to confess and do penance for a sin committed in childhood, and if that brother heard that forgiveness for one grave sin forgotten would have been denied after death if absolution had not been granted legitimately beforehand—what will be the final punishment for those who conceal sins because of shame or because they loathe a severe penance or, what is more dangerous than these, because they have confidence in a long religious life? "Truly it is a fearful thing to fall into the hands of the living God" [Heb 10:31], for "the Lord is terrible in his judgments upon the sons of men" [Ps 65:5]. So it is indispensable for all, and especially for those who profess religious life, to reflect in bitterness of soul on the passing years and to judge themselves without dissimulation, confessing their sins orally and with contrition of heart as well as the doing of good works if they do not want to be condemned with this world. Remember that "the way which leads to life is narrow" [Matt 7:14] and even those who are free from all burdens and bonds pass along it only with difficulty,[46] for, as it is written, "the just shall scarcely be saved" [1 Pet 4:18]. Those weighed down and distracted by the cares and pleasures of the world cannot walk on it. Anyone who wants to enter through the gate of life must humiliate himself, for it is a horrible evil if anyone exceeds the height of the lintel by a finger's width because he will crack his head and collapse.[47]

We must trust in the Lord Jesus because if anyone has in his youth abandoned himself to laxness of life or committed crimes and wicked deeds, and if, having been aroused by him who said, "Lazarus, come forth!" [John 11:43], he avoids the traps of death and strives to return to the right way and examine his conscience with fear and care and sincerely confess all he finds there, not once, but many times, even for the rest of his life, then he will not lose the fruit of repentance. He should confess to God, in prayer with tears and groans of penitence, as many of the sins he can remember among those which he had by chance forgotten, humbling himself continually because of them. For the rest, as the Apostle

---

[46] Piesik, *Exordium Magnum Cisterciense*, 2.421n299, discusses *dilatatus* (which we have translated as "free from") and notes its connection to Deut 32:15 and Ps 128:32. See Bernard of Clairvaux, Asspt 2.3 (SBOp 5:233; SBS 3:226).

[47] Bernard of Clairvaux, SC 37.7 (SBOp 2:13; CF 7:186).

said, "one who does not know will not be known" [1 Cor 14:38], so if anyone refuses to seek the great mercy of the Lord [Ps 50:3] for his many iniquities, mercy will forget about him [Job 24:20]. And as we may justifiably fear, whoever he may be, he will suffer a severe judgment, as much for those sins which he remembers as for those he had forgotten.

CHAPTER TEN

*A Final Summary of What This Volume Contains*

We have finished everything which we considered necessary to write concerning the beginning of the Cistercian Order and about the reverend and outstanding religious life of those who shone in Cîteaux and Clairvaux. It also seemed to me right to give, in appropriate places, similar examples and stories at the end of the book. We ask readers, if they find anything that will inspire them with hatred of vice and love of virtue in the pages of this little work, to thank God, the first author of all good, and to be grateful to our fathers for the industriousness through which these documents have reached us. And for myself, who undertook this modest work not without pain, I ask the help of your holy prayers. As we said at the beginning [EM 1.10], we have not written all this as if we were writing something new but have gathered together in this volume what our assiduous fathers had already put in writing. It is their notes scattered here and there that I have put together so as to give a more extended knowledge of the things they thought worth remembering and to bring these things within reach of a great number of readers. Nevertheless, I have taken care to interweave into the piece a few chapters which I learned in reliable reports from religious and trustworthy people, thus chopping and cooking pottage for the children of the prophets from herbs collected in the field [2 Kgs 4:39] of the venerable fathers in such a way as carefully to avoid adding the laxative of falsity as if it were poisonous hellebore. The consideration of two points have driven us to this degree of concern: first, that we might hand down a certain knowledge of our Order from its inception to our brothers who, having professed our Order in the more remote parts of the world, closely embrace the holy house of Cîteaux, as the head and mother of all of us, and likewise the holy house of Clairvaux, on account of blessed Bernard, and that we might make known for their edification how sublime and how worthy of imitation was the life which the first fathers of each house lived; and, second, that we might remove the occasion of calumny from the monks of the black Order, who openly slander our Order to seculars and to those ignorant of the facts, saying that it began from presumption and that our fathers who first came from Molesme had left without the permission of their abbot.[48] How false this is the beginnings of this book amply prove, as if presumption, which is the mother of ruin and the enemy of stability, could have had a part in such a praiseworthy plan as that of the servants of God whose willing sacrifice was approved by reason and inspired by faith. Struggling by hard work and through many trials, they did not let themselves be discouraged; they did not hesitate daily to offer themselves on the altar of the cross as living sacrifices, pleasing to God [Rom 12:1], as they tried by their own labor and industry to raise the purity of the monastic order from the squalor of dissolution and the pit of lies into which it had fallen and restore it to its ancient discipline and so, by the help of God, to secure the salvation of many.

The chief and standard bearer of these valiant athletes of Christ was Dom Stephen of blessed memory, of whom we spoke earlier [EM 1.21–31]. It was nearly ten years after the foundation of Cîteaux that he accepted the office of pastoral care there. Despite his ardent desire to spread and propagate holy religion, he was very distressed for fourteen years because the number of monks remained small. At last, in the fifteenth year, by the inspiration of divine grace, the most blessed Bernard, the apostle of our times, came with his group of brothers and companions to be received and undertake spiritual training. And from that day forward the

---

[48] See EM 1.10 for note on the "black Order," i.e., the Cluniac Benedictines.

Lord poured his lavishly abundant blessings upon the Cistercian Order, which spread throughout all the lands of the West. This most venerable Father Stephen, after a few years, sent blessed Bernard's brothers to found the house of Clairvaux and made him abbot. Although he was still young, he had more wisdom and maturity than many who had grown old in the wisdom and virtues of religious life. We believe that Stephen foresaw by a revelation of the Holy Spirit that a great and beautiful cedar tree would grow in this paradise of the Church of God and that a great crowd would come from every part of the world to rest under its thick foliage, that is to say, that they would seek in the shadow of the merits of the saint a sure refuge from the illicit passions of the flesh. Who would have guessed how immense the multitude of this blessed army would be, or from how many provinces and lands they would be recruited! To say nothing about the Mediterranean provinces of Italy, Germany, and Gaul, those distant islands like Ireland, Britain, Denmark, and Sweden, which are at the edge of the world, and which sent a great number of people to join this army, and they venerated the place because it had been sanctified by this holy abbot. And I have not even mentioned the lay brothers, who were more numerous than the monks, and for whom, after the death of the blessed man, were found eight hundred eighty-eight documents of profession and that there were no doubt many more that could not be found through negligence and the long passage of time.[49] When certain members of this holy army, cultivated by the ploughshare of discipline and having received the seeds of virtue, had blossomed and it was hoped that they could be of use to others, just as they had been gathered from diverse regions, so they were sent out to diverse regions to build monasteries. And this explains how it was that although the number of novices often exceeded ninety or sometimes even a hundred, that holy monastery never seemed too small for so large a number.

---

[49] "Charter of profession" is a technical term for the charter signed and placed on the altar at monastic profession.

Dom Henry of holy memory, the first abbot of Vitskøl,[50] founded in Denmark from Clairvaux, liked to tell the following story about when he was a novice at Clairvaux with ninety recruits being formed in the novitiate under the training of blessed Bernard. One day while they were at table, this most loving father came in to visit his sons and was followed by a lay brother who carried a basket filled with pieces of cheese. He came up to the aforesaid Henry, since he was the senior novice, and he took one of the scraps of cheese from the basket and cheerfully gave it to him with his own dear hand, saying, "Eat this, my brother, for you have a long way to go" [1 Kgs 19:7]. Then this faithful minister of the great Father of the family, who makes his servants sit down and serves them himself [Luke 12:37], distributed this little pittance of charity to each of them with the same words and joyfully refreshed their bodies and filled their souls with zeal for the straight and narrow way [Matt 7:14; EP Prol.] which they had begun to follow.

Although men of virtue were frequently sent out from the sacred community of Clairvaux to plant the austere discipline of the Cistercian Order throughout different climates of the world, never were the heat of Spain, the horror of the Scythian cold, or other hostile climates able to divert their souls from heaven, so that whatever usage they had learned at Clairvaux about clothing, food, and other bodily necessities, they kept with a virile constancy. The beautiful words of Horace could be applied to them: "constant souls, who do not change with changing places."[51] Not only did bishops and lords of various countries ask that monasteries following the discipline of the man of God be founded in their districts, but the people of great towns chose their bishops and archbishops from among his disciples, thinking themselves happy to have pastors for their souls from such a source of perfection.

---

[50] Vitskøl (*Vitae-Schola*) in the Diocese of Viborg in Jutland, Denmark. Henry was first abbot of Varnhem in 1150, then abbot of Vitskøl in 1158. Compare Januschek, 120, 141; Cottineau 2:3452; McGuire, *Cistercians in Denmark*, 58–59; France, *Cistercians in Scandinavia*, 63–76.

[51] This passage has not been found in Horace. The earlier reference to "Scythian cold" refers to the ancient Roman province of Scythia on the northwestern shore of the Black Sea, to whose people Horace did refer in *Odes* 4.5.10.

Moreover, their leader, the most perfect of this perfect throng, had obtained grace from God and men to keep clear of such high dignities. More than anyone, he deserved it, and he was elected more than once to vacant bishoprics and archbishoprics, but he would never let himself be deprived of his beloved poverty, and he would not be forced to accept these posts against his will.[52] But why speak only of the different cities, when the capitol of the world itself, the mother of all churches, the holy Roman Church, chose her pope from among the humble society of the children of this blessed Bernard and conferred on him the full papal authority, and many monks were called to surround the pope as cardinals of the apostolic Curia in order to assist him in his responsibilities?[53] Lord Christ, this is your work; you so exalt those who glorify you and keep your commandments that your servants, who according to the precept of your apostle have subjected themselves to every human creature for your sake [1 Pet 2:13], are by you exalted above all mortal nature by the judgment of your love.

Moreover, after thirty-one years, that Clear Valley sent its first and clearest abbot to the court of the King of heaven.[54] He is the more powerful as an intercessor insofar as he is more closely contemplating the face of the Most High. After him the vigor of holy religion was maintained intact in that glorious house through his worthy successors whose virtues we have already described, and thanks to the favor of God we too were allowed to experience it under the venerable Dom Peter, that great servant of God, and his

---

[52] Regarding "beloved poverty," see Bernard of Clairvaux, V Mal 21 (SBOp 3:331–32; CF 10:39–40).

[53] A reference to Pope Eugene III (r. 1145–53), who had been abbot of Tre Fontane, a daughter house of Clairvaux. In all, there were seventy bishops from the Cistercian Order before 1200 and twelve cardinals before 1300; see Joel Lipkin, "The Entrance of the Cistercians into the Church Hierarchy, 1098–1227: The Bernardine Influence," *The Chimæra of His Age*, ed. E. R. Elder and J. R. Sommerfeldt, CS 63 (Kalamazoo, MI: Cistercian Publications, 1980), 62–75. See also Newman, *Boundaries of Charity*, 141–70, 247–51.

[54] Following Grießer (EM, 367n4), *Le Grand Exorde*, 400n17, remarks that the number of years here is incorrect; it should be thirty-eight (1115–53). As only one of the manuscripts Grießer used had the correct number, thirty-one seems to be an early scribal error. "Clear valley" and "clearest abbot" is a wordplay on Clairvaux.

successor Dom Garnier, who was afterward bishop of Langres.[55]
The Lord is our witness that since we were subject to the claustral
discipline and holy observances of Clairvaux, which we mentioned
above, and since we have seen such piety, purity, and holiness, we
may say, exalting in our heart for the grace of God, that if our
legislator and most blessed Father Benedict, whose rule we have
professed, were still alive and could take over the governance of this
community, he could not guard his own holy precepts in this holy
place more faithfully. At Clairvaux there is no place for carelessness, light-mindedness, or laxity, which is the ruin of the Order,
but the holy emulation of blossoming virtue and fraternal charity
thrive there. What is even more admirable, there is no need for
superiors to compel individuals to maintain these ideals with any
harsh reproof, for this blessed congregation possesses as its heritage
the avoidance of vices and the application to virtue. Also we saw
there seniors from among the disciples of Saint Bernard inspiring
in the intensity of their manner, the integrity of their observance,
and their prudence and simplicity: Dom Gerard, prior of blessed
memory [EM 2.29]; Dom Geoffrey, secretary of that same holy
abbot and much beloved by him;[56] Dom Hugh of Mont-Félix;[57]
Dom Peter of Châlons and others—monks as well as lay brothers—who from the time of that blessed man until our own day
are models of piety and fervor for all, and with the rest of this holy
community they show by their conduct the plenitude of perfection that was to be found at Clairvaux in the first days, inasmuch
as the devotion of a few has been able to imitate the energy of the
seniors in observing the exercises of the holy Order.

But even as we have been speaking about the purity of religion
and how in those early days many advanced to the height of perfection not only at Clairvaux but at Cîteaux and the other well-
regulated houses of the Cistercian Order, we remember with great

---

[55] Peter Monoculus, 1179–86; see note in EM 2.32; and Garnier of Rochefort,
1186–93.

[56] Geoffrey of Auxerre, author of books 3–5 of the *Vita Prima*; see note at
EM 2.24.

[57] An Augustinian priory in the diocese of Soissons.

fear and trembling what we once heard the aforementioned venerable man, Dom Gerard, say in the chapter at Clairvaux. He had,
on the one hand, been encouraging us with gentle admonitions
to serious conduct and careful discipline when he also mentioned
how in earlier times the souls of some of the departed brothers
had appeared to a certain spiritual man, a monk of that monastery.
They lamented with sorrow that they had been sent to the place
of punishment, not because they had committed serious sins, but
because they had been less careful than they should have been in
avoiding daily negligences. If, then, in those blessed times when
negligence scarcely entered through tiny cracks yet the censure of
the stern judge wiped away the rust of guilt by punishment and
removed it with great care, what, then, should be our concern over
our unhappy times when negligence breaks through, not by cracks,
but by clefts, or rather by chasms of tepidity? Let us be afraid that
from such negligence and careless sloth deadly wickedness and iniquity will enter through our windows because these times destroy
everything and even weaken religion, inclining men to follow vice
rather than virtue. Let us do all we can against the listlessness that
obliterates our strength and walk courageously in the footsteps of
our forefathers, meditating on their memory in our hearts, and
often and willingly reread the accounts of their actions, so that by
their good conduct we may reflect on the confusion of our ways
as if in a very clear mirror[58] and so that we may learn to mingle
salutary shame with the good we do, rejecting all imperfection and
always longing for greater perfection in righteousness.

If there is anyone who truly wants to make a great deal of progress but is getting nowhere and finds himself acting more carelessly
through a feeling of frustration, let such a one listen to what the
holy Father Bernard says: "I do not want instantly to attain the
heights, but I want to keep going forward little by little."[59] The poet
also, with very eloquent and witty words in excellent verse, invites

---

[58] On good conduct, Piesik (*Exordium Magnum Cisterciense* 2:422n320) notes
the connection with Bernard of Clairvaux, Sent 2.20 (SBOp 6/2:29–30; CF
55:145) and Gregory the Great, Mor 37.

[59] Bernard of Clairvaux, SC 3.4 (SBOp 1:16; CF 4:18).

the crude and hard minds of men to learn right conduct, showing them that no one should despise making a little progress of whatever kind and ought not to give in to difficulties, since a constant upright intention overcomes everything. He says:

> Though you cannot rival Lynceus in keenness of eye,
> you would not disdain using ointment for an inflammation;
> Nor because you despair of overcoming the strength of Glycon,
> does your body have to be knotted with gout.[60]

And if in our desire to advance, our efforts do not find success immediately, while it seems that some can progress, "one has to go forward if one has not yet reached the limit."[61] Not to want to go forward is to open the door to total negligence and dissoluteness which ends in death and damnation.

I beseech those who read this book, by our Lord Jesus Christ, that they not read it just out of curiosity but that they think with diligent consideration how far their way of life is from the norm of righteousness which shone out so clearly in the holy fathers and that whatever they discover in their way of life that is contrary to the ways of true religion, they will hasten to bring back to the standard of truth in their daily conflict between vice and virtue. Everyone would judge a man to be extremely stupid if he were to come to a tree covered with green leaves and rich fruit and fill his stomach with useless leaves, leaving the useful fruit untouched. In the same way someone would be thought very stupid if, coming to this beautiful and rich account of the strenuous conduct of the holy fathers, he read them like a chronicle of events or the annals of a king, solely out of curiosity for information, and did not let anything he read about enkindle in him the fervor of compunction, cleanse his conscience from rust, and balance the inequalities of his life with the hand of holy devotion. The laudable deeds of

---

[60] Horace, *Epistles* 1.1.28-31. Glycon was an undefeated athlete and the rival of Lynceus, the lynx-eyed Argonaut. Bernard of Clairvaux used the lynx-eyed imagery in Ep 285.2 (SBOp 8:201; James Ep 412.2, p. 482); and Epi 2.4 (SBOp 4:303; SBS 2:19).

[61] Horace, *Epistles* 1.1.32.

our forefathers are described here, not to satisfy vain and restless curiosity, but to instruct the unlearned, strengthen the weak, prune away the burden of lasciviousness, pierce the hard heart, inform the devout for perfection, and, by edification and consolation of the readers, strengthen the whole Church, and, by the action of grace, to amplify the praise of God who gives us all good things. Moreover, there is one matter for which we ask pardon of the careful reader: sometimes we have summarized the words or the meaning of what was said, and we have been careful to restate summaries in suitable language. In regard to those things themselves, we have taken great care, as far as we could, that not even the least detail is other than the truth. Far be it from me to wound my conscience by willful lying.

The Eternal God, Son of the Eternal God, our Lord Jesus Christ, who in the days of his humiliation made sacred the sacrament of perfect penance, laid the foundation of true religious observance when he said, "Let him who will come after me deny himself and take up his cross daily and follow me" [Luke 9:23]. In these last days, when the world is growing old and many are shaken in faith, wavering in hope, growing cold in love, he has filled many hearts with his own burning love through the purity of the Cistercian Order, and in that holy Order, he erected at Clairvaux a very splendid column in our most reverend father Saint Bernard. May our God and our Lord, I say, by the merits and intercession of our holy fathers, of whose life and conduct we have written for the edification of our successors, grant us so as to follow in their footsteps and to keep to their simplicity and innocence and to be so strengthened in true humility by the mortification of the flesh that we may deserve to come to that glory of eternal blessedness at which we believe our holy fathers have undoubtedly already arrived. And may even we come to that blessedness
by the help of God's grace and with the support
of our Lord Jesus Christ,
who with the Father and the Holy Spirit,
lives and reigns,
God through ages without end.
Amen.

# Glossary

| | |
|---|---|
| abbot | Chosen leader of a monastery of at least twelve monks. From *abba*, father. |
| acolyte | A server (*q.v.*) tending to nonpriestly duties (e.g., lighting candles) or assisting the celebrant at Mass. |
| antiphon | A refrain, usually a psalm or Scripture verse appropriate to the liturgical season, chanted before and after psalms and canticles in the Divine Office. |
| bloodletting | Bleeding was considered therapeutic and was usually done at an abbey (not at granges) routinely four times a year. Blood and other bodily fluid were considered to be "humors" whose proper balance maintained health. It was the most common medical practice performed by doctors from antiquity up to the late nineteenth century. |
| cantor | The monk who intones, or begins, the singing. |
| cellarer | The monastic official charged in RB 31 with oversight of the physical plant, including the guesthouse and infirmary. |
| chancel | The eastern end of the church containing the altar and the choir. |
| Chapter | A daily meeting of the professed community which began with the reading of a chapter of the Rule, discussed common business, and administered discipline. |
| chapter house | A large room off the cloister, quite near the entrance to the church in the east range, in which Chapter was held. Lay brothers, when present, usually stood in the cloister, listening through the apertures. |
| choir | The monks who chanted the Divine Office; also the part of the church in which the choir stalls were located. |
| *collatio*, collation. | A light supper taken in summer, so called because it was followed by readings from the *Collations*, or *Conferences*, of John Cassian. See RB 42. |

| | |
|---|---|
| commendation of a soul | The prayers recited as someone is dying. |
| Compline | The final choir Office of the day, a formalized night prayer with unvarying psalmody. The term comes from *completorium*, finished. |
| convent | The community; professed members of a monastic community. |
| Conventual Mass | The formal sung eucharistic celebration attended by the entire community. |
| *conversi* | The Latin term for Cistercian lay brothers; singular, *conversus*, meaning "convert"; a term applied among Benedictines to adult recruits, as distinct from *oblati*, those offered in childhood. As the Cistercians did not accept children, the term was appropriated for the lay brothers. |
| conversion | The decision to enter monastic life; living the monastic life. The term appears both as *conversio* and as *conversatio*. |
| crozier | The staff, resembling a shepherd's crook, which indicates the pastoral authority of an abbot or a bishop. |
| Divine Office | The seven daytime and one night worship services of monks and nuns, laid out in detail in RB 8–18. |
| Ember Days | Four periods throughout the year, occurring near the changes of seasons, consisting of three days marked by special prayers for vocations to clerical and religious life. |
| eremitical (adj.) | The lifestyle of solitaries, hermits. |
| familiar brothers | Men who lived within the monastic precincts but took no vows; members of the household. |
| father abbot | The abbot of the monastery which founded the daughter house of which he is the father abbot. His obligation to make an annual visitation of daughter houses is outlined in the Charter of Charity. |
| filiation | The relationship between father abbots and abbots of daughter houses gave rise to a system whereby all Cistercian abbeys were traced back on a "family tree" to one of the five protoabbeys: Cîteaux, La Ferté, Pontigny, Clairvaux, or Morimond. |

| | |
|---|---|
| General Chapter | The originally annual meeting of all, or, as the Order expanded, as many, Cistercian abbots as possible, to reestablish good order in the monasteries, to confirm peace, to safeguard charity, and to oversee general discipline, as well as to legislate for the Order as a whole. |
| Germania Prima, Secunda | Imperial Roman divisions of the vast northern European landmass. |
| grange | Land belonging to a monastery but often not contiguous with it. Under the authority of the cellarer, a laybrother was placed as grange master in charge of each grange, usually farmland, to free the monks for choir. |
| hebdomadary | The monk assigned to a particular task for the space of a week; usually applied to the monk who officiated at the Divine Office during a particular week. |
| homily | A sermon or address preached by the abbot on major feast days. |
| infirmarian | The monk who oversees the infirmary. |
| infirmary | Area of the monastery set aside for those who were ill or aged. It usually contained its own chapel and its own kitchen and refectory, in which meat was allowed. |
| interval | The period between Offices, or between Office and work. |
| invitatory | The recitation of Psalm 94 (Hebrew: 95) with antiphon at the beginning of the Night Office. |
| Lauds | Also called Matins (*q.v.*); the major morning worship service, sung at daybreak. |
| Matins | Alternative term applied sometimes to Lauds (*q.v.*) (RB 16.5) and sometimes to the Night Office or Vigils. |
| Maundy | From Latin *mandatum*, "commandment," Maundy refers both to the Thursday of Holy Week and to alms given that day. |
| meridiem | An afternoon nap which followed the main, in winter the only, meal of the day. |
| mixt | Light refreshment allowed to someone reading during the meal and, therefore, eating later. |

| | |
|---|---|
| None | The short midafternoon Office, often recited from memory; with Terce and Sext (*q.v.*) referred to as "the little hours." |
| observance, observances | The regulations and customs which governed the monks' activities. These included keeping one's place in rank in choir, processions, and at table; when and how to bow; and when to cover one's head with the hood. |
| oil, holy oil | Oil mixed with herbs and blessed, used to anoint ordinands and the sick. |
| Order, order | Originally a designation of one's place in the social structure, a clerical order, lay order; it became a legal term indicating the religious organization to which religious belonged. |
| Parasceve | Holy Saturday, the day before Easter. |
| parlor, *auditorium* | A room off the cloister in which necessary speaking was allowed. |
| pittance | An allowance of food, in addition to the two cooked vegetables and bread allowed in RB 38 for the community on special occasions or for monks having special needs. |
| presbytery | The area of the church in which the altar was located; also called chancel. |
| Prime | The short Office recited as dawn began to break, named—like Terce, Sext, and None (*q.v.*)—after the first hour (third, sixth, ninth hours) of the Roman day. |
| prior | The monastery's second-in-command who attended to internal discipline, freeing the abbot to deal with external affairs. |
| proclaim (verb) | To accuse another monk of breach of discipline. |
| profession | The formal lifelong commitment to serve God in monastic or religious life. |
| prostration | Lying face down on the floor as a sign of humility or repentance. |
| province | Ecclesiastical. A geographical area containing several dioceses and under the authority but not necessarily the jurisdiction of an archbishop. |

| | |
|---|---|
| refectory | The monks' dining hall, set in the south range of an east-facing abbey. |
| regulations | Written directions for the manner in which things are to be done within the monastery; in Latin: *Instituta*. |
| religious (noun) | Those who had bound themselves (*religare*) by vow to serve God in monastic or religious life. |
| response | A short reply made to a versicle (*q.v.*) within a liturgical ceremony. |
| rule | The authoritative written document governing the daily life of a community or an Order. Cistercians follow the Rule of Saint Benedict. |
| sanctuary | See "presbytery," "chancel." |
| sermon | See "homily." |
| server | Someone who "serves" at Mass (see "acolyte") or at table. |
| Sext | The short midday Office. See "Terce" and "None." |
| sign[s] | Wordless communication by means of hand signals to preserve the claustral silence. |
| solemnity | A major feast day on the liturgical calendar. |
| stall | Choir seat. |
| subprior | The prior's assistant. |
| table of the dead | Latin: *tabula mortuorum*. The table or platform, usually of stone, used to wash the bodies of those who had died before their funeral rites and burial. |
| Terce | The short midmorning Office. See "Sext" and "None." |
| unction | Formal anointing of the sick with holy oil. See "oil." |
| versicle | A short phrase in liturgical worship which is answered by a response (*q.v.*). |
| Vespers | The chief late afternoon Office which ends the working day, usually sung as the sun sets and lamps are lighted. |
| vestiarian | The monk in charge of the wardrobe, including sewing and mending clothing. |
| Vigil | The liturgical anticipation of a major feast. |

Vigils                  The Night Office, sometimes called Nocturns, recited
                        during the darkness of night and consisting of "nocturns"
                        or sections of readings with responses. See RB 9–10.

vows                    Lifelong promises made to God. Cistercians, like all
                        Benedictines, make a lifelong commitment of obedi-
                        ence to the Rule and the abbot "who is believed to
                        hold the place of Christ in the monastery" (RB 2.2),
                        conversion to the monastic way of life, and stability of
                        place. See RB 58.17.

Work of God             *Opus Dei*, Benedict's term for the Divine Office, the
                        monks' chief and distinctive responsibility, "to which
                        nothing is to be preferred" (RB 43.3).

# Bibliography

## Primary Sources

*Conrad of Eberbach: Texts*

*Exordium magnum cisterciense.* PL 185:995–1198; also 415–54.

*Exordium magnum cisterciense sive Narratio de initio cisterciensis ordinis.* Edited by Bruno Grießer. Series scriptorum s. ordinis Cisterciensis 2. Rome: Editiones Cistercienses, 1961.

*Exordium magnum cisterciense sive Narratio de initio cisterciensis ordinis.* Edited by Bruno Grießer. CCCM 138. Turnhout, Belgium: Brepols, 1994 [1997].

*Thesaurus Fontium Cisterciensium*, vol.1: *Exordium Magnum*. Series A—Formae. Corpus christianorum. Thesaurus patrum latinorum. CETEDOC, Catholic University of Louvain. Turnhout, Belgium: Brepols, 1998. (Microfiche.)

*Conrad of Eberbach: Translations*

Conrad of Eberbach. *Le Petit et le Grand Exorde de Cîteaux.* Soligni-La Trappe, Orne: Imprimerie de la Grande-Trappe, 1884. [An anonymous translation, based on PL edition.]

*Conrad d'Eberbach, Le Grand Exorde de Cîteaux ou Récit des débuts de l'Ordre cistercien.* Traduit du latin par Anthelmette Piébourg. Introduction de Brian P. McGuire. Avec la collaboration de Marie-Gérard Dubois, Pierre-Yves Emery, Placide Vernet, Daniéle Choisselet, Jacques Berlioz, Claude Carozzi, et Pascal Collomb. Ourvrage publié sous la direction de Jacques Berlioz. Brepols/Cîteaux Commentarii cistercienses, 1998.

*Exordium Magnum Cisterciense oder Bericht von Anfang des Zisterzienserordens.* Translated, with commentary, by Heinz Piesik. Unter Mitwirkung von Hildegard Brem, Alberich Martin Altermatt, and Bruno Robeck. 2 vols. Quellen und Studien zur Zisterzienserliteratur, Bd. 3. Langwaden: Bernardus-Verlag, 2000, 2002.

*Other Primary Sources*

*Acta Sanctorum.* Antwerp: Joannes Nicolas vander Beken, 1643ff. Reprint edition, Brussels: Éditions Culture et Civilisation, 1965–.

Bernard of Clairvaux. *Sancti Bernardi Opera.* Edited by Jean Leclercq, C. H. Talbot, and H.-M. Rochais. 8 vols. Rome: Editiones Cistercienses, 1957–77.

———. *St. Bernard's Sermons for the Seasons and Principal Festivals of the Year.* Translated by A Priest of Mount Melleray [Ailbe Luddy]. 3 vols. Westminster, MD: Carroll Press, 1950.

See also "Works of Saint Bernard of Clairvaux," below.

*Bibliotheca Hagiographica Latina antiquae et mediae aetatis.* Ediderunt Socii Bolandiani. Brussels: Society of Bollandists, 1898–1901.

Caesarius of Heisterbach. "Die Fragmente der Libri VIII mirculorum des Caesarius von Heisterbach." Edited by Aloys Meister. *Römische Quartalschrift für christliche Altertumskunde und Kirchengeschichte,* supp. 14. Rome: Herder/Spithoever, 1901.

Caesarius of Heisterbach. *Dialogus miraculorum textum.* Edited by Joseph Strange. 2 vols. Cologne-Bonn-Brussels: J. M. Heberle, 1851. Reprint, Ridgewood, NJ: Gregg Press, 1966.

———. *The Dialogue on Miracles.* Translated by H. von E. Scott and C. C. Swinton Bland. 2 vols. London: George Routledge & Sons, 1929.

Canivez, Josephus-Maria, ed. *Statuta Capitulorum Generalium Ordinis Cistercienses, 1116–1786.* 8 vols. Louvain: Bureaux de la Revue, 1933–41.

*Carta caritatis.* Edited and translated by Chrysogonus Waddell, *Narrative and Legislative Texts from Early Cîteaux,* 442–52. Also translated by Bede K. Lackner, Louis J. Lekai. *The Cistercians: Ideals and Reality,* 442–66. Kent, OH: Kent State University Press, 1977.

Cicero. *De oratore.* In *On the Ideal Orator.* Translated by James M. May and Jacob Wisse. New York: Oxford University Press, 2001.

*Collectaneum exemplorum et visionum Clarevallense e codice Trecensi 946.* Edited by Olivier Legendre, CCCM 208, Exempla medii aevi, 2. Turnhout, Belgium: Brepols, 2005.

Cottineau, Laurent H. *Répertoire topo-bibliographique des abbayes et prieurés.* 3 vols. Mâcon: Protat Frères, 1939. Reprint, Turnhout, Belgium: Brepols, 1970.

Ecclesiastica Officia. *Les Ecclesiastica Officia cisterciens du XIIe siècle.* Texte latin selon les manuscrits édités de Trente 1711, Ljubljana 31 et Dijon 114, version française, annexe liturgique, notes, index et tables. Edited by Danièle Choisselet and Placide Vernet. Documentation cistercienne 22. Œlenberg: Documentation cistercienne, 1989; Turnhout, Belgium: Brepols, 1993.

————. *Gebräuchebuch der Zisterzienser aus dem 12. Jahrhundert: lateinischer Text nach den Handschriften Dijon 114, Trient 1711, Ljubljana 31, Paris 4346 und Wolfenbüttel Codex Guelferbytanus 1068.* Edited by Hermann M. Herzog and Johannes Müller. Langwaden: Bernardus-Verlag, 2003.

Herbert of Clairvaux. *Liber miraculorum.* PL 185:1271–1384; with additional fragments in PL 185:453–66.

Isidore of Seville. *Etymologiarum.* Edited by W. M. Lindsay. Vol. 1 of *Isidori Hispalensis episcopi etymologiarum sive originum.* Oxford: Clarendon Press, 1911.

Lenssen, Seraphin. *Hagiologium Cisterciense.* 3 vols. Tilburg, Holland: Mon. B. M. de Villa Regia, 1948–51.

Manrique, Angel. *Annales Cistercienses.* 4 vols. Lyon, 1642.

Migne, J.-P., ed. *Patrologia cursus completus, series latina.* 221 volumes. Paris, 1844–64.

Quintilian. *Institutiones oratoriae.* Vol. 2 of *The Orator's Education,* edited and translated by Donald Russell. Loeb Classical Library 125. Cambridge, MA: Harvard University Press, 2001.

*RB1980: The Rule of Saint Benedict in Latin and English with Notes.* Edited by Timothy Fry. Collegeville, MN: Liturgical Press, 1981.

*Regula magistri. La Règle du Maître.* Edited and translated by Adalbert de Vogüé. Sources Chrétiennes 105–7. Paris: Cerf, 1964–65.

*The Rule of the Master.* Translated by Luke Eberle. Cistercian Studies Series 6. Kalamazoo, MI: Cistercian Publications, 1977.

Spahr, Kolumban. *Das Leben des hl. Robert von Molesme.* Freiburg, Switzerland: Paulusdruckerei, 1944.

Veilleux, Armand, trans. *Pachomian Chronicles and Rules.* Pachomian Koinonia, 2. Cistercian Studies Series 46. Kalamazoo, MI: Cistercian Publications, 1981.

*Vita prima sancti Bernardi* by William of Saint Thierry (Book 1), Arnold of Bonneval (Book 2), and Geoffrey of Auxerre (Books 3–5). PL 185:221–368. Book 6, an account of Bernard's miracles in Germany is ascribed in PL to Geoffrey and Philip of Clairvaux.

Waddell, Chrysogonus, ed. *Narrative and Legislative Texts from Early Cîteaux: Latin Text in Dual Edition with English Translation and Notes.* Studia et Documenta, 9. Brecht: Cîteaux—Commentarii cistercienses, 1999.

————. *Twelfth-Century Statutes from the Cistercian General Chapter: Latin Text with English Notes and Commentary.* Studia et documenta 12. Brecht: Cîteaux—Commentarii cistercienses, 2002.

## Works of Saint Bernard of Clairvaux: Editions and Translations

*Apologia ad Guillelmum abbatem.* SBOp 3.63–108. Translated by Michael Casey with introduction by Jean Leclercq. "Cistercians and Cluniacs: Saint Bernard's Apologia to Abbot William." *Bernard of Clairvaux: Treatises I.* CF 1. Spencer, MA: Cistercian Publications, 1970. Pp. 3–69. Reprint, *Cistercians and Cluniacs: St. Bernard's Apologia to Abbot William.* Cistercian Studies Series 1A. Kalamazoo, MI: Cistercian Publications, 1986.

*De consideratione libri v.* SBOp 3.393–493. *Five Books on Consideration: Advice to a Pope.* Translated by John D. Anderson and Elizabeth T. Kennan. CF 37. Kalamazoo, MI: Cistercian Publications, 1976.

*Epistola de moribus et officii episcoporum.* SBOp 7.100–131. *Bernard of Clairvaux: On Baptism and the Office of Bishops,* translated by Pauline Matarasso, 11–82. CF 67. Kalamazoo, MI: Cistercian Publications, 2005.

*Epistolae. Letters.* SBOp 7 and 8. Trans. Bruno Scott James (see below).

*Homelium super* Missus est *in laudibus virginis matris.* SBOp 4.13–58. "In Praise of the Virgin Mother," in *Magnificat: Homilies in Praise of the Blessed Virgin Mother by Bernard of Clairvaux and Amadeus of Lausanne,* translated by Marie-Bernard Saïd and Grace Perigo, 3–58. CF 18. Kalamazoo, MI: Cistercian Publications, 1979. Reprint, *Bernard of Clairvaux: Homilies in Praise of the Blessed Virgin Mary.* CF 18A. Kalamazoo, MI: Cistercian Publications, 1993.

*Liber de diligendo Deo.* SBOp 3.119–54. "On Loving God," in *Bernard of Clairvaux: Treatises II,* translated by Robert Walton, 85–132. CF 13. Kalamazoo, MI: Cistercian Publications, 1974; and *Bernard of Clairvaux: On Loving God.* CF 13B. Kalamazoo, MI: Cistercian Publications, 1995.

*Liber ad milites templi (De laude novae militiae).* SBOp 3.207–39. "In Praise of the New Knighthood," in *Bernard of Clairvaux: Treatises III,* translated by Conrad Greenia, 127–67. CF 19. Kalamazoo, MI: Cistercian Publications, 1977. Revised edition, *Bernard of Clairvaux: In Praise of the New Knighthood.* CF 19B. Kalamazoo, MI: Cistercian Publications, 2001.

*Liber de gradibus humilitatis et superbiae.* SBOp 3.13–59. "The Steps of Humility and Pride," in *Bernard of Clairvaux: Treatises II,* translated by M. Ambrose Conway, 1–82. CF 13. Washington, DC: Cistercian Publications, 1974. Reprint, *Bernard of Clairvaux: The Steps of Humility and Pride.* CF 13A. Kalamazoo, MI: Cistercian Publications, 1989.

*Liber de praecepto et dispensatione.* SBOp 3.243–94. "On Precept and Dispensation," in *Bernard of Clairvaux: Treatises I*, translated by Conrad Greenia with introduction by Jean Leclercq, 73–150. CF 1. Spencer, MA: Cistercian Publications, 1970.

*Parabolae.* SBOp 6/2.259–303. *The Parables and the Sentences*, translated by Michael Casey, 11–102. CF 55. Kalamazoo, MI: Cistercian Publications, 2000.

*Sententiae.* SBOp 6/2.3–255. *The Parables and the Sentences*, translated by Francis R. Swietek, 105–458. CF 55. Kalamazoo, MI: Cistercian Publications, 2000.

*Sermo in adventu domini.* SBOp 4.160–96. Translations in SBS 1.1–52 and *Bernard of Clairvaux: Sermons for Advent and the Christmas Season.* Translated by Irene Edmonds, et al. CF 51. Kalamazoo, MI: Cistercian Publications, 2007, pp. 3–42.

*Sermo in ascensione domini.* SBOp 5.123–60. Translation in SBS 2.227–85 (does not include the short sermon 5; SBS sermon 5 corresponds to SBOp *Sermo* 6). In *Bernard of Clairvaux, Sermons for Lent and the Easter Season,* trans. Irene Edmonds, CF 52. Collegeville: Cistercian Publications, forthcoming.

*Sermo in assumptione BVM.* SBOp 5.228–61. Translation of four of six sermons in SBS 3.218–57. In *Bernard of Clairvaux, Sermons at Year's End,* trans. Irene Edmonds, CF 54. Collegeville: Cistercian Publications, forthcoming.

*Sermo in circumcisione domini. Sermones per annum.* Sermon for the feast of the circumcision. SBOp 4.273–91. Translation in SBS 1.423–46; and *Sermons for the Advent and Christmas Seasons,* 133–53. CF 51. Kalamazoo, MI: Cistercian Publications, 2007.

*Sermo de conversione ad clericos.* SBOp 4.69–116. *Sermons on Conversion: A Sermon to Clerics and Lenten Sermons on the Psalm "He who dwells,"* translated by Marie-Bernard Saïd, 11–79. CF 25. Kalamazoo, MI: Cistercian Publications, 1981.

*Sermones de diversis.* SBOp 6/1.59–406. Sixteen of these sermons are translated in SBS 3.397–552. *Bernard of Clairvaux: Miscellaneous Sermons,* translated by Daniel Griggs. CF 68. Collegeville: Cistercian Publications, forthcoming.

*Sermo in cena domini.* SBOp 5.67–72. *Sermo in dedicatione ecclesiae.* SBOp 5.370–98. Translation in SBS 2.385–433. Translated in *Sermons for Lent and the Easter Season.* CF 52. Collegeville: Cistercian Publications, forthcoming.

*Sermo in epiphania domini.* SBOp 4.291–309. Translation in SBS 2.1–29
and *Sermons of the Advent and Christmas Seasons*, 154–75. CF 51.
Kalamazoo, MI: Cistercian Publications, 2007.

*Sermo in obitu domni Humberti.* SBOp 5.440–47. Translation in SBS
3.61–72. In *Sermons at Year's End*, CF 54. Collegeville: Cistercian
Publications, forthcoming.

*Sermo in festivitate Omnium Sanctorum.* SBOp 5.327–70. Translation in
SBS 3.330–96. In *Sermons at Year's End*, CF 54. Collegeville: Cistercian Publications, forthcoming.

*Sermo in festo sancti Michaëlis.* SBOp 5.294–303. Translation in SBS
3.315–29. In *Sermons at Year's End*, CF 54. Collegeville: Cistercian
Publications, forthcoming.

*Sermo in die paschae.* SBOp 5.73–111. Translation in SBS 2.162–208
(the first three of four sermons). In *Sermons for Lent and the Easter
Season*, trans. Irene Edmonds, CF 52. Collegeville: Cistercian Publications, forthcoming.

*Sermo in dominica I post octavam epiphaniae.* SBOp 4.314–26. Translated
in SBS 2.35–54 and *Sermons for the Advent and Christmas Season*,
176–93. CF 51. Kalamazoo, MI: Cistercian Publications, 2007.

*Sermo in Quadragesima.* SBOp 4.353–80. Translation in SBS 2.68–111. In
*Sermons for Lent and the Easter Season*, trans. Irene Edmonds, CF 52.
Collegeville: Cistercian Publications, forthcoming.

*Sermo in Septuagesima.* SBOp 4.344–52. Translation in SBS 2.55–67.

*Sermo in vigilia nativitatis domini.* SBOp 4.197–244. Translation in SBS
1.309–80; *Sermons for the Advent and Christmas Season*, 43–98. CF 51.
Kalamazoo, MI: Cistercian Publications, 2007.

*Sermo super Cantica canticorum.* SBOp 1 and 2. *Bernard of Clairvaux: On
the Song of Songs*, translated by Kilian Walsh and Irene M. Edmonds.
4 vols. CF 4, 7, 31, 40. Kalamazoo, MI: Cistercian Publications,
1971–80.

*Sermo super psalmum* Qui habitat. SBOp 4.382–492. "Lenten Sermons
on the Psalm 'He Who Dwells,'" in *Sermons on Conversion: A Sermon
to Clerics and Lenten Sermons on the Psalm "He who dwells,"* translated
by Marie-Bernard Saïd, 83–261. CF 25. Kalamazoo, MI: Cistercian
Publications, 1981.

*Vita sancti Malachiae.* SBOp 3.297–378. *The Life and Death of Saint
Malachy the Irishman*, translated by Robert T. Meyer, 15–93. CF 10.
Kalamazoo, MI: Cistercian Publications, 1978.

## Works by Other Medieval Authors: Editions and Translations

*Aelred of Rievaulx*

The *Oratio pastoralis*. *Opera Omnia I. Opera Ascetica*. Edited by C. H. Talbot. CCCM 1. Turnhout, Belgium: Brepols, 1971. Translated by R. Penelope Lawson, "The Pastoral Prayer," *Aelred of Rievaulx: Treatises 1*, 103–18. CF 2. Spencer, MA: Cistercian Publications, 1971. *For Your Own People. Aelred of Rievaulx's Pastoral Prayer*. Critical Edition, Introduction, and Annotations by Marsha L. Dutton. Translated by Mark DelCogliano. CF 73. Kalamazoo, MI: Cistercian Publications, 2008.

*Sermones I–XLVI. Collectio Claravallensis prima et secunda*. CCCM 2A. Edited by Gaetano Raciti. Turnhout, Belgium: Brepols, 1989. *Aelred of Rievaulx: The Liturgical Sermons 1. Sermons One to Twenty-Eight* (The First Clairvaux Collection). Translated by Theodore Berkeley and M. Basil Pennington. CF 58. Kalamazoo, MI: Cistercian Publications, 2001. *Aelred of Rievaulx: The Liturgical Sermons 2. Sermons Twenty-Nine to Seventy-Eight* (The Second Clairvaux Collection and the Durham Collection). Translated by Marie Anne Mayeski and Martha Krug. CF 77. Collegeville, MN: Cistercian Publications, forthcoming.

*Speculum caritatis*. In *Opera Omnia, 1: Opera ascetica. CCCM 1*. Edited by C. H. Talbot, xv–161. Turnhout, Belgium: Brepols, 1971. *The Mirror of Charity*. Translated by Elizabeth Connor. CF 17. Kalamazoo, MI: Cistercian Publications, 1990.

*Gregory the Great*

*Dialogorum libri iv. Grégoire le Grand: Dialogues*. Edited by A. de Vogüe. SCh 251, 260, 265. Paris: Les Éditions du Cerf, 1978, 1979, 1980. *St. Gregory the Great: Dialogues*. Translated by O. Zimmermann. Fathers of the Church 39. New York: Fathers of the Church, Inc., 1959.

*Moralia in Job*. Edited by Marci Adriaen. CCSL 143–43B. Turnhout, Belgium: Brepols, 1979–85. Books 1–29 in *Morales sur Job*. Edited and translated [into French] by Aristide Bocobnano. SCh 32, 212, 221, 467. Paris: Éditions du Cerf, 1950–2003. Books 1-10 in *Moralia in Job*, translated by Brian Kerns, CS 249. Collegeville: Cistercian Publications, forthcoming.

*Guerric of Igny*

*Sermo in nativitate domini.* Edited and translated [into French] by John Morson, et al., 164–237. SCh 166. Paris: Éditions du Cerf, 1970. *Guerric of Igny: Liturgical Sermons, 1,* translated by Monks of Mount Saint Bernard Abbey, 37–67. CF 8. Spencer, MA: Cistercian Publications; Shannon, Ireland: Irish University Press, 1971.

*Sermo in die sancto pentecostes.* Edited and translated by John Morson, et al., 282–313. SCh 202. Paris: Éditions du Cerf, 1973. *Liturgical Sermons, 2,* translated by Monks of Mount Saint Bernard Abbey, 109–22. CF 32. Spencer, MA: Cistercian Publications, 1971.

*Sermo in purificatione BVM.* Edited and translated by John Morson, et al., 306–85. SCh 166. Paris: Éditions du Cerf, 1970. *Liturgical Sermons, 1,* translated by Monks of Mount Saint Bernard Abbey, 99–132. CF 8. Spencer, MA: Cistercian Publications; Shannon, Ireland: Irish University Press, 1971.

*Sermo in rogationibus,* SCh 202.260–71. Translation in *Liturgical Sermons,* 98–103. CF 32. Spencer, MA: Cistercian Publications; Shannon, Ireland: Irish University Press, 1971.

*John Cassian*

John Cassian. *De institutiones. Institutions cénobitiques.* Edited and translated by Jean-Claude Guy. SCh 19. Paris: Éditions du Cerf, 1965. *John Cassian: The Institutes,* translated by Boniface Ramsey. Ancient Christian Writers 58. New York: Newman, 2000. Also translated in *A Select Library of Nicene and Post-Nicene Fathers.* Second series. Vol. 11. Reprint, Grand Rapids, MI: Eerdmans, 1991.

## Secondary Works

Auberger, Jean-Baptiste. *L'Unanimité cistercienne primitive: mythe ou réalité?* Cîteaux, Studia et Documenta, 3. Achel: Administration de *Cîteaux: Commentarii cistercienses,* Editions Sine Parvulos, 1986.

Bär, Hermann, and Karl Rossel. *Diplomatische Geschichte der Abtei Eberbach im Rheingau.* 3 vols. Wiesbaden: Auf kosten des Vereins gedruckt, 1851–58.

Berman, Constance Hoffman. *The Cistercian Evolution: The Invention of a Religious Order in Twelfth-Century Europe.* Philadelphia: University of Pennsylvania Press, 2000.

Bouton, Jean de la Croix, and Jean Baptiste Van Damme, eds. *Les plus anciens textes de Cîteaux. Cîteaux: Commentarii cisterceinses*. Studia et Documenta 2. Achel: Saint-Remy, 1974.

Bredero, Adrian H. *Bernard of Clairvaux: Between Cult and History*. Grand Rapids, MI: W. B. Eerdmans, 1996

———. "The Canonization of Bernard of Clairvaux." In *Saint Bernard of Clairvaux: Studies Commemorating the Eighth Centenary of his Canonization*, edited by M. Basil Pennington, 63–100. CS 28. Kalamazoo, MI: Cistercian Publications, 1977.

Bremond, C., and J. LeGoff. *L' "exemplum,"* Typologie des sources du moyen âge occidental 40. Turnhout, Belgium: Brepols, 1982.

Canivez, Josephus-Maria. "Conrad d'Eberbach." *Dictionnaire d'histoire et de géographie ecclésiastique*, edited by Alfred Baudrillart, et al. Vol. 13:482. Paris: Letouzey et Ané, 1956.

———, ed. *Statuta Capitulorum Generalium Ordinis Cistercienses, 1116–1786*. 8 vols. Louvain: Bureaux de la Revue, 1933–41.

Casey, Michael. "Bernard and the Crisis at Morimond: Did the Order Exist in 1124?" *Cistercian Studies Quarterly* 38 (2003): 119–75.

———. "Towards a Methodology for the *Vita Prima*: Translating the First Life into Biography." In *Bernardus Magister*, edited by John R. Sommerfeldt. Cistercian Studies Series 135. Kalamazoo, MI: Cistercian Publications, 1992.

———. "Herbert of Clairvaux's *Book of Wonderful Happenings*." *Cistercian Studies Quarterly* 25 (1970): 37–64.

Constable, Giles, ed. *Apologiae Dvae*. CCCM 62. Turnhout, Belgium: Brepols, 1985.

———. "Past and present in the eleventh and twelfth centuries: Perceptions of time and change." *L'Europa dei secoli XI e XII fra novità e tradizione: Sviluppi di una cultura. Atti della decima Settimana internazionale di studio, Mendola, 25–29 agosto 1986*. Miscellanea del Centro de studi medioevali 12. Milan: Pubblicazioni dell'Università cattolica del Sacro Cuore, 1989. Reprinted in Giles Constable, *Culture and Spirituality in Medieval Europe*, Aldershot and Brookfield, VT: Variorum [Ashgate Publishing Limited], 1996.

———. *Three Studies in Medieval Religious and Social Thought*. Cambridge: Cambridge University Press, 1995.

Damier, M.-A. "Eberbach." *Dictionnaire d'histoire et de géographie ecclésiastique*, edited by R. Aubert and E. Van Cauwenbergh. Vol. 14:1281–85. Paris: Letouzey et Ané, 1960.

Donnelly, J. S. *The Decline of the Medieval Cistercian Laybrotherhood.* New York: Fordham University Press, 1949.

Elder, E. Rozanne, ed. *The New Monastery: Texts and Studies on the Earliest Cistercians.* Cistercian Father Series 60. Kalamazoo, MI: Cistercian Publications, 1998.

France, James. *The Cistercians in Scandinavia.* Cistercian Studies Series 131. Kalamazoo, MI: Cistercian Publications, 1992.

Freeman, Elizabeth. *Narratives of a New Order: Cistercian Historical Writing in England, 1150–1220.* Medieval Church Studies 2. Turnhout, Belgium: Brepols, 2002.

————. "What Makes a Monastic Order? Issues of Methodology in The Cistercian Evolution." *Cistercian Studies Quarterly* 37 (2002): 429–42.

Gastaldelli, Ferruccio. "A Critical Note on the Edition of the *Exordium Magnum Cisterciense.*" *Cistercian Studies Quarterly* 39 (2004): 311–20.

Gerlich, A. "Eberbach." *Lexikon des Mittelalters.* Vol. 4:1511–12. Munich: Artemis, 1989.

Goodrich, W. E. "The Cistercian Founders and the Rule: Some Reconsiderations." *Journal of Ecclesiastical History* 35 (1984): 358–75.

Grießer, Bruno. "Herbert von Clairvaux und sein *Liber miraculorum.*" *Cistercienser Chronik* 54 (1947): 21–39, 118–48.

————. "Probleme der Textüberlieferung des *Exordium Magnum.*" *Cistercienser-Chronik* 52 (1940): 161–68, 177–87; and 53 (1941): 1–10, 84–85.

Hüffer, G. *Der heiligen Bernard von Clairvaux: eine Darstellung seines Lebens und Wirkens.* Munich: Aschendorffschen, 1886.

Hümpfner, Tiburtius. *Exordium cistercii cum Summa cartae caritatis et fundatio primarum quattour filiarum cistercii.* Vàc, 1932.

————. "Der bisher in den gedruckten Ausgaben vermisste Teil des *Exordium Magnum* S. O. Cist." *Cistercienser-Chronik* 20 (1908): 97–106.

James, Bruno Scott, trans. *The Letters of St. Bernard of Clairvaux.* Chicago: Henry Regnery, 1953. Reprint with new introduction and indices, Kalamazoo, MI: Cistercian Publications; Stroud: Sutton, 1998.

Janauschek, Leopold. *Originum Cisterciensium Tomus I.* Vienna: Hoelder, 1877.

King, Archdale A. *Cîteaux and Her Elder Daughters.* London: Burns & Oates, 1954.

Knowles, M. David. *Great Historical Enterprises.* London: Nelson and Sons, 1963.

Kompatscher-Gufler, Gabriela. *Herbert von Clairvaux und sein Liber miraculorum: Die Kurzversion eines anonymen bayerischen Redaktors.* Bern-New York: Peter Lang, 2005.

Lackner, Bede. *The Eleventh-Century Background of Cîteaux.* Cistercian Studies Series 8. Washington, DC: Cistercian Publications, 1972.

Leclercq, Jean. *The Love of Learning and the Desire for God.* Translated by Catherine Misrahi. New York: Fordham University Press, 1961.

————. "Monastic Historiography from Leo IX to Callistus II." *Studia Monastica* 12 (1970): 58–62.

Lekai, Louis J. *The Cistercians: Ideals and Reality.* Kent, OH: Kent State University Press, 1977.

————. *The White Monks.* Okauchee, WI: Our Lady of Spring Bank Abbey, 1953.

Lubac, Henri de. *Medieval Exegesis.* Volume 1, translated by Marc Sebanc. Volume 2, translated by E. M. Macierowski. Grand Rapids, MI: Eerdmans, 1998, 2000.

Marilier, Jean. "Le vocable *Novum Monasterium* dans les premiers documents cisterciens." *Cistercienser-Chronik* 57 (1950): 81–84.

————, ed. *Chartres et documents concernant l'Abbaye de Cîteaux.* Rome: Editiones Cistercienses, 1961.

McGuire, Brian Patrick. "The Cistercians and the Rise of the Exemplum in Early Thirteenth Century France: A Reevaluation of Paris *BN MS lat. 15912.*" *Classica et Mediaevalia* 34 (1983): 211–67.

————. "Caesar of Heisterbach and the Cistercians as Medieval People." *Noble Piety and Reformed Monasticism,* edited by E. Rozanne Elder, 81–108. Cistercian Studies Series 65. Kalamazoo, MI: Cistercian Publications, 1981.

————. "Cistercian Storytelling—A Living Tradition: Surprises in the World of Research." *Cistercian Studies Quarterly* 39 (2004): 281–309.

————. *The Difficult Saint: Bernard of Clairvaux and His Tradition.* Cistercian Studies Series 126. Kalamazoo, MI: Cistercian Publications, 1991.

————. "The First Cistercian Renewal and a Changing Image of St. Bernard." *Cistercian Studies Quarterly* 24 (1989): 25–49.

————. *Friendship and Community: The Monastic Experience, 350–1250.* Cistercian Studies Series 95. Kalamazoo, MI: Cistercian Publications, 1988. Second edition, Ithaca, NY: Cornell University Press, 2010.

————. "An Introduction to the *Exordium Magnum Cisterciense.*" *Cistercian Studies Quarterly* 27 (1992): 277–29. An English translation of his Introduction to *Le Grande Exorde.*

————. "A Lost Clairvaux *Exemplum* Collection Found: The *Liber visionum et miraculorum* Compiled under Prior John of Clairvaux (1171–79)." *Analecta Cisterciensia* 39 (1983): 27–62.

————. "Structure and Consciousness in the *Exordium Magnum Cisterciense*: The Clairvaux Cistercians after Bernard." *Cahiers de l'Institut du Moyan-âge Grec et Latin* 30. Copenhagen, 1979. Pages 33–90.

————. "Was Alberic the Real Founder of Cîteaux?" *Cistercian Studies Quarterly* 34 (1999): 139–56.

————. "Who Founded the Order of Cîteaux?" In *The Joy of Learning and the Love of God: Studies in Honor of Jean Leclercq*, edited by E. Rozanne Elder, 389–413. Cistercian Studies Series 160. Kalamazoo, MI: Cistercian Publications, 1995.

————. *The Cistercians in Denmark: Their Attitudes, Roles, and Functions in Medieval Society*. Cistercian Studies Series 35. Kalamazoo, MI: Cistercian Publications, 1982.

Morrison, Karl F. *History as a Visual Art in the Twelfth-Century Renaissance*. Princeton, NJ: Princeton University Press, 1990.

Mula, Stephano. "Twelfth- and Thirteenth-Century Cistercian *Exempla* Collections: Role, Diffusion, and Evolution." *History Compass* 8 (2010): 903–12.

Müller, Reinhard. "Konrad von Eberbach." In *Deutsches Literatur-Lexikon: Biographische-Bibliographisches Handbuch*, edited by Bruno Berger and Heinz Rupp. Vol. 9:216–17. Bern: Franke, 1984.

Newman, Martha. *The Boundaries of Charity: Cistercian Culture and Ecclesiastical Reform, 1098–1180*. Stanford: Stanford University Press, 1996.

Partner, Nancy. *Serious Entertainments: The Writing of History in Twelfth-Century England*. Chicago: University of Chicago Press, 1977.

Ray, Roger. "Rhetorical Skepticism and Verisimilar Narrative in John of Salisbury's *Historia Pontificalis*." In *Classical Rhetoric and Medieval Historiography*, edited by Ernst A. Breisach, 61–102. Kalamazoo, MI: Medieval Institute Publications, 1985.

Savage, Paul M. "History, *Exempla*, and *Caritas* in the *Exordium Magnum*." Ph.D. diss., University of Notre Dame, 2000.

Schaefer, Karl. *Die Abtei Eberbach im Mittelalter*. Berlin: E. Wasmuth, 1901.

Schneider, A. "Eberbach." In *Dizionario degli istituti di perfezione*, edited by G. Pelliccia and G. Rocca. Vol. 3:1006–7. Rome: Edizioni Paoline, 1976.

Smalley, Beryl. *The Study of the Bible in the Middle Ages.* 3rd ed. Oxford: Blackwell, 1983.

Söhn, J. *Geschichte des wirtschaftlichen Lebens der Abtei Eberbach in Rheingau.* Veröffentlichungen der historische Kommission für Nassau VII. Wiesbaden: Bergmann, 1914.

Spahr, Kolumban. "Konrad." *Neue Deutsche Biographie.* Vol. 12:536. Berlin: Duncker & Humbolt, 1980.

Taylor, John. *English Historical Literature in the Fourteenth Century.* Oxford: Clarendon Press, 1987.

Tissier, Bertrand. *Bibliotheca Patrum Cisterciensium.* Vol. 1. Bonnefontaine, 1660.

Tubach, Frederic C. *Index exemplorum: A Handbook of Medieval Religious Tales.* FF Communications 204. Helsinki: Suomalainen Tiedeakatemia Aademia Scientiarum Fennica, 1969.

Vacandard, E. *Vie de Saint Bernard.* 4th ed. 2 Vols. Paris: Gabalda, 1927.

Van Damme, Jean-Baptiste. *The Three Founders of Cîteaux: Robert of Molesme—Alberic—Stephen Harding.* Translated by Nicholas Groves and Christian Carr. Cistercian Studies Series 176. Kalamazoo, MI: Cistercian Publications, 1998.

Van Houts, Elisabeth M. C. *Local and Regional Chronicles.* Turnhout, Belgium: Brepols, 1995.

Waddell, Chrysogonus. "The *Exordium Cistercii* and the *Summa Cartae caritatis*: A Discussion Continued." In *Cistercian Ideals and Reality*, edited by John R. Sommerfeldt. Cistercian Studies Series 60. Kalamazoo, MI: Cistercian Publications, 1978.

———. "The *Exordium Cistercii*, Lucan, and Mother Poverty." *Cîteaux: Commentarii cistercianses* 46 (1984): 379–88.

———. "The Myth of Cistercian Origins: C. H. Berman and the Manuscript Sources." *Cîteaux: Commentarii cistercienses* 51 (2000): 299–386.

———. "Toward a New Provisional Edition of the Statutes of the Cistercian General Chapter, ca. 1119–1189." In *Studiosorum Speculum: Studies in Honor of Louis J. Lekai, O. Cist*, edited by Francis R. Swietek and John R. Sommerfelt, 389–419. Cistercian Studies Series 141. Kalamazoo, MI: Cistercian Publications, 1993.

———, ed. *The Twelfth-Century Cistercian Hymnal.* Cistercian Liturgy Series 1–2. Trappist, KY: Gethsemani Abbey (distributed by Cistercian Publications), 1984. Available online at http://www.wmich.edu/library/digi/collections/liturgy/series.

Waha, Michel de. "Aux Origines de Cîteaux: Rapports entre
l'*Exordium Cistercii* et l'*Exordium Parvum.*" In *Lettres latines du moyen
âge et de la Renaissance*, edited by Guy Cambier, Carl Deroux, and
Jean Préaux, 152–82. Collection Latomus 158. Brussels: Revue
d'Études Latines, 1978.

Ward, Benedicta. "Enthusiasm in the *Exordium Magnum Cisterciense.*"
*Cistercian Studies Quarterly* 7 (1972): 154–59.

———. *Miracles and the Medieval Mind: Theory, Record and Event, 1000–
1215.* Rev. ed. Philadelphia: University of Pennsylvania Press, 1987.

Ward, John. "Some Principles of Rhetorical Historiography in the
Twelfth Century." In *Classical Rhetoric and Medieval Historiography*,
edited by Ernst A. Breisach, 103–65. Studies in Medieval Culture 19.
Kalamazoo, MI: Medieval Institute Publications, 1985.

Williams, Watkin. "The *Exordium Magnum Cisterciense.*" *Monastic Studies*,
52–60. Manchester: Manchester University Press, 1938.

———. *Saint Bernard of Clairvaux.* Westminster, MD: Newman Press,
1952.

Worstbrock, F. J. "Konrad von Eberbach." In *Die deutsche Literatur des
Mittelalters Verfasserlexikon*, edited by Kurt Ruh, et al. Vol. 5:156–59.
Berlin: De Gruyter, 1985.

# Index of Scriptural References

*Note:* Numbers on the right refer to the Book and Chapter number in *The Great Beginning of Cîteaux*.

# Index of Classical References

**Homer**

*Odyssey*
12          5.12, 5.13

**Horace**

*Epistles*
1.1.28–31   6.10
1.1.32      6.10
1.11.27     6.1
1.18.71     3.5, 3.19,
            5.19
1.18.84     1.9

*Odes*
1.3.8       3.11

4.5.10      6.10

*Satires*
1.3.25–26   1.9
2.2.80–81   2.2
2.7.86      3.6

**Ovid**

*Fasti*
1.218       5.14

*Heroides*
2.85        1.15

*Metamorphoses*
1.87–162    3.7

3.466       1.10

*ex Ponto*
4.10.5      1.9

**Persius**

*Satires*
1.27        6.2

**Virgil**

*Aeneid*
1.216       5.11
1.387–88    5.21
3.56        5.15
4.373       3.10
6.853       2.31

# Index of Patristic and Medieval References

# General Index

Aachen, synod (817), 1.4 (note).

Aaron, brother of Moses, 5.7.

Abbey church, at Clairvaux, 4.34; at Foigny, 5.11.

Abbot, Prol; 1.6; 1.8-24; 1.27-35; 2.14; 2.19-34; 3.1; 3.3; 3.4; 3.6; 3.8; 3.9; 3.10; 3.12; 3.15; 3.16; 3.20; 3.22; 3.25; 3.29-31; 4.1; 4.13; 4.14; 4.16; 4.18; 4.19; 4.25; 4.26; 4.27; 4.28; 5.1; 5.2; 5.4-6; 5.10; 5.11; 5.13; 5.15; 5.17; 5.20; 5.21; 6.2-5; 6.8; 6.10. Abbot understood that blood-letting was dangerous, 4.29. Abbot holds the place of Christ, 4.29.

Abraham, biblical patriarch, 3.18.

Abraham, abbot of La Prée, 5.2.

Abraham, cellarer of a monastery in Sweden (possibly Alvastra), 4.28.

Abstinence, 1.32; 3.2; 3.16; 5.20. See Fasting.

Achard, novice master, noble who entered Clairvaux, 3.22.

Acolytes, 3.23.

Adam, 3.11. Children of Adam, 1.1; 5.4; 5.7. Sons of Adam, 3.5. The first Adam, 3.18. Sin of Adam, 5.13.

Adder, 3.22.

Adelbert, archbishop of Mayence, 5.17.

Admission to Clairvaux, 3.11.

Adolescence, *see* Youth.

Adultery, 3.27.

Æbelholt, house of canons regular, Denmark, 1.9 (note).

*Agaonitheta*, 5.12.

Agony, 2.15; 2.24; 2.28; 2.31; 4.1; 4.6; 5.1; 6.3. *See* Death agony.

Agriculture, *see* Land.

Ailment, 4.27.

Ainay (in Lyon), *see* Joceran of Ainay.

Alan, monk of Clairvaux, bishop of Auxerre (1152–67), 4.47.

Alba, bishopric, 2.30.

Alberic, prior of Molesme, a founder and abbot of Cîteaux (1099–1109), 1.12; 1.16; 1.16; 1.19; 1.20; 2.34.

Alexander, canon of Cologne, monk of Clairvaux, abbot of Grandselve (1149), abbot of Cîteaux (1166–75), 1.33.

Alexander III, pope (1159–81), 1.32; 2.29; 5.17; 6.3.

Alexandria, 5.14; 6.3.

Alexis, saint, 6.7.

All Souls Day, 1.8 (and note); 3.16; 6.3.

Alleluia, 4.16; 5.17.

Alms, 1.28; 3.28; 4.3; 5.5; 5.12; 6.6.

Alps, 4.34.

Alquirin, monk of Clairvaux, 4.1.

Altar(s), 1.9; 1.20; 2.6; 2.24; 2.27; 2.29; 2.33; 3.8; 3.11; 3.15; 3.16; 3.18; 3.23; 3.25; 3.28; 4.2; 4.3; 4.4; 4.7; 4.11; 4.29; 5.5; 5.12; 5.14; 5.15; 5.17; 5.18; 6.1; 6.2; 6.10.

Alvastra, Cistercian monastery, 4.28 (note).

Ambition, 3.11; 4.17; its nature and signs, 5.7.

Ambrose of Milan, saint, 5.13.

Amen, 6.5; 6.7.

Amo, Cluniac monk, 6.7.

Anacletus II, antipope, 2.11 (and note); 4.34 (note); 6.2 (note). *See* Peter Leoni.

Ananias, 4.24; 6.22.

Anathema, 3.27; 5.11. *See* Excommunication.

Andrew, archdeacon of Verdun, monk of Clairvaux, 2.21.

5.17; 5.18; 6.2; 6.4-7; 6.10. Church
of the Pater Noster, 3.28.
Cinnamon, 5.6.
Cistercian(s), 1.10; 1.15; 1.17; 2.24; 3.18;
3.21, *passim.*
Cistercian Order, 1.9; 1.10; 1.12; 1.13;
1.15; 1.16; 1.19-23; 1.29; 1.32; 2.18;
2.20; 2.25; 2.34; 3.10; 3.12; 3.15; 3.26;
3.28; 4.5; 4.6; 4.25; 4.30; 5.2; 5.3; 5.7;
5.15; 5.17; 5.18; 5.20; 6.3; 6.8; 6.10.
Cîteaux, Prol; 1.10; 1.13; 1.15; 1.16;
1.19-23; 1.27-30; 1.32-35; 2.1; 2.20;
2.24; 2.34; 3.1; 3.10; 3.11; 3.27; 4.24;
4.30; 5.8; 5.20; 6.4; 6.10. Cîteaux, as
"New Monastery," 1.15; 1.18; 1.20.
Clairvaux, Prol, 1.10; 1.23; 1.32; 1.33;
2.1; 2.2; 2.7; 2.9-13; 2.15; 2.19-24;
2.26-34; 3.1; 3.4; 3.6-8; 3.10; 3.12;
3.13; 3.15-23; 3.25-31; 3.33; 4.1;
4.4; 4.6; 4.7; 4.9; 4.12-21; 4.23-5;
5.1-4; 5.6; 5.10; 5.11; 5.17; 5.19;
5.21; 6.1; 6.3-5; 6.10. Clairvaux as
"clear valley," Prol, 5.2; 6.10.
*Clementissime Domine,* 6.3.
Clerk(s), 1.20; 1.35; 2.13; 2.21; 3.19;
3.27; 4.6; 4.30; 5.12; 5.14; 5.16; 5.20;
6.5.
Clermont, 2.24; 2.26.
Cloak, 1.20; 2.15; 3.22. Cloak of
immortality, 4.27.
Clock, 5.7; 5.18.
Cloister, 1.6; 1.20; 1.31 (note); 2.23;
2.27; 2.29 (note); 3.6; 3.17; 4.1; 4.5;
4.22; 5.17; 5.19; 6.1; 6.6.
Cloth, 3.11; 5.2. Altar cloth, 1.21; 3.11.
Grave cloths, 5.5.
Clothing, 1.32; 1.33; 2.20; 2.29; 2.33;
3.1; 3.5; 3.6; 3.11; 3.13; 3.16; 3.17;
3.19; 3.22; 3.27; 4.1; 4.14; 4.15; 4.19;
4.26; 4.29; 4.35; 5.2; 5.3; 5.6; 5.15;
6.10. *See* Garments.
Cluniacs, 1.2 (note); 3.12; 6.6 (and
note).
Cluny, 1.6; 1.8-10; 6.7. Cluny in
Bernard's day, 3.10-12; 3.24.
Coat, 1.20.
Coffin, 2.20.
Cold, 1.28; 2.32; 3.5; 3.11; 6.10.

Collects, 6.5. *See* Liturgical prayer.
Cologne, 1.33; 2.27; 5.16.
Common life, 1.2; 1.3; 2.30; 3.2; 3.18;
5.15.
Community, Prol; 1.7-10; 1.14-16; 1.18-
23; 1.29; 1.34; 1.35; 2.1; 2.9; 2.21;
2.24; 2.25; 2.31; 3.4; 3.7; 3.11; 3.13;
3.17; 3.18; 3.20; 3.32; 4.1; 4.4; 4.7;
4.13; 4.20; 4.25; 4.27; 4.28; 4.35; 5.3;
5.7-10; 5.14; 5.19; 5.20; 6.3-5; 6.10.
Compassion, 1.8; 2.20; 2.33; 3.4; 3.13;
3.26-28; 4.27-29; 4.35; 5.6; 5.10;
5.12; 5.14; 6.3; 6.5; 6.6; 6.8.
Compline, 1.23; 2.9; 2.25; 2.30; 3.13;
3.14; 5.10. *See* Divine Office.
Compostella, 1.35 (note). *See* James, saint.
Compunction, 1.13; 3.11; 3.12; 3.17;
3.18; 3.27; 4.2; 4.4; 4.21; 4.35; 5.7;
5.9; 5.13-15; 5.21; 6.1-3; 6.5; 6.10.
*See* Contrition.
Confession, 1.11; 2.22; 2.26; 2.31; 2.33;
3.5; 3.19; 3.32; 4.2, 5.2; 4.16; 4.22;
4.24; 4.25; 5.2; 5.3-5; 5.7; 5.9; 5.10;
5.12-5.15; 6.3; 6.8; 6.9. *See* Penance,
Repentance.
Confessor, 2.31; 5.5; 5.12; 6.8.
Conrad, abbot of Corbie, 5.11.
Conrad, noble from Mayence, 5.17.
Conrad II, German King, Holy Roman
Emperor (1024/27–39), 1.33.
Conscience, 1.4; 1.7; 1.13; 1.20; 1.21; 2.3;
2.5; 2.14; 2.27; 2.28; 2.31; 3.2; 3.5;
3.8; 3.9; 3.11; 3.15-17; 3.19; 4.2; 4.3;
4.18; 4.19; 4.24; 4.25; 4.27; 5.2; 5.5;
5.9-15; 5.21; 6.1; 6.2; 6.6; 6.9; 6.10.
Consecration (of Eucharist), 3.15; 3.26;
5.14; 6.1; 6.2. *See* Eucharist, Host.
Consistory, 2.29.
Conspiracy, 5.10. *See* Rebellion, Revolt,
Scandal.
Constantine, Roman Emperor, 2.27.
Constantine I of Lacon, judge at
Torres, 3.26.
Constantinople, 1.3.
Constantius, brother in Clairvaux, 2.15.
Constitution (Cistercian), 1.28; 1.30;
5.10. *See* Customs, Institutes,
Observances, Statutes.

2.15; 2.19; 2.20; 2.23-31; 2.33; 3.1;
3.3-5; 3.7; 3.11; 3.13-19; 3.22; 3.24-
28; 3.30; 3.33; 3.34; 4.1; 4.14; 4.17-
20; 4.35; 5.2; 5.3; 5.5; 5.7; 5.9; 5.10;
5.12; 5.18; 6.2; 6.3; 6.5; 6.7; 6.8;
6.10. Dying at Clairvaux, 2.10; 3.25;
3.30; 4.28; 4.29; 6.3; 6.4. *See* Agony,
Death agony.
Death agony, 1.8; 1.31; 2.28; 2.31; 3.14;
3.19; 3.33; 4.1; 4.6; 4.18; 5.1; 5.9;
6.1; 6.5. *See* Agony, Death.
Debts, 4.6; 4.33. Metaphorical use of
debt, 2.33; 3.18; 5.5; 5.9; 5.12; 5.21.
Decrepit, 2.14; 3.4; 4.27.
Dedication of churches, 3.7 (note);
3.8 (note); 5.8; 6.7 (and note).
Of church at Clairvaux, 3.25. Of
church at Foigny, 5.11.
Delirious, 3.19; 5.9.
Demon(s), 1.13; 2.2; 2.20; 2.22; 2.28;
2.31; 3.15; 3.22; 3.27; 4.4; 4.28;
4.31; 4.34; 5.1; 5.2; 5.5-10; 5.12;
5.13; 5.14; 5.17; 5.18; 5.20; 6.2. As
Ethiopian (or black), 3.22, 4.4; 4.31;
5.8; 5.12; 5.18, 5.20. Demons flee
from prayer to Mary and the sign of
the cross, 4.4; flee from calling on
Christ, 4.34. *See* Devil, Satan.
Denmark, 2.31; 3.27; 3.28; 4.27; 4.29;
4.35; 6.10.
Desert, Prol (and note); 1.13-16; 2.21;
3.10; 3.11; 3.18; 4.6.
Desert Fathers, Prol; 1.2; 1.3; 1.4; 4.4
(note); 4.26; 4.29 (note); 5.3; 5.18.
Desire(s), Prol; 1.1; 1.5; 1.7; 1.9-11;
1.13; 1.16; 1.20; 1.21; 1.29; 1.31;
1.32; 1.34; 2.6; 2.10; 2.12; 2.13; 2.16;
2.24-28; 2.30; 2.31; 3.2-5; 3.9-11;
3.15-17; 3.20; 3.25; 3.26; 3.28; 3.30;
3.32; 4.5-7; 4.12; 4.18; 5.4; 5.6; 5.7;
5.9; 5.12; 5.15; 5.19; 5.21; 6.1-4;
6.8; 6.10.
Devil(s), Prol, 1.19; 1.27; 2.2; 2.6; 2.15;
2.19; 2.21; 2.22; 2.27; 2.28; 2.33;
3.9; 3.11; 3.16; 3.22; 3.26; 4.4; 4.22;
4.31; 5.1; 5.2; 5.5; 5.8; 5.10; 5.12;
5.13; 5.15; 5.18; 5.20; 6.1. Devilish art, 5.12. Devilish spirits, 2.27;

5.10; 5.12. Noonday devil, 5.12. *See*
Demon, Satan.
Diet, meat eating, 3.16.
Dinner, 3.16; 5.11. *See* Meal.
Discernment, 1.4 (and note); 1.6; 1.11;
2.28-2.32; 3.5; 3.6; 3.11; 4.3; 4.27;
4.28; 5.3; 5.10; 5.12; 5.13; 6.2; 6.9.
Discipline, 1.4-6; 1.9; 1.14; 1.16; 1.20;
1.21; 1.29; 2.12; 2.13; 2.20; 2.25;
2.30; 2.31; 2.34; 3.2; 3.5; 3.6; 3.8;
3.14; 3.27; 3.29; 3.34; 4.2; 4.26-30;
4.32; 5.3; 5.9; 5.10; 5.12; 5.13; 5.17;
5.19; 6.2-4; 6.9; 6.10.
Disease/diseased, 1.13; 2.33; 4.16.
*See* Sick.
Dish(es), 2.21; 5.2. *See* Bowl.
Disobedience/disobey, 1.10; 1.15; 2.31;
3.9; 3.11; 3.19; 4.25; 4.29; 5.5; 5.8;
5.9.
Divine Office, 1.25; 2.2; 2.12; 2.28;
2.33; 3.5; 3.16; 3.22; 3.23; 3.25; 4.1;
4.4; 4.13; 4.35; 5.6; 5.9; 5.12; 5.13;
5.15-20. Office for the faithful
departed, 1.8. Office for the commendation of the soul, 5.10; 6.5.
*See* Compline, Lauds, Matins, None,
Prime, Sext, Terce, Vespers, Vigils.
Dog(s), 4.35; 5.8; 5.11.
Domitian, Roman emperor, 5.12.
Donkey, 2.8.
Door(s), 1.6; 1.20; 1.26; 1.32; 2.13; 2.20;
2.22; 2.23; 2.29; 3.11; 3.17; 3.21-23;
3.27; 3.29; 3.32; 4.1; 4.4; 5.3; 5.6;
5.8; 5.12; 5.17; 6.2; 6.5; 6.6. Door
of paradise open to all, 3.32.
Dormitory, 2.9; 2.28; 2.31; 3.17; 4.22;
4.28; 5.6; 5.8; 5.10.
Doubt, 1.21; 2.18; 2.29; 3.26; 3.29; 4.23;
4.31; 5.7; 5.9; 5.10; 5.12 (note); 6.1;
6.5.
Dragon, 1.9; 5.8; 5.10; 5.12.
Drainage, 3.1.
Dream, 3.17; 4.18; 5.7; 5.10; 5.18.
*See* Vision, Visitation.
Drunk, 1.21; 1.29; 5.15.
Dunes, les, Cistercian abbey, 2.21.
Dung, 3.11; 3.33; 4.6; 5.6. Dunghill,
1.9; 1.16.